Exploring Art

Gene Mittler, Ph.D.
Professor Emeritus
Texas Tech University

Rosalind Ragans, Ph.D.
Associate Professor Emerita
Georgia Southern University

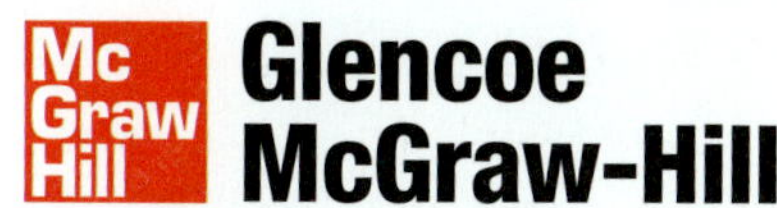

New York, New York Columbus, Ohio Chicago, Illinois Peoria, Illinois Woodland Hills, California

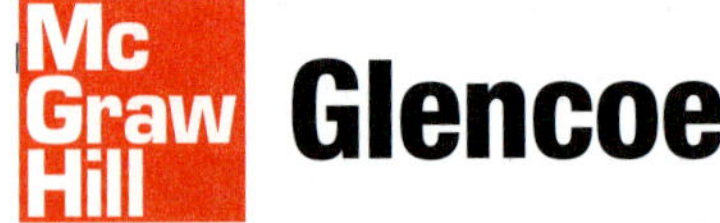

The McGraw·Hill Companies

Printed in the United States of America.

Send all inquiries to:
Glencoe/McGraw-Hill
21600 Oxnard Street, Suite 500
Woodland Hills, CA 91367

ISBN 0-07-846514-1 (Student Text)
ISBN 0-07-846519-2 (Teacher Wraparound Edition)

6 7 8 9 027/043 08 07 06

About the Authors

Gene Mittler

Gene Mittler is one of the authors of Glencoe's middle school art series, *Introducing Art, Exploring Art,* and *Understanding Art.* He is also author of *Art in Focus,* a chronological approach to art for Glencoe's senior high program, and *Creating and Understanding Drawings.* He has taught at both the elementary and secondary levels and at Indiana University. He received an M.F.A. in sculpture from Bowling Green State University and a Ph.D. in art education from the Ohio State University. Dr. Mittler is currently Professor Emeritus at Texas Tech University.

Rosalind Ragans

Rosalind Ragans is one of the authors of Glencoe's middle school art series, *Introducing Art, Exploring Art,* and *Understanding Art.* She serves as senior author on the elementary program of *Art Connections* for the SRA division of McGraw-Hill, and wrote the multilevel, comprehensive *ArtTalk* text for Glencoe's senior high program. She received a B.F.A at Hunter College, CUNY, New York, and earned a M.Ed. in Elementary Education at Georgia Southern College and a Ph.D. in art education at the University of Georgia. Dr. Ragans was named National Art Educator of the Year for 1992.

About Artsource®

ART SOURCE ARTSOURCE

The materials provided in the Performing Arts Handbook are excerpted from *Artsource®: The Center's Study Guide to the Performing Arts,* a project of the Music Center Education Division. Based in Los Angeles, the Music Center is one of the three largest performing arts centers in the United States. It established the Education Division in 1979 as part of its commitment to engaging new and diverse audiences in the arts—in the center's theatres, in schools and throughout the community. The Music Center Education Division is dedicated to providing opportunities for lifelong learning in the arts and advancing quality arts education as integral to the core curriculum in Southern California schools. For additional information, visit www.musiccenter.org/artsource.

Editorial Consultants

Jean Morman Unsworth
Art Consultant to Chicago Archdiocese Schools
Chicago, Illinois, Texas

Faye Scannell, M.A.
Specialist, Technology
Bellevue Public Schools
Bellevue, Washington

Contributors/Reviewers

Donna Banning
Art Teacher
Orange Unified School District
Orange, California

Jeff Bender
Art Teacher
Plaza Park Middle School
Evansville, Indiana

Gordon Grant, MA. Ed.
Assistant Principal
Asheville Middle School
Asheville, North Carolina

Cris Guenter, Ed.D.
Professor, Arts Education/Curriculum & Instruction
California State University, Chico
Chico, California

Annette Loy
Art Teacher
Jefferson County High School
Dandridge, TN

Gloria McCoy
Art Supervisor
Spring Branch Independent School District
Houston, Texas

Bruce Sifrit
Art Teacher
Ed Irons Junior High
Lubbock, Texas

Lisa Vihos
Curator of Education
John Michael Kohler Arts Center
Sheboygan, Wisconsin

Performing Arts Handbook Contributors

Mark Slavkin
Vice President for Education, The Music Center of Los Angeles County

Michael Solomon
Managing Director, Music Center Education Division

Melinda Williams
Concept Originator and Project Director

Susan Cambigue-Tracey
Project Coordinator

Arts Discipline Writers:
Dance—Susan Cambigue-Tracey, Diana Cummins, Madeleine Dahm, Carole Valleskey
Music—Rosemarie Cook-Glover, Barbara Leonard
Theatre—Barbara Leonard, Susan Cambigue-Tracey

Studio Lesson Consultants

Acknowledgements: The authors wish to express their gratitude to the following art coordinators and specialists who participated in the field test of the studio lessons.

Lori Battaglia
Hebron Christian Academy
Dacula, GA

Lydia Bee
Redding School of the Arts
Redding, CA

Carrie Brooks (Brady)
Dacula Middle School
Augusta, GA

Cassandra Appleby
Glen Oaks Elementary
McKinney, TX

Deborah Dudley
Dacula Middle School
Dacula, GA

Jackie Ellet
Dacula Middle School and
Fort Daniel Elementary
Dacula, GA

Jessica Fisher
Porter Middle School
Granada Hills, CA

Donald Gruber
Clinton Junior High School
Clinton, IL

Cathy Kayrouz
Stuart Middle School
Louisville, KY

Suzanne Kunkle
Bob Courtway Middle School
Conway, AR

Amanda Linn
Harmony Grove School
Benton, AR

Lynn Ludlam
Memorial Middle School
Houston, TX

Joan Maresh
George Washington Carver
High School
Houston, TX

Tegwin Matenaer
Redding School of the Arts
Redding, CA

Eileen McClellan
Westbriar Middle School
Houston, TX

Gerald Obregon
Norland Middle School
Miami, FL

Marilyn Polin
Cutler Ridge Middle School
Miami, FL

Rosanne Stutts
Davidson Fine Art School
Augusta, GA

Chris Vigardt
J.P. McConnell Middle School
Loganville, GA

Jane Wells
Kitty Hawk Middle School
Universal City, TX

Student Contributors

Fig. 1–13, Kaitlin Bishop, Hoschton, GA; Fig. 2–18, Laura Sutherland, Westbriar Middle School, Houston, TX; Fig. 2–24, Savannah Ankerick, Dacula, GA; Fig. 2–28, Nicole Amendola, Glen Oaks Elementary, McKinney, TX; Fig. 3–5, Kyle Wilson, J.P. McConnell Middle School, Loganville, GA; Fig. 3–11, Simone Moss, Cutler Ridge Middle School, Miami, FL; Fig. 3–16, Paul Willey, Bob Courtway Middle School, Conway, AR; Fig. 4–23, Chelsea King, Redding School of the Arts, Redding, CA; Fig. 5–8, Michelle Piven, Cutler Ridge Middle School, Miami, FL; Fig. 5–12, Andra Steinbergs, Redding School of the Arts, Redding, CA; Fig. 6–5, Paige Schulte, Westbriar Middle School, Houston, TX; Fig. 6–9, Kasey Givens, Glen Oaks Elementary School, McKinney, TX; Fig. 6–15, Davalena Napolitano, Porter Middle School, Granada Hills, CA; Fig. 7–8, Trish Crago, Redding School of the Arts, Redding, CA; Fig. 7–10, Laura Lynch, Memorial Middle School, Houston, TX; Fig. 7–13, Korina Steinbergs, Redding School of the Arts, Redding, CA; Fig. 8–10, Heather V. Moore, Dacula Middle School, Dacula, GA; Fig. 8–12, Winter Fox Frank, Redding School of the Arts, Redding, CA; Fig. 8–14, Elyse Pate, Dacula Middle School, Augusta, GA; Fig. 9–8, Allyson Cunningham, Stuart Middle School, Louisville, KY; Fig. 9–10, Molly Boyd, Bellevue Public School, Bellevue, WA; Fig. 9–12, Winter Fox Frank, Redding School of The Arts, Redding, CA; Fig. 10–9, Joya Bush-Hopgood, Davidson Fine Arts School, Augusta, GA; Fig. 10–11, Brianna Ruch, Kitty Hawk Middle School, Universal City, TX; Fig. 10–13, Nora Pinnell, Norland Middle School, Miami, FL; Fig. 11–7, Adam Kyle Fiddler, Dacula Middle School, Dacula, GA; Fig. 11–9, Amanda Ray, Redding School of the Arts, Redding, CA; Fig. 11–11, Emily Morris, Victoria Hammond, Britt Pecht, Kate Guadagno, Kyle Irby, Kevin Roberts, Sarah Blythe Butler, Katie Hubbell, Hebron Christian Academy, Dacula, GA; Fig. 12–10, Jose Gomez, Westbriar Middle School, Houston, TX; Fig. 12–12, Colby Newton, Dacula Middle School, Dacula, GA; Fig. 12–14, Thomas Hanson, Harmony Grove High School, Benton, AR; Fig. 13–11, Dennis Mosley, Davidson Fine Arts School, Augusta, GA; Fig. 13–14, Kaitlin Bishop, Hoschton, GA; Fig. 13–16, Kody Knoth, Clinton Junior High School, Clinton, IL; Fig. 14–8, Jordan Maze, Redding School of The Arts, Redding, CA; Fig. 14–11, Samantha Wells, Stuart Middle School, Louisville, KY; Fig. 14–14, Carol Carranza, Porter Middle School, Granada Hills, CA; Fig. 15-7, Martin Casper, George Washington Carver High School, Houston, TX; Fig. 15–9, Brianna Ruch, Kitty Hawk Middle School, Universal City, TX; Fig. 15-11, Brad Conklin, George Washington Carver High School, Houston, TX.

Contents

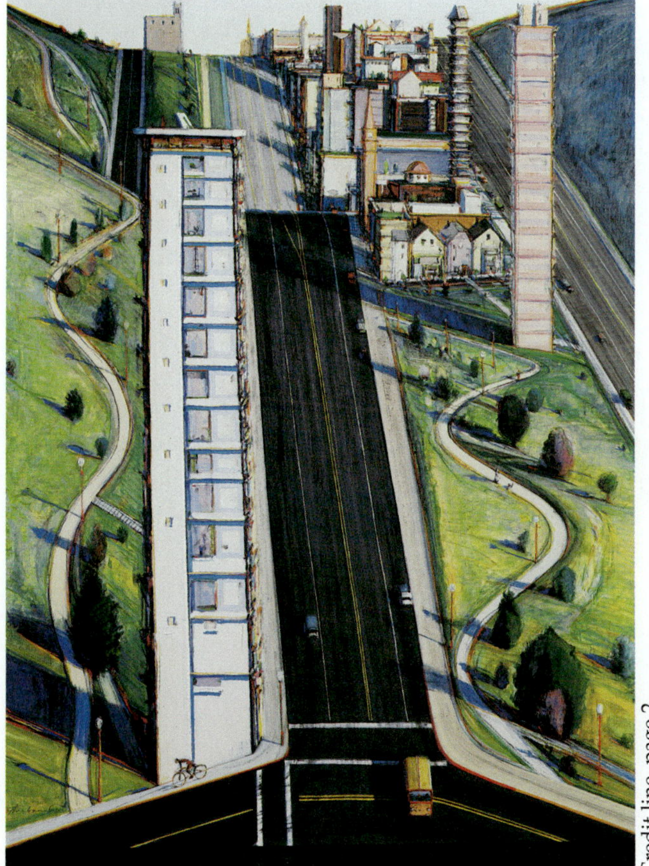

Credit line, page 2

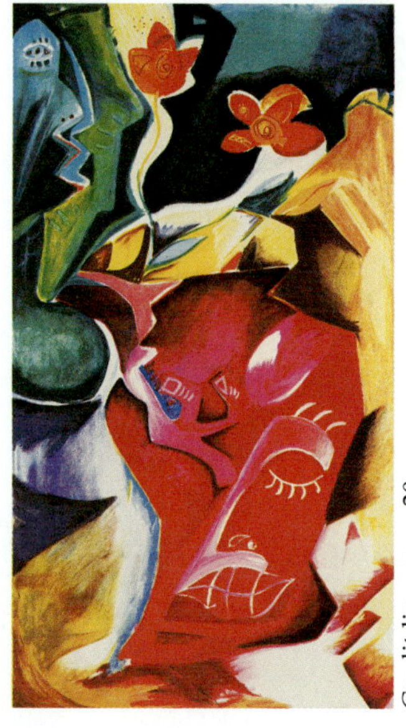

Credit line, page 20

Chapter 3

The Principles of Art 46

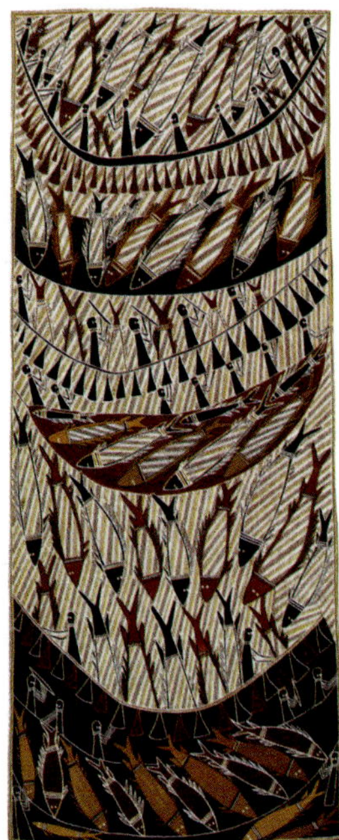

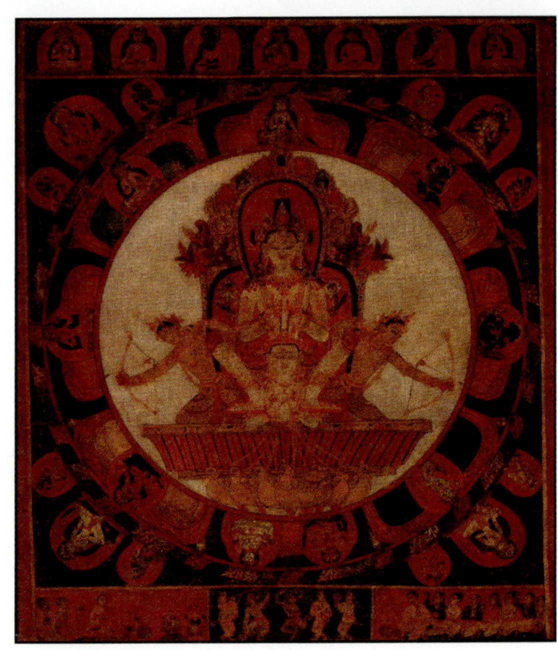

Chapter 4

Exploring Art Media 66

Chapter 5

Art Criticism and Aesthetics

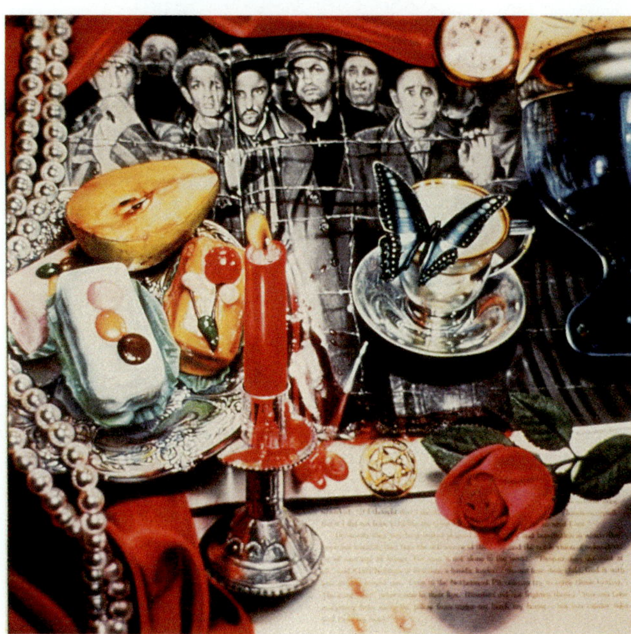

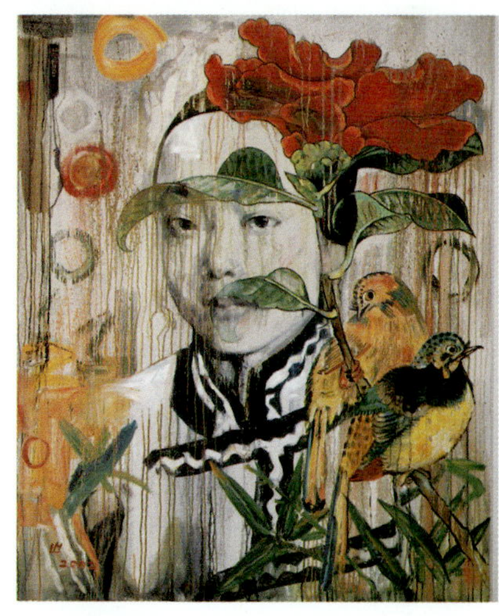

Chapter 6

Art History and You

Chapter 7

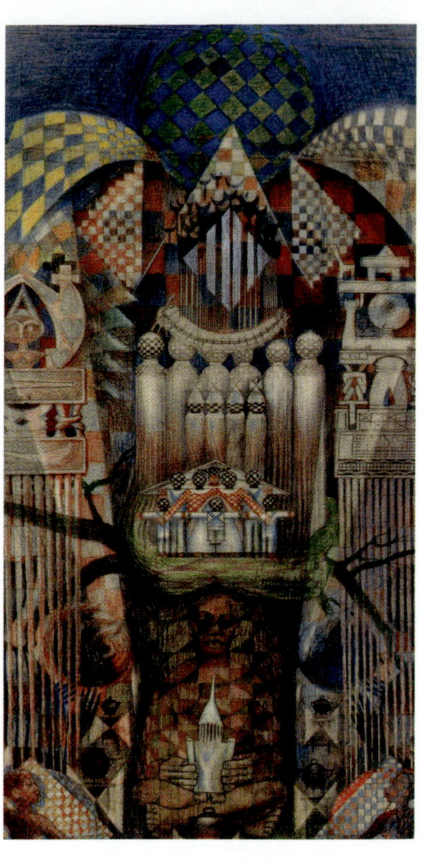

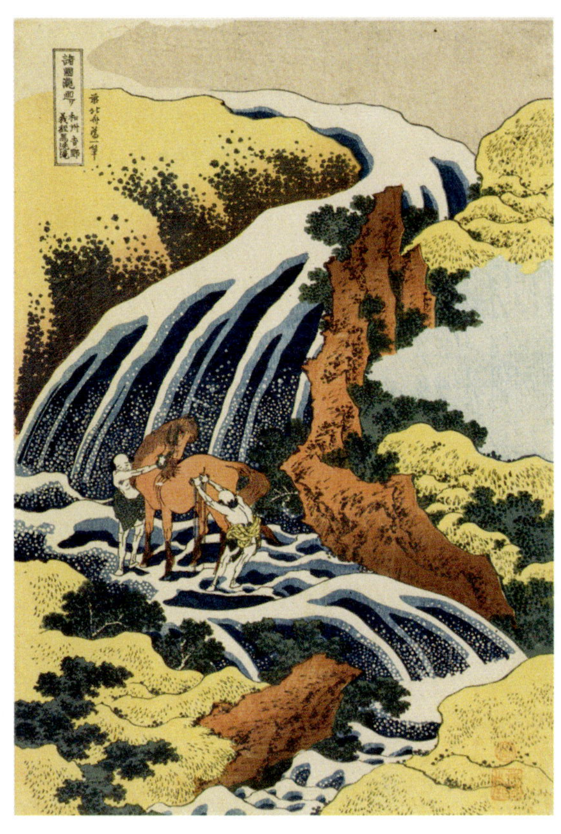

Chapter 8

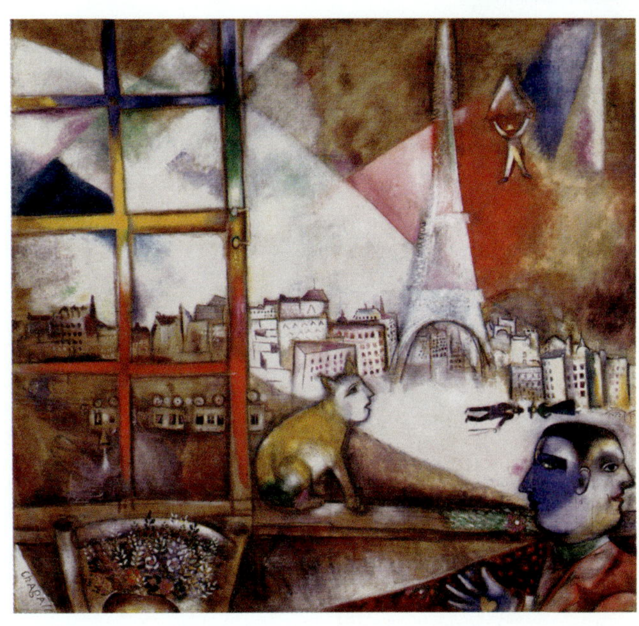

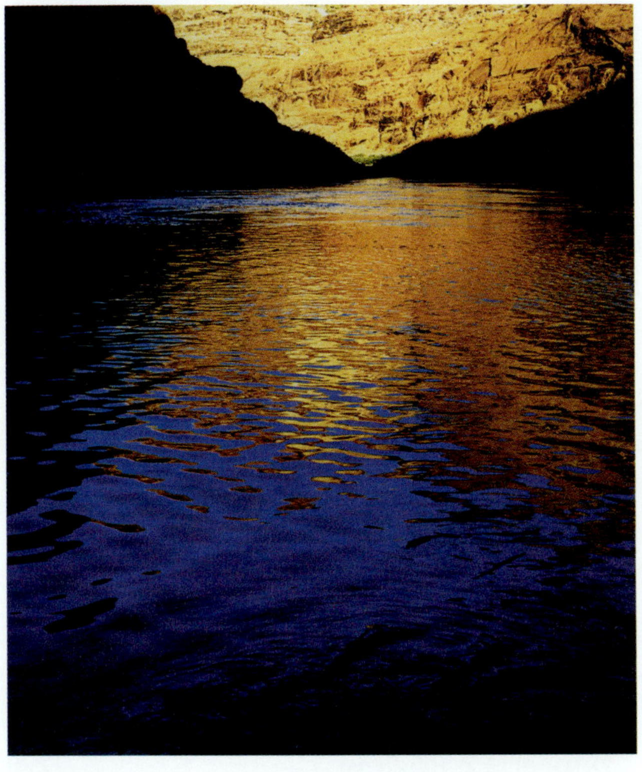

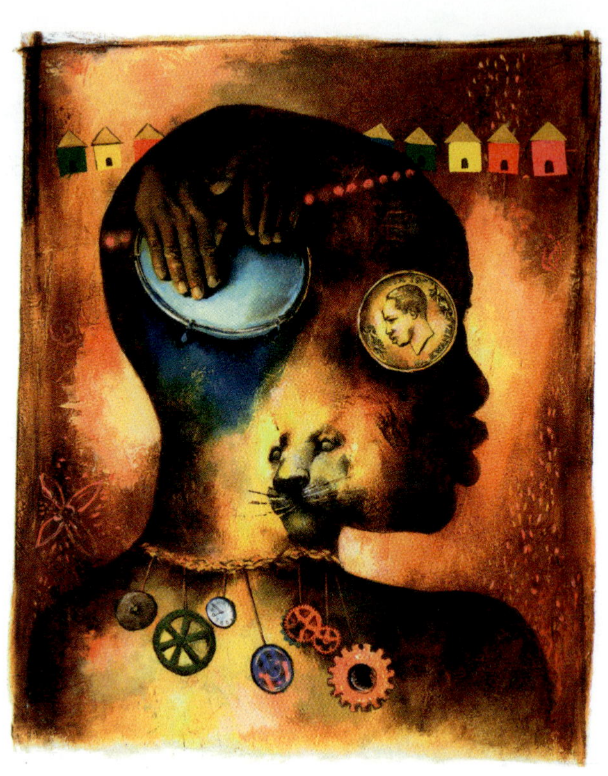

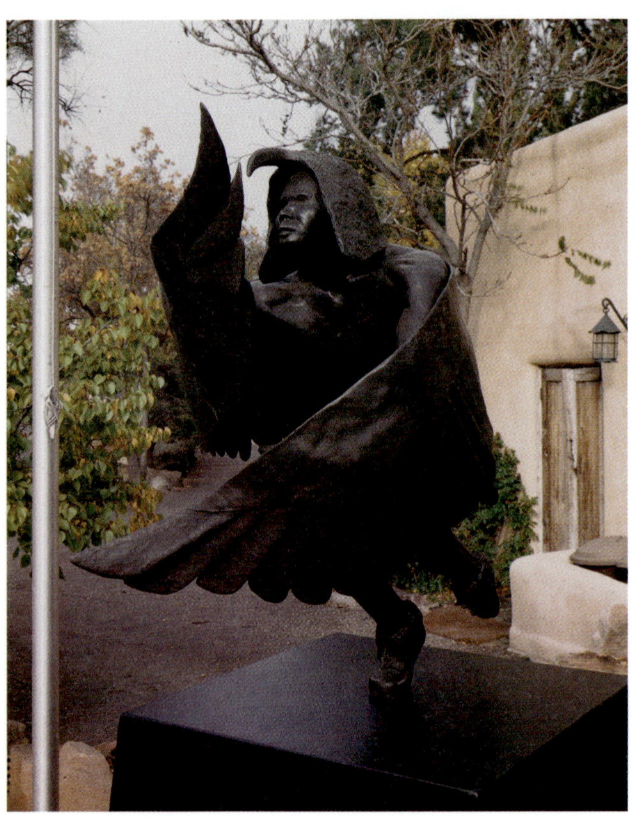

Chapter 13

Crafts

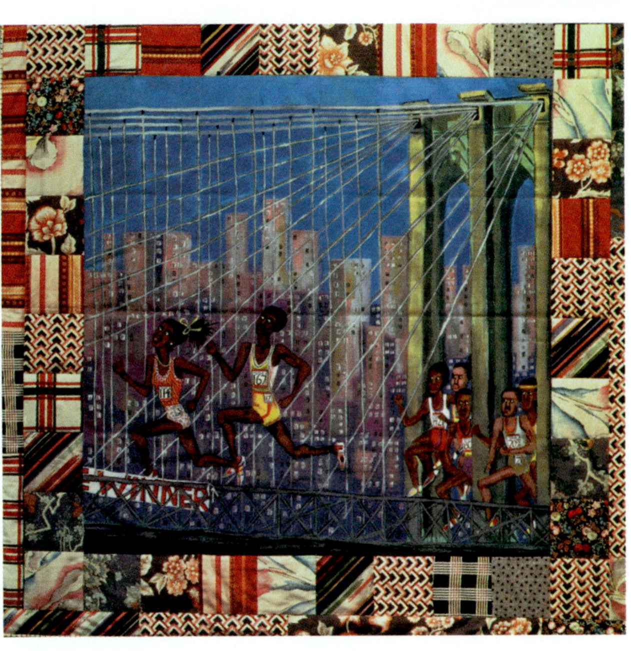

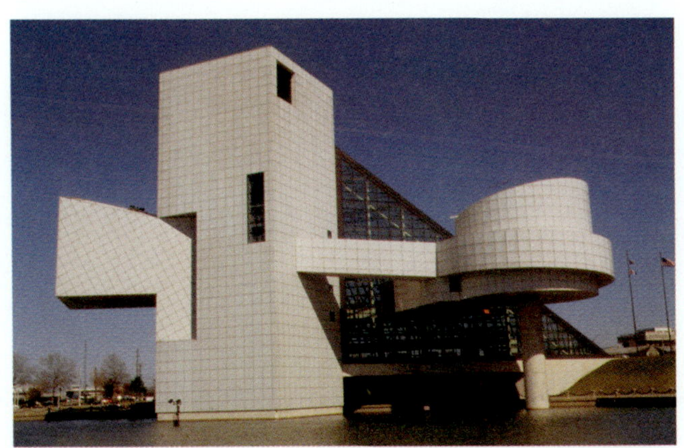

Chapter 14

Architecture

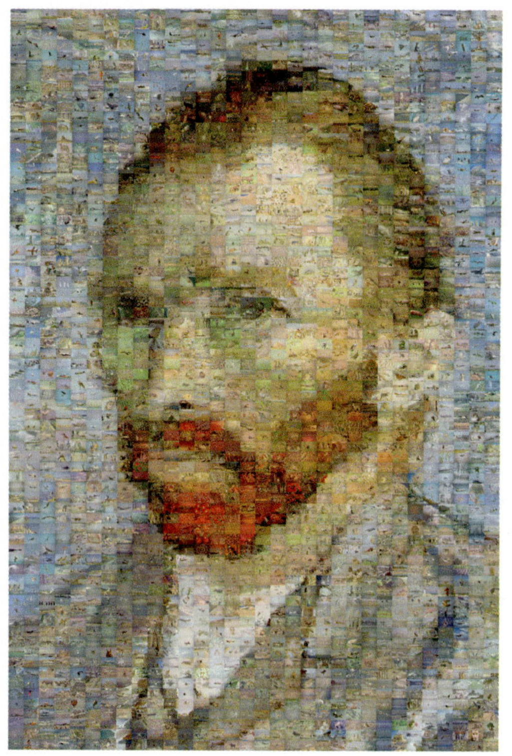

Handbook

Studio Lessons by Media

Acrylics and Oil Pastels

Chalk

Ceramic and Plaster

Electronic Media

Fiberart

Paper

Pencil, Pen, Charcoal, and Markers

Photography

Printmaking

Tempera

Watercolor

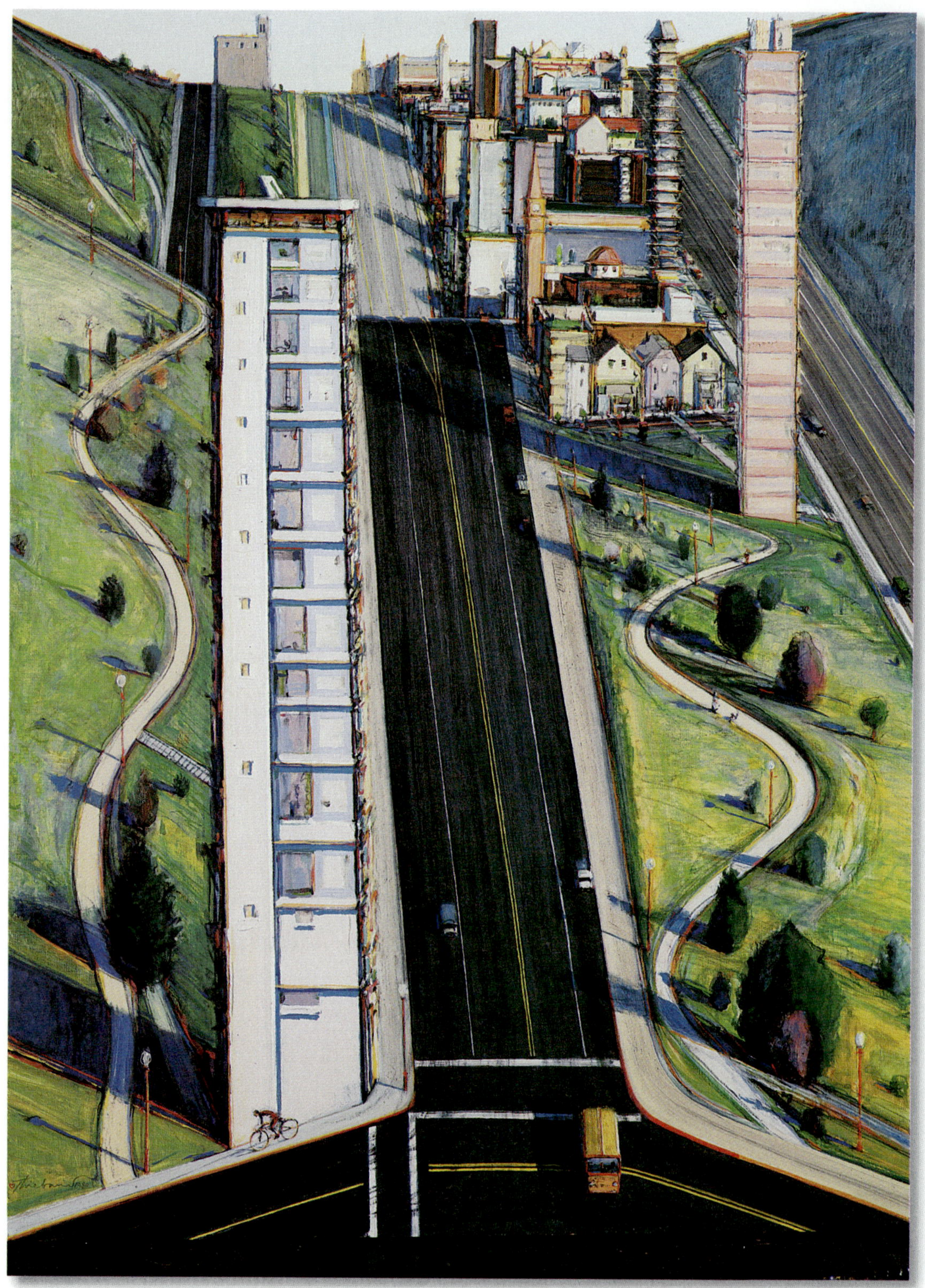

Focus On ◆ **Figure 1–1 Examine this painting. Then read the artist's comment on the opposite page. What feeling do you think the artist is trying to capture?**

Wayne Thiebaud. *Down Eighteenth Street.* 1980. Oil and charcoal on canvas. 122 × 91.1 cm (48 × 35⅞″). Hirshhorn Museum and Sculpture Garden, Smithsonian Institution, Washington, D.C. Museum purchase with funds donated by Edward R. Downe, Jr., 1980. © Wayne Thiebaud/Licensed by VAGA, New York, NY.

Chapter 1

Art in Your World

> *"To capture the swooping sense of space in San Francisco, you have to feel it in the pit of your stomach."* — **Wayne Thiebaud (b. 1920)**

Art is like a well-written story. Like a writer, an artist starts out with an interesting idea, event, or thought. He or she then captures this idea and expresses it in a way that often communicates strong feelings or emotions. What feeling do you get when you look at the painting on the left? What would it feel like to run or skateboard down this hill?

After completing this chapter, you will be able to:

- Develop perceptual skills.
- Identify avocational and career opportunities in art.
- Identify characteristics of fine art and applied art.
- Explain how artists create artworks based on direct observation, personal experience, and imagination.
- Analyze ways that international, historical, and political issues influence artworks.
- Discuss how subject, composition, and content relate to works of art.

Quick Write

Interpreting the Quote Read the quote by the artist, Wayne Thiebaud. Then look again at his painting in **Figure 1–1.** Write a descriptive paragraph that captures the idea expressed in the quote and the painting.

KEY TERMS

art
perceive
artists
fine art
applied art
patrons of the arts
portfolio
collage
subject
nonobjective
composition
formal properties
content
credit line

What Is Art?

You are about to enter an exciting world. This is a world of amazing ideas and baffling puzzles. It's a world in which cultural and historical heritage is expressed. It is a place to explore your creativity and challenge your problem-solving skills. At the same time, you will become more aware of your environment. The images and objects you encounter will stir your imagination. This is the world of art.

What exactly *is* art? There are many definitions of this term. In this book, **art** will be described as *a visual statement that communicates an idea, expresses a feeling, or presents an interesting design.* Artists make these visual statements using many different tools, materials and methods. Some artists paint, while others create sculpture. Sometimes they use cameras or computers as tools for creating art.

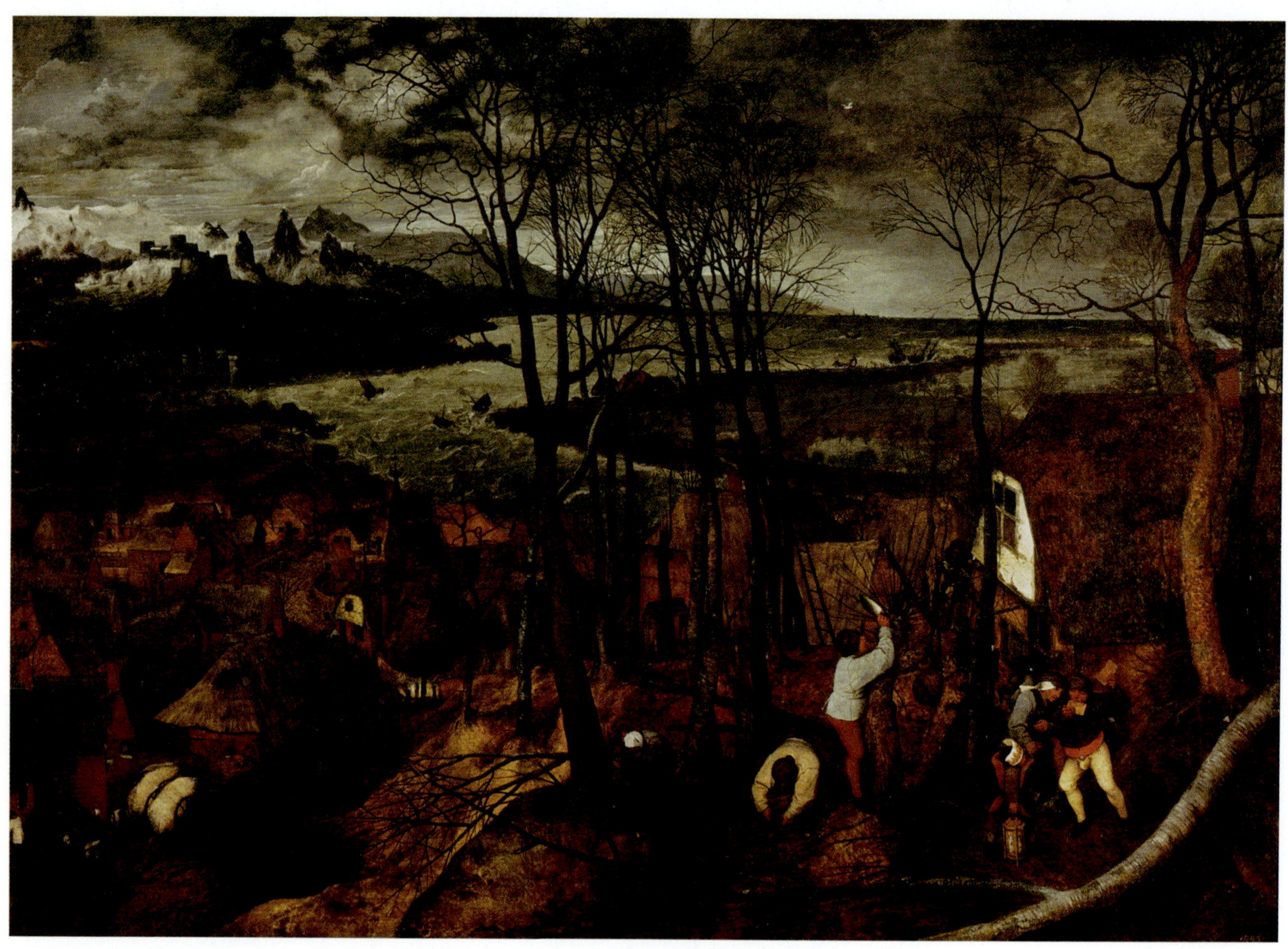

◆ **Figure 1–2** **Did you notice that this storm has already dumped snow on the mountains in the background? What do you think it would feel like to be the people in the foreground of this painting?**

Pieter Bruegel the Elder. *Gloomy Day.* 1565. Wood. 118 × 163 cm (46½ × 64$^{3}/_{16}$″). Kunsthistorisches Museum, Vienna, Austria.

Developing Perceptual Skills

Learning about art involves more than just looking at an object. It involves seeing, or *perceiving*. To **perceive** is *to become aware through the senses of the special nature of objects.* These perceptual skills can be developed by increasing visual awareness. This can be done by closely studying an object or scene and examining the details.

To understand the difference between looking and perceiving, examine **Figure 1–2**. How would you describe this painting? You might note that this is a skillfully done picture of a coastal village. You might add that there are several people working outdoors, yet there is much more going on in this painting. Look again, and focus your attention on the trees. Notice that the branches are bare. This observation provides a clue to the time of year: the scene is set in the fall or early winter.

Next, look at the sky. Its appearance gives clues about the weather. Dark clouds have gathered overhead, signaling the approach of a storm. In fact, the storm has already reached portions of the town below. Notice the choppy seas toward the center of the painting. Waves toss boats about, causing some of them to capsize.

This is no ordinary storm. Nor is this a simple painting of an outdoor scene. It depicts people securing their homes minutes before a storm. It is a visual tale in which people prepare for the power of nature.

Learning from Art

Art has the power to challenge our minds and stir up our feelings. The ability to interpret art can be learned with practice. This art program will prepare you to use your eyes and mind to analyze many different kinds of art. As each new art experience unfolds, your ability to perceive and create art will increase.

You can always learn from art, whether or not you choose to pursue art as a vocation, or career. Studying or creating art as a hobby also helps you gain knowledge of and appreciation for art.

Avocational and Career Opportunities

There are many *avocational* opportunities in art. Avocational means not related to a job or career. Creating paintings, jewelry, fiber-art, or ceramics can be fun and rewarding.

Pursuing art for personal enjoyment can teach you life skills as well. It can help strengthen your problem-solving skills. For example, you can use the elements and principles of art to come up with a design solution for a project. Creating art for recreation also allows you to experiment with a variety of tools, materials, and techniques.

Creating art as an avocation can sharpen your interpersonal skills, which involves working and communicating with others. For example, you might participate in a group critique after creating a studio project in the classroom. This can improve your ability to analyze works by peers and others. It can also help provide insight into your personal artworks.

You may wish to pursue art as a career. To find out more about various art careers, refer to the **Career Spotlights,** *Handbook* pages 302–308.

You can also visit **art.glencoe.com** for a more extensive list of career opportunities or choices.

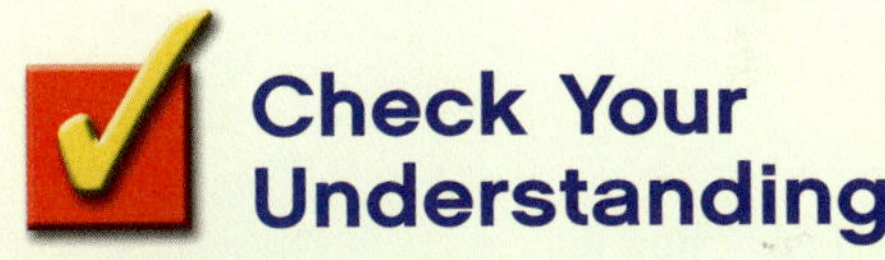

Check Your Understanding

1. Identify ways you can improve your perceptual skills.
2. Identify avocational opportunities or choices in art.

LESSON 2

Examining Artworks

When you see an interesting movie, do you keep the experience to yourself, or do you tell your friends about it? This eagerness to share experiences and feelings with others is a typical human trait. It is also a reason why artists like to make art. **Artists** are *people who use imagination, creativity, and skill to communicate ideas in visual form.* Artists often use problem-solving skills to effectively communicate their ideas. These ideas may represent experiences, feelings, or events in the artist's life.

Artists and Their Work

Artists are creative thinkers who often use their problem-solving skills. Artists combine a knowledge of art materials, tools, and methods with a rich imagination and deep sensitivity. They use this combination to present their views of and reactions to the world around them.

Fine Art

Have you heard the expression "Art for art's sake"? This expression refers to *art valued for its visual appeal or success in communicating ideas or feelings.* Such art is known as **fine art.**

Fine art can be made with a variety of materials. The sculpture in **Figure 1–3** is made of bronze, the one in **Figure 1–4** of stones. **Figure 1–5** is an oil painting. The artist who made it applied paint to canvas. What materials were used by the artist who did the painting that opened this chapter on page 2?

Applied Art

In contrast to fine art, **applied art** is *art made to be functional as well as visually pleasing.* Many of the objects used in daily life can be

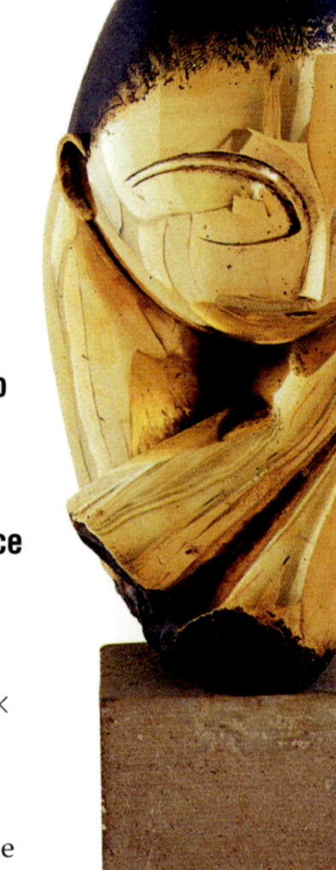

◆ **Figure 1–3** **How do you think this sculpture would feel to the touch? What role might this have played in the artist's choice of materials?**

Constantin Brancusi. *Mlle Pogany.* (Margin Pogany). 1913. Bronze. 43.8 × 21.5 × 31.7 cm (17¼ × 8½ × 12½). Museum of Modern Art, New York, New York. Acquired through the Lillie P. Bliss Bequest. © 2003 Artists Rights Society (ARS), New York/ADAGP, Paris.

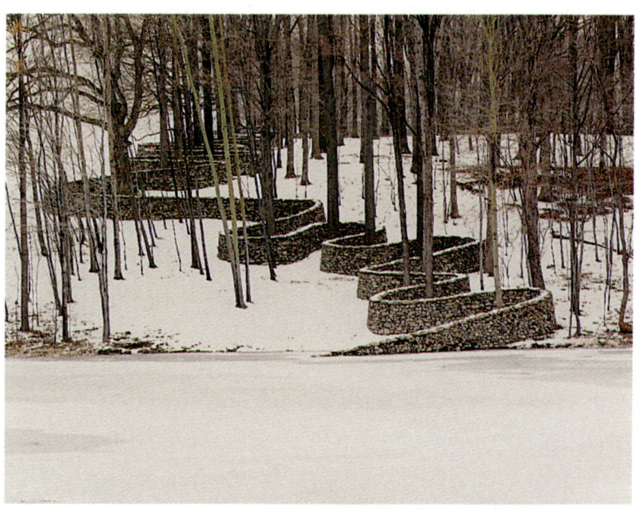

◆ **Figure 1–4** **The artist gathered stones to create this artwork. What materials in your community might you use in your own art?**

Andy Goldsworthy. *Storm King Wall.* Field stone. Approx. 1.5 × 694.5 m (5′ × 2,278′6″ overall). Storm King Art Center, Mountainville, New York. Photograph by Jerry L. Thompson.

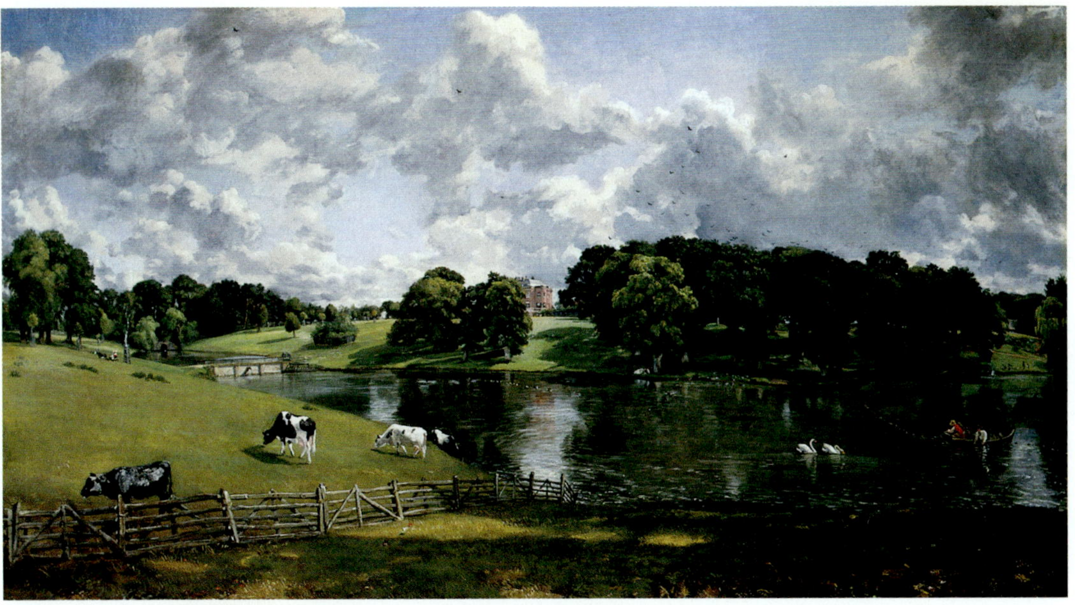

◆ **Figure 1–5** **What time of year is depicted in this nature scene? How can you tell?**

John Constable. *Wivenhoe Park, Essex.* 1816. Oil on canvas. 56.1 × 101.2 cm ($22\frac{1}{8} \times 39\frac{7}{8}''$). National Gallery of Art, Washington, D.C. Widener Collection.

classified as applied art. Jewelry, pottery, and furniture are examples of applied art.

Another example is the "art object" in **Figure 1–6.** You probably have one of these items in your home. It's a teapot. Look closely at this particular teapot. Notice the unusual design of the pot. Examine the painting on its surface. Did you notice the lizard that is perched below the teapot's spout? This teapot can be classified as applied art because it serves a practical purpose and is visually pleasing. How does it compare to the teapot in your home?

Today the distinction between fine and applied art is fading. The teapot you just examined is displayed in a museum. As you will learn in the chapter on crafts, various items such as drinking vessels, pitchers, and bowls, have come into their own as fine art.

◆ **Figure 1–6** **Why do you think the artist gave this object the name he did?**

Kurt Weiser. *Blue Horizon.* 1992. Porcelain, china paint. The Mint Museums, Charlotte, North Carolina. Museum purchase: Delhom Service League Fund. 1993. 5a–b

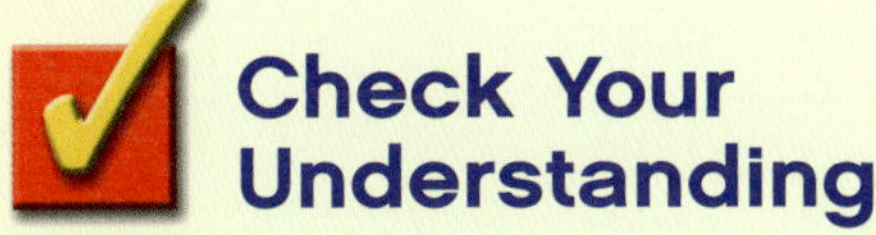

Check Your Understanding

1. What is an *artist?*
2. What is *fine art?* Name two pieces of fine art shown in this lesson.
3. What is *applied art?* Can any teapot be classified as applied art? Why or why not?

LESSON 3

Artists and Ideas

Artists, by nature, have strong perceptual skills and vivid imaginations. They might pass by a pile of pebbles on the beach and see the shape of a snail. An artist may see a simple boat docked in the water differently from other people. He or she might notice the grainy texture of the wooden boat or the way light plays upon the water's surface. Using their skills and talents, artists will then bring such images to life.

Sometimes, artists will go beyond their imaginations in search of inspiration. In this lesson, you will explore some of the sources they turn to. Later on, as you create art of your own, you may want to turn to some of these sources as well.

Sources of Inspiration

The ancient Greeks prayed to special goddesses called Muses (**myooz**-uhz) to inspire them with ideas. They even built shrines to honor the Muses. In more recent times artists have looked elsewhere to get their inspiration. These are sources you may want to turn to for inspiration:

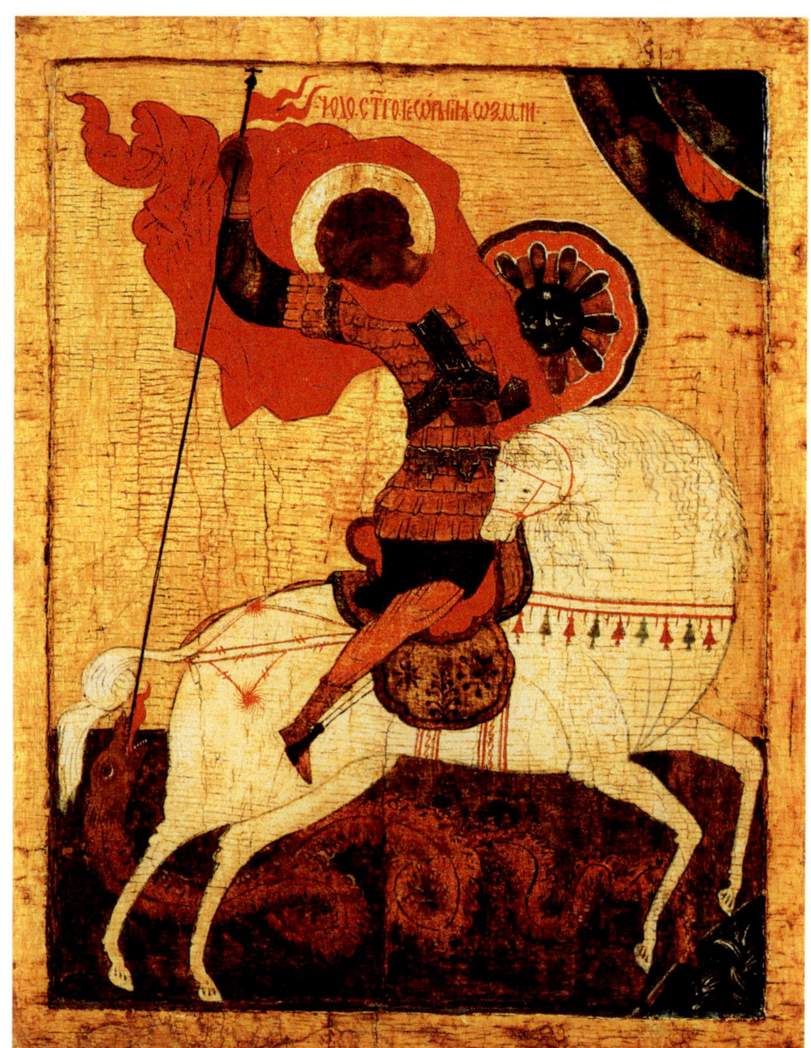

◆ **Figure 1–7** **What other myths and legends can you think of? What characters and other details would you show if you were an artist portraying one of these legends?**

St. George the Dragonslayer. Novgorod School. Early fifteenth century. 82 × 63 cm (32¼ × 24¾"). Tretiakov Gallery, Moscow, Russia.

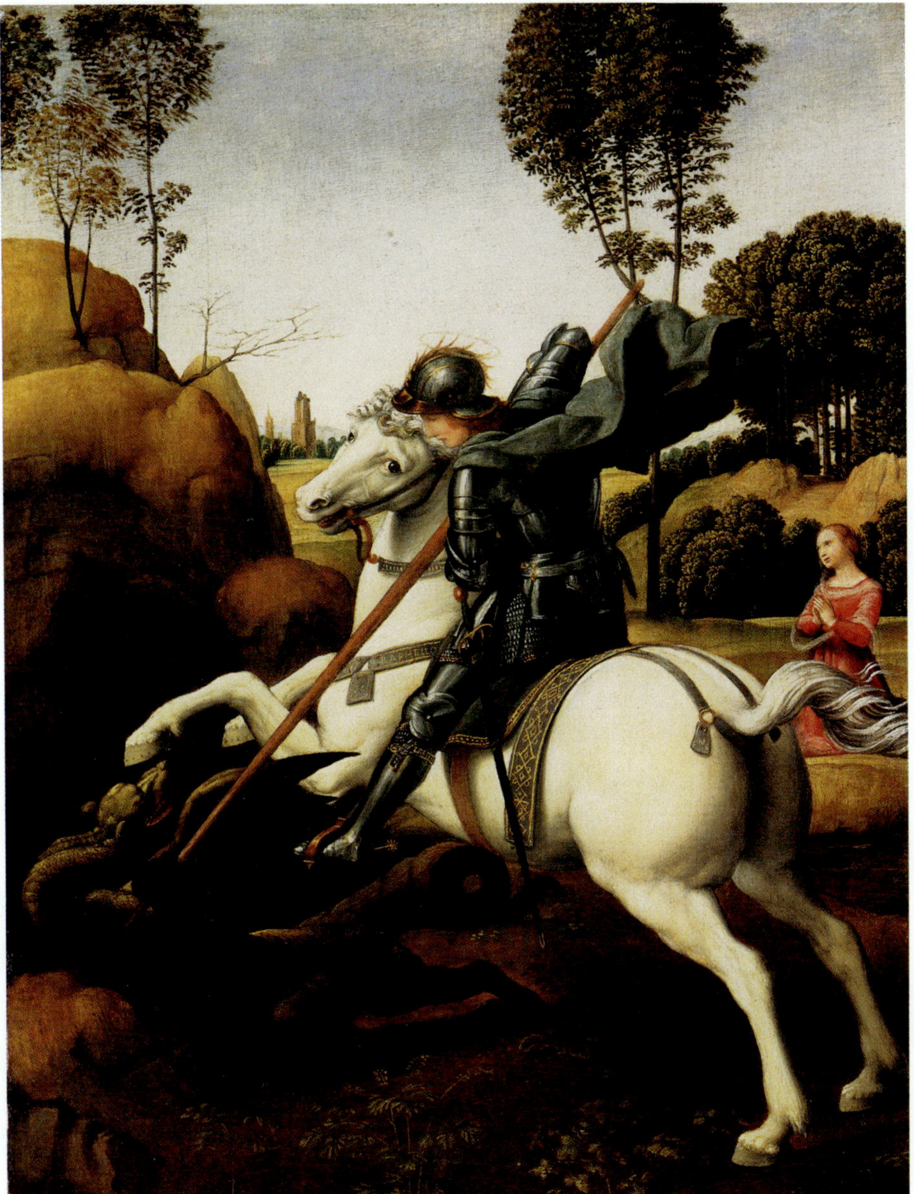

◆ **Figure 1–8** **How does this painting differ from the one shown in Figure 1–7, which was created in the previous century? What similarities do you notice?**

Raphael. *St. George and the Dragon.* 1504–06. Oil on wood. 28.5 × 21.5 cm (11⅛ × 8⅜″). National Gallery of Art, Washington, D.C. Andrew W. Mellon Collection.

- **Nature.** Look through this book, and you will find numerous paintings and other artworks depicting the outdoors. Many of the artists responsible for these works were inspired by nature and recorded what they saw. As an example, look again at Figure 1–5 on page 7. What are some natural features shown in this painting?
- **Myths and legends.** Some artists borrow ideas from literature or legend. The anonymous artist who made the painting in **Figure 1–7** based his work on the story of Saint George and the Dragon. Are you familiar with this famous tale?
- **Artists of the past.** Art is not made in a vacuum. Artists of a particular time period often influence later generations, who build on the work of those who came before them. Does the painting in **Figure 1–8** look at all familiar? It should. It is based on the painting you just examined in Figure 1–7.

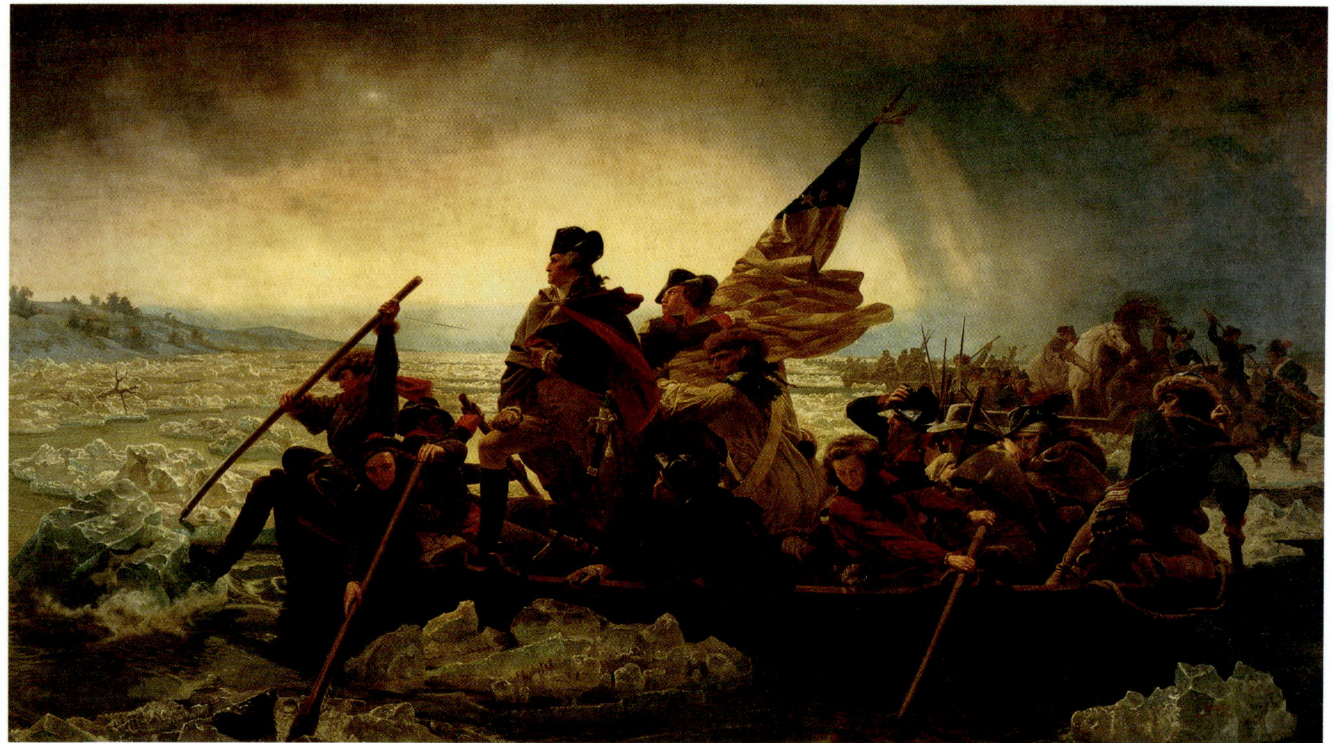

◆ **Figure 1–9** **Analyze ways that historical and political issues may have influenced this artwork.**

Emanuel Leutze. *Washington Crossing the Delaware.* 1851. Oil on canvas. 387.5 × 644 cm (149 × 255″). The Metropolitan Museum of Art, New York, New York. Gift of John Stewart Kennedy, 1897.

- **International, historical, and political issues.** The painting in **Figure 1–9** depicts an event from the Revolutionary War. Do you recognize the person standing in the boat? What historical event is depicted in this painting? Now analyze Figure 6–1 on page 112, which incorporates a black-and-white photograph in the background. What international issue is depicted in this painting? Political issues can also be used as subjects for artworks. Identify the political issue portrayed in Figure 7-14 on page 146.

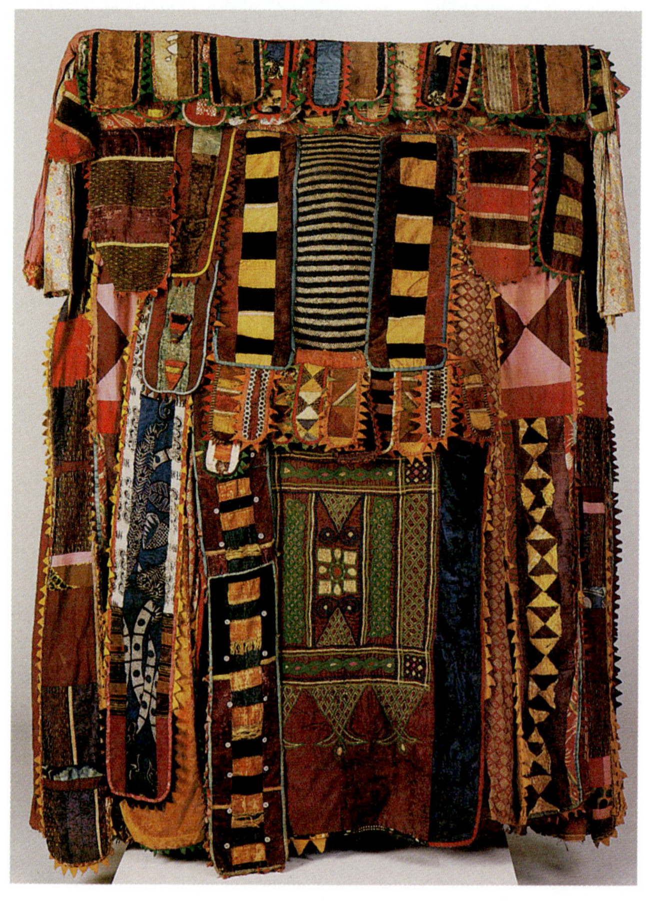

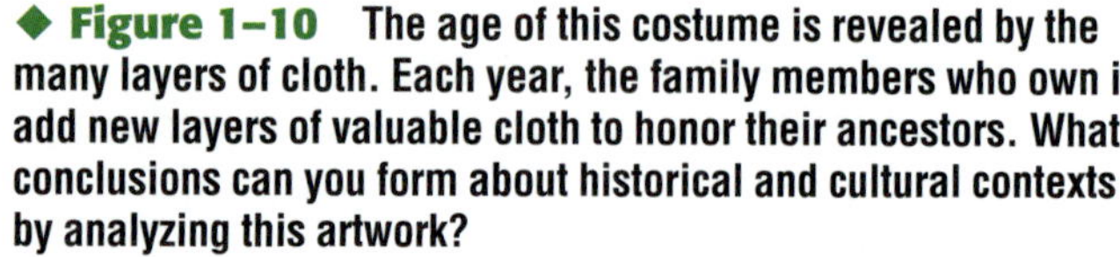

◆ **Figure 1–10** **The age of this costume is revealed by the many layers of cloth. Each year, the family members who own it add new layers of valuable cloth to honor their ancestors. What conclusions can you form about historical and cultural contexts by analyzing this artwork?**

African, Yoruba, Nigeria. *Egungun from Ogbomoso.* Twentieth century, front. Cloth, wood, and buttons. Height: approx. 152.4 cm (60″). North Carolina Museum of Art, Raleigh, North Carolina. Purchased with funds provided through a bequest from Lucille E. Moorman. 97.5.3

- **Spiritual and religious beliefs**. Artists of every culture use their skills to create objects and images to express spiritual beliefs. The elaborate costume in **Figure 1–10** is worn during a special ceremony to honor deceased ancestors of the Yoruba people.
- **Ideas commissioned by employers**. Many individuals or organizations can hire artists to create works of art. Such employers are called *patrons*. **Patrons of the arts** are *sponsors, or supporters, of an artist or art-related events such as exhibitions.* Look carefully at the work in **Figure 1–11.** Did you notice the two figures in the mirror on the back wall? These were the artist's patrons, the king and queen of Spain. Why do you suppose the artist chose to include their likenesses in this work?

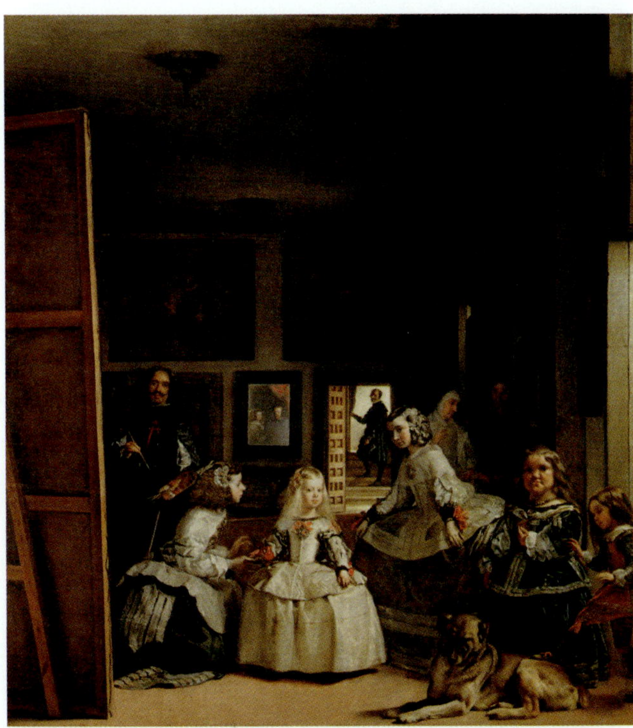

◆ **Figure 1–11** **The figure at the left side of the painting holding the brush and palette is the artist. Why do you think he included himself in this artwork?**

Diego Velázquez. *Las Meninas (with Velázquez self-portrait) or the Family of Philip IV.* 1656. Oil on canvas. 318.7 × 276 cm (10′ 5½″ × 9′ ¾″). Museo del Prado, Madrid, Spain. Art Resource, New York.

Studio Activity

Creating a Portfolio

Your personalized portfolio. A **portfolio** is *a carefully selected collection of artwork kept by students and professional artists.* Portfolios are used to hold a selection of your most outstanding works. They may also contain written observations, self-reflection, favorite reproductions, sketches, and teacher comments. A portfolio allows you to keep track of improvements in your work.

Because portfolios can be expensive, a handy alternative is to make your own. Cut a 14- x 22-inch rectangle out of each of two pieces of cardboard or poster board. Line up the rectangles lengthwise on a flat surface. Leave a gap between them about the thickness of a pencil. Cut a strip of packing tape 22 inches long. Carefully place the tape so that it covers the gap and connects both rectangles. Place a second piece of tape on the opposite side. You now have a hinged portfolio. Decorate the outside using color markers.

Include the following information with each new addition to your portfolio: your name, the date the work was completed, the medium, and your source or sources of inspiration.

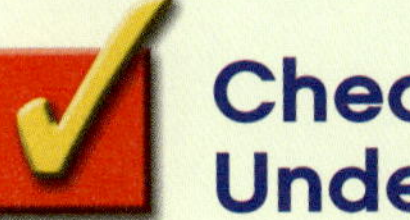

Check Your Understanding

1. Name and describe four sources of inspiration that can be used to develop your perceptual skills.
2. What are *patrons of the arts?*

Making a Collage

Artists constantly look for new forms of self-expression. The art form in **Figure 1–12,** for example, was created by Romare Bearden. It is a **collage** (kuh-**lahzh**), *an artwork made up of cut or torn materials pasted to a surface.* Most of Bearden's artworks focus on African American urban life. Typical of his work, Figure 1–12 combines photos with clippings from books and magazines, painted paper, and fabric.

What You Will Learn

You will produce a fiberart collage by selecting and using a variety of appropriate art materials and tools in traditional and experimental ways. You will interpret a subject or theme when producing this collage that illustrates a character from a story. You will use objects and shapes cut from newspapers and magazines. You will combine these with scraps of wallpaper, wrapping paper, and fabric.

What You Will Need

- Sketch paper, pencils, and erasers
- Magazines, newspaper, wallpaper, fabric, and wrapping-paper scraps
- Envelopes or sandwich bags
- 12 × 18-inch tag board, scissors
- White glue, paper towels
- Oil pastels or crayons (optional)
- Felt-tip fine-line marker (optional)

What You Will Do

1. Look closely at Figure 1–12. Notice how the people are made up of parts that do not necessarily match because they are cut from a variety of materials. Notice how simple flat shapes are used.
2. Brainstorm with your classmates about characters from stories you have read. What are some unique traits that make these characters stand out? What colors

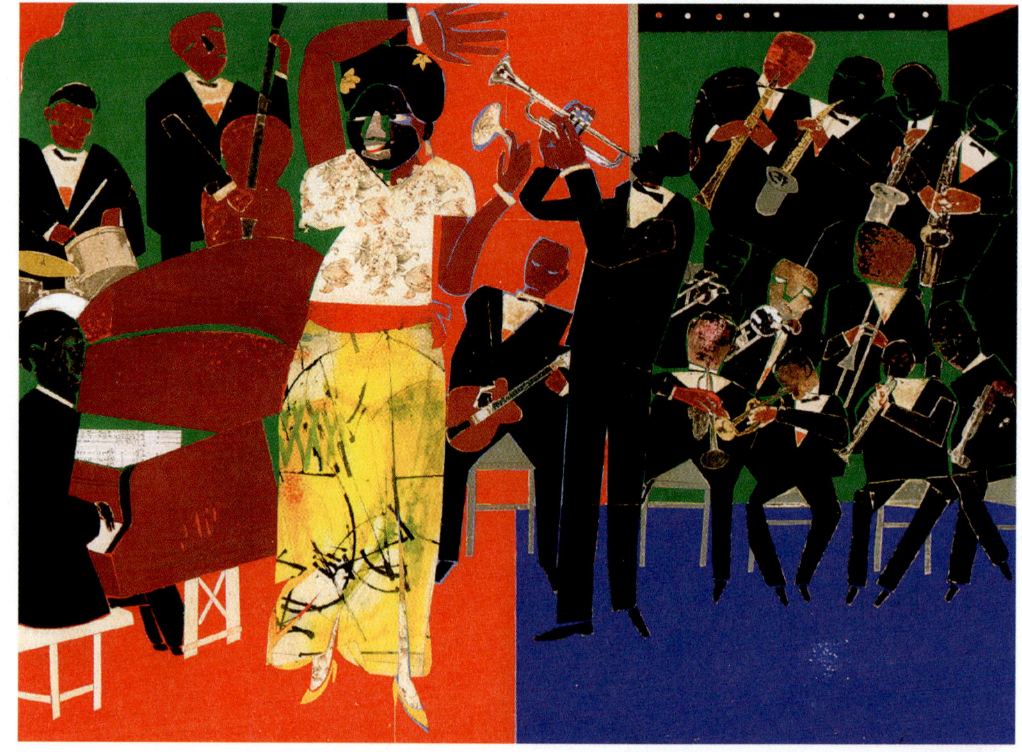

◆ **Figure 1–12** **Notice how some areas in this collage, such as the musicians' faces, look like they were cut from painted paper. Other areas, such as the singer's blouse, are cut from papers with designs.**

Romare Bearden. *Empress of the Blues.* 1974. Paper collage. 91.4 × 121 cm (36 × 48″). The National Museum of American Art, Smithsonian Institution, Washington, D.C. Museum purchase in part through Luisita L. and Franz H. Denghausen Endowment. Art Resource, New York. © Romare Howard Bearden Foundation, Inc./Licensed by VAGA, New York, NY.

would best represent their personalities? Are there any special objects associated with them?

3. Select a character that interests you. Make two or three sketches using flat simple shapes. Include any objects associated with your character.
4. Transfer the figure of your sketch onto another piece of sketch paper. Cut this out to use as a pattern to trace on your collage.
5. Collect newspapers, magazines, wallpaper, wrapping paper, construction paper, and fabric scraps. Choose colors that best represent your character. Use solid blocks of colors for the background. Arrange your cut pieces on your tag board until you are pleased with the composition, then glue them down. Keep the background simple so as not to compete with your figure.
6. Place your cut out pattern onto your selected fabrics and papers, trace and cut these out. A skirt may be one piece of paper, a shirt another. Use the photo images to create the head. Cut excess paper away from features such as eyes, nose, and mouth. Glue your figure and objects onto your background once you have them arranged to your satisfaction.
7. Experiment by using oil pastels or crayons to embellish your collage. A felt-tip fine-line marker can be used to add details.
8. Give your completed collage a title and display in a class exhibition.

Evaluating Your Work

- **Describe** What is the name of the story and character you chose? What objects and shapes did you choose to portray your character? What colors did you use to help convey your character's personality?

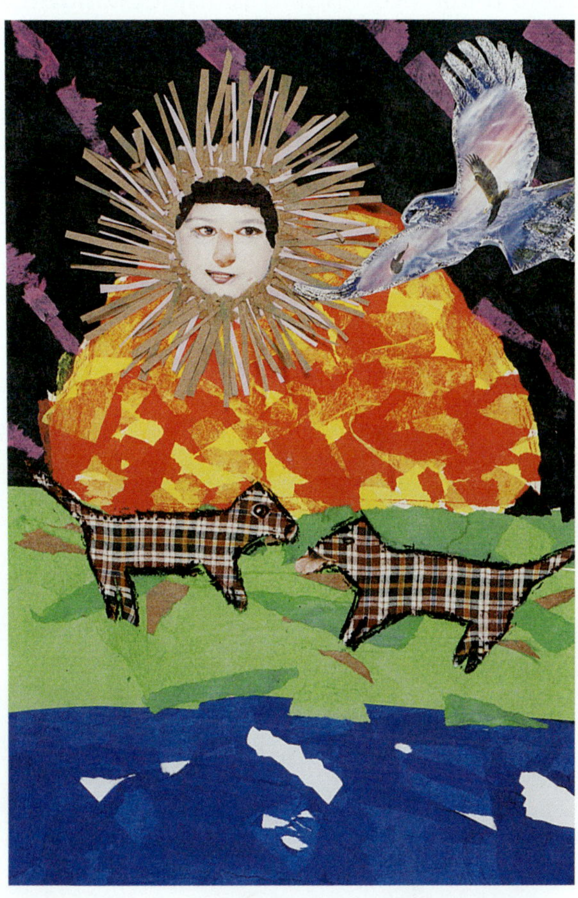

◆ **Figure 1–13** **Student work. Fiberart collage.**

COMPUTER OPTION

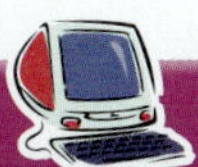

Produce electronic media-generated art by selecting and using a variety of appropriate art materials and tools in traditional and experimental ways. Look through clip-art files to interpret themes. For example, you might choose a sports or nature theme. Import or Copy the images for a collage into a computer art program. Adjust the size according to your design. Add color and textures to blend or to add contrast. Title, save, and print.

Visual Art Journal

A visual art journal can be a place to record your observations and thoughts about personal artworks and the artworks of others. For example, what clues does Bearden's collage give about his cultural heritage? Write down your thoughts in your journal.

Understanding Art

You may recall learning in literature that there are three ways to examine a short story: character, setting, and plot. Each answers a question that is critical to an understanding of the work. Character, for example, answers the question "Who is this story about?" Setting tells when and where the story takes place. Plot is the plan, or main story, of a literary work.

Just as with works of fiction, there are three ways to examine works of art. These are *subject*, *composition*, and *content*. Each of these answers a question central to a complete

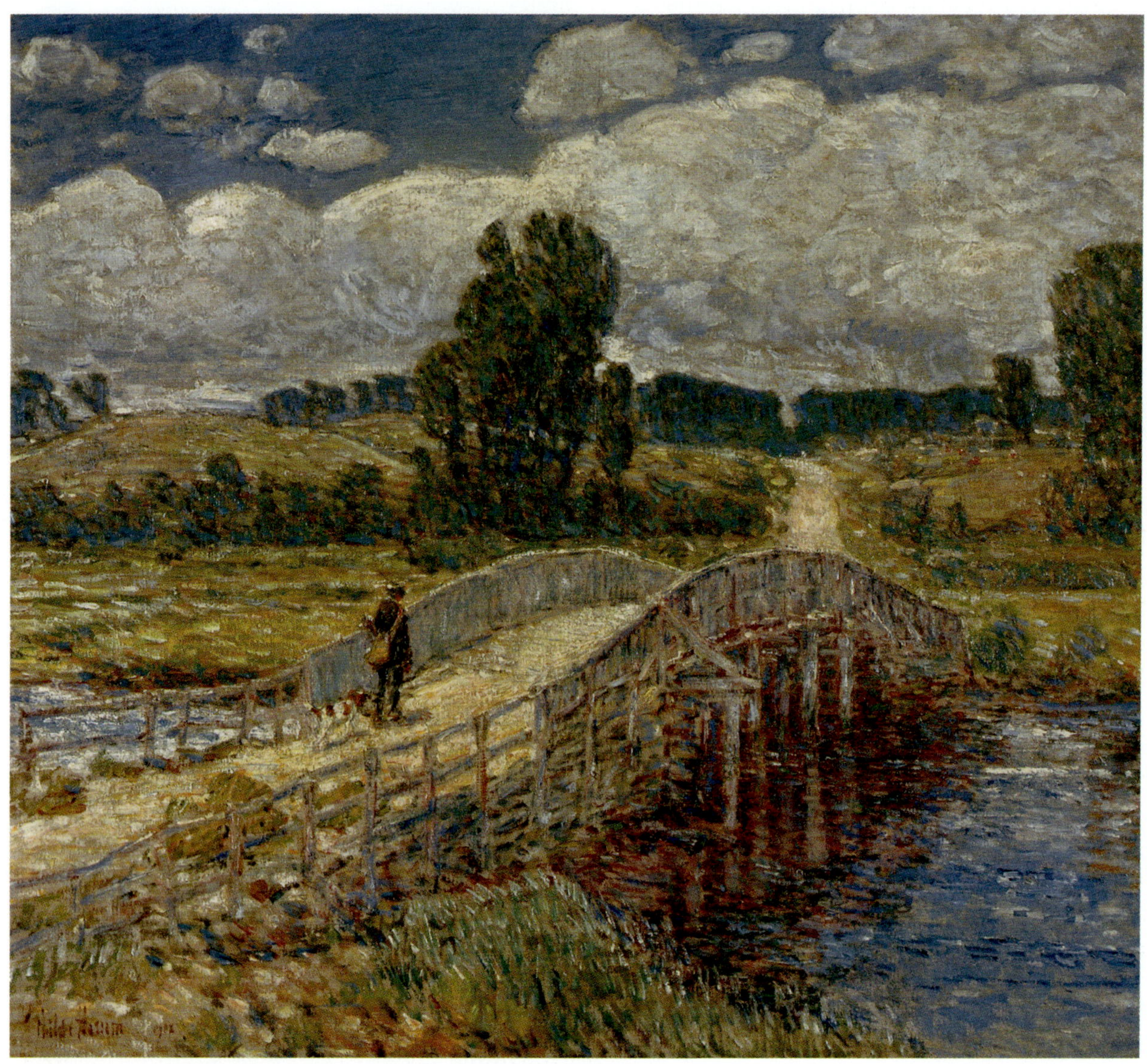

◆ **Figure 1–14** **What do you see in this painting? What might be going on here?**

Childe Hassam. *Bridge at Old Lyme*. 1908. Oil on canvas. 60 × 65.1 cm ($23\frac{5}{8} \times 25\frac{5}{8}$"). Georgia Museum of Art, University of Georgia, Athens, Georgia. Eva Underhill Hollbrook Memorial Collection of American Art, gift of Alfred H. Hollbrook.

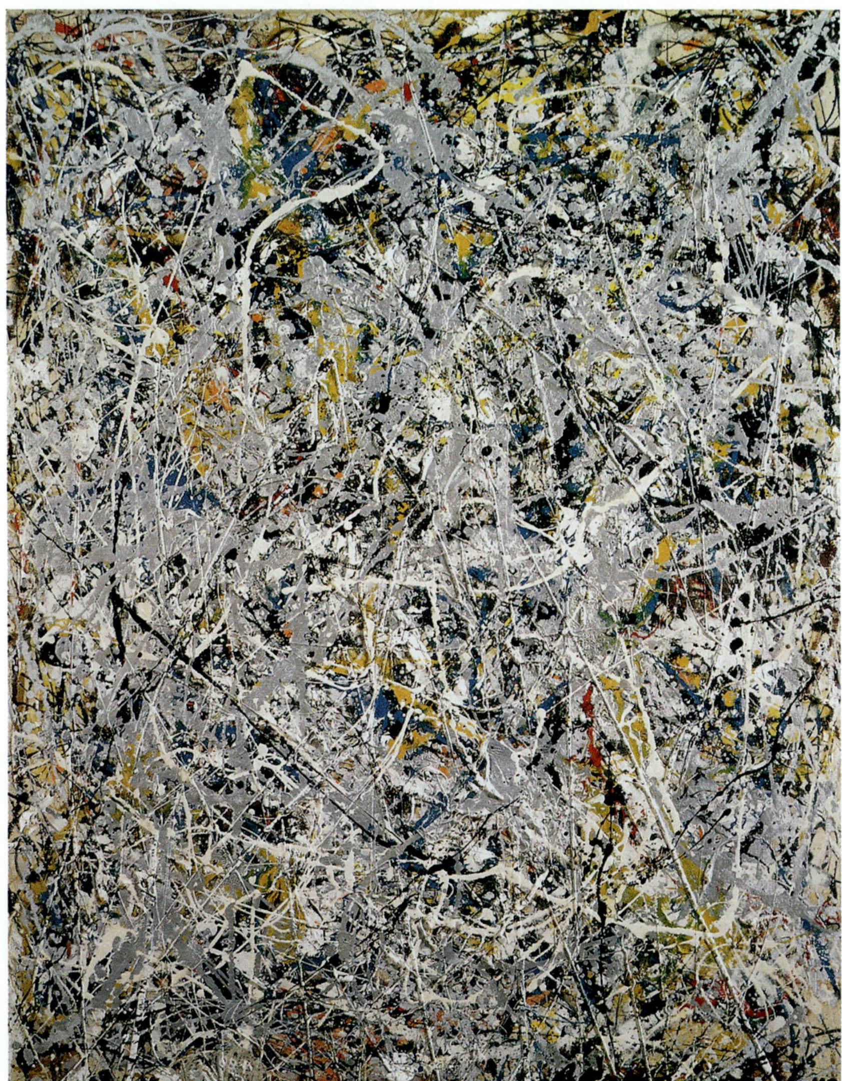

◆ **Figure 1–15** **The artist created nonobjective paintings like this by splashing and dripping paint onto a canvas.**

Jackson Pollock. *Number 9.* 1949. Oil on canvas. 112.1 × 86.7 cm (44¼ × 34″). Wadsworth Athenaeum Museum of Art, Hartford, Connecticut. Gift of Tony Smith. © 2003 Pollock-Krasner Foundation/Artists Rights Society (ARS), New York.

understanding of the work. In this lesson, you will learn about these ways to examine artworks. You will also learn about the credit line, which gives details about the artwork.

The Subject

In grammar, the subject of a sentence is the part that does the action. In an artwork, the **subject** is *the image that viewers can easily identify.* The subject answers the question, "What do I see when I look at this artwork?" As in grammar, an artwork's subject may be a person, place, thing, or event.

To better understand this point, examine the painting in **Figure 1–14.** The subject is easily recognized. The painting shows a simple country scene. Trees seem to sway gently under a blue sky thick with fleecy clouds. A grassy meadow on the left side slopes gently upward. A small wooden bridge is the only structure made by people. It crosses a quiet stream and connects a narrow dirt road.

The focal point of the subject is a human figure standing at the foot of the bridge on the near side. The person's age is impossible to determine because his or her back is to us, the viewers.

At the beginning of the twentieth century, some artists began creating works without subjects. An example of such a work is shown in **Figure 1–15.** Such art is known as **nonobjective.** The term means *having no recognizable subject matter.*

The Composition

When you combine sentences, you have a composition. In art, composition is also the result of combining units into a logical whole. Instead of individual words, artists use visual units called *elements of art.* Instead of rules of grammar, artists use *principles*—rules of visual design. The elements of art, which will be discussed in Chapter 2, include line, color, and shape. The principles, which will be covered in Chapter 3, include harmony, emphasis, and proportion. **Composition** in art, then, is *how formal properties are used to create unified artworks.* **Formal properties** refer to *the way the elements of art are organized by the principles of art.* Artists use these formal properties to create unified artworks.

Look at the detail of Figure 1–14 below. Find the large tree at the center of the work. Its green coloring and distinctive shape make it stand out vividly against the sky. Using your finger, trace down along the line formed by the tree's left edge. Where does this line take you? It leads you to the figure mentioned in the previous section. The lines that form the road and bridge do the same. All converge on and emphasize this sole human figure. The artist directs your eye to the painting's main focus by using the elements of shape, color, and line, and the principle of emphasis.

The Content

A successful written composition should have solid content. The same may be said of composition in art. In art, **content** is defined as *the message, feeling, or idea an artwork communicates.* Content answers the question, "What does the artwork mean or say?"

Sometimes, the content of an artwork is clear. At other times, the artist purposely leaves the viewer wondering and guessing. Look once again at Figure 1–14. The person in the painting appears to have stopped during a journey. The figure seems to be gazing out at something—but what? Maybe the person is caught up in the beautiful surroundings and has paused to admire the glory of nature. Possibly, the person is

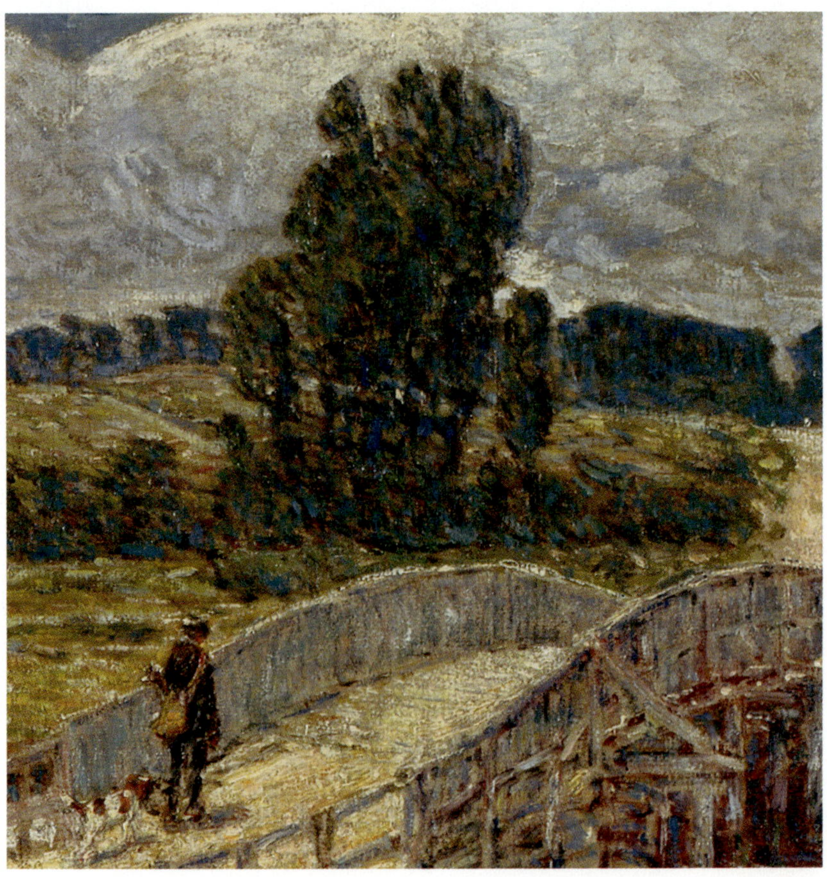

◆ **Figure 1–16** **Detail of Figure 1–14.**

Childe Hassam. *Bridge at Old Lyme.* (Detail).

heading home after suffering a personal tragedy or setback.

Perhaps the explanation is far simpler and less emotional than either of these interpretations. Maybe this person has been walking for hours and is just plain exhausted. He or she may be looking ahead wearily at the road, which stretches on forever. Since we cannot see the person's face, we can never know for sure. Yet, it is precisely this range of content possibilities that enhances the painting's richness. Because we don't know the person's state of mind, we are free to invent our own meaning.

Be mindful that even artworks without subjects can have expressive content. Reexamine the painting in Figure 1–15. Do you find your eye darting wildly from one place to another? The painting seems hectic and confusing. There is no rest or calm in this busy, congested work. The viewer's eye, rather, is in a constant state of motion.

The Credit Line

Look one last time at Figure 1–14. Do you know the name of the artist who created this work? Do you know the title of the work? Answers to these and other questions can be found in the credit line appearing alongside the work. A **credit line** is *a listing of important facts about an artwork.*

Every artwork in this book has a credit line. It is there to inform you of the basic facts about the artwork.

Reading a Credit Line

Most credit lines are made up of six facts. These facts, in the order in which they appear, are as follows:

- **The artist's name**. This information always comes first. So, who is the artist of the painting in Figure 1–14? How about the work in Figure 1–15?
- **The title of the work**. Many titles give useful information about the subject or content. Some are meant to arouse viewers' curiosity. Do you remember the title of the painting that opened this chapter (Figure 1–1, page 2)? Can you find a work in this chapter with the title *Wivenhoe Park, Essex*? Who painted it?
- **The year the work was created**. In the case of older works, *c.* may appear before the year. This is an abbreviation for *circa*, which means "around" or "about" in Latin. Which work in this lesson was created in 1656? What is its title?
- **The tools and materials used in creating the work**. Artists, as you will learn, use many different materials to create works of art. Watercolor paint is one of these materials. Pencil is another. How many works in this chapter were made using oil on canvas?
- **The size of the work**. Size helps you imagine how the work would appear if you were seeing it in person. Height, in centimeters as well as in inches, is always listed first. The width is listed second. A third number refers to depth if the artwork is three-dimensional. What is the height of the painting in Figure 1–15 by Jackson Pollock?
- **The location of the work**. Location includes the name of the gallery or museum where the work is housed. City and state are also provided, along, sometimes, with country. To what city would you need to travel to view the painting by Pieter Bruegel the Elder? In what city is the Hirshhorn Museum and Sculpture Garden located?

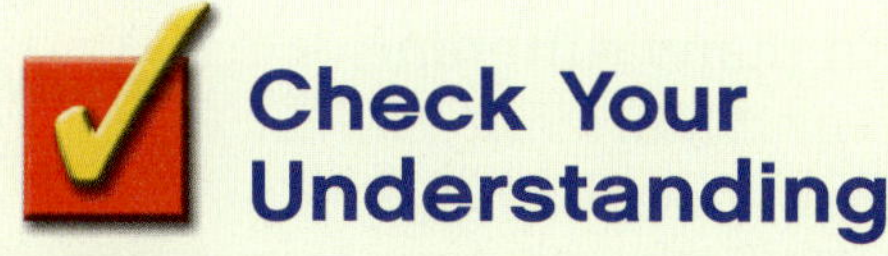

Check Your Understanding

1. What is meant by the term *nonobjective?*
2. What is the *content* of a work of art?
3. Name four pieces of information given in a *credit line.*

A Picture and a Thousand Words

Artist Barbara Kruger looks to the world around us for inspiration.

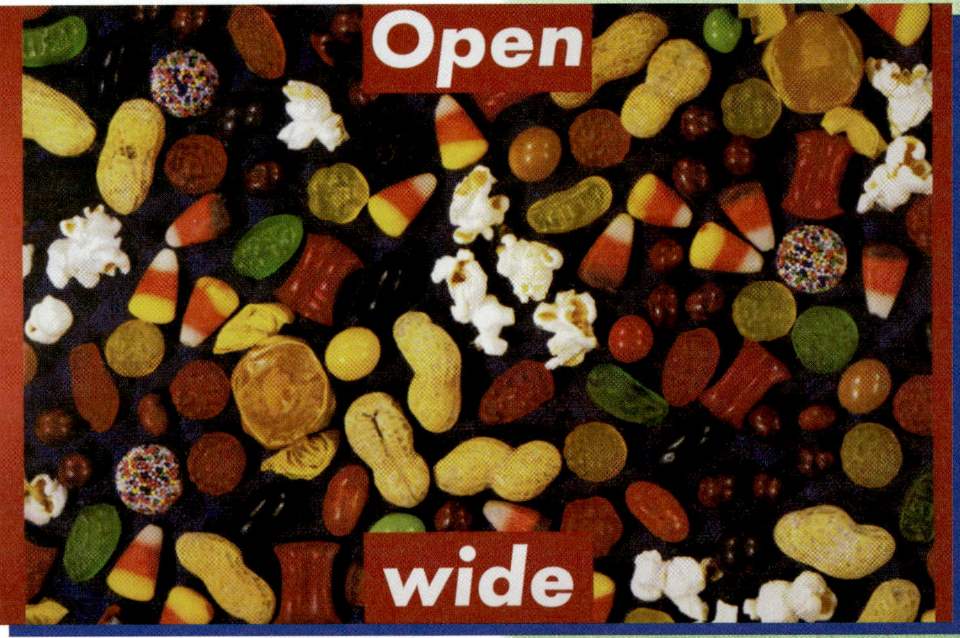

BARBARA KRUGER

Barbara Kruger. *Untitled.* 2001.
How does the image Barbara Kruger uses relate to her text? What do you think the original photograph was meant to communicate?

Some art makes us think. Some art makes us look at our world in a different way. Barbara Kruger, born in 1945, creates compelling pieces that do both.

Kruger's early career as a graphic designer and picture editor for a magazine is evident in her own artistic work today. Kruger borrows already existing images, typically using old magazine advertisements. Kruger first re-shoots and then enlarges the photos. Finally, she adds her own text, which puts a thought-provoking spin on these old ads.

Kruger's clever matching of words and images makes people question many different aspects of American consumer society and culture. Her words manage to transform the seemingly unremarkable images into art. As a result, her art often urges us to think deeply about the world in which we live.

TIME TO CONNECT

- **Cut out one advertisement from a magazine or newspaper that contains an interesting image.**
- **Study the image. What ideas or messages does the image communicate regardless of what it is advertising?**
- **Review how Kruger uses her own words—both in terms of what she says and the way she places them on top of her images.**
- **Create your own text and arrange it with the advertisement image you cut out to create a "Kruger-like" work of your own.**
- **Trade pieces with a classmate and share your responses, supporting your ideas with specific reference to the artwork.**

Chapter 1 Review

BUILDING VOCABULARY

Number a sheet of paper from 1 to 14. After each number, write the term from the list that best matches each description below.

applied art	formal properties
art	nonobjective
artists	patrons of the arts
collage	perceive
composition	portfolio
content	subject
credit line	
fine art	

1. To become aware through the senses of the special nature of objects.
2. People who use imagination and skill to communicate ideas in visual form.
3. A listing of important facts about an artwork.
4. Art valued for its visual appeal or success in communicating ideas or feelings.
5. Art made to be functional as well as visually pleasing.
6. Art made up of cut and torn materials pasted to a surface.
7. Sponsors, or supporters, of an artist or art-related events such as exhibitions.
8. A carefully selected collection of artwork kept by students and professional artists.
9. A visual statement that communicates an idea, expresses a feeling, or presents an interesting design.
10. How the art principles are used to organize the art elements.
11. The image that viewers can easily identify.
12. Art that has no recognizable subject matter.
13. The message, feeling, or idea an artwork communicates.
14. The way the elements of art are organized by the principles of art.

REVIEWING ART FACTS

Number a sheet of paper from 15–22. Answer each question in a complete sentence.

15. What are some of the ways people can benefit by looking at art?
16. Name two kinds of fine art.
17. Name a type of applied art.
18. Who were Muses? What role did they play for the ancient Greeks?
19. Name six sources to which artists turn for ideas.
20. What are patrons of the arts?
21. Where did Bearden get his idea for his collage, *Empress of the Blues?*
22. Define *composition* as it is used in art.

CROSS-CURRICULUM CONNECTIONS

23. **Social Studies.** Browse through a copy of today's newspaper, noting headlines. Skim through articles about political issues. Select one as the basis for an original artwork.
24. **Language Arts.** Survey and identify avocational and career opportunities or choices in your community. Create a flyer advertising ways that teens can pursue art as a career.

Web Museum Activity

The J. Paul Getty Museum, Los Angeles, California

Some artists use nature to create art, such as nontraditional sculptor Andy Goldsworthy. View more of his work at the Getty Museum's site at **art.glencoe.com**. Browse the online interactive lesson about Art & Ecology.

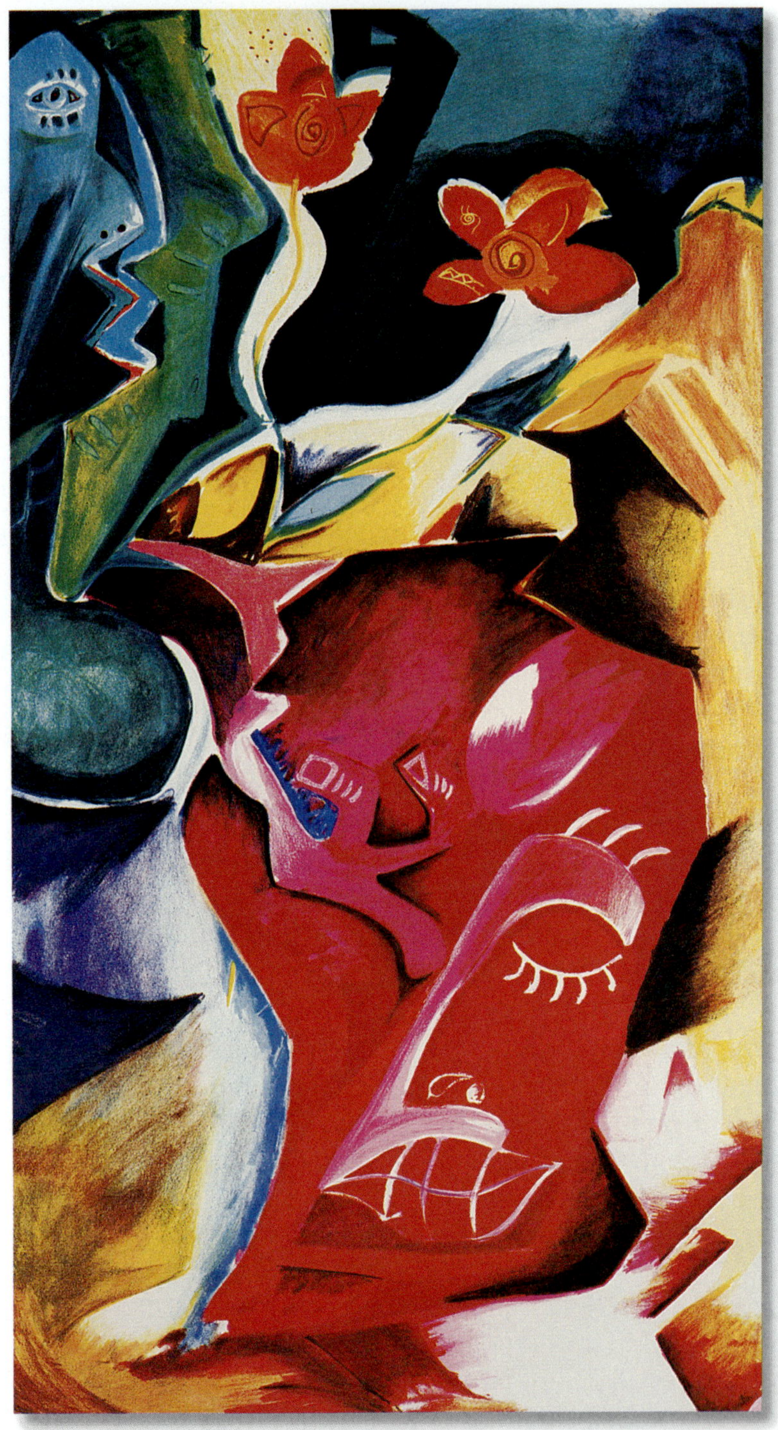

Focus On ◆ **Figure 2–1** **This artist is a child prodigy who had her first exhibit at the age of nine. In this work, created at the age of ten, she paints a story about a gardener. The face on the vase symbolizes the gardener, who adds life by putting flowers in the vase. Why do you think she has painted the gardener with green colors?**

Alexandra Nechita. *My Gardener.* 1995. Oil on canvas. 182.9 × 91.4 cm (72 × 36″).

Chapter 2

The Elements of Art

"I try to see colors with my eyes closed. When I open them and look at the canvas, I know exactly what color is needed." —Alexandra Nechita (b.1987)

You don't have to be a chemist to know the formula for water is H_2O. Water, in other words, is made up of the elements hydrogen and oxygen. Did you know that art also has elements? As in science, art elements are basic units. Some of these art elements are line, color, and shape. Which colors were used by the artist who painted **Figure 2–1?** What other elements of art can you find in this painting?

After completing this chapter, you will be able to:

- Name the seven elements of art.
- Explain how line can be used to create movement.
- Identify the three properties of color.
- Explain the difference between shapes and forms.
- Explain the use of space in art.
- Explain how we experience texture.
- Create artworks integrating themes found through personal experience.

Quick Write

Interpreting the Quote
Read the quote. Close your eyes and try picturing colors. What colors did you picture? Write a short paragraph explaining your reaction to this activity.

KEY TERMS

element of art
line
color
color wheel
hue
value
intensity
complementary colors
monochromatic colors
analogous colors
shape
form
space
landscape
point of view
texture

LESSON 1

The Language of Art

Do you know any languages besides English? After you read this lesson you will. The new language that you will learn has no words. Yet, it has the power to communicate feelings and moods. It is the "language" of art. An artist's success in communicating depends on his or her skill at this language.

The Visual Language

You may have heard the expression that a picture is worth a thousand words. When it comes to art, this saying certainly holds true. To see the relationship between words and pictures, read the following passage:

> *Tommy was waiting for his big brother to meet him. The street was deserted. Everyone else had gone home, and Tommy was getting nervous. The wind blew the trash along the sidewalk, and Tommy was getting cold. The tall, new skyscraper towered over this old building in his neighborhood. He noticed how the stucco had peeled off the building's surface to reveal the bare bricks. The shadow of the skyscraper fell on the condemned building.*
>
> *Tommy took out his flute. Music always made him feel better. He made up a tune to push away the fear. He continued playing and the environment became his rhythm section. The wire around the column rattled like castanets and the broken doors slammed a steady beat. The trash brushing along the sidewalk became the rustling of snare drums. He didn't care how long it took his brother to finish practice. Tommy wasn't nervous anymore as he waited for his brother. He had his music to keep him company.*

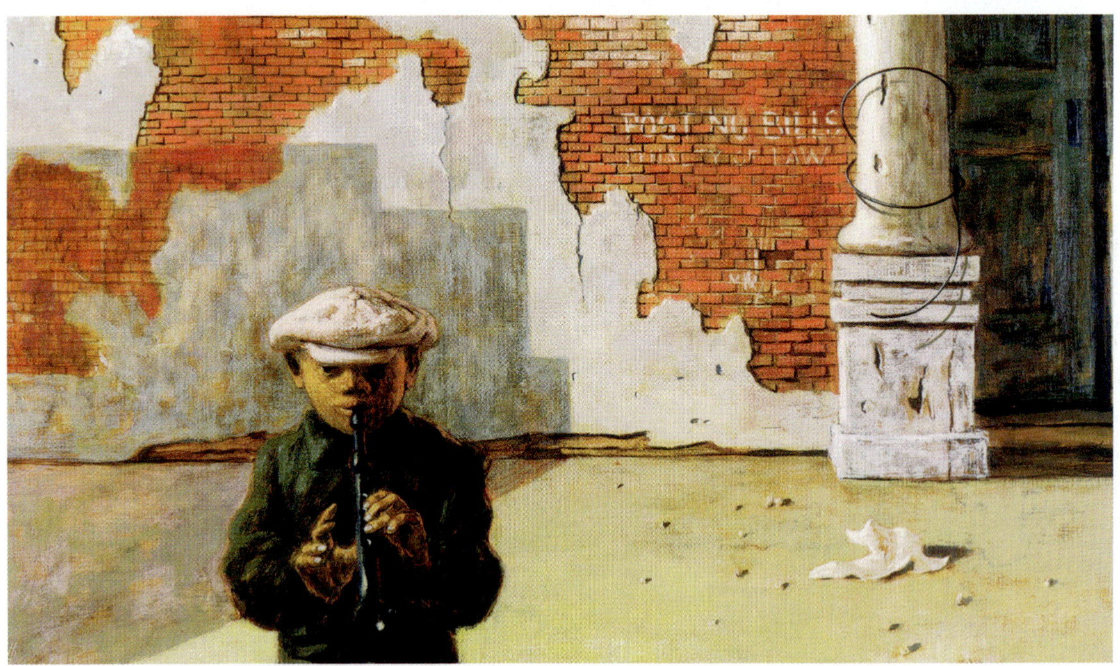

◆ **Figure 2–2** **Notice how the boy in this painting stands alone playing his flute. What mood has the artist created?**

Hughie Lee-Smith. *The Piper.* Oil on canvas. 55.9 × 89.5 cm (22 × 35″). Detroit Institute of Arts, Detroit, Michigan.

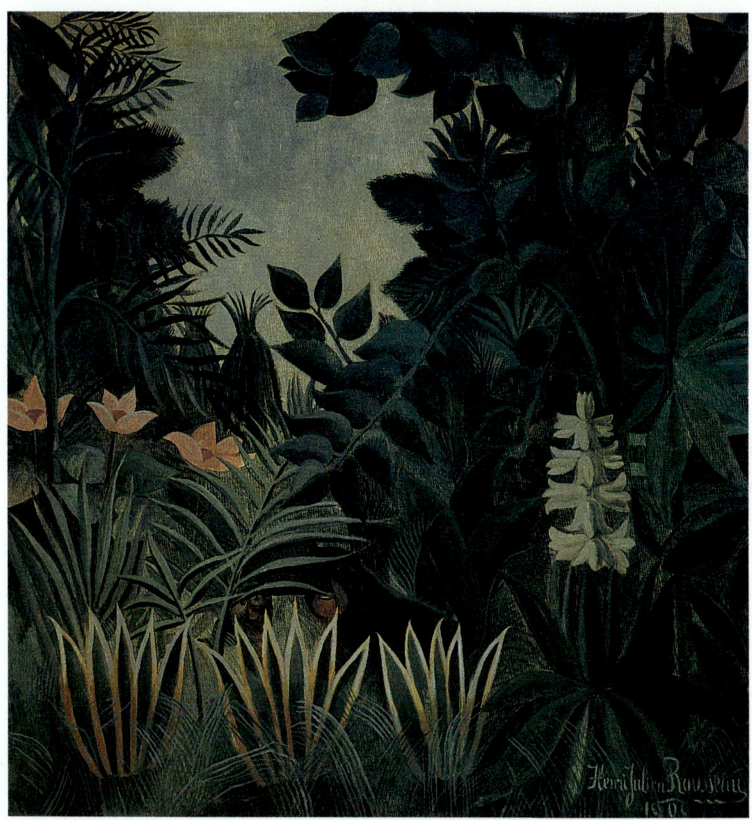

◆ **Figure 2–3** **What elements of art can you find in this painting? How does the artist use these elements?**

Henri Rousseau. *The Equatorial Jungle.* 1909. Oil on canvas. 1.4 × 1.3 m (55¼ × 51″). National Gallery of Art, Washington, D.C. Chester Dale Collection.

Now look at the painting in **Figure 2–2.** Compare the image it depicts with the description you just read. You will probably agree that what took the writer many words to describe, the artist depicted in a single painting.

The Elements of Art

As you are aware, every language has its own vocabulary. Before a person can speak the language, he or she must know some of the words in its vocabulary.

The language of art, too, has a vocabulary. Instead of words, however, the "vocabulary" of art consists of seven visual elements. An **element of art** is *a basic visual symbol an artist uses to create visual art*. These seven elements are line, color, value, shape, form, space, and texture.

How a given element is used greatly affects the way we perceive an artwork. To see this for yourself, look at **Figure 2–3.** Compare this work to the one shown in Figure 2–2. Notice how differently the two artists use color in their paintings. What feeling or mood is communicated by the colors in Figure 2–3?

Using the Elements of Art

When you first learned to read, you did not start with an entire book. You began by learning one word at a time. That is how you will learn the language of art: one element at a time.

Because these elements are so important, they will be discussed in the remaining lessons of this chapter. Once you have studied these elements you will be on your way to "speaking" the language of art.

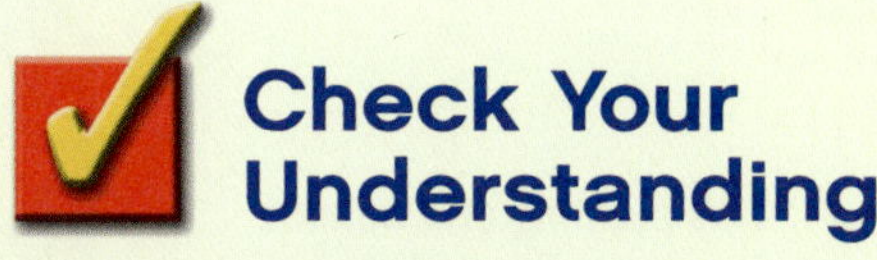

Check Your Understanding

1. In what way does art have a specialized vocabulary?
2. Define an *element of art.*
3. List the elements of art.

Line

"Cut along the dotted line." "Do not cross the center line." "Stay in line." Instructions like these are common in everyday life. They reveal how much we depend on lines.

Art, too, depends heavily on lines. Artists use lines to create pictures and to outline drawings for sculptures. In this lesson, you will learn about the element of line. You will recognize its importance in works of art.

The Meaning of Line

Take a pencil and move it across a sheet of paper. What happened? The moving point of the pencil made a path of connected dots on the paper. In other words, it made a line. This definition of the element **line**—*a continuous mark made on some surface by a moving point*—is a good one to remember. It reminds you that it takes movement to make a line and vice versa. When you see a line, your eye usually follows its movement. A trained artist uses lines to control the movement of the viewer's eyes. Lines can lead the eyes into, around, and out of visual images in a work of art. To understand this, look at the artwork in **Figure 2–4.** Do you find your eye moving haphazardly

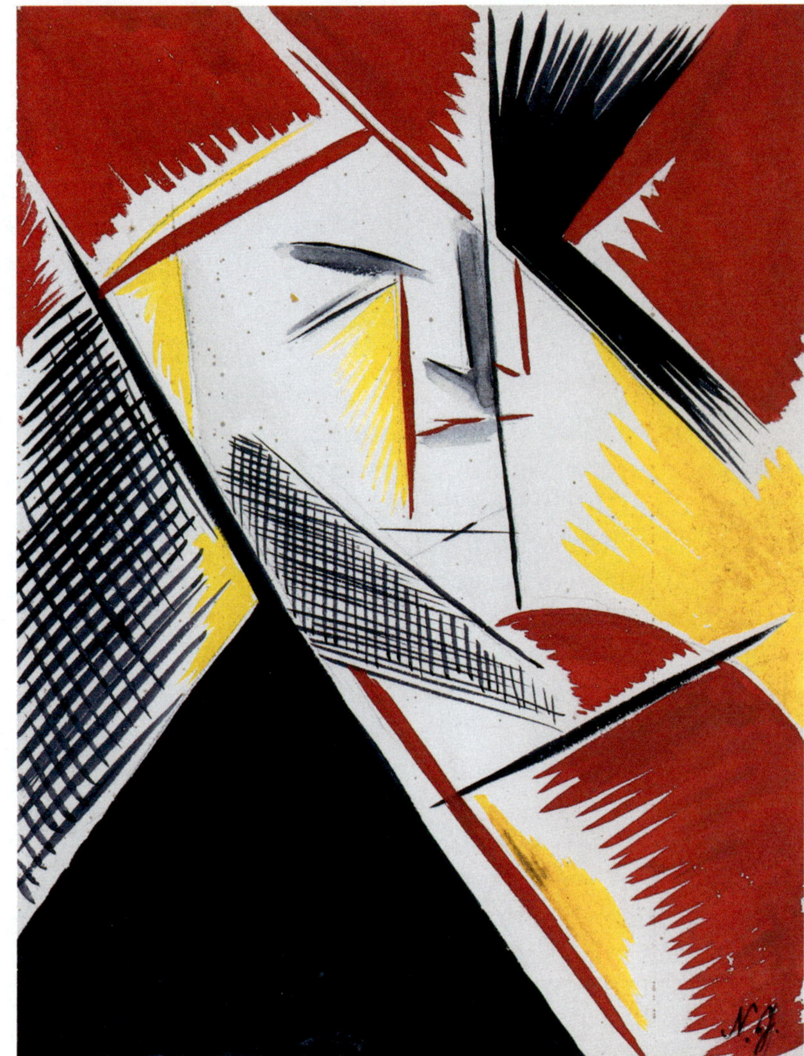

◆ **Figure 2–4** **This painting of a woman putting on makeup is done in the early twentieth century Russian style called "Rayism." The artist focuses on the rays of light and color radiating from the woman. This creates a work with lines that seem to explode from the surface.**

Natalia Goncharova. *Maquillage.* 1913–14. Gouache on paper. 16.2 × 12.1 cm (6⅜ × 4¾″). Dallas Museum of Art, Dallas, Texas. General Acquisitions Fund.

◆ **Figure 2–5** Horizontal lines lie parallel to the horizon.

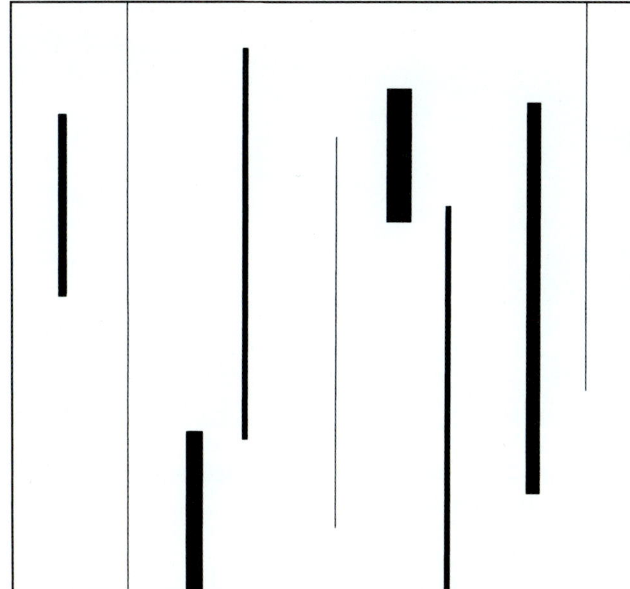

◆ **Figure 2–6** Vertical lines move straight up and down.

throughout this busy work? That is precisely what the artist had in mind. You are reading the chaotic lines, just as she intended.

Kinds of Line

There are five main kinds of line: horizontal, vertical, diagonal, curved, and zigzag. Each type is capable of communicating a different message or feeling to the viewer.

Horizontal Lines

Horizontal lines (**Figure 2–5**) run parallel to the ground. They do not slant. When you lie flat on the floor, your body forms a horizontal line.

Horizontal lines in art seem at rest. Other words that come to mind in connection with them are *quiet* and *peaceful.* Horizontal lines make the viewer feel comfortable, calm, and relaxed.

Vertical Lines

Vertical lines (**Figure 2–6**) move straight up and down. They do not lean at all. When you stand up straight and tall, your body forms a vertical line.

In art, vertical lines appear to be at attention. Artists use them to show dignity, formality, and strength.

Diagonal Lines

Diagonal lines (**Figure 2–7**) slant. They are somewhere between a vertical and a horizontal line. Imagine standing straight up and then, with your body stiff, falling to the floor. At any point during your fall, your body would form a diagonal line.

To the artist, diagonal lines generally signal action and excitement. Because they

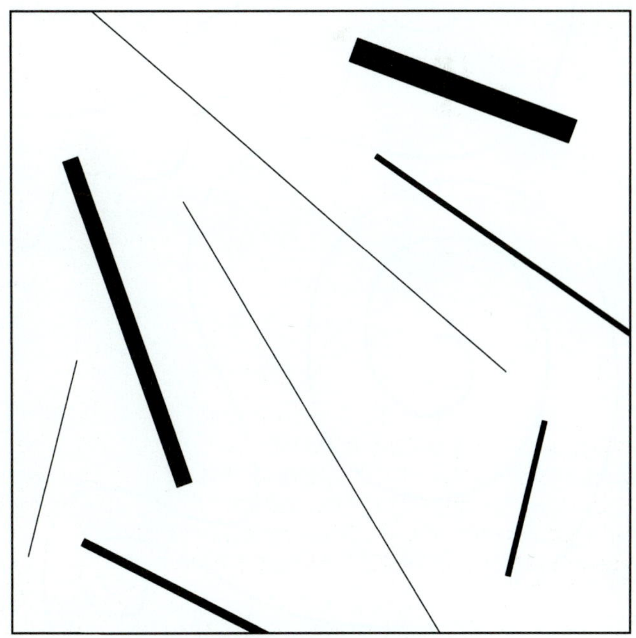

◆ **Figure 2–7** Diagonal lines slant.

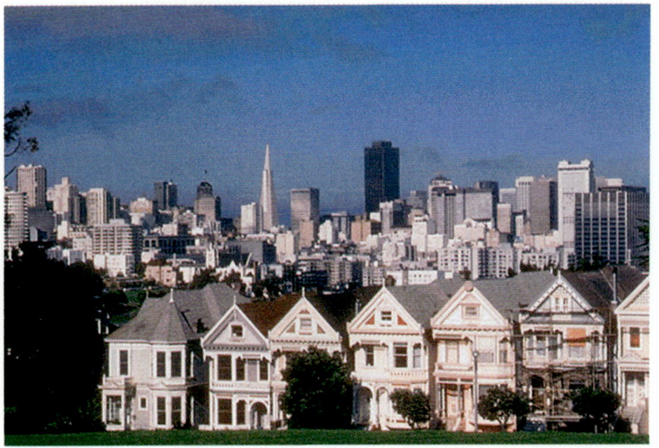

◆ **Figure 2–8** Row houses with gabled roofs, San Francisco, California.

appear to be either rising or falling, diagonals sometimes make a viewer feel tense and uncomfortable. Look again at Figure 2–4 on page 24. Do you find this work restful and relaxing? Probably not! The amount of diagonals has almost a dizzying effect on the viewer.

One exception to the above rule is diagonal lines that meet at a single point. Examine the photograph in **Figure 2–8.** Notice how the diagonals that form the roofs of the houses appear firm and unmoving. The lines seem almost to hold each other up.

Curved Lines

Curved lines (**Figure 2–9**) change direction gradually. When you draw wavy lines, you are actually linking a series of curves. Spirals and circles also begin with curves.

Like diagonal lines, curved lines express movement, though in a more graceful, flowing way. The amount of movement in a curve depends on how tightly the curve bends.

Zigzag Lines

Zigzag lines (**Figure 2–10**) are made by combining diagonal lines that change directions. The diagonals form sharp angles and change direction suddenly.

Zigzag lines can create confusion. They suggest action and nervous excitement. Sometimes zigzags move in even horizontal patterns, like those at the top of a picket fence.

Line Quality and Thickness

In addition to direction, lines may be categorized in terms of:

- **Quality.** The term *line quality* is used to describe the unique character of any line. Line quality can be affected by the tool or medium used as well as by the motion of

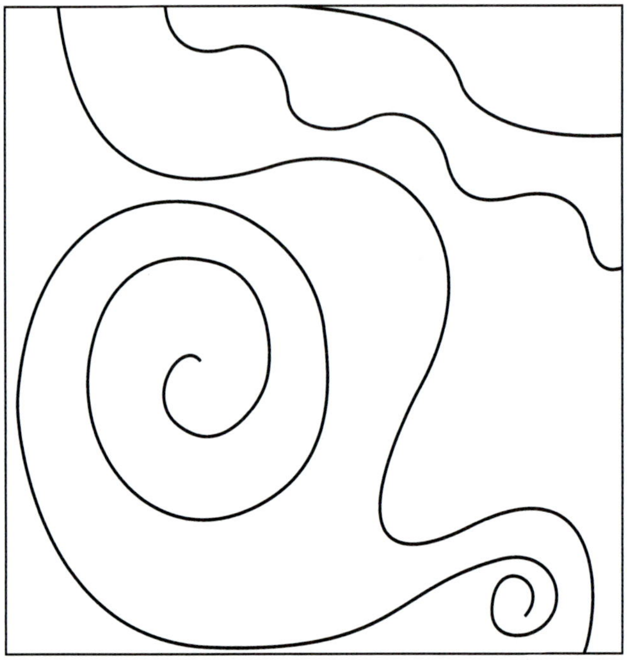

◆ **Figure 2–9** Curved lines change directions gradually.

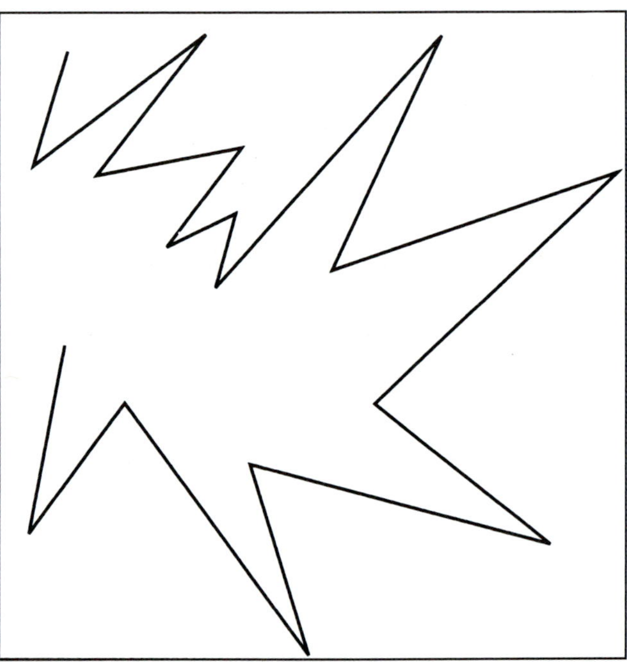

◆ **Figure 2–10** Zigzag lines are combinations of diagonals.

the artist's hand. It is line quality that determines whether a line appears smooth or rough, continuous or broken, sketchy or controlled. See **Figure 2–11.**

- **Thickness.** The thickness of a line determines how dark and heavy it appears. At one end of the thickness spectrum are *hairlines.* These are lines that are very thin and light. At the opposite end are thick, heavy lines such as the wide line shown in Figure 2–11.

Length. Lines can be long or short.

Width. Lines can be thick or thin.

Texture. Lines can be rough or smooth.

◆ **Figure 2–11** Line variations.

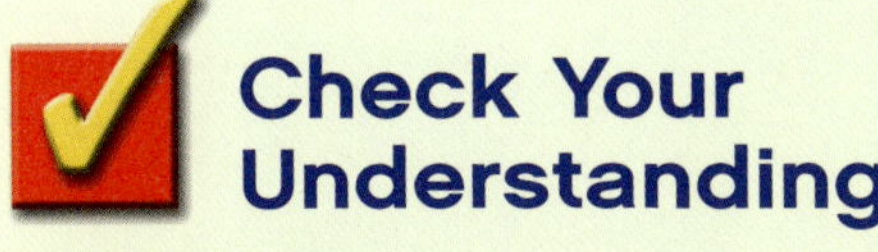

Check Your Understanding

1. What is the meaning of the term *line* as it is used in art?
2. Describe how line can be used to create movement.
3. Name five kinds of line.
4. What affects line quality?

Studio Activity

Creating an Idea Bank

Interpret themes. Find five envelopes. Label one *Noun,* one *Adjective,* one *Verb,* one *Adverb,* and one *Theme.* Think up words for each part of speech and ideas for themes (such as fairy tales, places, events, etc.). Use a dictionary and your art and literature books for ideas. Write each of your words on a separate slip of paper. Place your slips in the correct envelopes. Share the contents of your envelopes with other class members to get more of a variety in the word combinations. These envelopes will be your idea bank for future art projects.

Select one slip from each envelope. Arrange your slips in this order: theme-adjective-noun-verb-adverb. Make the words form an interesting idea. Select appropriate art materials and tools to interpret this theme when producing your drawing. On a sheet of white 9 × 12-inch paper, sketch your idea in traditional and experimental ways. The sketch should illustrate the subject (theme), idea (noun), action or what is happening (verb), and details (adjective and adverb) named.

Portfolio

Keep the four parts of speech that you selected for your first sketch. Select a new theme from your Idea Bank and make a new sketch. Compare how your new sketch is different from the first. Be sure to write the five words you selected on the back of both sketches. Keep your comparisons in your portfolio.

Color

Look up the word *color* in a dictionary, and you will find many different meanings. One of the definitions will be something like the following: *Color (verb): To brighten, add life to, or make more interesting.*

This definition of *color* sums up its role as an element of art. It adds life to art and enhances a work's visual interest. For many artists, color is the most important element of all. In this lesson, you will learn more about color and its many uses.

What Is Color?

Color is *the element of art that is derived from reflected light.* White light from the sun is actually a combination of all colors. When light passes through a wedge-shaped glass called a *prism,* the beam of white light is bent. The light is then separated into bands of color called the *color spectrum.* The colors of the spectrum always appear in the same order: red, orange, yellow, green, blue, and violet.

When light falls on an object, some of the light is absorbed by the object. The rest of the light bounces off. Color is what the eye sees when light bounces off an object.

Sometimes artists use colors in bold and shocking ways (**Figure 2–12**). At other times they use them in serious ways (**Figure 2–13**). Look back at the painting that opened this

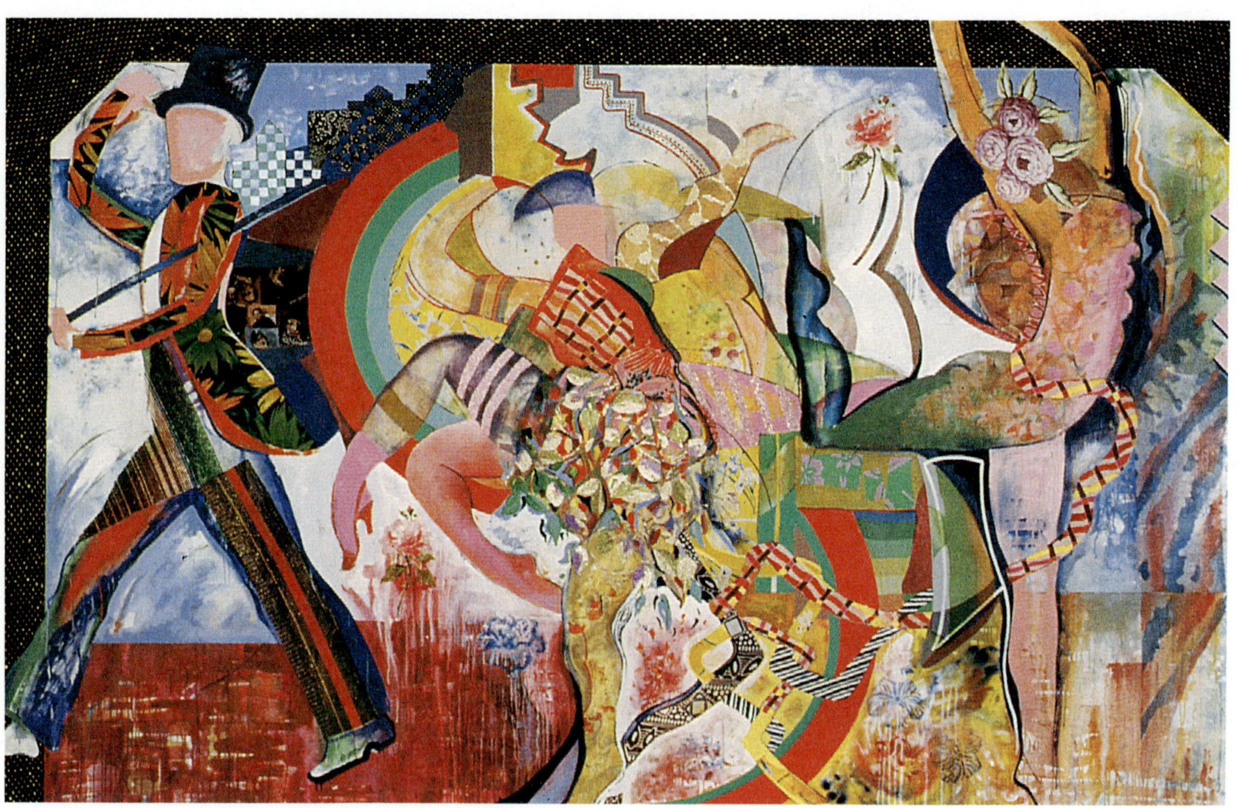

◆ **Figure 2–12** **Miriam Schapiro calls her works "femmages" because she pays tribute to the arts of women. In every city she visits, she searches for unique fabrics at flea markets and fabric shops.**

Miriam Schapiro. *I'm Dancin' as Fast as I Can.* 1985. Acrylic and fabric on canvas. 229 × 365 cm (90 × 144″). Courtesy of the artist.

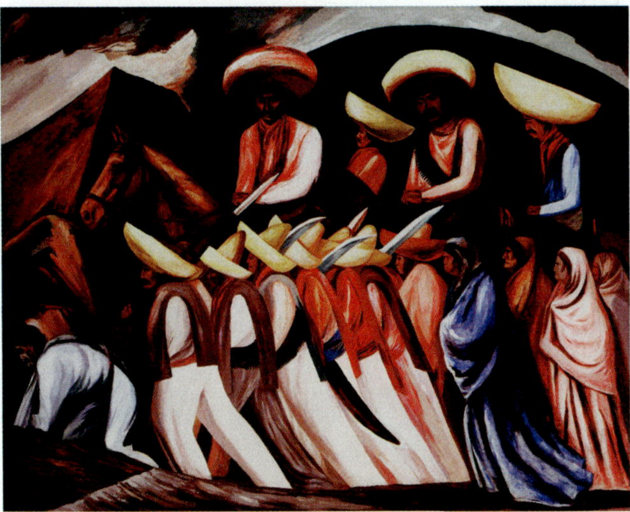

◆ **Figure 2–13** **Orozco used diagonal lines and dark colors to express the emotions of these Mexican peasants. The peasants are shown marching into battle with their leader, Emiliano Zapata.**

José Clemente Orozco. *Zapatistas.* 1931. Oil on canvas. 114.3 × 139.7 cm (45 × 55″). Museum of Modern Art, New York, New York. Given anonymously. © José Clemente Orozco. Scala/Art Resource, New York

chapter, Figure 2–1 on page 20. How would you describe the use of color in this artwork?

The Color Wheel

In the eighteenth century, Sir Isaac Newton organized the colors of the rainbow into a color wheel. The **color wheel** is *an arrangement of hues in a circular format.* Examine the color wheel in **Figure 2–14.** Notice that it shows the name and relationships among the various hues. Later in the chapter, you will learn more about the color wheel and its use.

Traits of Color

To achieve different results, artists must understand the three properties—or traits—of colors as they appear on the color wheel. Three of the most important traits are hue, value, and intensity.

Hue

Hue is *a color's name.* Red, yellow, and blue are the primary hues. They are always equally spaced on the color wheel. These colors are called *primary* (meaning "first")

Studio Activity

Creating Value

Drawing From Personal Experiences. Think of an outdoor scene you have experienced. On a sheet of paper, illustrate your ideas from personal experience by drawing the scene and include such natural features as trees, hills, and mountains. Select one hue from the color wheel. Using either a paint palette or paper plate, mix your hue with white to create tints and black to create shades. What happens when you mix your hue with gray? Paint your picture using this range of values, making sure that no two values touch. (See Value on page 30 for information about tints and shades.)

PORTFOLIO

Make a scale showing five values of one hue. (See Figure 2–15 on page 30.) Write a brief description about the process of mixing tints and shades and keep it in your portfolio.

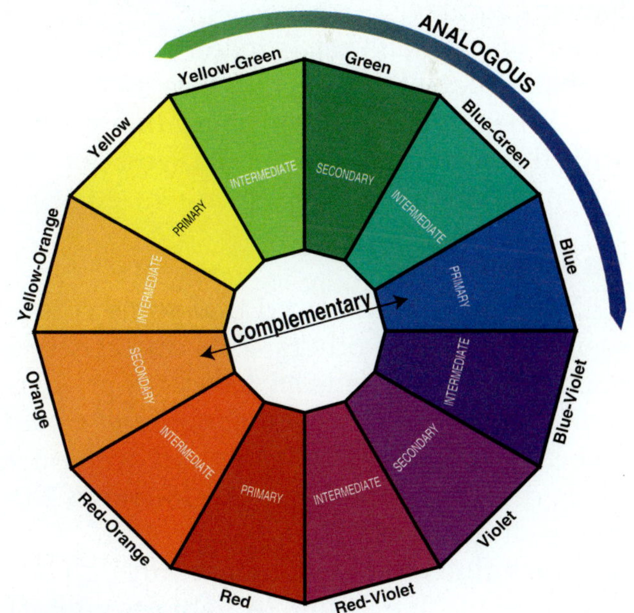

◆ **Figure 2–14** **Color wheel.**

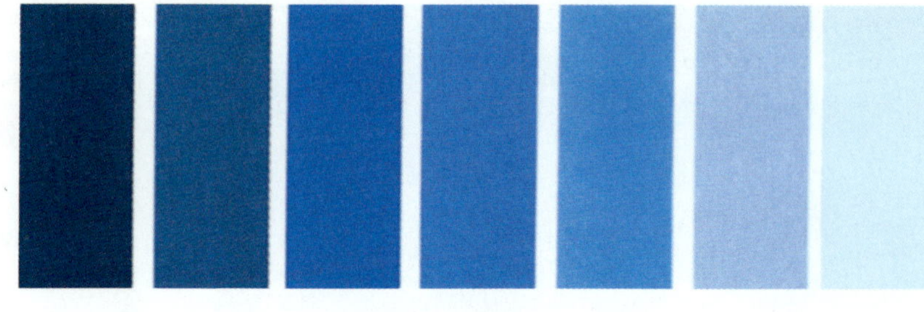

◆ **Figure 2–15** Values of blue.

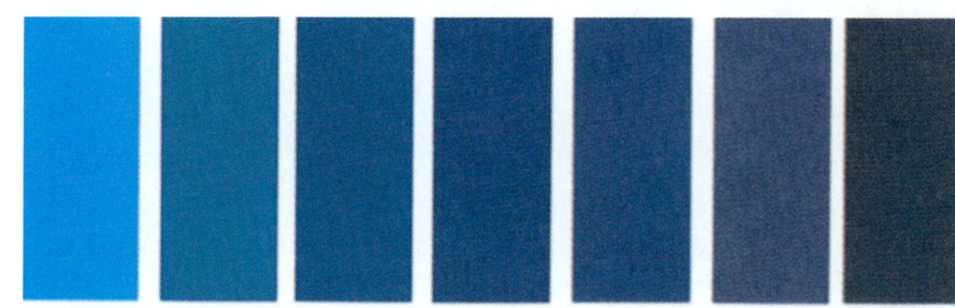

◆ **Figure 2–16** Intensities of blue.

because they can be mixed to make all the other hues. The *secondary hues*—green, orange, and violet—are made by mixing two primary hues. To get orange, for example, you mix equal parts of red and yellow. Can you identify the colors that you would mix to obtain the other two secondary hues? The painting in Figure 2–12 on page 28 uses primary and secondary hues. Notice how striking these colors are. Notice how they seem to add to the frenzied pace of the dancing figures.

An *intermediate hue* is made by mixing a primary hue with its neighboring secondary hue. When you mix the primary hue yellow with the secondary hue green, you get the intermediate hue yellow-green.

Value

You may have noticed that some colors seem lighter than others. This difference is one of value. **Value** is *an element of art concerned with the lightness or darkness of a hue.* Pale lavender is light in value, and deep purple is dark in value. **Figure 2–15** shows the values of blue.

The value of a hue changes through additions of black or white. A light (or whiter) value of a hue is called a *tint.* Pink, which is a mixture of red and white, is a tint of red. A dark (or blacker) value is called a *shade.* Maroon is a mixture of red and black. It is a dark shade of red. Be careful when using these art terms. In everyday language, the word *shade* is often used to describe both light and dark values of a hue.

Intensity

Some hues strike the eye as bright and lively. Others appear dull or muddy. The difference has to do with the color's intensity. **Intensity** is *the brightness or dullness of a hue.* A bright hue is said to be high in intensity. A dull hue is said to be low in intensity. Bright yellow is high in intensity. Mustard yellow is low in intensity.

Look again at the color wheel on page 29. Red and green are **complementary colors,** *colors opposite each other on the color wheel.* Adding a hue's complementary color lowers the hue's intensity. (See **Figure 2–16.**) If you mix equal parts of two complementary colors, you get a neutral color such as brown or gray.

Combining Colors

Colors are like musical instruments. Just as each instrument has its own special sound, so every color has its own "personality."

Combining colors in just the right way can lead to striking results. The following are some common color schemes that artists use:

- **Monochromatic color schemes. Monochromatic** (**mah**-nuh-kroh-**mat**-ik) **colors** are *different values of a single hue.* A color scheme using dark blue, medium blue, and light blue is monochromatic. This type of scheme tightly weaves together the parts of an artwork. A danger in using a monochromatic scheme, however, is that it can bore the viewer.
- **Analogous color schemes. Analogous** (uh-**nal**-uh-gus) **colors** are *colors that are side by side on the color wheel and share a hue.* Red-violet, red, and red-orange are analogous colors that share the hue red. Analogous colors in an artwork can tie one shape to the next.
- **Warm or cool color schemes**. Red, yellow, and orange remind us of sunshine, fire, and other warm things. For this reason, they are known as warm colors. Blue, green, and violet make us think of cool things, like water and grass. They are known, therefore, as cool colors. When used in an artwork, warm colors seem to move toward the viewer. Cool colors appear to recede, or move back and away.

Studio Activity

Understanding Intensity

Create Paintings Based on Direct Observation. You will produce paintings using a variety of art materials and tools in traditional ways. Select an object from within your classroom such as a plant or vase. On a sheet of paper use direct observation to draw a large image of your object. Select bright colors to paint your object. Paint your background using dull colors. You can dull a color by adding its complement a little at a time.

PORTFOLIO

Make another painting of the same image, but this time experiment by reversing the color intensities. Use dull colors for your object and bright colors in your background. Participate in an individual critique by comparing relationships in your artworks. What differences do you notice? Write a short paragraph comparing and contrasting the changes you observed when using different intensities of color. Place your reflection and the two paintings in your portfolio.

Check Your Understanding

1. What are the three primary hues?
2. Describe how value is changed with tints and shades.
3. Define *intensity.*
4. What are *complementary colors?* Give an example.
5. Describe an analogous color scheme.

Creating an Optical-Illusion Painting

Artists use color to create special effects in works of art. Color schemes can make a painting look vibrant or can create the illusion of movement. Consider the painting in **Figure 2–17.** Do the squares approaching the center of the painting appear to bulge toward you in a big semicircle? That is precisely the effect the artist set out to achieve. It is worth noting that he creates this illusion of three dimensions using the element of color. Notice which values of red, yellow, and blue the artist uses near the center of the circle. What values of these colors does he use near the outer edge of the bulge, or perimeter?

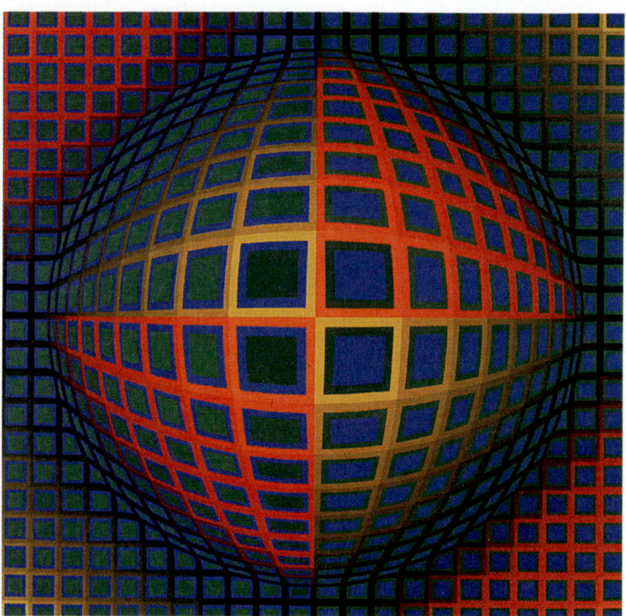

◆ **Figure 2–17** **This composition represents the expansion of the universe. It is one of many paintings the artist named after the distant star "Vega." He added "Noir" to make the title different from other paintings of Vega.**

Victor Vasarely. *Vega-Noir.* 1969. Oil on canvas. 200 x 200 cm (78¾″ × 78¾″). Albright-Knox Art Gallery. Buffalo, New York. Gift of Seymour H. Knox Jr. 1969.

What You Will Learn

You will create an optical-illusion painting similar to the one in Figure 2–17. You will organize geometric shapes to create the illusion of depth. You will paint your work with a color scheme of two or three bright hues with their tints and/or shades. Your goal will be to create the illusion of movement.

What You Will Need

- Pencil and eraser
- 18-inch ruler and compass
- Tag board scraps, scissors
- 16 × 16-inch heavy white drawing paper
- Tempera paints and mixing tray
- Water container, paint brushes in various sizes
- Paper towels, newspaper
- Optional: colored pencil, markers, oil pastel or crayons

What You Will Do

1. In *Vega-Noir* Vasarely uses distorted geometric shapes and vibrant colors to create the illusion of movement. What shapes do you see? What happens to the shapes as they move away from the center of the painting? Do you recognize the color scheme? Can you see how the painting can be divided into four equal sections, each a mirror image of itself? Do you recognize any of the color schemes?
2. Begin by creating a 2-inch grid on your 16 × 16-inch white paper. Start by lining up your ruler flush against the top edge of the paper. Mark off a dot with your pencil every 2 inches. Repeat this on the other three edges of the paper.

3. Next, connect the dots. Align your ruler along the left-most dots on the top and bottom of your paper. Draw a line connecting the dots. The line should be vertical. Connect the remaining dots in the same fashion. Now do the same with the dots on the left and right side to make horizontal lines.
4. Measure and cut two 2-inch squares from the tag board scraps. Draw a different geometric shape on each square. One square might have a diamond, the other a circle. Use a ruler and/or compass to make your shapes precise. Carefully cut out the shapes along the outlines.
5. Center one of the two outline shapes in the top left square of your grid. Using a pencil, trace around the shape. Move one square to the right, and repeat this process, this time using the second shape "template." Continue in this fashion, alternating templates until every square has a shape in it.
6. Select a color scheme that uses two or three bright hues. Begin painting your work. Use tints and/or shades of the colors you have chosen to create the illusion of depth. Mix the tints and shades of each color before you use them in the painting. Analyze your artwork in progress with peers and participate in a group critique.
7. Give your completed painting a title and display it in a class exhibition.

Evaluating Your Work

- **Describe** What shapes and colors did you use in your optical-illusion painting? Explain your procedures.
- **Analyze** What shapes did you use to create your template? Which color scheme did you use to enhance the optical illusion in your painting?

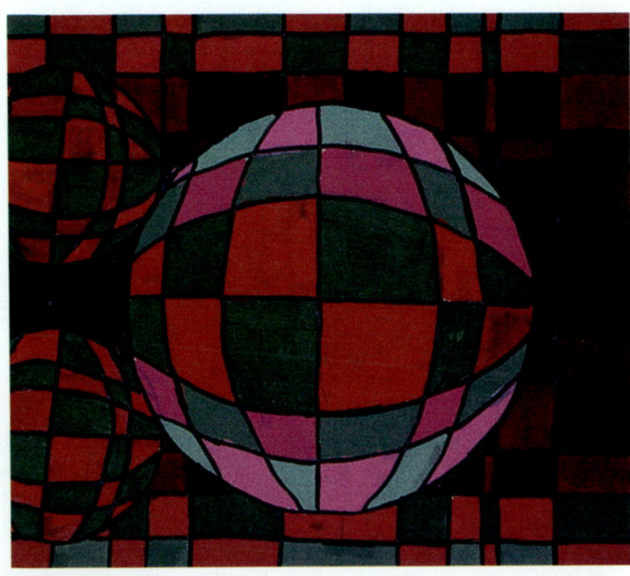

◆ **Figure 2–18** **Student work. Optical-illusion painting.**

REFLECTIVE THINKING

Critical Evaluation. Analyze the original artworks of your peers in the class exhibition. Examine the optical-illusion paintings they created and form conclusions about formal properties and intent. For example, did the use of shape and color enhance the optical illusion of the artwork? Is it what they intended?

Visual Art Journal

Experiment with different shapes and colors to create a variety of optical illusions. Define a variety of concepts directly related to these art elements using vocabulary accurately. For example, concepts relating to color include color properties and color schemes. Write your thoughts in your journal.

Shape, Form, and Space

The world around you exists in three dimensions. Every object—a tree, a house, your friend—has height, width, and depth. Imagine awaking one day to the discovery that depth had vanished. You would still be able to identify the *shapes,* or outlines, of objects. You would not, however, be able to see their *forms*—their three-dimensionality.

These terms, *shape* and *form,* play an important role in the language of art. Along with a third term—*space*—they represent three related art elements. In this lesson you will learn more about this relationship. You will also learn—and see—how these elements are used in works of art.

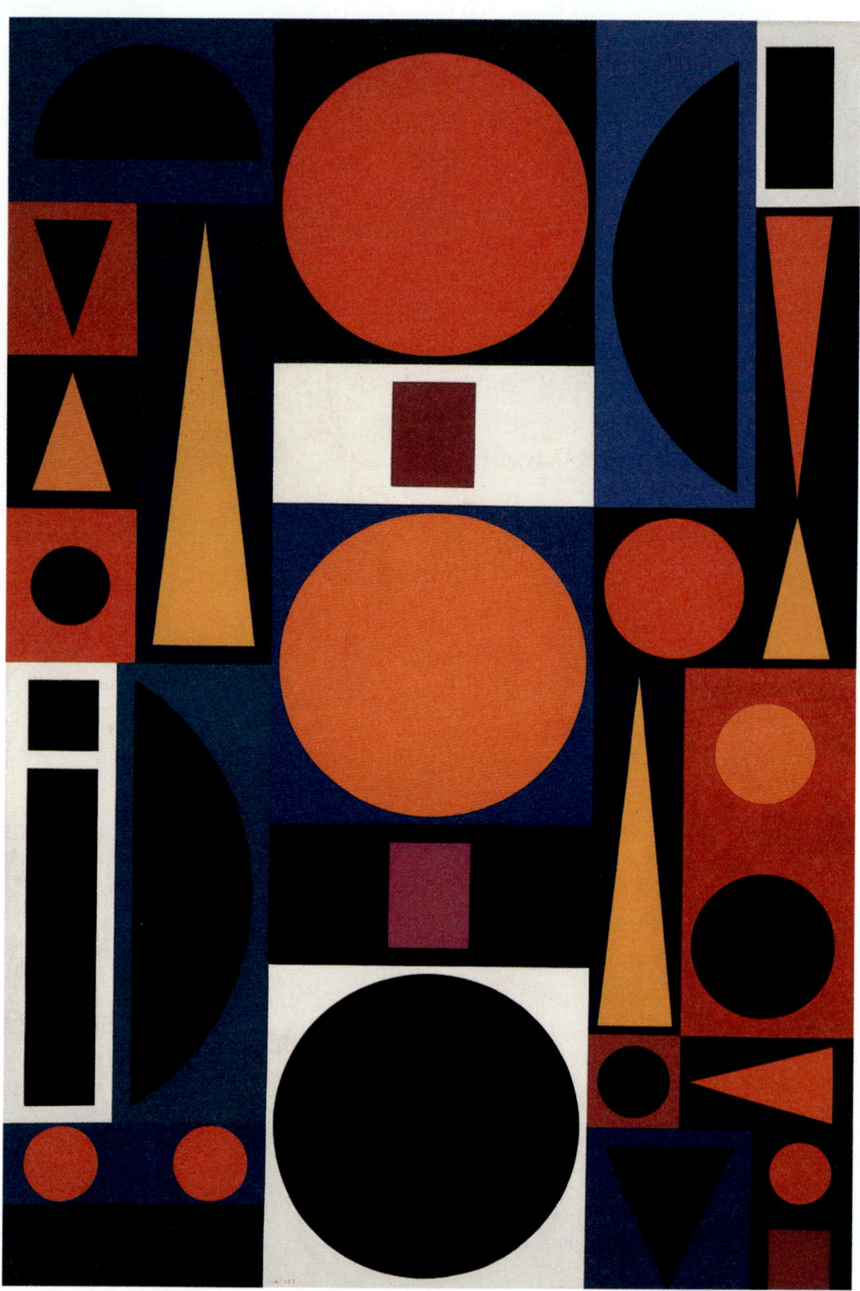

◆ **Figure 2–19** **Herbin shunned the use of objects in his work. He used bright colors and geometric shapes to create art that expressed his intellectual attitude toward painting. His work influenced the Hard Edge and Op art painters of the 1960s.**

Auguste Herbin. *Life No. 1.* Oil on canvas. 144.8 × 96.5 cm (57 × 38″). Albright-Knox Art Gallery, Buffalo, New York. Gift of the Seymour H. Knox Foundation, Inc. 1966.

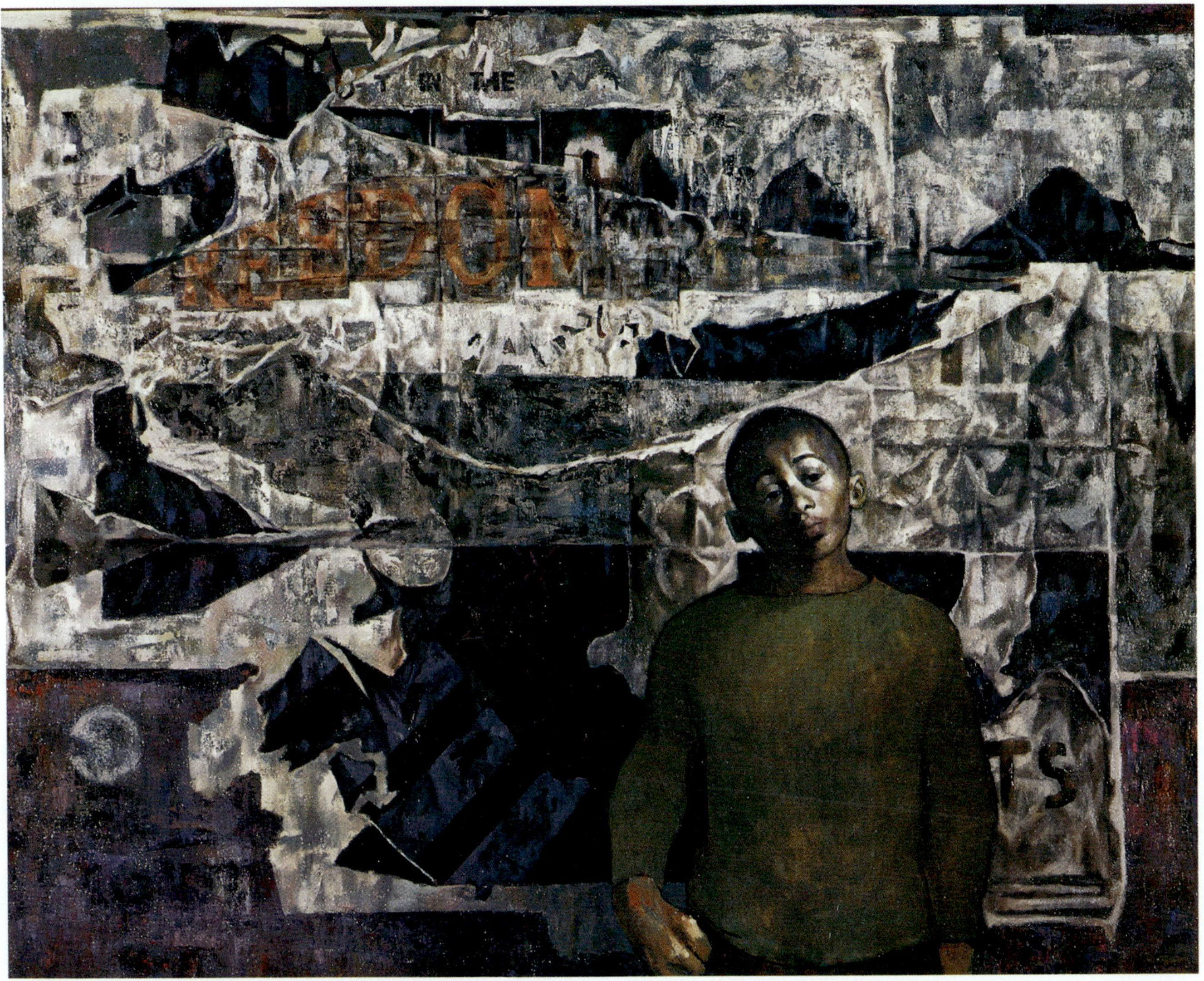

◆ **Figure 2–20** **The young man depicted is an organic, free-form shape. The torn paper in the background is made of free-form, irregular shapes.**

Charles White. *Freedom Now.* 1966–67. Oil on canvas. 102.9 × 127.6 cm (40½ × 50¼″). J. Paul Getty Museum, Los Angeles, California. Collection of the California African American Museum.

SHAPE

In art a **shape** is *an element that refers to an area clearly set off by one or more of the other six visual elements of art.* Shapes are flat. They are limited to only two dimensions: height and width. A ball's shape is a circle. A shape may have an outline or boundary around it. Some shapes show up because of color. Others are set off purely by the space that surrounds them. Shapes may be thought of as belonging to one of two categories:

- **Geometric shapes.** These are precise shapes that look as if they were made with a ruler or other drawing tool. The square, the circle, the triangle, the rectangle, and the oval are the five basic geometric shapes. The painting shown in **Figure 2–19** is made up largely of geometric shapes.
- **Organic shapes.** These are not regular or even. Their outlines curve to make free-form shapes. Organic shapes are often found in nature. Objects in the painting shown in **Figure 2–20** are based on organic, free-form shapes.

Form

Like shapes, forms have height and width. Forms, however, have a third dimension: depth. In fact, **form** is defined as *an element of art that refers to an object with three dimensions.* A tree is a three-dimensional form. So are you.

As with shapes, forms are grouped as either geometric or organic. Examples of geometric forms are a baseball and a child's building block. Examples of organic forms are a stone, a leaf, and a person.

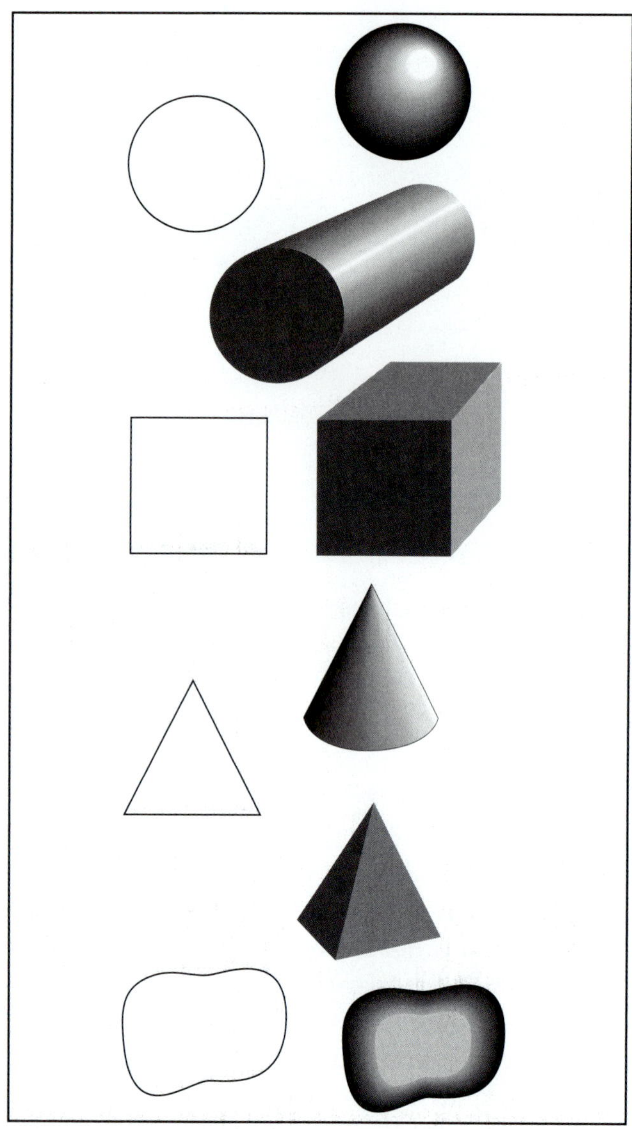

◆ **Figure 2–21** **Form-shape relationships.**

Shapes and forms are closely linked in art (**Figure 2–21**). The end of a cylinder is a circle. One side of a cube is a square. A triangle can "grow" into a pyramid.

Space

Space *is an element of art that refers to the distance or area between, around, above, below, and within objects.* Space is empty until objects fill it. All objects take up space. You, for instance, are a living, breathing form moving through space.

Space occurs in both two- and three-dimensional art. In a two-dimensional work such as a painting or drawing, space is often represented as *areas of color between and around shapes.* Such space is known as *negative space.* In three-dimensional artworks, such as sculpture, space is real. The space in and around a freestanding sculpture, like the one in **Figure 2–22,** permits the viewer to move around the work and see it from different angles.

Creating the Illusion of Space in Two-Dimensional Art

Although drawings and paintings are created in two dimensions, they can be made to appear three-dimensional. Artists have developed techniques for giving the feeling of depth in paintings and drawings. These include:

- **Overlapping.** Having one shape cover part of another shape.
- **Size.** Making distant shapes smaller than closer ones. Look again at Figure 1–2 on page 4.
- **Focus.** Adding more detail to closer objects, less detail to distant objects.
- **Placement.** Placing distant objects higher up in the picture, closer ones lower down.

- **Intensity and value.** Using colors that are lower in intensity and lighter in value for objects in the distance.
- **Linear perspective.** Slanting the horizontal lines of buildings and other objects so they seem to come together at a point on the horizon.

Check Your Understanding

1. What is shape?
2. What are the two types of shapes?
3. What is form?
4. What are the two types of forms?
5. Name two techniques that artists use for creating a feeling of space.

Meet the Artist

Henry Moore (1898–1986)

Historical Connection. What do underground bomb shelters have in common with the art of Africa? Both played a role in shaping the sculpture of Henry Moore. Moore was born in England and served in the British army in World War I. After the war, he attended art school on grant money issued to war veterans. As a student, he developed a keen interest in African tribal sculpture. He would later adopt features of this style in his own abstract sculpture. On the brink of World War II, Moore received an unusual request from the British government. They asked him to create drawings depicting life in underground bomb shelters. From 1940 to 1943, he focused almost entirely on drawing. These drawings, mostly of families or rounded forms of people, had an enormous impact on his later sculptures.

◆ **Figure 2–22** **This is the earliest of Moore's reclining figures. This work shows Moore's fascination with the human form.**

Henry Moore. *Reclining Figure.* 1935–36. Elmwood. 48.3 × 93.3 × 44.5 cm (19 × 36¾ × 17½"). Albright-Knox Art Gallery, Buffalo, New York. Room of Contemporary Art Fund, 1939.

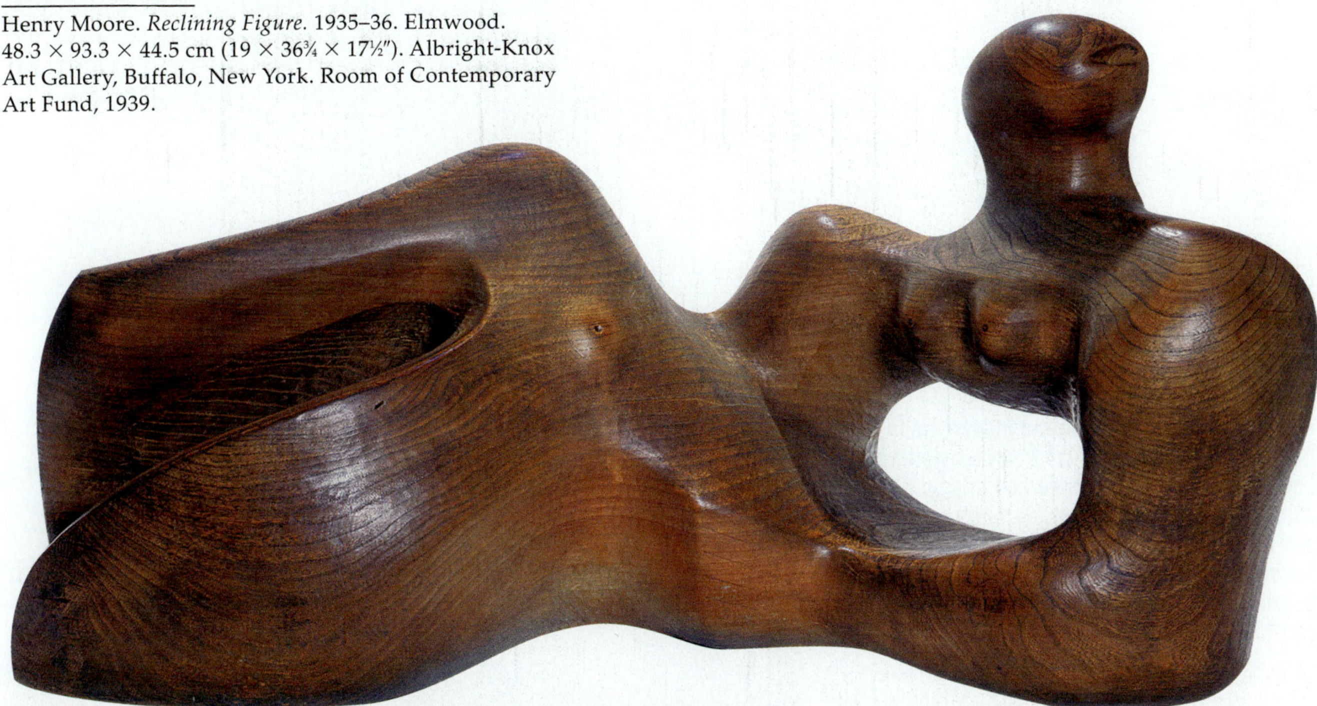

LESSON 6

Making a Landscape Painting

Her real name was Anna Mary Robertson Moses. You may know her better as "Grandma" Moses. She is considered a leading American folk painter of the twentieth century. She painted landscapes. A **landscape** is *a drawing or painting of mountains, trees, or other natural scenery.* Look closely at the painting in **Figure 2–23.** Moses organized her landscape using foreground, middle ground, and background. The foreground is the area closest to the viewer. Background is the most distant area. Moses captured the feeling of depth by making the animals and people larger in the foreground and placed them in front of the white house.

What You Will Learn

Using a variety of art materials and tools in traditional and experimental ways, you will create a landscape painting based on an event from personal experience. Your artwork will integrate a theme found through personal experiences such as the changing of the seasons. Your landscape will be divided into a foreground, middle ground, and background. You will use at least three of the six perspective techniques discussed on pages 36 and 37 to create depth.

What You Will Need

- Sketch paper, pencil, and eraser
- 12 × 18-inch heavy white drawing paper
- Tempera paints, mixing tray
- Water container, paint brushes in various sizes
- Cotton swabs
- Paper towels, newspaper

What You Will Do

1. Look again at Figure 2–23. Notice the **point of view** Grandma Moses has chosen. The point of view is *the angle from which the viewer sees the scene.* Beyond the fence are the fields of a farm. Some of the fields have horses, cows, and people. Farther back, at the horizon, is a range of mountains. Notice how size and color are used to suggest distance.

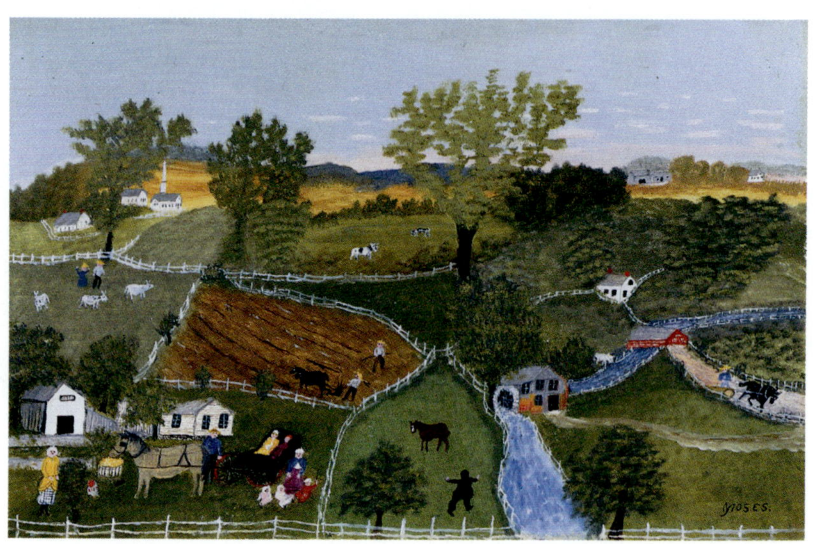

◆ **Figure 2–23** **Grandma Moses made memory paintings. This work shows visitors coming to call in their horse and buggy. It also shows fields being plowed, animals grazing, and buildings in the distance. The artist became a celebrity in the 1940s because her paintings helped people recall a time when life was simpler.**

Grandma Moses. *Callers.* 1959. Oil on pressed wood. 40.6 × 61 cm (16 × 24″). The Montclair Art Museum, Montclair, New Jersey. © Grandma Moses Properties Co., New York. Renewed 1987.

2. Integrate a theme found through personal experiences by illustrating an outdoor event that you would like to portray. The event might be a picnic, a lawn party, or a hiking trip. Picture the natural setting—the landscape features—in which this event took place. Make notes and pencil sketches about this event. In your sketch, illustrate the landscape features, such as mountains, clouds, and plant life, as well as people, animals, and objects. Be sure to note the time of year.
3. Plan the areas for foreground, middle ground, and background.
4. Refer to your notes and sketches. Draw the landscape details on your drawing paper. Paint your sky and the land. Remember to use three of the six techniques shown on pages 36 and 37. Think about the colors you will need in order to portray the season. Experiment by mixing colors on a piece of scrap paper with your tempera paint.
5. Allow the background features of your work to dry. Then add people, animals, and objects, including trees.
6. Display your work alongside those of your classmates. Can you find similar stories? Can you tell the season in which the various stories take place? Compare and contrast the use of space in your work with the work of your classmates.

Evaluating Your Work

- **Describe** What personal event did you choose to illustrate? Which people, animals and objects did you include in this work? What season did you depict?
- **Analyze** Identify how you used foreground, middle ground, and background. Explain which perspective techniques you used to create the feeling of depth. Explain how your use of color helped convey the season in which your event took place.

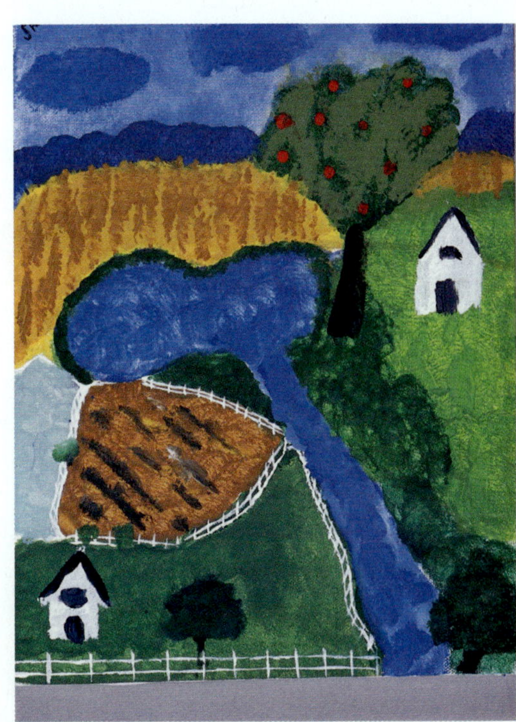

◆**Figure 2–24** **Student work. Landscape painting.**

PORTFOLIO IDEAS

Analyzing Artworks. Looking at portfolios of others can often provide inspiration for your own. Analyze portfolios by peers and others, such as your teacher or older students. Form conclusions about formal properties, historical and cultural contexts, intents, and meanings. For example, what principles of art are used to organize the elements of art? What clues do the artworks included in the portfolios provide about the artists' historical and cultural heritage?

Visual Art Journal

Create another landscape painting, this time experimenting with different colors. Use different perspective techniques. Compare the relationship between color choices and perspective techniques in your experimental painting and your first landscape. Write your notes in your visual art journal.

Texture

Rub your fingers lightly over the bottom of your shoe. How would you describe the way it feels? **Texture** is *the element of art that refers to how things feel, or look as though they might feel, if touched.* Think about the textures you find pleasant to the touch. Do you like them because they are smooth? How would you describe the textures you avoid touching?

In this lesson you will learn about the two ways texture work as an element of art.

Texture in Your Environment

Sandpaper, glass, a block of concrete—each has its own special texture, or feel. Have you ever tried on a piece of clothing—perhaps a sweater—that you thought looked

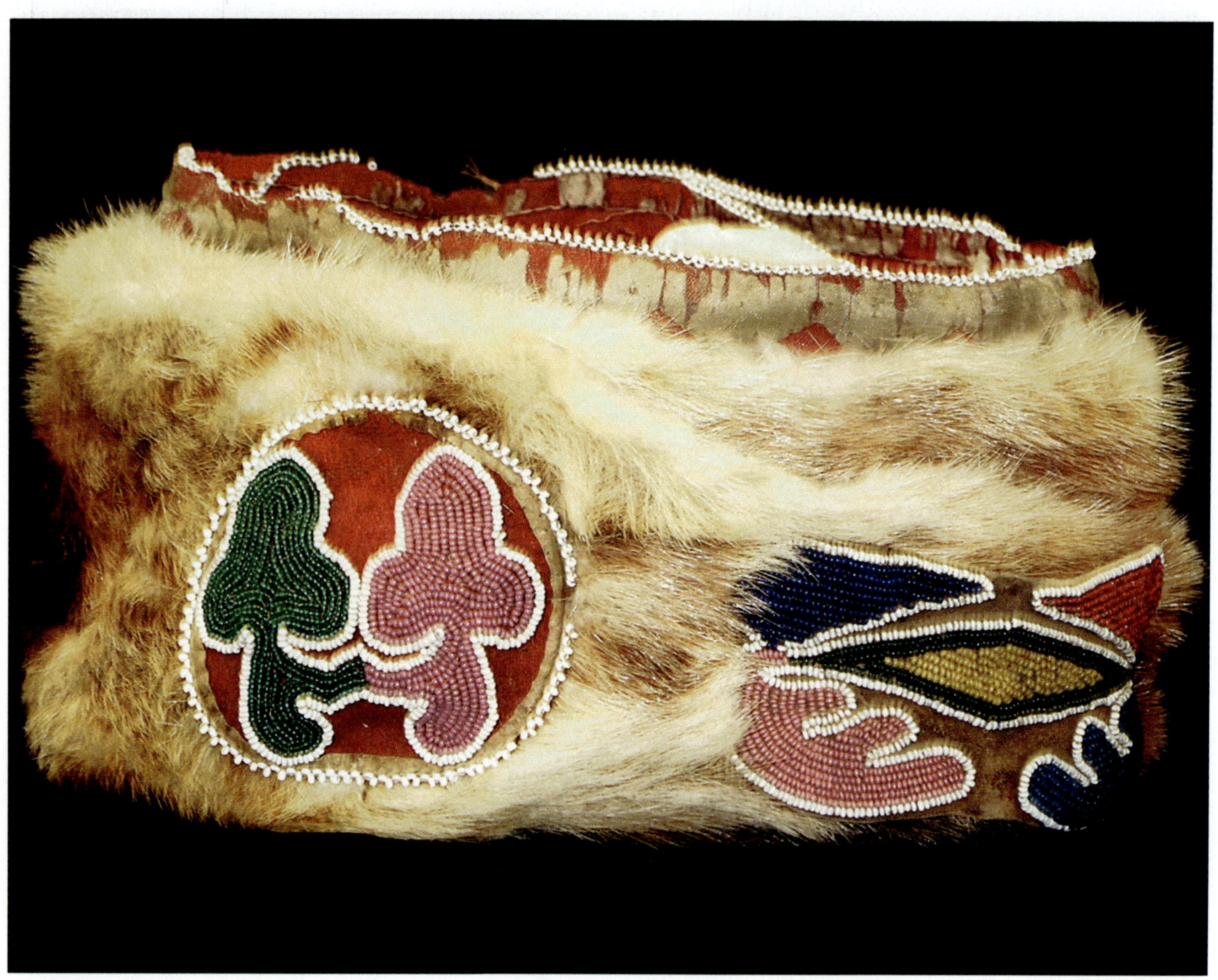

◆ **Figure 2–25** **The shadows in the fur tell your eyes that it must have a rough texture. The fine hairs of the fur remind you that this turban will feel silky and pleasant to the touch. Rubbing the fur might feel like petting a Persian cat.**

Potawatomi Turban. Wisconsin. c. 1880. Otter pelt, silk ribbon, and glass beads. Height: 15.9 cm (6¼″). Cranbrook Institute of Science, Bloomfield Hills, Michigan. 3146

itchy, only to find it was not? Such things are possible because we experience texture through two of our senses. We experience texture with our sense of sight. We also experience it again—and sometimes differently—with our sense of touch.

When you look at the artworks in **Figures 2–25** and **2–26**, you see patterns of light and dark. These patterns call to mind memories of how those objects feel when touched. When this happens you are experiencing "*visual texture*." If you touch these items on the page, they feel smooth and flat. It is your eyes that add the softness of the fur or the coarseness of the fiber. Actual, or real texture, on the other hand, is what you experience when you touch the object itself, not the photograph. It is the message that your fingers send to your brain.

Time & Place

Hupa People

Cultural Contexts. The people of California's Hupa Valley settled along the Trinity River in the northwestern part of the state. They were among the state's first settlers. There are no written records to suggest when the first Hupas arrived in the area. Available evidence suggests this may have been as early as A.D. 1000. The first contact between Hupas and Americans of European descent did not occur until the 1800s. In 1864, a Peace and Friendship Treaty was negotiated with the United States. Much of the history of this people survives, thanks to a rich oral tradition. The Hupas' art has also provided a glimpse into their past and customs. Analyze Figure 2–26 to determine cultural contexts. What clues does the artwork provide about Hupa culture?

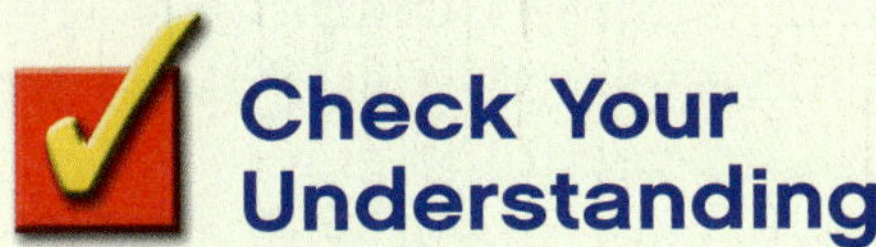

Check Your Understanding

1. What is *texture?*
2. Through which two of your senses do you experience texture?
3. Compare and contrast visual texture and actual texture.

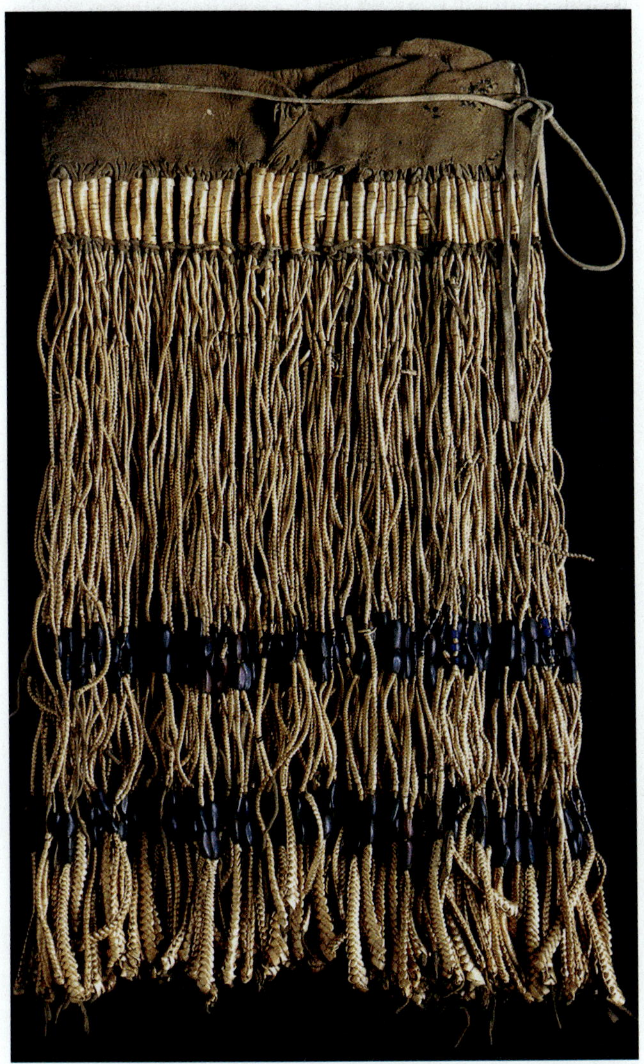

◆ **Figure 2–26 The Hupa women wear these skirt panels on their lower backs as they dance. The rough braided fibers make a musical sound when the fibers rub against each other.**

Hupa People. Klamath River Region. *California Dance Skirt Section.* Late nineteenth century. Braided squaw grass with pine nuts and blue beads on buckskin. 68.6 × 50.8 cm (27 × 20″). Museum of International Folk Art, Santa Fe, New Mexico. Neutrogena Collection. Photo by Pat Pollard.

Making an Arpillera Wall Hanging

Look at the artwork in **Figure 2–27.** This is an example of a Peruvian arpillera (ahr-pee-**yehr**-ah). These are works of art created in the Andes, a mountain range in South America. They include everyday scenes, such as harvesting crops, weddings, and religious celebrations. They are depicted in three dimensions. Arpillera means "piled on." A variety of textural materials—fabrics, straw, wood, and sometimes leather—are combined using appliqué techniques and stitchery. Today, arpilleras are found in many countries throughout South America.

What You Will Learn

In this studio lesson you will design a fiberart wall hanging illustrating a special place you have visited. You will use traditional appliqué techniques to create your work. You will experiment with a variety of textured objects and fabrics to depict a place. You will organize the elements of line, shape, color, form, and texture to create a three-dimensional composition in the manner of Peruvian arpilleras.

What You Will Need

- Sketch paper, pencil, and eraser
- A variety of textural materials, fabrics, felt scraps, yarn
- Foam for stuffing 3-D objects
- Large envelopes or plastic bags
- Fabric for the background
- Fabric scissors, straight pins
- Embroidery floss, sewing thread, and needles
- Thin dowel rod
- Optional: pinking shears

What You Will Do

1. Begin by collecting fabrics, yarn, buttons, ribbons, threads, and other textured items to construct your arpillera. Look closely at the arpillera in Figure 2–27. Notice how the three-dimensional figures are "piled on" the appliquéd background.
2. Start by creating an idea list with your classmates of special places you have been. This could be a place in your community or somewhere you went on vacation. Are there any special buildings or objects that are associated with them? Select an idea that interests you and make two or three sketches of that place. Use flat simple shapes to represent objects and people in that special place.

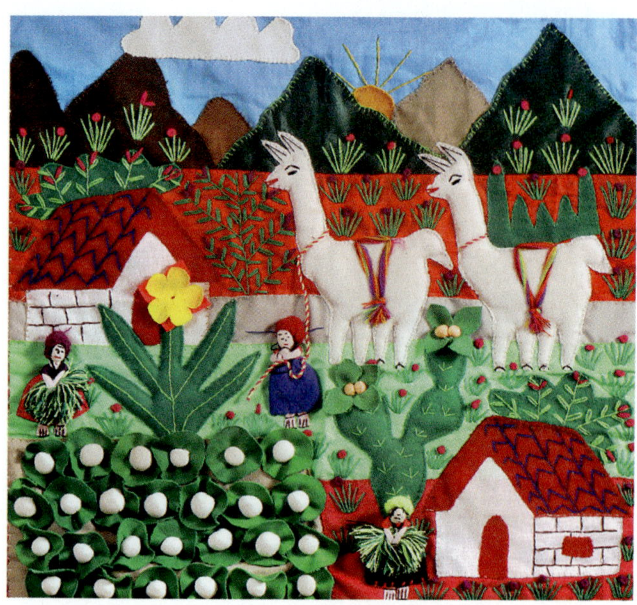

◆ **Figure 2–27 The various fabrics and fibers of this arpillera create a texturally appealing surface.**

Peruvian *Arpillera.* c. 1990. Felt, thread, and scrap fabrics. 51 × 51 cm (20 × 20″). Private Collection.

3. Choose your best sketch. Select a fabric that will be used as the support. Hem the sides according to your teacher's directions. Finally, fold over the top edge and sew to make a tube through which a thin dowel rod can be inserted to hang your work.
4. Collect several pieces of scrap fabric to create background shapes, such as grass, mountains, hills, and so forth. Draw the background shapes of your scene onto the scrap pieces of fabric with a pencil and cut them out. Experiment by arranging the cut pieces onto the support fabric until you are pleased with your composition. Then pin the pieces down. Glue or sew your pieces to your support fabric. Using a variety of fabrics and textured items, begin "piling on" the people and objects needed to complete your arpillera.

Evaluating Your Work

- **Describe** List the materials you used in your arpillera. Describe the place you depicted. List the objects in your work.
- **Analyze** Compare and contrast the use of art elements in your arpillera. Using vocabulary accurately, explain how you used those elements to create a three-dimensional composition.

5. Give your arpillera a descriptive title and display with those of your classmates.

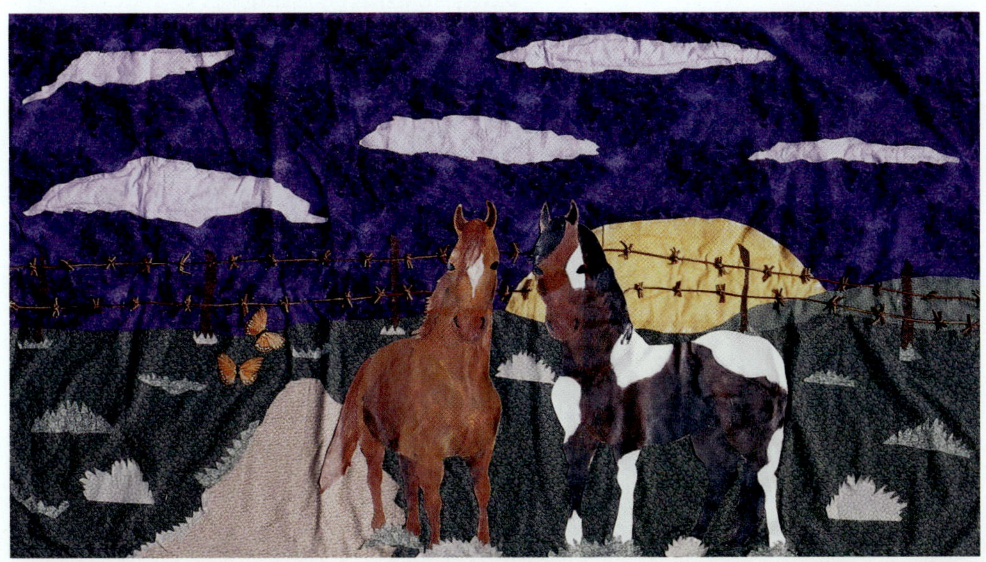

◆ **Figure 2–28** Student work. Arpillera wall hanging.

STUDIO OPTION

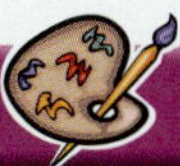

Think of a design for a new fiberart arpillera and illustrate your ideas based on experiences at a school or community event. Experiment by using different colors, shapes, and textures to enhance the design. Complete your arpillera and display in a school exhibit.

Art Online

Go to Web Links at **art.glencoe.com** to learn more about South American arpilleras. There you will also find:

- Artist Profiles
- Interactive Games
- Student Art Gallery

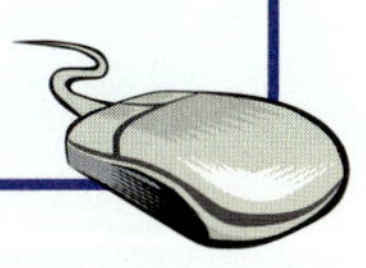

TONY VACCARO/GETTY IMAGES
INSET: GEORGIA O'KEEFFE/ART RESOURCE

Georgia O'Keeffe. *Trees in Autumn.* 1920–21.

NATURE BY COLORS

Artist Georgia O'Keeffe uses color and shape to capture the land.

American painter Georgia O'Keeffe (1887–1986) used art as a visual language. She once said, "I found that I could say things with color and shapes that I couldn't say in any other way—things I had no words for."

O'Keeffe's shapes typically related to objects in nature. However, she wasn't interested in capturing exact details in her close-up views of subjects ranging from flowers to bleached cow skulls. Rather, O'Keeffe used intense, non-naturalistic colors to create an almost abstract beauty. With her subjective colors and simplified shapes, O'Keeffe wanted her paintings to portray what she called "magical realism."

O'Keeffe grew up on a farm in Wisconsin in the 1890s. As a young girl, O'Keeffe decided that she was going to be an artist, an unusual goal for women at the time. She began her career as a painter in New York City, but O'Keeffe eventually settled in the Southwest. The tantalizing colors and shapes inspired by O'Keeffe's beloved New Mexico remained the focus of her canvases for three decades.

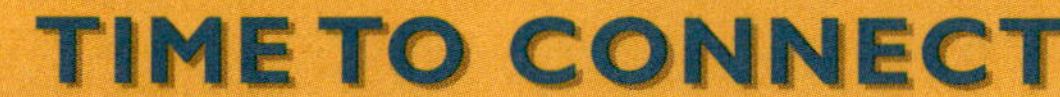

- **Look at O'Keeffe's paintings. What feelings or emotions do they convey? How did O'Keeffe use colors and shapes to create these emotions?**
- **Now as a poet, "paint" one of the landscapes with words. Use a thesaurus to find the most fitting adjectives and adverbs to make the poem vivid.**
- **Share your poem with a partner and revise your work based on her or his feedback. Then share with the class.**

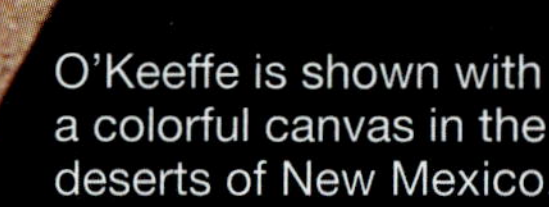

O'Keeffe is shown with a colorful canvas in the deserts of New Mexico.

Chapter 2 Review

BUILDING VOCABULARY

Number a sheet of paper from 1 to 16. After each number, write the term from the list that best matches each description below.

analogous colors	landscape
color	line
color wheel	monochromatic colors
complementary colors	point of view
element of art	shape
form	space
hue	texture
intensity	value

1. Colors opposite each other on the color wheel.
2. An area clearly set off by one or more of the other six visual elements of art.
3. Different values of a single hue.
4. A color's name.
5. An object with three dimensions.
6. The brightness or dullness of a hue.
7. The lightness or darkness of a hue.
8. Colors that are side by side on the color wheel and share a hue.
9. The distance or area around, between, above, below, and within objects.
10. How things feel, or look as though they might feel, if touched.
11. A continuous mark made on some surface by a moving point.
12. Angle from which the viewer sees the scene.
13. Arrangement of hues in a circular format.
14. A basic visual symbol an artist uses to create visual art.
15. An element of art that is derived from reflected light.
16. A drawing or painting of mountains, trees, or other natural scenery.

REVIEWING ART FACTS

Number a sheet of paper from 17 to 20. Answer each question in a complete sentence.

17. How does a trained artist use line?
18. How can an artist vary the quality of a line?
19. What effect can be achieved by using analogous colors together?
20. What is the relationship between shape and form?

CROSS-CURRICULUM CONNECTIONS

21. **Science.** One way artists develop perceptual skills is by changing the distance from which they view an image. As an object is viewed through a microscope, greater detail is observed and the image changes. Try drawing leaves and other objects while looking at them through a microscope.

22. **Language Arts.** Create a list of school and community events you could portray in a drawing. Using the elements of art, create a drawing that illustrates ideas from your experiences at one of these events.

Web Museum Activity

The Minneapolis Institute of Arts, Minneapolis, Minnesota

Click on The Minneapolis Institute of Arts site at **art.glencoe.com**. Test your knowledge of the art elements by viewing the examples on the museum's site. Create your own work of art using the online activity. How many art elements can you identify in your work?

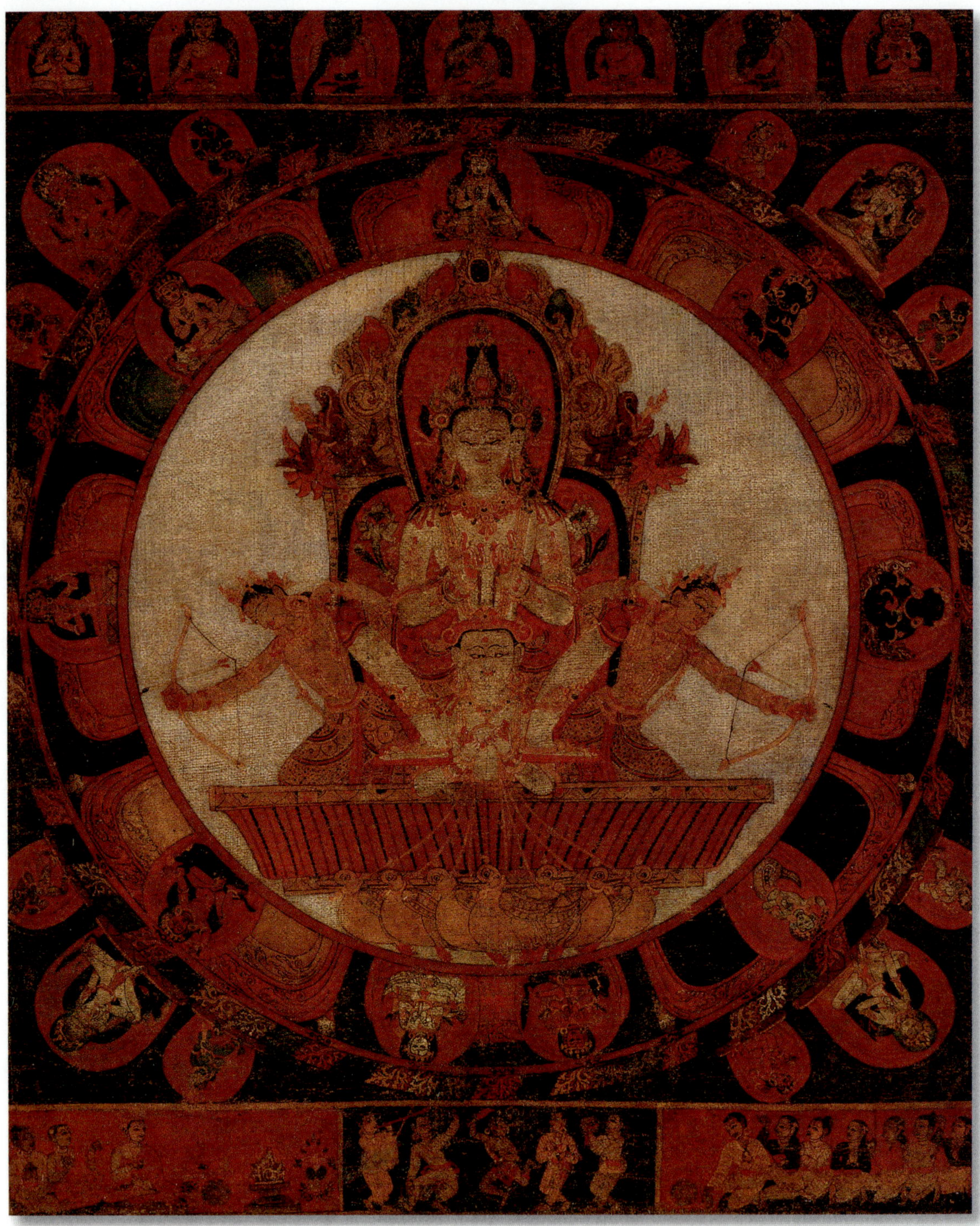

Focus On ◆ **Figure 3–1** **Mandalas are ritual diagrams studied during prayer by Hindus and Buddhists. This one depicts Chandra, the Hindu God of the Moon. He is seated on his chariot, which is drawn by seven geese. On each side, a female attendant shoots arrows to push away the darkness of night. In front, the charioteer holds the reins of the geese. In the first circle around Chandra, the nine planets are represented.**

Nepali. *Mandala of Chandra, God of the Moon.* Late fourteenth to early fifteenth century. Panel: Opaque watercolor on cloth. 40.6 × 36.2 cm (16 × 14¼"). The Metropolitan Museum of Art, New York, New York. Gift of Mr. and Mrs. Uzi Zucher, 1981.

Chapter 3

The Principles of Art

> *"Art is the expression of the profoundest thoughts in the simplest way."*
>
> **—Albert Einstein, German scientist (1879–1955)**

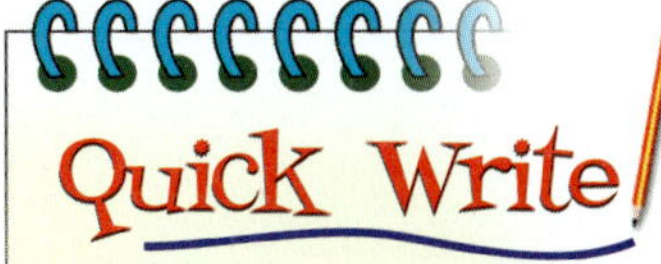

Interpreting the Quote Read the quote. Look up the word *profound* in a dictionary. Then decide whether you agree or disagree with the quote. Write at least three sentences supporting your view.

Have you ever gazed at a work of art and wondered what the point was? Take a moment to study the centuries-old art object at the left. Can you guess what goal or purpose the artist had in mind when setting out to create this object? Notice the ornate arrangement of figures and shapes. What "rules" of design, if any, might this artist have followed?

After completing this chapter, you will be able to:

- Define the term *principles of art*.
- Explain the three kinds of balance.
- Analyze how artists use the principles of variety, harmony, emphasis, proportion, pattern, movement, and rhythm.
- Explain what unity does for an artwork.
- Practice organizing the elements and principles in original artworks.

KEY TERMS

principles of art
balance
informal balance
variety
harmony
emphasis
proportion
pattern
movement
rhythm
unity

LESSON 1

The Language of Design

As a speaker of English, you are aware that every language has rules of grammar. These rules govern the way separate words are combined to form sentences.

In much the same way, the "language" of art has rules. Just as we use guidelines in language, artists use rules to create artworks. Known as **principles of art,** these are *guidelines that govern the way artists organize the elements of art.* There are eight art principles in all. They are balance, variety, harmony, emphasis, proportion, pattern, movement, and rhythm. In this lesson you will learn about the first of these principles—balance.

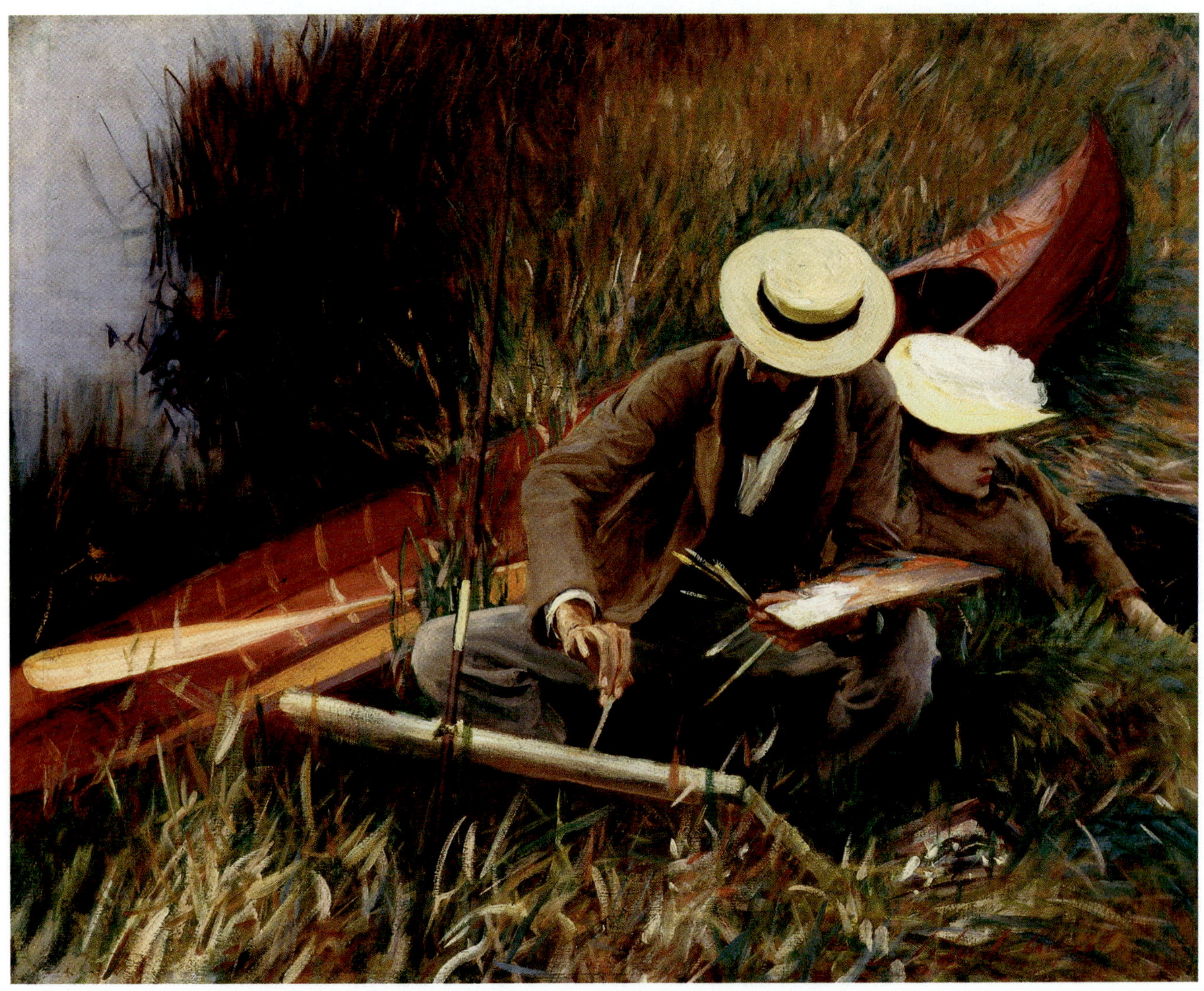

◆ **Figure 3–2 Informal balance makes this painting look as if the artist painted it quickly on the scene. The creation of many sketches, however, tells us that this was carefully planned and produced in the artist's studio.**

John Singer Sargent. *Paul Helleu Sketching His Wife.* 1889. Oil on canvas. 66.4 × 81.6 cm (26⅛ × 32⅛"). The Brooklyn Museum, Brooklyn, New York.

Balance in Art

Do you recall learning to skate or ride a bicycle? You may recall having an occasional spill when you leaned too far in one direction or another. As your self-confidence and balance improved, these falls probably became less frequent.

In art, as in life, balance is also important. **Balance** is *concerned with arranging art elements in an artwork so no one part of that work overpowers, or seems heavier than, any other part.* In the real world, balance can be measured on a scale. If you put too much weight on one side of the scale it will not balance. In art, balance is a function of "visual weight." The art elements are the visual weights in an artwork.

Artists use three kinds of balance. These are formal balance, informal balance, and radial balance. Every work of art, as you will see, has one or another type of balance.

Formal Balance

Formal balance occurs when one half of a work mirrors or closely resembles the other half. Also called symmetrical balance (suh-**meh**-trih-kuhl), formal balance is the easiest type to notice. Look again at **Figure 3–1,** which opened this chapter on page 46. If you draw a line down the center of the work, each half would "mirror" the other.

Informal Balance

Informal, or asymmetrical (**ay**-suh-**meh**-trih-kuhl), **balance** *involves a balance of unlike objects or elements.* A small shape painted bright red, for example, will have the same visual weight as a larger shape painted a duller hue. Consider the painting in **Figure 3–2.** Find the canoe paddle and light-blue patch of water on the left side of the work. Notice how the lighter values of these objects balance the muted colors of the two large figures on the right.

Informal balance is often used to create interesting, true-to-life visual statements. Arranging objects or the elements of art informally can be very complicated. Yet, it can create strong visual interest when used skillfully.

Radial Balance

Radial balance occurs when elements of art or objects in an artwork are positioned around a central point. An example of radial balance in art may be seen in **Figure 3–3.**

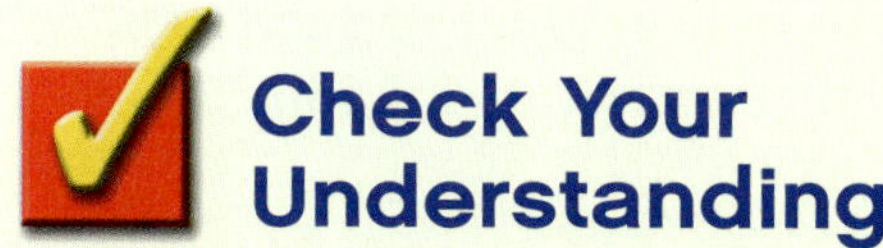

Check Your Understanding

1. What are the *principles of art?*
2. List the eight principles of art.
3. What is *balance?*
4. Compare and contrast how the three kinds of balance are used in artworks.

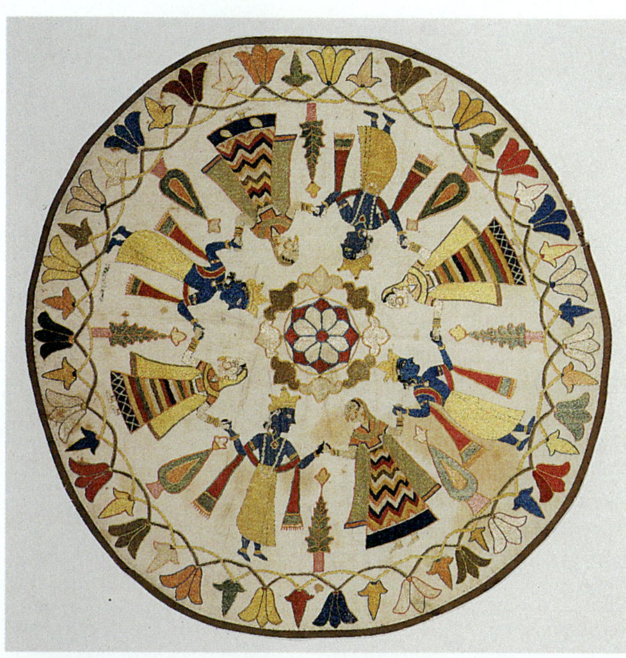

◆ **Figure 3–3 An identical pattern is repeated in this cloth; nevertheless it holds our eye. Why?**

Ceremonial Cloth (Chamba Rumal). India, Himachal Pradesh. c. 1875–1925. Cotton with colored embroidery (silk). 68.6 cm (27″) diameter. Philadelphia Museum of Art, Philadelphia, Pennsylvania. Purchased with funds contributed by Ann McPheil and anonymous donors. 1991–48–1.

Creating a Radial Design

Look closely at **Figure 3–4.** These gold chest ornaments were made by the Asante people, who live along the Gold Coast of western Africa. Known as "soul disks" or "soul washers' badges," these disks act as good luck charms. People who act as caretakers of their dead chieftain's soul wear them around their necks. Notice how your eye is drawn to the center of each disk. What type of balance accounts for this?

What You Will Learn

You will create a radial design using art materials and tools in traditional ways. You will create a focal point in the center of your design using geometric or organic shapes. You will use repeated lines and shapes to create a pattern radiating from a central point. Finally, you will choose a color scheme and use colored pencils or markers to enhance your design.

What You Will Need

- Pencil and eraser
- Compass and ruler
- 12 × 12-inch heavy white drawing paper
- Fine-line black permanent marker
- Colored pencils or markers

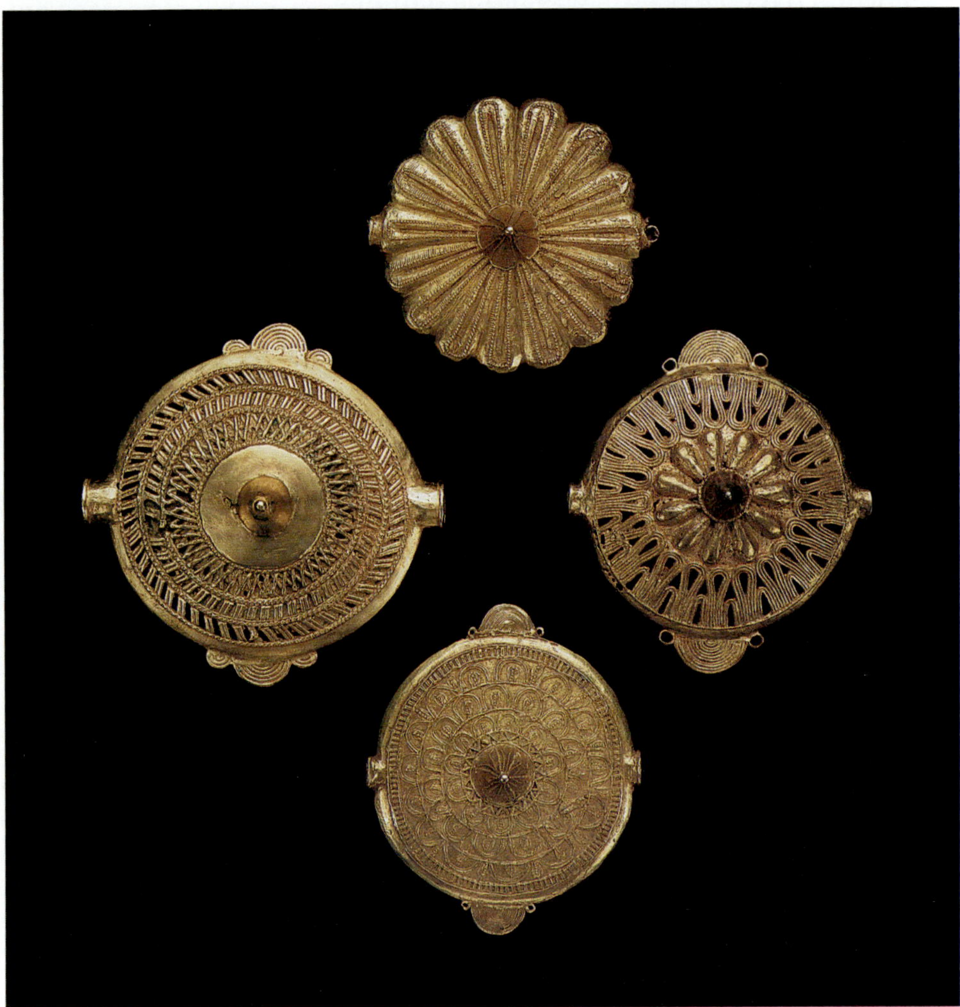

◆ Figure 3–4 Analyze and compare relationships, such as function and meaning, in these discs. How does the intended function of these objects relate to their meaning? The radial designs on the discs represent the roads that lead to the chief, who is symbolized by the central point.

African, Akan. Artist Unknown. Asante. *Pectoral.* Twentieth century (?). Gold. Largest diameter: 11.4 cm (4½″). The Museum of Fine Arts Houston, Houston, Texas. The Glassell Collection of African Gold, gift of Alfred C. Glassell Jr. (Museum # 97.1541. 97.1324. 97.1541.1. 97.1332)

What You Will Do

1. Analyze the Asante soul disks in Figure 3–4. Notice the various ways in which the artists used repeated lines and shapes to create radial balance. What shapes do you see? What types of lines are repeated? What happens to the shapes and lines as they move out from the central point? What objects in nature do you think inspired these designs?
2. Draw a 6-inch circle using a compass.
3. Divide your circle into eight evenly spaced pie shapes that fan out from your central point. Do this by drawing four diameters across your circle. Your lines should all meet at your central point.
4. Create a focal point by drawing a geometric or organic shape around the central point. Next draw a shape or design in one of the pie shapes. Repeat that same shape/design on the other radii as you turn your circle. Your design will begin to "radiate" out from the center. Continue adding more shapes on your radii in this manner. Make sure that you maintain radial symmetry as you develop your design.
5. With your fine-line black marker, trace carefully over your radial design. Review color schemes on page 31. Select one color scheme that uses three or more colors and add color to your radial design.
6. Give your completed radial design a title and display it with those of your classmates. Do all of the radial designs have the same visual effect?

Evaluating Your Work

- **Describe** How did you create your radial design? What shape did you use as your focal point? Explain your procedures.
- **Analyze** How did you use art materials and tools in traditional ways? What kinds of lines and shapes did you use to create patterns in your radial design? Which color scheme did you select? Tell how your use of line, shape, and color added to the creation of a focal point in your radial design.

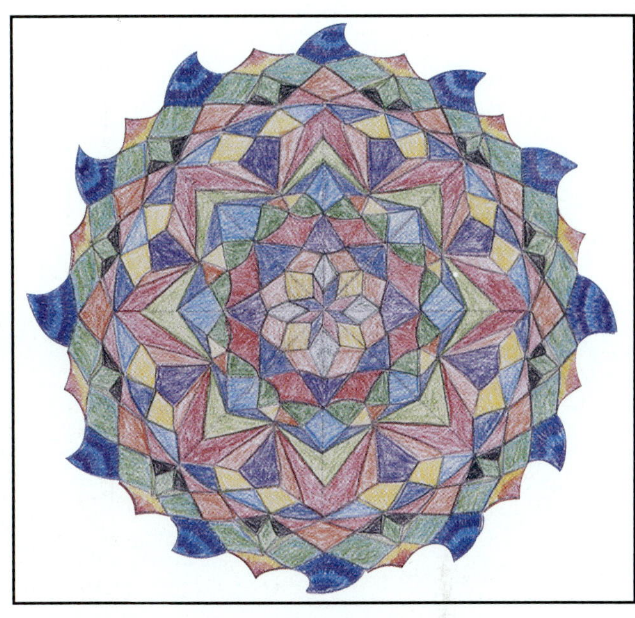

◆ **Figure 3–5** **Student work. Radial design.**

Reflective Thinking

Historical and Cultural Heritage. Soul discs are used as good luck charms in the Asante culture. Analyze Figure 3–4 to determine cultural contexts. What do these discs tell you about the Asante culture? What might you create to honor, symbolize, or depict your cultural heritage?

Visual Art Journal

Compare and contrast the use of balance in Figures 3–1 and 3–3. Now compare these artworks to the one you just created noting similarities and differences. Write your response in your journal, using vocabulary accurately.

Variety, Harmony, Emphasis, and Proportion

"Variety," it is said, "is the spice of life." It might also be said that variety is the spice of art. As an art principle, variety makes artworks interesting and pleasing to view. In this lesson you will learn how variety, as well as three other principles—harmony, emphasis, and proportion—are used in art.

Variety in Art

Imagine listening to your favorite song, not once, but over and over for perhaps 25 or 50 times. No matter how much you liked the sound, eventually you would probably grow tired of hearing it. You might even begin to dislike it!

The explanation for this has to do with the human need for variety—for an occasional change in routine. Art, too, depends on variety. As a principle of art, **variety** *is concerned with combining art elements by adding slight changes to increase visual interest.* By giving a work variety, the artist heightens the visual appeal of the work.

Variety may be introduced in many ways. Light values of a color, for example, may be

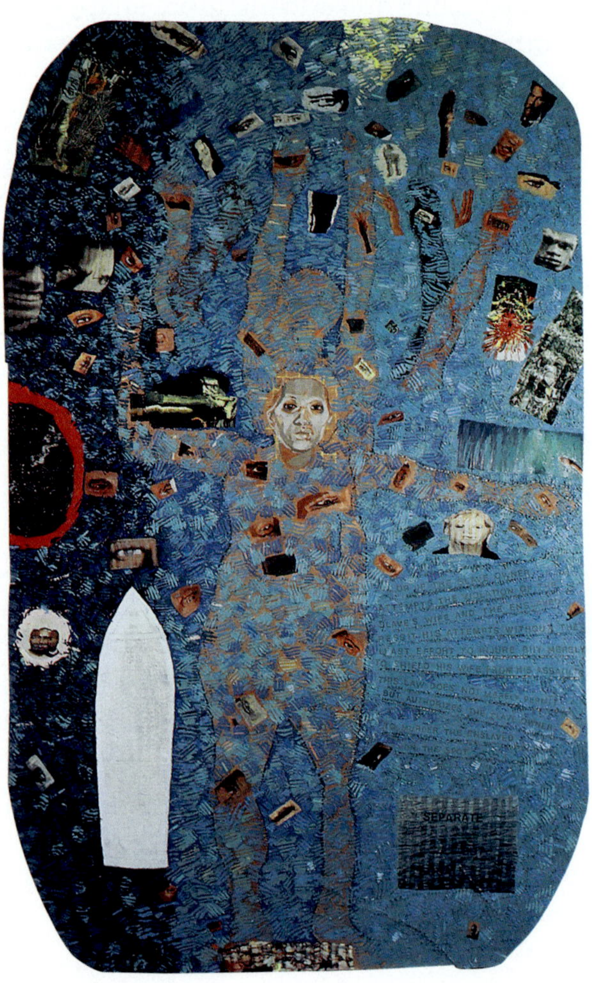

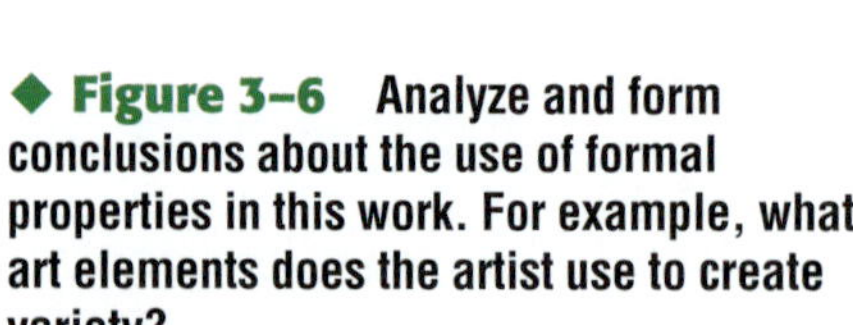

◆ **Figure 3–6 Analyze and form conclusions about the use of formal properties in this work. For example, what art elements does the artist use to create variety?**

Howardena Pindell. *Autobiography: Water/Ancestors/Middle Passage/Family Ghosts.* 1988. Acrylic, tempera, cattle markers, oil stick, paper, polymer. 300 × 43.2 cm (118 × 17″). Wadsworth Athenaeum Museum of Art, Hartford, Connecticut. The Ella Gallup Sumner and Mary Catlin Sumner Collection Fund.

used to create interest in a painting that is made with dark colors. Straight lines can be a welcome change in a work mainly made up of curved lines. Compare and contrast the use of different textures the artist has used in **Figure 3–6.** What other elements contribute to a sense of variety in this unique painting?

Harmony in Art

Picture a coin with the word *variety* on its face. The word on the flip side of such a coin would be *harmony.* You know the term *harmony* from music, where it refers to two or more instruments or voice parts combining to create a pleasant sound. In art, **harmony** is *the principle of art concerned with combining similar art elements to create a pleasing appearance.* In **Figure 3–7** O'Keeffe has used analogous colors to create harmony. Skilled artists use the principles of variety and harmony to successfully blend the art elements. Too much variety and too little harmony in a work can make it complicated and confusing. Focusing only on harmony, on the other hand, can make a work humdrum and uninteresting. Notice how the artist of the work in Figure 3–7 combines the two principles.

Emphasis in Art

When you want to call attention to an important word in a sentence, what do you do? You underline or italicize the word. This makes it stand out visually from the rest of the words on the page. It gives the word emphasis. In art, emphasis has almost the same meaning. **Emphasis** is *the principle of art concerned with making an element or object in an artwork stand out.* The use of this principle helps the artist control what part of a work the viewer looks at first. It also helps the artist control how long the viewer will spend looking at each of the different parts. Emphasis can be created by contrast or extreme changes in an element of art.

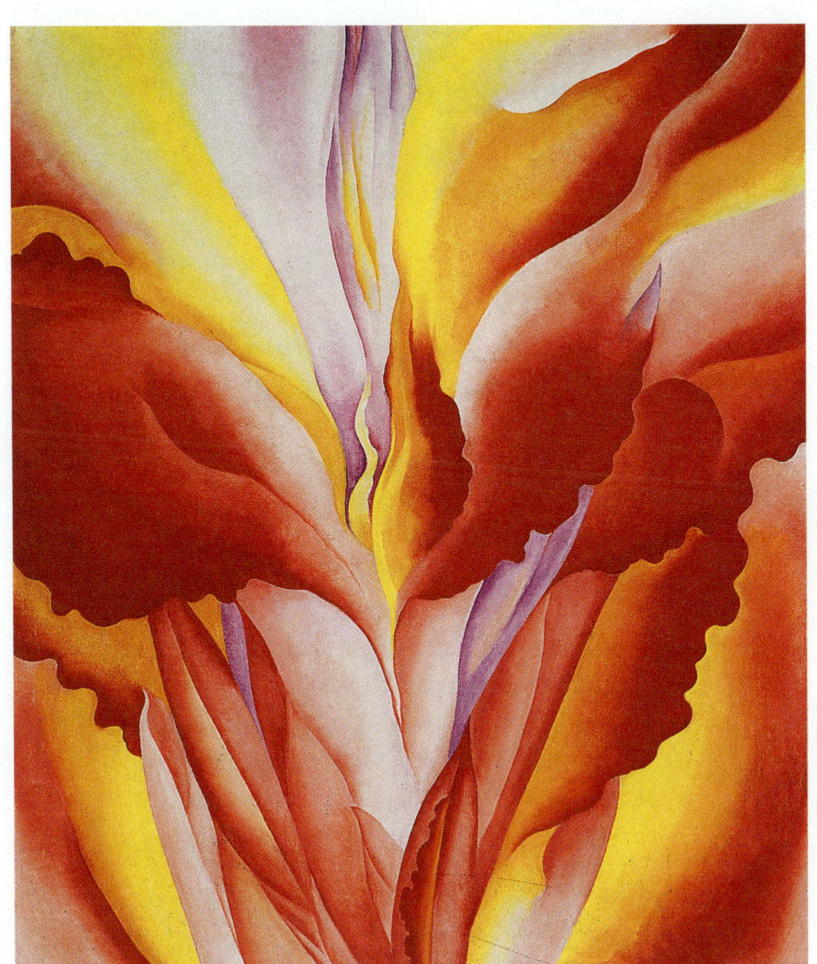

◆ **Figure 3–7** **O'Keeffe has used five related hues to create this work. How has the addition of white and black affected these hues?**

Georgia O'Keeffe. *Red Canna.* ca. 1923. Oil on canvas mounted on masonite. 91.4 × 76 cm (36 × 29⅞"). The University of Arizona Museum of Art, Tucson, Arizona. Gift of Oliver James. © 2003 The Georgia O'Keeffe Foundation/ Artist's Rights Society (ARS), New York.

◆ **Figure 3–8** **It looks like a spotlight is shining on the figure in this work. From what direction is the light shining?**

Rembrandt van Rijn. *Lady with a Pink.* Early 1660s. Oil on canvas. 92.1 × 74.6 cm (36¼ × 29⅜"). The Metropolitan Museum of Art, New York, New York. Bequest of Benjamin Altman, 1913.

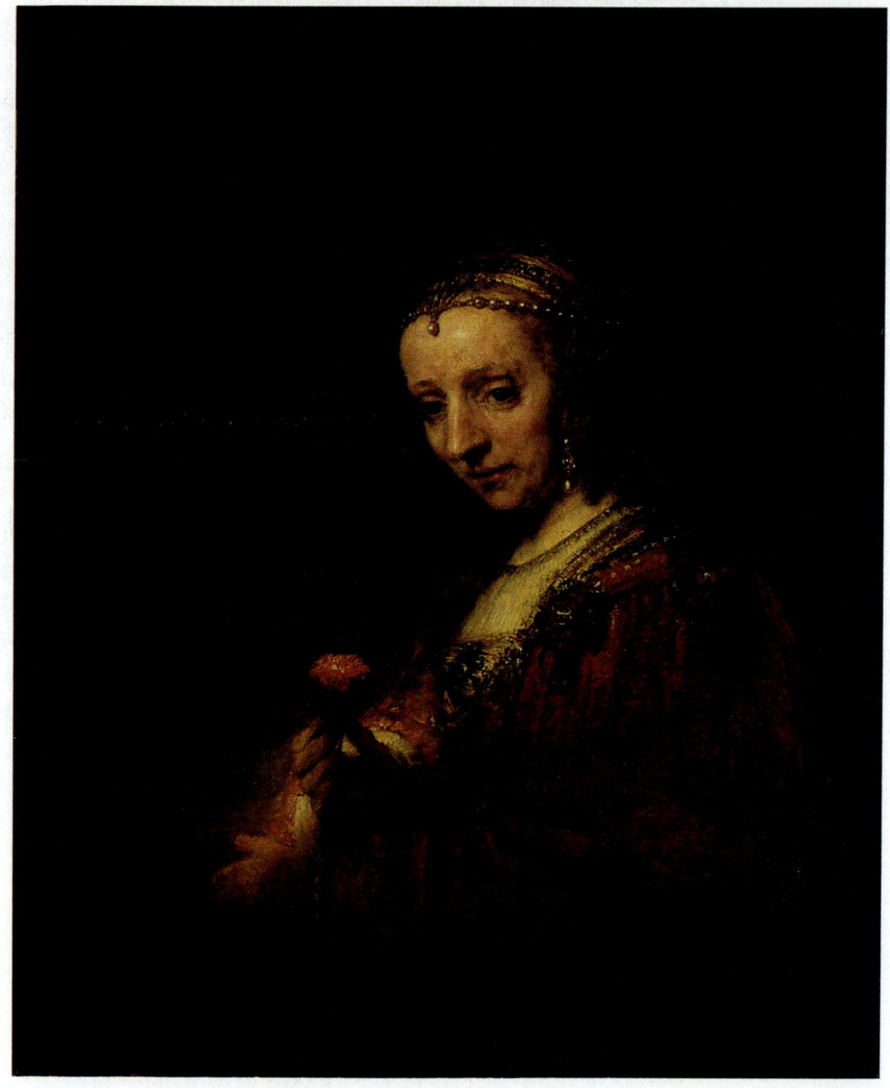

Examine the portrait in **Figure 3–8.** The painting was done by Rembrandt. What do you notice first in this painting? Most likely, your attention was drawn to the woman's face, the flower, or both. Notice that these areas are accentuated by the use of light. They stand out in vivid contrast to the rest of the painting, which is in shadow.

Proportion in Art

Have you ever tried on a piece of clothing and found that it made you look shorter or taller than you actually are? Perhaps the issue was one of proportion. As a principle of art, **proportion** is *the manner in which the parts of a work relate to each other and to the whole.*

Consider the artwork in **Figure 3–9.** The large central figure is the Buddha, founder of the Buddhist faith. Did you notice the other human figures in the work? Two of them are found on either side of the base. They are much smaller than the Buddha, but their servants, kneeling on the ground, are smaller still.

It is important to note that as an art principle, proportion is not just limited to size. Elements such as color can also be used in varying proportions.

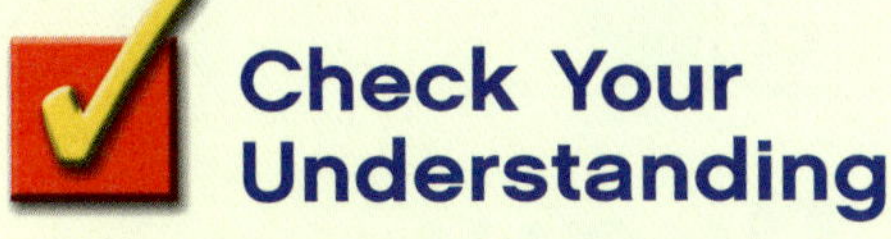

Check Your Understanding

1. Name two ways artists can achieve variety in works of art.
2. How do artists achieve harmony in works of art?
3. What is *emphasis?* What two things does using this principle enable an artist to do?
4. What is *proportion?* Compare and contrast how artists use proportion in artworks throughout this chapter.

Meet the Artist

Rembrandt van Rijn (1606–1669)

Historical Connection. Few names in art are as well known as that of Rembrandt. Born Rembrandt van Rijn (**ryn**) in the Dutch town of Leiden, the artist was a genius in every sense. Rembrandt's first love was painting. At age 14, he began studying with the foremost Dutch artist of the day. Within six months, the student had surpassed the teacher. Rembrandt soon became a brilliant painter, etcher, and draftsman. His portraits especially show his keen eye and attention to detail. Rembrandt is celebrated for his remarkable use of light and shadow, which can be seen in Figure 3–8. Analyze this artwork to form conclusions about formal properties. For example, how does Rembrandt use dark and light values to create an area of emphasis?

◆ **Figure 3–9 Hierarchal proportion is used in artworks of many cultures. That means the most important figure is the largest, and the least important are the smallest. Analyze this artwork to determine cultural contexts. What clues does the artwork provide about this culture in the eighth century?**

Kashmir or northern Pakistan. *Crowned Buddha Sakyamuni.* Eighth century. Brass with inlays of copper, silver, and zinc. Height: 31.8 cm (12½″). Asia Society, New York, New York.

LESSON 4

Using Proportion to Draw a Portrait

Artists have been creating portraits since ancient times. You can often find clues about historical and political influences of a culture by examining its artwork. The Egyptians idealized their kings in sculptural monuments, for example. The Greeks created profiles of rulers for use on coins. The portrait in **Figure 3–10** is by twentieth-century painter Alice Neel. Neel began creating portraits as a way to depict the physical and emotional characteristics of a person. This portrait is of her son Hartley. Hartley seems confident and relaxed as he sits quietly. Can you tell something about his personality in this painting?

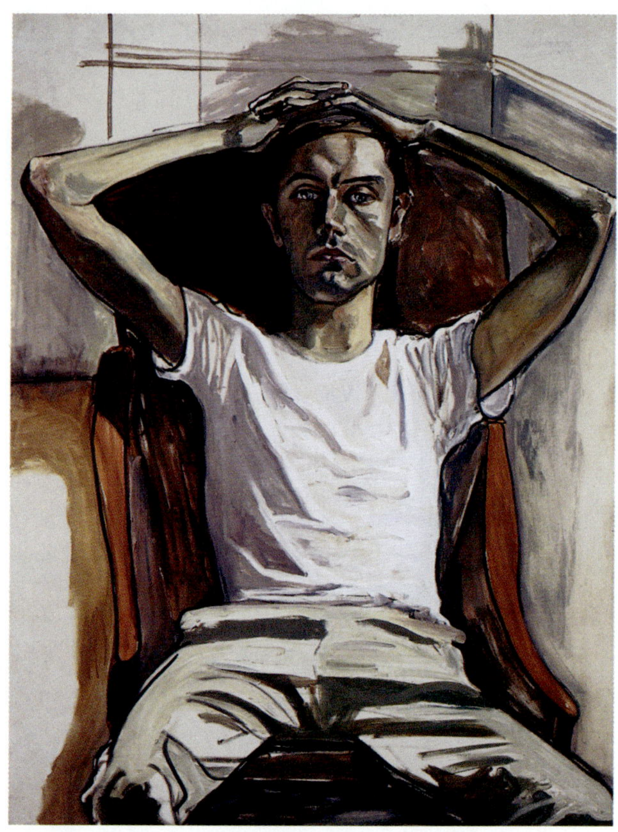

◆ **Figure 3–10** **While other artists changed styles through the middle of the twentieth century, Neel never wavered. She always painted expressive portraits. She was finally recognized in the 1970s for her depiction of character in her portraits of people.**

Alice Neel. *Hartley*. 1965. Oil on canvas. 127 × 91.4 cm (50 × 36″). National Gallery of Art, Washington, D.C. Gift of Arthur M. Bullowa, in honor of the 50th Anniversary of the National Gallery of Art.

What You Will Learn

Using traditional and experimental techniques, you will use direct observation to create a portrait using pencil, charcoal, or oil pastels. Your portrait should accurately emphasize the expressive facial features of your subject. You may draw the rest of the person accurately or experiment with loose lines in the manner of Neel's work. You will organize lines, colors, shapes, and textures to emphasize your subject's personality. The portrait should communicate both the physical and emotional characteristics of your model.

What You Will Need

- Sketch paper, pencil, and eraser
- 12 × 18-inch heavy white or black drawing paper
- Charcoal and/or oil pastels
- Cotton swabs or blending sticks (optional)
- Paper towels

What You Will Do

1. Look again at Figure 3–10. Notice how the eyes divide the oval-shaped head in half. All parts of the face look like they are the right size in relation to each other. Alice Neel used accurate proportion when painting the face. The top of the

head or hair, the forehead, nose, and the mouth and chin are all equally spaced apart. Look at your own face or those of your classmates. Notice how the features are spaced. Neel painted the face realistically, but she painted the arms and body by using loose, simple shapes.

2. Choose a family member, friend, or celebrity to draw. If possible have that person sit for you so that you can use direct observation to make several sketches for your drawing. If the actual person is not available, select a photograph or picture from a magazine.
3. Next, make several quick sketches of your subject. Make a list of at least three personality traits of the person you will draw. Choose one you would like to communicate in your portrait. Experiment with the principles of emphasis and proportion. For example, emphasis can be shown by use of color or by exaggerating the size of a feature. A smile can be enlarged to emphasize a cheerful or outgoing personality. Lips could be colored brightly and drawn in a twisted grin to depict a mischievous person.
4. Select your best sketch and plan your composition. Lightly transfer your best sketch to your sheet of white drawing paper. Think about how you will organize colors, lines, shapes, and textures to emphasize your subject's personality. Choose either pencil, charcoal, or oil pastels to complete your portrait. Analyze with the teacher your portrait in progress, using critical attributes. Step away from your work periodically and view it from a short distance to see if you are capturing the personality trait as you had planned.
5. Title your work and display it with those of your classmates.

Evaluating Your Work

- **Describe** Who is the person in your portrait? Explain why you chose that person. What media did you use to create the portrait? What elements of art did you use to convey the personality of your subject?
- **Analyze** How did you experiment with the elements of art to emphasize the expressive facial features of your subject?

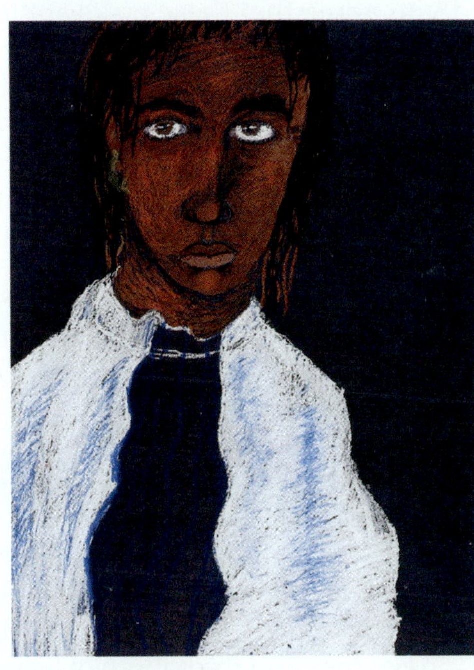

◆ **Figure 3–11** **Student work.**

REFLECTIVE THINKING

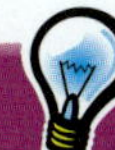

Analyze the original artworks of your classmates. Form conclusions about formal properties and intent. Does their artwork convey the physical and emotional characteristics of the model? Is the end result what the artist intended?

Art Online

To view other examples of portraits, visit **art.glencoe.com**. There you will also find:

- Artist Profiles
- Interactive Games
- Web Links

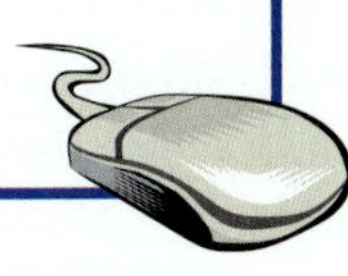

LESSON 5

Pattern, Movement, and Rhythm

Imagine trying to learn a dance in which every step was different from the one before it. Alternatively, imagine what it would be like to dance rhythmically without moving. Would you agree that these tasks are impossible to do? The reason rests with three related concepts—pattern, movement, and rhythm. In this lesson you will learn about these three concepts as principles of art.

Pattern in Art

In art, a **pattern** refers to *a two-dimensional decorative effect achieved through the repetition of colors, lines, shapes, and/or textures.* Repetition plays a major role in creating patterns that add visual interest to a work of art. Each repeated unit in this type of design is called a *motif* (moh-**teef).**

In **Figure 3–12** the clothing of the noblewoman is covered with patterns. Notice the bands around her white sleeves. Notice also the stripes on her shirt and the pattern of leaves embroidered with them. The ruffles of her collar and the flowers in her hair provide more decorative patterns. Analyze Figure 3–12 to determine cultural contexts. Do you think working-class people of her time had ornate patterns on their clothes?

Movement in Art

We are living in an age of special effects. Movies today feature impossible events and scenes. These images are possible thanks to special effects and the creative minds behind them.

In art, special effects are nothing new. Artists have been using them for centuries. One such effect is movement. **Movement** is *the principle of art used to create the look and feel of action and to guide the viewer's eye throughout a work of art.* Artists create movement through a careful blending of elements such as line and shape.

Through the principle of movement, the artist is able to guide the viewer's eye from one part of a painting to the next. Take a look at **Figure 3–13.** Notice how the railroad tracks, which start at the lower left, pull your eye into and through the painting. Additional movement is created by the other diagonal and horizontal lines that converge near the horizon in this unusual "landscape."

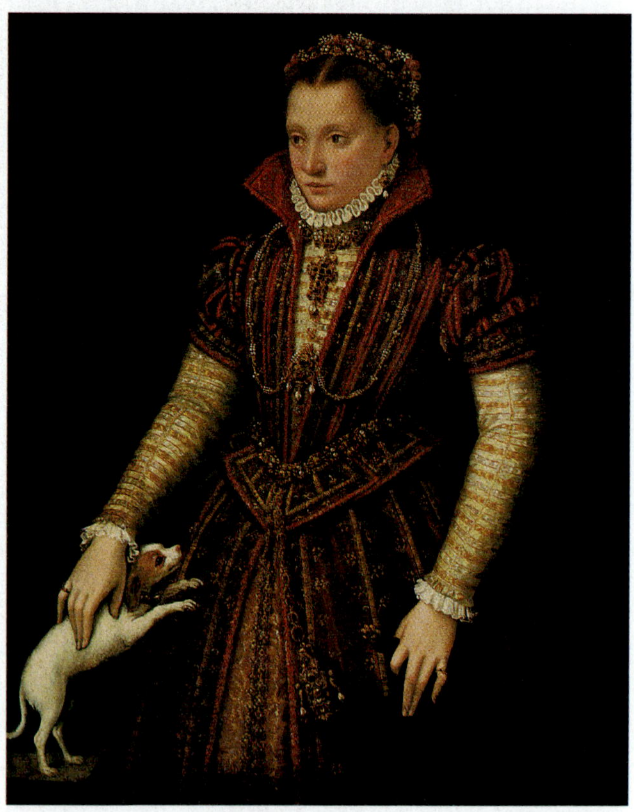

◆ **Figure 3–12** **Fontana is believed to be the first woman in western Europe to develop a professional career as an artist. Her husband acted as her assistant and managed their large household, which included eleven children.**

Lavinia Fontana. *Portrait of a Noblewoman.* c. 1580. Oil on canvas. 115.6 × 89.5 cm (45¼ × 35¼″). National Museum of Women in the Arts, Washington, D.C. Gift of Wallace and Wilhelmina Holladay.

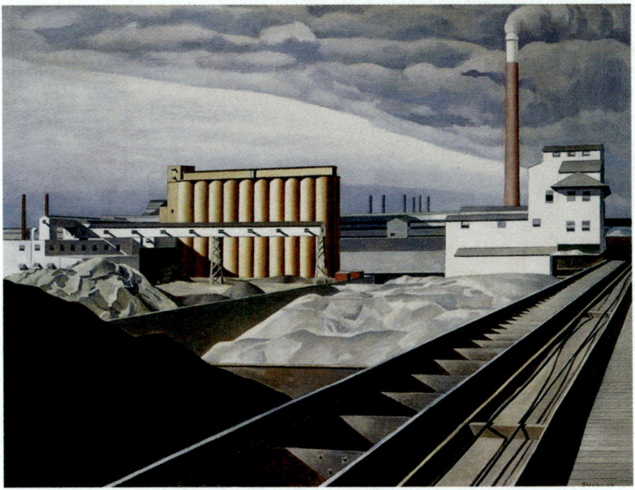

◆ **Figure 3–13** **Notice how Sheeler distinguishes between man-made and natural shapes.**

Charles Sheeler. *Classic Landscape.* 1931. Oil on canvas, 62.9 × 81.9 cm (24¾ × 32¼″). National Gallery of Art, Washington, D.C. Collection of Mr. and Mrs. Barney A. Ebsworth.

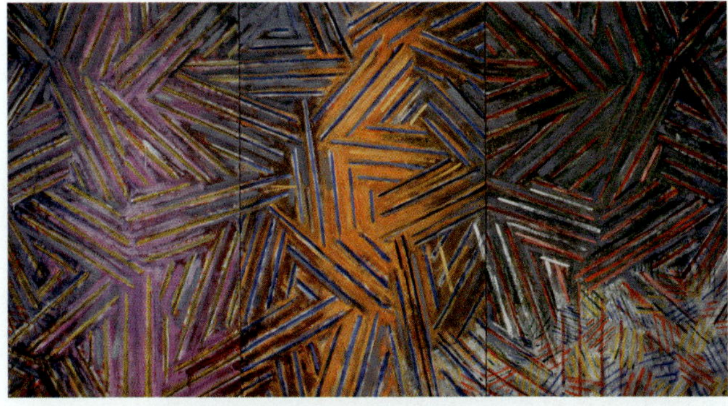

◆ **Figure 3–14** **Which element does the artist incorporate with rhythm to give the painting a "beat"?**

Jasper Johns. *Between the Clock and the Bed.* 1981. Encaustic on canvas, three panels, overall. 183.2 x 321 cm (72⅛″ × 126⅜″). Museum of Modern Art, New York, New York. Gift of Agnes Gund. © 1998 Jasper Johns/Licensed by VAGA, New York, NY.

STUDIO ACTIVITY

Making a Motif

Using Pattern to Create Prints. In this studio activity, you will produce a print using a variety of art materials and tools in traditional ways. Create a motif on a piece of 3 x 3-inch mat board or poster board. Do this by gluing cut shapes from scraps of poster board or construction paper and lines from bits of string onto your background board. A small paper clip or similar object can be used in your motif as well. Place your motif under a 9 x 12-inch piece of paper and, using crayons in either cool or warm colors, make a rubbing to create a print of your motif. Repeat making rubbings of your motif to create a pattern.

PORTFOLIO

Share your work with the other students who sit at your table. Take turns analyzing and critiquing each other's pattern rubbings and motifs. Form conclusions about formal properties in your artwork and in those of your classmates. Take notes on the comments made about your work, attach it to your rubbing, and keep it in your portfolio with your motif.

RHYTHM IN ART

You may recall learning about harmony in Lesson 2. Another musical term, rhythm, also plays a vital role in art. In art, **rhythm** is *the repetition of an element to make a work seem active.* You sometimes "feel" rhythm in a work of art as strongly as you see it. As an example, look at **Figure 3–14.** The artist uses rhythm to make his painting come alive. By carefully mixing shapes and values, he moves the viewer's eyes to the painting's beat.

Sometimes, to create rhythm, artists will repeat not just elements but the same exact objects over and over. When they do this, a pattern is formed.

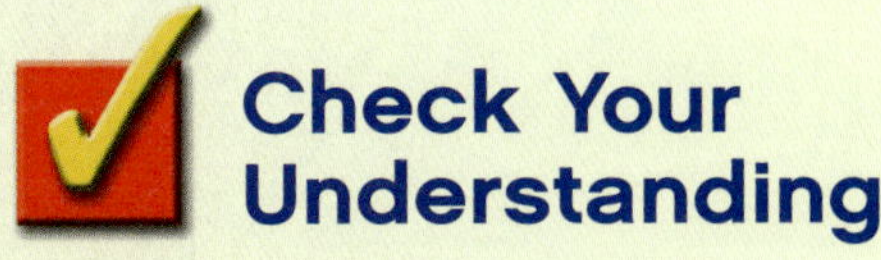

Check Your Understanding

1. What does an artist create by repeating an object again and again?
2. What is *movement?*

Creating Movement with Rhythm

Look closely at the woodcut in **Figure 3–15.** The work shows two formations of birds, one white, one black. Yet there is more to this print than first meets the eye. Find the lead bird in either formation. Notice that the birds behind the leader are created with progressively less detail. Eventually the black birds fade into the negative space between the white birds and vice versa. This occurrence is, of course, impossible. The artist, M. C. Escher, was known for his ability to blend geometry and art. When combined, the two create fantastic worlds that look real—until you study them carefully.

What You Will Learn

Look again at Figure 3–15. Do you see how Escher has altered the elements of shape and space to create his effect? Now it is your turn. You will produce a drawing in which one geometric shape gradually changes into a recognizable free-form object. You will select and use a variety of appropriate art materials and tools to experiment with the elements of line, shape, and space and the principle of rhythm. Use a black marker and colored pencils to create contrast and positive and negative shapes in your work.

What You Will Need

- Sketchbook, pencil, and eraser
- 12 × 18-inch white drawing paper
- 18-inch ruler, compass
- Thin- and medium-line permanent black markers
- Colored pencils
- Mat board or poster board (optional)

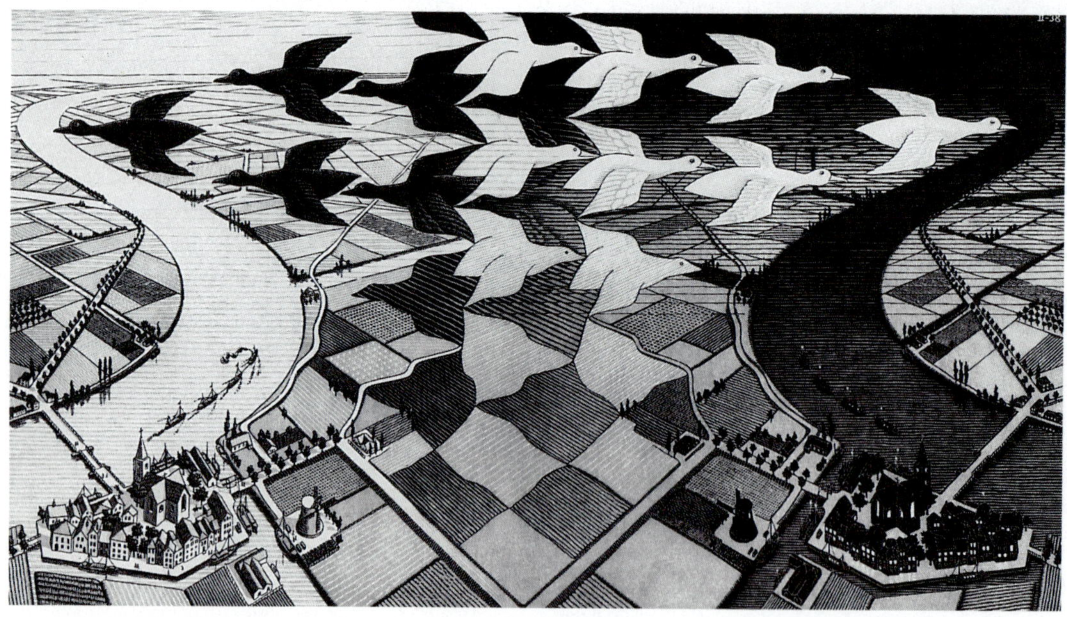

◆ **Figure 3–15** **Some have called Escher "The Poet of the Impossible." When you look at this work in which night becomes day, you can understand the title. He makes impossible transformations of shapes into space seem real.**

M. C. Escher. *Day and Night.* 1938. Woodcut in black and gray, printed from two blocks. 39.1 × 67.7 cm (15⅜ × 26⅝″).

What You Will Do

1. Study Figure 3–15 closely. Notice how the geese slowly become unrecognizable free-form shapes. What other changes do you notice in the sky and ground? How does Escher create contrast?
2. As a class, observe and discuss how shapes in nature change gradually. An example is a flower opening from a closed bud. In your sketchbook experiment by gradually changing one geometric shape into a recognizable free-form object. Do this in five to six steps. It may be helpful to think of the object you want to draw. Practice changing different geometric shapes in this manner.
3. Select the sketch you like the most. Begin by using your pencil and ruler to measure your squares or rectangles on your white drawing paper. Lightly transfer your design onto your prepared grid with a pencil. You may need to use a ruler or compass to draw your geometric shape.
4. Outline your drawing with your black markers. Add color to create contrast and to complete your project.
5. Mat or mount your finished work and display in a class exhibition. Give your work a title. Look at the works of your classmates. Discuss the variety of approaches used to create movement through gradual changes.

Evaluating Your Work

- **Describe** Explain the steps you took to create gradual movement in your drawing. What object did your shape evolve into?
- **Analyze** How did you experiment with the elements of art? What geometric shape did you use in your drawing? What negative spaces were created by your positive shapes?

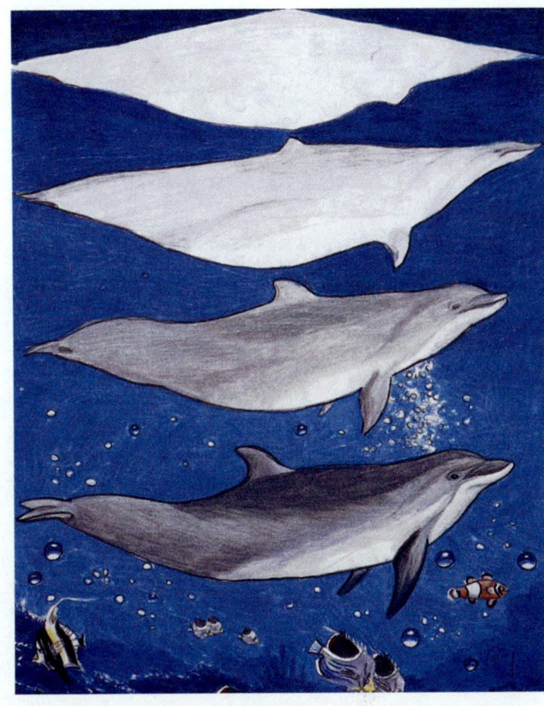

◆ **Figure 3–16** **Student work.**

Portfolio Ideas

Analyze portfolios by your classmates and others, such as those of upper-grade students or your art teacher. Participate in a group critique. Take turns explaining your intent and meaning behind the artworks in your portfolio. Then take turns explaining your conclusions about how the formal properties are used. List the comments made about your artworks and keep them in your portfolio.

Visual Art Journal

Analyzing exhibitions. Analyze the class exhibition by your peers. Form conclusions about formal properties, such as how the elements of line, shape, and space are used with the principle of rhythm. Summarize your conclusions in your journal.

Unity in Art

Are you familiar with our country's motto? It's *E Pluribus Unum*—Latin for "Out of many, one." It celebrates the unity, or oneness, of a nation made up of many cultures.

Unity is also celebrated as a property in art. Every artist strives to combine the parts, or elements, of a work into a meaningful whole. In this lesson, you will learn how artists go about unifying a work.

Unity in Art

Unity is *the arrangement of elements and principles with media to create a feeling of completeness*. Unity in an artwork is like invisible glue. You can't point to it as you can an element or principle. However, you can sense it. You can also sense when it is missing. Look at **Figure 3–17.** The painting seems to display a sense of completeness. Can you name the principles shown in this artwork that contribute to that unity?

Plotting Unity on a Chart

Explaining how the parts of an artwork fit together can be difficult. Using a design chart **(Figure 3–18)** makes the task easier.

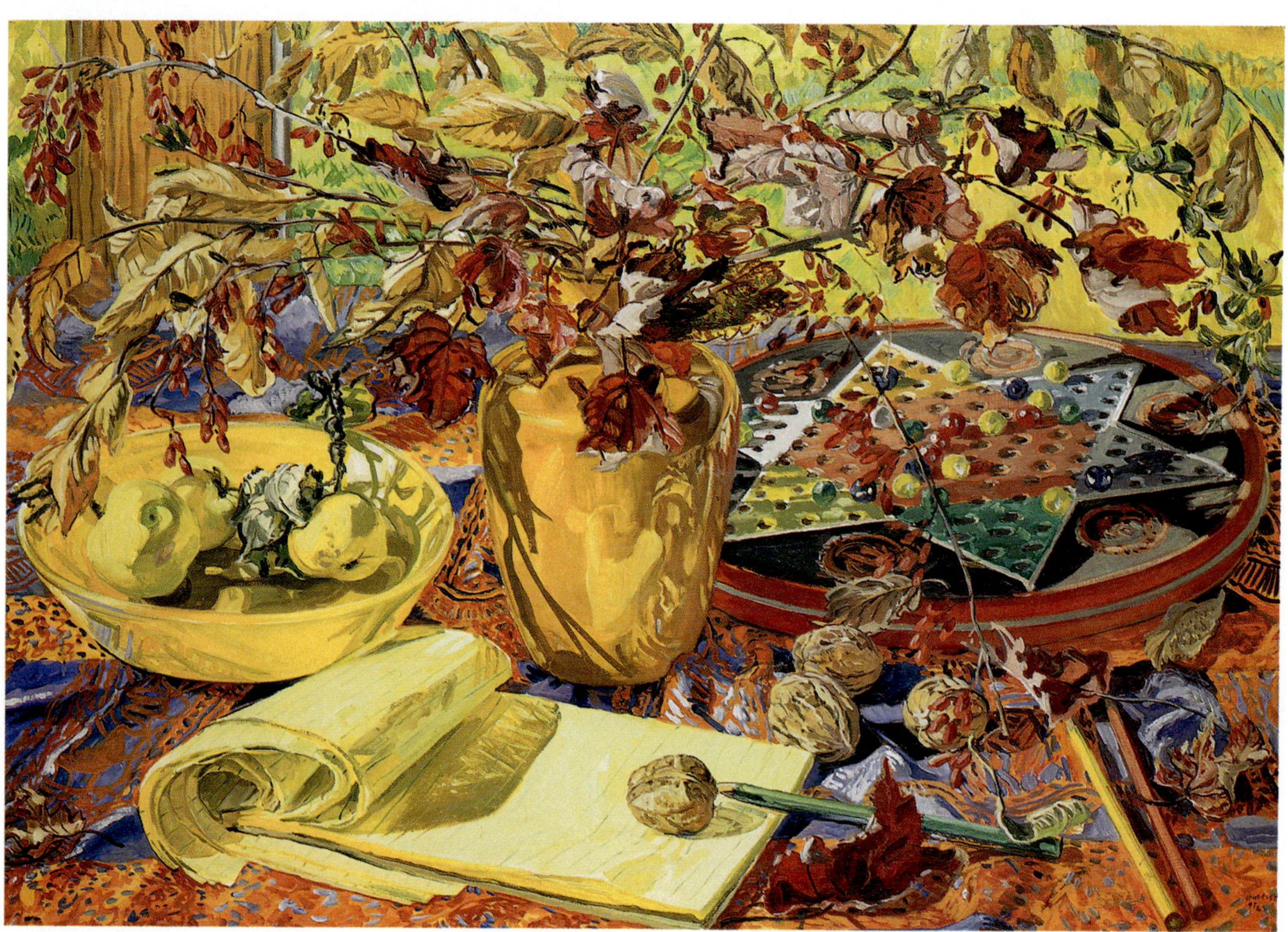

◆ **Figure 3–17 Analyze and form conclusions about the use of formal properties in this work. For example, how has Fish used the element of color to unify her painting?**

Janet Fish. *Yellow Pad*. 1997. Oil on canvas. 91.4 × 228.6 cm (36 × 50″). The Columbus Museum of Art, Columbus, Ohio. © Janet Fish/Licensed by VAGA, New York, NY.

DESIGN CHART	PRINCIPLES OF ART						
ELEMENTS OF ART	Balance	Variety	Harmony	Emphasis	Proportion	Pattern	Movement/ Rhythm
Line							
Color: Hue							
Intensity							
Value							
Shape/Form							
Space							
Texture							

Unity

◆ **Figure 3–18** **Design chart.**

Notice that the chart shows the elements of art along the side and the principles of art along the top. Think of each square where an element and principle meet as a design question. Here, for example, are some questions that might be asked about hue:

- Is the balance of the hues formal, informal, or radial?
- Do the hues show variety?
- Is a single hue used throughout to add harmony?
- Is hue used to emphasize, or highlight, some part of the work?
- Is the proportion, or amount of hue, greater or lesser than that of other elements?
- Does hue add to a sense of movement?
- Do hues repeat in a rhythmic way that add actions to the work?

Think about what questions you might ask about each of the remaining elements.

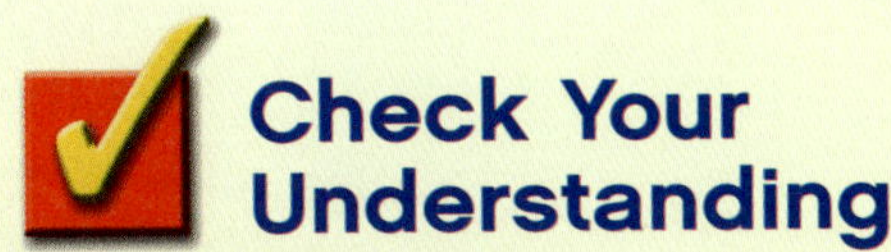

Check Your Understanding

1. What is *unity* in art?
2. What does a design chart help you do?

J Mays Puts You in the Driver's Seat

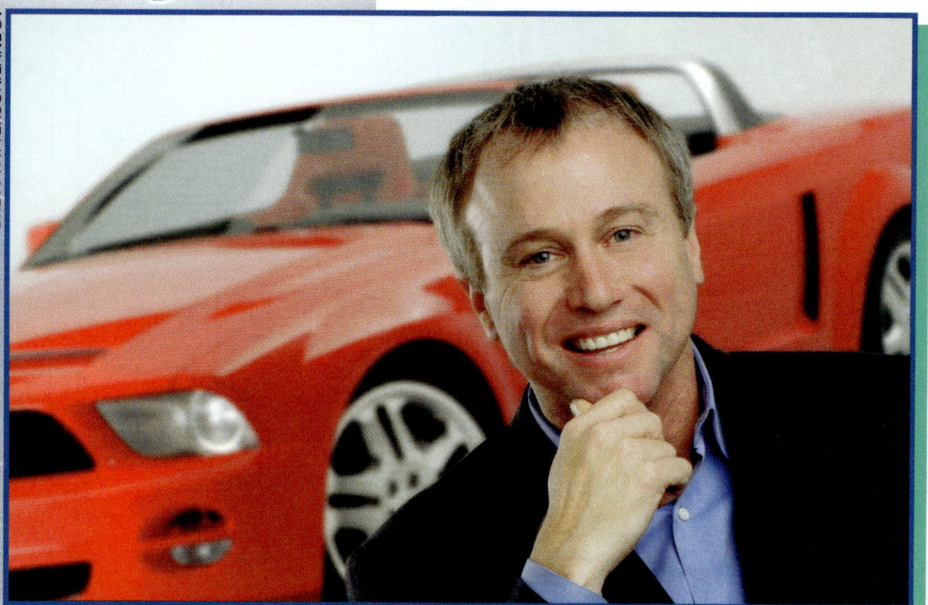

BRETT PATTERSON/LANDOV

J Mays poses with one of his famous designs: a Mustang GT convertible coupe. Car designers like J Mays are responsible for the overall design as well as the exterior colors and interior fabrics.

An industrial designer gives people what they want.

J Mays is a real big wheel in Detroit, Michigan. He is part of the new generation of industrial designers—people who design consumer products from trash cans to cars. This new generation of designers wants to give the public what it wants, not what designers think the public should have.

How do you design something people will like? Mays explains that you must "get inside their brains!" You talk with them, asking questions about their needs and their dreams. You check out current music and television shows. Mays also seeks inspiration from current fashion, architecture (for example, buildings by Mies van der Rohe and Frank Gehry), and products that he thinks are well designed.

For Mays, design is about connecting with people. "It's the battle for their heartstrings," he says. That's why he tries to appeal to people's feelings and emotions, as well as their wallets.

A huge design success for Mays was a car he created, the 2001 Thunderbird. Its interior and exterior reveal his spare, elegant style. Each element fits seamlessly together to create a unique, sleek, and satisfying object. Mays explains that he is not just building a car—he's "trying to design an experience."

TIME TO CONNECT

- **Imagine you are on the marketing team selling a new car. You have to write a press release for a newspaper describing why people will like the car.**
- **Choose a car model that appeals to you. Draft, edit, and revise a statement that explains why its design works so well.**
- **Describe how its design uses the elements and principles of art, such as color, shape, and proportion. Be sure the press release creates an understanding of, and a desire for, the car you are advertising.**

Chapter 3 Review

BUILDING VOCABULARY

Number a sheet of paper from 1 to 11. After each number, write the term from the list that best matches each description below.

balance	principles of art
emphasis	proportion
harmony	rhythm
informal balance	unity
movement	variety
pattern	

1. Guidelines that govern the way artists organize the elements of art.
2. What a work has when no one part overpowers any other.
3. Combining art elements by adding slight changes to increase visual interest.
4. Combining similar art elements in a pleasing way.
5. Making an element or object in a work stand out.
6. The way parts of a work relate to each other and to the whole.
7. The principle that leads a viewer to sense action or guide the eye through a work.
8. The repetition of an element to make a work seem active.
9. Combining elements, principles, and media to create a feeling of completeness.
10. A two-dimensional decorative effect achieved through the arrangement of colors, lines, shapes, and/or textures.
11. A balance of unlike objects or elements.

REVIEWING ART FACTS

Number a sheet of paper from 12 to 20. Answer each question in a complete sentence.

12. What kind of balance is shown in a work where one half mirrors the other?
13. What is another name for asymmetrical balance? For symmetrical balance?
14. Some artists think of radial balance as a complicated form of what other type of balance?
15. What can happen to a work when an artist overuses harmony?
16. What principle will an artist use to control which part of a work a viewer's eye sees first?
17. Is proportion in art limited to size of objects? Explain.
18. What principle will an artist use to carry the viewer's eye from one part of a work to the next?
19. What is a pattern?
20. What is another name for oneness?

CROSS-CURRICULUM CONNECTIONS

21. **Science.** Find examples from nature that represent formal, informal, and radial balance. Create drawings of the examples based on direct observation. Try looking at them through a microscope. Group your drawings according to the type of balance. Think about the different principles of art. How do they relate to the designs found in nature?

Web Museum Activity

The Smithsonian Institution, Washington, D.C.

What is a mandala, like the one shown in Figure 3–1? What kind of balance is used in creating a mandala? To find out the answer to these and other questions, visit The Smithsonian Institution online. Click on the museum's link at **art.glencoe.com** to see how a mandala is created.

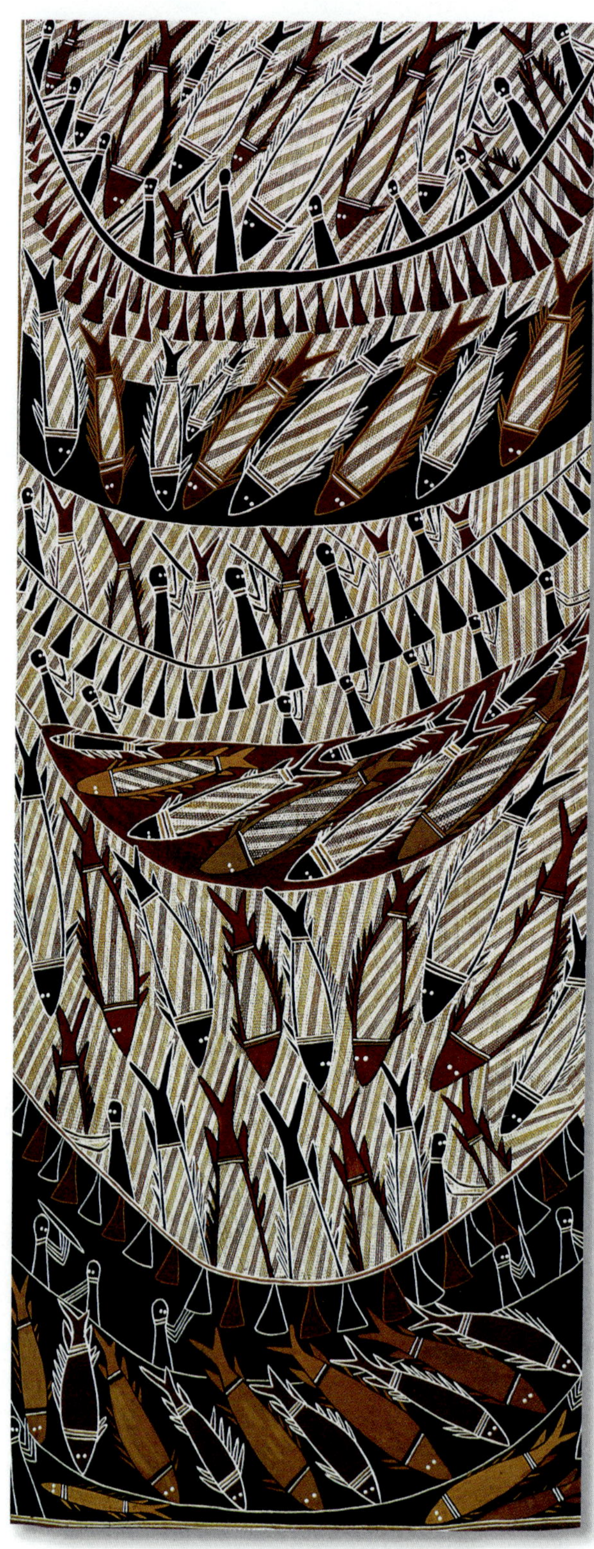

Focus On ◆ **Figure 4–1** **This image is one part of a triptych, or a work made of three panels. It conveys this Australian artist's childhood memories. Why do you think he depicted the fish larger than the people? What clues does this artwork provide about the artist's cultural heritage?**

George Milpurrurru. *Fishing Net.* Natural pigments on eucalyptus bark. 226 × 90 cm (89 × 35$\frac{7}{16}$"). University of Virginia, Charlottesville, Virginia. Kluge-Ruhe Collection. © 2003 Artists Rights Society (ARS), New York/VISCOPY, Sydney.

Chapter 4

Exploring Art Media

"*The medium is the message.*"

—Marshall McLuhan, social commentator (1911–1980)

When they hear the word *artist,* many people think "painter." It is true that paint and brushes are among the most commonly used art tools. Certainly they are among the oldest. Yet, these are far from being the *only* tools available to the creative mind and hand.

As you will discover in the lessons in this chapter, artists use a wide variety of materials and techniques in traditional and experimental ways in their work.

After completing this chapter, you will be able to:

- Define the term *art media*.
- Name the different kinds of media used in drawing, printmaking, painting, sculpting, and electronic media-generated art.
- Learn how drawing, printmaking, painting, sculpting, and digital media are created in traditional and experimental ways.
- Use computers to create an electronic media-generated artwork.

Quick Write

Interpreting the Quote Read the quote and examine the artwork in **Fig. 4–1**. The medium in this work is natural pigments on eucalyptus bark. Do you think the work would give a different message if it were made of smooth marble? State your opinion in a brief paragraph.

KEY TERMS

art media
printmaking
fine art print
edition
pigment
binder
solvent
sculpture
freestanding
relief
digital art
resolution
rendering

The Media of Art

Every work of art begins with a thought or idea. Every work ends with a realization of that starting concept. What happens in between is a result of many choices the artist makes.

Some of the most important choices are the tools and materials that will be used to create the artwork. For some projects, the materials may include clay and sculpting tools. For others, the tools of choice may be crayons and paper. A computer screen and a mouse might be used by others. These and other *tools and materials used to create works of art* are known collectively as **art media.**

It is worth noting that that term—*art media*—is plural. It refers to more than one material or tool. When referring to a single art material or tool, you use the term *art medium.*

Art Media and Processes

Some art, as you have learned, is created in two dimensions. Paintings, drawings, and photographs are examples of two-dimensional art. The images they provide can be seen only when looked at directly, or head-on.

Other art is made to be appreciated in three dimensions. Statues and most objects of applied art fall into this category. They are made to be seen from different sides and angles. The same is true of works of architecture.

Like art itself, the media and processes used in its creation can be categorized as being two- or three-dimensional.

- **Two-dimensional media and processes.** These include tools and materials used in the various processes of picture making. Among these tools are pencils, pens, pastels, and paint brushes. Materials, or surfaces, on which the two-dimensional image appears include paper, parchment, and canvas. Figure 4–1, which opened this chapter on page 66, was made using fairly uncommon two-dimensional media. These include natural pigments and eucalyptus bark. What medium was used for the two-dimensional artwork in Figure 3–10 on page 56?
- **Three-dimensional media and processes.** These include tools and materials used in the processes that

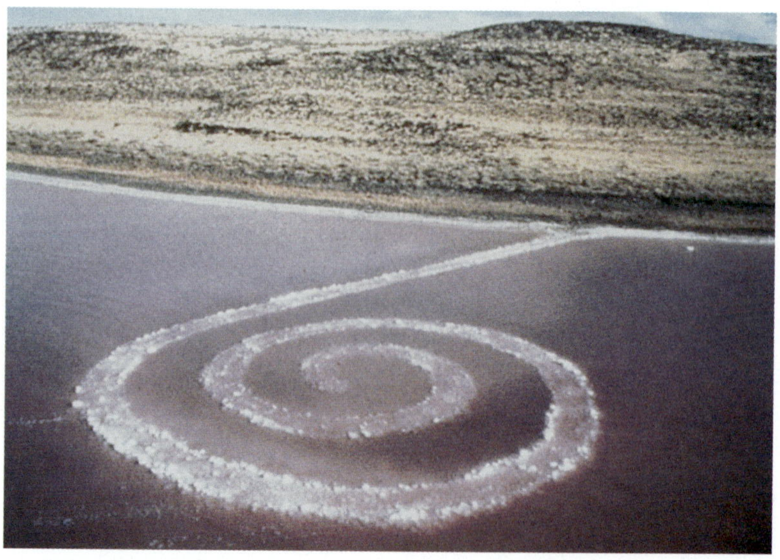

◆ **Figure 4–2** ***Spiral Jetty*** **was created when the water in the lake was low. It is always visible from the sky, but it disappears when the water is high and reappears when the water is low. What is its status in this picture?**

Robert Smithson. *Spiral Jetty.* Long-term installation in Rozel Point, Box Elder County, Utah. 1970. Black basalt rocks and earth from the site. The coil is 460 m (1,500′) long and 4.6 m (15′) wide. Photo: Nancy Holt. Collection: Dia Art Foundation. Art © Estate of Robert Smithson/Licensed by VAGA, New York, NY

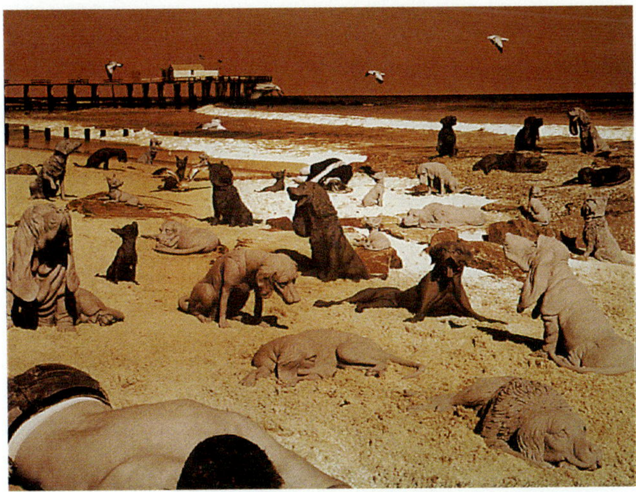

◆ **Figure 4–3** **Skoglund first created the dog sculptures for this piece and then installed them on this beach site. The two people in the scene were part of her plan. After photographing the installation, she made lithograph prints from the photos at a printmaking studio.**

Sandy Skoglund. *Dogs on the Beach.* © 1992. Lithograph printed in color on Ragcote paper. 62.9 × 56.8 cm (24¾ × 22⅜″). Smith College Museum of Art, Northampton, Massachusetts.

produce art in three dimensions. Among these tools are chisels, knives, and mallets. Among the materials are marble, bronze, and wood. Examine **Figure 4–2.** The "media" used by the artist included a bulldozer and other heavy digging and earth-moving equipment. What media were used by the sculptor of the work shown in Figure 1–3 on page 6?

Unconventional Art Processes

Sometimes, the line between the processes used to make an artwork and the finished work itself becomes blurred. This is especially true in some contemporary art. Consider the fantasy work in **Figure 4–3.** The process behind this unusual creation had several steps. First, the artist sculpted the dogs. Then she photographed this beach scene, which includes two live models. Finally, she made a series of fine art prints from the photo.

You will learn more about printmaking and other processes in the lessons that follow. The Studio Activity on this page will give you practice making a print of your own.

Studio Activity

Making a Leaf Print

Experimenting with Art Media. In this activity, you will select and use a variety of appropriate art materials and tools in experimental ways. You will try your hand at using an ordinary leaf to create an artwork.

Find and bring to class several leaves with raised veins. Choose the most interesting leaf as your subject to interpret. Lightly coat the veins of the leaf with cold, melted candle wax. Be careful not to get wax on the rest of the leaf's surface. Set the leaf aside, wax-side up, for about 10 minutes. This will give the wax a chance to harden slightly. Dip the leaf, wax-side down, in a shallow pan containing ¼ inch of printer's ink or acrylic paint. Press the inked side of the leaf against a sheet of scrap paper to absorb excess ink or paint. Now press the leaf carefully on a sheet of drawing paper. Make additional prints.

PORTFOLIO

Write a paragraph comparing and contrasting the use of pattern in the first and later prints. Which best captured the design of the leaf? Which did you like best? Why? Save your favorite design with your notes and keep in your portfolio.

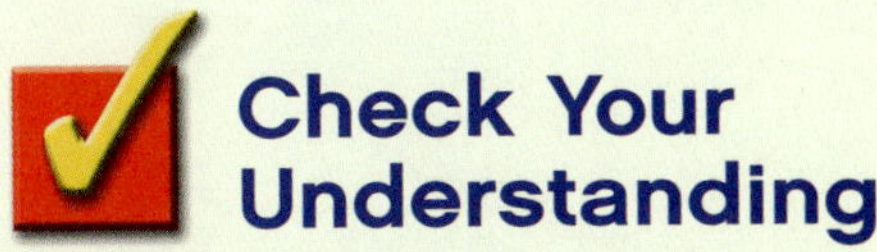

Check Your Understanding

1. Name three media used in two-dimensional art.
2. Compare and contrast two media used in three-dimensional art.

Drawing

Have you ever watched a small child scribbling with crayons? Although you may not have known it at the time, you were witnessing drawing media in action. The media used in drawing are many and varied. In this lesson, you will learn about several. You will also learn about special ways in which artists use these media. Later, you will experiment using some of them yourself.

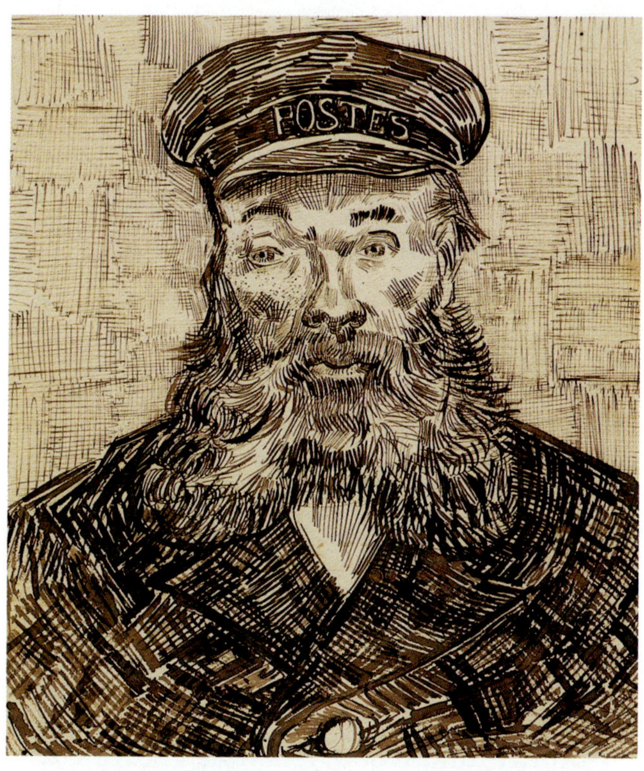

◆ **Figure 4–5** **Many of van Gogh's paintings are famous for their strokes of color, but this drawing comes alive with the strokes of his pen. Notice how the lines seem to dance around the face of the man.**

Vincent van Gogh. *Portrait of Joseph Roulin.* 1888. Reed and quill pens, brown ink, black chalk. 32 × 24.4 cm (12⅝ × 9⅝″). The J. Paul Getty Museum, Los Angeles, California.

The Media of Drawing

The media of drawing are among the most extensive of any area of art. Many of these media coincide with writing materials you use every day. For example, pencils are considered drawing media and so is classroom chalk.

Some of the other tools used in drawing are shown in **Figure 4–4.** How many of these have you used at one time or another? Which of these tools was used in the creation of **Figure 4–5?** Of **Figure 4–6?**

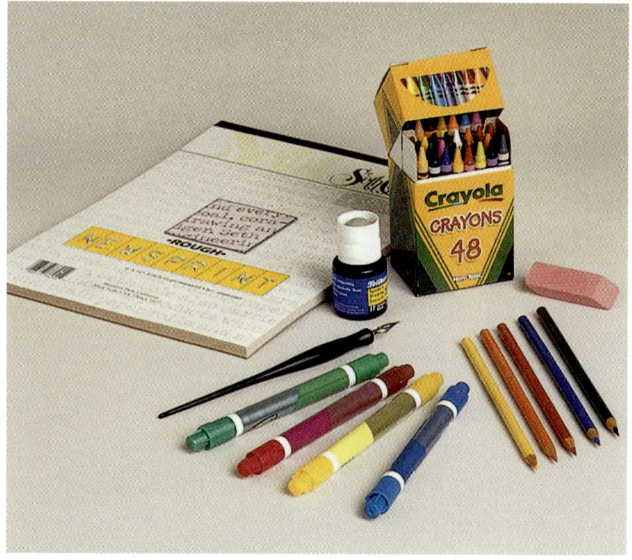

◆ **Figure 4–4** **There are many kinds of drawing media. Can you name other media?**

The Role of Drawing in Art

Before you can play ice hockey, you need to be able to skate. Excelling at ice-skating is a stepping-stone to the sport.

In much the same way, improving your drawing skills is a stepping-stone to almost all types of art production skills. Fashion designers make drawings of a design before patterns can be made for cutting fabric. Architects need to draw detailed plans, or blueprints, before the actual building of a house can begin. Some painters make sketches, or preliminary drawings, before they put a brush to canvas.

Look again at the drawings in Figures 4–5 and 4–6. Both were created as finished works of art. Each was completed by an important artist of the past two centuries.

Van Gogh used a flexible reed pen that made his lines look like brushstrokes. Look closely at Klee's drawing. Which do you think he made first, the lines or the colors?

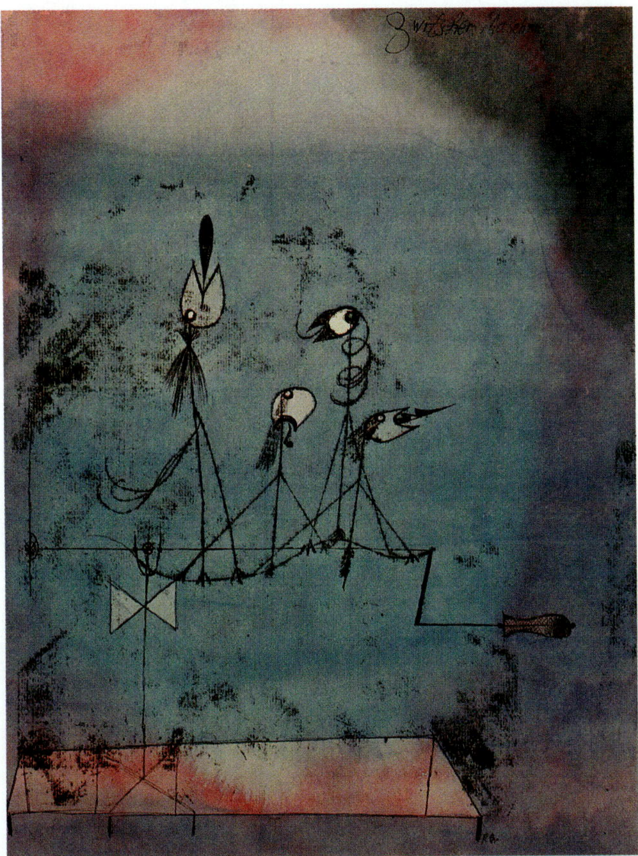

◆ **Figure 4–6** **It is difficult to classify Klee in a specific group of artists, but fantasy is a common theme in his work.**

Paul Klee. *Twittering Machine.* 1922. Watercolor, pen, and ink on oil transfer drawing on paper mounted on cardboard. 64.1 × 48.3 cm (25¼ × 19″). Museum of Modern Art, New York, New York. © 2003 Artists Rights Society (ARS), New York/ VG Bild-Kunst, Bonn.

Meet the Artist

Paul Klee (1879–1940)

German-Swiss artist Paul Klee (**klay**) was born into a family of musicians. His childhood love of music would remain an important force in his life and work. He was a talented violinist, and Lily Stumpf, the woman he married, was a pianist.

Music played a particularly vital role in Klee's art. Klee studied at the Academy of Fine Art in Munich and produced roughly 8,000 works in his lifetime. His goal as an artist, he said, was "to learn to improvise freely on the keyboard of colors." He approached each new work in much the way a composer would plan a new musical composition. Klee's artwork may look childlike, but he carefully organized the elements and principles of art. Look closely at Figure 4–6. Notice the handle attached to the machine. How do you think the birds would move if you turned the handle?

Compare and Contrast

Analyze Figure 4–6, paying close attention to Klee's use of line, shape, and space. Compare and contrast the use of these elements in Klee's watercolor with the image in Figure 4–1. What similarities do you notice? What are the differences?

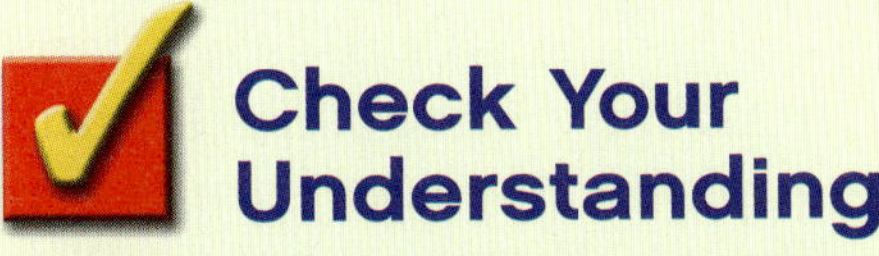

Check Your Understanding

1. Compare and contrast the effects of three media that are used in drawing.
2. How is drawing used by an architect?
3. How is drawing used by a painter?

Printmaking

Most people would have trouble finding art in a dirty paw print. Yet the action of a dog tracking mud is not unlike the one used in printmaking. **Printmaking** is *an area of fine art in which an inked image is transferred to a surface.*

In the art of printmaking, an artist creates an image on a flat surface. Ink is then applied, and the surface is pressed against paper or fabric. A **fine art print** is *an artwork created by the printmaking process.* An artist who makes prints is known as a printmaker. A number of printmaking tools appear in **Figure 4–7.**

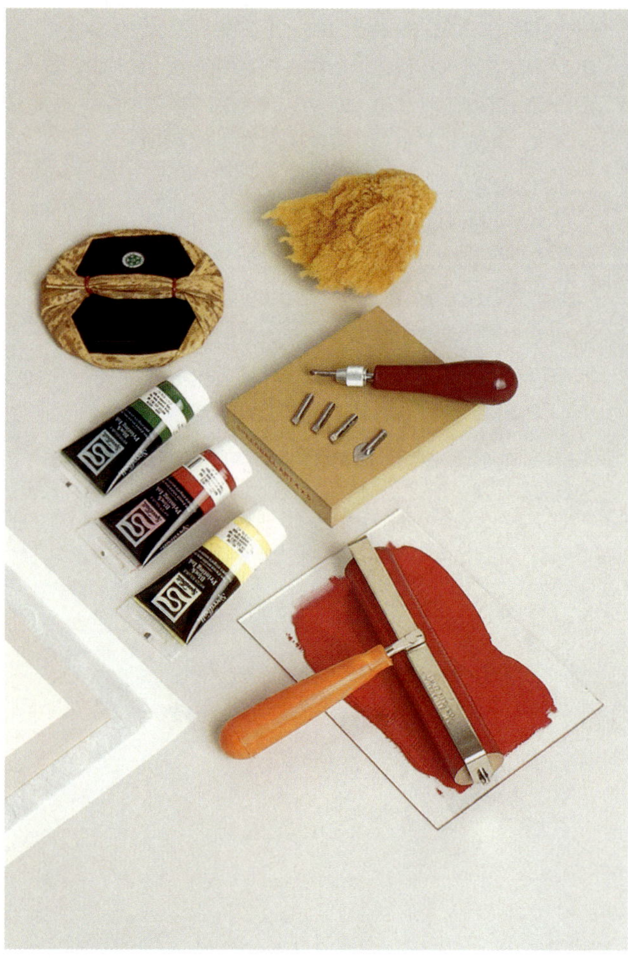

◆ **Figure 4–7** **This photo shows printmaking materials. How do drawing and printmaking materials differ? What are their similarities?**

Prints versus Reproductions

Like other types of art, printmaking allows artists to produce an image on various surfaces. In printmaking, though, an artist can produce multiple copies of the original work. Each print, such as the one shown in **Figure 4–8,** is signed by the artist. After the set of prints is complete, the original plate is destroyed and no more images can be made of that print.

Notice that a print is not the same as a fine art reproduction. A fine art reproduction is a high-quality copy of an artwork made using commercial photographic processes. Fine art reproductions, which are often done as posters, frequently use good-quality paper. The fine art images in this book are reproductions. The difference between these and prints is that prints are originals and reproductions are copies of artworks.

Printmaking Processes

The process of printmaking involves three basic steps:

- **Creation of the plate.** The printmaker creates a printing plate by altering a surface to create an image.
- **Inking the plate.** Next, the printmaker applies ink to, or *inks,* the plate.
- **Transferring the image.** Finally, the printmaker transfers the ink to the paper or cloth by pressing the paper or cloth against the plate. Then the paper or cloth is pulled off the plate.

This set of steps may be repeated many times for a given plate. *A series of prints that are all exactly alike* is called an **edition.** The printmaker signs his or her name, usually in the bottom margin. He or she writes a number on each print with the form "10/20." The first number identifies the number of this

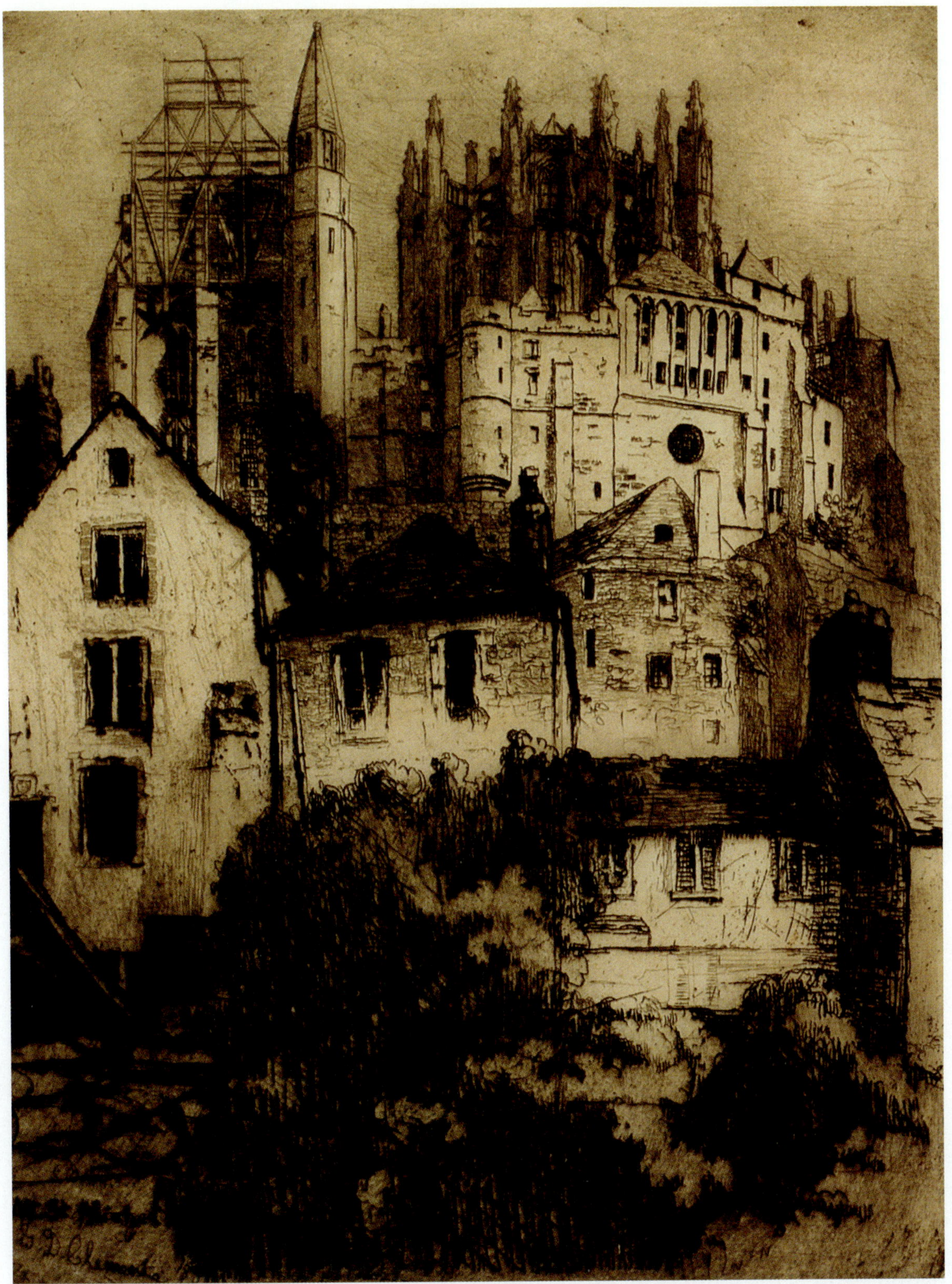

◆ **Figure 4–8** **The lines for this print were scratched and etched into the metal plate. Marin also used drypoint techniques, an engraving process that produces a soft effect. Compare and contrast the difference in line quality between this work and the woodcut in Figure 4–9.**

Gabrielle de Veaux Clements. *Mont St. Michel.* 1885. Etching on paper. 21.6 × 16.2 cm (8½ × 6⅜″). National Museum of Women in the Arts, Washington, D.C. Gift of Wallace and Wilhelmina Holladay.

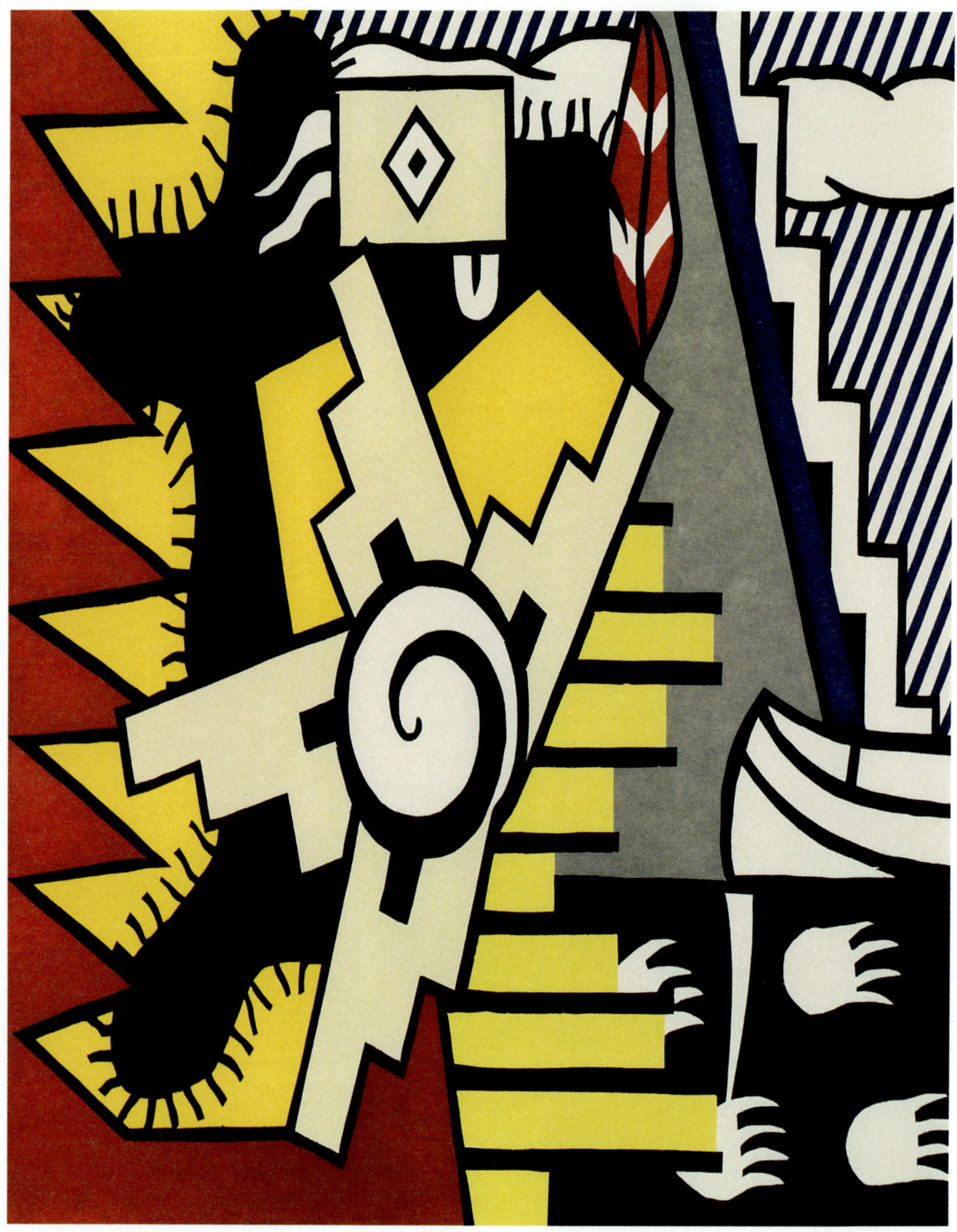

◆ **Figure 4–9**
Notice the quality of the lines carved from wood. Analyze this woodcut to determine cultural contexts. For example, how many symbols from Native American art and life can you find in this print?

Roy Lichtenstein. *American Indian Theme II.* 1980. Woodcut, printed in color. 61 × 72.7 cm (24 × 28⅝″). Museum of Modern Art, New York, New York.

particular print in the edition. The second number reveals the total number of prints in the edition. A print labeled "10/20" means that this particular print is the tenth print out of 20 printed from one plate.

Printmaking Media

As noted earlier, the printmaker uses a number of tools and materials in making a print. (See Figure 4–7.) Plates are usually made of linoleum, wood, stone, or metal. Sometimes other materials are used. Often prints are done in color. To make a print with more than one color, the printmaker usually uses a separate plate for each color.

The final appearance of a print will depend on the media, colors, and techniques the printmaker used. Different combinations will give different results. Compare Figure 4–8 with **Figure 4–9.** Figure 4–8 is an etching. The lines and shapes were scratched into a metal plate with a sharp, pointed tool. In contrast, Figure 4–9, done by American "Pop" Artist Roy Lichtenstein, is a woodcut. Lichtenstein used wood for his printing plate. He carved away the background, leaving raised lines and shapes to be inked. This is a relief print.

In relief printing, the image to be printed is raised from the background. After the raised portion is inked, paper is laid on it. Pressure is applied and ink is transferred to the paper.

Printing with carved wooden blocks originated in China. In the seventeenth century the process spread to Japan, where it became a highly developed art form.

Meet the Artist

Roy Lichtenstein (1923–1997)

Roy Lichtenstein, a founder of the Pop Art school, began making works that were abstract in style. In the early 1960s, he met sculptor Claes Oldenburg, who was experimenting with art that reflected everyday life. Lichtenstein's paintings were often inspired by comic strips and advertisements. He viewed these images as "threatening characteristics of our culture." He also noted that they had a powerful effect on Americans of the twentieth century. Lichtenstein's inspiration apparently came from one of his children who challenged him to paint "as good as" a comic strip artist. *American Indian Theme II* (Figure 4–9) was done in the late part of Lichtenstein's career. What medium did he use in this work?

Studio Activity

Creating a Pattern

Experimenting with Prints. Select and use a variety of appropriate art materials and tools to produce an experimental print. Each student in the class is to select a different letter of the alphabet as the subject for the print. Place a thin sheet of paper over a thick pad of newspaper. Pressing down hard, draw your letter on the thin sheet. Turn the paper over, and you will see your letter in reverse. Using the image as a model, carve a stamp from a cube of modeling clay. Apply paint to your stamp with a brush. On a sheet of paper, make a pattern by pressing your stamp several times. Does each image in your pattern look the same, or do they differ? Does this make your pattern more or less interesting? Explain your answers.

PORTFOLIO

On a separate sheet of paper, evaluate your stamp. Ask: Does the stamp make the image I intended? What did I do well? What could I do better? Did I make a good mirror image? Keep the stamped patterns and your self-assessment together in your portfolio.

Check Your Understanding

1. Compare and contrast how an original print differs from a fine art reproduction.
2. Explain the three basic steps in printmaking.
3. What is an *edition?* What is the meaning of the numbers an artist writes on a print?
4. Name two materials that can be used to make plates in printmaking.

Painting

Painting, in some form, is believed to be the earliest form of art. Wall paintings discovered in caves in Spain, France, and Africa date as far back as 10,000 B.C. These early works were created by cave dwellers. Their materials included plant oils and animal blood for binding and natural earth pigment for color. Chewed soft branches were used like brushes and hollowed sticks were used to blow paint onto a surface.

In the years since, painting media have come a long way. In this lesson, you will learn about painting media and their many uses.

How Paint Is Applied

Painting is the process of covering a surface with color. You may recall finger painting as a young child. The fingers are just one tool used to apply paint to a surface. The most common tool among professional artists is

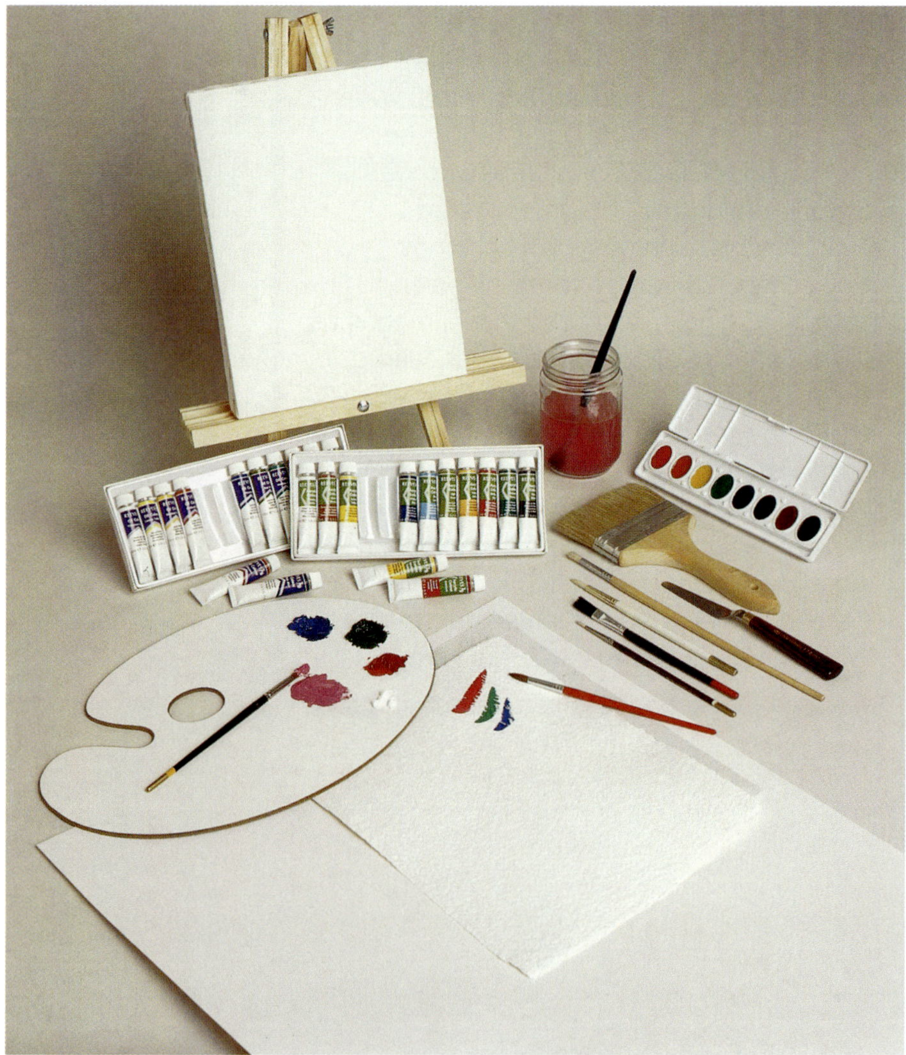

◆ Figure 4–10 **This photo shows some painting tools and media. What other media can you think of that are not shown here?**

the brush. Brushes come in many different sizes, or brush heads. The finer the bristles and smaller the head, the finer the detail the brush is able to capture.

Other tools for applying paint include a palette knife and roller. Sometimes paint is made into a mist. It is then blown onto a surface by means of an airbrush. Some of these tools are shown in **Figure 4–10.** As you take on new and more challenging art projects, you will become familiar with many of these.

Painting Media

Before a painter begins a work, he or she chooses a type of paint and an appropriate surface on which to work. Paints are selected for different qualities they exhibit. These include drying time, appearance in finished works, and how well colors blend.

The surface is the material to which the paint is to be applied. Canvas, paper, or silk are three examples. The look of a finished painting has much to do with the combination of materials. A painting made by applying oil paint on canvas with a knife has a look very different from a painting made by dabbing watercolor on paper with a soft brush. To appreciate this, compare the paintings in **Figures 4–11** and **4–12.** The one in Figure 4–11 is a watercolor. The work has a slightly bright, transparent look to it. The white portions of the work are the paper's color showing through. The painting in Figure 4–12 appears more opaque. Compare and contrast the use of color in Figures 4–11 and 4–12.

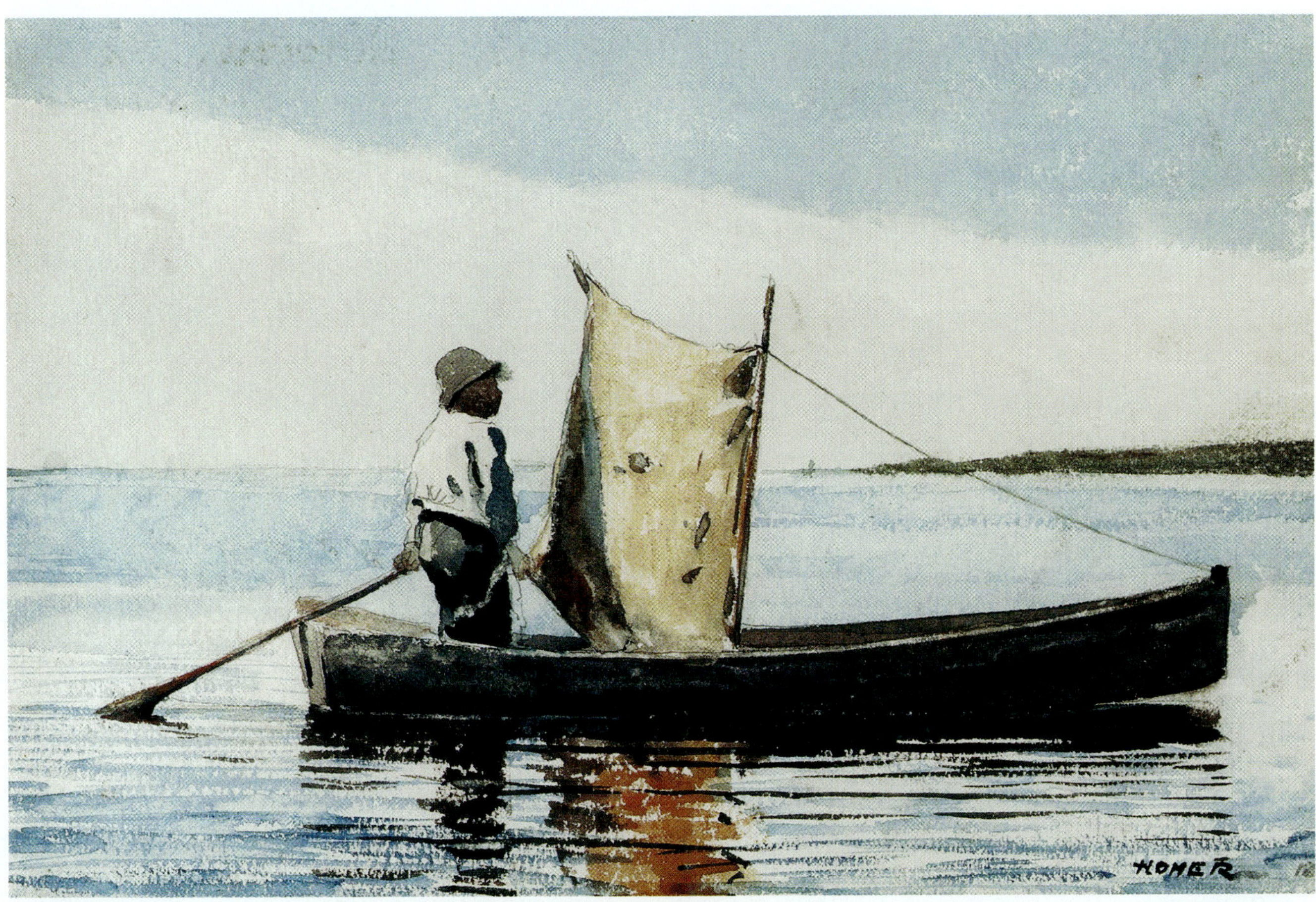

◆ **Figure 4–11** **Notice how the use of white fills this scene with the quality of intense sunlight.**

Winslow Homer. *Boy in a Dory.* c. 1880. Watercolor on paper. 24.8 x 35 cm (9¾ × 13¾″). Wadsworth Atheneum Museum of Art, Hartford, Connecticut. Bequest of Charles C. Cummingham. 1980.6.

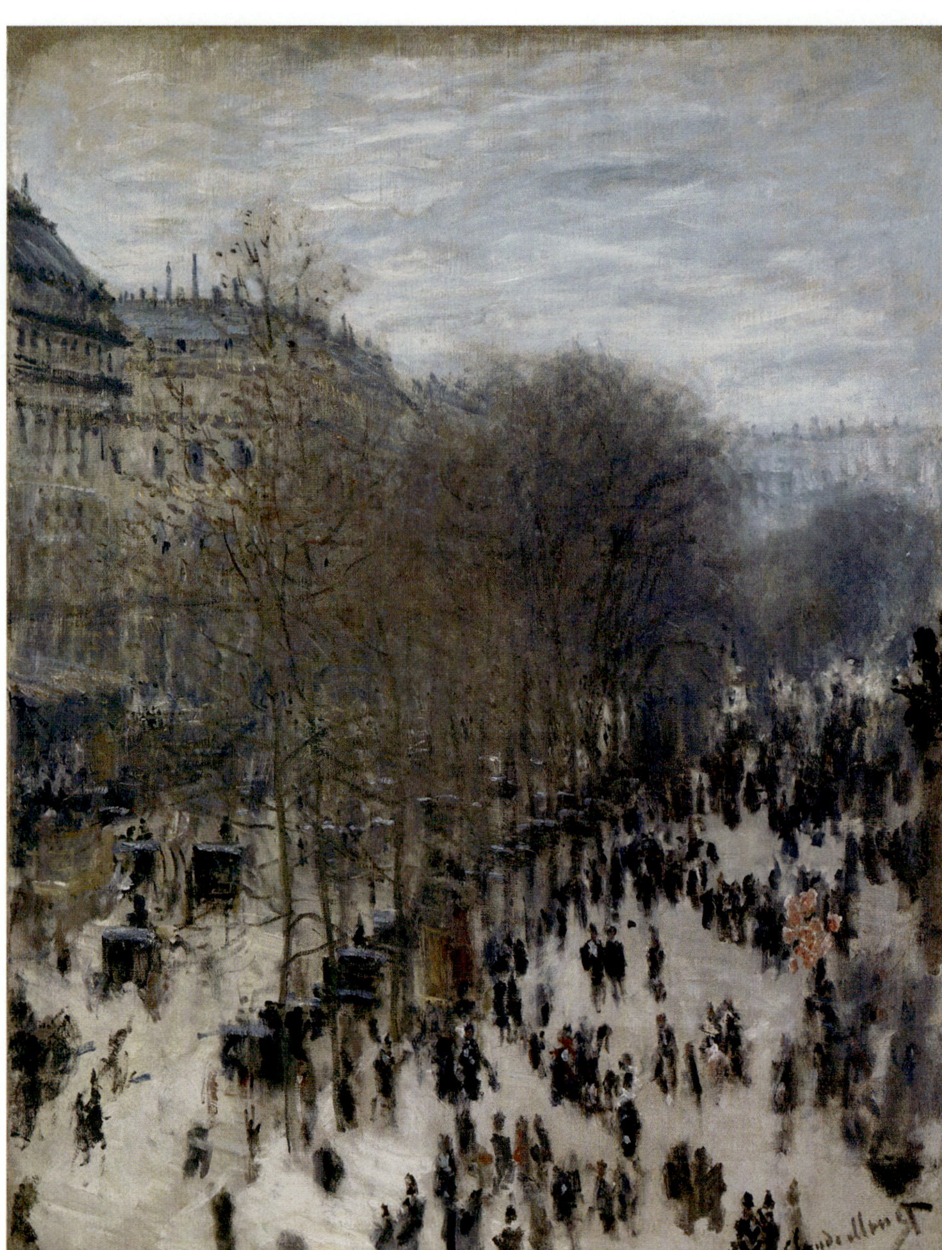

◆ **Figure 4–12** **The thick dabs of opaque, white paint in this work make the sunlight appear as if it is dancing around the people.**

Claude Monet. *Boulevard des Capucines.* 1873–74. Oil on canvas. 80.4 × 60.3 cm (30$\frac{5}{8}$ × 23$\frac{3}{4}$″). The Nelson-Atkins Museum of Art, Kansas City, Missouri. Purchase acquired through the Kenneth A. and Helen F. Spencer Foundation Acquisition Fund. F72–35.

All paints used in art are made up of three basic ingredients:

- **Pigment** is *a finely ground, colored powder that gives paint its color.*
- **Binder** is *a liquid to which the dry pigment is added.* The binder makes it possible for the pigment to stick to a surface. Linseed oil is the binder for oil paints. Gum arabic (**air**-uh-bik) is the binder for watercolors.
- **Solvent** is *a liquid that controls the thickness of the paint.* Turpentine is the solvent in oil paints. Water is the solvent in watercolors. Solvents are also used to clean brushes.

Painting Styles

When painters finish works of art, they usually sign their names to them. In a way the signature of the artist is already there, in his or her individual style. *Style* is an artist's personal way of expressing ideas in a work. Style is like a fingerprint. No two are exactly alike. Two artists may start off with exactly the same media. They will end up, however, with works that look totally different. Compare and contrast Figures 4–12 and 4–13. Both are oil paintings; one is done on canvas, the other on wood. Both were created in the late

1800s. The vibrant street scene in Figure 4–12 shows lively dabs of paint and bright colors. Figure 4–13, on the other hand, has a soft dreamy quality to it. What other differences between painting techniques of the two works can you detect?

Check Your Understanding

1. What are the three types of ingredients found in every type of paint?
2. What is *pigment?*
3. What is an artist's style?

STUDIO ACTIVITY

Interpreting Subjects

Experimenting with Pigments. Pigments were originally made from natural sources such as earth, minerals, and vegetation. Make your own earth pigments by collecting different colors of dirt, clay, and sand. You can use them as you find them, or grind them for a finer texture. Create a binder by mixing one part white school glue with one part water. Using a paper plate, experiment mixing a little of the glue mixture with some of your pigment. Test the various colors. Once you have finished experimenting, paint a small picture interpreting a subject, such as a portrait or a still life, using the various colors you have made.

◆ **Figure 4–13** **Ryder's works are always full of mystery. The way he applies paint creates this foggy, fantasy effect.**

Albert Pinkham Ryder. *Moonlight.* 1887. Oil on mahogany panel, cradled. 40.4 × 45 cm (15$\frac{15}{16}$ × 17$\frac{2}{3}$″). The National Museum of American Art, Smithsonian Institution, Washington, D.C. Gift of William T. Evans. Art Resource, N.Y.

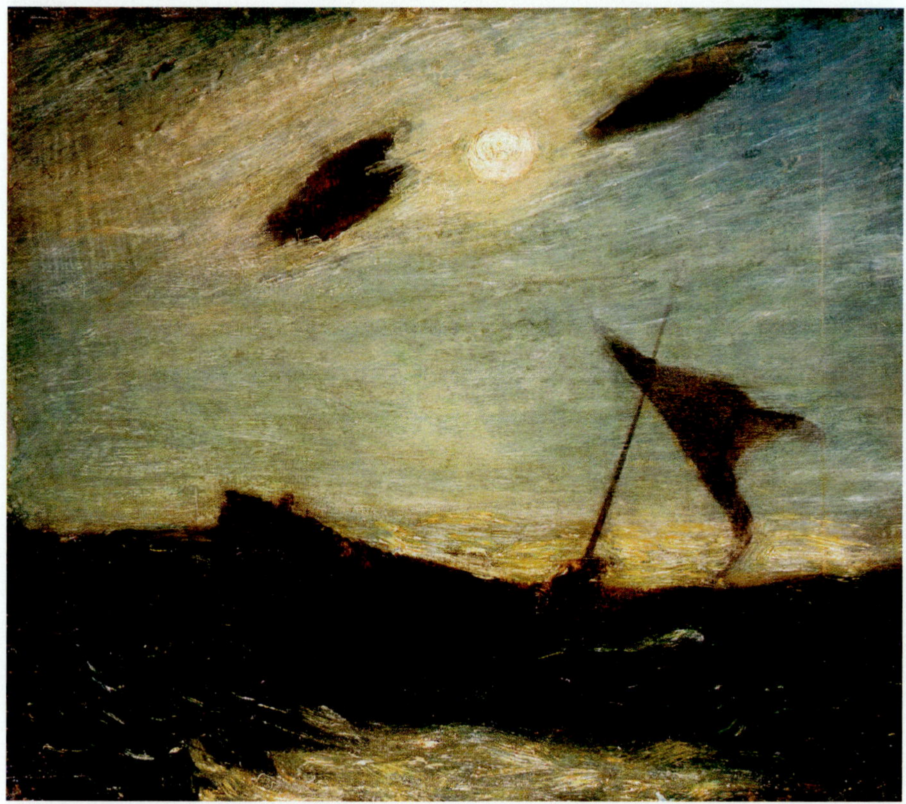

Sculpture

What do stone, wood, and sand share in common? All may be used as media in sculpture. Even water can be sculpted so long as it is frozen.

The *art of creating three-dimensional works* or **sculpture** dates back to prehistoric times. In this lesson, you will learn about the materials used to make sculpture. You will also learn about the processes used by artists working in this area.

The Media of Sculpture

An artist who works in sculpture is called a sculptor. Sculptors work with a great many materials and tools. One sculpting medium that you have probably used is clay. Some others are shown in **Figure 4–14.** How many of these can you name? How many have you used?

Types of Sculpture

As an art form, sculpture exists in one of two states:

- **Freestanding.** Also known as "in the round," the word **freestanding** means *surrounded on all sides by space.* Statues of people are examples of freestanding sculptures. Every side of a freestanding sculpture is sculpted and finished. In order to see the work as the sculptor meant it to be seen, you have to move

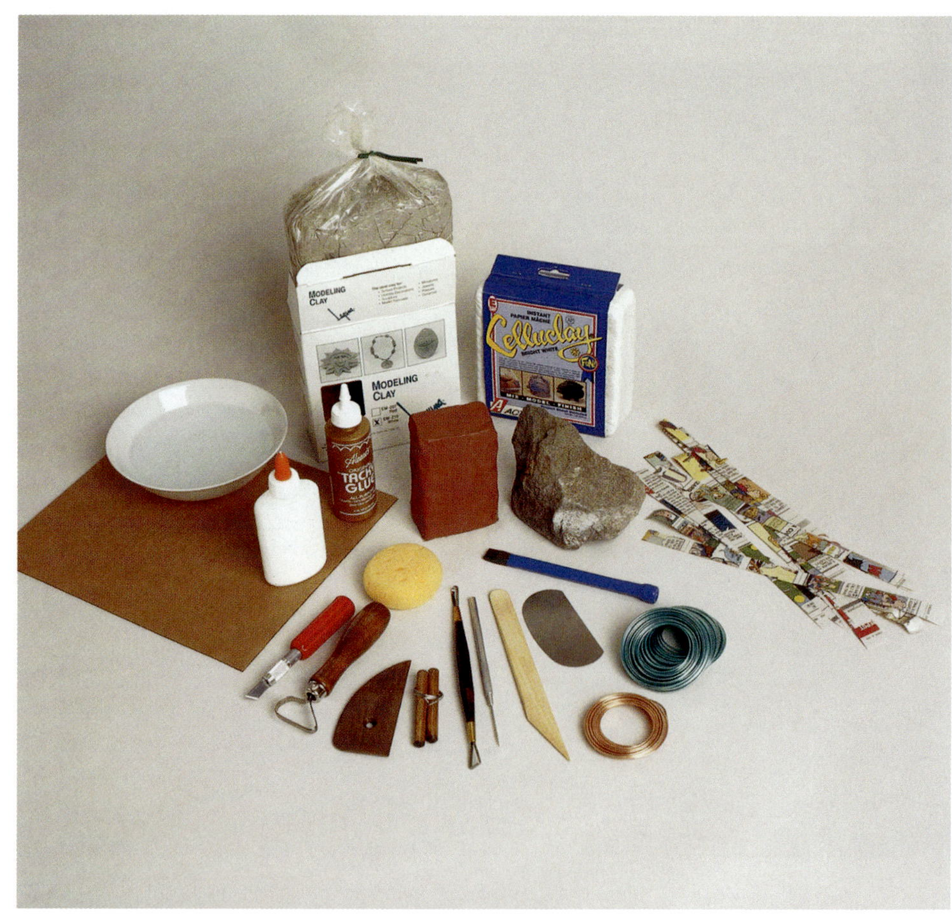

◆ **Figure 4–14** There are many kinds of sculpture tools and media. Can you name some others not shown in this photo?

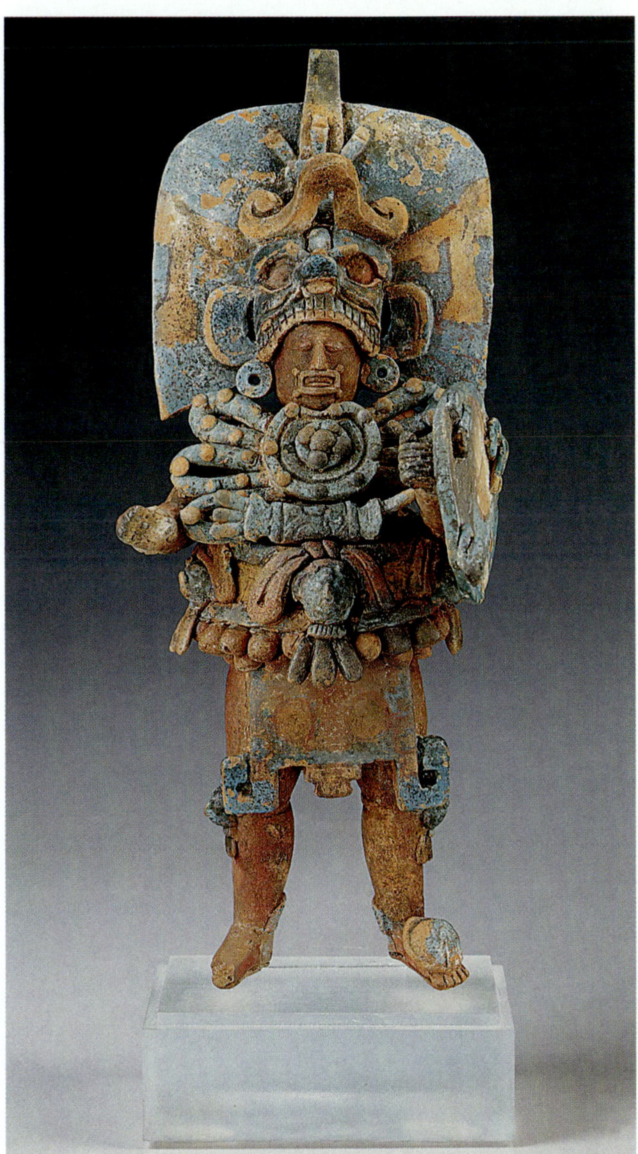

◆ **Figure 4–15** **This Mayan ruler is dressed to imitate a mythical person. What kind of dance movements do you think he would make wearing this costume? What kind of a beat would the dance have?**

Precolumbian, Maya. *A Ruler Dressed as a Chac-Xbi-Chac and the Holmec Dancer.* c. A.D. 600–800. Ceramic with traces of paint. Height: 24.1 cm (9½″). Kimbell Art Museum, Fort Worth, Texas.

around it. The sculpture of a Mayan ruler in **Figure 4–15** is an example of a freestanding sculpture.

- **Relief.** This is *a type of sculpture in which forms and figures project only from the front.* It is flat on the back. You can see large reliefs on buildings and small reliefs on items such as jewelry. The artwork in **Figure 4–16** is an example of a relief sculpture.

Analyze and compare the sculptures in Figure 4–15 and Figure 4–16. Form conclusions about historical and cultural contexts. For example, what clues does each piece provide about its culture?

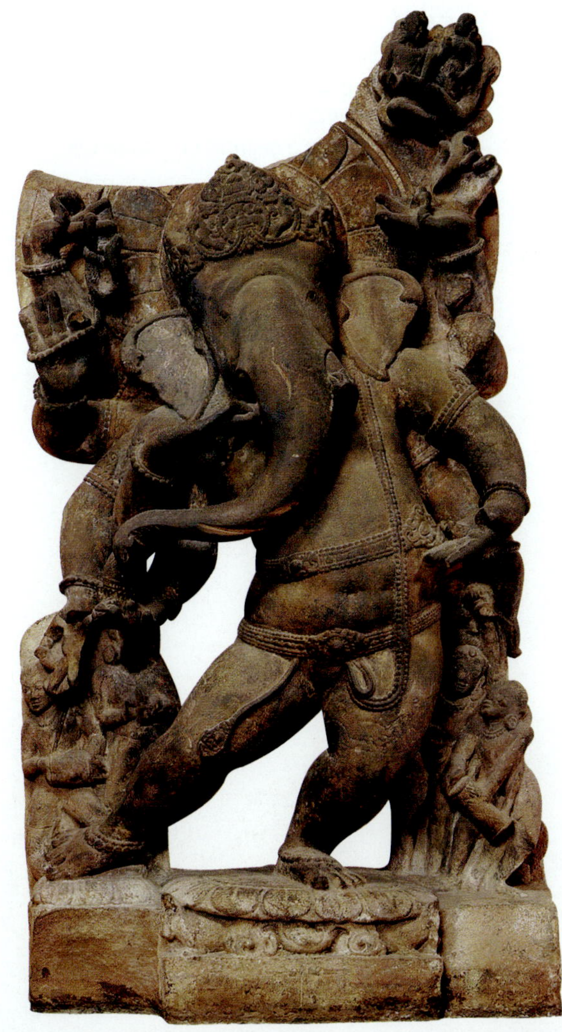

◆ **Figure 4–16** **Lord Ganesha is a very popular god in India. He is believed to be a remover of obstacles. Another sculpture of this god appears in Figure 12–15 on page 226.**

India, Uttar Pradesh. *Ganesha.* Sandstone. Height: 125.7 cm (49½″). Asia Society, New York, New York.

Sculpting Methods and Processes

There are four basic methods for making sculpture. These are:

- **Carving.** In carving, the sculptor starts with a block of material and cuts or chips a shape from it. Often a hard material like stone is used. Look again at the sculpture in Figure 4–16. This work was carved from sandstone.
- **Casting.** In casting, the sculptor starts by making a mold. He or she then pours in a melted-down metal or some other liquid. Eventually, the liquid hardens. The mold is broken to reveal the newly created work within. One of the most commonly used media in casting is bronze. An example of a copper casting can be found in **Figure 4–17.**
- **Modeling.** In modeling, the sculptor builds up and shapes a soft material. Clay and fresh plaster are two such materials. The ancient Mayan sculpture you viewed in Figure 4–15 was the result of modeling. Notice the materials used in this ancient artwork.

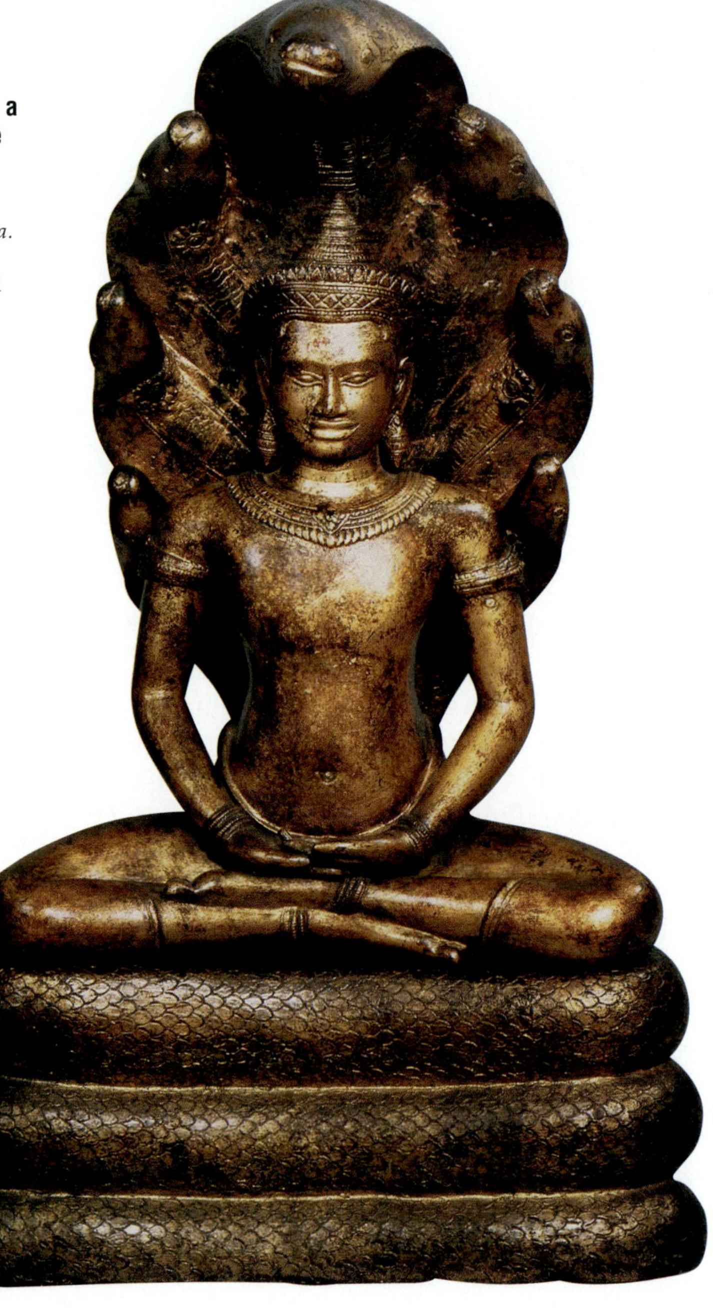

◆ **Figure 4–17** **This Buddha is seated in a pose of meditation. Notice the position of the hands forming a gesture of meditation.**

Cambodia. Angkor period. *Crowned Buddha Seated in Meditation and Sheltered by Muchilinda.* Probably twelfth century. Copper alloy with recent covering of black and gold lacquer and gold leaf. Height: 73 cm (28¾″). Asia Society, New York, New York.

- **Assembling**. In assembling, also known as constructing, the sculptor glues or in some other way joins together pieces of material. The sculpture in **Figure 4–18** was made by assembling pieces of wood.

Modeling and assembling are known as *additive* methods of sculpting. Works created by these methods are built up or added to. Carving is a *subtractive* method. In works created in this fashion, the artist takes away or removes materials.

Check Your Understanding

1. What is another term that has the same meaning as *freestanding?*
2. Name two media used by sculptors.
3. Describe the four basic sculpting methods.
4. What is meant by the term *additive* as it is used in sculpture? Which two basic methods of making sculpture are additive?
5. What is meant by the term *subtractive* as it is used in sculpture? Which basic method of making sculpture is subtractive?

Studio Activity

Environmental Sculpting

Illustrate Ideas from Imagination. Collect a variety of natural objects such as rocks, sticks, leaves, and grasses, which are not much larger than your hand. Illustrate ideas from your imagination by arranging these to create a three-dimensional environmental sculpture. Your work can be nonobjective or a recognizable object, such as a building or animal. Use the elements of line, shape, color, and texture to help you in arranging your natural objects in experimental ways. Share your environmental sculpture with your classmates. You may choose to do this activity as a group or individually.

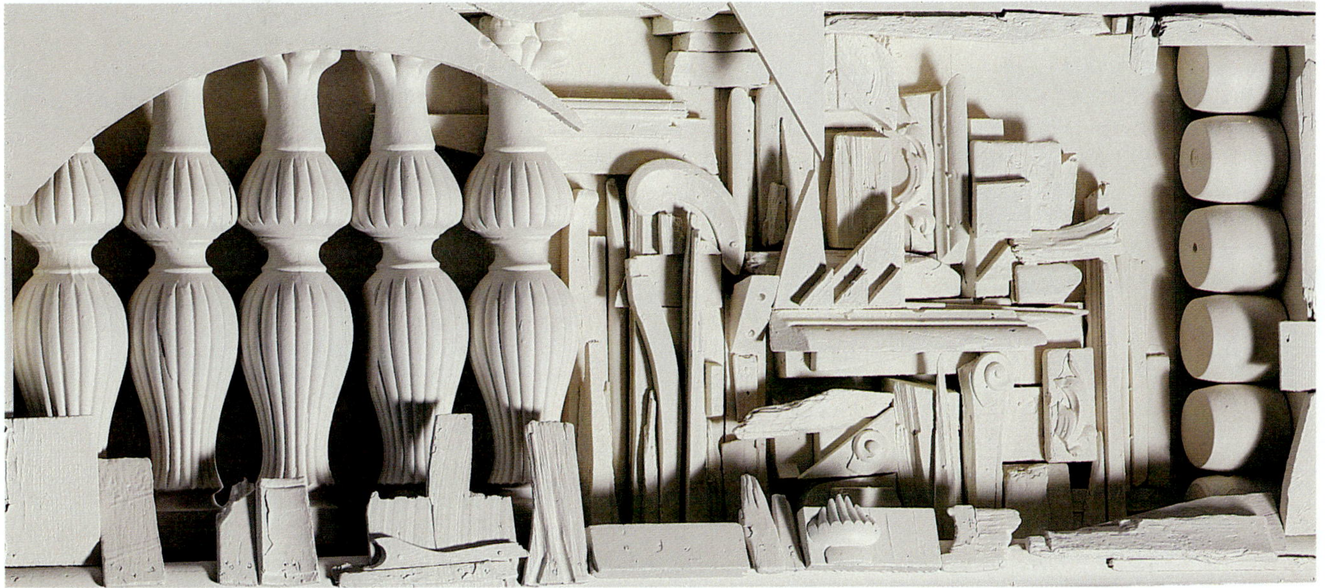

◆ **Figure 4–18** **This sculpture was part of a large installation called *Dawn's Wedding Feast.* It was a complex arrangement of 85 separate reliefs, boxes, and columns.**

Louise Nevelson. *Case with Five Balusters.* 1959. Wood paint. 70.2 × 161.6 × 24.1 cm (27⅝ × 63⅝ × 9½"). Walker Art Center, Minneapolis, Minnesota. Gift of Mr. and Mrs. Peter M. Butler, 1983. © 2003 Estate of Louise Nevelson/Artists Rights Society (ARS), New York.

Digital Media

The invention of the camera in the 1800s brought with it a new art medium. That medium was photography. Toward the end of the 1900s, another technological invention emerged and expanded the media available to artists. That invention was the personal computer.

Look at the digital painting in **Figure 4–19.** The artist, Susan Le Van, was inspired by Pablo Picasso's painting of a boy and a horse. She says the computer "encourages playfulness and experimentation in ways that just can't be imagined with conventional media." Think about ways you might experiment with digital media.

Art made using electronic media is known as **digital art.** This is *art made in part or whole using computer hardware and software.* In this lesson, you will read about some of the tools used to create digital, or electronic media-generated art.

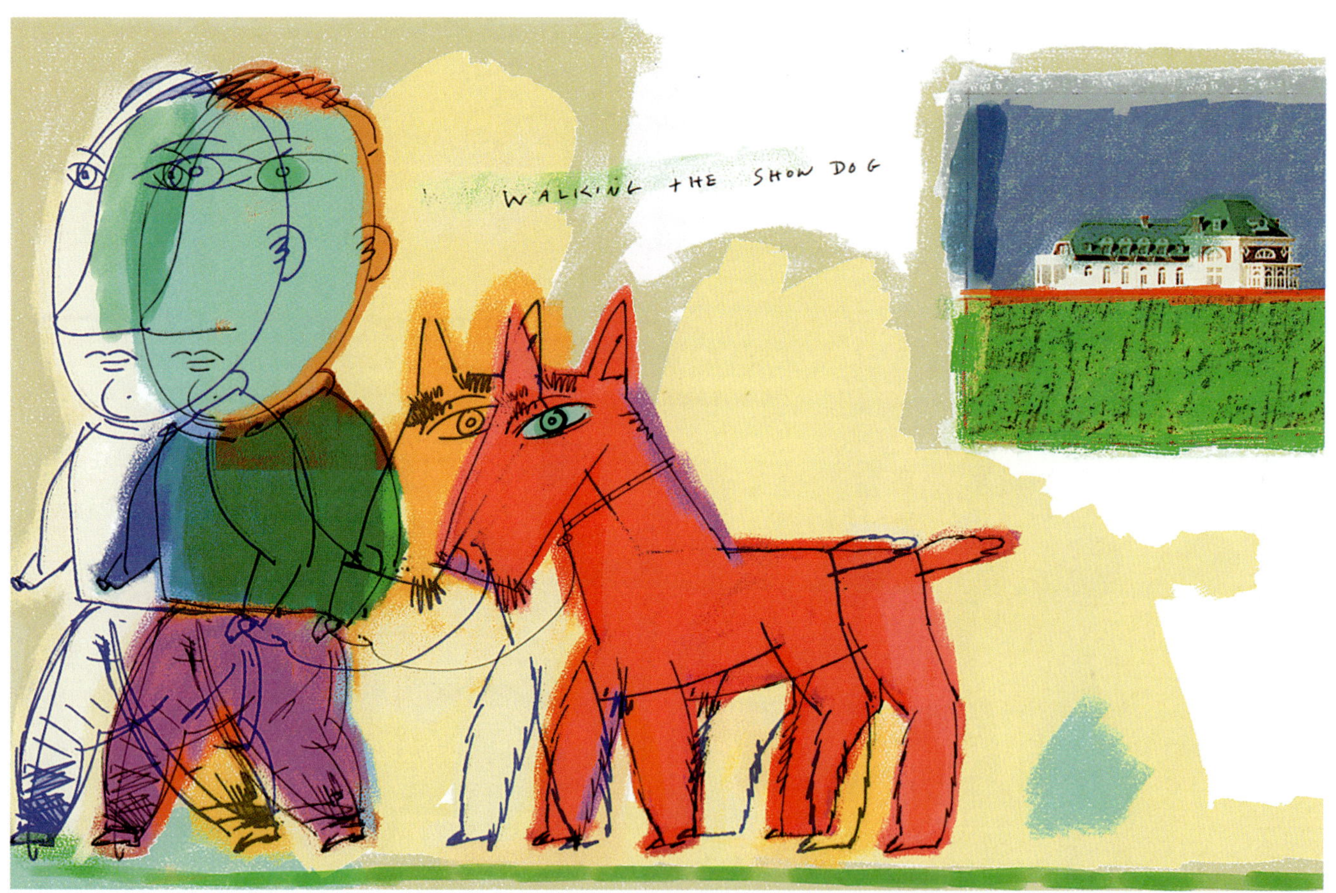

◆ **Figure 4–19** **This was an image created for the artist's portfolio. It combines a digital photo of a house with a simple drawing of a man and a dog. The artist used a paint program and a graphics tablet.**

Susan Le Van. *Walking the Show Dog.* 1998. Digital painting. Photo: Ernest Barbee Le Van/Barbee Studio.

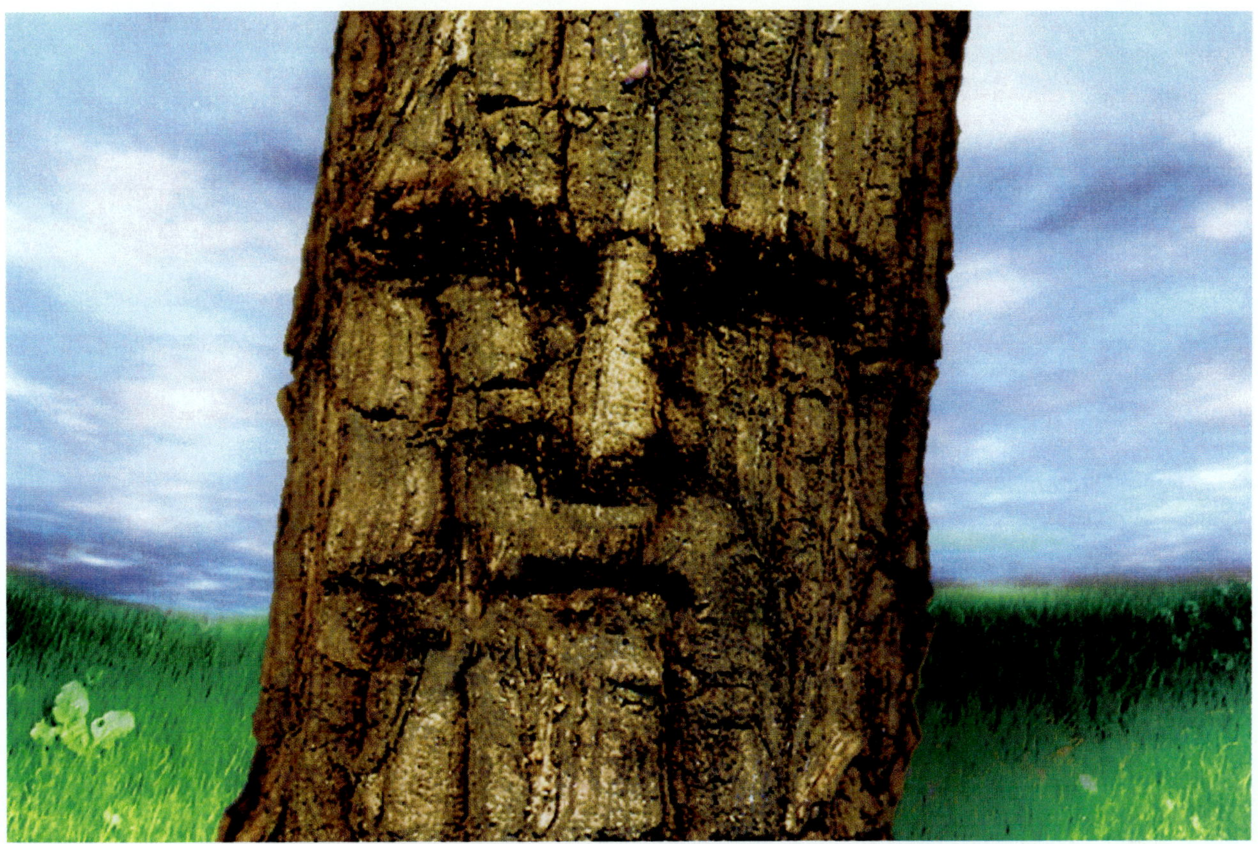

◆ **Figure 4–20** **Analyze ways in which electronic media have influenced artworks. In particular, how did the use of digital media affect the visual look of this image?**

Tom Ledin. *Tree*. 2003. Digital photo manipulation.

Digital Art Hardware

At one time, digital art was made exclusively using a computer keyboard and a two-color screen. Then came the mouse and the high-resolution monitor. **Resolution** is *the fineness of detail that can be distinguished in an image*. The resolution of a digital image is measured in dpi (dots per square inch). Resolution is expressed in terms of "bits," or *binary digits*.

Since the invention of the personal computer, the technology has grown by leaps and bounds. For the digital artist, this has meant an abundance of "virtual" tools. These include the following:

- **Graphics tablet.** This tool is a high-tech equivalent of drawing paper or a painter's canvas. Artists paint on graphics tablets using an electronic pen, or stylus. In the early 1990s, a *pressure-sensitive* stylus was introduced. The device responds to pressure from the hand, much like a real art tool.
- **Scanner.** A scanner is a device that "reads" an image printed on paper. It then sends a digitized copy of the image to the computer's memory. From there the image may be sent to a software application, saved, manipulated, or printed.
- **Digital camera.** Digital cameras record images on a hard drive, so film is not required. Digital photography has opened the doors to a new field of art. An example in this medium appears in **Figure 4–20.** This is a digitally enhanced image. The artist, Tom Ledin, started out by photographing a tree and then his own face. What you see here is the result of his skill and imagination.

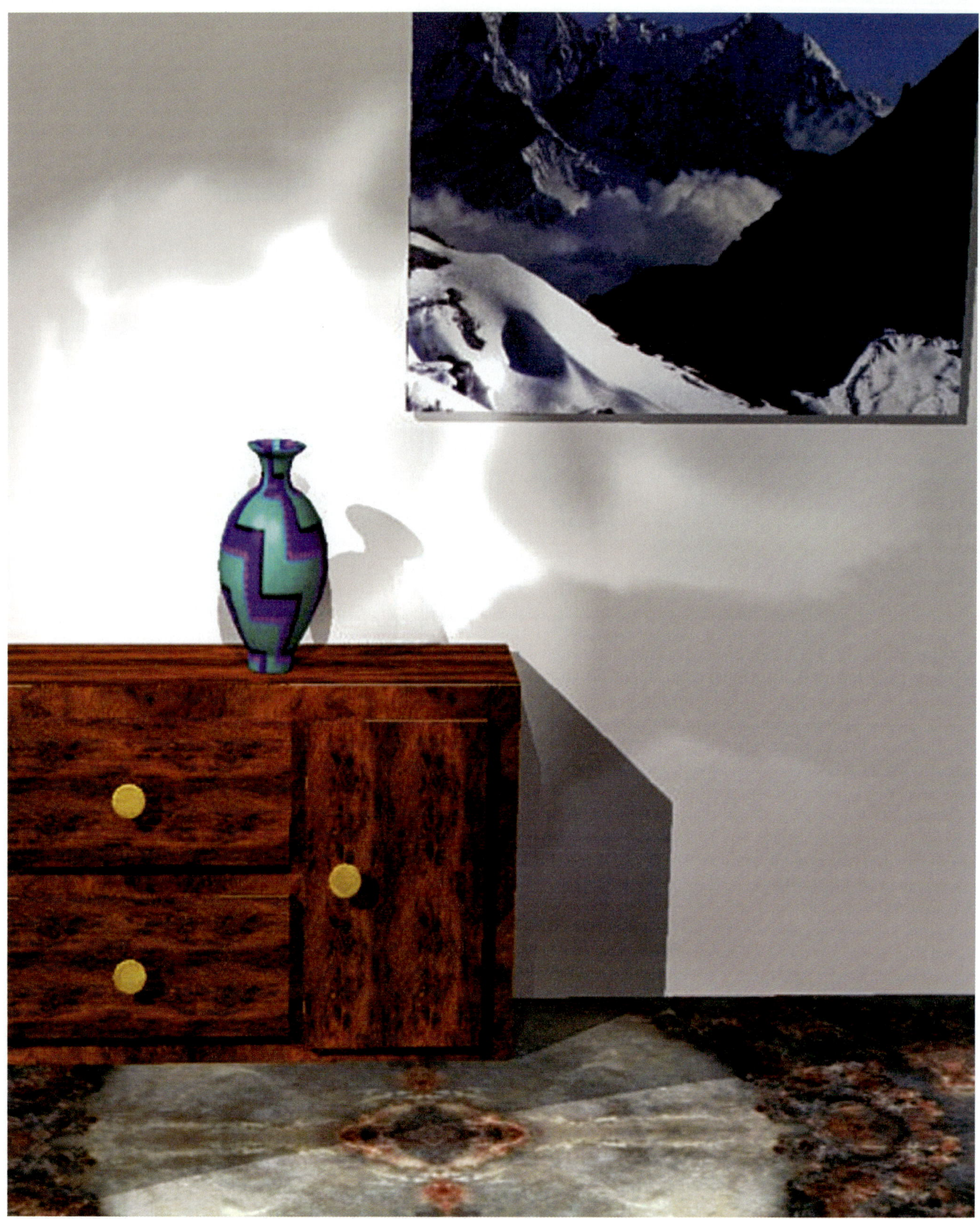

◆ **Figure 4–21** **Using vocabulary correctly, compare and contrast the use of texture in this digital artwork and the one shown in Figure 4–20.**

Kevin J. Bepp. *Still Life with Vase and Painting*. 1997. Ray tracing. Copyright © HPES.

Digital Art Software

Digital art also relies on software. Among the most basic software applications are *paint* and *draw* programs. The main difference between the two is the way they store images. Paint programs, which are the most widely used by digital artists, store images as *bitmaps*. These are collections of tiny digital units known as *pixels*. Paint programs are used both for the creation of original art and for editing photos.

Figures 4–19, 4–20, and **4–21** were created using a paint program. In Figure 4–19, the photo of the house was taken using a digital camera.

In contrast to paint programs, draw programs store images as mathematical expressions called *vectors*. This enables the images to be enlarged or shrunk without distortion.

Recent Digital Software

The last decade has introduced a new generation of digital software. Several of these innovations have been used widely on the Internet. Two of the most commonly used of these new applications are:

- **3-D rendering software.** Like draw programs, 3-D rendering programs use vectors as the basis of working images. These images are sculpted, then posed on a virtual stage on the computer screen. The artist is able to control the "camera angle" from which the image is shot. Lighting can also be adjusted to make a scene dramatic. Once the stage is set, the working image is converted to a final rendered image. **Rendering** is *a process by which a vector-based image is converted to a bitmap*. The still life in Figure 4–21 was created in a 3-D rendering program. The objects, textures, and shadows are all virtual creations of the digital artist.
- **Digital frame animation software.** Digital frame animation software is used in many computer games. It is also widely used in television, where it got its start. Images, which can include photos, are imported from paint and other programs. So are sounds. An assortment of preset and user-defined tools allow the digital artist to create the illusion of movement. Objects appear to spin, fade in or out, grow, and shrink. All of these effects are the result of internal mathematical computations.

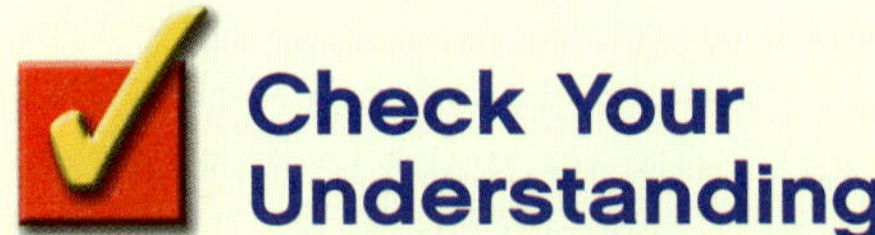

1. What is *resolution?* Why is it important to the appearance of digital art?
2. Name and describe two pieces of hardware used by the digital artist.
3. Compare and contrast paint programs and draw programs.
4. What is *rendering?* In what type of digital-art application is rendering used?
5. What type of digital-art software is used to create many computer games?

Computer Cartooning

Cartoons represent objects with simple lines, shapes, and colors. Cartoon characters can be humans, animals, or objects. They often appear as exaggerated caricatures portrayed with human characteristics. Cartoonists usually combine characters, action, setting, and a message in one or more frames.

Humorous cartoons often focus on politics, mysteries, everyday events, or superhuman feats. Today, computers have streamlined the cartoon-making process. A frame from a computer cartoon appears in **Figure 4–22.** This cartoon was created by digital artist Mike Pantuso. He creates his pictures using simple shapes and primary and secondary colors.

What You Will Learn

You will produce electronic media-generated art by selecting and using a variety of appropriate art materials and tools in traditional and experimental ways. You will create an original cartoon character on the computer, using simple lines and shapes. Add setting and details to depict a humorous event. You will start by drawing your character using conventional art media. You will then scan your character into your computer. Once the image is on the screen, you will manipulate it.

What You Will Need

- Pencil and sketchbook
- Computer, scanner, and paint application
- Color printer (for black-and-white printer, add color with pen, pencils, or markers)

What You Will Do

1. Choose a favorite animal or figure for your sketch. Think of the characteristics you want to express. Is your character bold, cunning, shy, or heroic? Make several sketches on paper. Use simple lines and shapes to draw the figure. Emphasize each characteristic by exaggerating proportion, shape, and size.
2. Scan your original sketch into the computer as line art. Title and save your work.
3. Open your paint program. Open a New File. First choose a setting or location that will serve as a backdrop for your

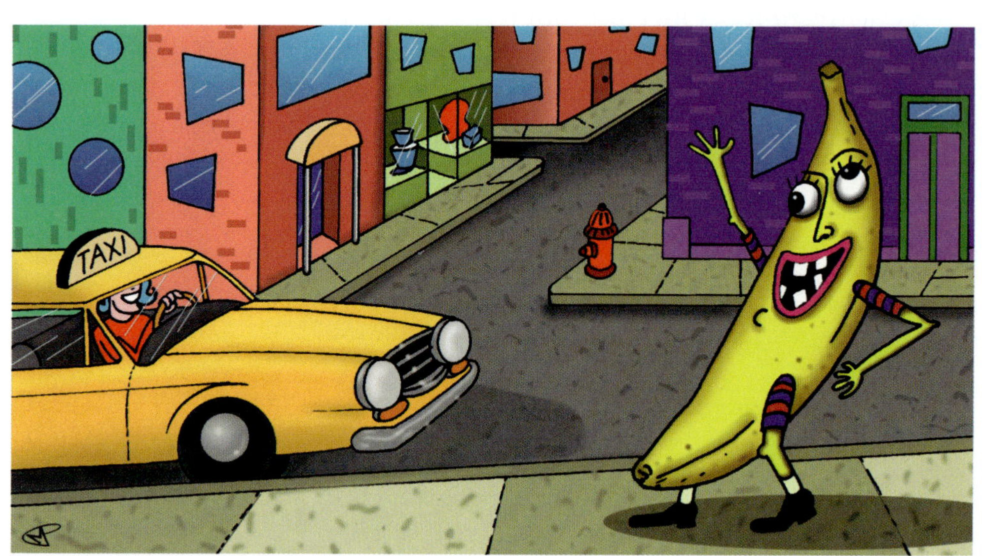

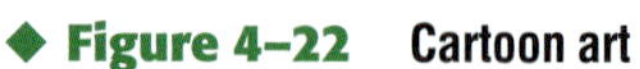

◆ **Figure 4–22** **Cartoon art**

Mike Pantuso. *Banana Man.* Computer art, appears in the following publication: *Adobe Photoshop, Creative Techniques.* Denise Salles, Gary Poyssick, and Ellen Behoriam. 1996. Macmillan Computer Publishing and Shepard Poorman Communications Corporation, Indianapolis, Indiana.

character. The location may be inside or outside. Determine the time of day, weather, and season. Draw the setting with a Pencil or small Brush tool. Add objects, figures, and details to help convey the message. Save your work.

4. Import your scanned image into the current file. Color your character. Select three or four primary and secondary colors. Experiment with the Bucket tool to flood-fill shapes and spaces with hues. If the color "leaks" into unwanted areas, immediately use the Undo command. Then choose the Zoom tool to find the missing pixels in the outline. Fill these in with the Pencil tool or a small Brush tool to close the outline. (Make sure the Opacity of your tool is set to 100 percent.)
5. Next, experiment by altering your electronic media-generated image using the special tools and filters available. You might, for example, add a gradient fill to part of your character. Another option would be to add a drop shadow. Use the Undo command to remove any effect you don't like. Continue to work in this fashion until you are satisfied with the result. Save your work.
6. Think of a message you want your cartoon to express. Include humor, if possible. Insert a dialog if desired, using the Text tool. Select a font, size, and style. Click the cursor where you want to begin the text. Type in your dialog.
7. Save and print your cartoon. Display in a group exhibit with your classmates.

Evaluating Your Work

- **Describe** Identify your cartoon character. Describe the setting. Identify the lines and shapes you used. Tell what tools and effects you used to produce your electronic media-generated artwork.
- **Analyze** Tell what elements you used to emphasize the character's personality. Show how you exaggerated the character's features.

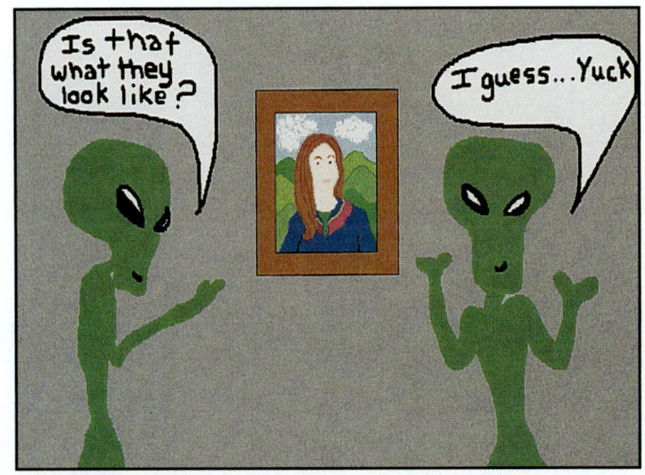

◆ **Figure 4–23** **Student work. Digital cartoon.**

PORTFOLIO IDEAS

Analyze portfolios by your peers and others, such as the artist whose work appears in Figure 4–19 on page 84. Form conclusions about historical and cultural contexts, intents, and meanings. For example, what can you determine about an artist's cultural heritage by analyzing his or her portfolio? What are the intended messages of some of the artworks?

Art Online

Visit **art.glencoe.com** to view more student artworks at the Student Art Gallery. There, you can also explore:

- Artist Profiles
- Career Corner
- Interactive Games

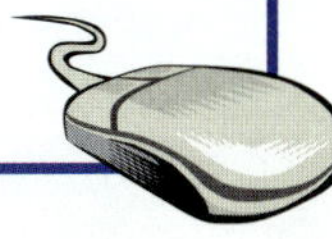

It's a Wrap!

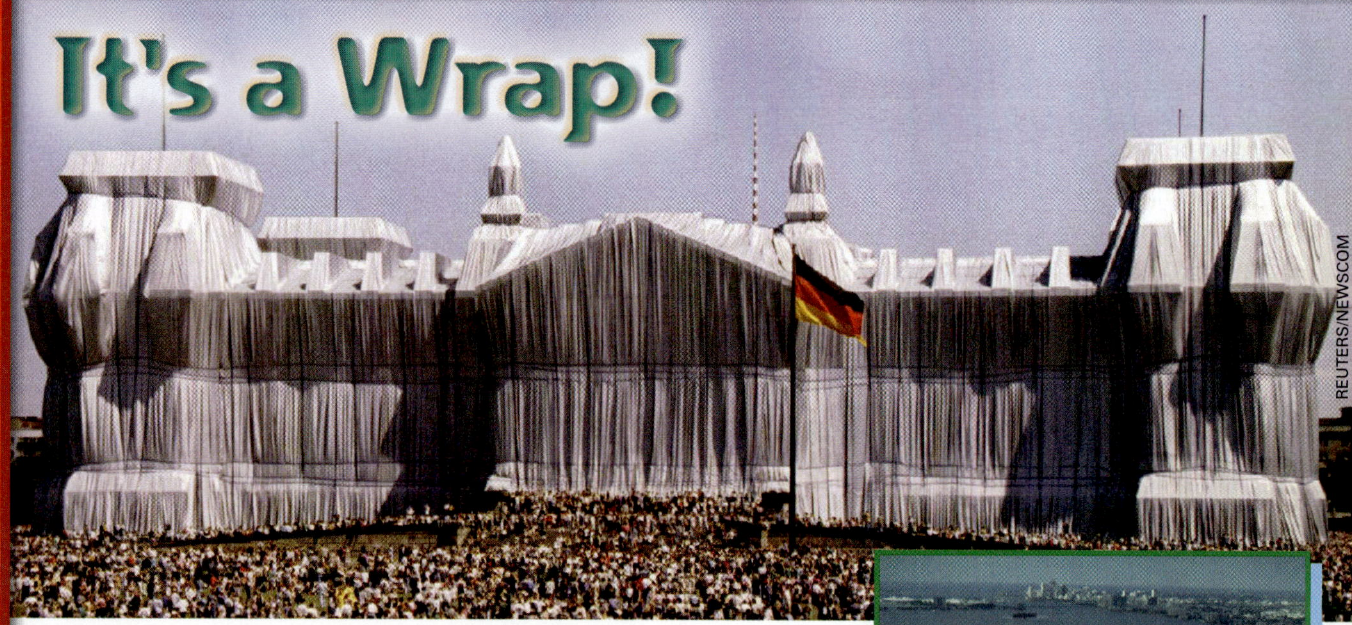
REUTERS/NEWSCOM

Christo and Jeanne-Claude's medium is measured in yards.

Wrapping an oddly shaped object isn't easy. If the object is enormous, it's even more challenging. Bulgarian-born Christo and his partner, Jeanne-Claude, have managed to turn this challenge into an art. The team has wrapped endless yards of fabric around government buildings in Germany, an ancient bridge in Paris, and even part of the California coastline.

Some people may think fabric is an odd medium with which to create art, but not this couple. They wrap soft fabric around odd corners and shapes, like a building's roof or a tree trunk. In fact, the folds, wrinkles, and creases of the fabric become elements of Christo and Jeanne-Claude's art. The elements serve as lines, shapes, and forms.

The artists' work is not just about the outside of the fabric. Draping an object also makes it mysterious. Fabric can either reveal the item's form or hide it. Either way, it sparks peoples' imaginations and gets them wondering just what is underneath the cloth.

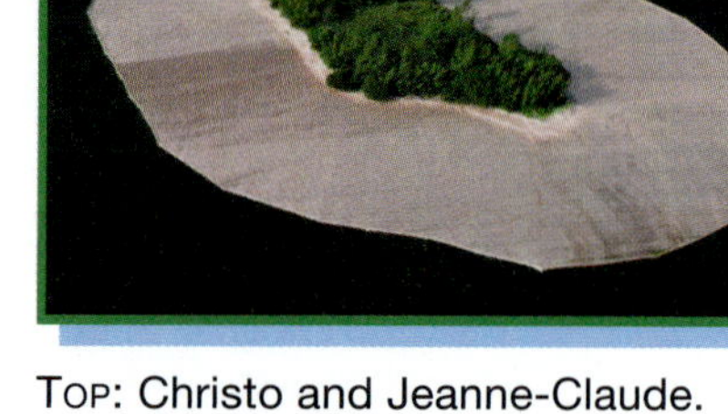
BETTMANN/CORBIS

TOP: Christo and Jeanne-Claude. *Wrapped Reichstag.* 1995.

ABOVE: Christo. *Surrounded Islands*. 1983. To wrap eleven islands in Miami's Biscayne Bay, the artist worked with scientists, construction workers, and cloth makers.

TIME TO CONNECT

- **Select a public site in your neighborhood and choose an object that you would like Christo and Jeanne-Claude to cover in cloth.**
- **Write the artists a letter fully describing why you selected the particular location, the object, and how you believe the wrapped item will look once the project is completed.**

Chapter 4 Review

BUILDING VOCABULARY

Number a sheet of paper from 1–13. After each number, write the term from the list that best matches each description below.

art media	printmaking
binder	relief
digital art	rendering
edition	resolution
fine art print	sculpture
freestanding	solvent
pigment	

1. Tools and materials used to create an artwork.
2. A type of fine art in which an inked image is transferred to a surface.
3. The art of creating three-dimensional artworks.
4. A finely ground powder that gives paint its color.
5. Surrounded on all sides by space.
6. An artwork created by the printmaking process.
7. Art made using computer hardware and software.
8. A type of sculpture in which the image projects only from the front.
9. A liquid to which dry pigment is added.
10. A liquid that controls the thickness or thinness of the paint.
11. A series of prints all exactly alike.
12. The fineness of detail that can be distinguished in an image.
13. A process by which a vector-based image is converted to a bitmap.

REVIEWING ART FACTS

Number a sheet of paper from 14–17. Answer each question in a complete sentence.

14. Name two drawing media.
15. What is the first step in printmaking?
16. How is freestanding sculpture meant to be seen?
17. What type of sculpture is flat on the back?

CROSS-CURRICULUM CONNECTIONS

18. **Communication.** Find three examples of printmaking in your daily activities. Think about how this art form has developed into an important medium for communicating ideas. Share your examples with the class.
19. **Industrial Arts.** In 1440 a German printer named Johannes Gutenberg invented a printing press with movable type. The effect of this invention was profound. Trace the development of the printing industry from 1440 through the present. Analyze ways that technological developments influence artworks.

Web Museum Activity

The Metropolitan Museum of Art, New York, New York

Test your knowledge about different art media by visiting The Metropolitan Museum of Art's site at art.glencoe.com. View the different artworks shown in the Explore & Learn section. Can you identify the correct media used in each image?

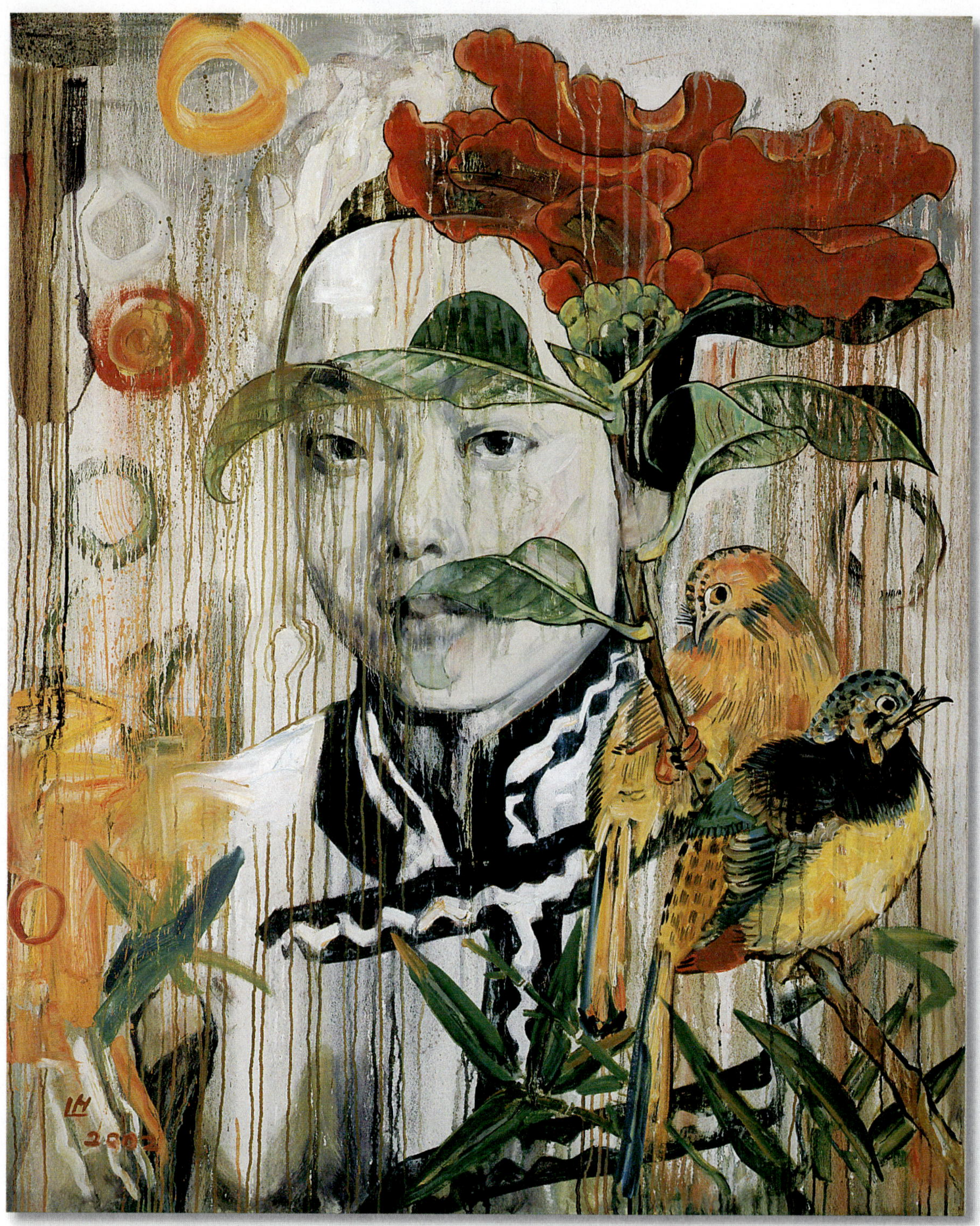

Focus On ◆ **Figure 5–1** **The artist, Hung Liu, enhances this work with a photograph. She also incorporates drawings of birds and a flower to create a mysterious story for the viewer to interpret.**

Hung Liu. *Hong Shancha: Red Camelia.* 2002. Oil on canvas. 152.4 × 121.9 cm (60 × 48″). Bernice Steinbaum Gallery, Miami, Florida.

Chapter 5

Art Criticism and Aesthetics

"Great art can communicate before it is understood."

— T. S. Eliot, poet (1888–1965)

Have you noticed the many kinds of books and movies that exist? There are fantasies, action adventures, sci-fi thrillers, and mysteries. The reason for this variety has to do with individual tastes. Some people enjoy one kind of book or film—others, another.

Like readers and moviegoers, art critics also exhibit wide-ranging tastes. Some prefer art that is true-to-life—that is realistic. Others like art that is well organized—that has a pleasing composition. Still other critics appreciate art that is expressive—that communicates strong emotions. What might each of these critics say about the painting in **Figure 5–1?**

After completing this chapter, you will be able to:

- Name the four steps used in art criticism.
- Describe objective and nonobjective works of art.
- Illustrate ideas from school and community events.
- Define *describing, analyzing, interpreting,* and *judging.*
- Apply art criticism to a work of art.

Quick Write

Interpreting the Quote Read the quote. Then look again at the painting in Figure 5–1. Write a short paragraph in which you summarize what this painting communicates to you.

Key Terms

art criticism
art critic
describing
analyzing
picture plane
interpreting
judging
aesthetics
aesthetic view

Describing Works of Art

What do you think of when you hear the words *art criticism?* Do you think of someone saying they like a painting because the colors are vivid or the scenery is realistic? It is more than saying you like or do not like a piece of art. **Art criticism** is *the process of gathering facts and information from artworks in order to make intelligent judgments about them.*

The Art Critic

A person whose career is art criticism is called an **art critic.** Art critics learn as much as possible from all kinds of artwork. They carefully study and examine works of art. They search for a meaning or message in the work. They gather facts that add to their understanding about the artwork. Then this information is

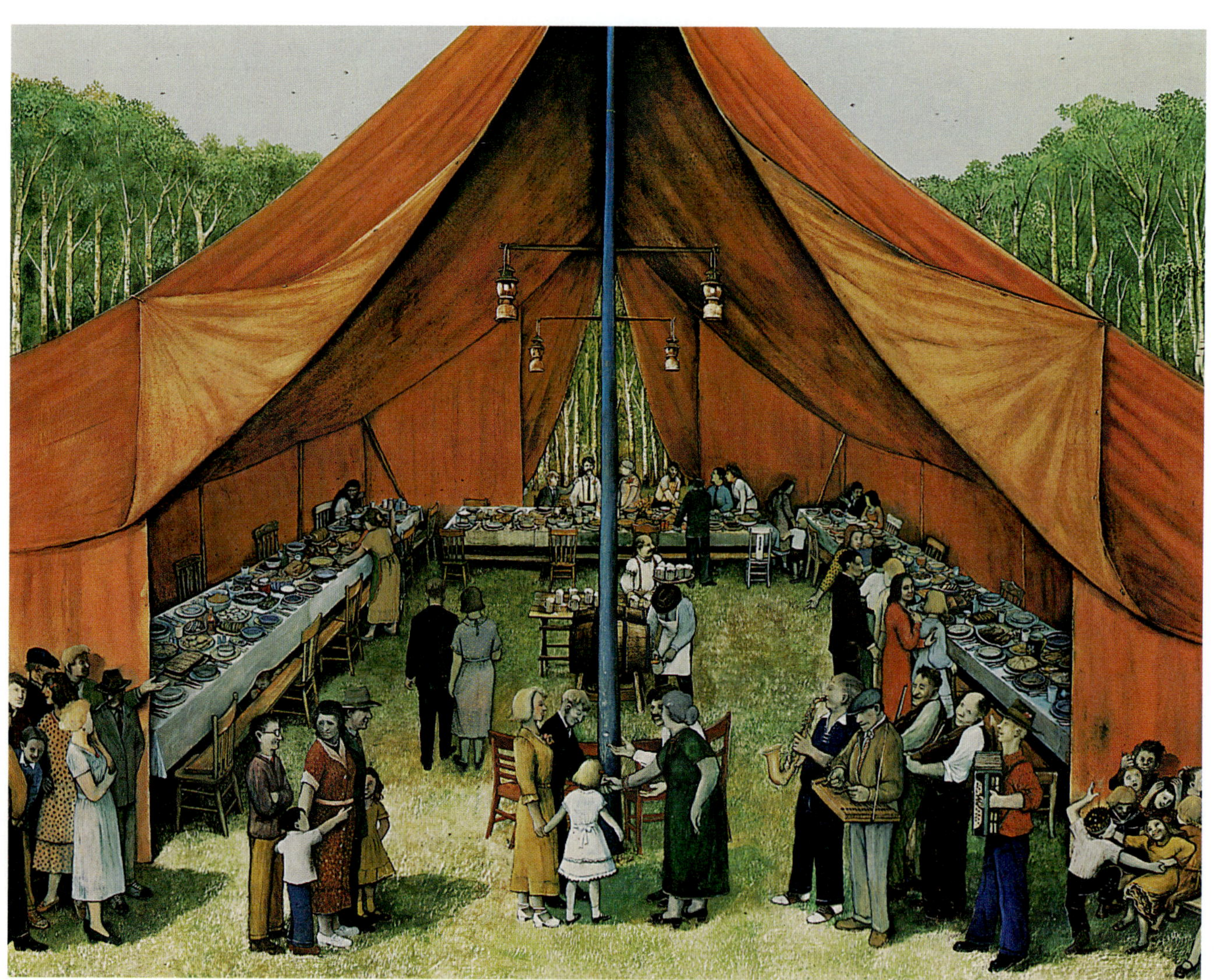

◆ **Figure 5–2** **In this painting Kurelek recalls a scene from his childhood in Manitoba, Canada.**

William Kurelek. *Manitoba Party.* 1964. Oil on masonite. 121.9 × 152.4 cm (48 × 60″). National Gallery of Canada, Ottawa, Canada.

used to help them form judgments that can be supported with solid reasons.

You, too, can practice art criticism. You will find that it can help you:

- Analyze and understand the artworks of others.
- Analyze your own artworks to determine how to improve them.
- Gain a better understanding and appreciation for all types and styles of art.

The Critique

Every art critique involves the same four-step process. The steps, which will be examined in detail in this and later lessons, are:

- **Describing.** In this stage, the critic is as careful and complete as possible. He or she makes detailed notes about what an artwork shows and how it was made.
- **Analyzing.** Analyzing is determining how an artwork is designed or put together.
- **Interpreting.** Interpreting is assigning a meaning or finding a message in an artwork.
- **Judging.** Judging states whether, how, and why an artwork is a success.

In this lesson you will learn about the first of these steps, describing.

Describing Artworks

When you describe a work of art, you ask yourself the question, "What do I see?" **Describing** is *making a careful list of all the things you see in the work.* In describing a work, you identify:

- The size of the work, the medium, and the process used.
- What people and objects you see and what is happening.
- The elements of art used.

In the describing stage, you report only the facts. You do not mention, for example, if the artist's use of color makes the painting confusing. That will come later.

Size and Medium

Describing the size and medium of a work is easy. This information is given in the credit line, which you learned about in Chapter 1. In museums, this information appears on a card or placard placed near the work. Remember that the height of a work is always listed before the width.

It is now time for you to begin your work as an art critic. Examine the credit line of the artwork in **Figure 5–2.** What is the size of this work? Visualize or measure how much space this would take up on a wall in your classroom. What medium was used?

Subject, Objects, and Details

The next phase of a description is listing people and objects and telling what is happening. Try this yourself. Look again at the painting in Figure 5–2. How many figures do you see? Where are they placed? What objects do you see in the work? How are the people interacting with each other? With the objects?

A critic answering these questions might note there are several people. Some are clustered in small groups. Some appear to be waiting outside a large pitched tent. Among this group, on the right side, is a small band of musicians. Beyond them is a small group of children.

The front flaps of the tent have been pulled back, revealing the interior. How would you describe the objects in the tent? The event depicted appears to be some sort of party or celebration. That fact is confirmed by the painting's title.

◆ **Figure 5–3** Art Elements Checklist

Art Element		Description
Color	Hue	
	Intensity	
	Value	
Line		
Shape/Form		
Space		
Texture		

◆ **Figure 5–4** **This painting was not meant to tell a story. It expresses feelings about death and loss.**

Robert Motherwell. *Elegy to the Spanish Republic.* 1960. Boucour Magna paint on canvas. 182.9 × 244.5 cm (72 × 96¼″). Modern Art Museum of Fort Worth, Fort Worth, Texas. © Dedalus Foundation, Inc./Licensed by VAGA, New York, NY

Describing the Elements of Art

The final step of the description phase is observing which elements of art have been used. To simplify this step, a critic might use a checklist. One possible format appears in **Figure 5–3.** Notice that a space for a brief description appears alongside each element.

Try describing the elements in Figure 5–2. What hues can you identify in this painting? Which hue predominates? In what object or objects is this hue found? Is it bright (high-intensity) or dull (low-intensity)? Is it light or dark in value? Continue in this fashion for each of the remaining elements. You may want to use a chart such as the one in Figure 5–3 to record your observations.

Describing Nonobjective Artworks

Look at the painting shown in **Figure 5–4.** As noted in Chapter 1, this type of art is known as nonobjective. In a nonobjective work, the art elements become the subject matter of the work. What colors has Motherwell used? Describe the lines, shapes, and textures you see. Remember, a critic's job is to describe what he or she sees. When an artwork has no objects, the critic focuses purely on the elements of art. The description is still valid because the critic is describing what the artist intended.

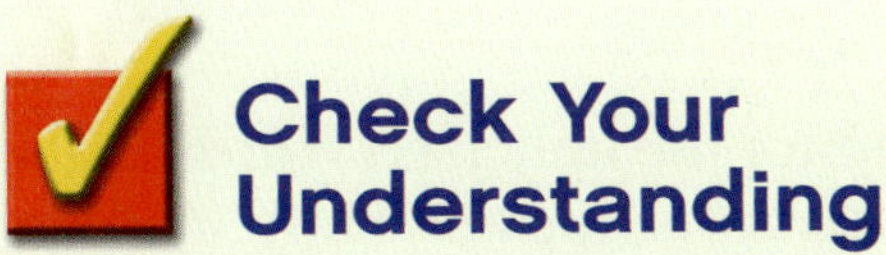

Check Your Understanding

1. What are the four steps of art criticism?
2. Describe one benefit of learning art criticism.
3. How would you go about describing a nonobjective work of art?

Studio Activity

Description Game

Download and print or photocopy a work of art. Look closely at the work. Write a description of it on an index card. Include all the aspects of a description mentioned in the lesson. On the bottom of the card, write your name. On the reverse side name the artist and title of the work.

Place your index card along with those of classmates in a shoe box. Display all the images so that everyone can see them. Form two teams. Taking turns, teams draw an index card from the box and read the description. The team has thirty seconds to identify the matching image. A point is awarded for each correct match.

Portfolio

At the game's end, reclaim your index card and reread your description. Think about the reaction your classmates had about your description. Then write answers to these questions: How well did I describe my selected work of art? What should I have explained in more detail? How did my description compare with those of my classmates? Keep your original description and your answers in your portfolio.

Analyzing Works of Art

Mathematics teaches that the whole is equal to the sum of its parts. This statement may work for numbers, but it does not necessarily hold true for art. In this lesson, you will *analyze*—take apart and reassemble—a work of art. You will discover that there is often more to an artwork than meets the eye.

During this step you are still collecting facts. You will analyze the work by looking at the separate elements of art and how the artist has organized them.

Analyzing Artworks

The second step in an art critique is the analysis. **Analyzing** is *noting how the art principles are used to organize the elements of art.* During this step, the critic looks at an artwork in terms of its composition. He or she answers the question, "How are the parts of this work arranged?"

Imagine yourself to be a critic reviewing the painting in **Figure 5–5.** Here is how you might begin your analysis:

- The subject of the painting is centered horizontally in the picture plane. The **picture plane** is *the flat surface of a painting or drawing.* Her figure casts a stylized blue shadow, disrupting the *balance.*
- A second, more realistic, shadow is cast by her left arm. The double *line* of the arm and its shadow lead your gaze upward to the girl's face. They help *emphasize* this *form.* So does the black *freeform shape* of the girl's hair.
- The girl's face is further *emphasized* by several *rhythmic* swirls of *color,* which frame it. These include the *pattern* of red and blue stripes on her blouse. They also include the curved *lines* of the flowered wallpaper behind her.

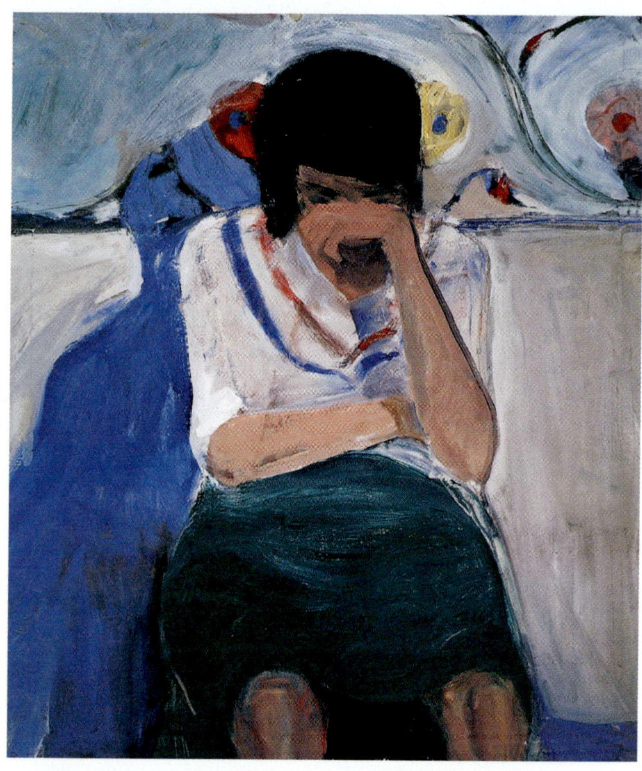

◆ **Figure 5–5** **Diebenkorn challenged himself by incorporating figures into his compositions. He created an interaction between the figure and the setting in which he placed it.**

Richard Diebenkorn. *Girl with a Flowered Background.* 1962. Oil on canvas. 101.6 × 86.4 cm (40 × 34″). The Modern Art Museum of Fort Worth, Fort Worth, Texas. Museum purchase, Sid W. Richardson Foundation Endowment Fund.

Did you notice the italicized words in the bulleted paragraphs above? They identify specific principles the artist, Richard Diebenkorn (**dee**-buhn-korn), used in this painting. They also indicate which elements these principles were used to organize.

Analyzing Nonobjective Art

This same type of analysis can be used with nonobjective works. Look at the painting in **Figure 5–6.** This work was also painted by Richard Diebenkorn. Even though the work has no recognizable subject, the artist carefully controls the viewer's reaction. See this for yourself by answering the following questions. Then compare your answers with those of classmates.

- Which shape in this painting first caught your eye?
- What is the color of that shape?
- What principle of art led your eye to this portion of the painting?

As with an objective artwork, a nonobjective work is analyzed with respect to composition. You note the elements used and the principles used to organize them.

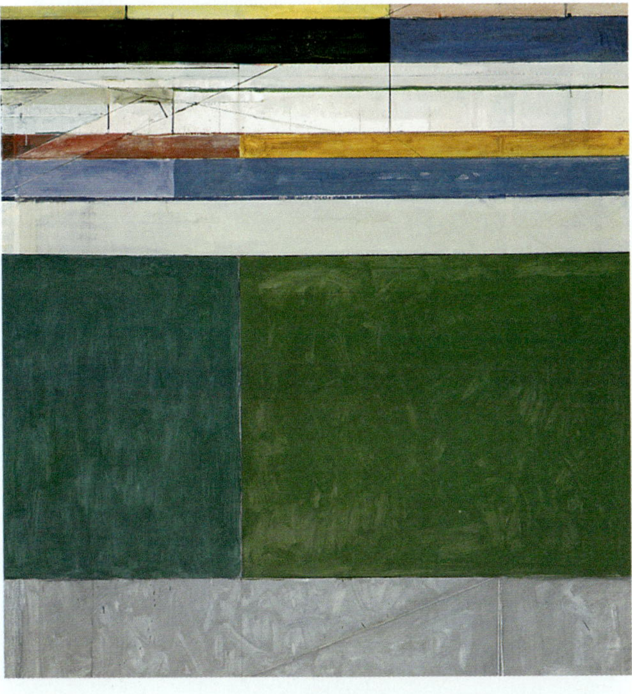

◆ **Figure 5–6** **When he moved from northern California to Southern California in 1967, Diebenkorn painted mostly abstract works. He created his Ocean Park series of abstract landscapes to reflect the sunlight and colors of southern California.**

Richard Diebenkorn. *Ocean Park #105*. 1978. Oil and charcoal on canvas. 253.7 × 236.2 cm (99⅞ × 93″). The Modern Art Museum of Fort Worth, Fort Worth, Texas. Museum purchase, Sid W. Richardson Foundation Endowment Fund and the Burnett Foundation.

Meet the Artist

Richard Diebenkorn (1922–93)

Some artists "reinvent" themselves throughout their careers. They constantly seek new forms of self-expression—new answers to the question, "What is art?" American artist Richard Diebenkorn was such an artist. Diebenkorn was born in Portland, Oregon, and studied art at the University of California at Berkeley. He then served in the United States Marine Corps. All the while he painted, experimenting with styles. His first exhibition was held in 1948. All of the paintings displayed were nonobjective. Over the next two decades, his work moved toward more realistic subjects. A degree of abstraction, however, was always visible in the artist's brushstrokes. Toward the end of his life, Diebenkorn returned to nonobjective art.

Compare and Contrast

The work in Figure 5–5 is from the end of Diebenkorn's middle period. The subject is recognizable, but details are abstract. Compare and contrast the use of art elements and principles in this painting with the one by Alice Neel in Figure 3–10 on page 56. Analyze each work to form conclusions about the artist's intent. How did each artist use line and movement to guide the viewer's eyes through the work?

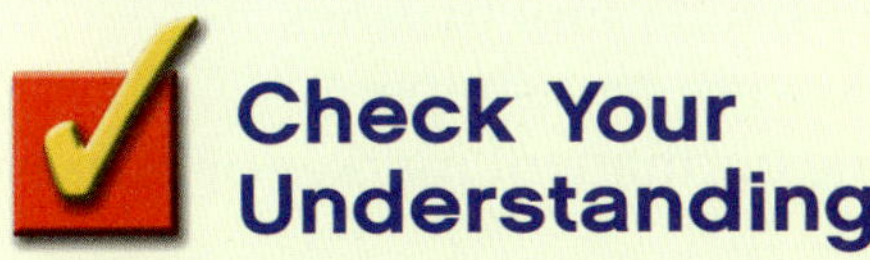

Check Your Understanding

1. What is the second step in art criticism?
2. What does an art critic do in the analysis stage of art criticism?

Recording Personal Events

Artists often create works of art as a reaction to a personal event. Leo Twiggs drew on his personal experiences with his sons when he painted *Blue Wall* (see **Figure 5–7**). Look at the image for clues. What are the two boys doing? Notice how the boys are facing away from one another, yet they are touching. Notice the curved lines that outline the two figures. What clues are given about the boys?

What You Will Learn

You will select and use a variety of appropriate art materials and tools to create a painting in traditional ways. Illustrate a reaction to a personal experience, such as a school or community event. You will apply design skills to effectively communicate ideas and thoughts in everyday life. Use the principle of rhythm to organize both positive and negative space in your work. Emphasize your positive shapes using warm colors. Create contrast by using cool or neutral colors in the negative spaces. Use balance to organize the art elements of shape and color.

What You Will Need

- Sketchbook, pencil, eraser
- 12 × 16-inch heavy white drawing paper or watercolor paper, water container
- Watercolor paints, mixing palette
- Various-sized paint brushes
- Paper towels, newspaper
- Fine-line permanent marker or oil pastels

What You Will Do

1. Look closely at Figure 5–7. Notice how the boys are drawn using simple shapes. They are both sitting quietly. Twiggs uses informal balance in organizing the shapes of the boys and the wall. Why do you think he left the negative space, or background, so simple? What do you think was his intent when creating *Blue Wall?*
2. Make a list of personal experiences or school and community events that have had an effect on you. For example, the watercolor shown in **Figure 5–8** conveys loneliness the student artist felt while attending a school dance. What clues does the student provide to show that emotion? Look over your list and select one experience. Think about the details of the event. Apply design skills by using the art elements and principles to communicate your ideas and thoughts. Make several sketches based on your selected experience. Use the principle of rhythm to organize the positive shapes and negative space in your composition. Use repeated shapes to create rhythm. Use formal or informal balance when you organize your shapes and colors.

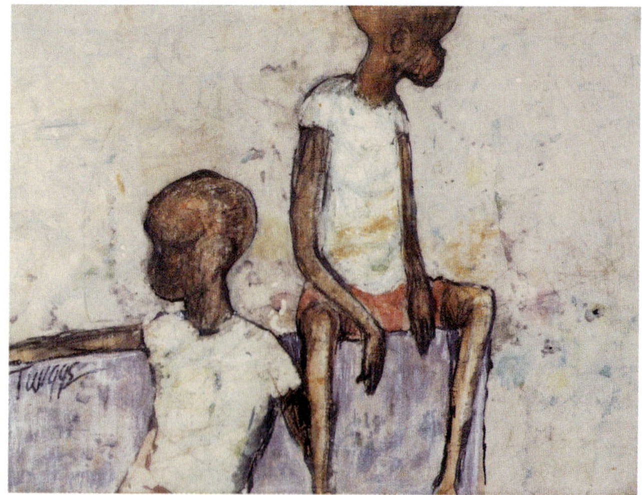

◆ **Figure 5–7 Twiggs creates his paintings using batik-dye and wax-resist techniques.**

Leo Twiggs. *Blue Wall.* 1969. Batik painting. 61 × 76.2 cm (24 × 30″). Private collection.

3. Select your best sketch and transfer it with pencil onto your paper. Use your fine-line marker or oil pastels to outline your image. Add warm colors in your positive shapes, using watercolors and a brush. Paint some areas of your painting with bolder colors by using less water with your paints. Use your palette to mix colors. Use a cool or neutral color in your negative space.
4. After your painting has dried, write a brief description of your intent on the back of your work. Explain the event and the emotions you experienced.
5. Title and display your work with those of your classmates in a group exhibit.

Evaluating Your Work

- **Describe** What personal experience did you choose to illustrate?
- **Analyze** How did you apply design skills to communicate ideas and thoughts in everyday life? How did you use the principle of rhythm to organize positive shapes and negative space? What colors were used to create contrast? What type of balance did you use to organize your shapes and colors? Which is the most important element in your work? Explain.

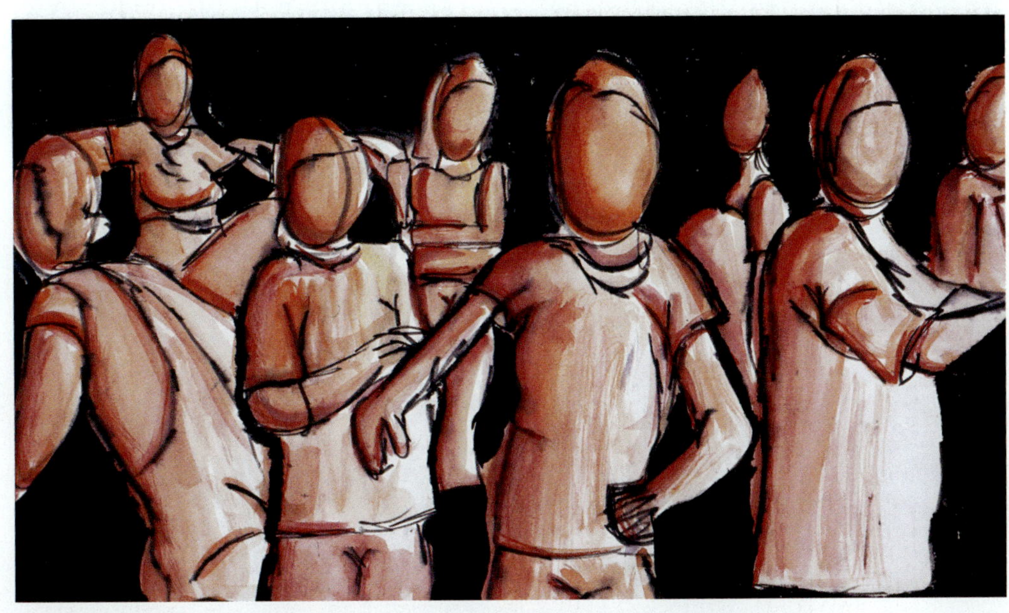

◆ **Figure 5–8** **Student work. A watercolor recording a personal event.**

REFLECTIVE THINKING

Critical Evaluation. Analyze the original artworks of your peers displayed in your class exhibition. Form conclusions about formal properties, historical and cultural contexts, intents, and meanings. Do the artworks reveal anything about the artists' culture? Discuss your responses with classmates. Ask your peers to explain their intents and the meanings of their works.

Art Online

Becoming an art critic is one art-related career you might choose. Survey and identify other career choices or opportunities in art at **art.glencoe.com**. There you will also find:

- Artist Profiles
- Interactive Games

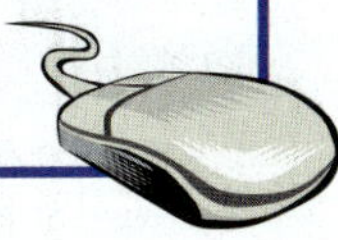

LESSON 4

Interpreting Works of Art

Interpreting is the third stage of art criticism. **Interpreting** is *determining and explaining the meaning, mood, or idea of the work of art.* It can be the most difficult step for some people. It can also be the most creative and rewarding. You must use your intelligence, imagination, and courage. You must not be afraid to make an interpretation that is different from someone else's. How you interpret a work of art will depend on what you have done and seen in your life. Your interpretation should be based upon the facts and clues collected during the first two steps. Your interpretation can express your feelings, but must be backed up by observation.

Interpreting Objective Artworks

When you interpret an objective work of art, you ask yourself two questions. The first is, "What do I believe is happening?" The second question is, "What idea, mood, or feeling does this artwork suggest?"

To see this, look back at the painting in Figure 5–5 on page 98. As noted earlier, the artist went to considerable lengths to emphasize the subject's face. Perhaps it should be said he emphasized the parts that are *visible.* The girl sits with her head lowered, her face buried in one hand. We can see only her forehead, plus the bottom of her chin. Her gesture, however, provides enough information

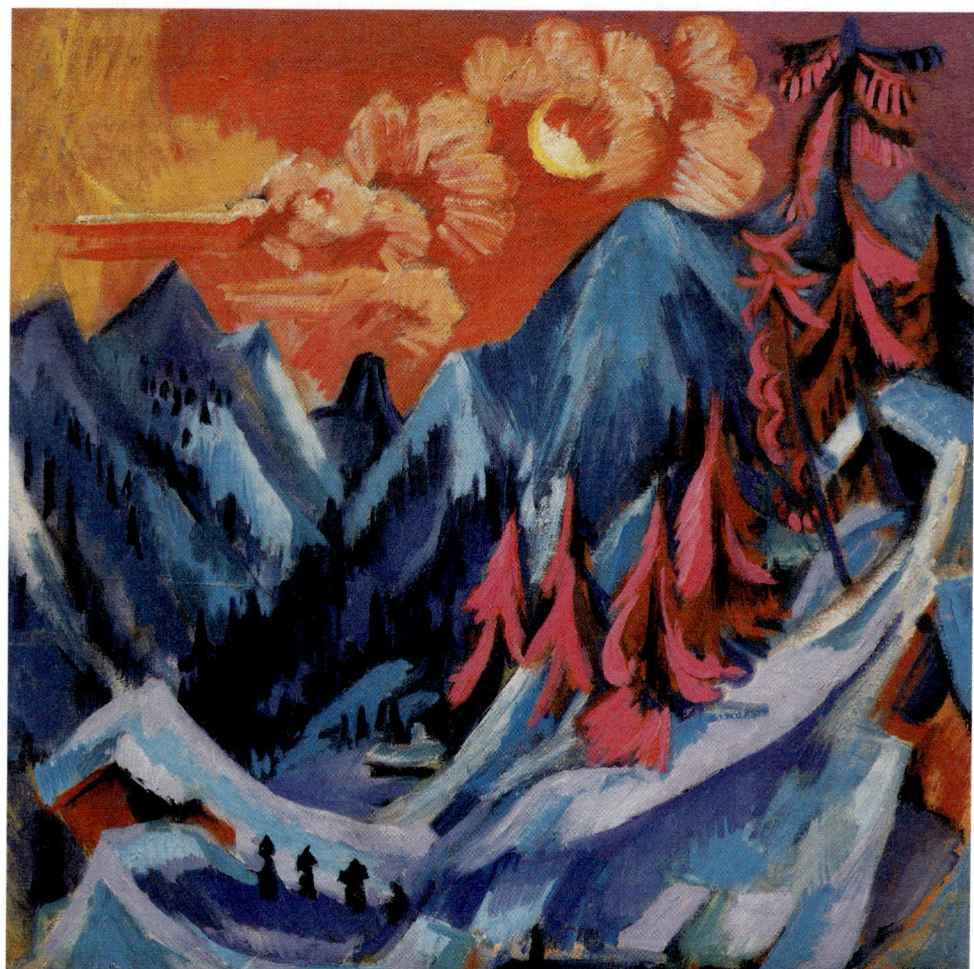

◆ **Figure 5–9** **Kirchner left architecture school in 1905 and formed a group called Die Bruke (The Bridge). The title indicated a desire to link revolutionary ideas with new art. The group's work expressed strong emotions through intense colors.**

Ernst Kirchner. *Winter Landscape in Moonlight.* 1919. Oil on canvas. 1.2 × 1.2 m (47¼ × 47¼″). Detroit Institute of Arts, Detroit, Michigan. Gift of Curt Valentin in memory of the artist on the occasion of Dr. William R. Valentiner's 60th birthday. Photograph ©1984, The Detroit Institute of Arts. 40.58.

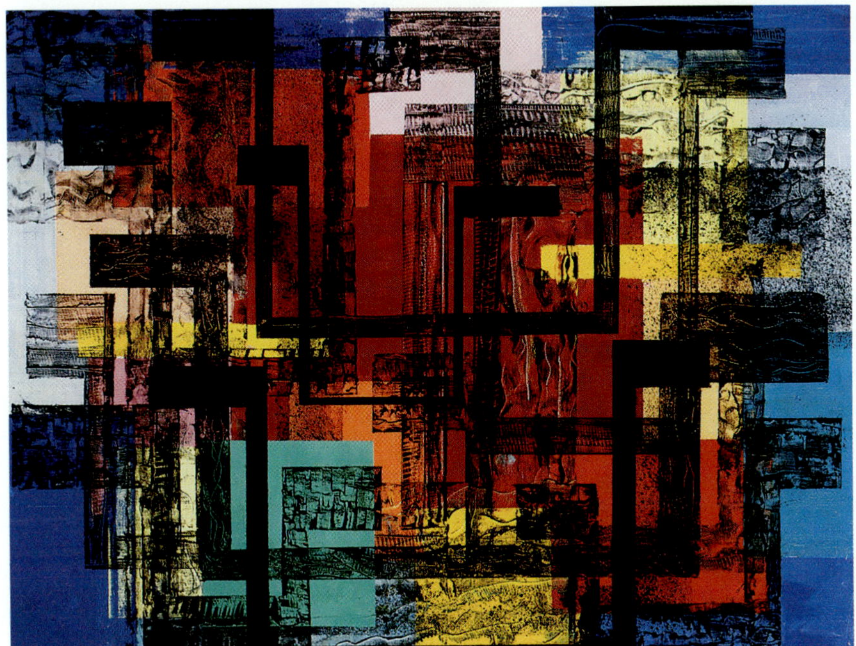

◆ **Figure 5–10** **Pereira creates textures layered over solid shapes to capture her ideas.**

Irene Rice Pereira. *Midnight Sun.* c. 1954. Oil on canvas. 101 × 126.4 cm (39¾ × 49¾″). Walker Art Center, Minneapolis, Minnesota. Gift of Mr. Harold Kaye and Art Center Acquisition Fund, 1959.

to enable us to "read" her mood. We don't have to see her eyes to know she is feeling despair. The dominant color in the painting, blue, supports that view. So does her "body language." Notice that her frame is limp, as though drained of energy. She sits with her arms wrapped about her, shoulders hunched. She seems to be withdrawing into herself and her own gloomy thoughts. What is this girl so sad about? That is impossible to say. What is central to this painting is how effectively the artist communicated this mood.

Now you try interpreting. Look once more at the painting in Figure 5–2 on page 94. What is the mood or feeling at this outdoor event? What clues lead you to this interpretation?

It is worth noting that not all interpretations are this clear. Look back at the work that opened this chapter on page 92. How do you read this unique painting? How do you interpret the brightly colored work shown in **Figure 5–9?** Don't be concerned if you don't have immediate answers to these questions. Some artists make you work to uncover the mood or message expressed in their works. You will find that the payoff is usually that much more rewarding. You will also find that your skill at interpreting improves with practice.

Interpreting Nonobjective Artworks

Pictures without subjects can also express ideas and feelings. Look at the painting in **Figure 5–10.** Notice how the many overlapping shapes keep your eyes moving throughout the artwork. Do you find yourself seeking relief from this busy work in the background patterns? All of these effects were part of the artist's overall plan. Analyze and compare the mood of this painting with the one in Figure 5–4 on page 96. What conclusions can you form about the intent of each artist?

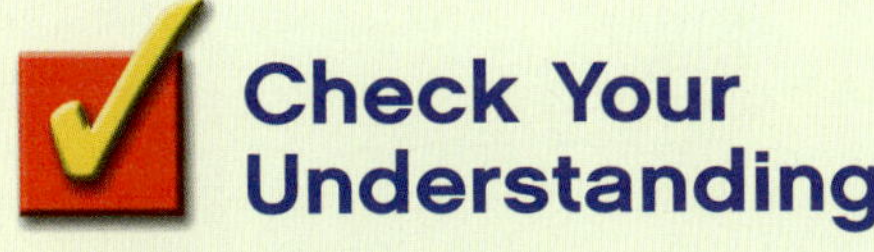

Check Your Understanding

1. Define *interpreting,* as the term is used in art criticism.
2. What two questions do you ask yourself when you interpret a work?

Mood Chalk Painting

Look at the work shown in **Figure 5–11.** This seascape, or painting of the sea, was done by the American artist Albert Pinkham Ryder. Notice that the work is made up of simple shapes and few colors. No object is clearly shown. There is hardly any detail. Yet the quiet, calm mood of this moonlit scene is almost impossible to miss.

What You Will Learn

You will select and use a variety of appropriate art materials and tools, such as sandpaper and colored chalk, to create another version of the seascape shown in Figure 5–11. Using traditional methods, you will repeat simple shapes of sailboats, the sea, the moon, and clouds to give the work harmony. Your seascape, too, will focus mainly on mood. Yours, however, will express a mood opposite that of the original. Look at **Figure 5–12** to see how a student captured an opposite mood from the original painting (Figure 5–11). You will choose four colors that help capture that mood. Repeating these colors will also add harmony to your work.

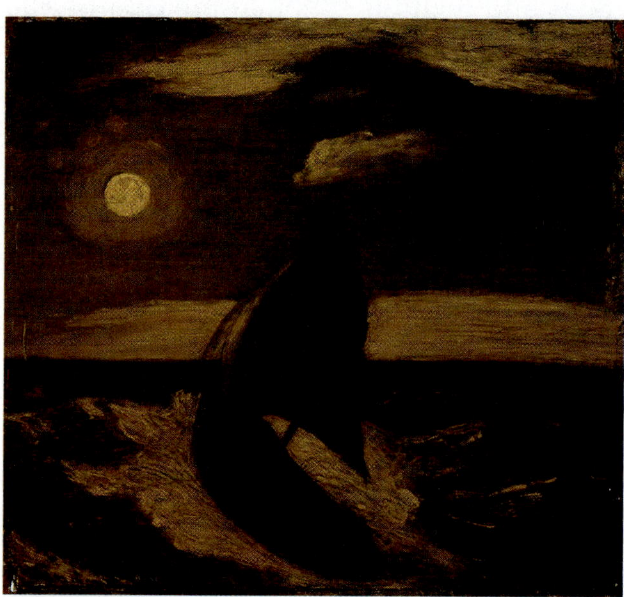

◆ Figure 5–11 **Ryder became an artist after an illness damaged his sight. He could not see details, so he painted large simple shapes filled with color to express feelings.**

Albert Pinkham Ryder. *The Toilers of the Sea.* ca. early 1880s. Oil on wood. 29.2 × 30.5 cm (11½ × 12″). The Metropolitan Museum of Art, New York, New York. George A. Hearn Fund, 1915.

What You Will Need

- Pencil
- Notepad
- Sketch paper
- Sheet of rough sandpaper, 10 × 12 inches
- Colored chalk

What You Will Do

1. After looking at Ryder's seascape in Figure 5–11, brainstorm with your classmates to come up with words meaning the opposite of quiet and calm. Two possibilities are stormy and rough. Try to come up with at least four more words. Write these on your notepad.
2. On a sheet of sketch paper, lightly draw shapes of sailboats, the sea, the moon, and clouds. Keep your shapes simple, like those in Figure 5–11. Add no details beyond those in the original work.
3. Review the list of terms you copied. Think of colors that capture the mood expressed by these terms. Write the names of four of these colors on your notepad. Look back at your sketch. Think of changes you could make in line and shape that would help express the new mood. Make those changes. Again, do not add any new objects or details.

4. Transfer your sketch to the sandpaper. Color in your shapes with the four colors of chalk you chose. Limiting your colors to four will help add harmony to your work.
5. Compare your finished seascape with those of your classmates. Can you identify the mood of each work? Which most successfully expressed a mood?

Safety Tip

Chalk, which creates dust, should be used in a room with good ventilation. Those with breathing problems should wear a dust mask or avoid using chalk altogether. Crayon or oil pastels can be used instead.

Evaluating Your Work

- **Describe** Point out the shapes of sailboats, the sea, the moon, and clouds in your work. Tell whether you added shapes and details that were not in the original. Identify the four colors you chose. Explain how you used a variety of art materials and tools to obtain different effects.
- **Analyze** Explain how your use of the same simple shapes in your work gives it a feeling of harmony. Tell how your use of four colors repeated throughout the work added to the feeling of harmony.
- **Interpret** Tell what mood your work communicates to the viewer. Explain what you did to communicate that mood to the viewer. Explain what you did to communicate a mood opposite of that communicated in Ryder's painting.

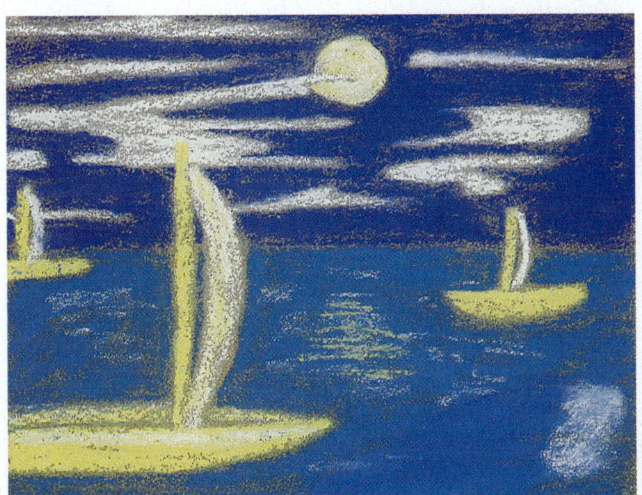

◆ **Figure 5–12** **Student work. A mood chalk painting.**

Studio Option

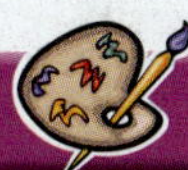

Create another mood seascape painting different from Ryder's nighttime scene. Select and use a variety of appropriate art materials and tools in experimental ways to interpret a seascape theme. Experiment with different - sized brushes to create a variety of visual effects. Choose only two or three hues, but include black and white paint to create the different hues. Does your painting evoke a certain mood? How did you achieve this?

Visual Art Journal

Examine your completed artwork. How did it illustrate your chosen mood? In your visual art journal, explain how you used the art elements line, shape, and color to create your mood chalk painting.

Judging Works of Art Using Aesthetics

Now it is time to give your opinion about the work. Judging is the fourth stage of art criticism. In this lesson, you will learn about the process of *judging* art.

Judging Artworks

Judging an artwork is *making a decision about a work's success and giving reasons to support that decision.* To make a good judgment you need to be honest with yourself.

There are two levels of judgment to be made. The first is personal. Do you like the work? No one can ever tell you what to like or dislike. You must make up your own mind. The second level of judgment is based on aesthetic views used by art critics. Here you decide if the work is successful according to generally acceptable aesthetic views.

Art and Aesthetics

Aesthetics (ess-**thet**-iks) is *the branch of philosophy concerned with the nature and value of art.* Physical beauty was once the only standard for judging the quality of art. Today, a good work of art is called *successful.* Critics no longer limit themselves to the standard of

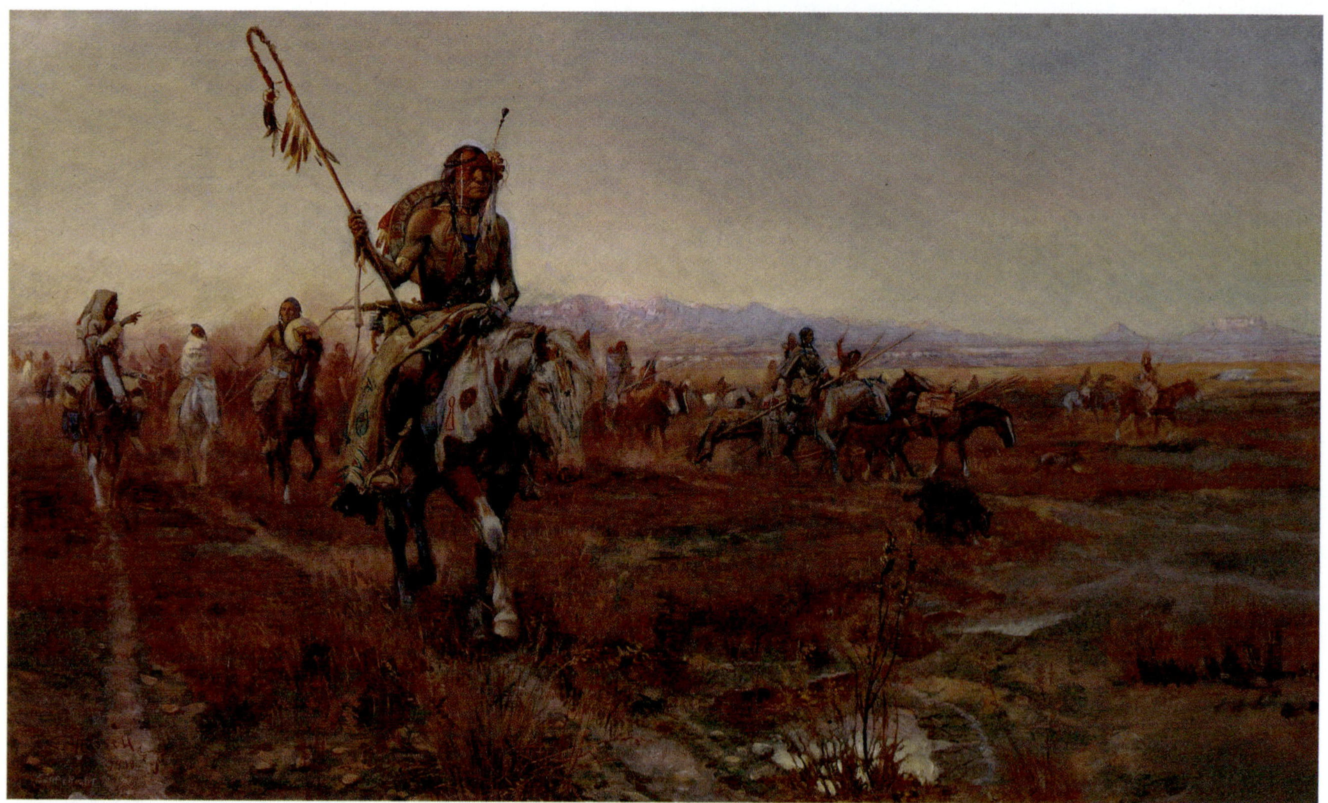

◆ **Figure 5–13** **This painting shows a group of Blackfeet Indians with a medicine man in the foreground. What cultural contexts can you determine from analyzing this artwork?**

Charles M. Russell. *The Medicine Man.* 1908. Oil on canvas. 76.2 × 122.2 cm (30 × 48″). Amon Carter Museum, Fort Worth, Texas.

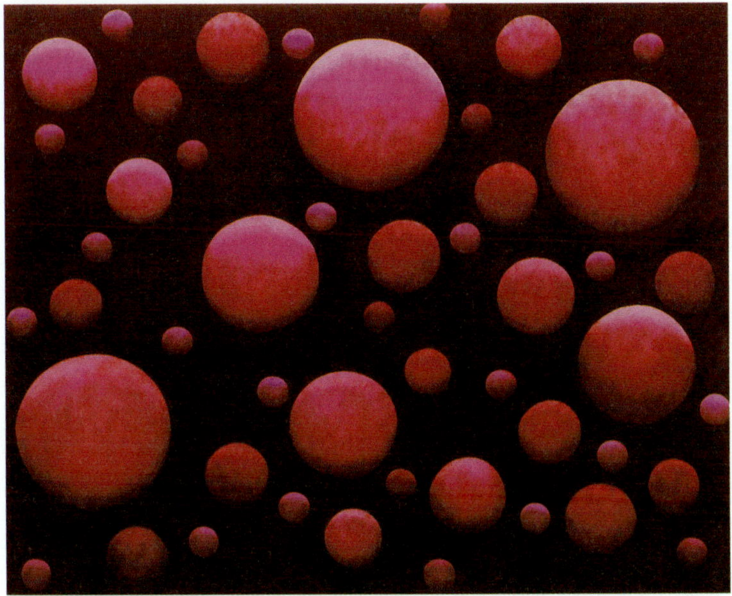

◆ **Figure 5–14** **This painting is part of a series the artist produced based on color names. The series started with the title Ruby Red Rumba. First he made up the name, then he created the visual image to illustrate the idea.**

Paul Brach. *Shocking Pink Polka.* 2001. Oil on canvas. 152.4 × 182.9 cm (60 × 72″). © 2003 Artists Rights Society (ARS), New York/VG Bild-Kunst, Bonn.

beauty to decide "What is art?" Some successful works of art may not look pretty, but they are well organized and interesting.

Over time many different ways of judging art have been developed. Among the most common are the three views described below. An **aesthetic view** is *an idea or school of thought on what is most important in works of art.*

View #1: Subject

In the subject view, art is considered successful if it imitates what we see in the real world. Supporters of this aesthetic view will place the most weight on whether an artwork looks lifelike. Analyze the painting in **Figure 5–13.** Notice how realistic the forms—the figures and objects—appear. Note the amount of detail the artist has included, such as the ruts from wagon wheels. Even the smallest rock casts a shadow. Art scholars subscribing to the subject view would praise this painting for being so true to life. Would you agree with them? What do you think a scholar maintaining this view would think of the work in Figure 5–2 on page 94?

View #2: Composition

In the second aesthetic view, what counts most in art is composition. In this view, the focus is on an artwork's formal properties. As you learned in Chapter 1, these properties refer to the organization of the elements of art by the principles of art. Look again at Figure 5–13. Supporters of the composition view would call this a successful painting. The artist has captured a strong sense of space using formal properties. Figures in the foreground overlap and are larger than those in the middle ground. The mountains at the horizon, meanwhile, are less detailed and lighter in value. Notice also how the placement of riders creates a sense of action and movement. Your eye is led across the entire panoramic painting.

Look once again at the painting in Figure 5–2. Note that the blue tent pole divides the work in half vertically. Notice how the flaps and sloping canvas are almost identical on either side. The work exhibits formal balance. What other details contribute to the strong sense of balance? How would art critics supporting the composition view judge this work?

It is important to note that some artists have paid more attention to composition than any other feature. How would art critics holding the composition view react to the painting in **Figure 5–14?** What elements of art might they refer to when discussing this work? What principles of art would they note?

View #3: Content

The third aesthetic view maintains that what is most important in an artwork is its content. In this view, a successful artwork is one with a clear message or feeling. Look back at Figure 5–5 on page 98. Read the work's title, if you haven't done so. The painting is titled *Girl with a Flowered Background.* The title makes no mention whatsoever of the subject's mental state. It doesn't need to. The work is so expressive that the viewer needs little help reading the emotion.

AESTHETICS AND THE ART CRITIC

You should be aware that few critics limit themselves to a single aesthetic view. Most agree that an open mind is the critic's most important asset. In approaching any artwork, they will attach equal importance to its subject, composition, *and* content. They agree that this is the only way of achieving a full understanding of art. You should follow their lead in your future encounters with art. Evaluating a work in terms of multiple aesthetic views can enhance the experience of judging art.

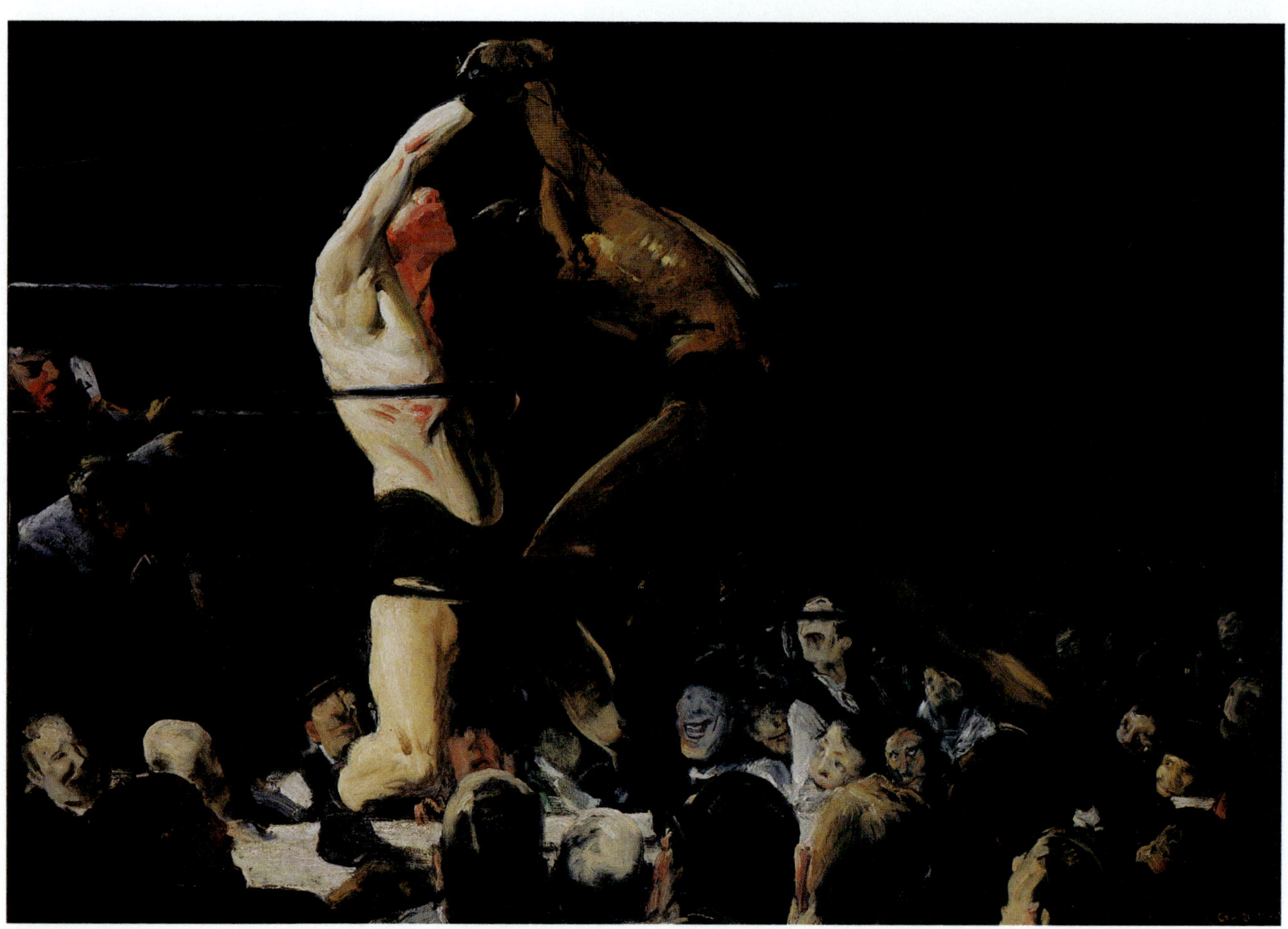

◆ **Figure 5–15** **The title of this painting is intended as ironic commentary. The boxers were fighting in a private club. The viewers are all regular members. The fighters were members only for the night they fought.**

George Bellows. *Both Members of This Club.* 1909. Oil on canvas. 114.9 × 160.3 cm (45¼ × 63⅛″). National Gallery of Art, Washington, D.C. © 1998 Board of Trustees. Chester Dale Collection.

Study the painting in **Figure 5–15.** First, note the realism with which the artist has faithfully recorded his subject. The work shows two prizefighters in the middle of a boxing match. Observe how every muscle strains, standing out vividly on the men's bodies. Shouting fans lean into the ring as the boxers slug away.

Next, look at the painting's composition. Find the diagonal line that begins in the leg of the boxer on the right. Follow that line upward through the man's torso and chest. It points to the head of his opponent, whose own body is dramatically highlighted. You may have noticed for the first time the stripes of red outlining this man's ribs.

Finally, notice the content. Observe how the sound of the crowd is almost audible. A look of agony registers in the face of the boxer on the left. His knees appear to buckle as his opponent's fist plows into his bruised midsection.

Far from a static image, this painting is a vivid action tale. The story is portrayed with accuracy and filled with color, movement, and noise.

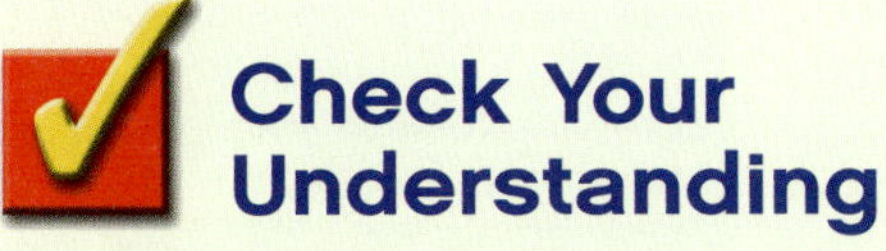

Check Your Understanding

1. What is aesthetics? What is the chief goal of aesthetics?
2. Briefly describe the three main aesthetic views presented in this lesson.
3. Why should you accept multiple aesthetic views?

Studio Activity

Judging Artworks

Creating Drawings Based on Direct Observation. Look in a magazine for a black-and-white photograph of an object viewed from the front. Cut out the photo and cut the object in half. Glue one half to a sheet of white paper. Use a pencil to complete the missing half of the object viewed. Before you begin, take one of the following views:

- My drawing will be as lifelike as I can make it.
- My drawing will focus on line and shape.
- My drawing will communicate a message, idea, or feeling.

Discuss your drawing with other students in the class. How many were able to identify the aesthetic approach you took? Were you able to identify the aesthetic approach they followed?

Recognizing Aesthetic Views

Which aesthetic view appeals to you? Write a paragraph that identifies that aesthetic view and explains why you like it best. Date your writing and keep it in your portfolio. Read it several times before the end of this course. See if your opinion changes. If it does, write that on the same sheet of paper.

What Is Your Junk Worth?

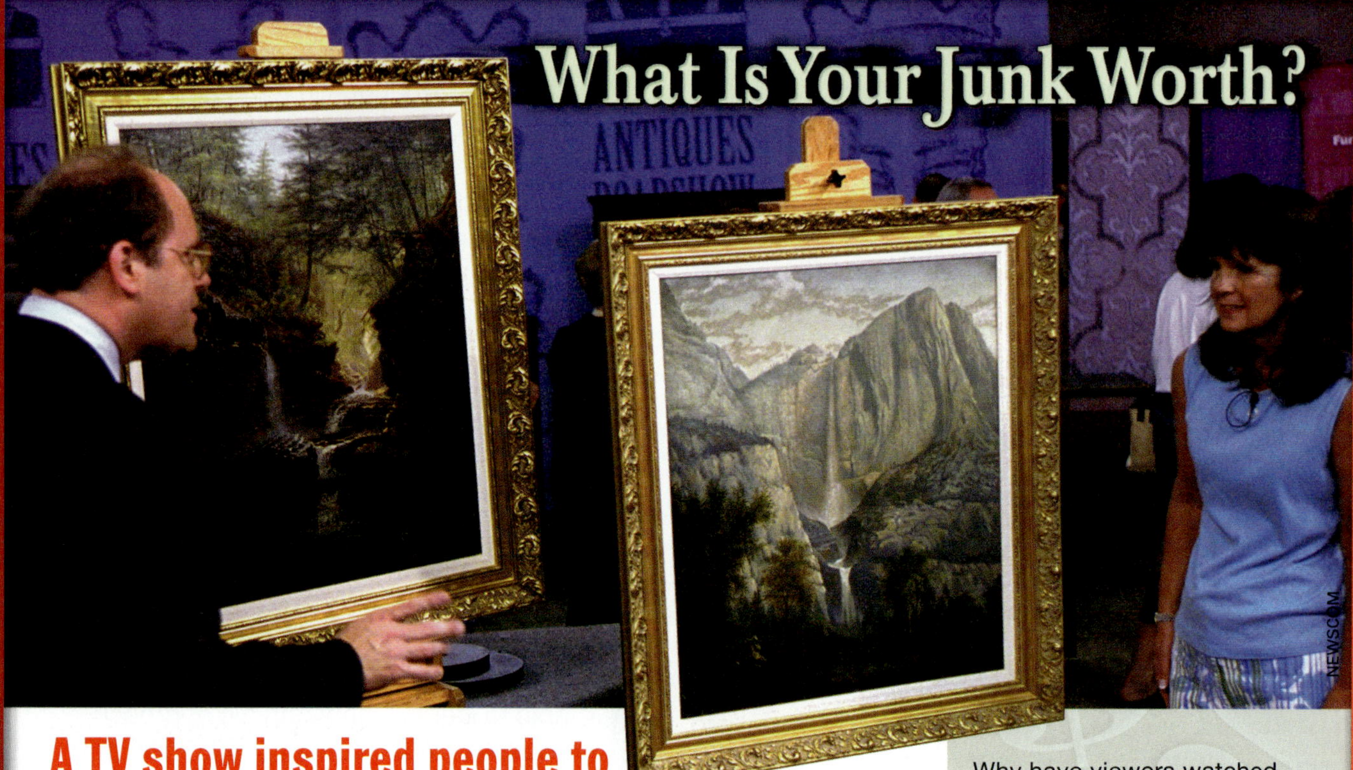

A TV show inspired people to search their attics for valuable items.

That "junk" your family has never thrown out could be worth a lot of money. A few years ago, Public Television launched *Antiques Roadshow*, a program that sent 10 million viewers searching their attics and closets, looking for the next valuable find.

Each week the show traveled to a U.S. city. Residents brought in items for expert appraisers to determine the object's worth. As many as 10,000 people entered with bags and boxes filled with miscellaneous items. The show focused on about 15 to 20 of the most interesting objects, such as furniture, baseball cards, old toys, and musical instruments.

Often the appraisers' judgments surprised the owners. A Houston man learned that his oil painting of the *Titanic* was worthless. The original menu from the ship's last meal pasted on the back of the canvas, however, was worth close to $100,000.

Maybe it's time to poke around your home and visit an appraiser. Who knows? That old portrait of your great aunt might be more than just a dust catcher!

Why have viewers watched people learning about the value of their old pieces? The show's executive producer, Aida Moreno, explained, "Every few minutes there's a cliff-hanger." People loved watching a growing look of amazement when someone was told Grandma's vase was valuable—or their look of disappointment when they were told that their prized antique was a fake. Viewers also learned how antiques were made and how to spot a fake antique from a genuine one.

TIME TO CONNECT

- **Look at the paintings in the photo.**
- **Critique them as to how well they use the elements and principles of art.**
- **From this basis, appraise, or estimate the value of, each painting and write an explanation that supports your decisions.**

Chapter 5 Review

BUILDING VOCABULARY

Number a sheet of paper from 1 to 9. After each number, write the term from the list that best matches each description below.

aesthetic views	describing
aesthetics	interpreting
analyzing	judging
art critic	picture plane
art criticism	

1. The process of gathering facts and information from works of art in order to make intelligent judgments about them.
2. One who practices the four steps in art criticism.
3. Making a careful list of all the things you see in a work of art.
4. Noting how the art principles are used to organize the elements of art.
5. The flat surface of a painting or drawing.
6. Explaining the meaning, mood, or ideas expressed by an artwork.
7. Telling if and why a work of art succeeds or fails.
8. A branch of philosophy concerned with the nature and value of art.
9. A school of thought on what is most important in works of art.

REVIEWING ART FACTS

Number a sheet of paper from 10 to 16. Answer each question in a complete sentence.

10. Name the four steps of art criticism.
11. In addition to describing the people, objects, and events shown in a work of art, name two other things you could identify in a description.
12. In which part of art criticism does a checklist of elements come in handy? Briefly tell how such a device is used.
13. What question does a critic answer during the analyzing stage?
14. In which step of art criticism would you explain the intent expressed in the artwork?
15. What is the key question asked by people who work in the field of aesthetics?
16. Why do many students of art accept more than one aesthetic view?

CROSS-CURRICULUM CONNECTIONS

17. **Music.** Music also has subject, content, and composition. Music may tell a story through instrumentation or through lyrics. Choose a type of music, such as rock, jazz, country, or classical, and analyze the piece for its subject, content, and composition.
18. **Language Arts.** Select an object from nature. Look at it closely and write a description of the object. Act as if you were describing a work of art. Use each element of art at least once in your description. Try reading your description to a classmate without telling what it is you are describing. Have your classmate draw the object as you describe it.

Web Museum Activity

National Gallery of Art, Washington, D.C.

To practice your art criticism skills, visit the online exhibition at the National Gallery of Art. Visit **art.glencoe.com** and click on the museum link for this chapter. Choose two of your favorite artworks and use the four steps of art criticism to critique the works. Form conclusions about formal properties, historical and cultural contexts, and intent.

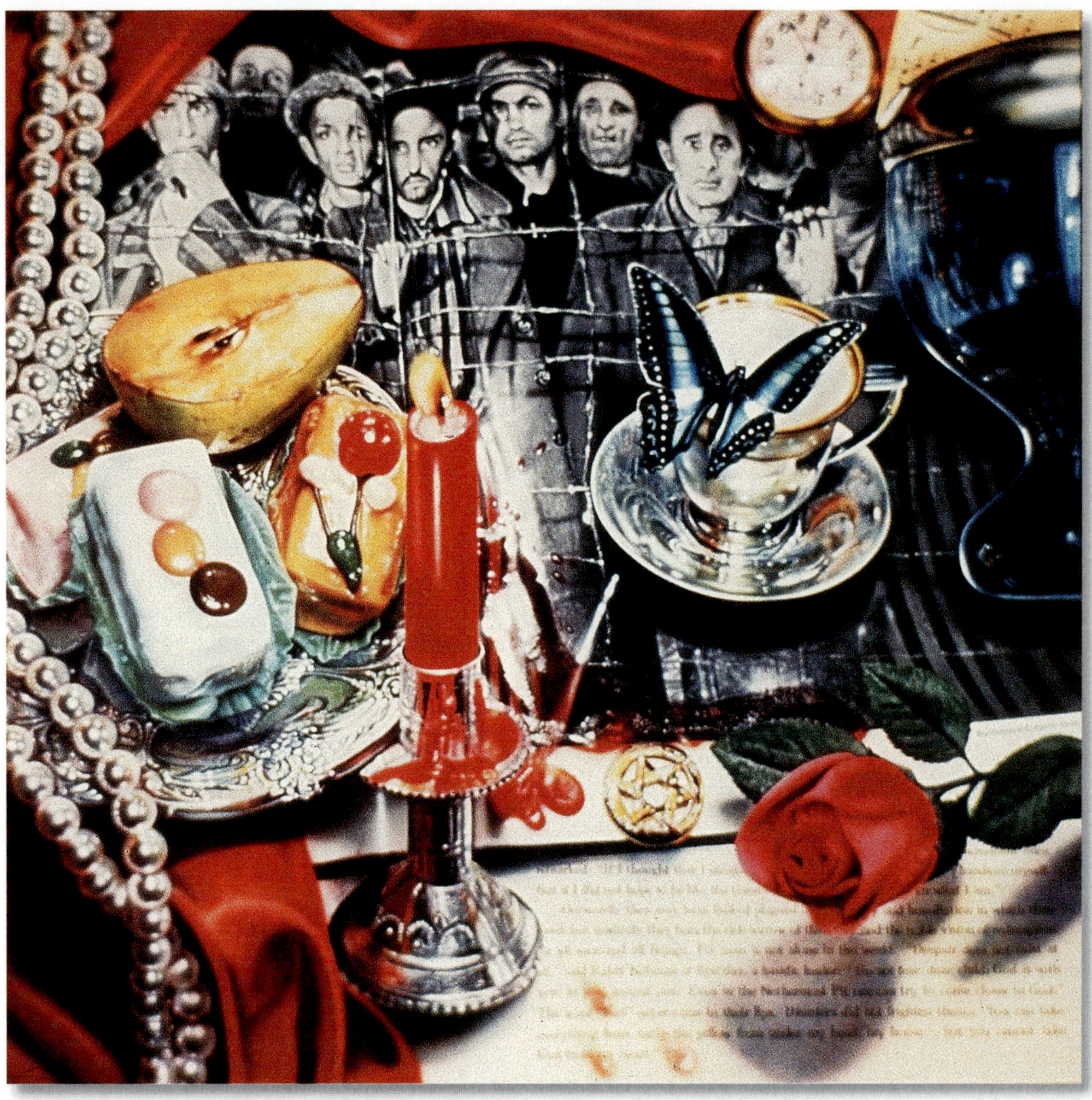

Focus On ◆ **Figure 6–1** **Audrey Flack composes a variety of seemingly unrelated objects into a unified whole. Which principles of art has she used to do this?**

Audrey Flack. *World War II (Vanitas)* incorporating a portion of the photograph *Buchenwald, April 1945,* by Margaret Bourke-White, © Time, Inc. 1976–77. Oil over acrylic on canvas. 243.8 × 243.8 cm (8 × 8′). Louis K. Meisel Gallery, New York, New York.

Art History and You

“*My intentions now are completely clear in my mind: I want to create healing energy.*”

—Audrey Flack (b.1931)

Quick Write

Interpreting the Quote Read the quote by the artist who created the painting in Figure 6–1. Read the title of the work. Does the artist “create healing energy” in her work? Write a paragraph explaining your thoughts.

Understanding art often requires looking *behind* the work—at when and why it was made. Look at **Figure 6–1.** If you were asked to describe this work, you might observe that it contains a number of seemingly unrelated objects, such as a candle, a butterfly, and a strand of pearls. You might notice that these objects have been painted realistically enough to pass for photographs. In fact, a representation of a photo appears in the background of the painting. It is a black-and-white image of people standing behind a barbed-wire fence.

In this chapter, you will learn about the meaning of this and other artworks as you explore art history.

After completing this chapter, you will be able to:

- Define *art history.*
- Explain what is revealed by each of the four parts of the art historian’s job.
- Explain how time and place influence a work of art.
- Use direct observation and personal experience to create works of art in the styles of different art movements.
- Identify how the Harlem Renaissance influenced art, poetry, and music.

KEY TERMS

- art history
- describing
- style
- analyzing
- art movement
- Pointillism
- Impressionism
- Fauvism
- interpreting
- Abstract Expressionism
- portrait
- Renaissance
- judging
- Cubism
- mobile

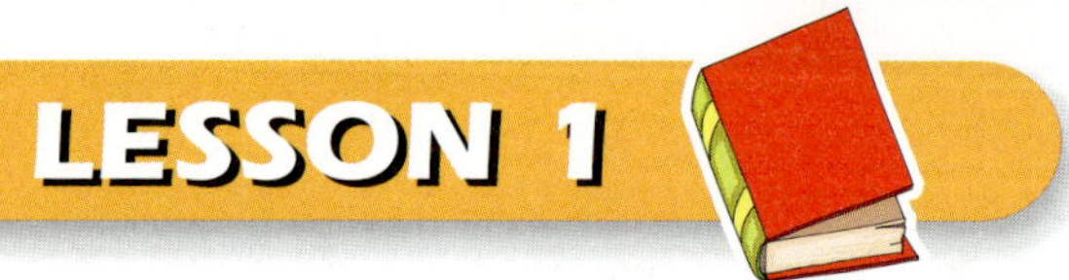

Describing—Who, When, and Where

History is sometimes symbolized as a *fabric*, a piece of woven cloth. There is some validity to this metaphor. History is not just a series of unrelated events. It is a continually unfolding tale or saga. Events of the past are interwoven with those of the present.

Art history is *the study of art from past to present*. It explores changes that occur in the field of art over time. It also looks at differences in the way art is made from place to place. People who work in the field of art history are called *art historians.*

Art History

Like art critics, art historians use a four-step process in their work. In fact, the steps have the same names—describing, analyzing,

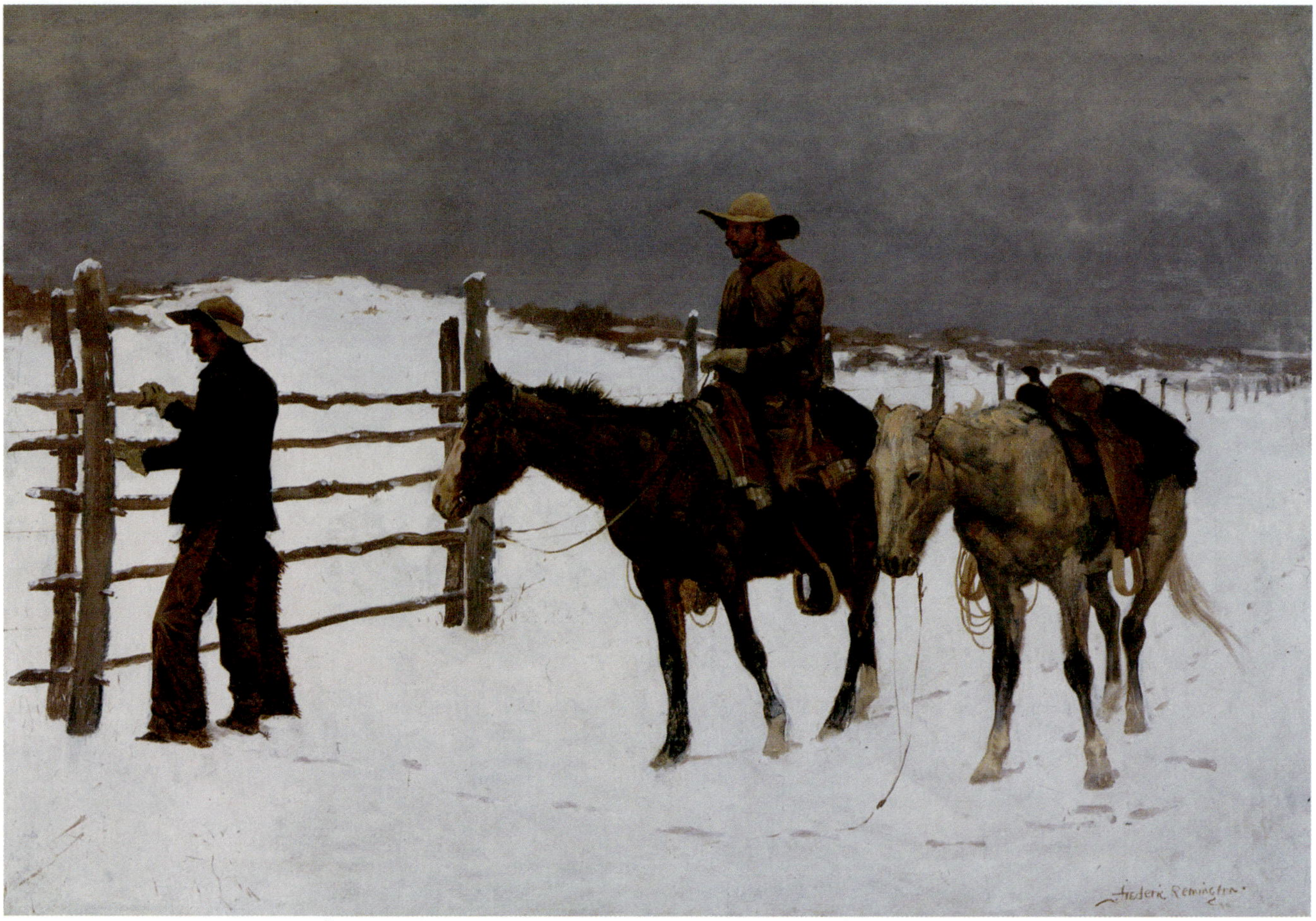

◆ **Figure 6–2** **Remington's paintings and illustrations created the image of the American cowboy that still endures today. In this work he used the fence to symbolize the end of the free lifestyle of the cowboy. Identify cultural ideas expressed in this artwork relating to social and environmental themes.**

Frederic Remington. *The Fall of the Cowboy.* 1895. Oil on canvas. 63.5 × 89.125 (25 × 35⅛″). Amon Carter Museum, Fort Worth, Texas.

interpreting, and judging. Unlike critics, the goal of art historians is not to learn *from* a work. Rather, it is to learn *about* a work.

In this chapter, you will see and practice the four steps used by art historians. In this lesson, you look at the first of these steps.

Describing a Work

During the **describing** step, the art historian identifies *when, where, and by whom the work was done.* Look at the painting in **Figure 6–2.** The art historian would first look for a signature on the work. The painting is signed in the lower-right corner. The signature reads "Frederic Remington."

Suppose the historian had never heard of this person. He or she would then turn to an art history book or search the Internet. Either would confirm that an artist by this name lived and worked in America in the late 1800s.

Exploring further, the historian might turn up these facts:

- As a young man, the painter traveled to the newly expanding "Wild West."
- The painting was done in 1895.
- The painter, who was 34 years old at the time, lived only till he was 48.

The historian might also learn that Remington was born in upstate New York, a near-wilderness region. He was a rugged outdoors person and adventurer from a young age. The cowboy and legend surrounding this American folk figure were constants in his art.

Now it is your turn to be an art historian. Study the painting of the two costumed figures in **Figure 6–3.** Before you do, cover up the credit line with your hand.

Can you identify the artist who painted this picture? If you look very closely, you might find his or her name on the work. It appears in the lower-left corner and starts with the letter *R.* Where could you go to find out the century when this work was done? What other things would you try to find out?

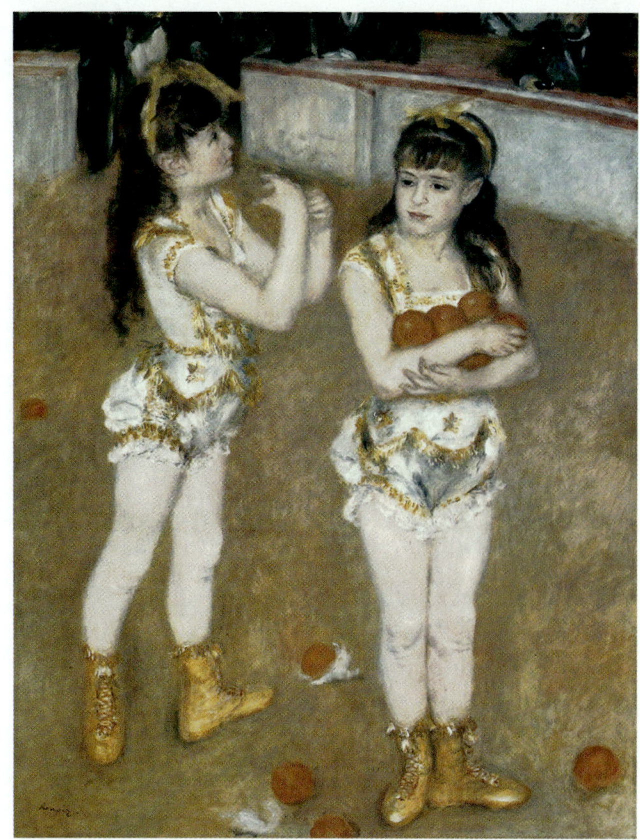

◆ Figure 6–3 **Renoir loved to capture the lights and colors of the moment. In this painting, he has placed himself on the same level with the performers. He brings us into the circus to see as the performers see.**

Pierre-Auguste Renoir. *Acrobats at the Cirque Fernando (Francisca and Angelina Wartenberg).* 1879. Oil on canvas. 131.5 × 99.5 cm (51¾ × $39\frac{5}{16}$"). The Art Institute of Chicago, Chicago, Illinois. Potter Palmer Collection. 1922.440.

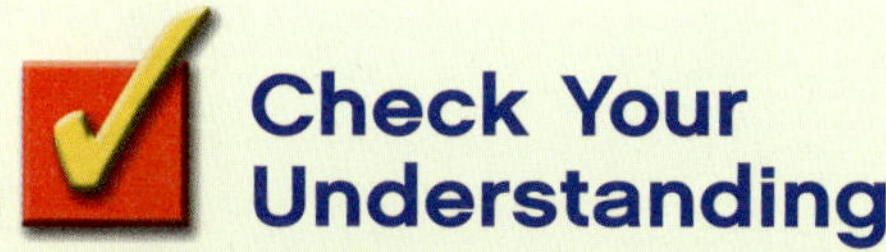

Check Your Understanding

1. What is *art history?*
2. What four steps do art historians use in their work?
3. Where might an art historian find details about an artist's life?

Painting in the Manner of the Aborigines

The Aborigines live in the Western Desert of Australia. They are the first people of the continent. In fact, the word *aborigine* means "from the beginning." Paintings like the one in **Figure 6–4** have been found on rocks dating back 40,000 years. Such works are called "Dream Time Paintings." The stories in them are an important part of the Aboriginal belief system. They often explain the origin of the world and natural occurrences.

The work shown here is by contemporary artist Munggurrawuy Yunupingu (mung-gah-**rah**-wee yoo-nah-**ping**-goo). Like his ancestors, Yunupingu uses line, color, patterns, and simple shapes. The stories he tells have been passed down to him and are usually based on myth. *The Crocodile Spreads Fire at Caledon Bay* tells the myth of the origins of fire. Did you notice the diamond shapes? They are symbols of the fire.

What You Will Learn

You will create a painting similar to the one by Yunupingu by selecting and using a variety of appropriate art materials and tools in traditional ways. You will interpret subjects or themes by creating symbols to illustrate a personal experience or a story you remember from childhood. You will use earth-tone colors in your painting. You will create harmony and unity by repeating lines, shapes, and colors in your composition.

What You Will Need

- Pencil and eraser, sketchbook
- 12 × 18-inch or larger heavy drawing paper in white or earth-tone colors
- Tempera or acrylic paints in earth tones, mixing trays
- Water container, paint brushes in various sizes, cotton swabs
- Paper towels, newspaper
- Optional: magazines, books, photos, and postcards of animals for reference

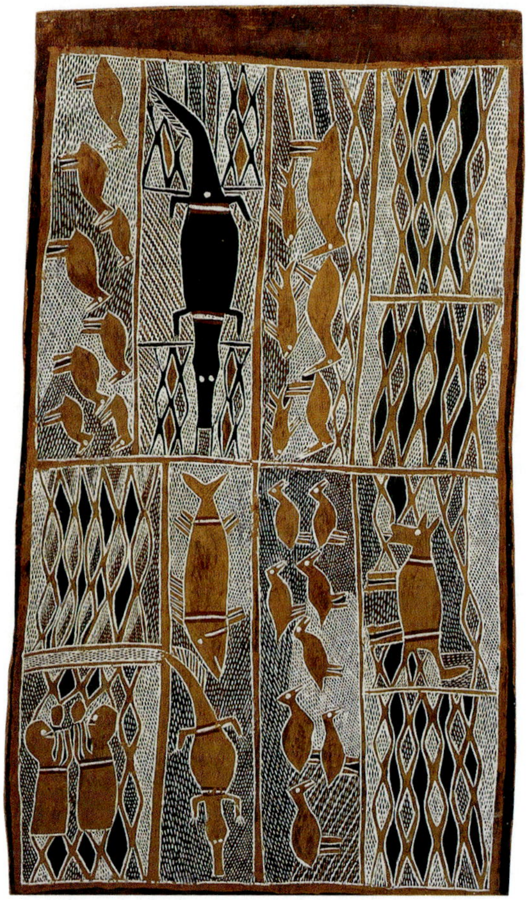

◆ **Figure 6–4** **To create this artwork, the artist painted the bark from a tree with earth pigments. Identify cultural ideas expressed in this artwork relating to environmental themes. For example, what can you tell about the artist's environment by analyzing this artwork?**

Munggurrawuy Yunupingu. *The Crocodile Spreads Fire at Caledon Bay.* 1961. Natural pigments on eucalyptus bark. 83 × 45 cm (32⅔ × 17¾"). University of Virginia, Charlottesville, Virginia. Kluge-Ruhe Collection.

What You Will Do

1. Look closely at Figure 6–4. Notice how the animals are simplified into flat shapes with little detail. Some figures are shown in profile (from the side), others from above. How has the artist divided up his composition?
2. Working in a group, brainstorm ideas for story paintings. Share stories from personal experience and those you remember from your childhood.
3. Decide on a story you want to illustrate. How will you create your Dream Time painting integrating themes found through personal experiences? Use your sketchbook to plan your simplified shapes and symbols. Next, make a rough sketch using those symbols and images to tell your story.
4. Transfer your rough draft to a sheet of drawing paper. Focus on the outlines and on filling the page with shapes.
5. Next, fill in your symbols and images with solid colors. Mix earth tones so that they are muted. Use a thin brush to create crosshatching and repeated lines in your background. Add simple details, such as stripes or dots. Use a cotton swab dipped in paint to create circles and patterns.
6. Allow your painting to dry completely. Title your finished work and place it in an exhibition with the Dream Time paintings created by your classmates.

Evaluating Your Work

- **Describe** What story did you select to illustrate from personal experience? What symbols and images did you use?
- **Analyze** Which elements of art did you use to create unity? How did you integrate themes found through personal experiences?
- **Interpret** What emotion do you feel when looking at your work?
- **Judge** Were you successful in creating a painting in the manner of the Aborigines? Explain.

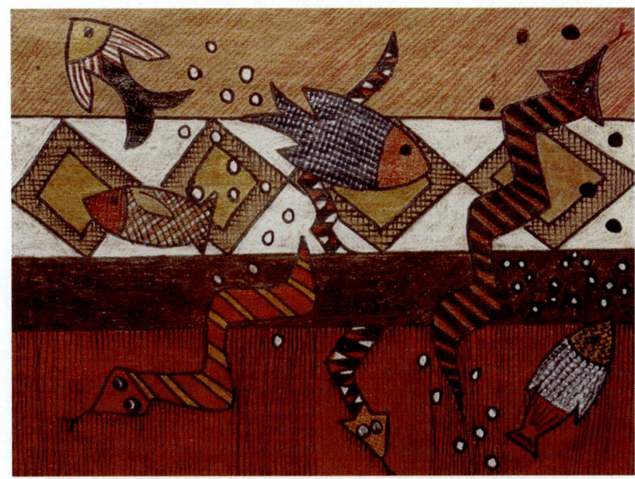

◆ **Figure 6–5** Student work. Using symbols to tell a story.

Reflective Thinking

Critical Response. Analyze the original artworks of your peers displayed in the class exhibition. Form conclusions about historical and cultural contexts of the paintings, such as symbols used and their meanings. What do their paintings reveal about their cultures?

Art Online

Visit **art.glencoe.com** to see more examples of student art at the Student Art Gallery. You will also find:

- Artist Profiles
- Interactive Games

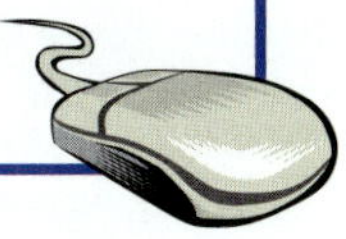

LESSON 3

Analyzing Artistic Style

Have you ever studied or compared fingerprints? No two people have exactly the same ones. Every person, rather, has his or her own unique prints.

This same observation holds true of artists. Each artist works in a manner that is at least slightly different from any other artist. Such differences form the basis of the second phase of the art historian's job. That stage is *analyzing.*

Analyzing a Work

During the describing stage, the art historian scans a work for a signature. Sometimes there is none. Then again, a signature is not always required. Sometimes the artist's distinctive stamp, or *style,* is right there in the work. **Style** is *an artist's personal way of expressing ideas in a work.* The art historian's task during this second stage is *to note the work's style,* or to **analyze** it.

Look back at the painting by Frederic Remington on page 114 (Figure 6–2). An art historian might note that the work has a lifelike or realistic style. The same might be said of the painting that opened this chapter in Figure 6–1. Which of these two works is the most convincingly lifelike?

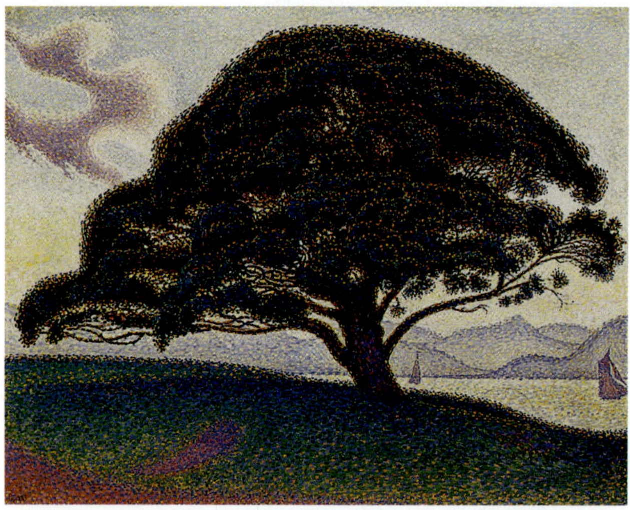

◆ **Figure 6–6** **Signac painted this tree soon after the death of his friend George Seurat. Seurat had started the Pointillist style, and Signac continued to use it for many years. Some say this tree is a memorial to his friend Seurat. Notice how the artist has created a solid form using only dots of color.**

Paul Signac. *The Bonaventure Pine.* 1893. Oil on canvas. 65.7 × 81 cm (25⅞ × 31⅞"). The Museum of Fine Arts, Houston, Texas. Gift of Audrey Jones Beck. © 2003 Artists Rights Society (ARS), New York/ADAGP Paris.

Art Movements

Sometimes *a group of artists with similar styles who have banded together* form an **art movement.** One such movement had its beginnings late in the 1800s in France. It was known as **Pointillism.** This is *a technique in which small dots of color are used to create forms.* The painting in **Figure 6–6** is by one of the movement's cofounders. His name was Paul Signac (seen-**yak**). Look closely at this work. The most prominent object is the large tree, which fills most of the canvas. Notice the colors of the dots used to make up the clusters of leaves. They include purple, orange, green, and red. Now try holding the book about a foot away from your face. What do you notice about the painting? Did the color of the leaf clusters appear to change, along with their form? This change in perception is one of the hallmarks of Pointillism.

Change in perception is also a defining feature of the painting in **Figure 6–7.** This painting also features trees as its subject. It, too, was done by a French painter. This artist, who lived and worked around the same time as Signac, was Claude Monet (moh-**nay**). Monet was cofounder of an art movement known as **Impressionism.** This is *a style of painting that attempts to capture the rapidly changing effects of sunlight on objects.* Do you see similarities between Monet's work and that of Signac? It should not be surprising if you do. Pointillism was an outgrowth of the Impressionist movement. Study Figure 6–7. Notice that this work, too, looks different when viewed from a distance. As in Signac's work, objects seem to acquire shape and form. Now look at the Monet painting up close. Instead of dots, Monet and his colleagues used dabs of color. The painting in Figure 6–3 on page 115 is by one of Monet's close associates. His name was Pierre-Auguste Renoir (pee-**air** oh-**goost** ren-**wahr**). He, too, was a cofounder of the Impressionist school. What similarities and differences do you detect between his work and Monet's?

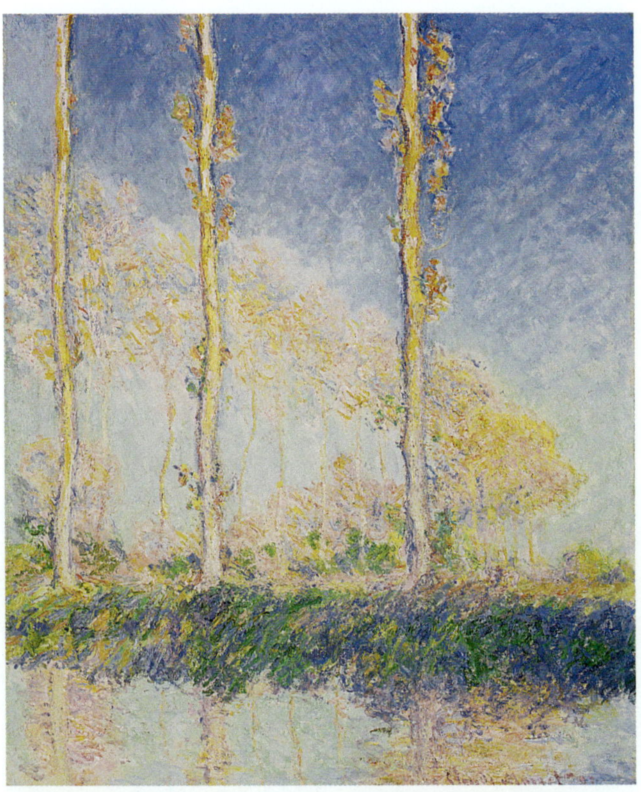

◆ **Figure 6–7 This is one of a series of paintings depicting poplar trees. Monet sat in a small boat and worked on several pictures at once. He exchanged one canvas for another as the light changed during the day.**

Claude Monet. *Poplars.* 1891. Oil on canvas. 93 × 74.1 cm (36⅝ × 29 3⁄16″). Philadelphia Museum of Art, Philadelphia, Pennsylvania. The Chester Dale Collection, 1951.

Studio Activity

Recognizing Impressionism

Drawing from Direct Observation. Take another look at Figure 6–7. Imagine you are Monet getting ready to paint this work. Look at the image and make a quick pencil sketch of this landscape. You will select a variety of appropriate art materials and tools to interpret your subject when producing a drawing traditionally. Use crayons or oil pastel to add color to your sketch. Imitate Monet's Impressionist style by using short choppy dashes and dabs of color. Begin in the center of the objects and work outward. Use complementary colors to make hues look dark. How did you illustrate your ideas from direct observation?

PORTFOLIO

Look again at the examples of Impressionism in this chapter. List characteristics of these paintings that are similar. Look at your sketch. Does it contain those characteristics you listed? Put a star beside those that are found in your sketch. Place your list with your sketch, and keep them together in your portfolio.

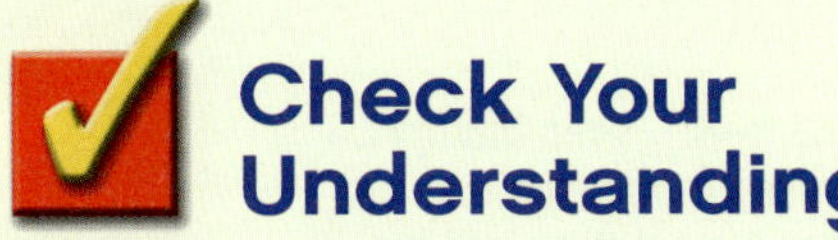

Check Your Understanding

1. Define *analyzing,* as the term is used by an art historian.
2. What is *style* as it relates to art?
3. Describe the features of an artwork done in the Pointillist style. Now describe them in the Impressionist style.

LESSON 4

Painting in the Fauve Style

Examine the painting in **Figure 6–8.** It represents an art style that rose to prominence twenty years after Impressionism. The style is known as **Fauvism.** This is *an art movement and painting style that made use of wild intense color combinations.* The name comes from *fauve* (**fohv**), the French word for "beast." The term was coined in 1905 by an art critic protesting the primitive style. This particular artwork is by Maurice de Vlaminck (vlah-**mink**), a major contributor to the movement.

What You Will Learn

You will paint an exterior scene or landscape in the Fauve style. Select and use a variety of appropriate art materials and tools to interpret nature themes in traditional ways. You will create your painting by illustrating ideas based on personal experiences and direct observation using simple shapes and bright, vivid colors. You will create a sense of harmony by repeating lines, shapes, and colors. Contrast will be achieved through both color and the use of geometric and free-form shapes. Short brushstrokes will create texture.

What You Will Need

- Pencil, eraser, and sketchbook
- 9 ×12-inch or larger heavy white drawing paper or canvas
- Acrylic paints in bold hues, mixing tray
- Water container, paint brushes in various sizes
- Paper towels, newspaper
- Optional: magazines, books, and postcards of outdoor scenes

What You Will Do

1. In Figure 6–8, Vlaminck combines geometric and free-form shapes. Geometric shapes are used for man-made structures. Free-form shapes are used for objects in nature. What color scheme has the artist used? Where in the painting have warm and cool colors been used?

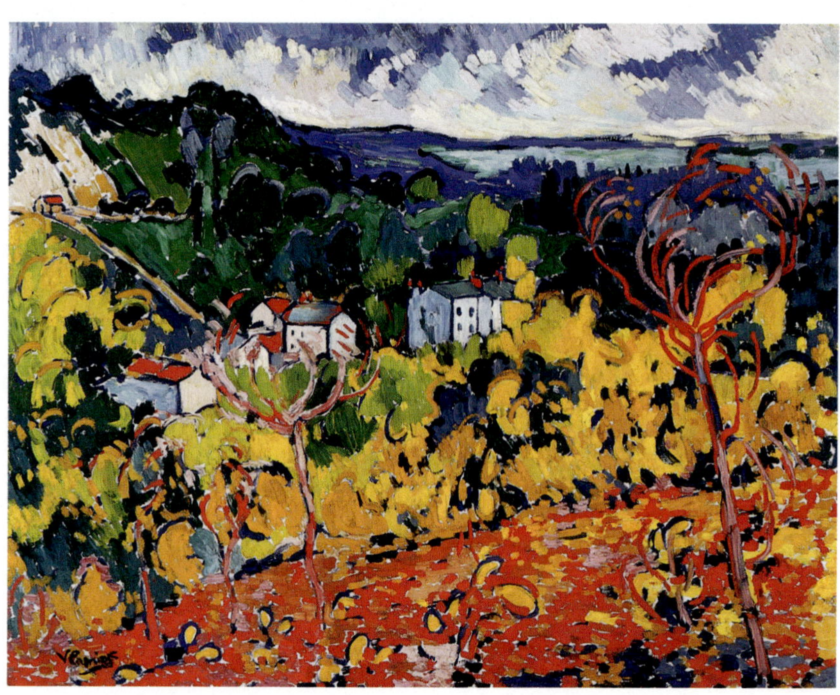

◆ **Figure 6–8 Even though the artist used intense colors, he still divided his painting into the traditional areas of foreground, middle ground, and background. Identify the colors he used in each area.**

Maurice de Vlaminck. *Bougival.* 1905. Oil on canvas. 82.6 × 100.7 cm (32½ × 39⅝"). Dallas Museum of Art, Dallas, Texas. The Wendy and Emery Reeves Collection. © 2003 Artists Rights Society (ARS), New York/ ADAGP, Paris.

2. Make two sketches of an exterior scene. Your subject may be a patio, a backyard, or a landscape focusing on a nature theme. If possible, create your sketches from personal experiences. You can also look through magazines, books, or postcards. Keep the shapes simple in your sketches.
3. Select your best sketch and transfer it onto your paper or canvas. Do not worry about whether your shapes look realistic.
4. Review warm and cool color schemes in Chapter 2 (page 31). Notice the way the two schemes are contrasted in Figure 6–8.
5. Select or mix bright bold colors in warm and cool hues. Using a medium-tipped brush, apply the paint in short brushstrokes, as Vlaminck has done. Remember that in many Fauve paintings brushstrokes were visible.
6. Periodically step back from your painting as you work. Are you repeating shapes and colors? Have you created contrast using both elements?
7. Allow your painting to dry. Give your completed painting a title. Share your finished work with your classmates.

Evaluating Your Work

- **Describe** What did you select from personal experiences as a nature theme?
- **Analyze** What shapes did you use in your composition? Which color schemes did you use to create contrast? How did you create harmony and texture?
- **Interpret** What emotion or mood does your painting elicit? Explain. Does the name of your painting express the emotion of the work? Why?
- **Judge** Do you feel you were able to successfully create a painting in the Fauve style? Why or why not?

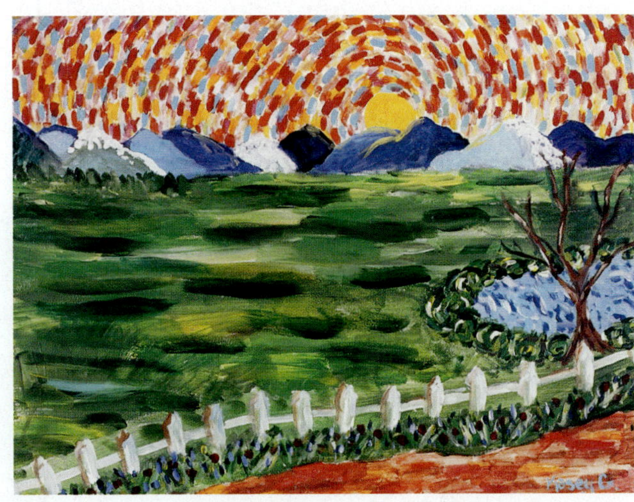

◆ **Figure 6–9** **Student work. Fauve-style painting.**

COMPUTER OPTION

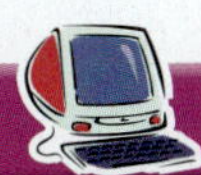

Select a variety of appropriate art materials and tools to interpret subjects in the Fauve style. Create an electronic media-generated landscape in experimental ways. Think about objects you will draw and the mood you want to express. Experiment with unusually bright colors. For instance, draw a purple tree or a blue dog. Use a variety of Brush and Shape tools and use unexpected colors for the objects, sky, and background. Title, save, and print.

Visual Art Journal

Analyze your painting in progress with the teacher or peers, using critical attributes. Critical attributes include your use of the elements and principles of art. Participate in individual and group critiques, making notes in your visual art journal.

LESSON 5

Interpreting Time and Place

When and where we live shapes our lives. Likewise, time and place also influence art. Artists living in wartime, for example, may create works different from those done in peacetime. Historical and cultural heritage often influence an artist's work as well. In art, time and place are central to the art historian's *interpretation* of works.

Interpreting a Work

Do you remember the three questions art historians ask when describing a work? Two of them are "when?" and "where?" In stage three, art historians follow up on their answers to those questions. **Interpreting** is *noting how time and place affect an artist's style and subject matter.*

Sometimes historians interpret a work by studying the impact of time and place on style. At other times, they focus mainly on the subject matter used. At still other times, an interpretation takes both style and subject matter into account.

Interpreting for Style

What do you make of the painting shown in **Figure 6–10?** Many people who say they don't like art often point to works like this. In order to be art, they contend, a painting has to *show* something. Yet supporters of the composition view of art might find much to praise in this painting.

The work, nevertheless, raises an interesting question: Why *do* artists create paintings

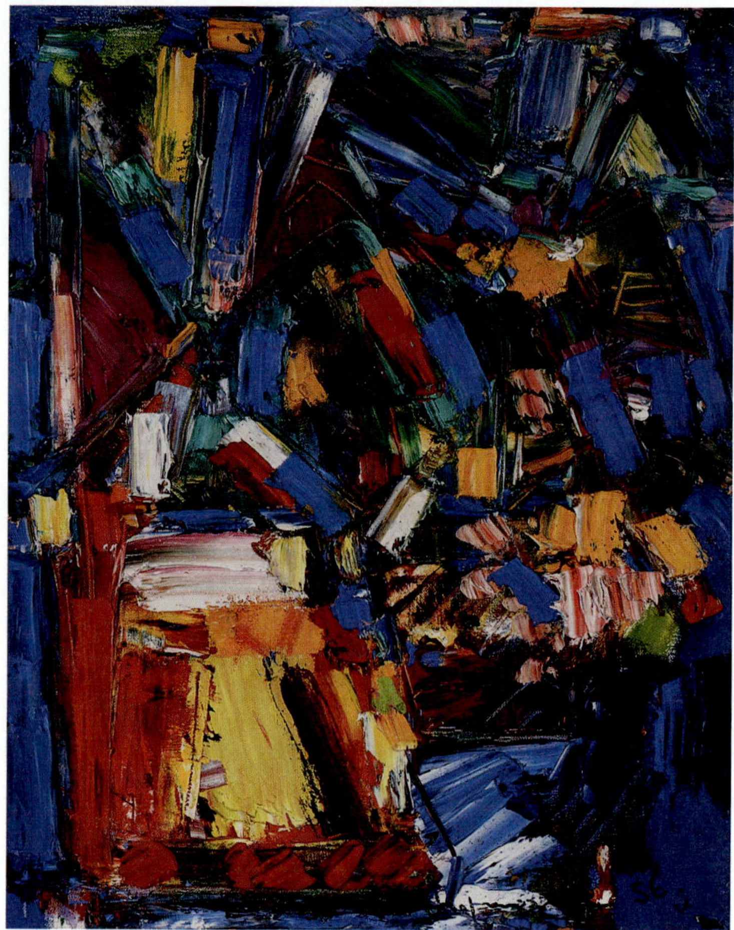

◆ **Figure 6–10** **Hofmann moved away from the tight realistic style he used at the beginning of his career. He then tried Cubism and moved on to Fauvism before he reached this style. Can you find traces of those two styles in this work?**

Hans Hofmann. *Scintillating Blue 38–30.* 1956. Oil on canvas. 96.5 × 81.3 cm (38 × 30″). Hunter Museum of Art, Chattanooga, Tennessee. Museum purchase with funds provided by Ruth S. and A. William Holmberg, Mr. and Mrs. Olan Mills II, Mr. and Mrs. Scott L. Probasco Jr., and Mr. and Mrs. Phil B. Whitaker. © 2003 Estate of Hans Hofmann/ Artists Rights Society (ARS), New York.

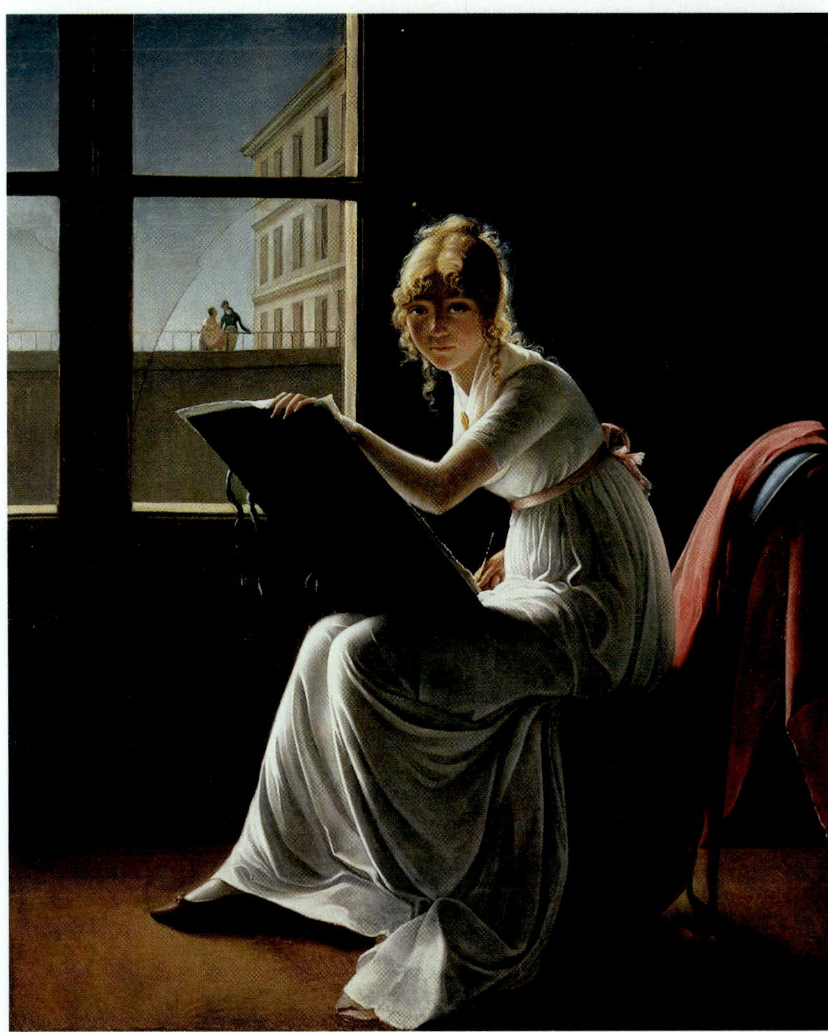

◆ **Figure 6–11** **This is a painting of mystery. Look closely at the window. Why do you think the artist has placed the couple out in the distance? Do you think they relate to the woman in some way? How?**

Marie-Denise Villers. *Young Woman Drawing.* 1801. 161.3 × 128.6 cm (63½ × 50⅝"). The Metropolitan Museum of Art, New York, New York. Mr. and Mrs. Isaac D. Fletcher Collection, Bequest of Isaac D. Fletcher, 1917.

like this? Was the artist of this work, Hans Hofmann, unable to paint realistically? The answer, as you might have guessed, is no.

Hofmann studied art formally in his native Germany and, later, in Paris. His earliest works, like that of most professional artists, were highly representational, or objective. In his late twenties he discovered Cubism, an abstract style popularized by Pablo Picasso. It was not until Hofmann was in his fifties that he began to make paintings like the one in Figure 6–10. Notice how the strong, often-clashing colors seem ready to leap off the canvas. This high-energy nonobjective style was typical of the movement Hofmann had become associated with. Its name was **Abstract Expressionism.** This is *an art movement that emphasized abstract elements of art and stressed feelings and emotions.*

Abstract Expressionism arose out of dissatisfaction with traditional painting. The Abstract Expressionists felt that art with representational subjects was too literal and confining. They wanted their works to distill raw human emotion. What emotions or feelings do you associate with the painting in Figure 6–10?

Interpreting for Subject Matter

Today when people make news, their pictures often appear in the newspaper. Sometimes, their pictures may appear on television. Where do you think pictures of famous people appeared before there was photography or television?

They appeared in paintings and other works of art. **Figure 6–11** is a **portrait,** *a visual representation of a person.* You may not recognize the young woman who posed for this painting. Then again, the artist chose not to identify the sitter. Most historians today believe this was a portrait of the artist herself.

Portraits are not the only example of art that keep records of people and events. Look once again at the painting in Figure 6–1. Read the work's title. The phrase before the colon identifies an event you have probably studied. The word *vanitas* is Latin for "vanity," which means a preoccupation with worldly or material objects. What is the connection between World War II and vanity? Start your quest for answers by examining the photographic imagery in the background of the painting. Observe the grim expressions on the faces of the figures. Notice also the drippings from the red candle that have spattered and stained the photo. They look almost like drops of blood—which is exactly what the artist intended. The effect calls to mind one of the most painful chapters in human history: the Holocaust. This was the senseless slaughter of 6 million innocent Jews by the Nazis. Before their execution, most of the victims were herded into concentration camps. This is why the faces peer out from behind barbed wire. An art historian interpreting this painting for meaning and intent would be mindful of this crime against humanity. Identify cultural ideas expressed in this painting relating to political themes.

Interpreting for Style and Subject Matter

A period of great cultural awakening occurred in Europe in the 1500s. This period is known today as the **Renaissance** (**ren**-uh-sahns). Renaissance is a French word meaning "rebirth." Before the Renaissance, artists were thought of as skilled craftspeople. Their work was no more important than that of

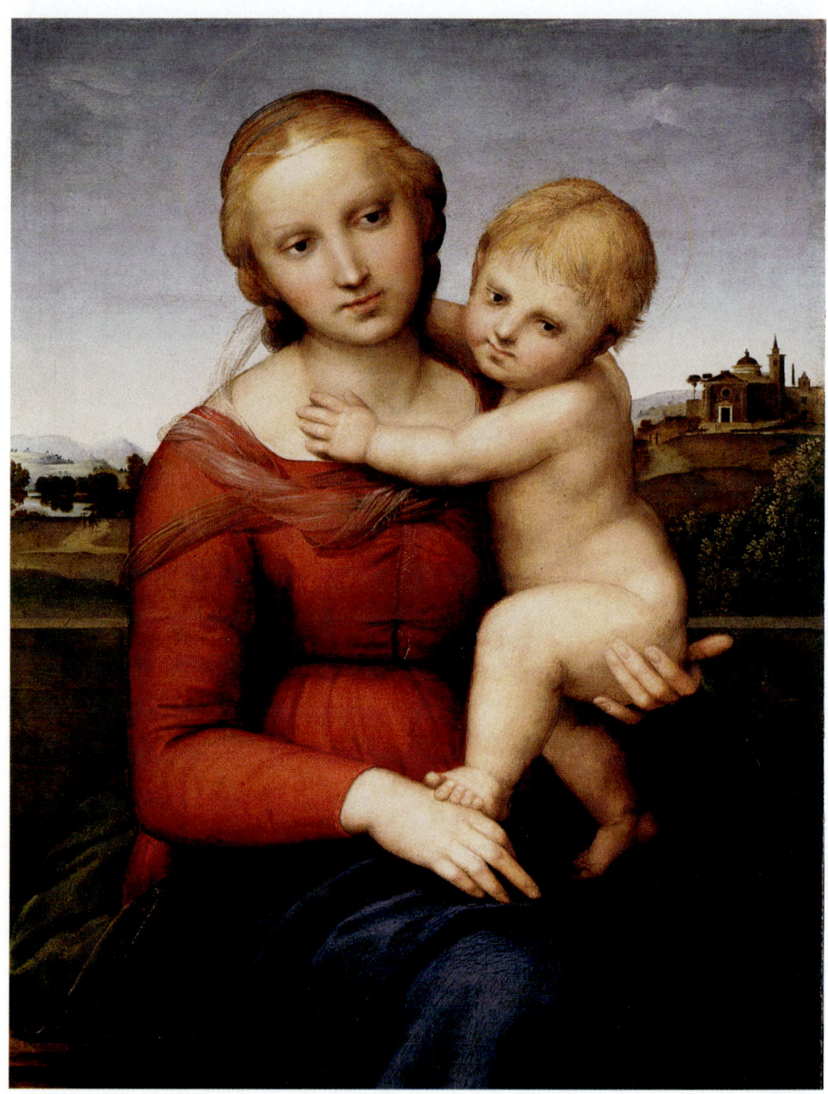

◆ **Figure 6–12** **Define a variety of concepts directly related to the art elements and principles in this painting, using vocabulary accurately. For example, note how the artist uses color and form to create emphasis.**

Raphael. *The Small Cowper Madonna.* c. 1505. Oil on panel. 59.5 × 44 cm (23⅜ × 17⅜"). National Gallery of Art, Washington, D.C. Widener Collection.

carpenters or stonecutters. During the Renaissance, however, artists suddenly gained new prestige. This was partly because of the enormous talents of many of the artists of the period. You have probably heard of Michelangelo (my-kuh-**lan**-juh-loh) and Leonardo da Vinci (lee-uh-**nahr**-doh duh **vin**-chee). Both of these highly gifted artists worked during the Renaissance.

Another artist of the period was a young painter named Raphael (**rah**-fah-el). Look at the painting by him shown in **Figure 6–12.** An art historian interpreting this work would notice two things. First, like most of Raphael's paintings, this one has a religious subject. Do you know the figures in the work? Reading about the Renaissance, an art historian might learn the following:

- The Catholic Church was a great patron of the arts.
- The Catholic Church hired artists to paint and sculpt scenes from the Bible.
- The artworks were used to decorate churches.
- Most people living in the 1500s were unable to read.
- Through these church paintings, the people were able to understand the story of Christ without reading it.

The second thing an art historian might notice is that the painting has a religious figure as a central theme or subject. During the Renaissance, the Madonna became a theme for many works of art. A *Madonna* is a work showing the mother of Christ. The word *madonna* means "my lady." Raphael alone painted over three hundred Madonnas. **Figure 6–13** shows a Madonna by another Renaissance painter. Compare and contrast this artwork with Raphael's. Notice the circles, or bands, framing the figures' heads. Do you know what these are called? How might you describe the looks on the faces of the figures? What other style features do the two works share? In what way are the works different?

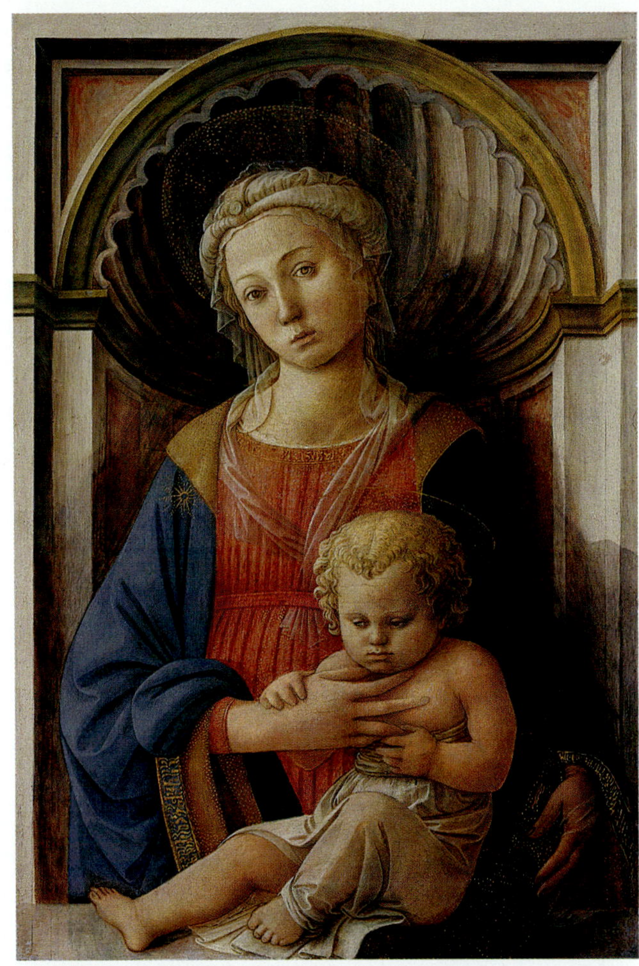

◆ **Figure 6–13** **Analyze this painting and the one shown in Figure 6–12 to form conclusions about historical and cultural contexts, and meanings.**

Fra Filippo Lippi. *Madonna and Child.* 1440–45. Tempera on panel. 79.7 × 51.1 cm (31⅜ × 20⅛″). National Gallery of Art, Washington D.C. Samuel H. Kress Collection.

Check Your Understanding

1. Define *interpreting,* as the term is used by an art historian.
2. What use did portraits have in the past?
3. What is a Madonna?
4. What and when was the *Renaissance*?
5. How were artists thought of before and during the Renaissance?

LESSON 6

Making a Time and Place Combine Painting

Compare **Figure 6–14** with Figure 6–1 on page 112. In both, time is a theme. Do the clocks in Figure 6–14 look real? Maybe that's because they *are.* This work is a *combine* (**kahm**-byne), an art form developed by American artist Robert Rauschenberg. These are mixed-media works in which three-dimensional objects are affixed to a two-dimensional painting. Look closely at *Reservoir.* Among the found objects the artist has used are wheels, clocks, cans, and cloth. Within the work is a clue about when it was created. The clock on the top left records the moment Rauschenberg began work on this combine. The bottom clock shows when it was completed. Do you think he completed the work in just over seven hours?

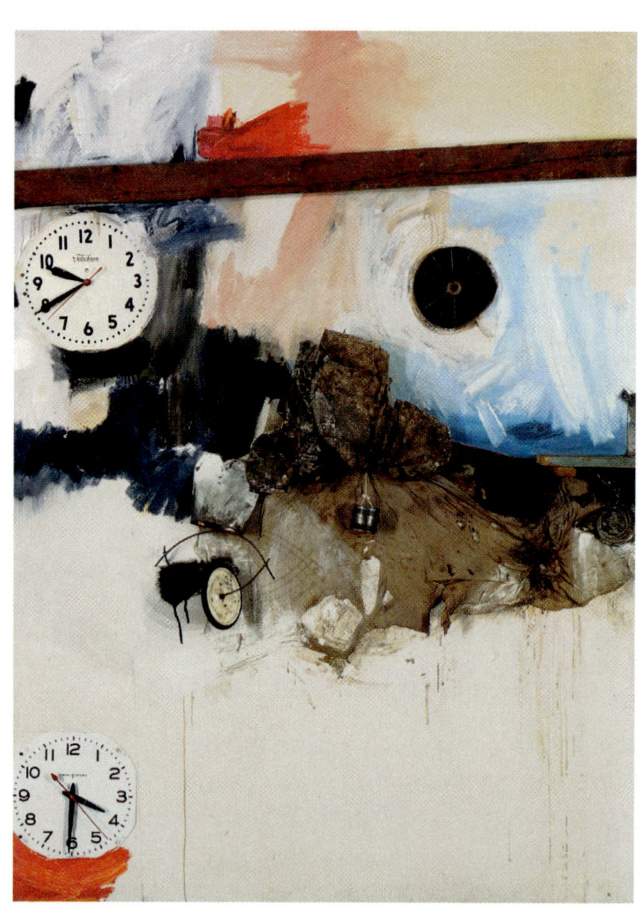

◆ **Figure 6–14 Rauschenberg stopped making combines in the 1980s. He experimented with printmaking and combinations of media, but his style remained the same.**

Robert Rauschenberg. *Reservoir.* 1961. Oil, wood, graphite, fabric, metal, and rubber on canvas. 217.2 × 158.7 × 37.4 cm (85½ × 62½ × 14¾″). The National Museum of American Art, Smithsonian Institution, Washington, D.C. Art Resource, NY. © VAGA, NY.

What You Will Learn

You will create a combine painting like the one in Figure 6–14 selecting and using a variety of appropriate art materials and tools in experimental ways. You will use found objects and add color to your composition. Your artwork should interpret themes that reflect today's visual environment. You will illustrate ideas from experiences at school and community events, and inspired by items that are associated with contemporary society. Added shapes and forms will be used to create variety. You will use contrasting colors to create emphasis.

What You Will Need

- 9 × 12-inch or larger mat board or cardboard
- Tempera or acrylic paints, mixing tray
- Water container, paint brushes in various sizes
- Scissors, wire-cutters, hole punch
- Craft glue, low-temp hot glue gun and glue sticks, wire, twine
- Paper towels, newspaper
- Miscellaneous collected objects
- Magazines, newspapers, calendars, discarded cards, personal photographs

What You Will Do

1. Brainstorm themes to interpret and illustrate from experiences at school and community events, and images that make up your *visual environment*. You might include computers, the Internet, specific songs, sports figures, and so on.
2. Collect used and found objects representing ideas on this list.
3. Study the combine in Figure 6–14. Notice how Rauschenberg paints over portions of the objects. This makes them part of the painting, not just additions.
4. Begin by looking through the objects you have collected. Select three objects to begin with; you can add more as you work on your combine. The objects and shapes you will be using will create variety in your work. Place these three objects on your mat or cardboard and study them for a moment. Cut and add photographic imagery to your arrangement from magazines or newspapers.
5. Add paint to your background. Use contrasting colors to emphasize important areas. Attach forms in the manner most fitting. Some things may be hanging from the board; others may be glued or attached with wire. As you attach items, continue layering your paint. Keep in mind that your images communicate your thoughts about your visual environment. Remember to include clues as to the time, date, or place.
6. Give your completed combine a title and display it in a class exhibition.

Evaluating Your Work

- **Describe** Which objects did you use? What event did you depict?
- **Analyze** What shapes and forms did you add to your combine to create variety? What colors were used to create emphasis in your composition?
- **Interpret** Write a paragraph describing the event your combine is based on.
- **Judge** Does your combine successfully communicate today's visual environment and the idea of time and place?

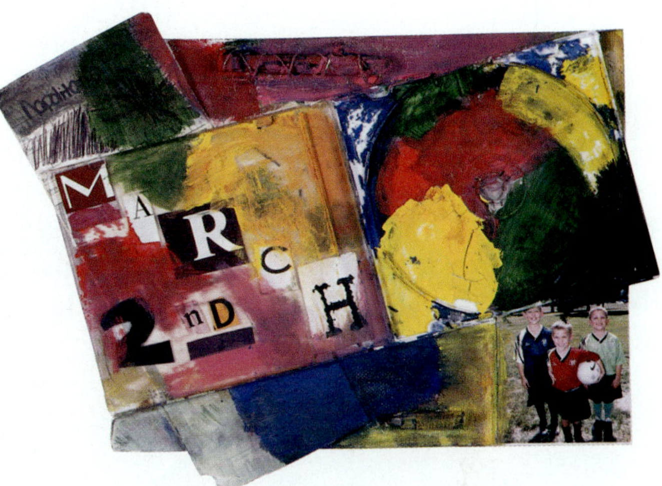

◆ **Figure 6–15** Student work. Time and place combine.

Reflective Thinking

Critical Evaluation. Analyze the original artworks of your peers in the class exhibition. Examine the combines they created and analyze the relationship between the objects chosen and the meaning of their work. What objects did they use? What is the meaning of these objects? Analyze and compare relationships in your combine with those of your peers.

Visual Art Journal

Review the work of your classmates. Compare and contrast the use of elements and principles, using vocabulary correctly. Share your thoughts with classmates. Write their comments about your artwork in your visual art journal.

LESSON 7

Judging Historical Importance

Can you recall something that happened years ago that seemed really important at the time? If the event changed the course of your life, then it still likely holds importance. If its impact was small or only momentary, you probably don't think about it that much.

The same is true of art. Some artists and art come and go with hardly a glance. Others have an impact on the art world that lasts through the ages. They influence the way art is thought about and created by future generations.

JUDGING A WORK

To art historians, **judging** is *determining an artwork's contribution to the history of art.* There are two chief ways in which a single artwork can have a lasting effect. One is by introducing a new style or revolutionizing an existing style. Another is by introducing a new technique or medium. Both are used by the art historian as measurements for judging any given work.

Judging for Style

Look at the painting shown in **Figure 6–16.** The work is by Pablo Picasso (pih-**cah**-soh) and exhibits an art style known as **Cubism.** This is *an art style in which a single object is shown simultaneously from multiple points of view.* The style was developed in the early 1900s by Picasso and a colleague, Georges Braque (brahk). Their common goal was to overcome a perceived limitation of conventional painting. Picasso and Braque felt that a two-dimensional picture was limited to one view of its subject. They felt such art failed to capture the essence of the subject. They reasoned that by visually shattering the subject, they could show all sides at once. Figure 6–16, for example, is a portrait of a man. It may be difficult to pick out his features. That is because all of them are shown simultaneously from multiple angles.

The effect of the Cubist movement on the history of art was enormous. It launched an era of artistic experimentation unparalleled by any before or since.

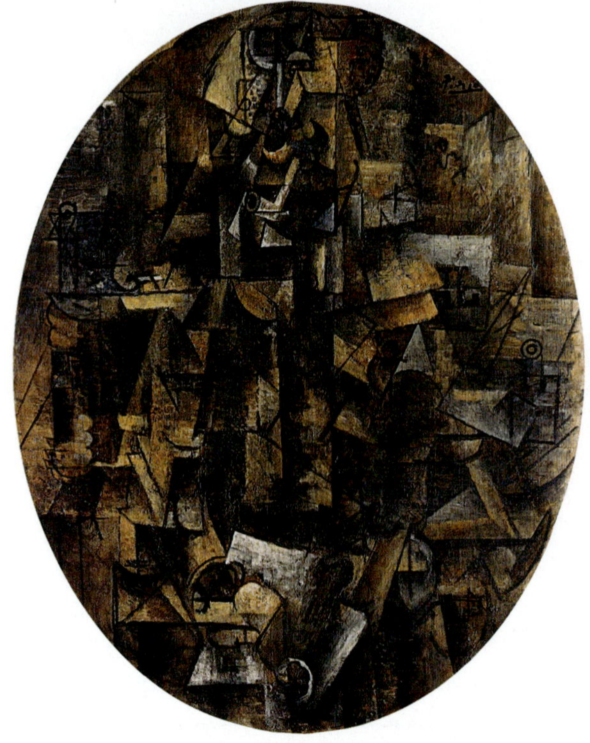

◆ **Figure 6–16** **In this work, shapes and forms have been reduced to lines and planes with transparent openings. Colors are limited to muted grays and dull browns. In later stages of Cubism, bright colors were used.**

Pablo Picasso. *Man with a Pipe.* 1911. Oil on canvas. Oval: 90.7 × 71 cm (35¾ × 27⅞″). Kimbell Art Museum, Fort Worth, Texas. © 2003 Estate of Pablo Picasso/Artists Rights Society (ARS), New York.

Judging for Technique

Another way a work of art can make a contribution is by introducing a new technique. Techniques are the ways an artist chooses to use art media. In Lesson 6, you learned about a novel way of using two- and three-dimensional media. This technique, you may recall, is the combine, brainchild of artist Robert Rauschenberg.

Another technique of the twentieth century is illustrated in **Figure 6–17.** This work is a **mobile**. It is *made up of objects that are delicately hung and balanced by other objects, permitting movement*. This technique was the creation of sculptor Alexander Calder. Calder's unique vision released sculptors from the constraints of traditional media. It influenced their work by encouraging them to experiment with different media.

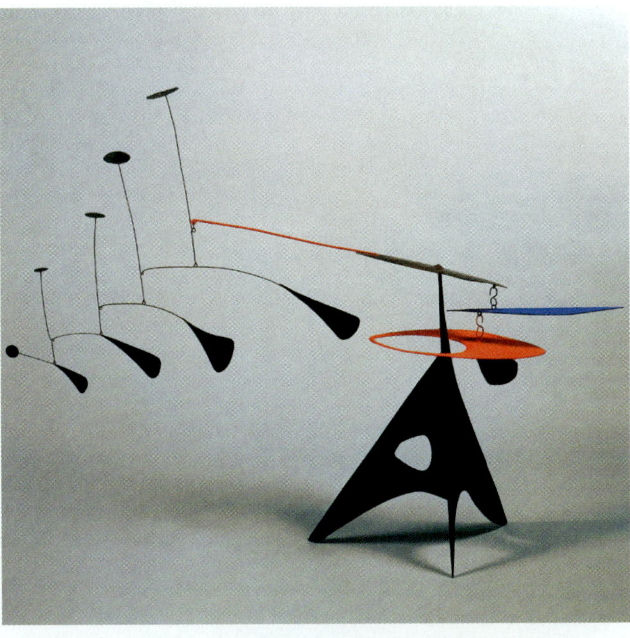

◆ Figure 6–17 **Looking at a Calder mobile is like watching a beautiful dancer. One shape moves, and in turn, its movement will cause the next shape to move. This is possible because of the loops of wire that he used to join one part to the next. Compare and contrast the use of the art element form in this sculpture with the one in Figure 6–14.**

Alexander Calder. *Blue Feather.* c. 1948. Sheet metal, wire, and paint. 106.7 × 139.7 × 45.7 cm (42 × 55 × 18″). Private collection. Art Resource, NY. © 2003 Estate of Alexander Calder/ARS, NY.

Meet the Artist

Pablo Picasso (1881–1973)

Historical Connection. Pablo Picasso was born Pablo Ruiz in Málaga, Spain, in 1881. It was obvious when he was still a toddler that he had a special gift. His father, himself an artist, nurtured his son's talents. He enrolled young Pablo in the Academy of Fine Arts in La Coruña, Spain. At the age of 14, Pablo graduated. At the age of 19, he went to paint in France. He remained there for most of his life. Picasso's professional career is divided into periods, each named for the type of art he produced. Cubism, represented by the painting in Figure 6–16, is the fourth of those periods.

Compare and Contrast

Picasso's earliest two periods are the Blue Period (1901–03) and the Rose Period (1904–05). Using print or online resources, research these periods. Compare and contrast the use of art elements and principles in a work from each period.

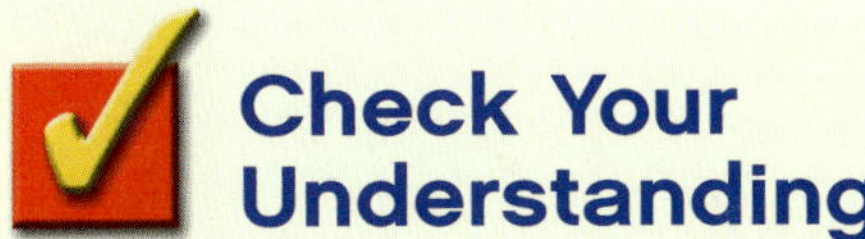

Check Your Understanding

1. Tell what the term *judging* means to an art historian.
2. What are two ways a work of art can make a contribution to the world of art?
3. Explain how the Cubist movement influenced the history of art.

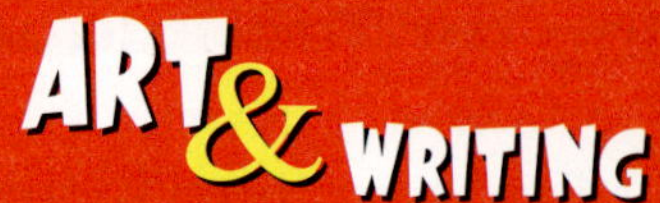

The Harlem Renaissance

Another historical movement that affected art history was the Harlem Renaissance. This movement occurred from 1919 through the middle of the 1930s. In the 1920s, the Harlem section of New York City experienced an influx of African Americans. Some came from the southern part of the United States, others from the Caribbean. These new arrivals brought with them the seeds of a culture previously unknown to the big city. By the middle of the decade, a full-blown cultural awakening had blossomed. It became known as the Harlem Renaissance.

The Influence of Jazz on Art

In art, William H. Johnson spearheaded this movement. The painting shown in **Figure 6–18** is by Johnson. It calls to mind another cultural legacy of the Harlem Renaissance—jazz. Jazz is a musical form featuring a complex and often irregular beat. The smiling couple in the painting is dancing to a jazz band. As the painting's title suggests, they are doing the jitterbug. Notice how the artist captures the couple's lively movements. He accomplishes this through the art principles of repetition and rhythm and the elements of line and shape. You can almost hear the music as you look at this joyful painting.

Analyze Figure 6–18 to form conclusions about formal properties. What elements of art does Johnson use to achieve the principles of rhythm and movement in this painting?

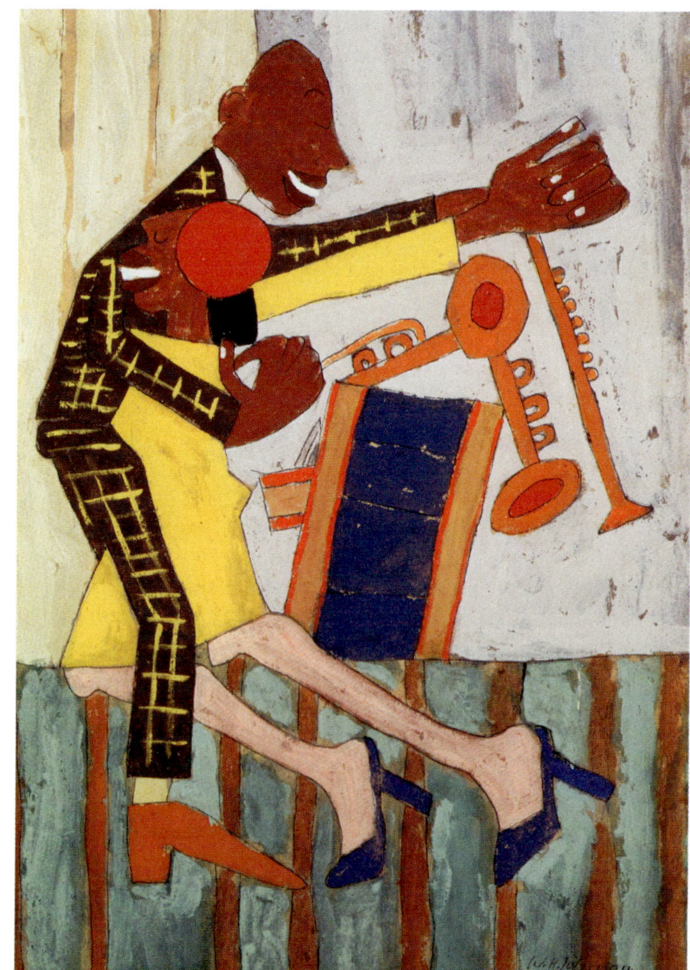

◆ **Figure 6–18** **Johnson was trained in the traditional school of academic realism. He was influenced by his exposure to African art, which changed his thinking, and he developed this unique style of painting.**

William H. Johnson. *Jitterbugs.* c. 1943. Oil on plywood. 61 × 39.1 cm (24 × 15⅜″). The National Museum of American Art, Smithsonian Institution, Washington, D.C.

Sounds of the Harlem Renaissance

In literature, the Harlem Renaissance was led by Johnson's friend, poet Langston Hughes. Like Johnson, Hughes attempted in his words to capture the essence of jazz. Read the poem by Hughes titled "Juke Box Love Song." As you read the poem, listen for the melody and beat. See if you can visualize the dancing couple. As you read the words glance at the image in Figure 6–18.

Juke Box Love Song

I could take the Harlem night
and wrap around you,
Take the neon lights and make a crown,
Take the Lenox Avenue buses,
Taxis, subways,
And for your love song tone their
rumble down.
Take Harlem's heartbeat,
Make a drumbeat,
Put it on a record, let it whirl,
And while we listen to it play,
Dance with you till day—
Dance with you, my sweet brown
Harlem girl.

◆ **Figure 6–19** **Notice how Langston Hughes uses rhyme in an unpredictable fashion in this poem.**

MAKE THE CONNECTION

Take Another Look

1. Read the poem closely in Figure 6–19. Sometimes, th poet makes successive lines rhyme—for example, *play* and *day* in lines 10 and 11. At other times, every fourth line rhymes. How many examples of this effect can you find in the poem?
2. Identify cultural ideas expressed in Figure 6–18 relating to social themes. Does the art seem to be celebrating this dance form?

ART & WRITING

Write a poem based on a painting. Another important artist of the Harlem Renaissance was Jacob Lawrence. One of Lawrence's paintings appears in Figure 9–4, on page 170. Compare and contrast this painting to the painting by Johnson. In what way is it different? Write a poem that captures the mood and subject of Lawrence's painting.

THE DRAW OF THE WEST

For some nineteenth-century painters, the American wilderness was a religious experience.

Exploring and settling North American land was an important part of the pioneer spirit. Still, it wasn't until the mid-nineteenth century that artists turned to nature as something to study and paint. These landscape artists created what was to become the country's first major art movement.

Thomas Cole (1801–1848) loved the freshness of America's wilderness and expressed that idea in his paintings. In his enormous works, such as *View from Mount Holyoke*, Cole questions the role of human progress. The farmland is boxed in by the vast, untouched land.

Other artists also did more than just capture the land on canvas. German-born Albert Bierstadt (1830–1902) mixed careful observation with spiritual awe at the beauty of nature. Light from the sky runs through his scenes of the wilderness, beckoning settlers to move west.

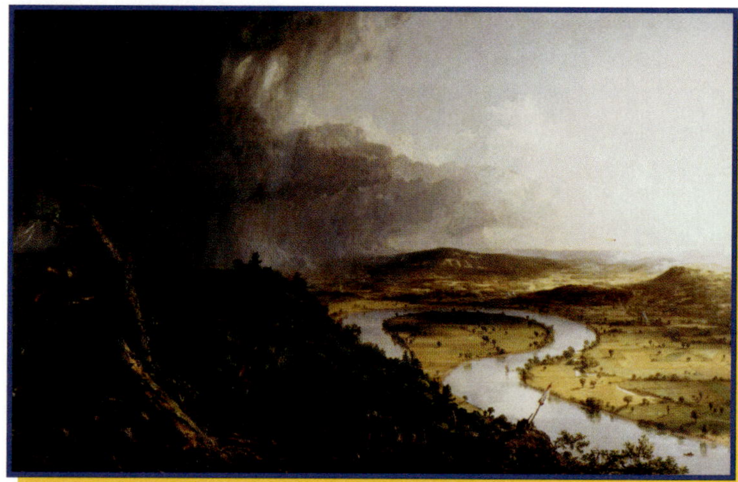

FRANCIS G. MAYER/CORBIS

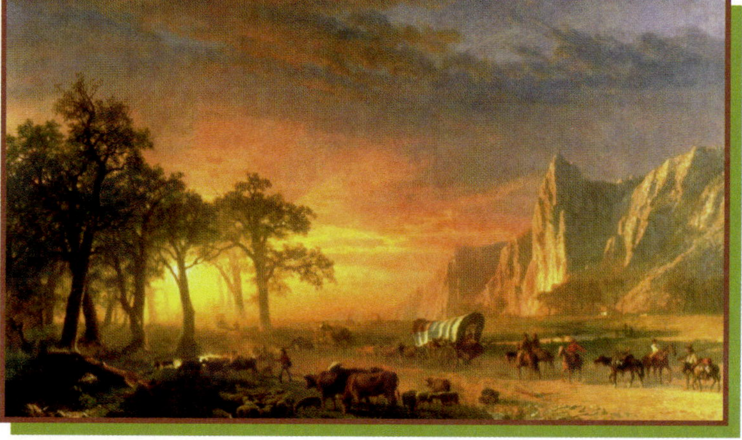

COLLECTION OF THE NATIONAL COWBOY HALL OF FAME

TOP: Thomas Cole. *View from Mount Holyoke, Northampton, Massachussetts, After a Thunderstorm—The Oxbow.* 1836.

Cole's landscape of the Connecticut River illustrates both the quiet and more dangerous sides of nature.

BOTTOM: Albert Bierstadt. *Emigrants Crossing the Plains.* 1867.

Bierstadt joined an 1859 expedition through the West, sketching views of the frontier for later paintings.

TIME TO CONNECT

- **Use textbooks, your school's media resource center, or the Internet to learn about Manifest Destiny. This was an important new idea in the United States when Bierstadt and Cole were working.**
- **Reread the last paragraph of the article. Discuss in small groups how Bierstadt's painting might relate to the idea of Manifest Destiny. To support your answer, use specific references to both the artwork and information you researched.**

Chapter 6 Review

BUILDING VOCABULARY

Number a sheet of paper from 1 to 15. After each number, write the term from the list that best matches each description below.

Abstract Expressionism	interpreting
analyzing	judging
art history	mobile
art movement	Pointillism
Cubism	portrait
describing	Renaissance
Fauvism	style
Impressionism	

1. The study of art from past to present.
2. Identifying who did a work of art, and when and where it was done.
3. A sculptural technique in which objects are delicately hung and balanced by other objects, permitting movement.
4. An art movement that emphasized abstract elements of art and stressed feelings and emotions.
5. Noting an artwork's style.
6. An artist's personal way of expressing ideas.
7. A group of artists with a similar style.
8. An art style in which a single object is shown simultaneously from multiple points of view.
9. French art movement in which artists used wild, intense color combinations.
10. Noting how time and place affect an artist's style and subject matter.
11. A period of great awakening in the arts in Europe in the 1500s.
12. A visual representation of a person.
13. Determining an artwork's contribution to the history of art.
14. A technique in which small dots of color are used to create forms.
15. A style of painting that attempts to capture the rapidly changing effects of sunlight on objects.

REVIEWING ART FACTS

Number a sheet of paper from 16 to 21. Answer each question in a complete sentence.

16. In what ways is an art historian's approach to art different from an art critic's?
17. In describing a work of art, where does an art historian look first for an answer to the question "who"?
18. Why is style like a person's signature?
19. What did the Fauves believe in?
20. What did the Impressionists believe in? Where did they work?
21. Name two great artists of the Renaissance.

CROSS-CURRICULUM CONNECTIONS

22. **Social Studies.** Art history provides a look into the past to show us what people did, the things they used, and the clothes they wore. Analyze artworks in this book and explain how they are influenced by international, historical, and political issues.
23. **Science.** Research information about radiocarbon dating, a technique used to determine the age of material. Explain how this technique helps art historians identify when an artwork was made.

Web Museum Activity

Louvre, Paris, France

Follow the link at art.glencoe.com to visit the Louvre, one of the world's most famous museums. Explore the online collection of paintings. Choose one of your favorite paintings to analyze and investigate the work as if you are an art historian. What facts did you learn about the piece? Write down your thoughts in a paragraph or two.

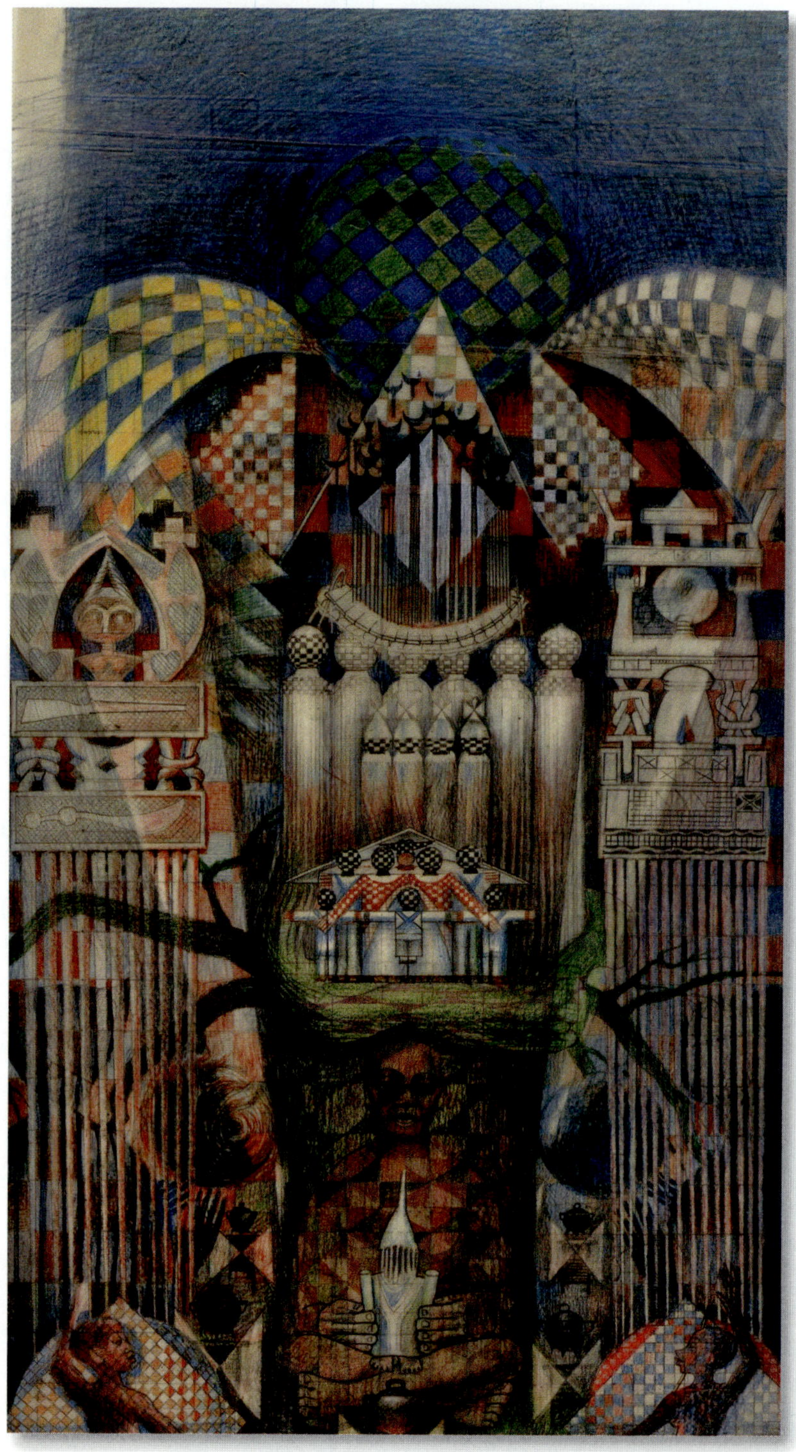

Focus On ◆ **Figure 7–1** **Biggers used a series of elaborate sketches, such as the one shown here, to plan a mural for the library at Hampton University. In them he wove together symbols of African and world mythology. The mural was his way of honoring his university.**

John Biggers. Sketch for the mural *Tree House*. 1989. Graphite and colored pencil on Mylar. 71.4 × 33.3 cm (28⅛ × 13⅛″). Hampton University Museum, Hampton, Virginia.

Chapter 7

Drawing

"*Paintings, lithographs, and drawings have come forth as I have wrestled with certain thoughts and images for mural projects.*" —John Biggers (1924–2001)

Drawing, in a sense, is the most basic of all the visual arts. It requires little in the way of tools or preparation. There are no paints to mix, no surfaces to prime, and no equipment to clean. Drawing is so basic, in fact, that many people do it without realizing it. They may scribble idly, for example, while talking on the phone.

Drawing seems so simple, in fact, that some people believe it is not art. The drawing shown in **Figure 7–1** defies that belief. In this chapter, you will view a number of masterpieces of drawing. You will also learn some of the secrets behind great drawing.

After completing this chapter, you will be able to:

- Name the three ways in which drawing is used in art.
- Define *shading*, and name four shading techniques.
- Create a gesture drawing, a contour drawing, and a presentation drawing in traditional and experimental ways.
- Identify and analyze how drawing is used in cartoons and comic strips.

Quick Write!

Interpreting the Quote Read the quote by John Biggers, the artist who created the work shown in Figure 7–1. Notice he uses the verb *wrestle* to describe his creative process. In a short paragraph, explain why you think he chose that word.

Key Terms

perception
studies
architectural rendering
shading
hatching
crosshatching
blending
stippling
gesture drawing
caricature
contour drawing
presentation drawing

The Art of Drawing

Who was the first artist to use drawing media? That is impossible to say because the individual lived before the dawn of art history. Can you picture some ancient cave dweller innocently scraping soft rock against flat stone? This may have been a chance occurrence. The person may have been surprised to discover that the process produced an image.

People have been drawing for centuries. Some draw purely for avocational, or recreational, enjoyment. Others draw for a career.

The Uses of Drawing

Drawing has many uses in art and art-related fields. It is helpful in planning projects, making finished artworks, and developing perception. **Perception** is *awareness of aspects of the environment through the senses.*

Planning Projects

Before you write a report or composition for school, you create an outline. You map out what you will say and the order in which you will say it. Artists plan out their work in a similar way. The main way they do this is by making **studies**. These are *preliminary artworks, often done as drawings*. Figure 7–1, which opened this chapter, is a study by John Biggers. It was done in preparation for a mural with the same subject matter. Notice the media the artist used in this elaborate preparatory drawing.

Because of the enormous scope and cost of the works they design, architects make drawings *throughout* a project. Each is presented to the client for approval. One type of preliminary drawing is called an **architectural rendering**. This is *a detailed, realistic, two-dimensional representation of a three-dimensional*

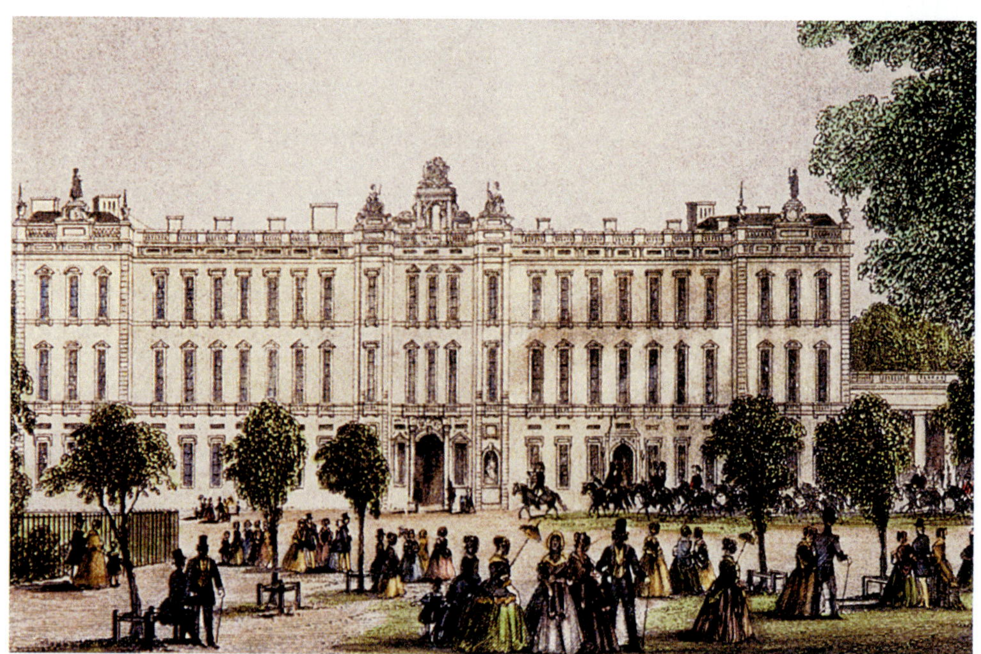

◆ **Figure 7–2** What feeling do you think this building was meant to communicate? Consider the type of balance in forming your answer.

Thomas Hosmer Shepherd. *Buckingham Palace*. Engraving.

structure. The rendering shown in **Figure 7–2** is by Thomas Hosmer-Shepherd. This drawing depicts Buckingham Palace in London, England.

Fine artists and architects are not alone in making preliminary drawings to plan projects. Applied artists, such as people who work with crafts, do this as well. Drawings for quilts and weavings may be sketched in detail before any work begins.

Developing Perceptual Skills

To artists, looking and seeing are not the same thing. Looking is simply noticing an object as you pass by it. Seeing, or perceiving, is closely studying the object. It is noticing every line and shadow. It is observing all the details.

Through drawing, artists sharpen their perceptual skills. Many artists use sketchbooks to record their surroundings and study objects. Another Renaissance master, Leonardo da Vinci, filled over a hundred sketchbooks in his lifetime. The drawing shown in **Figure 7–3** is from one of them. What is the subject of this sketch? How did the artist use line to create movement?

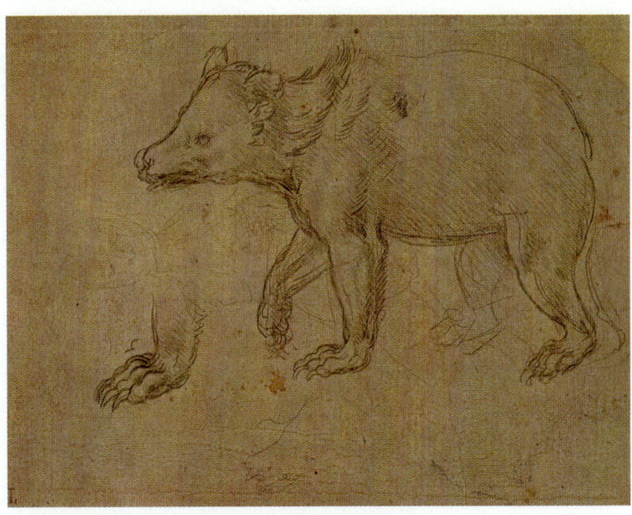

◆ **Figure 7–3** **Notice which details the artist focused most of his attention on. What can you learn from examining studies like this?**

Leonardo da Vinci. *A Bear Walking*. c. 1490. Silverpoint on light buff prepared paper. 10.3 × 13.3 cm ($4\frac{1}{16} \times 5\frac{1}{4}''$). The Metropolitan Museum of Art, New York, New York. Robert Lehman Collection, 1975.

Making a Finished Artwork

For some artists, drawing is not just the first step in the creative process. Drawing is also used to make finished artworks. Among artists who use drawing in this fashion are book and magazine illustrators. The drawing in **Figure 7–4** was created by English illustrator John Tenniel (**ten**-yuhl). Without looking at the credit line, can you tell what story this illustration is from?

Another finished artwork appears in **Figure 7–5** on page 138. What artist is responsible for this drawing? What medium did she use?

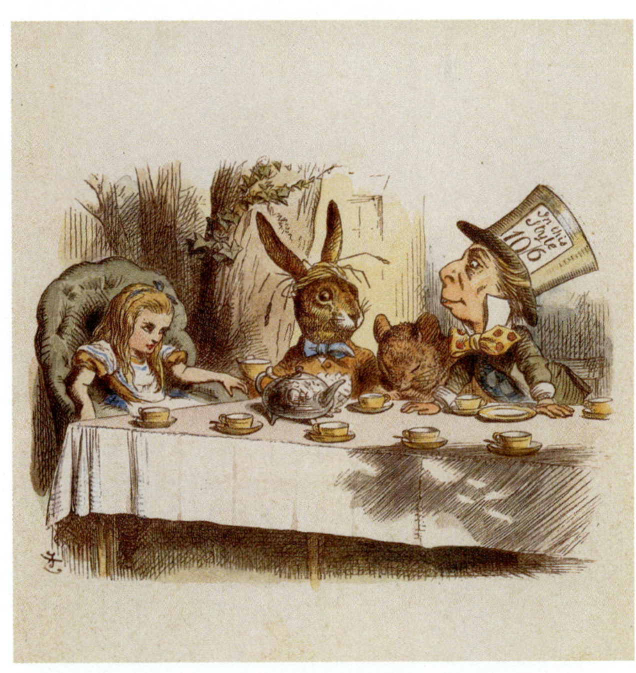

◆ **Figure 7–4** **Do you think the artist's objective was to record his subject matter in a lifelike fashion? Why or why not? What conclusions can you form about his intent?**

Sir John Tenniel. *The Mad Tea Party*. Proof for *The Nursery Alice*, by Lewis Carol. c. 1889. Hand-colored proof. The Morgan Library, New York, New York. Art Resource, NY.

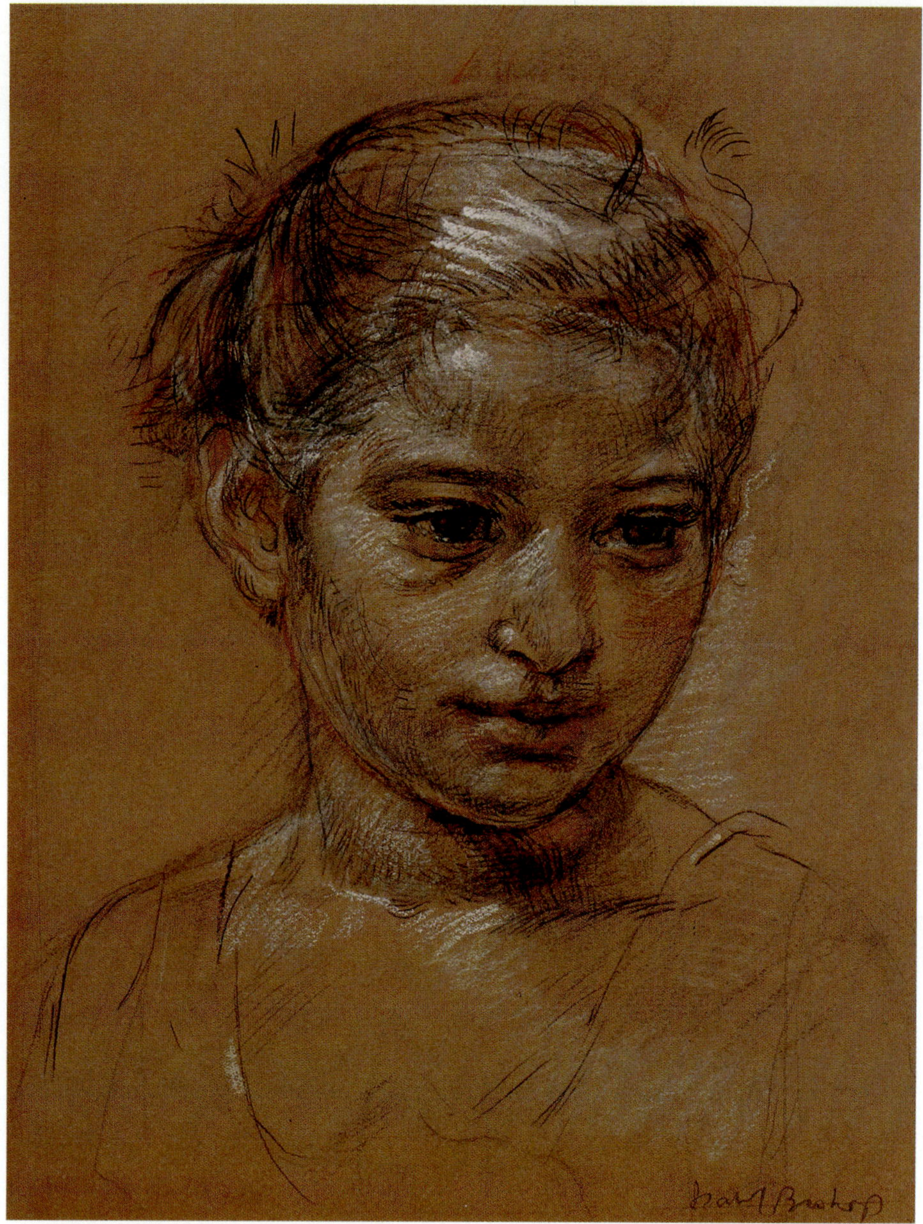

◆ **Figure 7–5** **Notice how Bishop has used white lines to indicate light areas on the head. She used warm brown lines to indicate color on the face. Black lines indicate shadows and lines of hair.**

Isabel Bishop. *Head,* #5. ca. 1902–53. Graphite, crayon, and chalk on paper. 29.8 × 20.8 cm (11¾ × 8$\frac{3}{16}$″). Wadsworth Atheneum, Hartford, Connecticut. Gift of Henry E. Schnakenberg.

Shading Techniques

Look at the drawing shown in Figure 7–5. Notice how the child's face has form and depth. Do you know how this is done? One technique the artist used to get this result is shading. **Shading** is *the use of light and shadow to give a feeling of depth.*

There are four basic shading techniques illustrated in **Figure 7–6.**

- **Hatching** is *drawing a series of thin lines all running parallel, or in the same direction.* Look again at the four drawings in Figures 7–2 through 7–5. Which of these show hatching?
- **Crosshatching** is *drawing lines that crisscross each other.* Can you find evidence of crosshatching in Figure 7–5? If so, where?

- **Blending** is *smoothly drawing dark values little by little by pressing harder on the drawing medium*. The drawing that opened this chapter in Figure 7–1 makes abundant use of blending. Can you identify any blended objects in Figure 7–4?
- **Stippling** is *creating dark values by using a dot pattern*. Look closely again at the works in this lesson. Do any show stippling? If so, which ones?

For more on how to use these shading techniques, see **Technique Tip 6**, *Handbook* page 283.

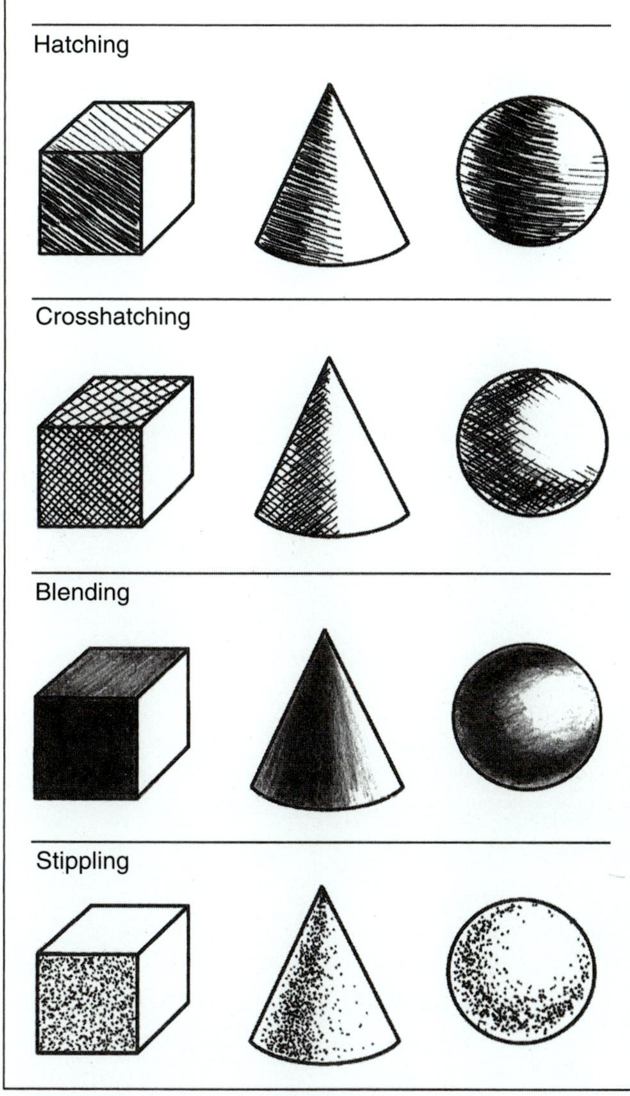

◆ **Figure 7–6** **Shading techniques.**

Studio Activity

Drawing Techniques

Experimenting with Shading. Select appropriate art materials and tools to interpret themes when creating a drawing. On a sheet of 9 × 12-inch white paper, make six rectangles. Each should be 1 × 5 inches. With a pencil, shade four of the rectangles using a different shading technique for each.

Demonstrate your control by changing values from pure white on the left to deep black on the right. Shade the two remaining rectangles using a fine-tipped pen. Use crosshatching for one and stippling for the other. Now, use shading techniques to create a drawing based on imagination or direct observation. Ideas for your drawing might include a still life or a grouping of imaginary objects.

PORTFOLIO

Analyze your final drawing and form conclusions about formal properties. Did you use the element of line to create form? Keep your analysis in your portfolio.

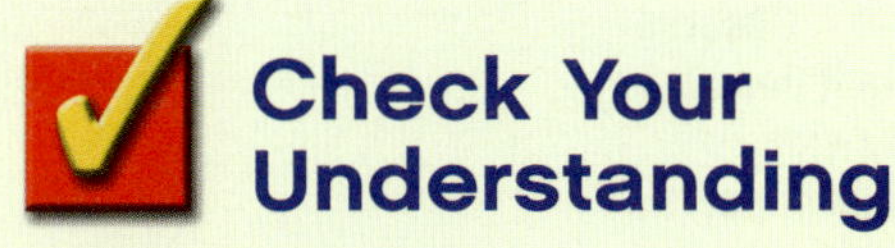

Check Your Understanding

1. What is *perception?* Why is developing perception important?
2. What is *shading?*
3. Name four techniques for shading. Describe each.

LESSON 2

Gesture Drawing

Look again at the drawing by da Vinci in Figure 7–3 on page 137. Notice that he has captured this bear in motion. The animal's right front leg is raised as it prepares to take its next step. The drawing in **Figure 7–7** captures a different sort of pose. The artist of this work has used a technique called gesture drawing. **Gesture drawing** is *drawing lines quickly and loosely to capture the form and actions of a subject*. Figure 7–7 was drawn by the great French painter Honoré Daumier (oh-noh-**ray** **doh**-mee-ay). Notice how the lines appear to have been drawn quickly to catch the action of the figure.

Using gesture drawing will help you break the habit of outlining everything you draw. In gesture drawing you use your whole arm, not just your hand. (See **Technique Tip 1**, *Handbook* page 282.)

What You Will Learn

You will illustrate ideas from direct observation to produce drawings using a variety of art materials in traditional ways. You will make a series of 30-second gesture drawings using charcoal, graphite, or crayon. You will focus on the movement of the figure, not on the likeness of the person.

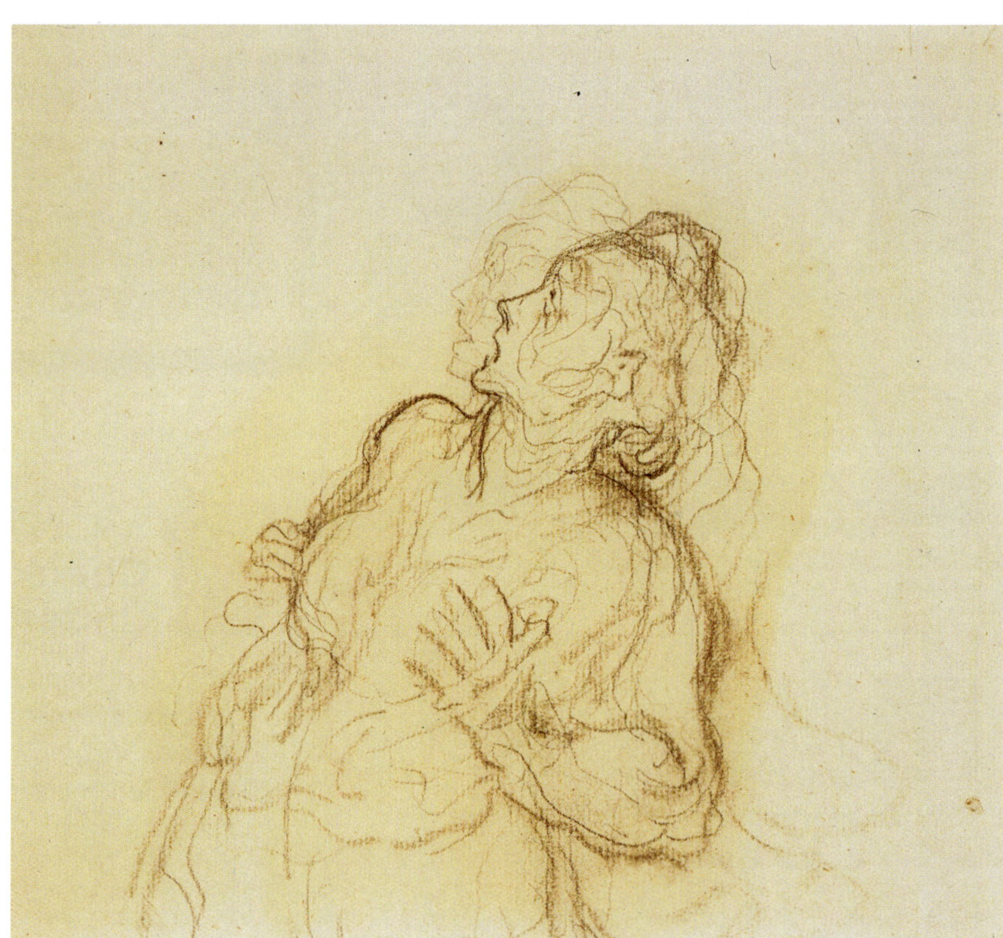

◆ **Figure 7–7 Observe the dark and light lines in this gesture drawing. Explain how movement is used in this work.**

Honoré Daumier. *Frightened Woman*. 1828–79. Charcoal with black crayon on ivory laid paper. 21 × 23.9 cm (8¼ × 9$\frac{7}{16}$″). The Art Institute of Chicago, Chicago, Illinois. Gift of Robert Allerton. 1923.944. Photograph courtesy of the Art Institute of Chicago.

What You Will Need

- Sticks of charcoal, soft graphite, or unwrapped crayon
- Sheets of white paper, 12 × 18 inches

What You Will Do

1. To create your drawing based on direct observation, you and your classmates will take turns acting as the model. Models should pretend to be frozen in the middle of an activity. This may be an everyday action, such as sweeping the floor or tying a shoelace. Dancing or acting out a sport are other possibilities. Each model will hold the pose for 30 seconds.
2. Using charcoal, graphite, or crayon, begin making gesture drawings. Do not hold the medium as if you were writing. Use the side of the drawing tool. Make loose, free lines that build up the shape of the person. (See **Figure 7–8.**) Your lines should be drawn quickly to capture movement. You can fit several sketches on one sheet of paper.
3. When you are done, display your last drawings in a class exhibition. Did your skill increase with practice?

Evaluating Your Work

- **Describe** Show the series of gesture drawings you made using charcoal, graphite, or crayon. Identify the action or pose you tried to capture in each.
- **Analyze** Point to the loose, sketchy lines in your gesture drawings. Explain why your lines were drawn this way. Tell how you showed movement.
- **Interpret** Explain how viewers will recognize that your figures are involved in some kind of action.
- **Judge** Tell whether you feel your drawings succeed in showing figures in motion. Explain your answer.

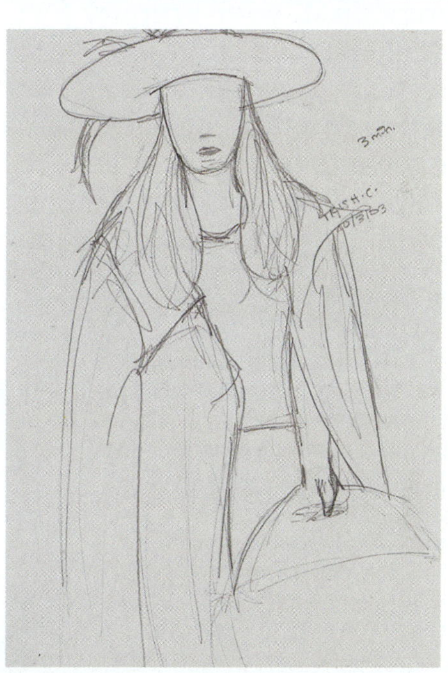

◆ **Figure 7–8** **Student work. Gesture drawings.**

Portfolio Ideas

Critical Evaluation Analyze the drawings in portfolios by your peers to form conclusions about formal properties, historical and cultural contexts, intents, and meanings. Do the images shown convey what the artists intended? Now analyze your own portfolio and compare relationships between what you intended and the meaning your peers found in your artworks. Choose only your best work to display in your portfolio.

Visual Art Journal

Analyze exhibitions. Analyze the original artworks by your peers in the class exhibition. Form conclusions about formal properties and intent. Write your analysis in your visual art journal.

LESSON 3

Contour Drawing

Lines, as you have learned, are powerful "tools" for artists. To see further proof, look at the drawing in **Figure 7–9.** This work is a **caricature** (**kehr**-ih-kuh-chur), *a drawing that exaggerates one or more facial or bodily feature.* This work is by noted twentieth-century caricaturist (**kehr**-ih-kuh-chur-ist) Al Hirschfeld. The drawing was made using the traditional technique of **contour drawing**. This is *drawing an object as though your drawing tool is moving along all the edges and the ridges of the form.* This technique helps you become more perceptive. In it, your primary focus is on drawing shapes and curves.

In contour drawing, your eye and hand move at the same time. Imagine that the point of your pen is touching the edge of the object as your eye follows the edge. You never take your pen off the paper. When you move from one area to another, you leave a trail. Look at the model and not at the paper.

What You Will Learn

You will select appropriate art materials and tools to interpret subjects when making a series of contour drawings with a felt-tipped pen. First, you will illustrate ideas from direct observation to draw different objects. Next, you will use your classmates as models. Finally, you will make a contour drawing of a classmate posed in a setting. (See **Technique Tip 2,** *Handbook* page 282.)

What You Will Need

- Felt-tipped pen with a fine point
- Sheets of white paper, 12 × 18 inches
- Selected objects provided by your teacher

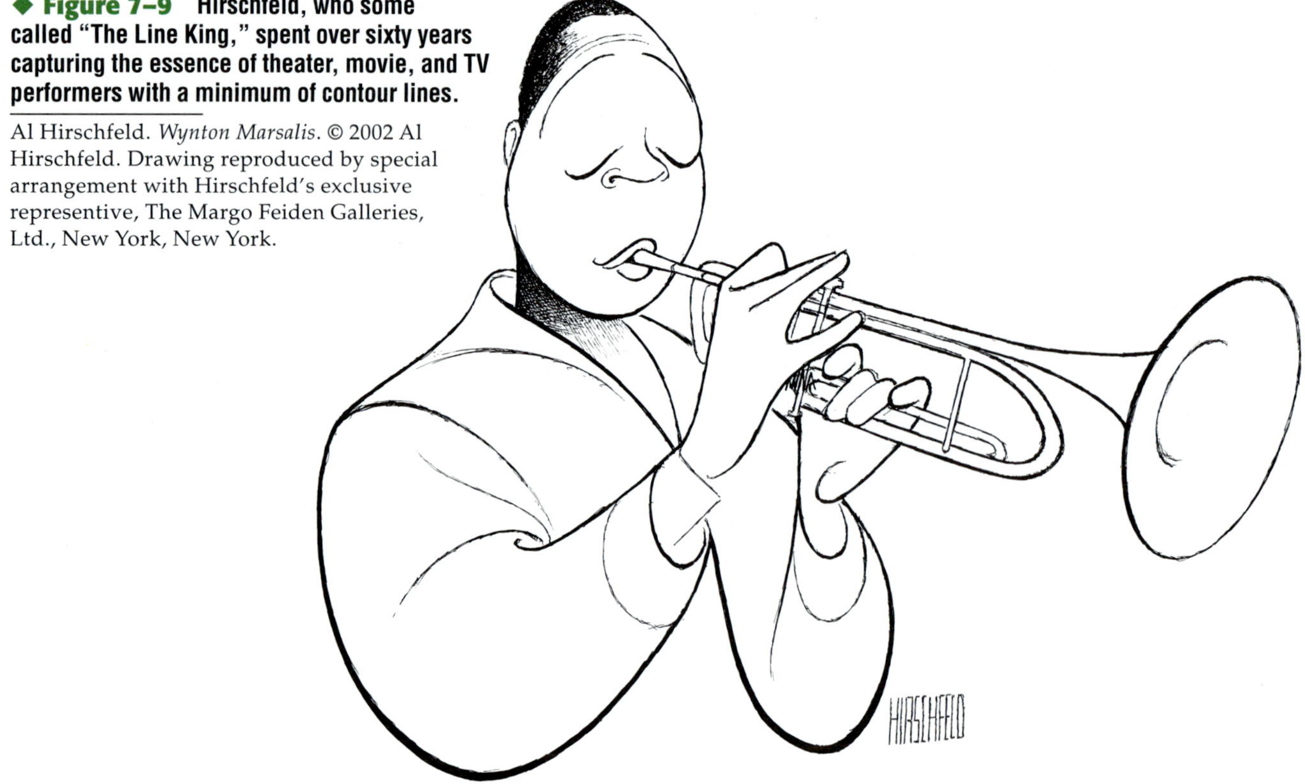

◆ **Figure 7–9** **Hirschfeld, who some called "The Line King," spent over sixty years capturing the essence of theater, movie, and TV performers with a minimum of contour lines.**

Al Hirschfeld. *Wynton Marsalis.* © 2002 Al Hirschfeld. Drawing reproduced by special arrangement with Hirschfeld's exclusive representive, The Margo Feiden Galleries, Ltd., New York, New York.

What You Will Do

1. Take one of the items from the collection on the display table. Place it on the table in front of you. Trace the lines of the object in the air on an imaginary sheet of glass. As you look at the object, you must concentrate and think. Notice every detail indicated by the direction and curves of the line.
2. Make a contour drawing of the object on a sheet of paper, using a felt-tipped pen. Do several more drawings on the same sheet of paper. Turn the object so you are looking at it from a different angle. Keep working until your drawings begin to look like the object.
3. Next, exchange objects with your classmates. Do a contour drawing of your new object. Do not worry if your efforts look awkward. Complete several drawings of different objects.
4. Work with a partner. Take turns posing for each other. Each model should sit in a comfortable pose. The first contour drawing may look distorted. Remember, you are drawing the pose. Work large and let the drawing fill the page.
5. Finally, make a contour drawing of one person sitting in a setting. Include background details. Try not to take your eyes off the model while drawing. You may stop and peek at the drawing, but do not take the pencil off the paper.
6. Display the final drawing. Discuss how contour drawing has improved your perceptual skills.

Evaluating Your Work

- **Describe** Show the different kinds of contour drawings you created. Identify the media you used.
- **Analyze** Compare your first contour drawing to your last. Explain how you interpreted your subject when creating your drawing. Tell how you created shapes using contour lines.
- **Judge** Evaluate your final contour drawing. Do you feel your work succeeds? Explain your answer.

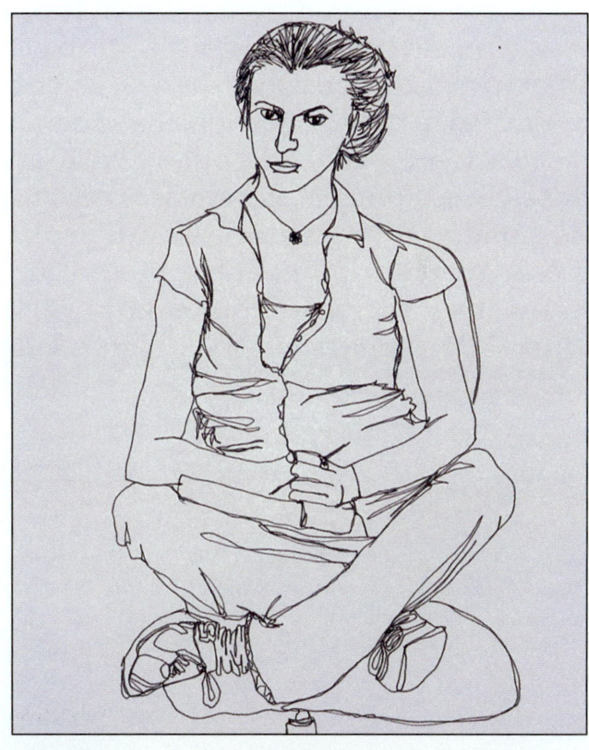

◆ **Figure 7–10** Student work. Contour drawing.

Reflective Thinking

Critical Evaluation Analyze portfolios by peers and others to form conclusions about formal properties, historical and cultural contexts, and intent. For example, how does the artist use line in his or her artworks? What can you determine about the artist's cultural heritage by analyzing his or her portfolio?

Art Online

Identify career choices that require drawing or illustration skills by visiting the Career Corners at **art.glencoe.com.** There you will also find:

- Interactive Games
- Student Art Gallery

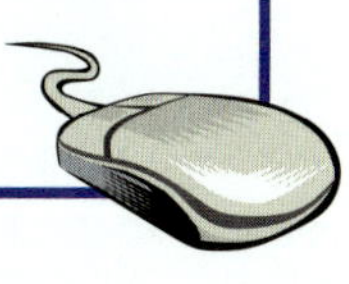

Presentation Drawing

As noted in Lesson 1, architects are required in their jobs to make numerous drawings. One of these, as explained, is the architectural rendering. A second type appears in **Figure 7–11.** This is a **presentation drawing**. Presentation drawings are *detailed sketches that show the final project in perspective.* They are created late in a project's planning stages. They might show the client different views of the work as it will appear upon completion.

The presentation drawing shown here is the work of environmental artist Christo who works with a collaborator, Jeanne-Claude. It was created in preparation for a huge curtain draped across a valley. Like other Christo and Jeanne-Claude projects, this one was designed on a grand scale. The work itself was in place for only 28 hours but has been preserved in photos. One of these photos appears in **Figure 7–12.** Compare it with Figure 7–11. How close did the artists come to realizing their vision in the finished work?

Imagine you have been asked to design a set of wrought-iron gates for the entrance to a zoo, garden, or playground.

What You Will Learn

You will select and use a variety of appropriate art materials and tools to interpret and integrate a theme found through imagination. Create a presentation drawing of a gate with two halves in traditional and experimental ways. The shape of the gate will be symmetrically balanced. You will unify your design within the shape of the gate by creating a symmetrical or asymmetrical design. You will incorporate design into your drawing of this artwork for use in everyday life. Your design will use lines and symbols that

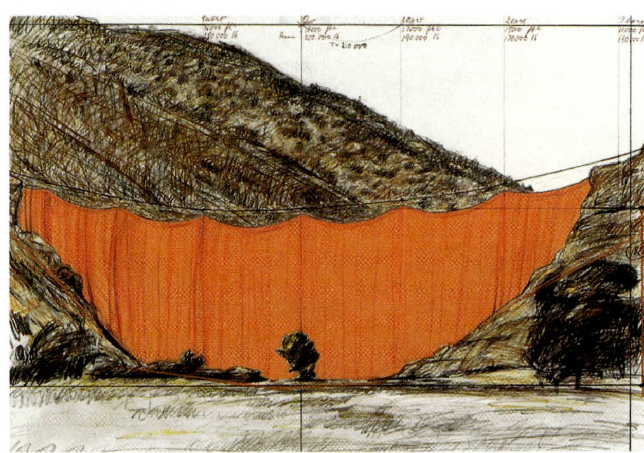

◆ **Figure 7–11** **Presentation drawing for the *Valley Curtain.***

Christo. *Valley Curtain.* Project for Rifle, Colorado. 1971–72. Collage: Pencil, fabric, pastel, charcoal, crayon, ballpoint pen 55.9 × 71.1 cm (22 × 28″). © Christo 1971. Photographed by Dimiter Zagoroff.

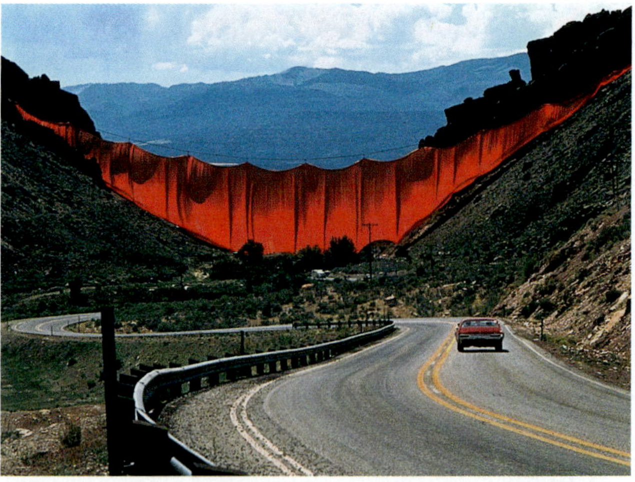

◆ **Figure 7–12** **Christo uses fabric in, over, through, and around natural objects and structures. *Valley Curtain* allows us to view the canyon's negative space. What interesting negative spaces can you find in your environment?**

Christo and Jeanne-Claude. *Valley Curtain.* Rifle, Grand Hogback, Colorado. 1970–72. 12,780 sq. m. (142,000 sq. ft) of woven nylon fabric. 49.8 tons of steel cables spanning 417 meters (1,368 ft). © Christo 1972. Photographed by Wolfgang Volz.

represent the place. Use the principles of rhythm and harmony to organize the lines.

What You Will Need

- Sheets of scrap paper
- Sheet of white paper, 12 × 18 inches
- Pencil and ruler
- Colored pencils or fine-line markers

What You Will Do

1. Choose a theme for your gates. Think about how you will incorporate design into your drawing of a gate to be used in everyday life. Make some rough sketches of designs that symbolize the theme. On scrap paper, experiment by making rough pencil sketches showing possible outline shapes for the symmetrical gate. Choose your best design, and set it aside.
2. Create pencil sketches of designs within the shape of the gate. Will the interior part of the gate represent symmetrical or asymmetrical balance?
3. With a pencil, carefully develop your best idea. Use a ruler to make all the straight lines. (See **Technique Tip 9,** *Handbook* page 284.)
4. Fill in the two sides of your gate with your best designs, using the ruler for straight lines. Repeat symbols to produce harmony.
5. Using the colored pencils or markers, add color to help give balance to the design.
6. Display your work in a class exhibition.

Evaluating Your Work

- **Describe** Show where you used the elements of line and in color in your presentation drawing.
- **Analyze** Explain how you used the principles of rhythm and harmony.
- **Interpret** Explain how you incorporated design into your drawing of an artwork for use in everyday life.
- **Judge** Explain whether you feel each of the gate halves succeeds as a design when viewed individually. Do they work together when they are closed?

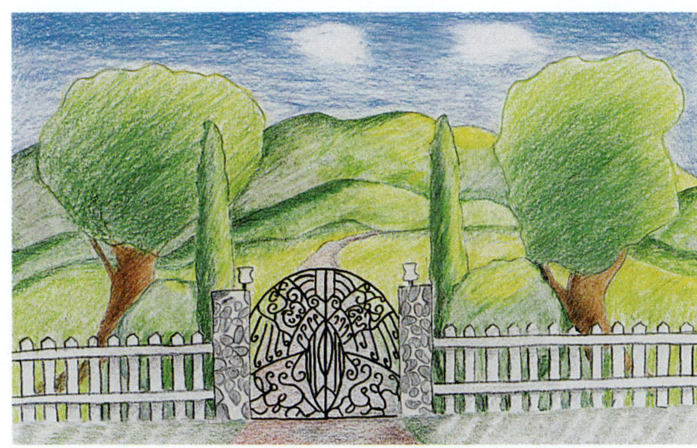

◆ **Figure 7–13** Student work. Presentation drawing.

Computer Option

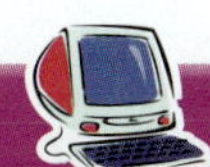

Produce electronic media-generated art to design an entryway for your school or a public building using traditional methods. Use the Symmetry tool and the small Brush tool to draw a balanced design. Choose the Straight Line tool and Shape tools to add windows and doors. Include details that capture the mood or theme of the building. Title, save, and print your line drawing. Use the Flood-fill tool to add color and texture. Retitle, save, and print. Display with the black-and-white line drawing. Include a description of the place and purpose of the design.

Visual Art Journal

Analyze Exhibitions. Analyze original artworks in exhibitions by your peers and others, such as high school students, art teachers, or local artists. Form conclusions about historical and cultural contexts, intents, and meanings. Write down your thoughts in your visual art journal.

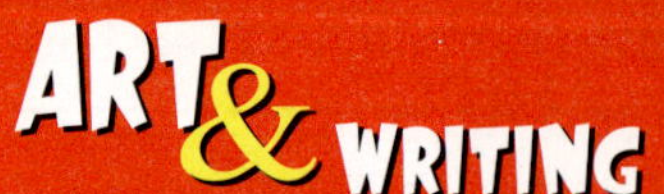

Cartoons and Comic Strips

Newspaper editors have a serious responsibility to their readership. One aspect of that responsibility is writing *editorials*. These are essays several paragraphs in length that focus on an important issue or opinion.

In addition to offering written editorials, many newspapers feature *editorial cartoons*. These are drawn by professional illustrators. Like written editorials, these cartoons present important political or social issues. Unlike written editorials, they use pictures to communicate an idea or opinion. Another difference is that these cartoons often take a humorous approach to the issue.

Politics in Pictures

Editorial cartoons are sometimes called *political cartoons*. That is because they often present a viewpoint about a political issue.

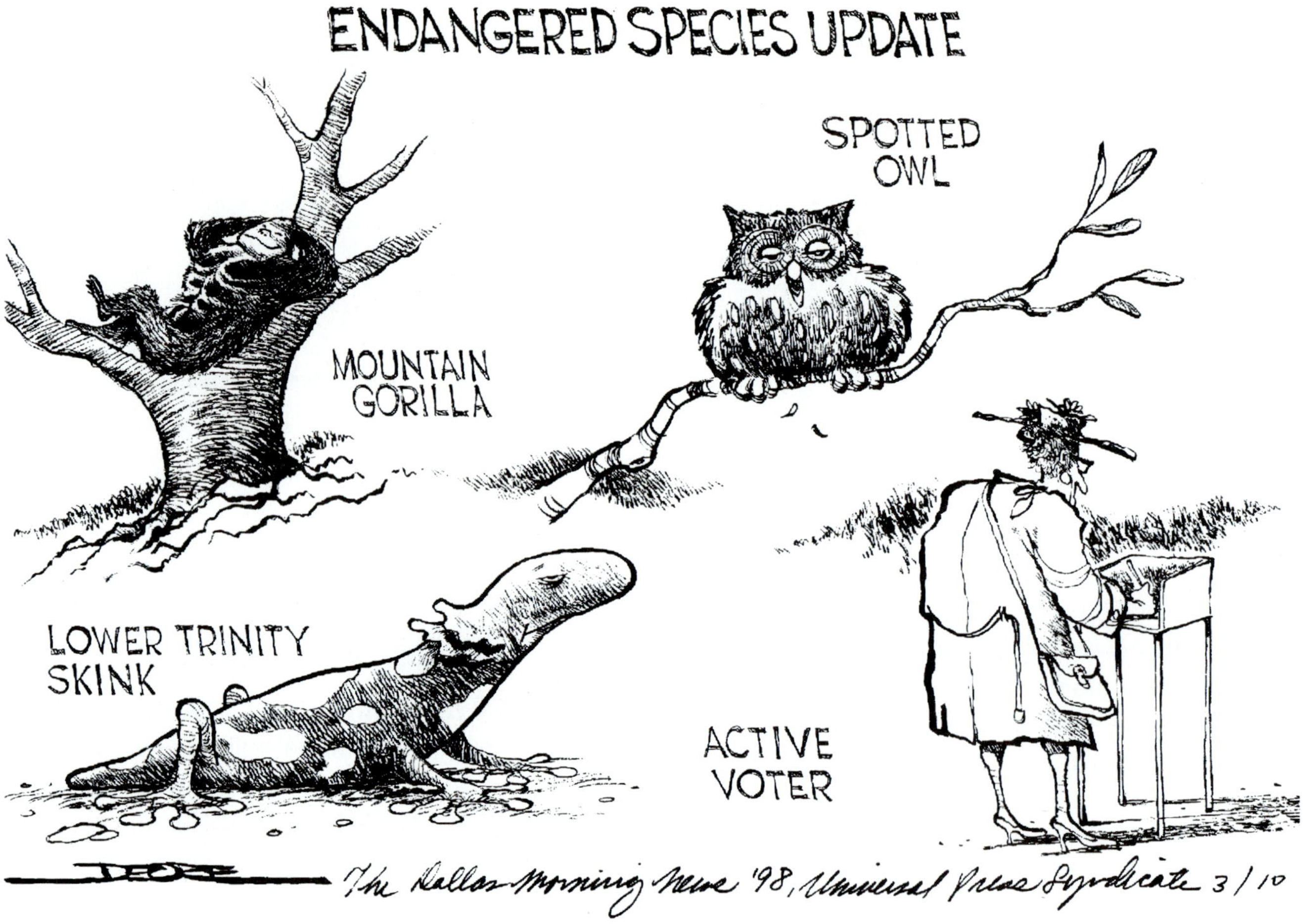

◆ **Figure 7–14** **How would you describe the style Bill Deore has used in this cartoon? Have the figures been presented realistically? Explain your reaction.**

Bill Deore. *The Dallas Morning News*, March 10, 1998. © 1998 *Dallas Morning News* with permission of Universal Press Syndicate. All Rights Reserved.

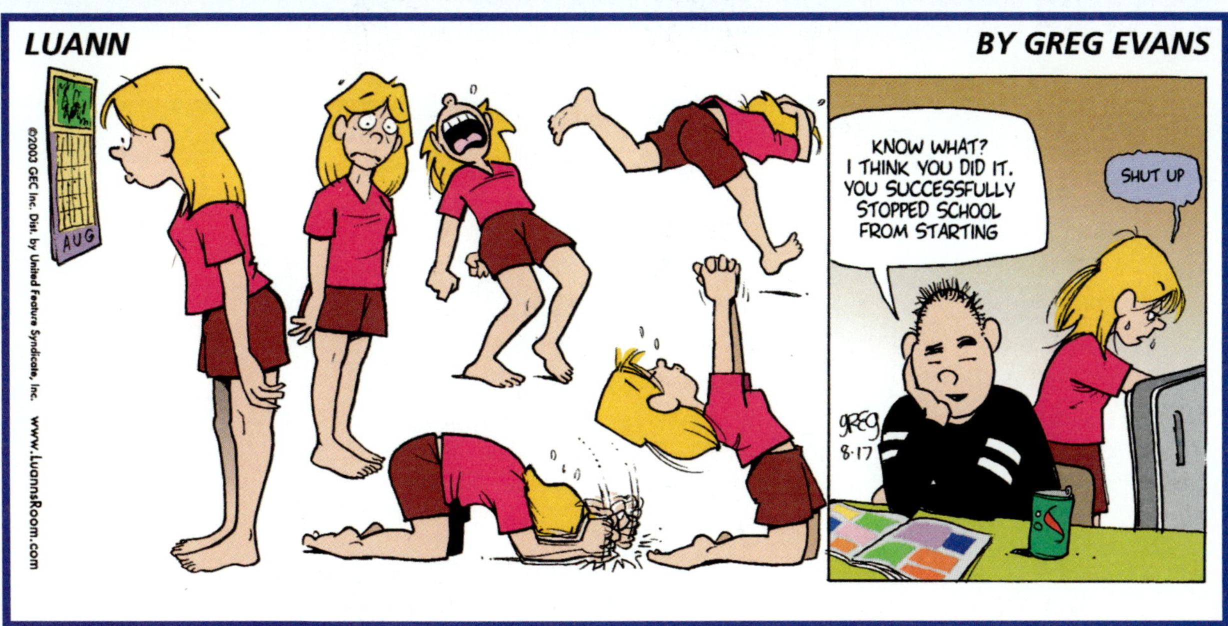

◆ **Figure 7–15** **Notice the different action poses the artist uses in this comic strip.**

Greg Evans. *The Ventura County Star,* August 17, 2003. LUANN reprinted by permission of United Feature Syndicate, Inc.

Sometimes a cartoon can make a statement about an important social issue. Examine the editorial cartoon in **Figure 7–14**. Can you pick up the message of this cartoon? It is subtle but clear.

The cartoon's headline reads "Endangered Species Update." You have probably learned about the concept of endangered species. These include animal populations that are disappearing from the planet. Now examine the four endangered species the artist has included in his cartoon. Begin in the upper-left-hand corner and read across left to right. Did you notice anything odd or darkly humorous about the last species shown? The cartoonist has identified this species as the "Active Voter." What statement is the artist making?

Comic Strips

Another feature seen in many newspapers is the *comic strip.* These are multipaneled illustrations set up in a series that tell a story. These stories can be dramatic, action-packed, or humorous, as in Figure 7–15. How does this comic strip differ from the editorial cartoon in Figure 7–14? How are they similar?

MAKE THE CONNECTION

Take Another Look

1. Think about Bill Deore's purpose in drawing the cartoon in Figure 7–14. Ask yourself: What statement did the artist set out to make? Analyze ways that political issues influence artworks.
2. Analyze the comic strip in Figure 7–15. Look at the different poses the artist uses to capture the girl's feelings. What do you think she might say using words? Write her thoughts down on a sheet of paper.

Art & Writing

Write an Editorial. Choose a social or political issue you feel strongly about. Now write an editorial at least three paragraphs in length. Swap your editorial with a classmate. Read his or her editorial and draw a cartoon about it, while your classmate does the same. Share your drawings with each other. Did you capture what your classmate intended? Did your classmate capture what you intended?

MAKING DRAWINGS MOVE

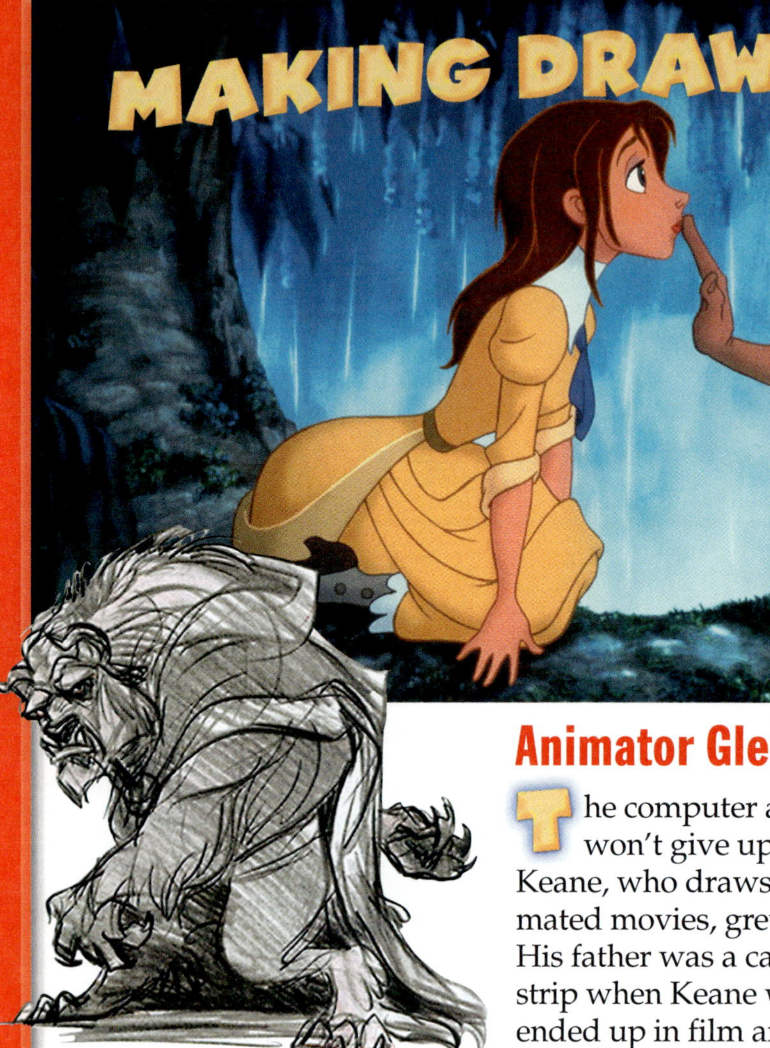

NEWSCOM

GLEN KEANE

TOP: Glen Keane helped create the animated movie *Tarzan* (1999).

ABOVE: Keane's sketch of the Beast from *Beauty and the Beast* (1991). This was the first animated feature film to be nominated for an Academy Award® for Best Picture.

Animator Glen Keane keeps his pencil.

The computer age is here, but animator Glen Keane won't give up drawing by hand any time soon. Keane, who draws many of the characters in Disney's animated movies, grew up with the smell of pencil shavings. His father was a cartoonist who began to draw a comic strip when Keane was five years old. Keane, however, ended up in film animation by chance. His application to graduate school was sent by mistake to the "film graphics" department. "I had no idea 'film graphics' was a fancy way of saying 'animation,'" Keane recalls. "I found out that animation was the thing I was born for."

Keane uses his whole body when drawing. A coworker says that Keane often leaves his office "smudged in charcoal dust and pencil soot."

"The character exists before you design it," says Keane. "When I start to draw, it reveals itself to me. But it's like I have to be touching the paper to get free of it. As that graphite point is breaking off the pencil, it feels like my imagination is being freed."

TIME TO CONNECT

- **Using the Internet, research information about computer-generated animation. Determine the major differences between traditional hand-drawn and computer-generated animation.**
- **Use this information to take on the voice of Glen Keane and discuss his feelings about the state of animation art today. Use this article to help you imagine what thoughts and attitudes he might have.**

Chapter 7 Review

BUILDING VOCABULARY

Number a sheet of paper from 1 to 12. After each number, write the term from the list that best matches each description below.

architectural rendering	hatching
blending	perception
caricature	presentation drawing
contour drawing	shading
crosshatching	stippling
gesture drawing	studies

1. The use of light and shadow to give a feeling of depth.
2. A detailed, realistic, two-dimensional representation of a three-dimensional structure.
3. A shading technique using thin lines all running in the same direction.
4. A shading technique using lines that criss-cross each other.
5. A shading technique in which dark values are added little by little.
6. A detailed sketch that shows the final project in perspective.
7. A shading technique in which dark values are created by using a dot pattern.
8. Drawing lines quickly and loosely to capture the form and actions of a subject.
9. Drawing an object as though your drawing tool is touching the edges and ridges of the form.
10. A drawing that exaggerates one or more facial or bodily features.
11. Awareness of the aspects of the environment through the senses.
12. Preliminary artworks, often done as drawings.

REVIEWING ART FACTS

Number a sheet of paper from 13 to 18. Answer each question in a complete sentence.

13. What are three main ways in which drawing is used by artists?
14. To an artist, how is looking at an object different from seeing, or perceiving, it?
15. How does drawing help artists "see" better?
16. Name three ways in which drawing might be used to plan a project.
17. What is a name for the rough sketch an artist uses to plan a painting?
18. Name one place where drawings of finished works of art are used.

CROSS-CURRICULUM CONNECTIONS

19. **Science.** Study the work of scientific illustrators shown in science books, field guides, and magazines. What type of images do they use to depict the natural world? Would da Vinci's drawings of animals be useful to scientists studying animal forms? Why or why not?
20. **Social Studies.** Starting with a drawing of your house and school, make a map showing the pathway of an imaginary journey. Include pictorial images to represent important landmarks. Show where you turn and how many blocks or miles you travel.

Web Museum Activity

Museum of Fine Arts, Boston, Massachusetts

Now that you've learned about different types of drawings, view them online! Visit this museum's site at **art.glencoe.com**. Analyze the online exhibition of drawings, noticing the different styles in each image. Form conclusions about historical and cultural contexts. For example, what clues does each artwork provide about the artist's culture?

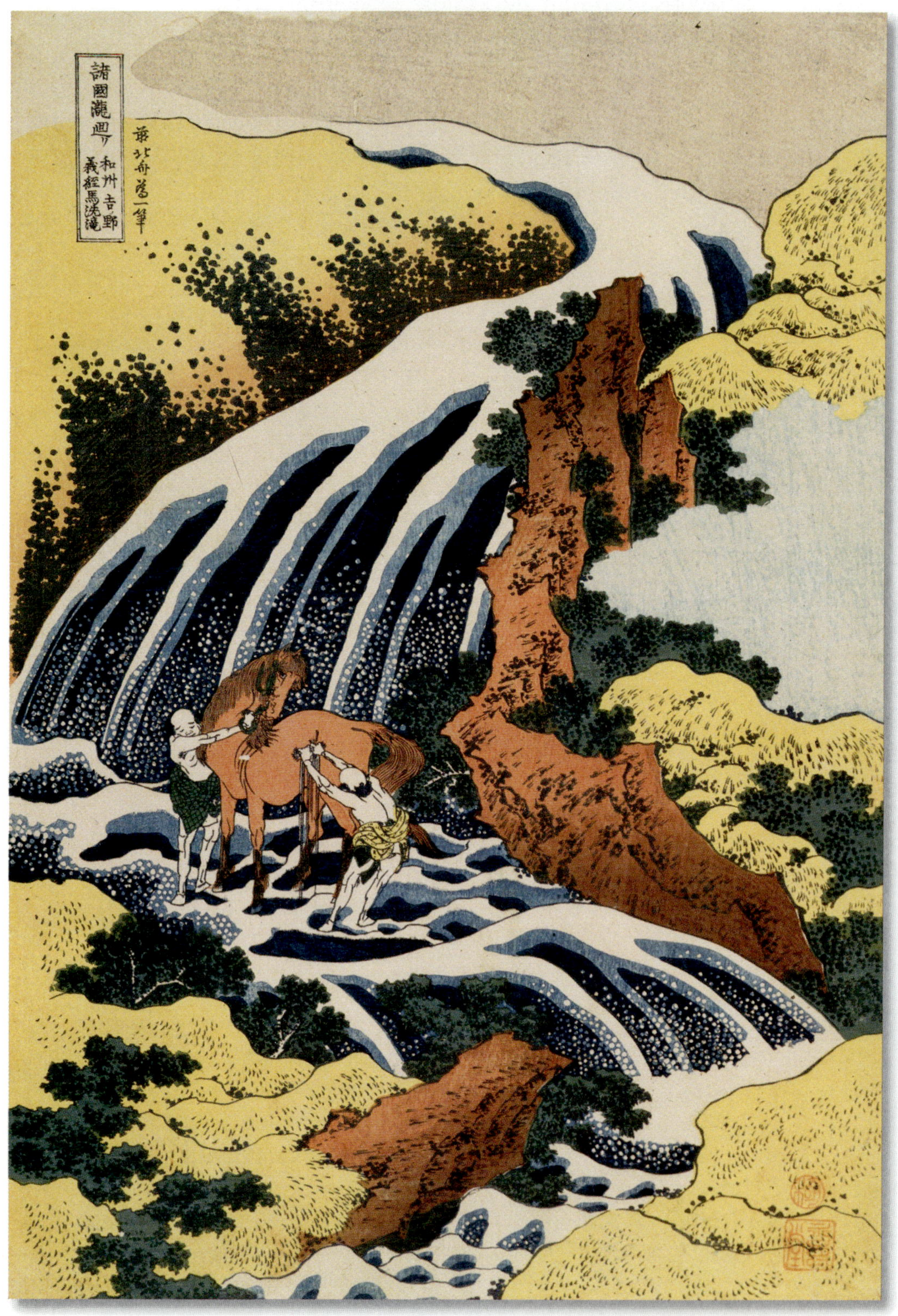

Focus On ◆ Figure 8–1 **The artist focused on scenes that showed the grandeur of nature. What natural wonder is the subject of this woodcut?**

Katsushika Hokusai. *The Waterfall at Yoshino Where Yoshitsuni Washed His Horse.* From "A Tour of Japanese Waterfalls." ca.1833. Woodblock print. 37.9 × 25.9 cm (15 × 10³⁄₁₆"). Honolulu Academy of Art, Honolulu, Hawaii. Gift of James A. Michener, 1969.

Chapter 8

Printmaking

"If I could live but ten more years or even five, I could become a true artist."

—Katsushika Hokusai (1760–1849)

In the first century A.D., the Chinese developed an exciting new art process. The process involved spreading ink onto a block of wood with an image carved in it. The block was then pressed onto another Chinese invention, paper.

Soon the process had spread all over Asia and, eventually, the world. It reached its high point in Japan in the early 1800s. During that period, an artist widely regarded as the greatest printmaker of all time lived and worked. One of his creations appears in **Figure 8–1**. Do you know the name of this artist? You will after reading this chapter. You will also learn more about the art of printmaking.

After completing this chapter, you will be able to:

- Explain the different ways in which printmakers work.
- Identify the steps in the printmaking process.
- Name the four chief methods for making prints.
- Create your own artworks using various printmaking methods in traditional and experimental ways.
- Create a haiku based on a Japanese woodblock print.

Quick Write

Interpreting the Quote Read the quote, which was made by the artist on his deathbed at age 89. What do his words reveal about his goals as an artist? Do you feel the print in Figure 8–1 achieves this goal? Write a brief paragraph defending your views.

Key Terms

printing plate
brayer
registration
relief printing
intaglio
lithography
lithograph
screen printing
serigraph
monoprinting

The Art of Printmaking

By the second century A.D., the Chinese had developed movable type. This made possible the printing of text. Text printing revolutionized long-distance communication so that many people soon forgot about picture printing. In art, however, picture printing—or *printmaking*—remains alive and well.

Steps in Printmaking

As explained in Chapter 4, all prints are made using three basic steps. The first of these is making the **printing plate**. This is *a surface onto or into which the image to be printed is cut or carved*. In preparing a plate, the artist makes a mirror image of the final print. Next the artist applies ink to the surface of the plate. Often this is done with a **brayer**, *a roller with a handle*. For a multicolor print, a separate plate is made for each color. The plates must be carefully aligned so that the colors appear in the correct areas. This *careful matching up of plates in prints with more than one color* is called **registration**.

The last step is the printing. This may be done either by hand or on a press. The surface on which the print is made is usually paper, though other media may be used.

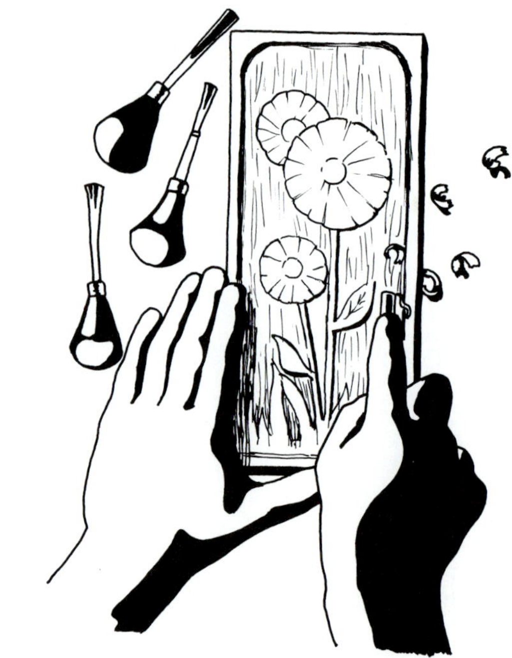

◆ **Figure 8–2** This drawing shows a woodcut being made.

Printmaking Techniques

Despite their variety, all prints are made using one of four basic techniques. These are relief printing, intaglio, lithography, and screen printing.

Relief Printing

If you have ever made a stamp print, you have made a relief print. In **relief printing**, *the image to be printed is raised from a background*. (See **Figure 8–2**.)

One popular medium used in relief printing is also the oldest—wood. Figure 8–1,

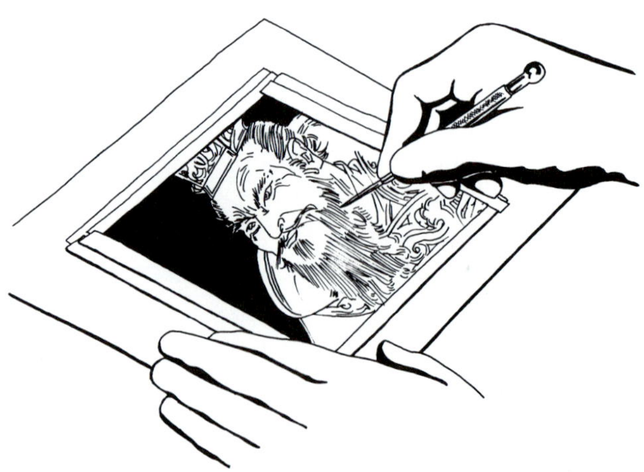

◆ **Figure 8–3** Using the intaglio technique, the image is cut or etched onto a surface with sharp tools.

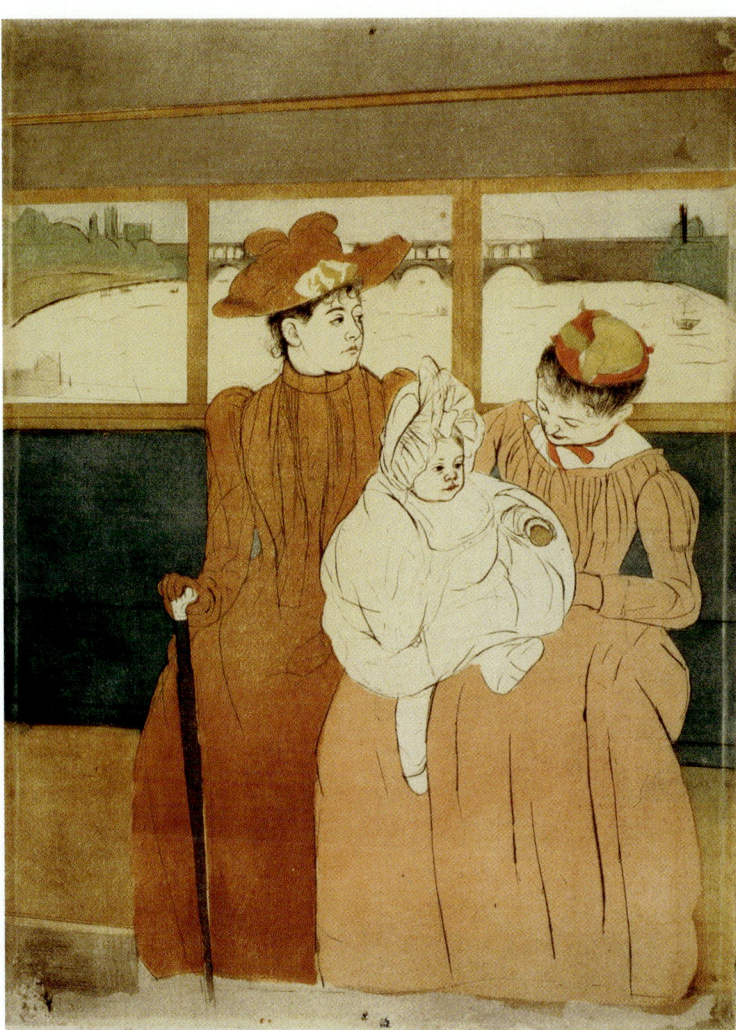

◆ **Figure 8–4** **Notice how delicate the lines of the figures and objects appear in this drypoint print.**

Mary Cassatt. *In the Omnibus* (*The Tramway*). 1891. Drypoint, soft-ground, and aquatint. 36.4 × 26.7 cm ($14\frac{5}{16} \times 10\frac{1}{2}$). The National Gallery of Art, Washington, D.C. Chester Dale Collection.

which opened this chapter, is an example of a woodblock print, or *woodcut*. This is one of many nature prints the artist made.

Intaglio

A second technique for making prints is, in a way, the reverse of relief printing. **Intaglio** (in-**tal**-yoh) is *a printmaking technique in which the image to be printed is cut or etched into a surface*. Sharp tools with tips of different thicknesses are used for this process (see **Figure 8–3**). In intaglio, the resulting grooves, or *undercuts*, are inked. Paper is then forced into the grooves. If you touch the surface of an intaglio print, you can feel the buildup of the ink.

As with relief printmaking, there are numerous intaglio techniques. One favored by many printmakers is *engraving*. In engraving, lines are scratched deep into a metal plate with an engraving tool. Another popular intaglio technique is *etching*. The artist begins by covering the metal printing plate with a thin protective coating. The drawing is scratched through the coating with an etching needle. The plate is then given an acid bath. The lines of the drawing are etched into the metal by the acid. The rest of the plate is protected from the acid by the coating. The print shown in **Figure 8–4** includes three printmaking techniques: drypoint, aquatint, and soft-ground. In *drypoint*, the image is simply scratched into the plate with a sharp needle. Notice the amount of detail the artist managed to achieve.

Lithography

Have you ever noticed that grease and water don't mix? This fact is at the root of lithography (lith-**ahg**-ruh-fee). Derived from a

German word meaning "stone," **lithography** is *a printmaking technique in which the image to be printed is drawn on limestone, zinc, or aluminum with a special greasy crayon.* When the stone is dampened and then inked, the greased area alone holds the ink. Paper is pressed against the plate to make the print. *A print made by lithography* is called a **lithograph** (**lith**-uh-graf).

The first step in making a lithograph is dampening the printing plate. The plate is then inked, as shown in **Figure 8–5**. The greased area containing the image alone holds the ink. Paper is pressed against the plate to make the print. Examine the lithograph in **Figure 8–6**. The work is by French artist Henri de Toulouse-Lautrec (ahn-**ree** duh too-**looz** low-**trek**), the first artist to create posters for commercial use. Compare and contrast the use of art elements and principles in this work and the one shown in Figure 8–8. In particular, what type of balance did each artist use? Describe the use of color in each artwork.

Screen Printing

You have probably used lettering stencils at one time or another. The same basic idea is at work in **screen printing**. This is *a printmaking technique in which a stencil with a design cut into it is placed over a fabric screen.* (See **Figure 8–7**.) Ink is forced through the part of the screen not covered by the stencil, onto paper or cloth to make a print. *A screen print that has been handmade by an artist* is called a **serigraph** (**sehr**-uh-graf). To make a color serigraph, the artist makes one screen—or plate—for each color. Some serigraphs may have as many as 20 colors. How many colors did the artist use to make the serigraph in **Figure 8–8?**

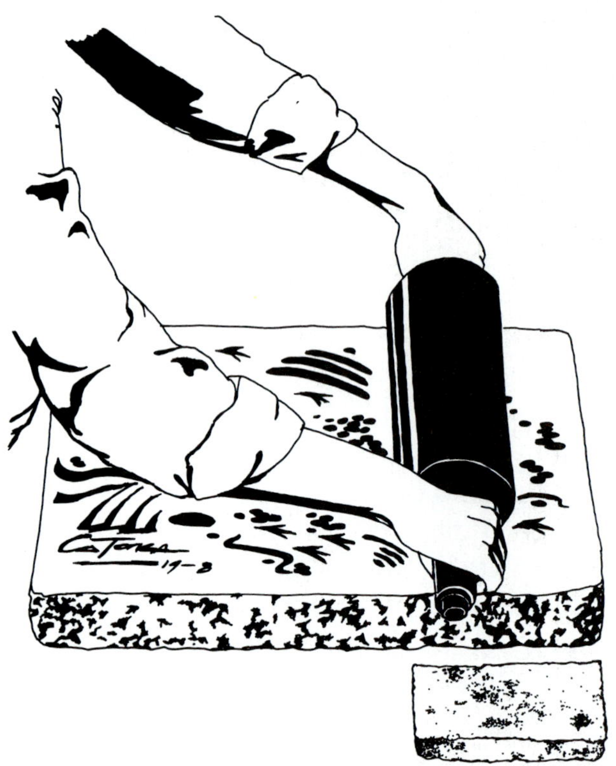

◆ **Figure 8–5** **The illustration above shows a lithography stone as ink is being applied with a brayer.**

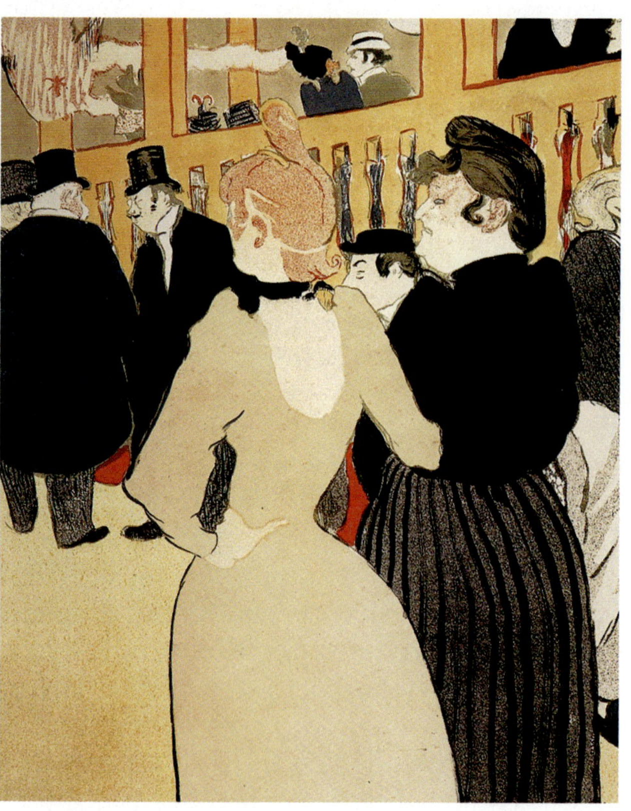

◆ **Figure 8–6** **A German actor and writer invented lithography in 1798. It reached its zenith as an art form in the late 1800s.**

Henri de Toulouse-Lautrec. *Au Moulin Rouge.* 1892. Color lithograph. 45.7 × 31.8 cm (18 × 12½″). Cincinnati Art Museum, Cincinnati, Ohio. Gift of Herbert Greer French.

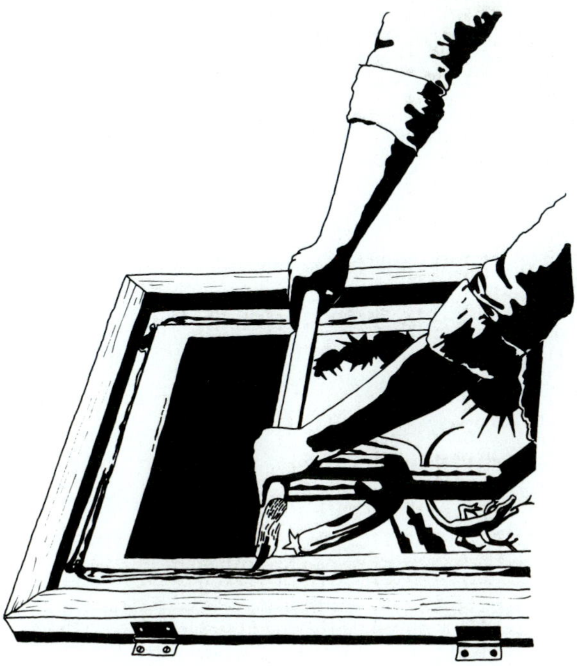

◆ **Figure 8–7** **Notice the detail of a screen print. How does it differ from the other printing plate details shown in Figures 8–2, 8–3, and 8–5?**

Meet the Artist

Henri Matisse (1869–1954)

Artist Henri Matisse (ahn-**ree** mah-**tees**) unveiled his artistic talents by chance. As a young adult, Matisse suffered an illness that required him to be bedridden. To pass the time, Matisse—a law student—began to paint. Within a decade, he had established himself as a leading French artist. By 1905, Matisse had developed a unique art style that used colors in a bold new way. Throughout his career he continued to forge new paths in art, which included printmaking. The serigraph in Figure 8–8 was completed toward the end of the artist's life.

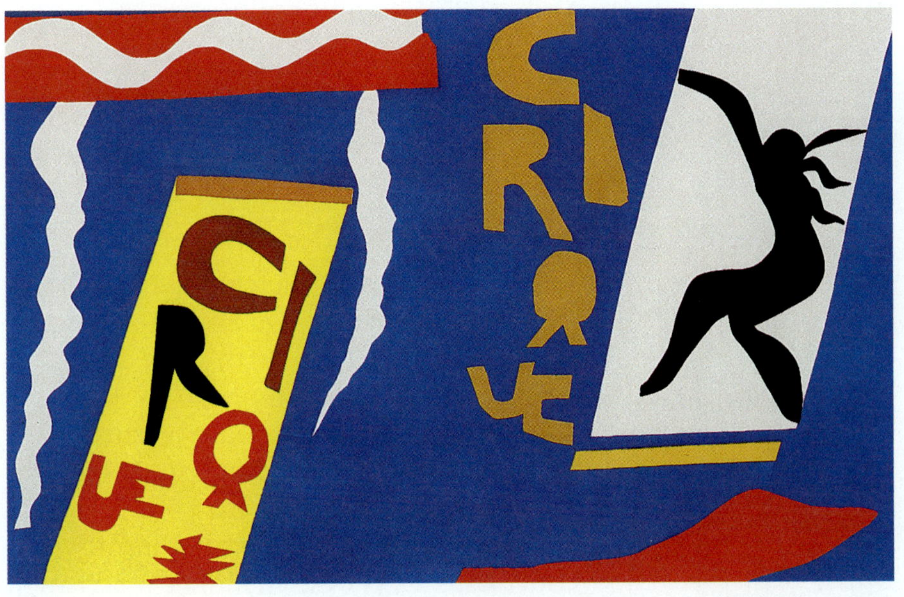

◆ **Figure 8–8** **This image is from a book that Matisse made about the circus.**

Henri Matisse. *Jazz (Cirque)*. 1947. Stencil prints in color on paper. 66.7 × 44.5 cm (26¼ × 17½″). New Orleans Museum of Art, New Orleans, Louisiana. Gift of Mr. and Mrs. Fritz Bultman. 66.13. z. © 2003 Succession H. Matisse, Paris/Artists Rights Society (ARS), New York.

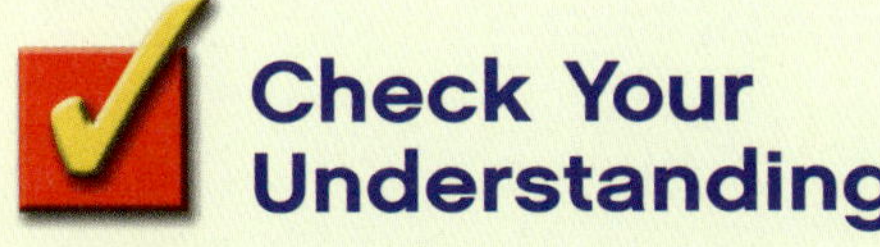

Check Your Understanding

1. Name the four main printmaking techniques.
2. Define the term *registration*.
3. Explain the difference between a lithograph and a serigraph.

Monoprints

Look at **Figure 8–9**. This is an example of a type of art called a monoprint. **Monoprinting** is *a printmaking technique in which the image to be printed is put on the plate with ink or paint and then transferred to paper by pressing or hand-rubbing*. A monoprint plate can be used only once. The paint is absorbed into the paper, and the original image is gone.

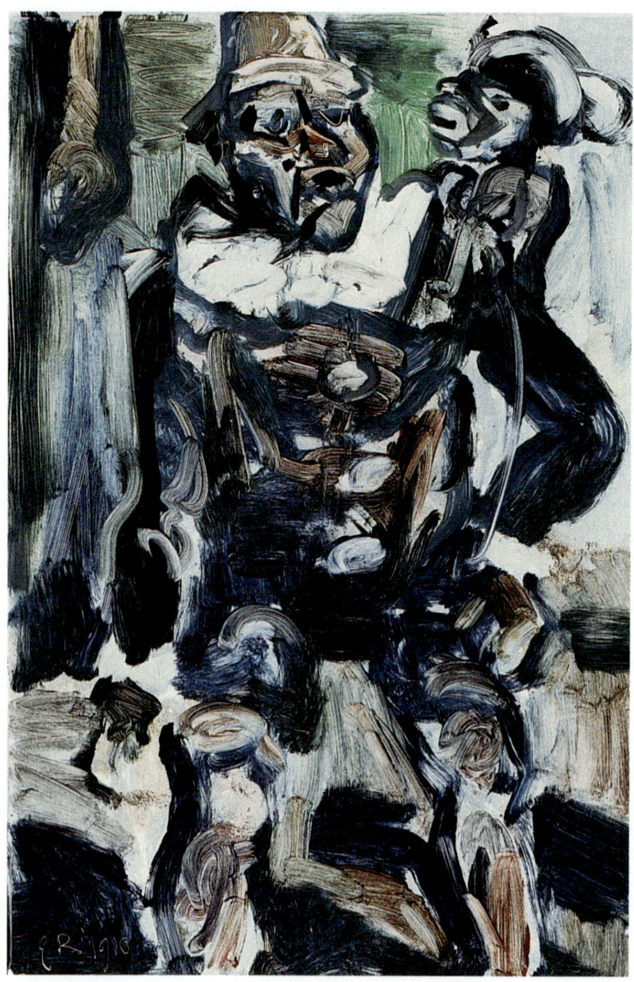

◆ **Figure 8–9** **A monoprint is actually a blot. Rouault painted his clown and monkey on glass and then pressed paper on it.**

Georges Rouault. *Clown and Monkey*. 1910. Monotype, printed in color. 57.5 × 38.7 cm (22⅝ × 15¼″). Museum of Modern Art, New York, New York. Gift of Mrs. Sam A. Lewisohn. © 2003 Artists Rights Society (ARS), New York/ADAGP, Paris.

What You Will Learn

You will produce a print by selecting and using a variety of art materials and tools in traditional ways. You will use a contour drawing process to interpret a subject by making a monoprint of a person. The image quality of the monoprint will help you understand the reversal process of printmaking. Create a mood within your work using the elements of line and color. The difference in line quality of a pencil and one made in a monoprint will become apparent.

What You Will Need

- Pencil and sheets of sketch paper
- Water-based printing ink
- Brayer
- Square of smooth vinyl flooring to be used as the printing plate
- Sheet of white paper

What You Will Do

1. Using a pencil and sketch paper, make blind contour drawings of the model. When you are happy with your drawing, move on to the next step.
2. Squeeze ink onto the square of vinyl flooring. This is to be your printing plate. Spread the ink evenly with your brayer.
3. Place the sheet of white paper lightly on your plate. Don't move it once it is down.

4. Supporting your hand so that it doesn't rest on the paper, use your pencil to draw a contour drawing that fills the paper. Be careful not to let anything but the pencil touch the paper. If a line looks wrong, draw it again. Do not erase a line.
5. Starting at two corners, pull your paper carefully from the plate. Do not stop once you begin pulling. Place your paper, image side up, in a safe place to dry.
6. Display your print once it has dried.

Evaluating Your Work

- **Describe** Show where you used contour drawing to create an image of a person. Explain how the monoprint came out the reverse of your pencil drawing.
- **Analyze** Explain how the quality of the monoprint line is different from a pencil line. Tell how you created contrast between the line of the print and the paper.
- **Interpret** Tell what mood your work creates. Explain how you interpreted a subject in your monoprint.
- **Judge** Tell whether you feel your work succeeds. Explain your answer.

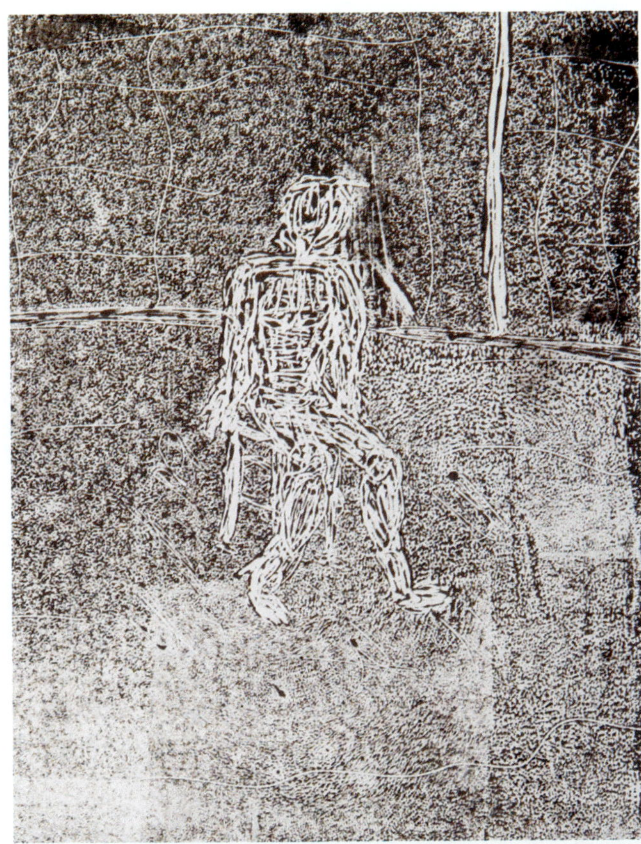

◆ **Figure 8–10** **Student work. A monoprint.**

STUDIO OPTION

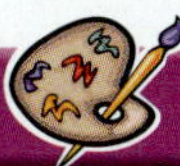

Use the techniques you have learned in this lesson by selecting and using a variety of art materials to produce a monoprint in experimental ways. For example, add cut-out cardboard shapes to your drawing by gluing them down on the paper. Gently roll the brayer across the surface. How does this technique affect the finished product? Did you create different patterns and textures?

Visual Art Journal

Compare and contrast the use of art elements in your monoprint with the one in Figure 8–9. Focus on the use of line and color or value. Summarize your analysis in your visual art journal using vocabulary accurately.

Inuit-Style Print

A Native American group that has been around since earliest times is the Inuit (**in**-yuh-wuht). You may know these people of Canada and Alaska as Eskimos. The name "Eskimo" was used by explorers from other lands. The Inuit have a tradition of carving bone, ivory, or stone to create abstract views of images from nature. This tradition is being upheld by artists working today. The print in **Figure 8–11** is by a leading Inuit artist named Kenojuak (kuh-**noh**-joo-ak).

What You Will Learn

You will produce a print by selecting and using a variety of appropriate art materials and tools to interpret a subject in traditional and experimental ways. You will design a print based on your school mascot or some other school symbol. You will apply design skills to effectively communicate ideas and thoughts in everyday life. Your print will be abstract in design and should use line and shape to express your feelings and thoughts about the animal. Create your print based on direct observations.

What You Will Need

- Pencil, eraser, and sheets of sketch paper
- 2 pieces of 8 × 10-inch corrugated cardboard
- Paper-cutting knife and white glue
- Colored water-based printing ink
- Shallow pan and soft brayer
- Paper for printing

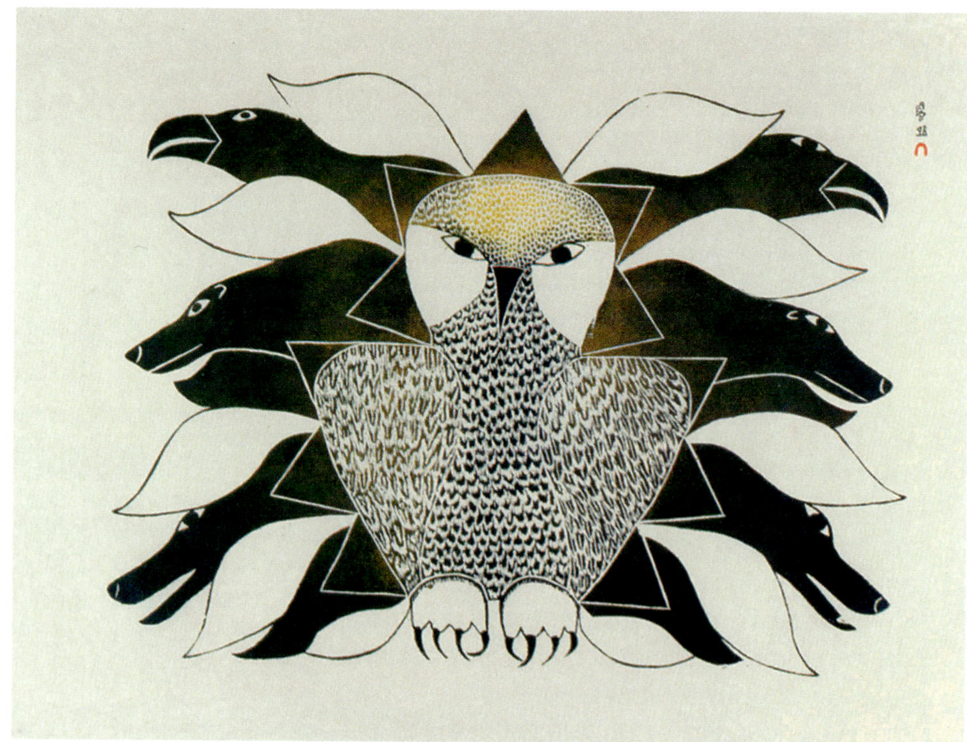

◆ **Figure 8–11** **Compare and contrast the use of the art element texture and the principle balance in this work and the student work in Figure 8–12. What art elements are used to create unity?**

Kenojuak. *Owls, Ravens, and Dogs.* Courtesy of Dorset Fine Arts, Toronto, Ontario, Canada. Reproduced with permission of the West Baffin Eskimo Cooperative Ltd., Cape Dorset, Nunawt.

What You Will Do

1. On sketch paper, draw the animal or symbol you chose. On a second sheet of sketch paper, use experimental ways to create an abstract design based on your first sketch. For example, leave out all unnecessary details, using line and shape to express feelings. Experiment by using round shapes to express gentleness. Diagonal lines can show danger or quick movement.
2. Transfer your design to a piece of corrugated cardboard. Using the paper-cutting knife, carefully cut out the design. Glue it to the second piece of cardboard to form a printing plate.
3. Squeeze out a small amount of colored ink into the pan. Roll the brayer back and forth in the ink to coat it evenly. Roll the brayer lightly over your printing plate. If you press down too hard, you might collapse the relief.
4. Place a clean sheet of paper on your plate. Gently rub the paper with the back of a spoon or your fingertips. Work quickly. Carefully remove the print. Set it aside to dry. Repeat the process twice more to make an edition of three prints. When all the prints are dry, sign them.
5. Display your best print alongside those of your classmates. Decide which design you feel best captures the appearance and spirit of your school mascot or symbol.

Evaluating Your Work

- **Describe** Identify the details you eliminated to create an abstract design.
- **Analyze** Explain how you experimented with shapes and lines. Tell which art elements stand out most in your design.
- **Interpret** State what feelings about your mascot or symbol your print expresses. What features help convey those feelings?
- **Judge** Tell whether you feel your work succeeds. If you could redo your work, tell what changes, if any, you would make.

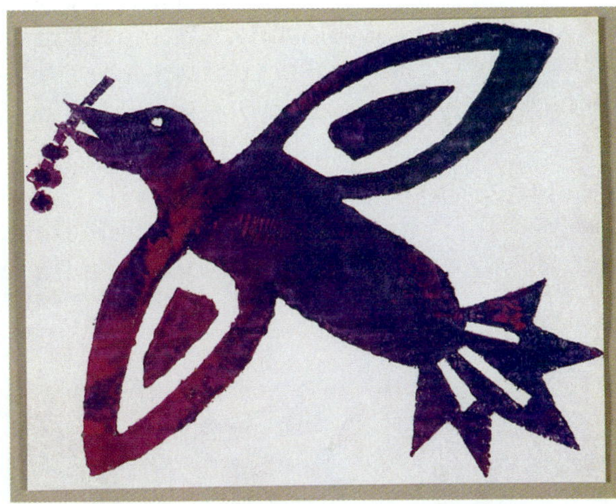

◆ **Figure 8–12** **Student work. Inuit-style print.**

Portfolio Ideas

Critically review the contents of your portfolio. Keep artwork that demonstrates your knowledge and skill with a variety of art media and techniques. You may add new artwork or remove less successful entries. Analyze and compare relationships, such as function and meaning, in personal artworks displayed in your portfolio. For example, do some of your artworks have similar meanings?

Visual Art Journal

Analyze portfolios. Analyze portfolios by your peers and others, such as high school students or your art teachers. Form conclusions about formal properties, historical and cultural contexts, intents, and meanings. Write a four-part analysis in your visual art journal.

Linoleum Block Print

Look at the print shown in **Figure 8–13**. This was done by the German artist Karl Schmidt-Rottluff. He was one of the founding members of an art movement called German Expressionism. This movement emphasized creating abstract art that expressed raw emotion. Schmidt-Rottluff's group was known as "Die Brucke" or "The Bridge." They saw their work as a bridge between traditional art and more futuristic methods. Members were greatly influenced by the angular lines and shapes of masks and Cubism. These characteristics are found in art of Die Brucke.

Landscape, the work shown in Figure 8–13, is a woodcut. The areas that appear white represent *negative* areas of the plate. These were carved away. Notice the interplay of light and dark in the print. The artist achieved this effect by controlling the thickness of lines and the distance between them.

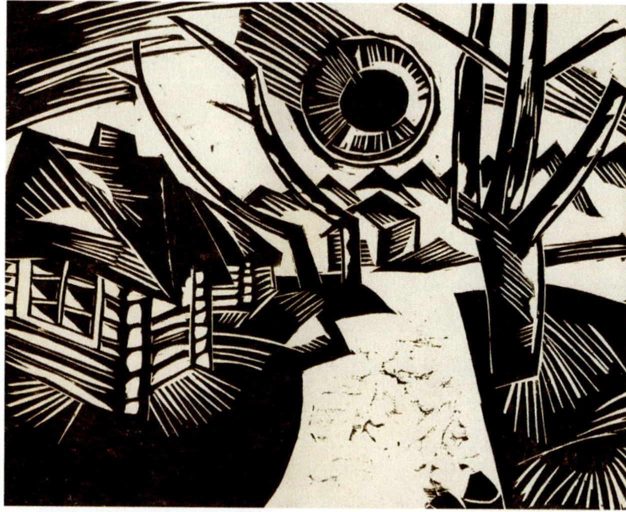

◆ **Figure 8–13** **Has the artist made this landscape an inviting place? Which elements of art contribute to the way you feel about this work?**

Karl Schmidt-Rottluff. *Landscape*. 1919. Woodcut. 49.1 × 59.8 cm (19⁵⁄₁₆ × 23⁹⁄₁₆"). Museum of Modern Art, New York, New York. © 2003 Artists Rights Society (ARS), New York/VG Bild-Kunst, Bonn.

What You Will Learn

You will make a linoleum block print by selecting and using a variety of appropriate art materials and tools to interpret a subject in traditional ways. You will use architecture as the subject. Your print will be a reverse image of your carving. You will use line, shape, and texture to create interest in your composition. You will use repeated lines to create light areas. You will use positive and negative space to create balance.

What You Will Need

- Sketchbook, 4 × 6-inch sketch paper, soft #2 pencil, eraser
- Scrap pieces of linoleum
- Linoleum cutting tool with different-sized blades
- Piece of 4 × 6-inch linoleum
- Black permanent marker and tape
- Crayon and scrap paper
- Inking plate and brayer
- Colored water-based printing inks
- Sheets of 9 × 12-inch white paper

What You Will Do

1. Using a linoleum scrap, experiment with the different blades. Practice cutting thin and thick lines, then carving out large areas.
2. Collect images of local architecture, personal photos, or postcards of buildings. Select two images to study closely. Make several quick sketches using simple lines and shapes. Use positive and negative space to create balance. Select your best sketch as your guide. Make your final design on your sketch paper, filling the page. Include a background with your building to create depth.

3. Transfer your image onto the linoleum by blackening the back of your drawing with a soft pencil. Tape your paper, image side up, onto your linoleum block. Trace over your lines and remove the paper.
4. Using a black marker, color in all areas of the linoleum that will not be cut away. These will be the raised lines that hold the ink during printing.
5. Using different blades, cut away the background. Stop from time to time and make a crayon rubbing of your plate. This will help you identify areas that need further carving.
6. Squeeze some ink onto the inking plate, and load the brayer. Roll the brayer over the linoleum block. Place the printing paper carefully on the block. Press the paper to the plate by rubbing it by hand or running it through a press. Lift your print carefully from the block. Notice how the image you carved is printed in reverse.
7. Make three prints, sign, and select one to display.

SAFETY TIP

Linoleum blades are very sharp and can cause serious cuts. Always cut away from your body and your other hand.

Evaluating Your Work

- **Describe** Show the details you used in your drawings. Explain why you used them.
- **Analyze** Explain how you used the art elements of line, shape, and texture in your composition. How did you interpret your subject in your print?
- **Interpret** What emotional quality does *Landscape* have? Does your print have the same emotional quality? Explain.
- **Judge** Were you able to successfully create three linoleum prints?

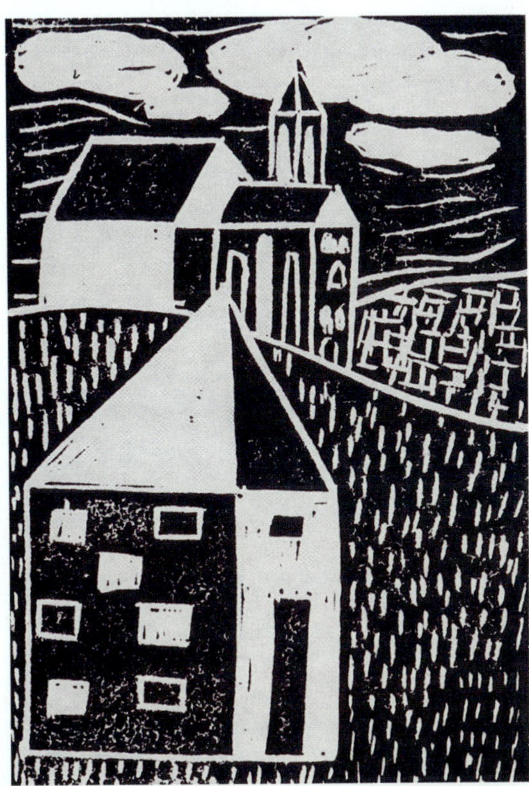

◆ **Figure 8–14** **Student work. Linoleum block print.**

STUDIO OPTION

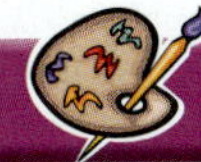

Use the techniques you have learned in this lesson to produce a linoleum block print in experimental ways. Illustrate ideas from imagination to create different possibilities in your print. For example, create negative space where you showed positive space in your first series of prints. Try experimenting with different ink colors.

Art Online

To learn more about printmaking, click on Web Links at **art.glencoe.com**. There you will also find:

- Artist Profiles
- Career Corner

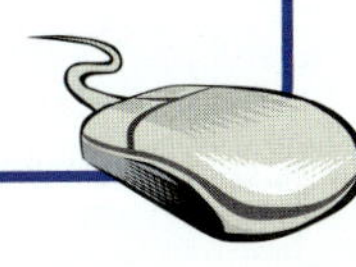

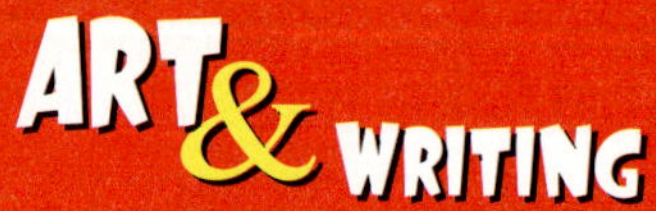

Haiku in Words and Pictures

Look back at the artwork that opened this chapter (Figure 8–1 on page 150). The work is a woodblock print. As noted, this is a form of creative expression for which the Japanese are famous. Another is the short verse form shown in **Figure 8–15.**

Do you know what this type of poem is called? It is a *haiku* (**hy**-koo), one of the most famous poetic forms ever created. This particular haiku is a translation from the Japanese. It was written by one of the undisputed masters of the medium. His name was Kobayashi Issa (**koh**-buh-**yah**-shee **ee**-suh) (1763–1827). This renowned haiku writer signed his works using his last name only.

Rules of Haiku

Read the haiku by Issa in Figure 8–15. Do not be fooled by its seeming simplicity. The haiku is a fairly complex poetic form that is governed by many rules. Some of these rules have to do with *meter*—the number of "beats" per line. Most haiku have 3 lines and 17 syllables distributed in 5, 7 and 5. Count the syllables in each line.

The theme and subject matter of haiku are also restricted. Haiku must celebrate the majesty of nature. There is usually a key word that implies or states the season of the year. There is also often a change in the viewpoint. What features of nature are mentioned in the poem?

In the city fields
Contemplating cherry trees
Strangers are like friends.

—Issa

◆ **Figure 8–15** Haiku by Issa.

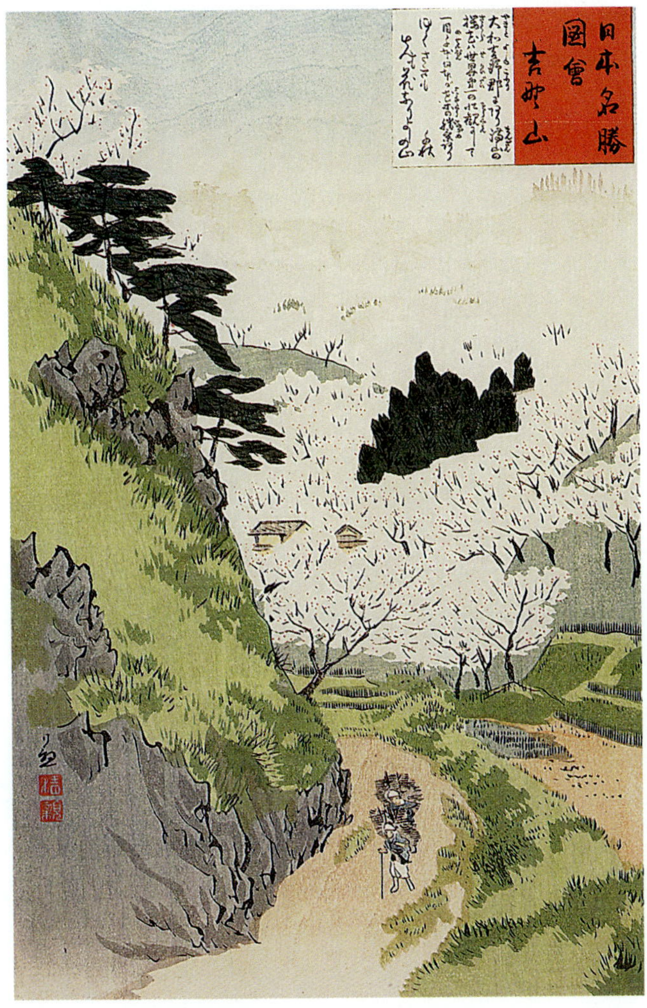

◆ **Figure 8–16** **What similarities and differences can you find between the haiku by Issa and this artwork?**

Kobayashi Kiyochika. *Mt. Yoshino, Cherry Blossoms.* 1897. Color woodblock print. 33.9 × 22.5 cm (13$\frac{3}{8}$ × 8$\frac{7}{8}$"). Sheet: 35.8 × 23.6 cm (14$\frac{1}{8}$ × 9$\frac{5}{16}$"). Los Angeles County Museum of Art, Los Angeles, California. Gift of Carl Holmes. m.71.100.96

Haiku in Visual Form

Haiku have been called *picture poems*. Like pictures, they capture a specific moment as a sensation or impression. The same may be said of the woodblock print in **Figure 8–16**. In fact, this work might be referred to as a haiku print. Like a haiku, the shapes and forms are simplified. Colors, too, are kept to a minimum. Even some of the same aspects of nature appear in this print. Can you guess the type of flowers shown blooming on the branches along the road? If not, examine the credit line for this artwork.

MAKE THE CONNECTION

Take Another Look

1. What words in Issa's haiku convey nature? What words depict people? Explain.
2. Haiku seldom have objects made by people in them. The woodblock print does. Where do you find these forms? Would you agree that they are depicted in the style of haiku? Explain your reaction.

ART & WRITING

Write a haiku. Look again at the rules for haiku writing. Familiarize yourself with these. Then write a haiku of your own based on the woodcut in Figure 8–16. Begin by choosing the objects of nature you will focus on.

For the Birds

Audubon's prints showed the beauty of our fine feathered friends.

Artists and scientists should be glad that John James Audubon (1785–1851) gave up an army career in France and moved to the United States. After failing in business, Audubon turned his passion for studying birds into a career. With little more than art materials and an assistant, Audubon set out to document North American wildlife in exact detail.

After drawing hundreds of lifelike pictures of birds, Audubon wanted to publish them in a book. No one in the United States was interested, so in 1826 he took his drawings and went to England. There, Audubon met English engraver Robert Havell. Impressed by Audubon's work, Havell agreed to make engravings of his spectacular watercolors. The four-volume *The Birds of America*, printed in 1838, contains 435 life-size engravings. The book measures 2 feet by 3 feet. The engravings illustrate 1,065 bird specimens from 489 species.

Wildlife historian David M. Lank explains what makes the publication so highly regarded: "The birds were absolutely alive. But it was Audubon's including the natural setting of the birds that was the real break from the past." For fans of wildlife, Audubon's famous book provides a look to the past—and to some birds that are now extinct.

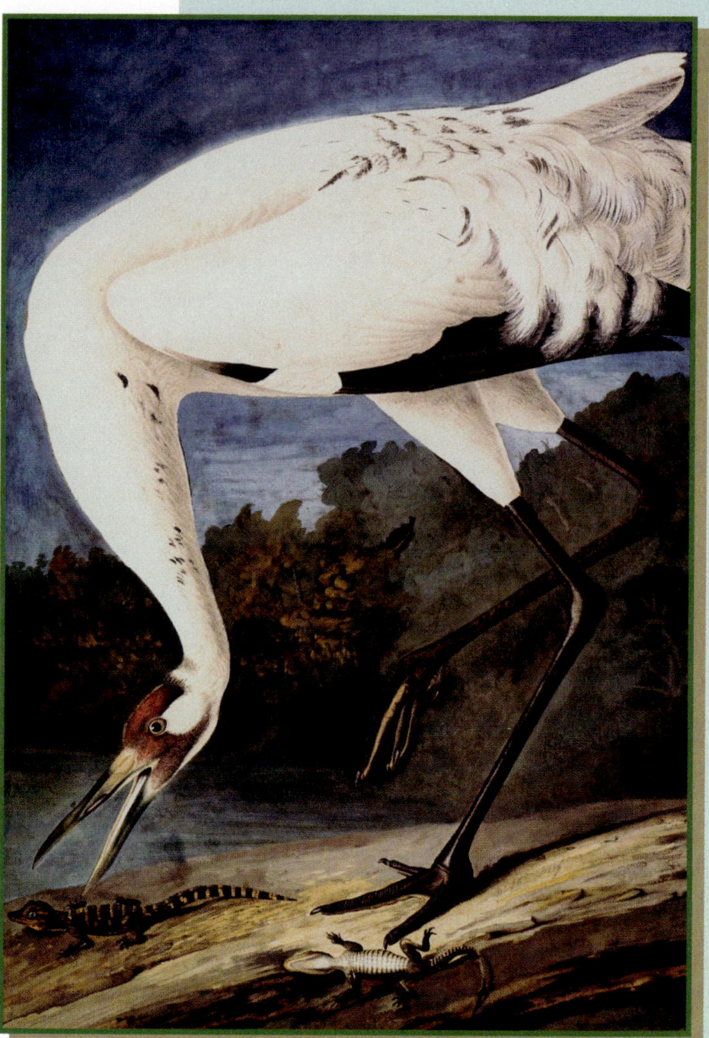

GEOFFREY CLEMENTS/CORBIS

John James Audubon. *Whooping Crane.* 1829. Many of the birds in Audubon's collection have become extinct. The whooping crane is currently on the endangered species list.

TIME TO CONNECT

- **Using the Internet, research the goals and mission of the Audubon Society.**
- **Write a well-developed draft of an essay that explains how and why John James Audubon's artwork might have inspired this group.**
- **Share your work with a partner. Together, peer-edit each other's essays for a logical presentation of ideas.**
- **Afterward, edit and revise your essay.**

Chapter 8 Review

BUILDING VOCABULARY

Number a sheet of paper from 1 to 10. After each number, write the term from the list that best matches each description below.

brayer	printing plate
intaglio	registration
lithograph	relief printing
lithography	screen printing
monoprinting	serigraph

1. The surface onto or into which the image to be printed is cut or carved.
2. A roller with a handle.
3. A technique in which the image to be printed is raised from the background.
4. The careful matching up of plates in prints with more than one color.
5. A technique in which the image to be printed is cut or etched into a surface.
6. A technique in which the image to be printed is drawn on limestone, zinc, or aluminum with a special crayon.
7. A print made by lithography.
8. A technique in which a stencil with a design cut into it is placed over a fabric screen.
9. A screen print that has been handmade by an artist.
10. A technique in which the image to be printed is put on the plate with ink or paint and then transferred to paper by pressing or hand-rubbing.

REVIEWING ART FACTS

Number a sheet of paper from 11 to 16. Answer each question in a complete sentence.

11. Why is being able to "think backward" important to a printmaker?
12. What is inking? What tool is often used in inking?
13. Which printmaking technique yields only one print?
14. What is a woodcut? What method of printmaking is used to make a woodcut?
15. Name one type of intaglio printing.
16. Which printmaking technique uses a stencil?

CROSS-CURRICULUM CONNECTIONS

17. **Social Studies.** Look at the colored woodcut by Hokusai on page 150. This is one of many waterfall prints the artist depicted. He also focused on other natural phenomena found in Japan. Look for other artworks by Japanese artists showing volcanoes, water, and islands and share them with the class. Why do you think these images play such an important part in Japanese works of art?
18. **Science.** The printmaking technique called *lithography* is based on the fact that oil and water do not mix. What other substances don't mix? Find out why.

Web Museum Activity

Museum of Modern Art, New York, New York

As you've learned in this chapter, there are several methods artists use to make a print. Now you can see those methods in action! Click on the museum's site at **art.glencoe.com** to view the interactive demonstrations. Analyze the online exhibition of prints by various artists and compare them with works shown in this chapter. Form conclusions about formal properties, historical and cultural contexts, intents, and meanings.

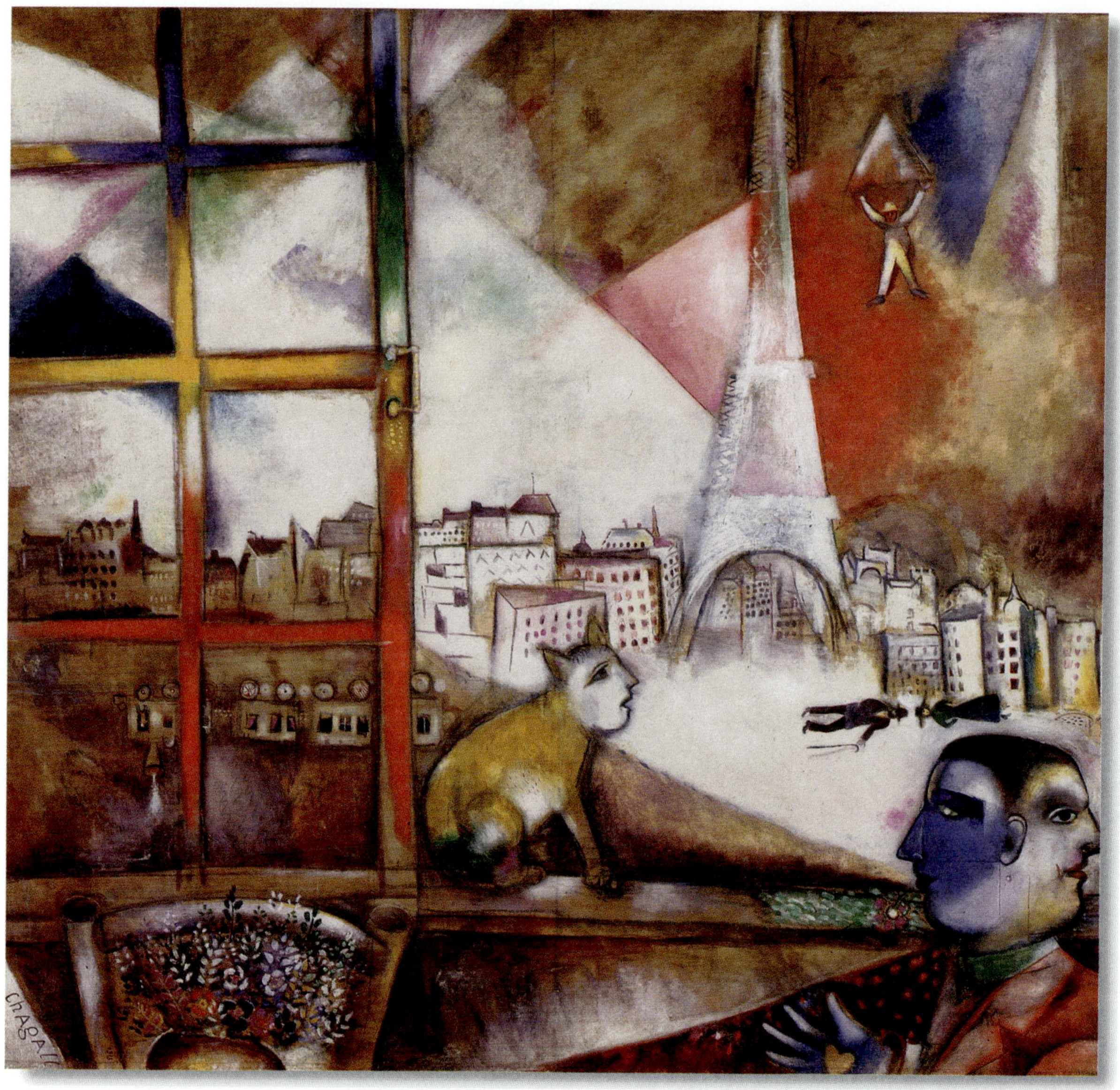

Focus On ◆ **Figure 9–1** **Is this a realistic view of the city named? What familiar symbols of Paris has the artist included?**

Marc Chagall. *Paris Through the Window*. 1913. Oil on canvas. 135.8 × 141.1 cm (53½ × 55½″). The Solomon R. Guggenheim Museum, New York, New York. Gift, Solomon R. Guggenheim, 1937. © 2003 Artists Rights Society (ARS), New York/ADAGP, Paris.

Chapter 9

Painting

> "*Art is the unceasing effort to compete with the beauty of flowers—and never succeeding.*"
>
> **Marc Chagall (1889–1985)**

Ask ten people to name a great artist, and many are likely to name a painter. For most people, painting is the most common type of all fine art. As an art form, it is also among the most varied. Compare the painting at the left with others you have seen. You may not have seen many with a style like this one. How would you describe this artist's style?

Don't be concerned if you can't answer the above question just yet. When you have finished reading this chapter, you will know much more about painting styles and media.

After completing this chapter, you will be able to:

- Name the basic ingredients of paint.
- Describe several important painting media.
- Use a variety of art materials and tools to create paintings in traditional and experimental ways.
- Write a personal reflection.

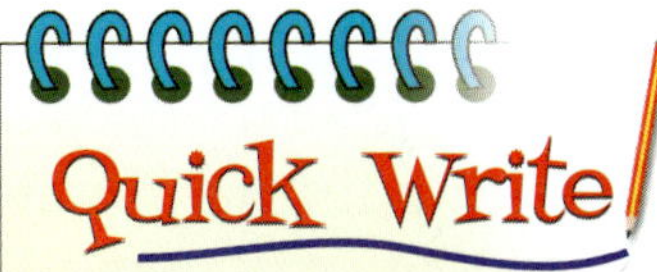

Interpreting the Quote Read the quote. The artist is hinting at a goal shared by all artists. Rewrite the quote in your own words, stating that goal.

KEY TERMS

encaustic
fresco
tempera
transparent
opaque
watercolor
palette
gouache
oil paint
impasto
glaze
synthetic paints
acrylic

LESSON 1

The Art of Painting

You may know that paints can be challenging. Paint can run and drip, and may smudge if touched while still wet. Then there's the matter of combining colors. More than one professional artist has had the experience of mixing red with green—and ending up with mud!

In this lesson you will learn all about the media of painting. In later lessons you will experiment with using several of these.

Painting Media

The media of painting include the tools of painting and the paint itself. The tools, as noted in Chapter 4, include brushes, palette knives, and even fingers. The paint has three ingredients. Two of these are pigment (powdered color) and binder (a liquid to which pigment is added.) The third component, solvent, is used to thin out paint that is overly thick. Solvent is also used for correcting mistakes in a painting and for cleanup afterward.

Many of the paints used today trace their roots to early times. Because artists are always looking for new means of self-expression, however, new media continue to appear.

Encaustic

One of the oldest known painting techniques is **encaustic** (en-**kaw**-stik). This is *a painting medium in which pigment is mixed into melted wax*. The wax, which is the binder, is kept liquid by heat. Heat is the "solvent." Works that are painted with encaustic seem to glow with light.

Fresco

Another painting technique developed long ago is *fresco*. Italian for "fresh," **fresco** (**fres**-koh) is *a painting medium in which pigment is applied to a wall spread with wet plaster*. The paint is applied while the plaster is still *fresh*, or "wet." Once the plaster dries, the painting becomes part of the wall.

In fresco painting, the plaster itself is the binder. Water is the solvent. This art form was revived in the twentieth century by Mexican muralist Diego Rivera (dee-**ay**-goh ruh-**vehr**-uh). **Figure 9–2** shows one of these works. Typical of his frescoes, this one is filled with images of hard-working people.

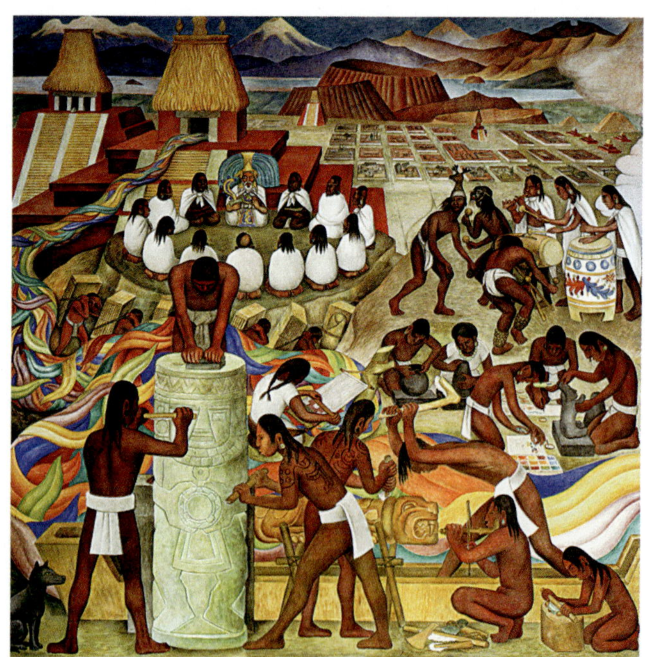

◆ **Figure 9–2 Notice that the people in this fresco are working together. Like other paintings by Rivera, this one emphasizes the importance of cooperation among people.**

Diego Rivera. *Pan-American Unity. The Creative Genius of the South Growing from Religious Fervor and a Native Talent for Plastic Expression* (one of ten panels). 1940. Fresco. 674.4 × 2,227.6 cm (22′1½″ × 73′1″) (Top five panels: 14′9″sq., bottom five panels: 7′4½″ sq.) Mural at City College of San Francisco, San Francisco, California.

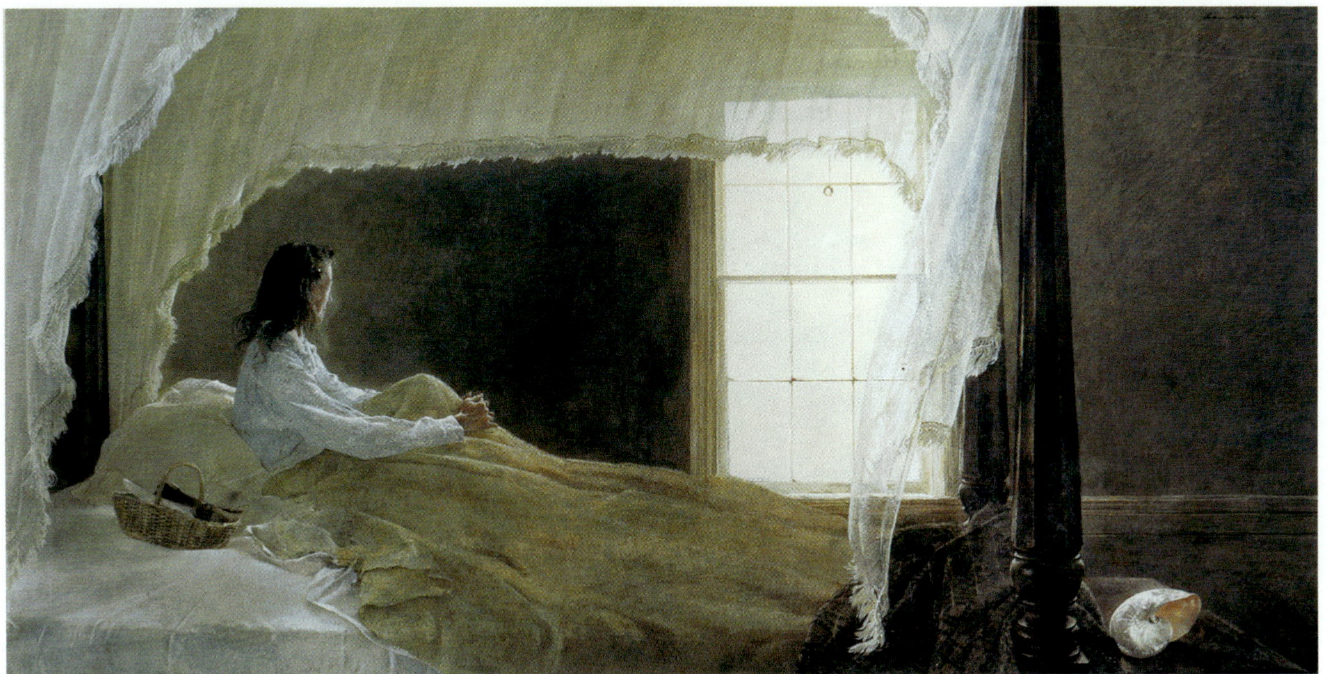

◆ **Figure 9–3** **Note the soft textures the artist was able to achieve using this medium. Compare and contrast this painting with the one in Figure 9–1. How does each artist use the art elements of color and space? How are these works similar? How are they different?**

Andrew Wyeth. *Chambered Nautilus*. 1956. Tempera on panel. 62.9 × 122.6 cm (24¾ × 48¼″). Wadsworth Atheneum, Hartford, Connecticut. Gift from the collection of Mr. and Mrs. Robert Montgomery. 1979.168.

Tempera

Another very old medium is **tempera** (**tem**-puh-ruh). This is *a painting medium in which pigment mixed with egg yolk and water is applied with tiny brushstrokes*. Tempera does not spread or blend well. Because of this, **transparent**, or *clear*, layers of color must be built up little by little. This can take time. Once dry, tempera is waterproof.

Tempera allows a painter to capture the details of a subject. Look at the painting in **Figure 9–3**. Observe how the medium enabled the artist to capture the transparency of the gauzy canopy.

Be aware that this kind of tempera is not the same medium as the tempera paint you use in school. The paint you use in your work is school tempera. This paint gives an opaque, matte finish. **Opaque** (oh-**payk**) means that it *does not let light pass through*. School tempera has a special chemical emulsion for its binder. This emulsion, unlike egg yolk, does not go sour.

Watercolor

Once used only for sketches, watercolor has become a favorite medium of serious painters. **Watercolor** is *a painting medium in which pigment is blended with gum arabic and water*. Watercolor takes its name from its solvent. For best results, watercolors are applied to good quality white paper. Blended colors are usually mixed on a palette before painting. A **palette** can be *any tray or plate on which paints are mixed before use*. A white palette allows you to see what color mixtures will look like against white paper before painting. A piece of white scrap paper can also be used to test colors for value and intensity before painting on good quality paper.

Watercolor can give a light, misty feel to paintings or can be intense and brilliant. Look at Figure 9–7 on page 172. The artist, Dong Kingman, has allowed the white of his paper to act as his white color. The work seems to glow with sunshine because he has allowed so many areas of white to represent the light.

◆ **Figure 9–4** **The artist, Jacob Lawrence, was a leading African American artist of the twentieth century. Analyze and compare relationships, such as meaning and subject matter, in this painting and the one in Figure 9–2.**

Jacob Lawrence. *Cabinet Makers.* 1946. Gouache with pencil underdrawing on paper. 55.9 × 76.4.cm (22 × 30¹⁄₁₆″). Hirshhorn Museum and Sculpture Garden, Smithsonian Institution, Washington, D.C. Gift of Joseph H. Hirshhorn, 1966. © 2003 Gwendolyn Knight Lawrence/Artists Rights Society (ARS), New York.

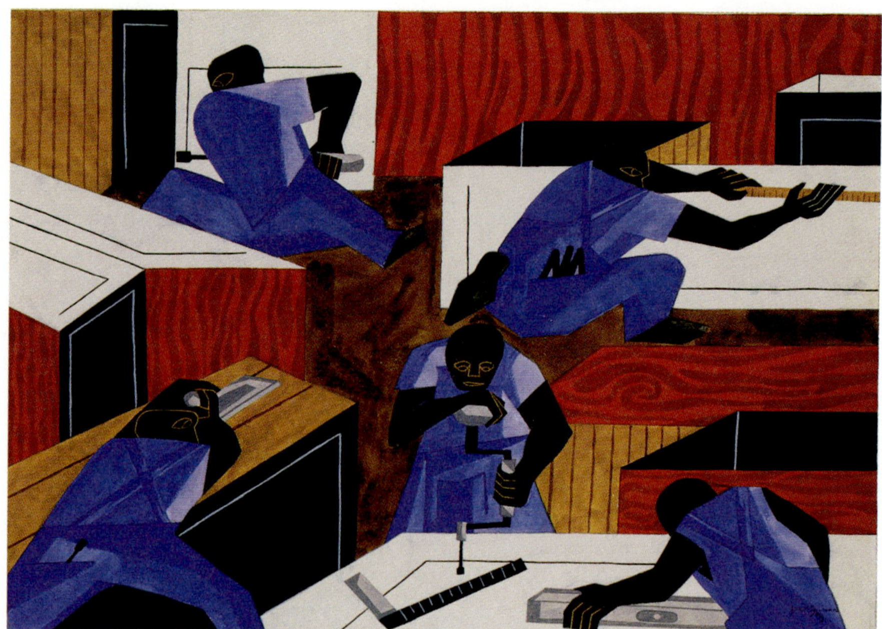

Gouache

Compare the painting in **Figure 9–4** with the one in Figure 9–7. Would you guess that the two works use closely related media? They do. Both are made with watercolor. The work in Figure 9–4 was created with **gouache (gwahsh)**, *an opaque water-based paint*. Also known as "body paint," gouache has a higher ratio of binder to pigment than ordinary watercolor. It produces a less wet-looking and more strongly colored picture. Because gouache does not undergo a chemical change when dry, it can be rewetted.

Oil Paint

Oil paint is *paint with an oil base*. Oil paint was first used in the 1400s and has continued to be one of the most popular media used today.

Linseed oil is the binder for oil paint, and its solvent is turpentine. Oil paint dries slowly. This allows artists to blend colors right on the canvas.

Oil paint can be *applied in thick, buttery layers,* called **impasto** (im-**pas**-toh), to make interesting textures. When applied thickly, oil paint is opaque. It can also be applied in *a thin, transparent layer*, called a **glaze**. A glaze allows dry color underneath to show through. Some artists make their works glow with light by building up layers of glaze. Look at **Figure 9–5**. Notice how the artist applied paint heavily in some areas, and thinly in others. On the cat, for example, there are areas of thin paint where the texture of the canvas shows through. On the paws, however, there is a thick layer of white paint.

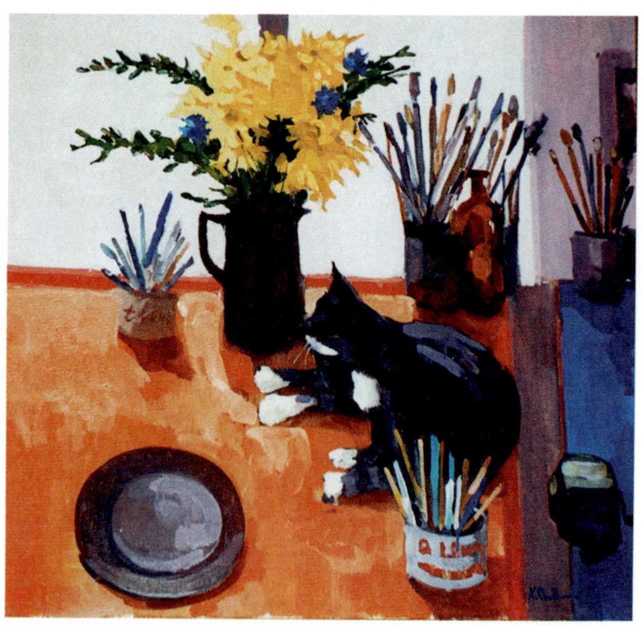

◆ **Figure 9–5** **Notice that the artist uses different values of the same hue to suggest shadow and depth. How many values of orange can you find in the table covering?**

Alfred Chadbourn. *Cat and Flowers on Studio Table.* Oil on canvas. 1983. 76.2 × 76.2 cm (30 × 30″). Private collection.

Acrylic

Advances in technology in the twentieth century have given artists new media choices. **Synthetic paints** are *manufactured paints with plastic binders*. They came onto the scene in the 1930s.

One of the most widely used paints today is **acrylic** (uh-**kril**-ik). This is *a quick-drying water-based synthetic paint*. Acrylic paint first appeared in the 1950s. One advantage of acrylic is the wide range of pure, intense colors it offers. (See **Figure 9–6**.) Another is that acrylic is versatile. Like oil paint, it can be applied both thickly and in thin glazes. Acrylic paints can even be diluted enough to be sprayed in a thin mist. Acrylic is less messy to use than oil paint. This is because the solvent for acrylic is water.

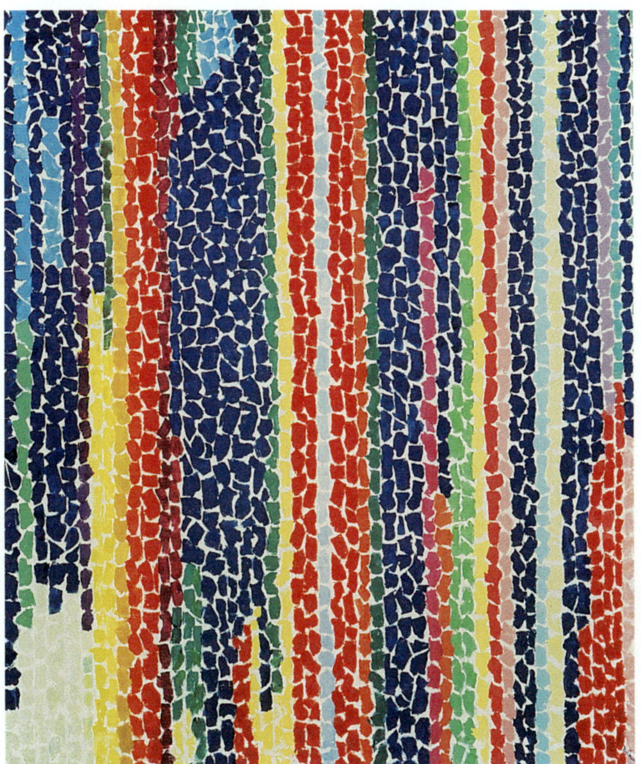

◆ **Figure 9–6** **The strong colors in the bands move up and down as well as across. Compare and contrast the use of the art element color in this painting to the way color is used in Figures 9–4 and 9–5.**

Alma Thomas. *Iris, Tulips, Jonquils, and Crocuses.* 1969. Acrylic on canvas. 152.4 × 127 cm (60 × 50″). National Museum of Women in the Arts, Washington, D.C. Gift of Wallace and Wilhelmina Holladay.

Meet the Artist

Alma Thomas (1891–1978)

Have you ever seen a field of flowers seem to dance as they moved in the breeze? Georgia-born artist Alma Thomas saw this frequently in her own garden. She also recorded this effect in the many abstract floral paintings she did. Thomas graduated from Howard University's Fine Arts program. She spent most of her life as a schoolteacher in Washington, D.C. and painted in her free time. After retiring from the classroom in the 1960s, she turned her attention to gardening. Then she noticed the "flower dance," and attempted to capture it visually. "I got some watercolors and some crayons, and I began dabbling," she once told an interviewer. "Little dabs of color that spread out very free . . . that's how it all began."

Check Your Understanding

1. What are the three main ingredients of paint?
2. How is *encaustic* different from *fresco?* How is it different from *tempera?*
3. How is *oil paint* different from *watercolor?* How is it different from *acrylic?*
4. What is *impasto?* What is a *glaze?*
5. What is a *synthetic paint?* When did synthetic paints first appear?

Watercolor Painting

Look at the painting in **Figure 9–7** by the artist Dong Kingman. Do you recognize the American city depicted in this work? What activity are these people taking part in? What words would you use to describe the mood of this painting?

Look more closely, this time at the medium. What kind of paint did the artist use to create this work? What is unusual about this use of white paper?

What You Will Learn

You will make a watercolor painting in the style of Dong Kingman by selecting and using a variety of appropriate art materials and tools in traditional ways. Illustrate ideas from experiences at school and community events. Use bright colors to emphasize some part of the event in which people are having fun. Use lines and color to create a feeling of excitement. You will leave areas of your work unpainted.

What You Will Need

- Pencil and sheets of sketch paper
- Watercolor paints, paper towels
- Palette for mixing colors
- Container for water
- Thin and thick watercolor brushes
- Sheet of good quality white paper, pressed board, or watercolor paper, 12 × 18 inches

What You Will Do

1. Brainstorm with your classmates to develop ideas for your work. Choose a festive occasion that is important to you, your school, or your community. Think of the particular part of the festival that represents the excitement. Think of special colors tied to the occasion and how those colors add to the festive mood.

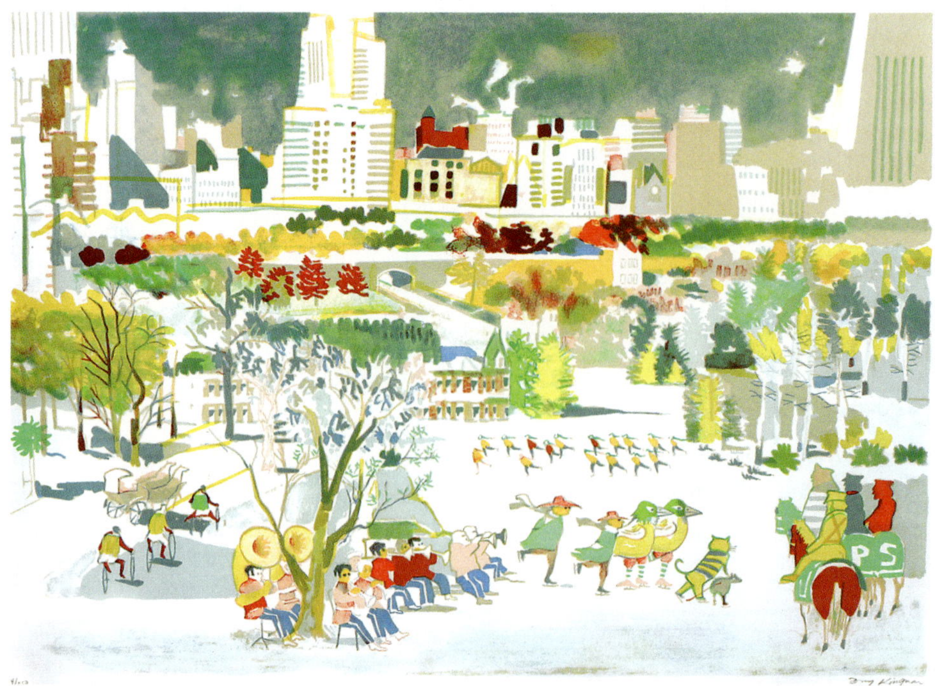

◆ **Figure 9–7** **What is the mood of this work? How does the medium help set the mood? How does the artist's attention to small details help?**

Dong Kingman. *Skaters in Central Park.* 1990. Watercolor. 71.1 × 91.4 cm (28 × 36″). Private collection.

2. Make pencil sketches to plan your work. Use line movements to create excitement. Choose your best idea.
3. Set up all your supplies before you begin. Watercolor is a quick-drying medium. Mix a light value of watercolor paint on your palette. (You create light values with watercolors by adding more water to the color you choose. This will allow more white from the paper to show through.) With the thin brush, draw your final sketch onto the sheet of good white paper. (See **Technique Tip 14,** *Handbook* page 286).

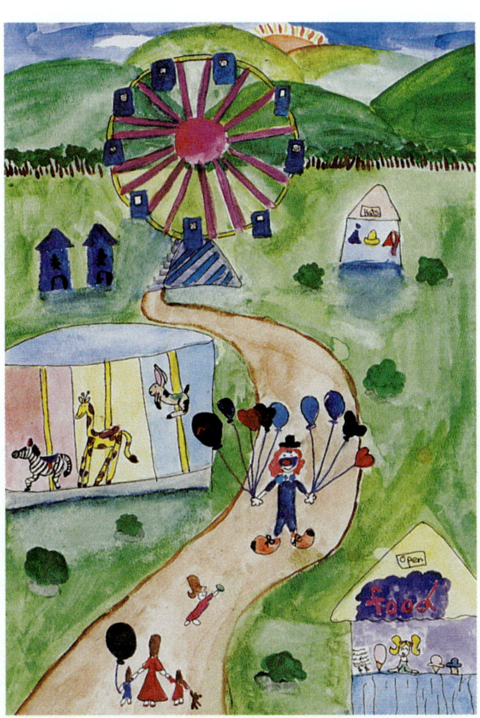

◆ **Figure 9–8** **Student work. A watercolor painting.**

Evaluating Your Work

- **Describe** Identify the experience at a school or community event you chose to paint. Tell what part of the event you focused on. Tell what colors and kinds of lines you used.
- **Analyze** Point to areas in which bright colors are used. Explain how you created contrast.
- **Interpret** Tell how a viewer might describe the mood of your painting. Explain how color and line are used to create this mood. Give your work a title based on its mood.
- **Judge** Tell whether you feel your work succeeds. What views of art would you use to defend your answer?

4. Decide which area of your work you will emphasize and paint this area with your brightest colors. Paint other areas in contrasting dull colors. Leave large areas of the white paper showing. Do not paint all your drawn objects. If you like, draw over some of your light lines using darker paint with a thin brush.
5. When your work is dry, display it. Discuss various ways classmates have achieved contrast and shown excitement using line and color.

COMPUTER OPTION

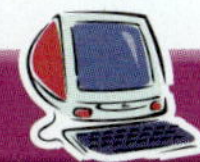

Select an activity or event to paint. Use the Pencil tool to produce an electronic media-generated artwork that interprets your subject. Experiment with a variety of tools, such as wet Brushes, transparent colors, and liquid effects. Choose smooth or rough paper, if available. Draw active lines to enhance the mood of the event. Apply bright colors directly by using a variety of Brushes. Leave some spaces white or off-white to make the painting lighter in value. Title, save, and print.

Visual Art Journal

Organize ideas from imagination. Illustrate ideas from imagination for an artwork that depicts an event. Imagine your favorite activities and people all at this fantasy event. Experiment with different types of paint media and colors to represent the event. Write down your thoughts in your visual art journal.

Nonobjective Painting

Look at the painting in **Figure 9–9**. The artist, Sonia Delaunay, believed color was the most important art element. With her artist-husband, Robert, she explored the expressive quality of color. Notice the rhythmic movement of the shapes along diagonal lines. Notice also the soft edges of the shapes.

What You Will Learn

You will produce a painting using a variety of art materials and tools in traditional ways. Your painting will show the repetition of geometric shapes. Like Delaunay's, yours will show rhythmic movement. You will use a color scheme based on primary or secondary colors.

What You Will Need

- Pencil, sketch paper, and ruler
- Round shapes of different sizes, such as jar lids, or precut cardboard patterns
- Paper towels
- Yellow chalk
- White paper, 12 × 18 inches
- Tempera paints, thin and thick brushes

What You Will Do

1. Using pencil and sketch paper, plan your work. Using the ruler, draw a diagonal line across the paper from top to bottom. With the ruler, make squares and/or rectangles so that their sides rest on the diagonal. Use the circle patterns to make

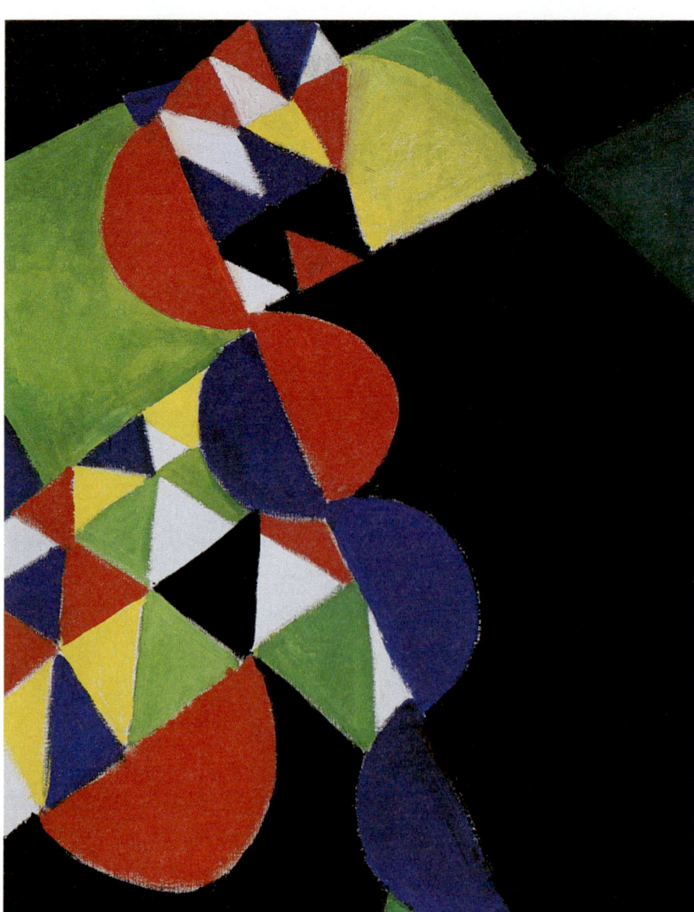

◆ **Figure 9–9** **Does your eye start at the top of this painting or at the bottom? Is the beat of the work a fast one or a slow one? Explain your answers.**

Sonia Delaunay. *Colored Rhythm No. 698*. 1958. Oil on canvas. 114.3 × 87 cm (45 × 34¼″). Albright-Knox Art Gallery, Buffalo, New York. Gift of Seymour H. Knox Jr., 1964.

a series of circular shapes in different sizes. These should meet and cross lines of the four-sided shapes. Repeating the different shapes will give a feeling of rhythm and movement to the design.

2. Using yellow chalk, draw your design on the sheet of white paper. Use the ruler and circle pattern. The edges of your shapes do not have to be perfect. Draw your design so that it touches at least three sides of the paper.
3. Choose a color scheme based on primary or secondary colors for the work. You may also use white. Repeat your colors in a way that adds to the sense of rhythmic movement.
4. Using a thin brush, paint the outline of each shape. Switch to a thick brush to fill in each shape with the same color you used for its outline. Since poster paints will run, be sure that one shape is dry before you paint a wet color next to it. (For more on using poster paints, see **Technique Tip 13,** *Handbook* page 286.)
5. When your work is dry, display it along with those made by other members of the class. Do any of the paintings look like yours? Are some completely different?

Evaluating Your Work

- **Describe** Identify the diagonal line that organizes the shapes in your work. Point out and name the different geometric shapes you used. Explain which color scheme you chose.
- **Analyze** Tell what colors and shapes you repeated to create rhythmic movement. Tell whether the "beat" of your work is steady or irregular. Show the path the viewer's eye follows through your work. Explain how you created contrast.
- **Interpret** Tell whether you feel your work succeeds. Explain your answer.

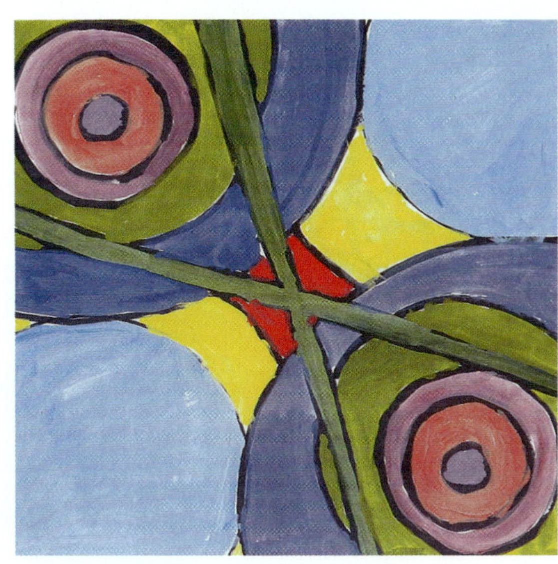

◆ **Figure 9–10** **Student work. A nonobjective painting.**

COMPUTER OPTION

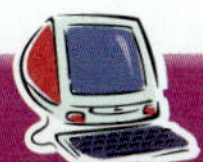

You will produce electronic media-generated art using a variety of tools in traditional ways. Choose the Straight Line tool and hold down the Shift key to draw two or three straight diagonal lines that intersect and touch the edges of the paper. Select geometric Shape tools and create a pattern by repeating the shapes using the Copy and Paste tools. Use the Transformation menu to Flip or Rotate the shapes. Title and save. Use the Flood-fill tool to add primary and secondary colors to all open spaces. Retitle, save, and print.

Visual Art Journal

Identify avocational choices. You've seen examples of work by artists who use a variety of media. Now, survey and identify avocational, or recreational, choices or opportunities in the art of painting. Would you choose to paint a mural in your room? Refer to page 5 in Chapter 1 to review avocational choices in art. Write down your thoughts in your journal.

LESSON 4

Expressive Painting

Sometimes artists use their works to speak about issues and social problems of the day. Look at the painting in **Figure 9–11** called *Differing Views*. It was done in the early 1980s by a contemporary artist. Study the two people in the painting. What do their expressions and their position within the room tell you about what might just have happened in this scene? What do you think will happen next in the scene?

What statement about human relationships might the artist be making in this work? Which elements and principles has he chosen to punctuate his statement?

What You Will Learn

You will learn to use social issues to influence a work of art. Select a social, political, or international issue that faces the world today. You will paint a close-up view of people to illustrate this issue. Colors and heavy lines will be used to emphasize the mood of your work. Distorting the proportions of shapes will also add to this mood. Free-flowing, loose brushstrokes will be used to show movement and add texture.

What You Will Need

- Pencil and sheets of sketch paper
- School acrylic paints
- Shallow tray with sides to mix paints
- Water (as a solvent)
- Bristle brushes, varied sizes
- Sheet of heavy white paper, 12 × 18 inches
- Water (to clean brushes) and paper towels

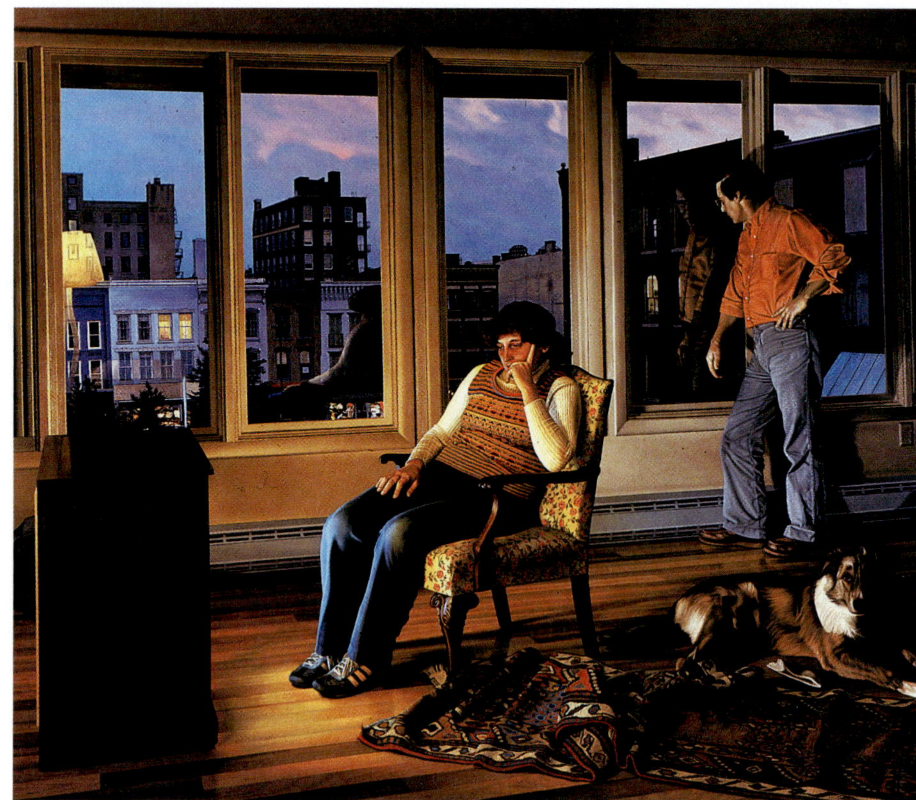

◆ **Figure 9–11** **Would you describe the mood of this painting as happy or lonely? How does the artist help you feel that mood? How does the medium help?**

James Robert Valerio. *Differing Views.* 1980–81. Oil on canvas. 234.3 × 261 cm (92¼ × 103¾″). Courtesy of George Adams Gallery, New York, New York.

What You Will Do

1. Brainstorm with your classmates, and list social, political, or international issues of the day. Some possibilities include pollution, drug abuse, the homeless, and war. Choose an issue you know about and that truly concerns you.
2. Think about a way you can create a painting that will make people think about the problem.
3. Make several pencil sketches for your composition. Use distortion and exaggeration to make your message strong. Do not put any words in balloons for your people to speak. The visual image must carry the message. Select the best sketch.
4. Decide on a color scheme. Think about what colors will help express your feelings. How can you use contrast?
5. Pour a little of a light-value paint into the shallow tray. Add enough solvent to make a thin paint. Using your ¼-inch brush, transfer the main shapes of your work onto the sheet of white paper.
6. Paint your composition. Using your 1-inch brush, add deeper hues to the shapes. Do not try to smooth over the brushstrokes. Let them show movement and create different textures. Use strong colors to emphasize your shapes.
7. Put your work on display. Can you and your classmates read the themes in each others' statements?

Evaluating Your Work

- **Describe** Identify the person or persons in your work. Tell what social, political, or international issue you chose to influence your work.
- **Analyze** Show where free-flowing, loose brushstrokes are used to create movement. How do heavy lines and brushstrokes add to the exaggeration and contrast?
- **Interpret** Tell what mood your painting expresses. Explain how the colors and distortion help express this mood. Give your work a title that sums up its meaning.
- **Judge** Tell whether you feel your work succeeds in making a social statement.

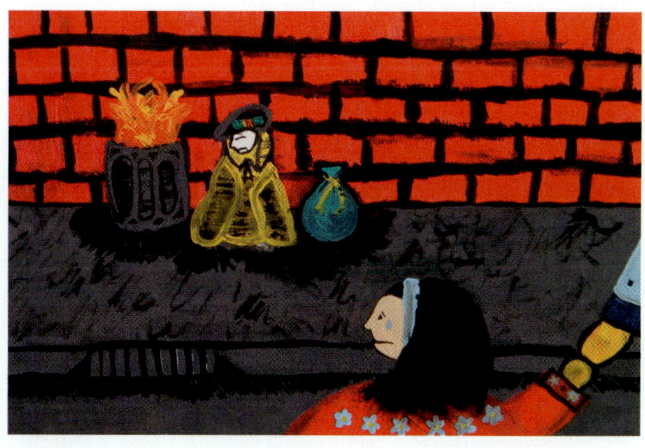

◆ **Figure 9–12** **Student work. An expressive painting.**

Reflective Thinking

Critical Response Analyze and compare relationships in the original artworks of your peers. Study the mood paintings they created and form conclusions about cultural contexts and their meanings. For example, does the artwork reveal anything about the artist's culture?

Visual Art Journal

Analyze your expressive painting and those of your classmates. How do social, political, or international issues influence artworks? Write your analysis in your visual art journal.

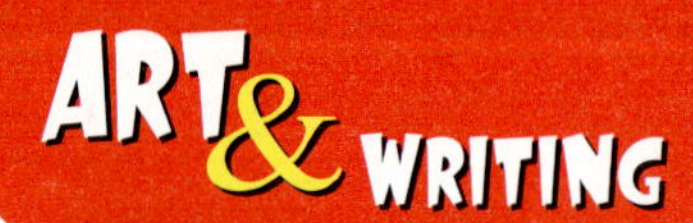

Dreams in Art and Life

Have you ever gazed up at clouds and seen objects in their shapes? That's what the two teens are doing in the painting shown in **Figure 9–13**. This warm painting, by artist Carmen Lomas Garza, recalls a fond memory from the artist's own childhood. One of the two figures shown is Garza herself at age 15. The other is her sister. They sit on the roof of their home, gazing at the evening sky. They are dreaming of the future and what it might hold in store. For Garza, the dream was to become an artist. Clearly, that dream has come true.

A Personal Reflection

Another individual whose dream came true is Olympic wrestler Rulon Gardner. In 2000, Gardner realized his dream—representing the United States in the Olympic Games. Rulon did more than just participate in the games. He won a Gold Medal in Greco-Roman wrestling.

The excerpt on page 179 is from an open letter Rulon has since written. It is addressed to high school students everywhere. Read the passage carefully. It contains some good advice you may want to follow.

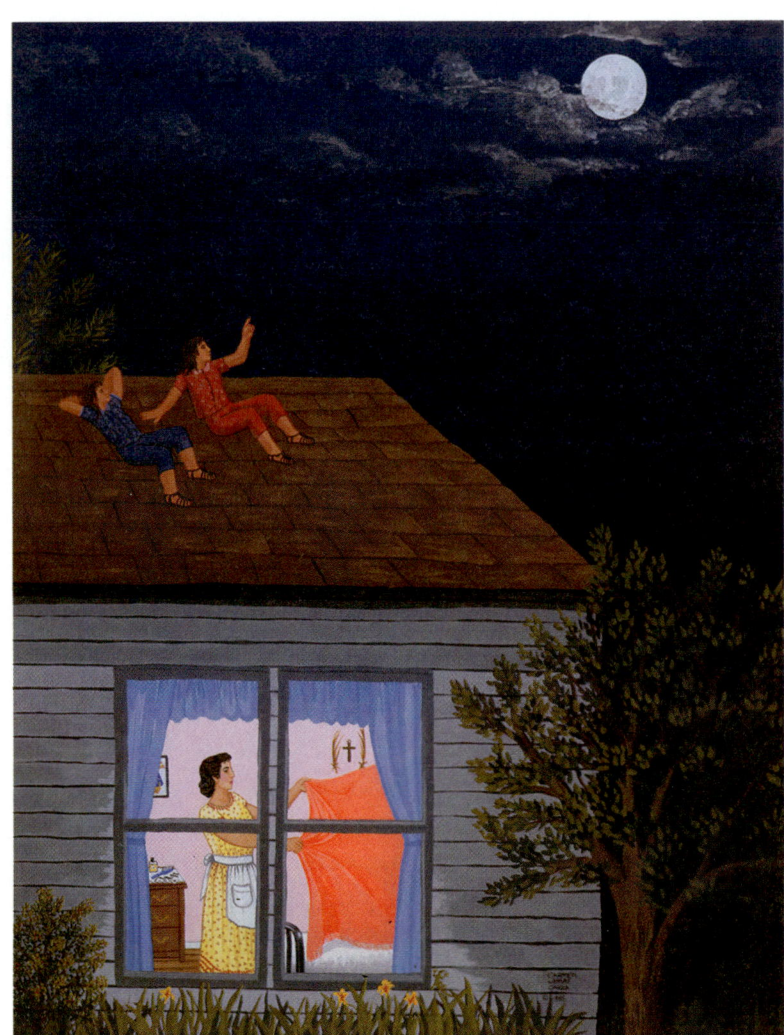

◆ **Figure 9–13** **How would you describe this scene? What do you suppose was the artist's reason for painting it?**

Carmen Lomas Garza. *Cama para Sueños (Bed for Dreams)*. 1985. Gouache. 71.8 × 52.1 cm (28¼ × 20½″). Museum of American Art, Smithsonian Institution, Washington, D.C.

Winning the Gold Medal was the culmination of many, many years of hard work and overcoming many, many challenges. What a thrill it was for me to be elected by teammates to carry the U.S. flag for the closing ceremonies.

For many years I have struggled with a learning disability, but with hard work, family support, and determination, I have been able to succeed despite my disability. Although I am very proud of my Olympic Gold Medal and my World Championship Belt, I have more satisfaction when I look at my diploma from the University of Nebraska.

I worked hard and utilized my resources to complete a very tough degree in physical education. I hope each of you will know all things are possible if you believe in yourselves and surround yourselves with good people. Remember that your families, teachers, and all of your support systems are on your team.

◆ **Figure 9–14** Excerpt from letter by Rulon Gardner.

MAKE THE CONNECTION

Take Another Look

1. Identify cultural ideas expressed in Figure 9–13 relating to social themes. For example, what clues does the painting provide about the artist's culture?
2. In Rulon Gardner's letter, he mentions members of "support systems . . . on your team." Make a list of people in your own life that fit this description. Tell what type of support each gives you.
3. Rulon overcame a disability. In a way, everyone has an obstacle of one sort or another to overcome. Examples include poor study habits and getting along with a brother or sister. Think of a personal obstacle in your life. Then develop a "recipe" for overcoming that problem.

ART & WRITING

Write a personal reflection. The inspirational letter by Rulon Gardner is an example of a *personal reflection.* This is a writing passage in which the writer takes inventory of his or her own life. Write your own personal reflection. In it, state your dreams for the future. Tell what steps you plan to take in order to make them come true.

PAINTING ON THE FLOOR

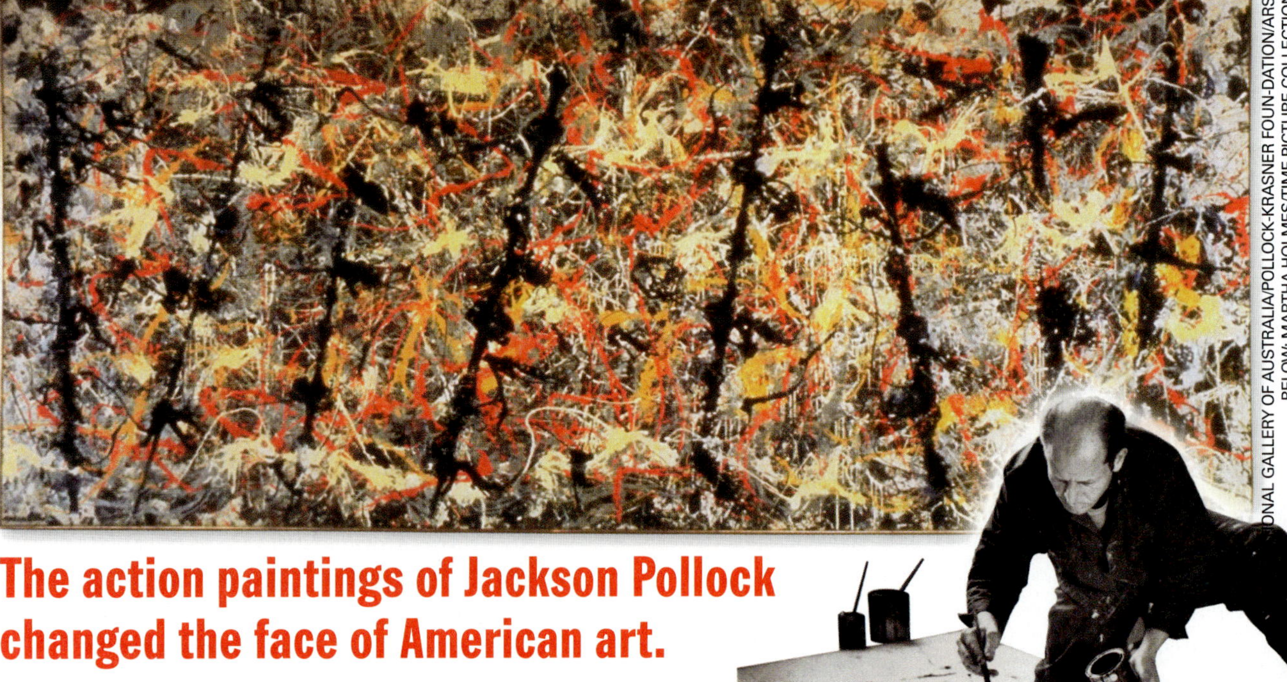

The action paintings of Jackson Pollock changed the face of American art.

Jackson Pollock (1912–1956) helped turn the art world on its head in the late 1940s and early 1950s. Pollock did something few other artists did. To paint, he put his canvas on the floor. Pollock discovered it was easier to control his signature drips, splatters, and splashes as he stood above the painting. Pollock didn't just stand there as he painted, however. He moved around the edge of the canvas, pouring, overlaying, and bleeding colors on the surface.

TOP: Jackson Pollock. *Blue Poles: Number 11.* 1952.

ABOVE: Pollock sometimes used wide brushes or poured paint right from the can, controlling the flow with a flip of his wrist.

Pollock belonged to a group called the Abstract Expressionists. As the name suggests, Pollock wanted his art to express feelings rather than illustrate them. As your eye follows his interweaving lines, you can almost feel the energy Pollock applied when laying down his sinuous, mesmerizing colors.

Pollock's canvases are visual records of his physical actions that remain as alive today as when he made them decades ago.

TIME TO CONNECT

- **Read the article and create a two-column chart. One column will lists fact about Pollock; the other will list your opinions about him.**
- **Research more information about Pollock using art books, your school media resource center, or the Internet. Add new facts and opinions to the appropriate column in your chart.**
- **Review the information and determine which facts and opinions support your own reactions to Pollock's artwork.**

Chapter 9 Review

BUILDING VOCABULARY

Number a sheet of paper from 1 to 13. After each number, write the term from the list that best matches each description below.

acrylic	opaque
encaustic	palette
fresco	synthetic paints
glaze	tempera
gouache	transparent
impasto	watercolor
oil paint	

1. A medium in which pigment is mixed into melted wax.
2. A medium in which pigment is applied to a wall spread with wet plaster.
3. A medium in which pigment mixed with egg yolk and water is applied with tiny brushstrokes.
4. Paint with an oil base.
5. An opaque water-based paint.
6. Thick, buttery layers of paint.
7. Clear.
8. A thin, transparent layer of paint.
9. A painting medium in which pigment is blended with gum arabic and water.
10. Manufactured paints with plastic binders.
11. Quick-drying water-based synthetic paint.
12. Does not let light pass through.
13. Any tray or plate on which paints are mixed before use.

REVIEWING ART FACTS

Number a sheet of paper from 14 to 18. Answer each question in a complete sentence.

14. What are the three ingredients of paint? What is the purpose of each ingredient?
15. What is the solvent in encaustic? In fresco?
16. Why is tempera paint hard to use? What is an advantage of using it?
17. What fact about oil paint allows an artist to blend colors on the canvas?
18. Name two different techniques for applying oil paint. Tell what result you get with each technique.

CROSS-CURRICULUM CONNECTIONS

19. **Language Arts.** Look again at Figure 9–7 on page 172. Think about what words you would use to describe the experience these skaters are having. Write a short descriptive paragraph that captures that feeling.
20. **Science.** Stare at a bright shape for a minute and then look away. What do you see? It's called an *afterimage,* and it has the same shape and size as the image you stared at but is a different color. Read about this illusion, or ask your science teacher to help you find information, then share what you learn with the class.

Web Museum Activity

The Museum of Fine Arts, Houston, Texas

As you have learned, different paint media produce different visual results. Click on **art.glencoe.com** to view paintings at this museum's online collection. Analyze the online exhibition to form conclusions about formal properties, historical and cultural contexts, intents, and meanings. For example, notice how each artist uses the art elements and principles. What can you determine about historical and cultural contexts in these artworks? Are the meanings of the artworks obvious? Can you interpret the artists' intents?

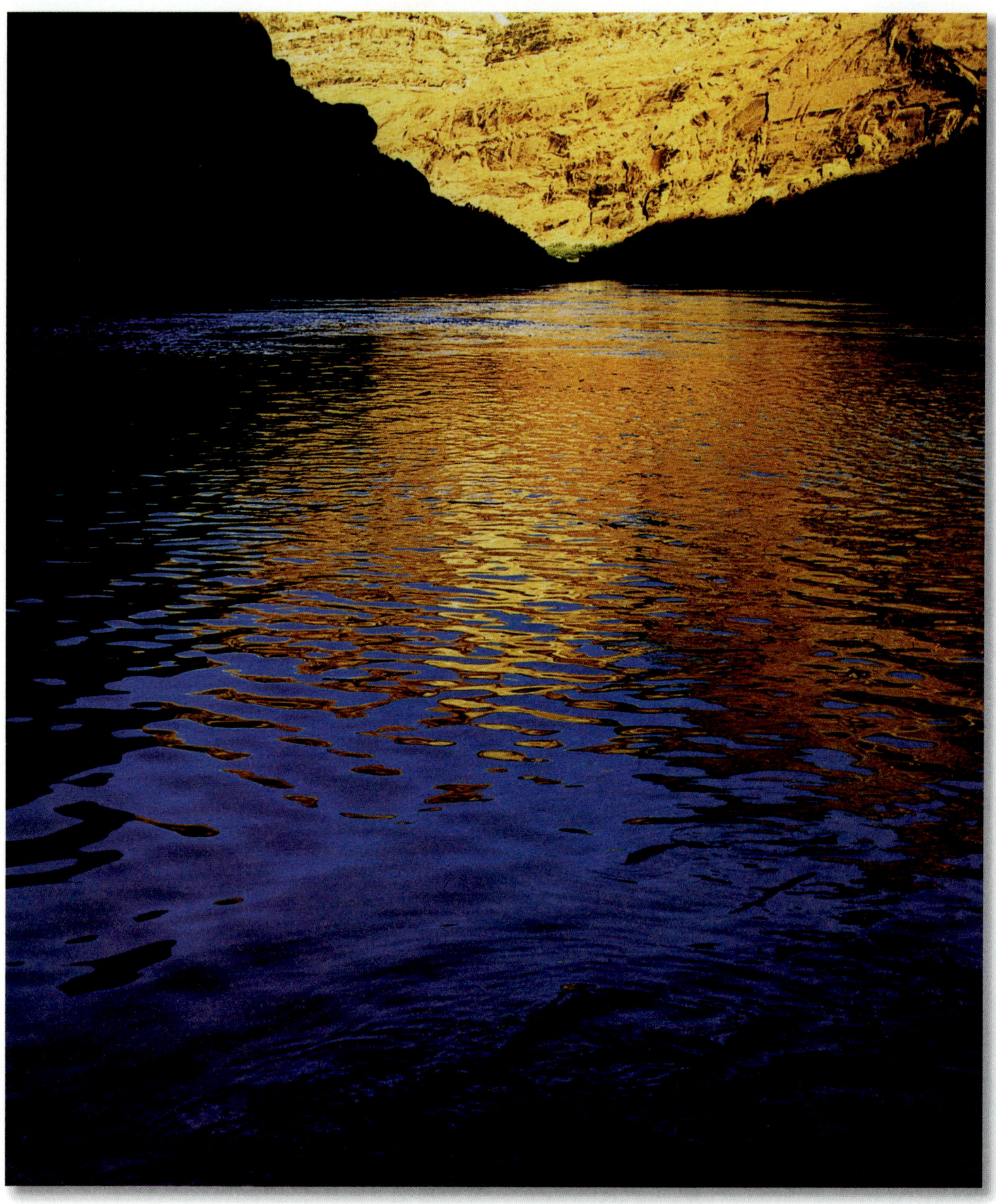

Focus On ◆ **Figure 10–1 To capture the complex look of Glen Canyon, Porter altered his style. He emphasized the art element of color to express his feelings about the canyon.**

Eliot Porter. *Sunrise on River: Navajo Creek, Glen Canyon, Utah, August 25, 1961.* 1961. Dye transfer print. 26 × 21.6 cm (10¼ × 8½″). Amon Carter Museum, Fort Worth, Texas. Bequest of the artist.

Chapter 10

Photography

"*My aim is increasingly to make my photographs look so much like photographs that unless one has eyes and sees, they won't be seen.*"

—Alfred Stieglitz, (1864–1946)

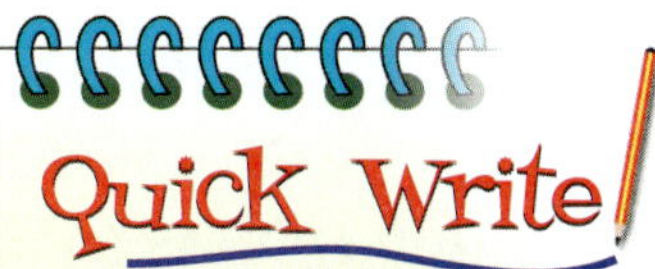

Interpreting the Quote Read the quote. The statement was made by a pioneer in the art of photography. What do you think Stieglitz meant by the second use of the verb *see* in this sentence? Paraphrase the quote in your own words.

The goal of some artists, as you have seen, is to create lifelike pictures. In the early 1800s, a device was perfected that made that goal easier than ever to achieve. The artwork in **Figure 10–1** was created using this new "medium." The work is, of course, a photograph.

In this chapter you will learn about the history and art of photography. You will also meet several artists who brought this art form to previously unimagined heights. You will discover that not all of them have shared the artistic goal of imitating life.

After completing this chapter, you will be able to:

- Define *photography*.
- Design and create a photogram and a photo essay.
- Experiment with photographic imagery and the process of hand-coloring photographs.
- Analyze ways that international, historical, and political issues influenced photography.

KEY TERMS

photography
camera
digital camera
daguerreotype
photogenic drawing
negative
photojournalism
translucent
photogram

LESSON 1

The Art of Photography

Today, we take for granted knowing what people in the news look like. That has not always been the case. Two centuries ago, people had no easy access to images of newsmakers or even celebrities. Such images are available to us today thanks to *photography*.

What Is Photography?

Photography is *the art of making images using light and other principles of science*. The word *photography*, which is Greek, means "drawing with light." The chief tool used in the art of *photography* is the **camera**. This is *a dark box with a hole controlling how much light enters*. Up until the late twentieth century, all modern cameras used film to record images. The arrival of the **digital camera** in the 1980s revolutionized picture taking. A digital camera *contains a tiny scanner, which converts visual information into computer-coded form*. Film is not needed. The image may be transferred to a computer and edited using computer software.

The Origins of Photography

Like every invention, photography was a collaborative effort, involving many individuals. The idea of capturing an image using light dates to the ancient Phoenicians. During the 1500s, the first device capable of achieving this effect was invented. That device was the *camera obscura*, a forerunner of the modern camera. This was a simple box with a pinhole on one side. On the opposite side was a glass screen. Light coming through the pinhole projected an image onto the glass screen. (See **Figure 10–2**.)

By 1800, scientists had refined the idea behind the camera obscura. These refinements led to two almost simultaneous breakthroughs.

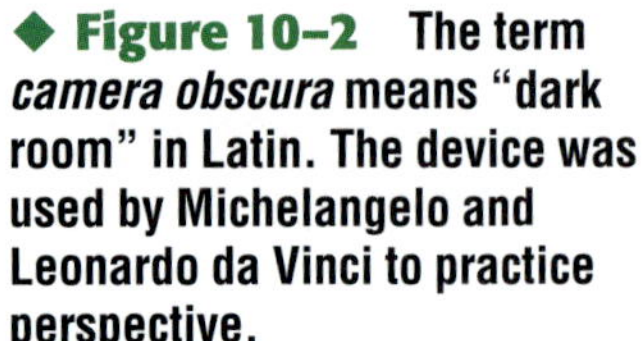

◆ **Figure 10–2** The term *camera obscura* means "dark room" in Latin. The device was used by Michelangelo and Leonardo da Vinci to practice perspective.

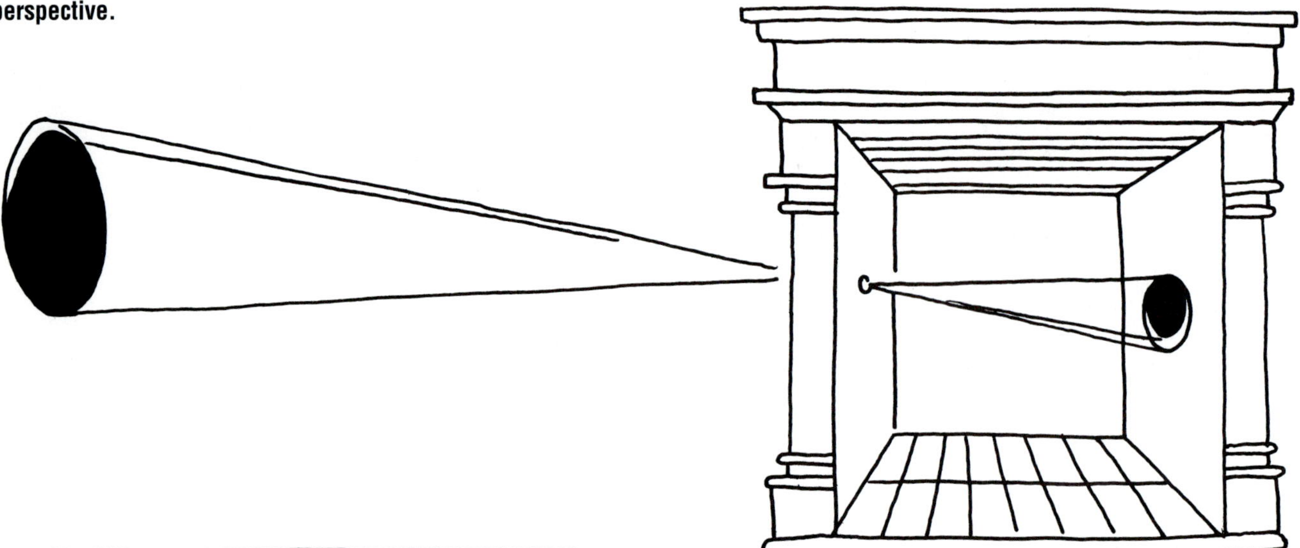

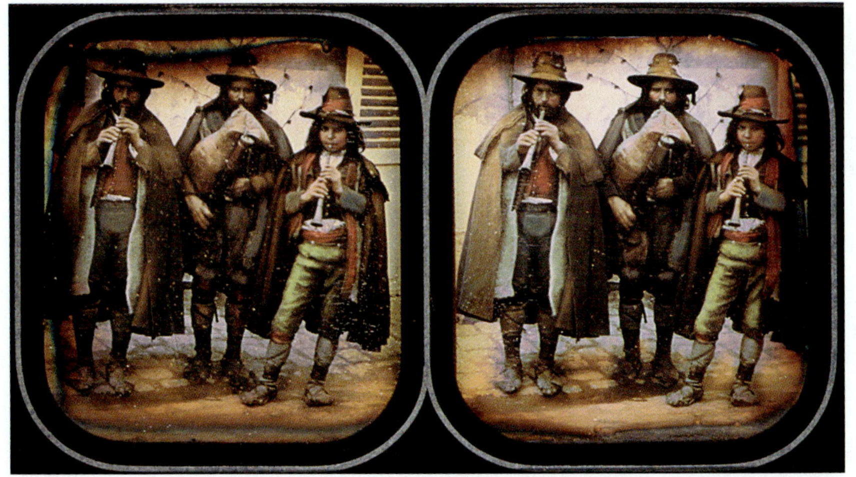

◆ **Figure 10–3** **Early photographs were hand-colored and viewed together in a stereopticon.**

Unknown/French. *Street Flutists*. c. 1852. Stereograph daguerreotype. 8.7 × 16.8 cm (3⅜ × 6⅝″). International Museum of Photography, George Eastman House, New York, New York.

One was by French theatrical designer Louis-Jacques Mandé Daguerre (loo-**we**-zhahk-mon-**day** duh-**gehr**), and his partner, Joseph Niépce (zhoh-**zef** nee-**ehp**-seh), a scientist. Their invention, the **daguerreotype** (duh-**gehr**-uh-typ), was *an image made on copper plates coated with highly polished silver*. **Figure 10–3** shows a daguerreotype. Notice how grainy the subjects appear.

The other breakthrough was made by English scientist William Henry Fox Talbot. His contribution, the *calotype*, was the result of a process he termed **photogenic drawing**. This was *the process of coating a sheet of drawing paper with silver chloride*. The paper was then placed inside a camera obscura. The main difference between the calotype and daguerreotype was that Talbot's process

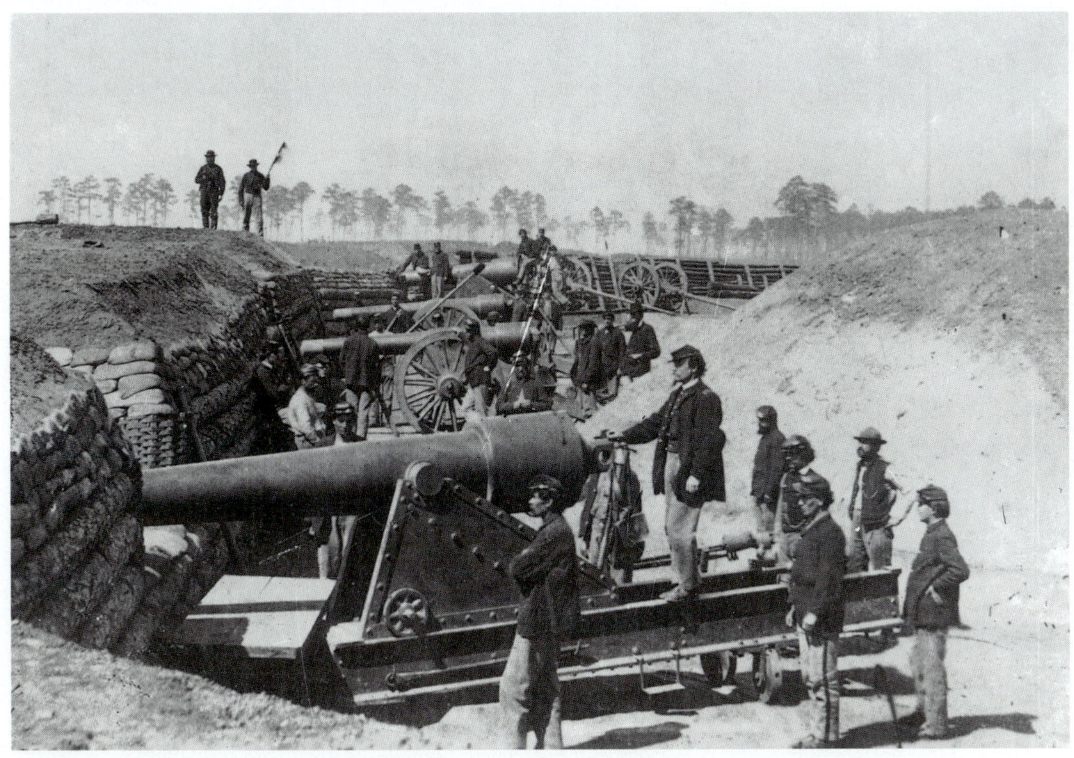

◆ **Figure 10–4** **Brady was one of the earliest photojournalists. He captured the reality of war with his camera to show people at home how horrible it really was. Up until the discovery of the camera, people had only seen glorified paintings of war.**

Mathew Brady. *Civil War*. c. 1865. Photograph. National Archives, Washington, D.C.

produced a **negative**. This is a *reverse image of the object photographed*. Film negatives are used to this day in photo processing.

Commercial Photography

By the mid-1800s, photography had come a long way. It was becoming increasingly common for newspapers to include photographs in their stories. The new field of **photojournalism** had been born. Photojournalism *is reporting a news event mainly or totally through photographic images*.

One of the first photojournalists is the man whose work appears in **Figure 10–4**. His name was Mathew Brady. This photo is one of many Brady took during the Civil War. **Figure 10–5** is a work by another pioneering photojournalist, Dorothea Lange. Lange worked during the era of the Great Depression. This was the period following the stock market crash of 1929. Many Americans lost their jobs; some were forced from their homes. Look closely at this photo. It shows a gaunt prairie woman in a dress made of burlap sacks. Words alone can't capture the sense of loss or uncertainty conveyed by this image.

Photography as Art

Not all early photographers were content merely to record events with their cameras. Some chose to photograph whatever captured their interest, to explore photography's potential as art. They took the time and care to compose their pictures, much like painters.

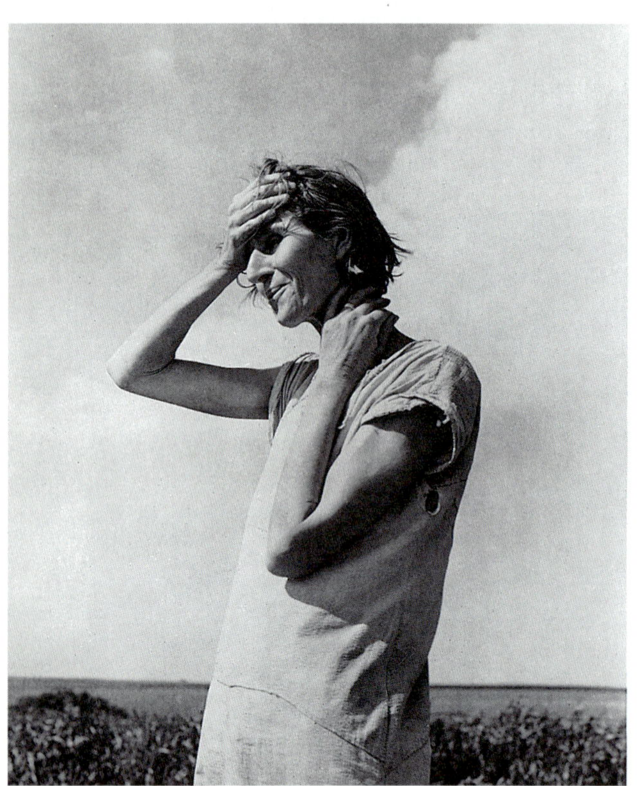

◆ **Figure 10–5** **This poignant photo was taken by Dorothea Lange, a photojournalist of the 1930s. What could pictures like these add to a news account that words alone could not?**

Dorothea Lange. *Woman of the High Plains, Texas Panhandle*. 1938. Photograph. The Dorothea Lange Collection, Oakland Museum of California, Oakland, California. Gift of Paul S. Taylor.

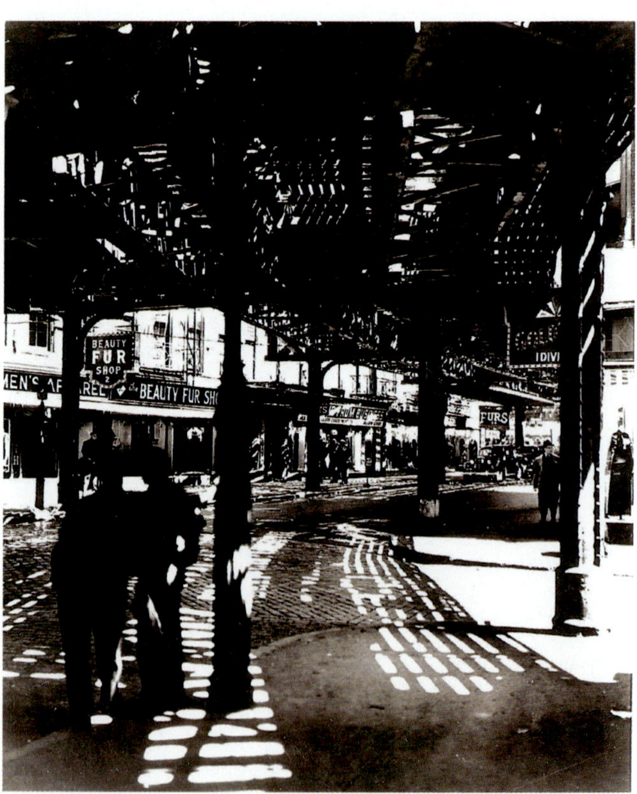

◆ **Figure 10–6** **This image was part of a series of photographs that Abbott called "Changing New York." The project was carried out between 1935 and 1939. The city she loved was changing, so she captured images of New York before they were replaced by more modern scenes.**

Berenice Abbott. *"El" Second and Third Avenue Lines; Bowery and Division Street, Manhattan* (from the series "Changing New York"). 1936. Gelatin-silver print. 24.4 × 19.9 cm ($9\frac{5}{8} \times 7\frac{13}{16}$"). The National Museum of American Art, Smithsonian Institution, Washington, D.C. © Berenice Abbott. Art Resource, NY.

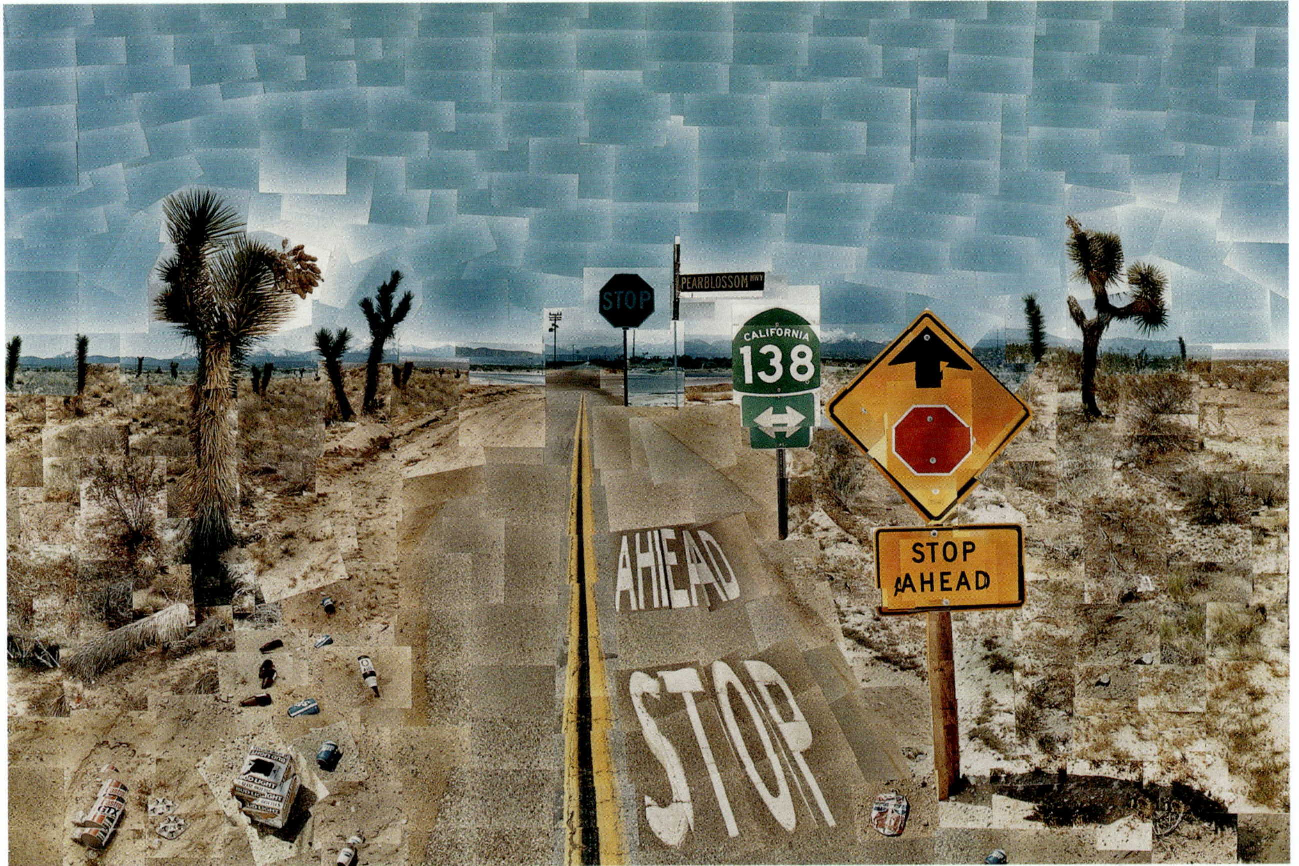

◆ **Figure 10–7** **Compare and contrast the use of art principles in this artwork. How is rhythm created by the individual photographs in this collage?**

David Hockney. *Pearblossom Hwy., 11–18th April 1986*, #2. April 11–18, 1986. Photographic collage of chromogenic prints. 198 × 282cm (78 × 111″).The J. Paul Getty Museum, Los Angeles, California.© 1996 David Hockney.

Two of the most important early photo artists were contemporaries of Dorothea Lange. Both were based in New York City, which served as a backdrop for their work. Their names were Berenice Abbott and Alfred Stieglitz. **Figure 10–6** shows one of Abbott's many shots of New York. The work depicts a store-lined street in the shadows of an elevated train trestle. Notice the pattern of contrasting light and dark shapes created by the sun filtering through the wooden slats.

In the twentieth century, artists broadened the horizons of photography as art. Look at the work in **Figure 10–7** by British artist David Hockney. Notice that this is not a single photograph. Rather, it is a photo collage made up of many shots taken during a trip along California's Pearblossom Highway. Hockney reassembled the photos to create a new art form. The work almost resembles a Cubist painting. What comment do you think the artist was trying to make by including images of litter in this artwork? What mood or feeling does this artwork convey?

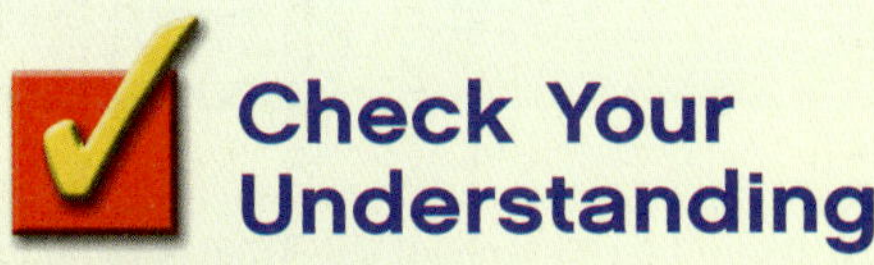

Check Your Understanding

1. Define *photography*.
2. Define *camera*.
3. When were the first real photographs made?
4. What were two methods of making photographs in the 1800s?

Photograms

The artwork shown in **Figure 10–8** is an example of a cyanotype (sy-**an**-oh-typ). This is a photographic process using images in tints and tones of blues. Notice how the plant image is white, and the negative space surrounding it is blue. Note also how the rounded leaf at the top appears almost to be "see-through." The leaf is **translucent**. This means *light is able to pass through*.

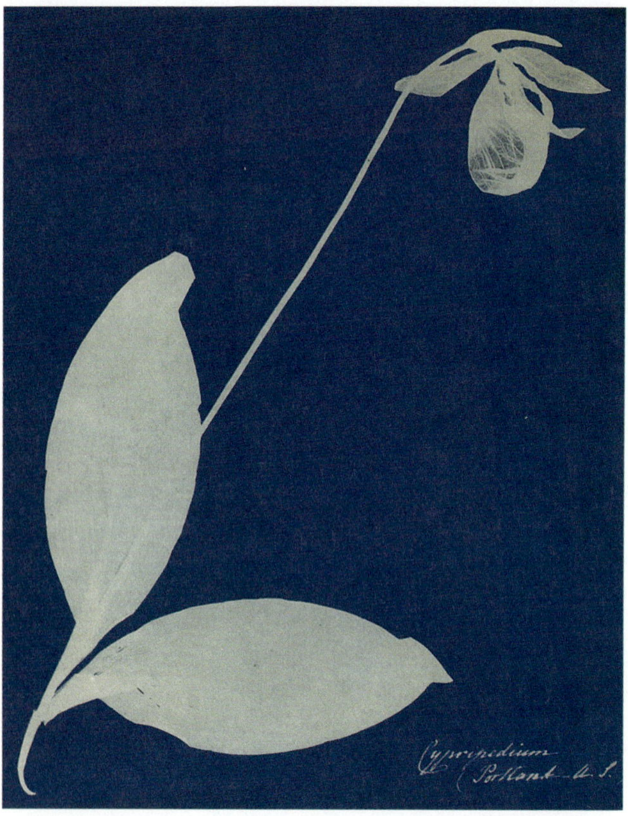

◆ **Figure 10–8** **The artists made a cyanotype to create this image for a scientific reference book. They established photography as an accurate medium for scientific illustration.**

Anna Atkins and Anne Dixon. *Pink Lady's Slipper (Cypripedium), collected in Portland*. 1854. Cyanotype. 25.8 × 20.2 cm (10¼ × 8″). The J. Paul Getty Museum, Los Angeles, California.

What You Will Learn

In this lesson you will select appropriate art materials and tools to interpret subjects in nature when producing photographic imagery in experimental ways. You will make a variant of a cyanotype called a **photogram**. This is *an image made using precoated paper that detects the presence of ultraviolet light*. You will use either natural or manufactured objects to create your print. You will use the principle of variety to arrange the art elements of line and shape. Positive and negative space will be equally important in your composition. You will use either formal or informal balance.

What You Will Need

- UV-sensitive paper (precoated paper)
- Various collected objects
- Cardboard slightly larger than paper
- White paper the size of the UV-sensitive paper
- Shallow pan with running water
- Acrylic sheet (optional)

What You Will Do

1. Begin by brainstorming a list of small objects that have interesting contours. Notice the negative space, or shapes formed around the objects. Collect as many objects as possible for your photographic imagery. Include at least one transparent and one translucent item in addition to opaque objects.
2. Place a sheet of white paper on a table. Arrange the objects in experimental ways. To create variety, arrange three to five of the items you collected on the paper. Think about the various lines and

shapes of the objects. Look at the positive and negative spaces in your arrangement. Decide on whether you will use formal or informal balance. Choose an arrangement you are pleased with, and begin your photogram.

3. Dim the lights and lower the blinds to keep your work space as dark as possible. Place your sun-sensitive paper on a piece of cardboard, blue side up. Rearrange your selected objects on the paper.
4. Place the grouping in direct sunlight until the paper turns almost white. This may take from 1 to 5 minutes, depending on the brightness of the day. Try not to overexpose the sun-sensitive paper.
5. Remove your objects. Rinse your paper in a shallow pan under slowly running water for 1 minute. Washing removes the unexposed soluble chemical. Handle the paper gently to avoid tearing it. Gently blot with a paper towel.
6. Carefully set out your photogram so that it dries flat. Where the sunlight shone on the paper, you will see blue. The areas where you placed the objects will appear white. Make several photograms and select one or two to mount and display.

Evaluating Your Work

- **Describe** How did you produce photographic imagery using a variety of art materials and tools?
- **Analyze** How does your photogram show variety? Explain how you used both negative and positive space in your composition. How did you arrange your objects in experimental ways?
- **Interpret** What mood or feeling is expressed in your photogram? Explain.
- **Judge** Do you feel your photogram is successful? Using one or more of the aesthetic theories explained in Chapter 5, defend your decision.

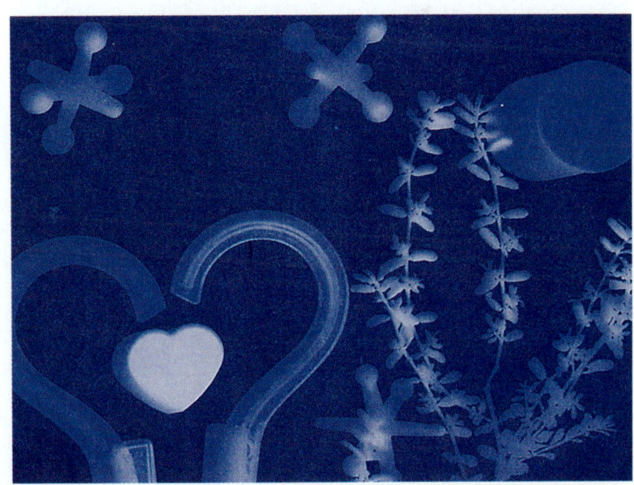

◆ **Figure 10–9** **Student work. Photogram.**

REFLECTIVE THINKING 

Critical Evaluation. Analyze the original artworks of your peers. Examine the photograms they created and form conclusions about formal properties and intent. For example, how did they organize the elements of art? Did their work convey what they intended?

Art Online

To view more photograms, check out the Student Art Gallery at **art.glencoe.com**. On our Web site you will also find:

- Artist Profiles
- Interactive Games
- Web Links

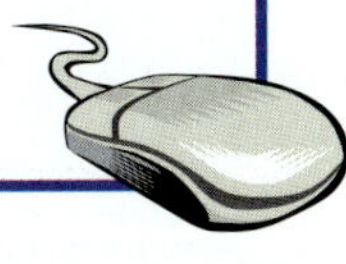

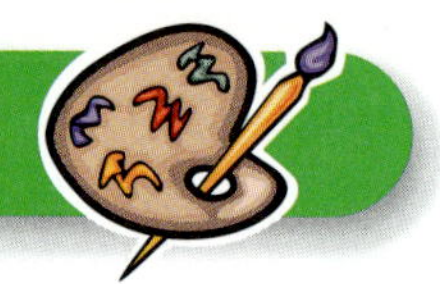

Photo Essay

Look closely at the six faces in **Figure 10–10**. What is unusual about these photographs? Describe the texture you see and the range of values used. Brazilian-born artist Vik Muniz created these images for his photographic series *Sugar Children*.

Muniz used the children of sugarcane workers as his models. He had met them while visiting the island of St. Kitts in the Caribbean. Each image was made by carefully sprinkling granulated sugar on black paper. Muniz then photographed each image, and wiped the black paper clean to begin his next "drawing."

Photo essays are used to tell a specific story. They often include more than one image so that the story can be told clearly.

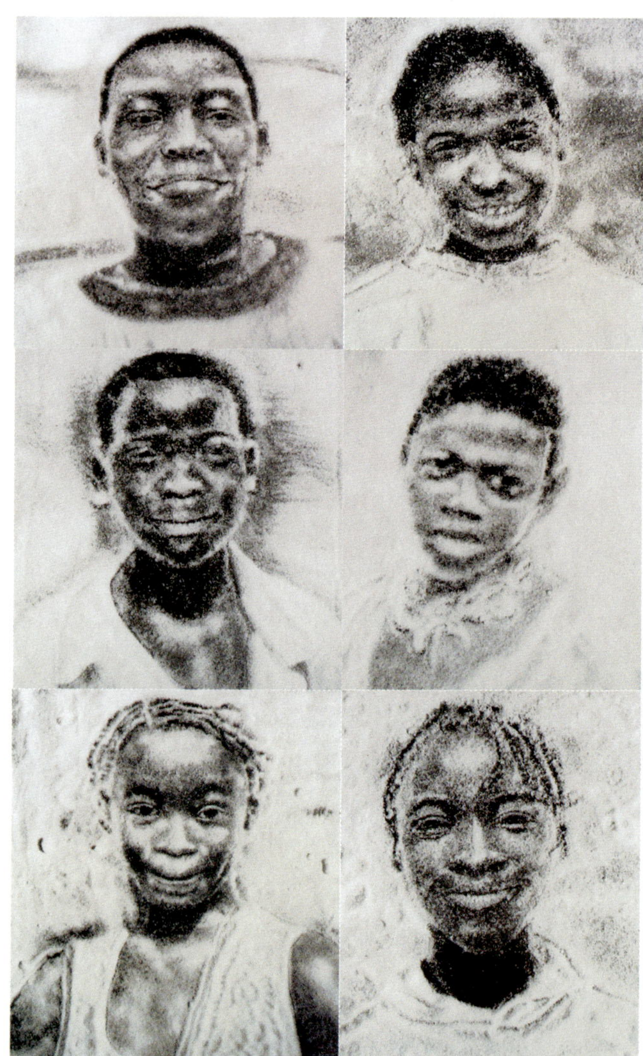

◆ **Figure 10–10 Analyze this artwork to form conclusions about intent and meaning. What story do you think the artist was trying to tell with these images?**

Vik Muniz. [Left column, top to bottom:] *Big James Sweats Buckets; Little Calist Can't Swim; Velentina, the Fastest* [Right column, top to bottom:] *Jacynthe Loves Orange Juice; Ten Ten's Weed Necklace; Valicia Bathes in Sunday Clothes*; from the series *Sugar Children*. 1996. Gelatin silver prints. Each 35.6 × 27.9 cm (14 × 11″). Museum of American Art, Smithsonian Institution, Washington, D.C. Museum purchase made possible by the Horace W. Goldsmith Foundation. © Vik Muniz/Licensed by VAGA, New York, NY. Photo credit: Smithsonian American Art Museum, Washington, D.C./Art Resource, NY. 1996.

What You Will Learn

You will select and use a variety of appropriate art materials and tools when producing a biographical photo essay using traditional methods. You will use no less than five photographs to tell a story about one person. Select either color or black-and-white film to tell your story. Give your essay variety and visual interest by how you arrange your photographs. You will use either formal or informal balance in your composition. Unify your photographs by cropping and arranging them on a single color background. Your photo essay will incorporate clues about historical and cultural contexts.

What You Will Need

- Sketchbook, pencil, and eraser
- Camera and a roll of 24- or 36-exposure color or black-and-white film
- Sheet of mat board (black or white)
- Scissors and white glue

What You Will Do

1. Ask a friend or relative to serve as the subject for your photo essay. Explain to that person that your photo essay will tell a story of some aspect of their life. Discuss with your subject what story you could tell about them, writing notes in your sketchbook. Discuss different poses and expressions he or she can make to convey meaning.
2. Have your model demonstrate different poses as you choose an angle from which to take each photograph. Decide if photographing from above or below eye level will add interest to the photo. Will you take photographs of items and environments without your model? This may provide clues about historical and cultural contexts.
3. Photograph your subject using the entire roll of film. Compose each photograph to capture the exact expressions, gestures, and poses needed to complete the story.
4. Lay out the developed photographs and select the best ones. Choose no less than five that tell a story about your subject.
5. Arrange your photographs on a sheet of black or white mat board. You may want to cut or crop your photographs. By overlapping, placement, and cropping, you can create variety and visual interest. Carefully glue the photographs in place.
6. Exhibit your photo essay along with those created by your classmates.

Evaluating Your Work

- **Describe** Did you include at least five photographs in your essay? Are there a variety of expressions and objects or places in your essay?
- **Analyze** How does your essay exhibit variety and visual interest? How do the photographs exhibit unity?
- **Interpret** Compare relationships, such as function and meaning, in your photo essay. How did you tell a story with your photo essay? What clues did you provide about historical and cultural contexts?
- **Judge** Do you feel your photo essay is successful?

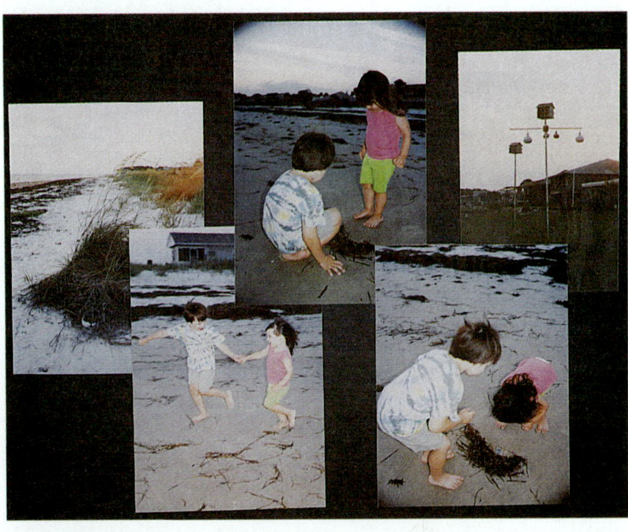

◆ **Figure 10–11** Student work. Photo essay.

Computer Option

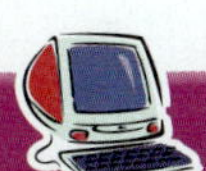

Produce photographic imagery and electronic media-generated art in traditional and experimental ways. Think of emotions you associate with color (for example, red/rage). Using either a conventional or digital camera, take a head shot of a friend, classmate, or relative. Ask your subject to show an emotion with a facial expression. Download or scan your image to the computer. Open the image into a paint or photo-editing program. Apply a tint to your subject's face that captures the emotion displayed.

Visual Art Journal

Historical and Cultural Heritage. Analyze the original photo essays of your peers to determine cultural contexts. What clues do their photo essays provide about the subject's cultural heritage? How might a photo essay convey your own cultural heritage? Write down your thoughts in your journal.

Hand-Colored Photography

The hand coloring of photographs began during the first half of the twentieth century. Its purpose was to make black-and-white photographs more interesting. Jessica Hines is a postmodern photographer who has turned to old techniques to create new and interesting works. Look at the photograph in **Figure 10–12**. Hines has used a variety of techniques to change the look of her hand-colored photograph. After shooting a roll of film, she chose one negative from which to create the initial print. Next, she altered the look of the print by exposing it to chemical toners. Finally she used semitransparent paints to add color to her work.

What You Will Learn

In this lesson you will select and use a variety of appropriate art materials and tools to interpret a subject when producing a hand-colored photograph. You will use color in experimental ways to create emphasis and value. Create a focal point by the use or absence of color.

What You Will Need

- Black-and-white matte finished photographs, watercolor paints
- Water-based color markers
- Colored pencils, eraser
- Cotton swabs and cotton balls
- Mixing tray, thin and medium brushes

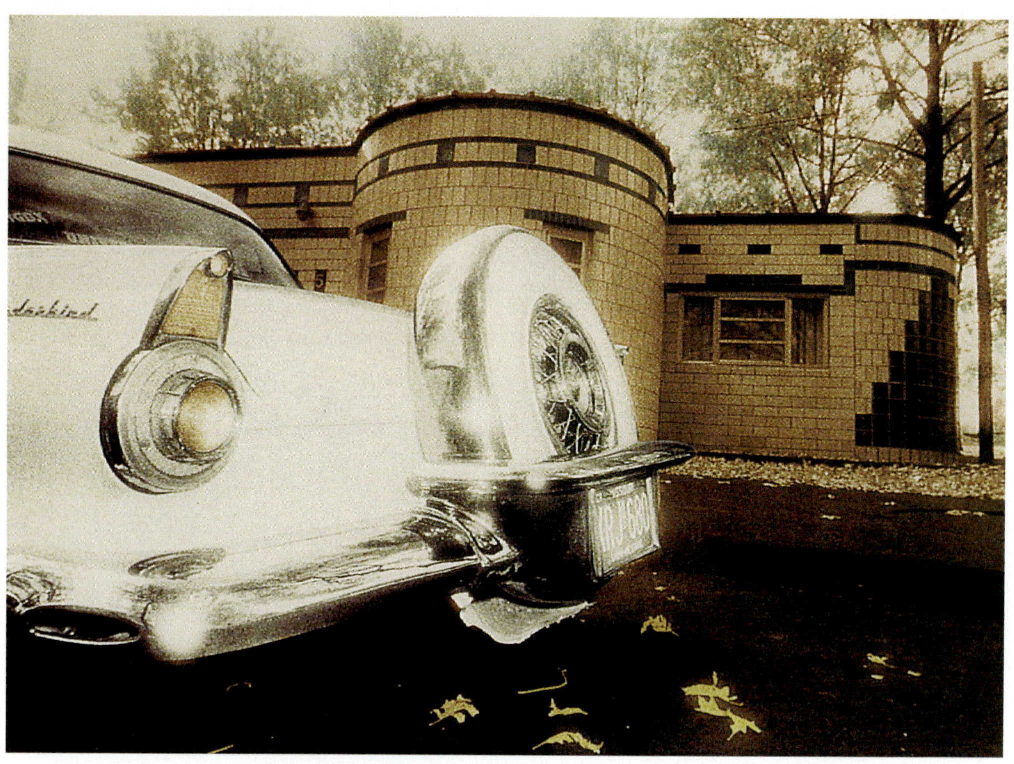

◆ **Figure 10–12 Photography and painting are combined in this artwork to create photographic imagery. How does this technique make the photograph more interesting?**

Jessica Hines. *Dream Series*. 1996. Hand-colored black-and-white photograph. 40.6 × 50.8 cm (16 × 20″). Private collection.

What You Will Do

1. Collect several black-and-white photographs that show a range of values.
2. Experiment with the color media you have selected to see how they will look when applied to the photograph. Practice applying light areas of watercolor to your photograph. Try overlapping and layering color. Colored pencils can also be layered and blended. Use a cotton ball or cotton swab to blend colors or keep the paint from running. Try creating texture by applying pressure when coloring with pencils. Use an eraser to remove unwanted lines. Try using water-based markers in one area of your photo. Notice how each material gives your photograph a different look.
3. Look closely at your hand-colored photograph. Which coloring technique did you like the best? Select an image for your final photograph. Decide which color media you will use. You may combine two coloring techniques.
4. Look closely at the composition and decide how you will use color to create a focal point, or area of emphasis.
5. Let the photograph dry if you used watercolor or markers. Mount or mat your photograph and display it with those of your classmates. How does hand-coloring affect the meaning of the photographs?

Evaluating Your Work

- **Describe** What is the subject matter of your photograph? Explain how you used a variety of art materials to color your photograph in experimental ways.
- **Analyze** Analyze relationships between the elements of art used in your photograph. How did you create a focal point in your photograph? How did you use color to emphasize that area?
- **Interpret** How did your hand-coloring technique affect the look and mood of your photograph? Explain.
- **Judge** Do you feel your final hand-colored photograph is successful? Explain why or why not.

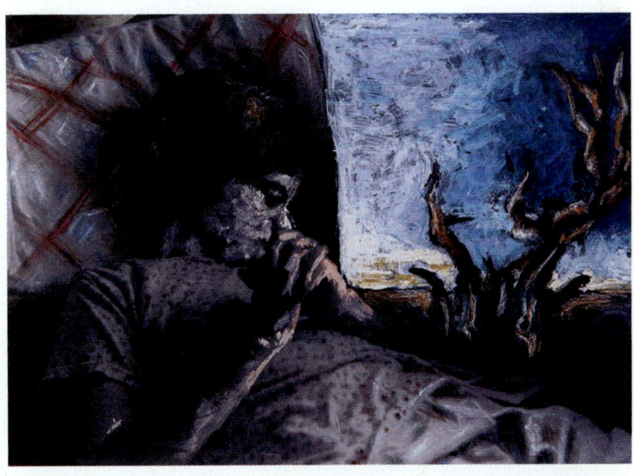

◆ **Figure 10–13** **Student work. Hand-colored photograph.**

STUDIO OPTION

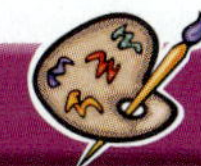

Produce photographic imagery using a variety of art materials and tools in traditional ways. Use traditional photography techniques to create a series of black-and-white photographs of a school or community event. Develop the film and choose your best print. Use the techniques learned in this lesson to hand-color your print.

Visual Art Journal

Identify Avocational Choices. You've seen examples of work by professional photographers. Now, identify avocational, or recreational, choices in the art of photography. Write down your thoughts in your visual art journal.

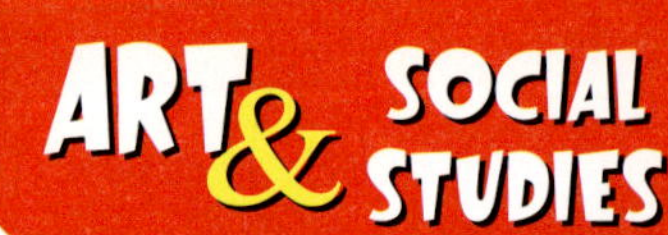

A Time Line of Photography and Film

Photography did not spring out of the mind of a single thinker. Rather, it has a long history and involves many contributors. Some of these contributions appear in the time line on this page and the next. So do key events in world history and culture. As you read through the time line in **Figure 10–14,** look for trends and relationships.

Events in Photography, Film and Broadcasting

◆ **Figure 10–14A** **Dorothea Lange's *Migrant Mother*. 1936.**

	1900	1910	1920	1930	1940	1950	1960
Events in Photography, Film and Broadcasting	**1900** First mass-marketed camera, the Brownie, cost $1	**1916** Charlie Chaplin's silent film *The Tramp* debuts	**1923** Kodak introduces 16mm movie film for amateur use **1927** Flashbulb invented **1928** Walt Disney's *Steamboat Willie,* first animated cartoon with spoken words	**1932** Ansel Adams founds Group f.64, dedicated to nature photography **1936** Dorothea Lange takes photograph titled *Migrant Mother* (Figure 10–14A)	**1940** Film debut of the *Grapes of Wrath*, adaptation of John Steinbeck's novel about Great Depression **1945** Alfred Eisenstaedt records "V-J Day," the end of the war **1948** First 35mm Nikon camera introduced	**1955** First all-color television series, *Howdy Doody,* begins.	**1964** Film *Mary Poppins* is released.
Events in World History and Culture		**1912** *Titanic* sinks **1914** World War I begins	**1920** Women in United States get right to vote **1929** Stock market crash causes Great Depression	**1931** Empire State Building opens. **1939** Hitler invades Poland, starting World War II	**1941** Japan attacks Pearl Harbor; United States enters WW II **1949** North Atlantic Treaty Organization (NATO) formed	**1957** Sputnik, the first satellite is launched.	**1969** Neil Armstrong is first person to walk on moon (Figure 10–14B)

Events in World History and Culture

◆ **Figure 10–14** Time Line.

Reprinted by permission of George Eastman House International Museum of Photography and Film. www.eastmanhouse.org.

1972 Pocket Instamatic Camera-110 introduced

1981 MTV begins broadcasting

1985 First digital camera marketed

1988 Robert Zemecki's *Who Framed Roger Rabbit?* combines cartoons with people

1993 Steven Spielberg's *Jurassic Park* uses computer-generated creatures.

1995 *Toy Story*, first full-length feature composed completely of computer animation.

1999 Bullet-time photography used in motion pictures

1970 1980 1990

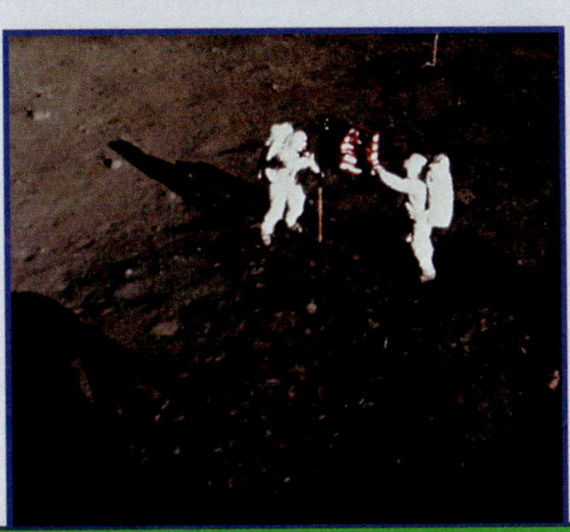

1989 Soviet bloc is dismantled, allowing film companies into eastern Europe for the first time

◆ **Figure 10–14B**
Neil Armstrong lands on moon. 1969.

MAKE THE CONNECTION

Take Another Look

1. What is the connection between the works of Charlie Chaplin (1916) and Steven Spielberg (1993)? Compare and contrast their contributions to the art of filmmaking.
2. How are the events of the following years related:
   a. 1929, 1936, and 1940?
   b. 1939, 1941, and 1945?
   c. 1928, 1988, and 1995?
3. Analyze ways that international, historical, and political issues influence artworks. For example, what historical event influenced the work of Dorothea Lange?

ART & SOCIAL STUDIES

Analyze an exhibition. Analyze a photography exhibition at a museum in your community, or visit one online. Analyze and compare relationships, such as function and meaning, in the photographs. Do the photographs function as a record of a place or event? Do they express a mood or have a symbolic meaning? Then form conclusions about historical and cultural contexts.

DOROTHEA LANGE

A photographer who had compassion and vision

Born in 1895, Dorothea Lange used her camera to alert Americans about the suffering of others. Lange was horrified by how ordinary Americans were struggling to survive the Great Depression in the 1930s. She photographed people waiting in endless lines for bread or searching for scarce jobs. Her photos also captured proud migrant workers who pitched their tents in fields or temporary camps hoping to find any kind of work. Lange's moving portraits became symbols of poverty and suffering during the 1930s.

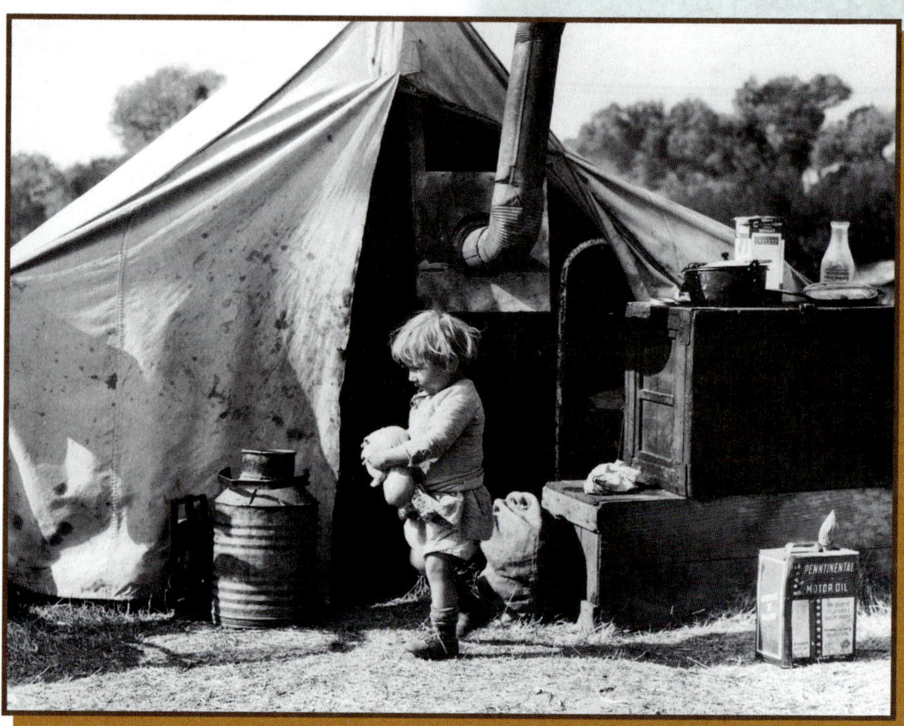

DOROTHEA LANGE/RESTTLEMENT ADMINISTRATION

This photo (1936) by Dorothea Lange shows the daughter of migrant farm workers outside the tent her family lived in. Photos like this documented a difficult time in the United States.

Lange desperately wanted her work to have an impact—and it did. Housing for the homeless was set up after a newspaper published her now-famous image *Migrant Mother*. The photo captured a widow with her children. The woman, who looked much older than her 32 years, kept her family alive on peas from farm fields and the wild birds her children could catch.

The power of Lange's work—and the people she portrayed—helped make Americans aware of the economic and physical challenges other people faced daily.

TIME TO CONNECT

- **Locate a picture of a person in a history book, newspaper, or magazine that moves you in some way.**
- **Identify what exactly in the photograph makes you feel this way.**
- **Write a short essay that describes the subject of the photograph and how you feel about that person. Make sure to use words that accurately convey your feelings and thoughts.**

Chapter 10 Review

BUILDING VOCABULARY

Number a sheet of paper from 1 to 9. After each number, write the term from the list that best matches each description below.

camera
daguerreotype
digital camera
negative
photogenic drawing
photogram
photography
photojournalism
translucent

1. A term that means light is able to pass through.
2. The art of making images using light and other principles of science.
3. Reverse image of the object photographed.
4. A device containing a tiny scanner, which converts visual information into computer-coded form.
5. An image made using precoated paper that detects the presence of ultraviolet light.
6. Reporting a news event mainly or totally through photographic images.
7. A dark box with a hole controlling how much light enters.
8. An image made on copper plates coated with highly polished silver.
9. The process of coating a sheet of drawing paper with silver chloride to produce a calotype.

REVIEWING ART FACTS

Number a sheet of paper from 10 to 13. Answer each question in a complete sentence.

10. Who is Louis-Jacques Mandé Daguerre? Compare his contribution to photography with that of William Henry Fox Talbot.
11. Who were the first important photojournalists? What subjects did they concentrate on?
12. Name and describe two pioneering photographers of the twentieth century. Tell what each contributed to photography as an art form.
13. What is a photo essay?

CROSS-CURRICULUM CONNECTIONS

14. **Social Studies.** Study the Brady photograph of the Civil War battlefield on page 185. Identify cultural ideas expressed in this artwork relating to environmental themes. For example, how does Brady document the destruction of war? What effect do you think war machinery had on the environment?
15. **Science.** Research the development of the Polaroid camera invented by Edwin Land. When did this camera come into existence? Analyze ways in which electronic media or technologies have influenced art. For example, how might the Polaroid camera have influenced professional photographers?

Web Museum Activity

Amon Carter Museum, Fort Worth, Texas

Learn about cowboy life through the lens of photographer Erwin E. Smith. View his work at the Amon Carter Museum by clicking on **art.glencoe.com**. Participate in the online lesson to learn more about cowboy culture. Learn more about Texas culture and history, too!

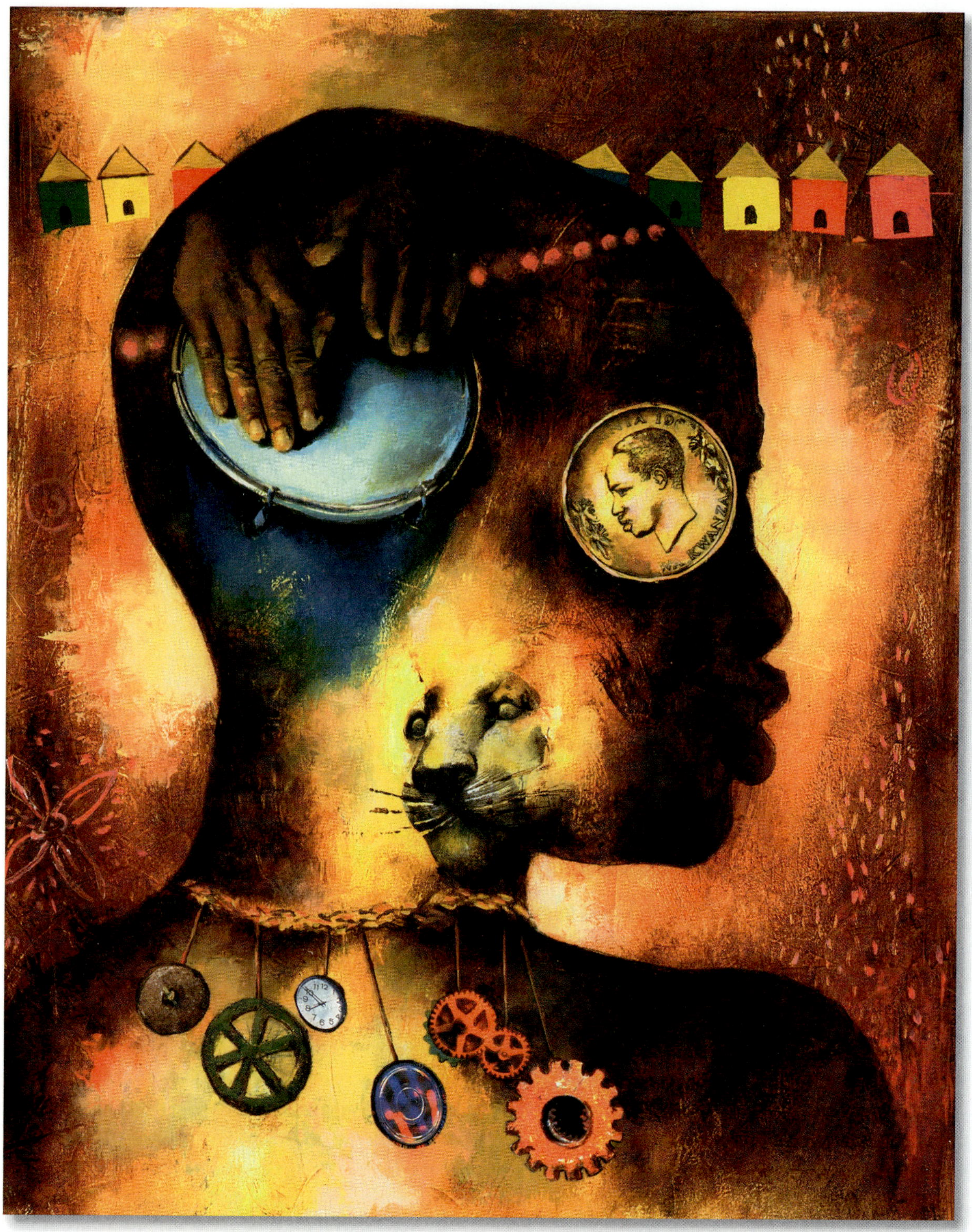

Focus On ◆ Figure 11–1 **What is the focal point of this illustration? Where are your eyes drawn to first?**

Clemente Botelho. *Emerging Africa*. 1998. Found and painted collage elements, acrylic underpainting with oil glaze finish. 43.2 × 34.3 cm (17″ × 13½″). Illustration for Harvard University's African Studies Department brochure. Harvard University, Cambridge, Massachusetts.

Chapter 11

Graphic Design

> *"I began playing with the idea of incorporating the image of an African youth to represent an emerging Africa, ready to mature in a new Global reality."*
>
> — **Clemente Botelho, (b. 1967)**

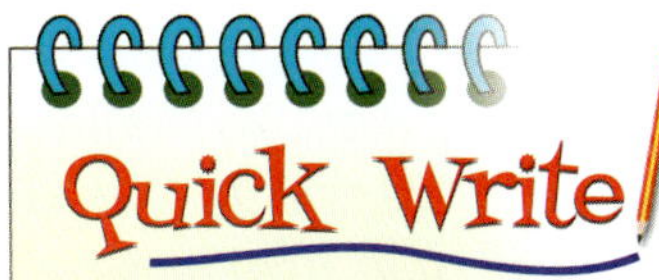

Interpreting the Quote Read the quote. Then write a short paragraph explaining how the comment relates to the brochure illustration in **Figure 11–1**.

KEY TERMS

graphic artists
graphic design
illuminations
layout designers
desktop publishing
advertising design
logo
Web designers

When you watch a TV program, you see only the "on-screen talent." These include actors, performers, hosts, and other celebrities. You don't see the many skilled behind-the-scenes personnel whose efforts went into the show.

The same is true of some artists. Their work oftentimes goes unsigned. The artwork at the left, for example, was created as an illustration for a brochure. Do you know the artist's name? After reading this chapter, you will. You will also know the names of other artists and the jobs they do.

After completing this chapter, you will be able to:

- Explain what graphic design is.
- Identify career choices in the field of graphic design.
- Define *layout*.
- Create a story illustration, design a concert poster, and create a package design using a variety of art materials and tools in traditional and experimental ways.
- Design and create an advertisement.

LESSON 1

The Art of Graphic Design

You live in a world filled with visual art. Artists create the television commercials you see and the packaging of products you use. Some artists create billboards, others posters. There was even an artist who designed the book you are holding.

These artists are known as **graphic artists**. They are *art professionals who work in the field known as graphic design*. **Graphic design** is the *field of art that uses pictures and words to instruct or communicate a specific message*. Look around your classroom. What graphic design symbols and images do you see?

Graphic Artists

Graphic artists have been around for as long as there has been written communication. The page from a prayer book shown in **Figure 11–2** dates to the late 1300s. It was printed and illustrated by an artist called an *illuminator*. Professional illuminators were considered craftspeople. The *illustrations in early handmade manuscripts* were called **illuminations**. The name comes from the media used, which often included gold leaf and paint made of crushed gems. These materials made the works glitter with light.

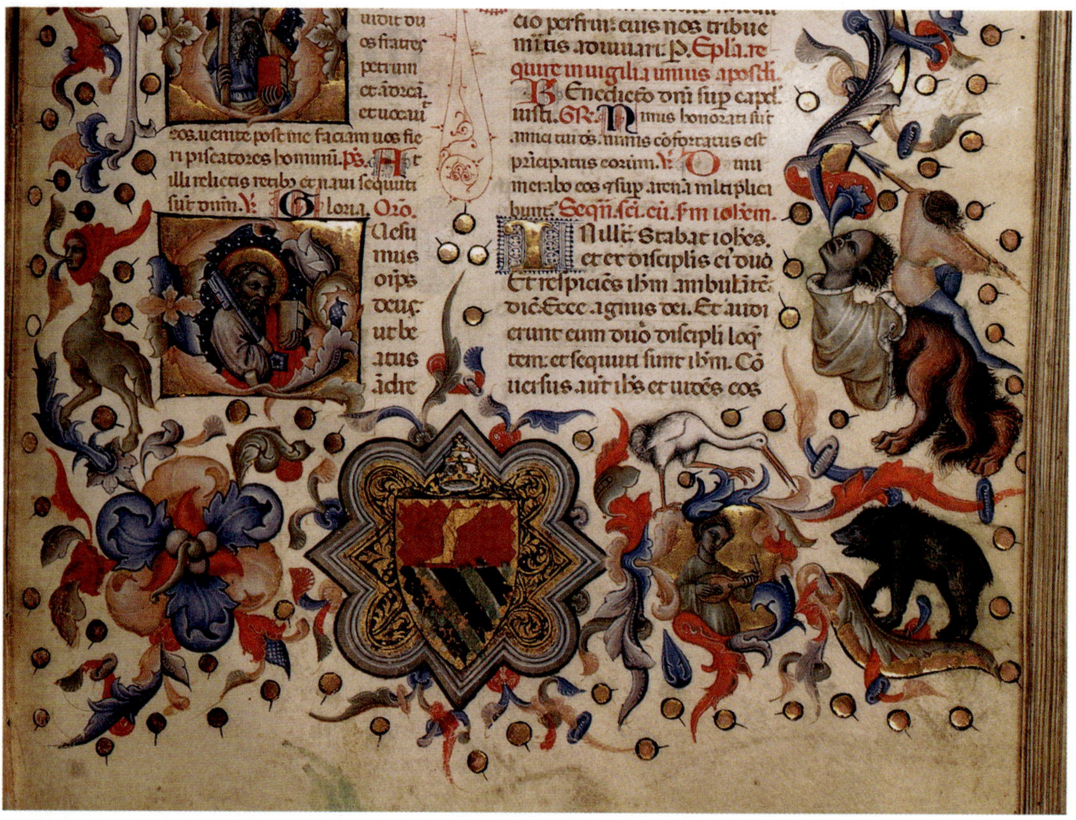

◆ **Figure 11–2** **Does this book page look at all like the one in your textbook? What similarities can you find?**

Italian (Bologna). *Missal*. 1389–1404. Vellum, 277 leaves. Tempera colors, gold leaf, gold paint, and ink on parchment, bound between wood boards covered with blind-stamped sheepskin. Illustration: Master of the Brussels Initials, *The Calling of Saints Peter and Andrew*. 33 × 24 cm (13 × 9⁷⁄₁₆″). The J. Paul Getty Museum, Los Angeles, California.

Graphic artists today work in many different fields. Each area has its own special tasks and job title. Some of these fields are publishing, illustration, advertising, and Web design. Sometimes graphic artists work together as members of a larger creative team. Most of them use computers to create their designs. What are some other career choices you can identify involving graphic artists?

Publishing

Like other art fields, graphic design has been influenced by advances in technology. One of these was the invention of the printing press in 1438. This advance made it possible to produce multiple copies of printed material at one time. It also gave rise to the branch of graphic art known as page layout. **Layout designers** are *graphic artists who arrange text and illustrations and prepare the material for printing*. Some of these designers work on books, while others work on magazines and newspapers.

Another more recent invention that has streamlined publishing design is the digital computer. It has given rise to **desktop publishing**. This is *the use of a computer and special software to combine text and graphics on a page*. Computers have allowed designers to do page layout in a fraction of the time it previously took.

Illustration

Illuminators were responsible for both text and illustrations in books. Today, graphic design is more specialized. Original images in books and other printed materials are the work of professional illustrators. Many times illustrators work closely with designers.

The color wheel on page 29 of this book (Figure 2–14) was drawn by an illustrator. So was the drawing in **Figure 11–3**. This is an example of a technical illustration. Notice the fine details that have been included in this drawing.

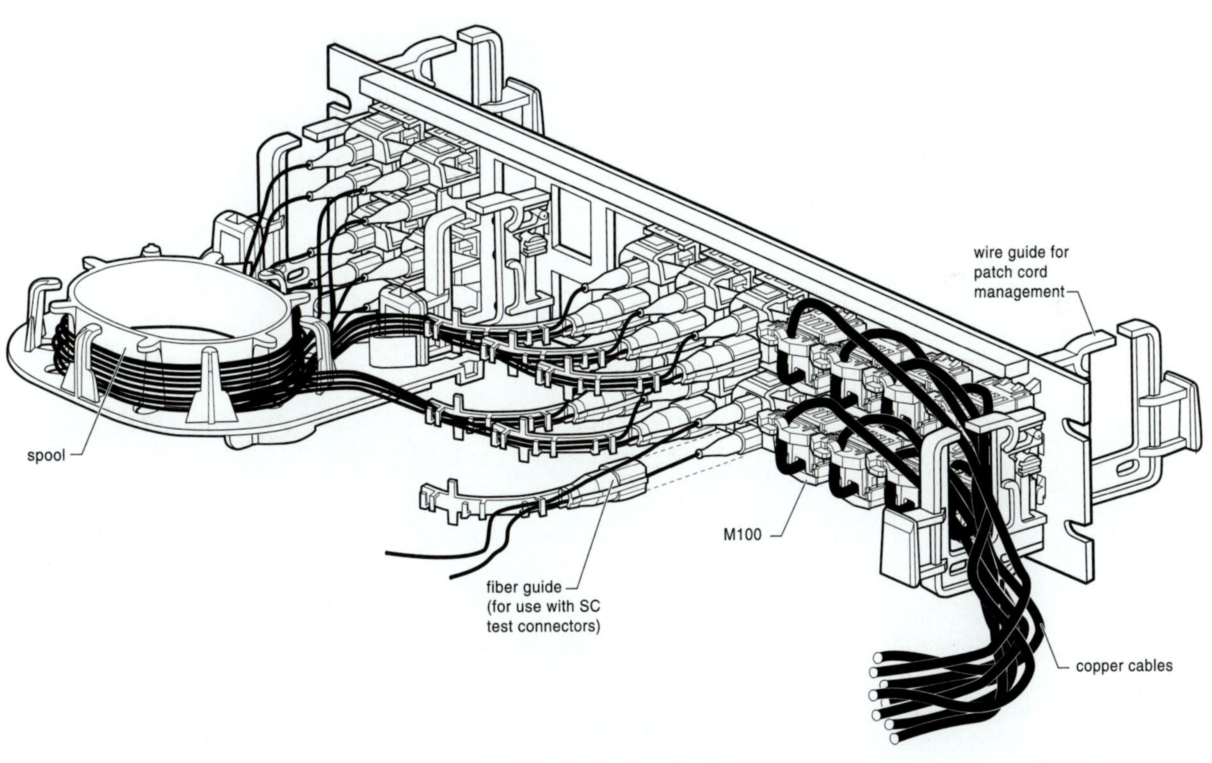

◆ **Figure 11–3** **How does this illustration differ from others in this chapter?**

Leane Wells. Technical line-art illustration for AT&T. 1998.

The artwork that opened this chapter (Figure 11–1) is another illustration. This one was used to introduce an article on African Studies in a college brochure. Compare the style of this work to the illustration in Figure 11–3. In addition, compare the media used. These differences show the wide range of art possibilities in the field of illustration.

Advertising Design

One field in which there is a great demand for creative art solutions is **advertising design**. This is *an area of graphic art whose goal is to help inform, sell, or promote products or services.* **Figure 11–4** shows an example of a work done in this field. Did you notice the boxed "M" that forms the tire tracks and the car's license plate? This is the advertiser's **logo**. Short for "logotype," a logo is *a special image representing a business, group, or product.*

Like publishing designers, advertising designers are concerned with layout. Some advertising designers work on newspaper or magazine ads. Others design commercials for

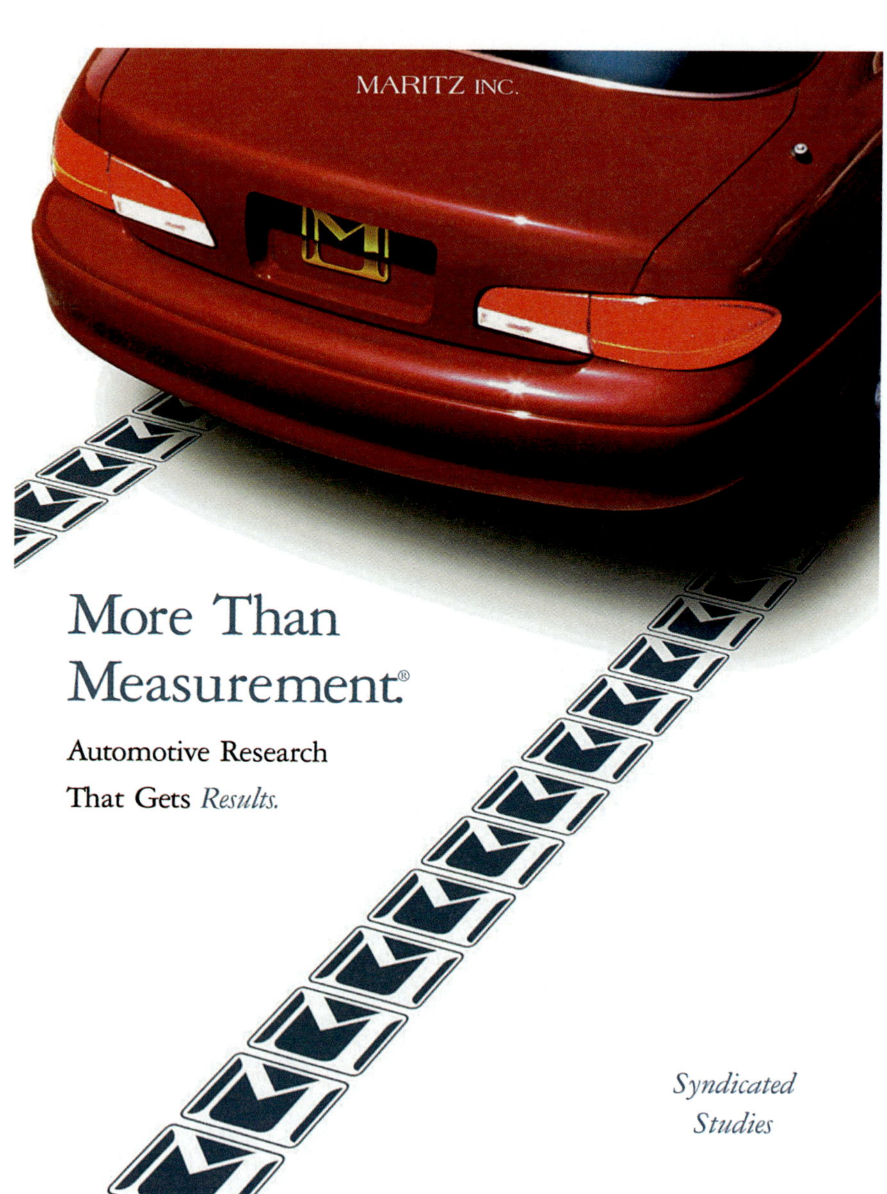

◆ **Figure 11–4** **Think of a recent advertisement you've seen in a newspaper or magazine. How is it similar to this image? How does it differ?**

Mary Baum. Maritz Automotive Research Group brochure. 1998.

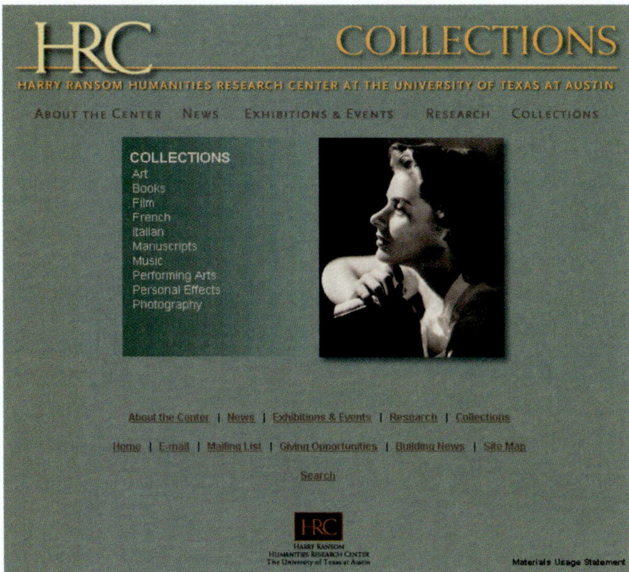

◆ **Figure 11–5 Notice the way in which images and text have been combined on this Web page. What has the designer done to get the user's attention?**

Web page for Harry Ransom Humanities Research Center, The University of Texas at Austin, Austin, Texas.

television. The success of their work is measured by the impact the message has on the viewer. Can you think of an advertisement that has left an impression on you?

Web Design

Another technological development that has impacted graphic design is the Internet. The arrival in the late 1980s of the World Wide Web created a new field called **Web design**. Like other graphic designers, **Web designers** are *artists who work with text and pictures to create Web sites*. Unlike other graphic designers, Web designers often use computer code in their creations. This enables the user to click on links that lead to another page or Web site. One commonly used code is HTML, short for *hypertext markup language*. **Figure 11–5** shows a page from a Web site. Can you find a logo appearing on this Web site?

Time & Place

Historical and Cultural Contexts

Look back at the prayer-book page in Figure 11–2. Analyze the artwork to determine historical and cultural contexts. For example, did you notice how much of the page space is taken up by pictures? There is a reason for this. Back in the fourteenth century, when this book was created, few people were educated. Many people had never learned to read. The pictures enabled them to follow the religious teachings despite being unable to read.

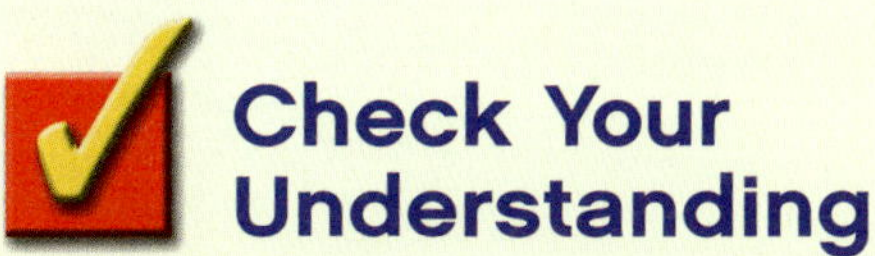

Check Your Understanding

1. Identify career choices in the field of graphic design.
2. What does a layout designer do?
3. Name two different media that an illustrator might use.
4. What do graphic artists who specialize in advertising do?
5. How does Web design differ from other areas of graphic design?

LESSON 2

Illustrating a Story

Illustrator N. C. Wyeth combined a story's action with character studies in his illustrations. Look at **Figure 11–6**. In this painting he captures the sadness of the mother and the determination of her son. Do you need to know the story of Robert Louis Stevenson's *Treasure Island* to know what is happening in this scene?

What You Will Learn

Select an action story or poem you have recently read and liked. You will illustrate ideas from imagination to paint an incident that took place in the story or poem. Your illustration will capture the setting, mood, and style of the whole work. Using traditional techniques, you will give your illustration formal or informal balance. You will decide whether to use realistic proportions for your figures or distortion.

What You Will Need

- Notepad, pencil, and eraser
- Sheets of sketch paper, paper towels
- Sheet of white paper, 12 × 18 inches
- School acrylic paint
- Bristle brushes, varied sizes
- Water container and water

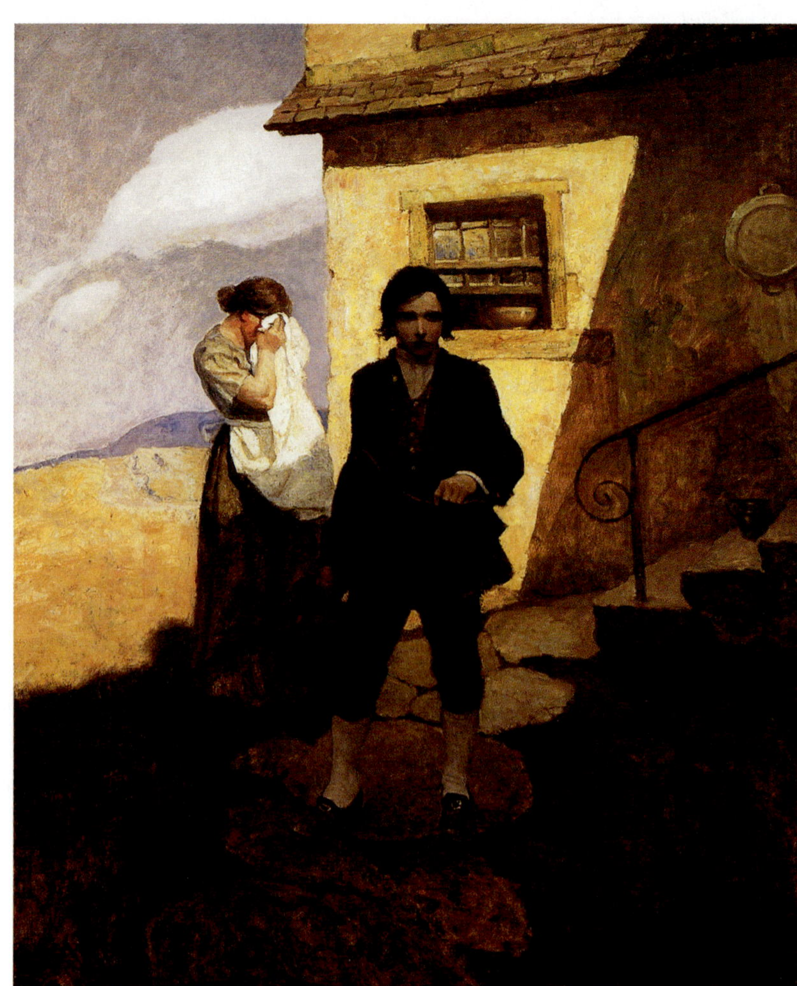

◆ **Figure 11–6** **What does the artist show in this illustration that the author might not convey with words?**

N. C. Wyeth. *I Said Good-bye to Mother and the Cove*. 1911. Oil on canvas. 120 × 91.8 cm (47¼″ × 36⅛″). Illustration for Robert Louis Stevenson's *Treasure Island* (New York: Charles Scribner's Sons, 1911). Collection of Brandywine River Museum, Chadds Ford, Pennsylvania. Acquisition made possible through the generosity of Patricia Wiman Hewitt, 1994.

What You Will Do

1. Think about a short story, novel, or poem you have read and liked. Decide what scene from this work you want to illustrate, using the main characters.
2. On the notepad, describe what the characters are doing. Using your imagination, write down information about their expressions, moods, and actions. Think of how you will integrate themes from the story in your illustration. List ways you will use the elements of art in your painting. Decide whether the proportions of your figures will be realistic or exaggerated. Will you then use emphasis to make a figure or object stand out? Your illustration will depict either formal or informal balance.
3. Make rough pencil sketches for your painting.
4. Lightly sketch your plan on the good paper. Use a 1/4-inch brush and a light-value paint to draw the main shapes of your illustration on the sheet of white paper. Use larger brushes to fill in shapes. Complete your painting.
5. Display your painting with those of your classmates in a group exhibition. Analyze the exhibition to form conclusions about formal properties, intents, and meanings. Try to guess the titles of the different stories and poems illustrated. Did you guess the title the artist intended to depict?

Evaluating Your Work

- **Describe** What is happening in the story you illustrated? Who are the characters? List the elements and principles of art you used.
- **Analyze** Does your work have formal or informal balance? Were the proportions of your figures used to make them look realistic or exaggerated?
- **Interpret** Explain how you illustrated ideas from imagination to capture the setting and mood of the story.
- **Judge** Tell whether you feel your work succeeds.

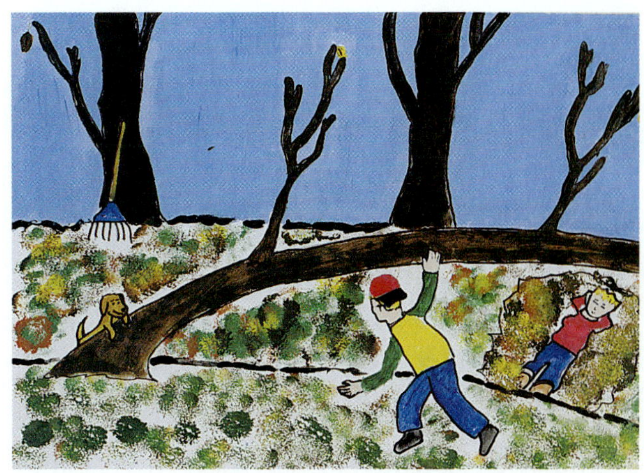

◆ **Figure 11–7** **Student work. Story illustration.**

COMPUTER OPTION

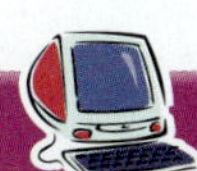

Produce electronic media-generated art to create a storybook for a younger class. Choose a page from a familiar story to illustrate. Sketch with the Pencil or a variety of Brushes and colors to capture the mood of the scene. Use the whole screen for your page. Choose the Text tool and Font, Size, and Style that match the original text. Remember to include the page number. Proofread, title, save, and print. Laminate and bind as a book.

Art Online

Survey and identify career choices or opportunities in graphic design. Explore them at the Career Corner at **art.glencoe.com**. There you will also find:

- Artist Profiles
- Student Art Gallery
- Web Links

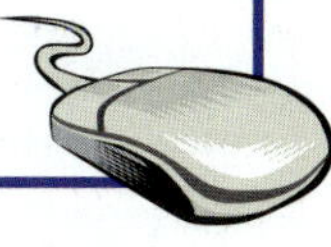

LESSON 3

Designing a Poster

In music, as in art, different artists have different styles. The style of today's most popular rock group is different from that of yesterday's group. Both are very different from the musical style of Mozart.

When graphic artists design concert posters for musical groups, they try to capture the musicians' style. Their works often reflect one of the three views of art you have learned about. Look at the concert poster in **Figure 11–8**. Which view is exemplified in this poster?

What You Will Learn

You will create a poster integrating themes found through imagination. Invent a musician or musical group and choose the style of music your imaginary artist makes. Then design a concert poster for that artist. Decide on a title for the group. The poster will include the title of the concert and name of the artist. You will select and use a variety of appropriate art materials and tools to interpret a theme in traditional and experimental ways. You will use the principles of balance, rhythm, and emphasis to organize the elements of color, line, shape, space, and texture in your design. You will produce photographic imagery in your design.

What You Will Need

- Notepad, pencil, sketch paper
- Any or all of the following: broad-line and fine-line colored markers, crayons, collage materials (magazines, photographs, newspapers, scissors, white glue, small brush)
- Sheet of heavy white paper
- Transparent tape, eraser and ruler

What You Will Do

1. Use your imagination to think of a musical style and name for your imaginary musician or group. Write down the name on your notepad. Create a title for the concert poster. Write a short description of your group.

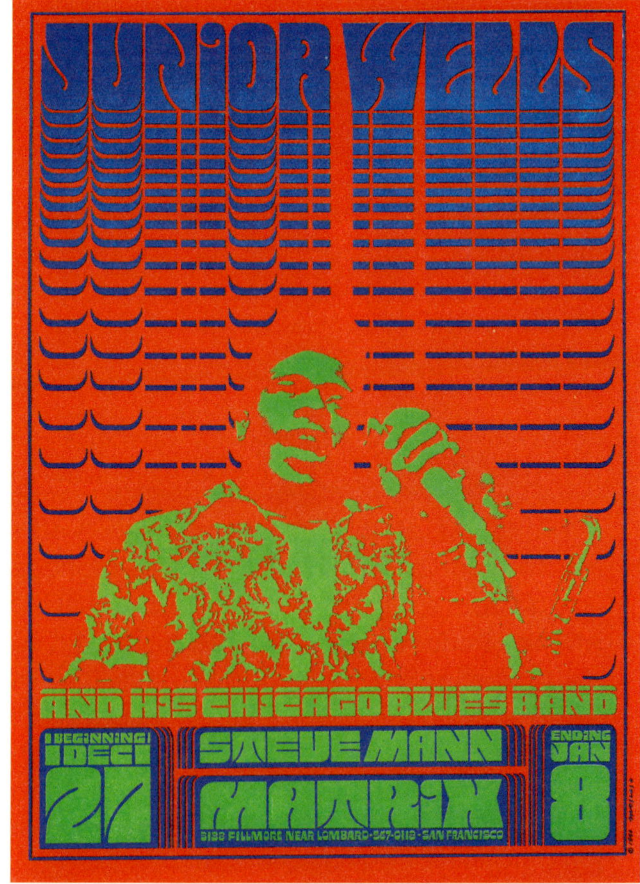

◆ **Figure 11–8 Describe the style of music of the poster. If you were interested in rock and roll, would this poster interest you?**

Victor Moscoso. *Junior Wells and His Chicago Blues Band*. 1966. Offset lithograph, printed in color. 50.5 × 35.6 cm (19⅞″ × 14″). Museum of Modern Art, New York, New York. Gift of the designer.

2. Create your own style or choose a style of lettering for the concert title and the artist's name. Decide where on the poster each will appear and decide how large each will be. Sketch them in.
3. Plan how you will fill the remaining space. If you plan to use collage materials, find and clip images found in magazines and newspapers. Produce photographic imagery in your design in traditional and experimental ways. You may choose to incorporate photos you've taken of people or events. Decide if you want your work to look realistic, to make a statement with design alone, or to express a feeling or mood.
4. Working lightly in pencil, place your title lettering, artist's name, and any images on the poster. (See **Technique Tip 5,** *Handbook* page 282)
5. Using markers or crayons, color in the letters and images. Using glue and brush, paste down any photos and magazine or newspaper clippings.
6. Display your concert poster. See how many of your classmates can tell the style of music your imaginary artist plays.

Evaluating Your Work

- **Describe** Point out the artist's name and the concert title. Tell what media you chose.
- **Analyze** Tell which principles you used to organize the elements. Explain how you used photographic imagery in traditional and experimental ways.
- **Interpret** Explain how your design helps a viewer understand the style of music.
- **Judge** Tell whether you feel your work succeeds. Identify the aesthetic view of art you used when making this decision.

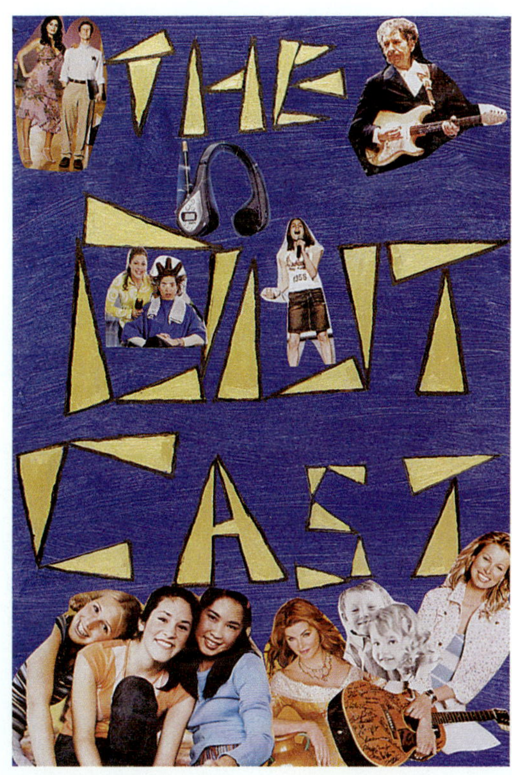

◆ **Figure 11–9** **Student work. A concert poster.**

REFLECTIVE THINKING 

Critical Response Analyze the original artworks of your peers. Examine the posters they created and form conclusions about formal properties, historical and cultural contexts, and intents. For example, do their posters provide any clues about the artists' cultural heritage?

Visual Art Journal

In your visual art journal, explain how your poster illustrates ideas from direct observation, imagination, and personal experience.

Package Design

A package designer is a graphic artist who produces containers that are attractive, functional, and safe. The package designer comes under the heading of industrial designer. This means he or she designs packaging for products sold to consumers. Package designers use form and color to make their packages unique and appealing. Look closely at **Figure 11–10**. Notice how the artist has used color contrast to create emphasis. She has organized the lines of text to make a circular design. She has used repeated curved lines to emphasize the small, round, yellow shapes.

What You Will Learn

The last time you were in a store, did any product attract you more than the others? What was it about the package that drew your attention? In this lesson, you will use your answers to those questions. You will incorporate design into an artwork for use in everyday life by creating a package design for a new product. You will incorporate the art elements of line, shape, color, and form into your design. Select one color for your background to create unity. Add one contrasting color to create emphasis.

What You Will Need

- Pencil eraser and rulers
- Sketchbook, existing containers
- Acrylic primer, acrylic paints
- Brushes in various sizes
- Water containers, paint palettes
- Paper towels, newspaper

What You Will Do

1. As a class, create a list of commonly used products. Ideas could be soft drinks, watches, shoes, and so on. Choose the product you like best.

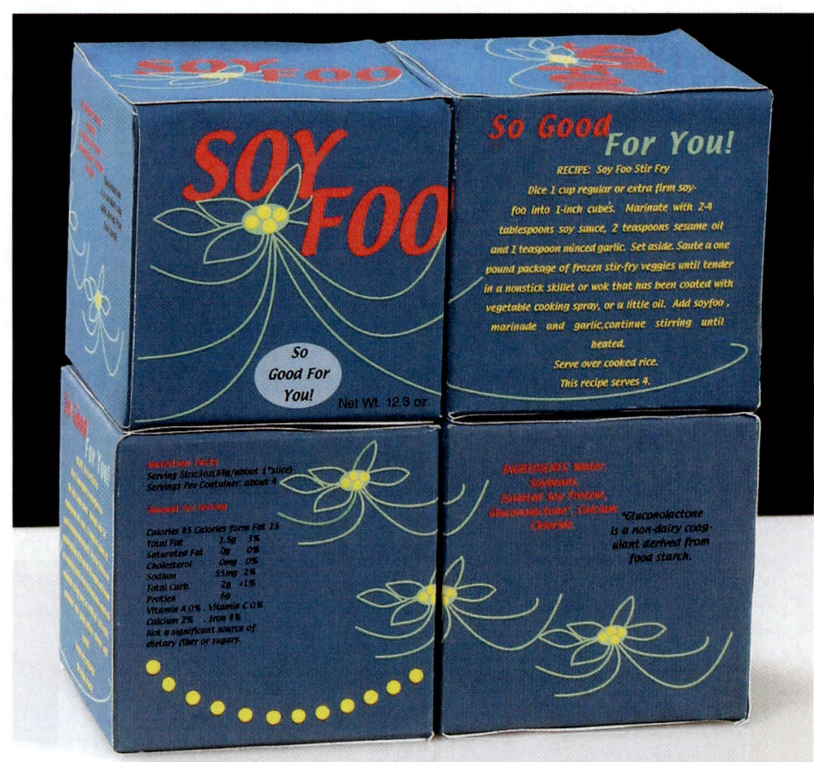

◆ **Figure 11–10** What are some of your favorite package designs?

Leslie McMains. *Soy Box.*

2. You have been selected to compete in designing a package for your product. The package must be appealing, unique, and it must contain information about the product. Ask these questions when incorporating design into your package: Who will use this product? What colors and images are associated with this product? What shape works best for this product?
3. Make several rough pencil sketches for your design. Incorporate the art elements of line, shape, color, and form. Select one color for your background to create unity. Add a contrasting color to create emphasis. Decide on an existing container shape to be used for your product. Since your container is three-dimensional, plan each surface area.
4. Prepare your selected container with acrylic primer. Once your primer has dried, carefully draw your design in pencil onto the container. Add color to your design with acrylic paints. Outline your shapes with a small brush, let dry, and then fill them in with a larger brush. Use your palette to mix colors.
5. Present your product to the class and display it with those of your classmates. What are some similarities in the designs? What are some differences?

Evaluating Your Work

- **Describe** What product did you choose for your package design? How did you incorporate design into your artwork for use in everyday life?
- **Analyze** What type of lines and shapes did you use in your design? What colors were used to create unity and emphasis?
- **Interpret** How might your design persuade someone to buy your product?
- **Judge** Do you feel your package design was successful? Use the aesthetic theories in Chapter 5 to defend your decision.

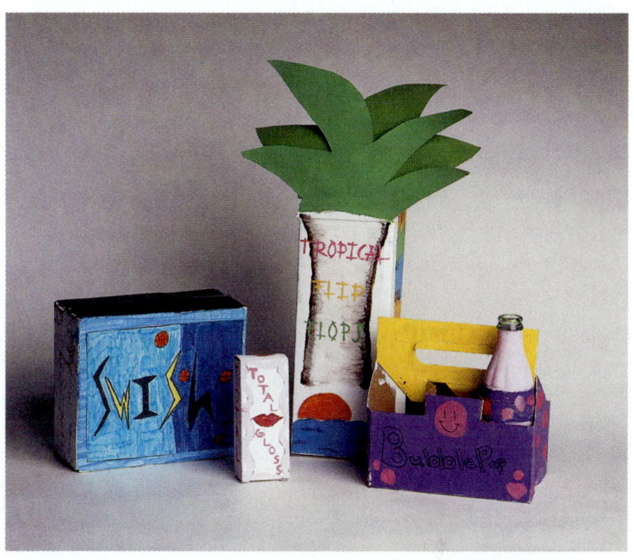

◆ **Figure 11–11** **Student works. Package designs.**

COMPUTER OPTION

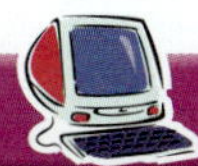

Create a compact disc cover for a musician you like. Select and use appropriate art materials and tools to produce your cover as electronic media-generated art. Using your graphics program, create a rectangle measuring $5\frac{1}{2} \times 4\frac{3}{4}''$, the standard size of a CD jewel case cover. Illustrate your cover by creating your photos or by downloading images from the Internet. Experiment with different layouts. Print your finished art and insert it into a blank jewel case.

Visual Art Journal

Incorporating Design. In this lesson you learned how design is incorporated into artworks for use in everyday life. How did the art elements of line and shape enhance your package design? Write down your thoughts in your visual art journal.

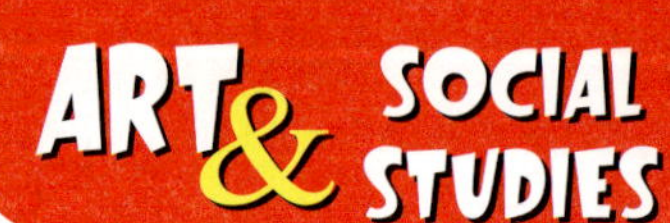

Art in Advertising

Do you recognize the art form in **Figure 11–12?** It is an example of the graphic art form known as *advertising.* Advertisements come in a variety of shapes, sizes, and forms. Some advertisements use art to depict a glamorous image while others may use art to shock or surprise you.

Advertising Techniques

According to industry estimates, the average consumer is exposed to 1,000 ads every day. Some of these take the form of TV commercials. Others come to us by means of radio, print material, and the Internet. You may view hundreds of advertisements every day, yet are you aware of the strategies behind them?

A variety of techniques are used in the advertising industry. One of these is known as the *rich-and-famous* technique. An example of this type of ad might be an image of an expensive car driven by an attractive person. The hidden message behind the ad is that you will feel glamorous, or rich and famous, if you use this product.

Some ads or commercials use a technique known as the *testimonial.* This technique portrays a celebrity using or endorsing a product. You may have seen a celebrity on the front of a cereal box, for example.

Regardless of the technique, however, the motivation behind advertisements is the same: to sell a product or service.

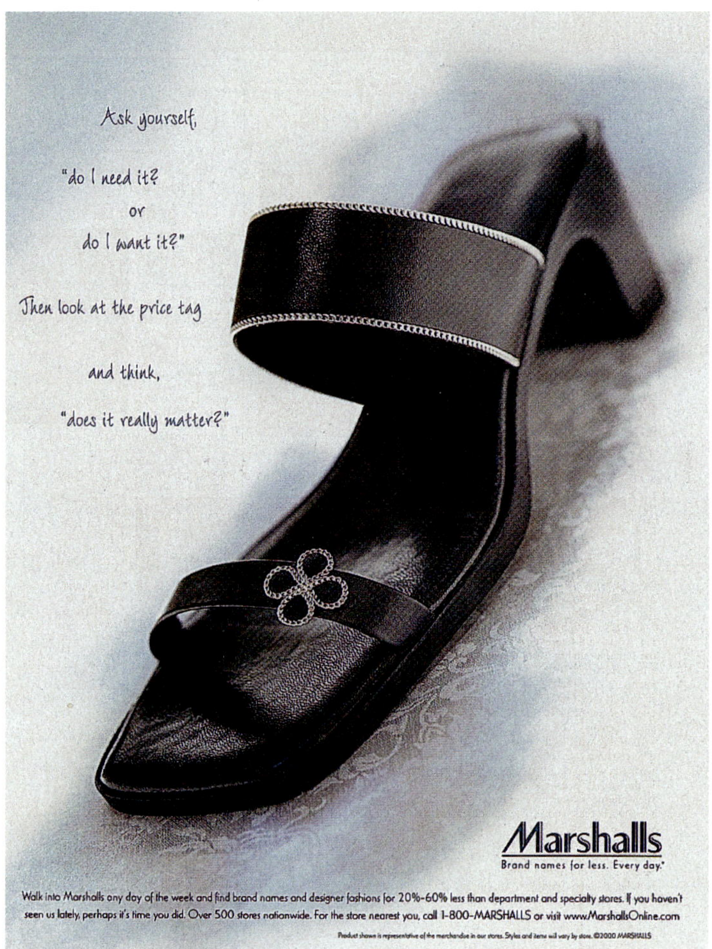

◆ **Figure 11–12** Notice how the designers who created this advertisement balance the use of text and images.

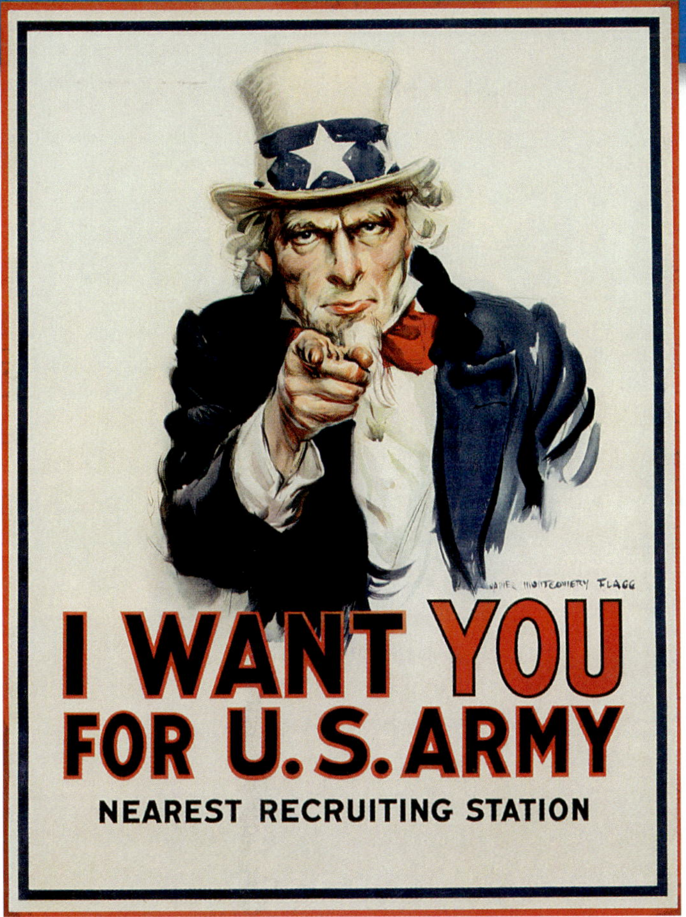

◆ **Figure 11–13** **How does this image differ from more modern advertisements, such as the one in Figure 11–12?**

James Montgomery Flagg. *I Want You for U.S. Army*. 1917. Chromolithograph. 100.4 × 73.8cm (39½ × 29⅛ in.). The National Museum of American Art, Smithsonian Institution, Washington, D.C.

Icons and Slogans

Some advertisements may use *icons,* or symbols of respect and admiration. Icons may show a figure, emblem, or image to represent an idea. Look at **Figure 11–13.** Do you recognize the icon used in the poster? The version of Uncle Sam shown in this poster is a self-portrait created by artist James Montgomery Flagg in 1917. What other icons have you seen in print advertisements or television commercials?

Often advertisements may use a *slogan,* or an attention-getting phrase, to sell a product or service. What slogan is used in the poster shown in Figure 11–13? Can you think of other slogans you've seen or heard in advertisements? Analyze ways that international, historical, and political issues influence artworks in advertising. For example, what issue might have influenced the artwork in Figure 11–13?

MAKE THE CONNECTION

Take Another Look

1. Look again at the print ad in Figure 11–12. What technique is used? What is the hidden message?
2. Look again at Figure 11–13. Where is your attention drawn? What elements of art has the artist used to achieve this emphasis?

ART & SOCIAL STUDIES

Create an ad. Think about some of your favorite advertisements or commercials. Make a list of features that you like about one of these ads. Then make a print ad of your own for a product of your choosing. Draw or find images for your ad. If you are working on a computer, choose typefaces for your ad. Include a slogan in your design.

WILD THING

Maurice Sendak's imagination has created a fantastic world.

JAMES KEYSER/TIMEPIX

Maurice Sendak (ABOVE) believes that illustration should add to the mystery of the story. Many wild characters in *Where the Wild Things Are*, like the one below, were inspired by Sendak's aunts and uncles. As a child, Sendak felt these adults, whom he loved, "looked like toothy monsters."

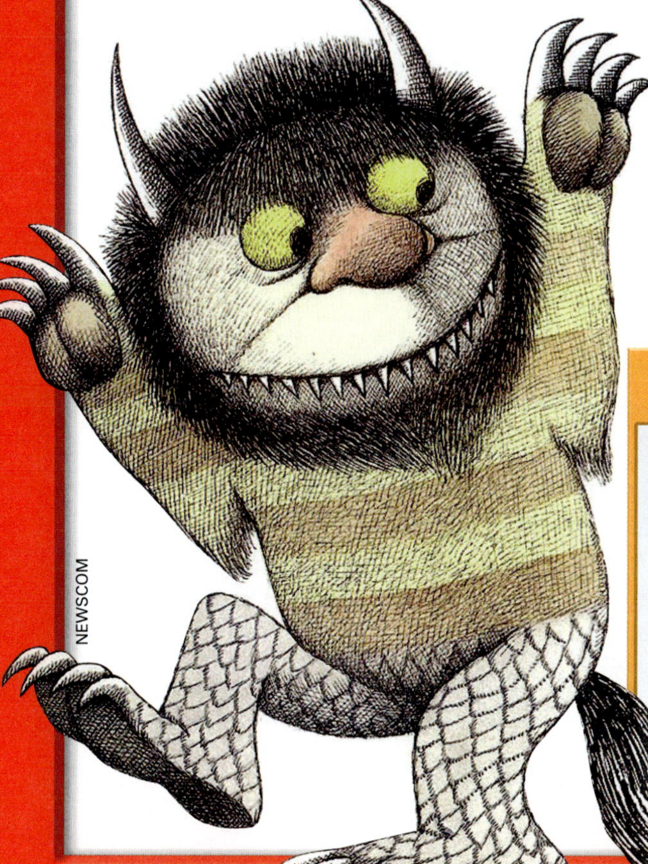

NEWSCOM

Maurice Sendak (b. 1928) has drawn mysterious fantasies and wild creatures since 1951. Adults didn't immediately like his now-famous book, *Where the Wild Things Are*. They were put off by monsters who "gnashed their terrible teeth and rolled their terrible eyes and showed their terrible claws." Children, however, loved the book, which helped make it one of Sendak's most popular.

Sendak's passion for books began as a young boy. Home a lot because he was often sick, Sendak escaped by reading. He also began to draw, allowing his imagination to take him places where he couldn't physically go. Max, the main character in *Where the Wild Things Are*, may be based on Sendak himself. After being sent to his room, Max creates in his mind a whole new world of strange places and monsters.

Sendak says, "I have been doodling with ink and watercolor all my life. It's my way of stirring up my imagination to see what I find hidden in my head. I call the results dream pictures, fantasy sketches, and even brain-sharpening exercises."

TIME TO CONNECT

- **Find a picture in a children's book or in an art book that is full of fantasy and which captures your attention.**
- **Develop a story inspired by the picture. Describe the scene and the character or characters.**
- **Outline a solid beginning, middle, and end. Then write a draft using effective transitions and precise wording for the greatest effect.**

Chapter 11 Review

BUILDING VOCABULARY

Number a sheet of paper from 1 to 8. After each number, write the term from the list that best matches each description below.

advertising design	graphic design
desktop publishing	illuminations
layout designers	logo
graphic artists	Web designers

1. The field of art that uses pictures and words to instruct or communicate a specific message.
2. The use of a computer and special software to combine text and graphics on a page.
3. Graphic artists who arrange text and illustrations and prepare the material for printing.
4. Illustrations in early handmade manuscripts.
5. Artists who work with text and pictures to create Web sites.
6. A special image representing a business, group, or product.
7. Art professionals who work in the field known as graphic design.
8. An area of graphic art whose goal is to help inform, sell, or promote products or services.

REVIEWING ART FACTS

Number a sheet of paper from 9 to 13. Answer each question in a complete sentence.

9. Name four areas of graphic design.
10. What invention spurred the beginning of the field of graphic design?
11. What are two responsibilities of a graphic artist?
12. In what way has desktop publishing streamlined the work of layout designers?
13. Name two places besides television where you can see the work of advertising designers.

CROSS-CURRICULUM CONNECTIONS

14. **Careers.** Analyze the images shown in this chapter and identify careers options that might fit those images. For example, the images shown on page 212 depict the work of Maurice Sendak, a famous children's book illustrator. Think of a career you might choose involving graphic design. Write a paragraph describing your job duties.
15. **Historical and Cultural Heritage.** Analyze ways that international, historical, and political issues influence graphic design. Determine the cultural contexts in three of the images displayed in this chapter. For example, the illustration in Figure 11–1 was made for Harvard University's African Studies Department brochure.

Web Museum Tour

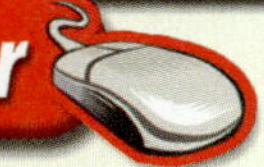

The American Sign Museum, Cincinnati, Ohio

Check out examples of signs from the past and present at the American Sign Museum. Click on the link at **art.glencoe.com** to view online images from the museum's collection. Notice how art media used to create signs has changed over the years. Illustrate ideas from imagination and direct observation to create a sketch of your own sign.

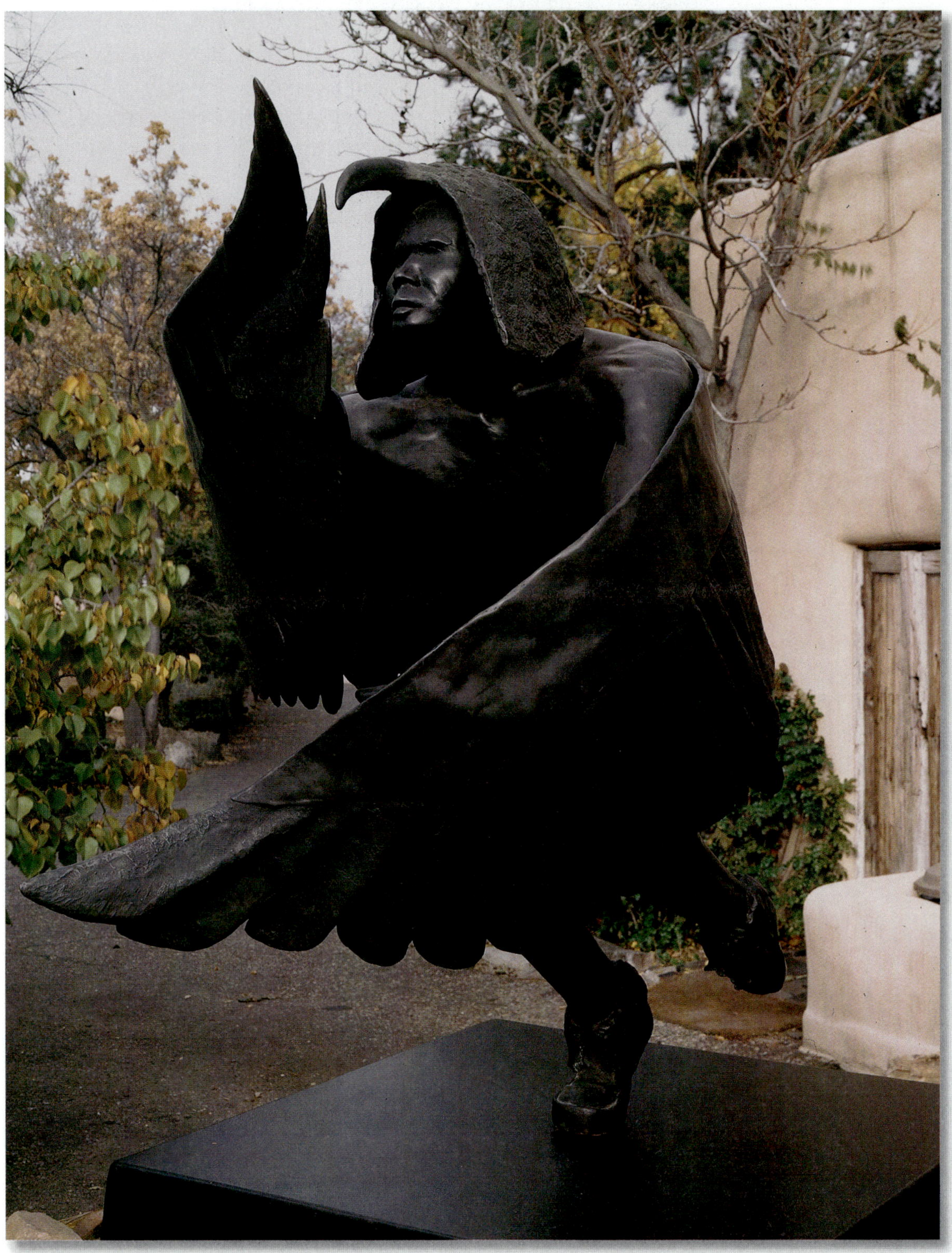

Focus On ◆ **Figure 12–1** **Michael Naranjo worked with clay as a child. After he was blinded in combat during the Vietnam War, he was told he could never be a sculptor. He was determined, however, and he has succeeded in becoming an internationally acclaimed artist who "sees" with his hands.**

Michael Naranjo. *Eagle Man.* 1996. Bronze, edition 3. 162.6 × 78.7 × 162.6 cm (64 × 31 × 64″). Collection of the artist.

Chapter 12

Sculpture

"It's like a picture puzzle or a chess game that's constantly changing. The challenge is retaining what I'm touching and transferring [that sensation] to what I'm working with."

—Michael Naranjo (b. 1945)

Quick Write

Interpreting the Quote Read the quote. Then write a one-paragraph essay titled "The Challenge of Creating." In it, detail challenges facing artists in general and this artist in particular.

Most artists create something from an idea. They start with a blank page or canvas and end up with an original creation. Some artists work in reverse. They start with a solid block of material that has height, width, and depth. When their work is done, there is less material than when they started. Such artists are sculptors. The sculpture in **Figure 12–1** was created by an artist facing a greater challenge. He is blind. He uses his hands to "see" and transfers his feelings and memories into sculpted forms.

After completing this chapter, you will be able to:

- Name and describe the four basic sculpting methods.
- Tell which sculpting methods are additive and which are subtractive.
- Create an abstract sculpture, a low-relief panel, and a plaster carving in traditional and experimental ways.
- Analyze and compare relationships, such as function and meaning, in symbolic sculptures.

KEY TERMS

study
cross-section
maquette
additive
subtractive
carving
casting
modeling
assembling
abstract
low relief
high relief

LESSON 1

The Art of Sculpture

The earliest known artists, cave dwellers, you may recall, made paintings. Were you aware that they made sculptures as well? Stone, horn, ivory, and bone were some media used by these early artists.

In this lesson you will explore some of the media used by sculptors today. You will also take a closer look at the four techniques by which sculptures are made.

Sculpting Preliminaries

Before a house can be built, the builders must have a blueprint. This is a detailed plan showing the exact dimensions of the walls and floors. Like architects, sculptors often create works in three dimensions that must stand on their own. Like architects, sculptors plan out such projects. Among the "blueprints" used by sculptors are the following:

- **Studies**. As noted in Chapter 7, a **study** is *a preliminary drawing or painting.* **Figure 12–2** shows a study by sculptor Claes Oldenburg. The drawing was made to plan the giant ice bag sculpture in **Figure 12–3.** Look closely at the study. It provides a **cross-section**, or *cutaway view*, of the intended form. Compare and contrast the study and the finished work. What part of the sculpture is represented by the circles in the diagram? What function is served by the diagonal structure resembling a pole inside the "bag"?

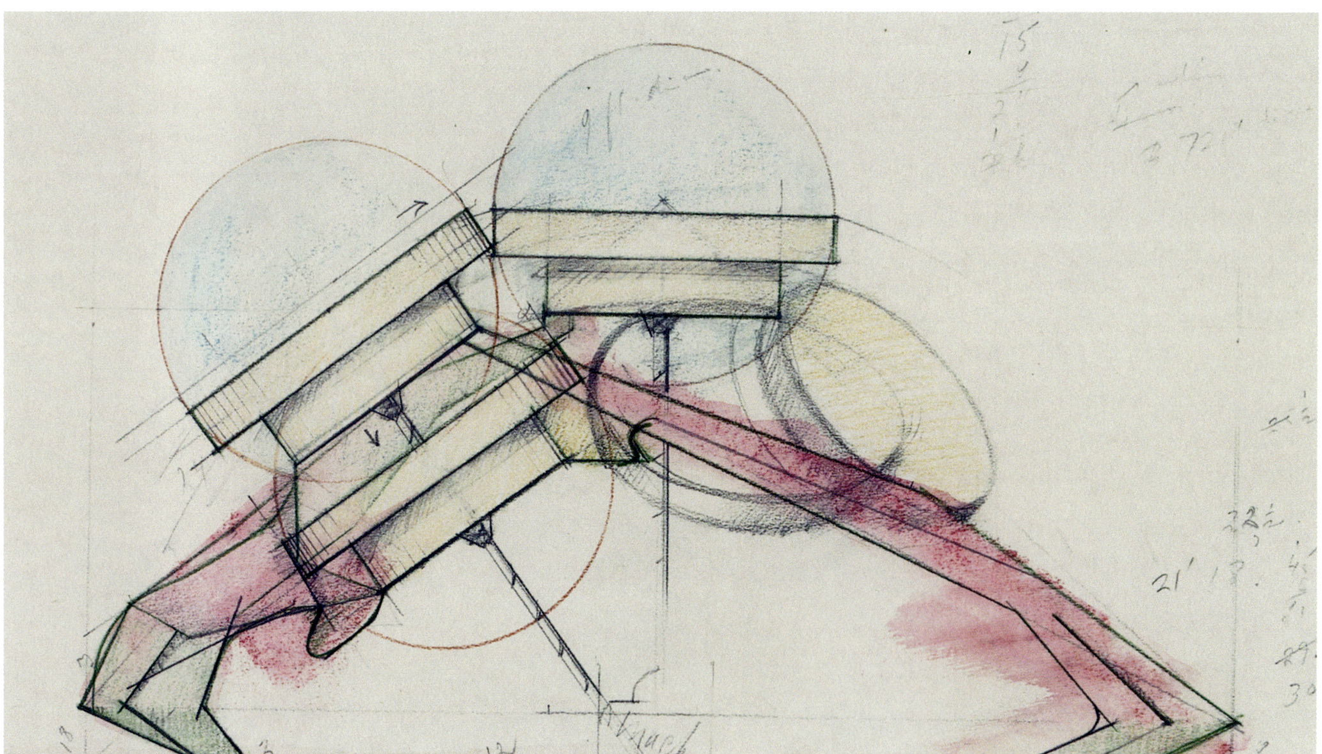

◆ **Figure 12–2** **This is a drawing that the artist made for the construction of the monumental sculpture in Figure 12–3.**

Claes Oldenburg. *Giant Ice Bag, Cross-Section View I, W.E.D.* 1969. Pencil, graphite and colored pencil on wove paper. 27.9 × 34.9 cm (11 × 13¼″). National Gallery of Canada, Ottawa, Canada. Purchased 1971.

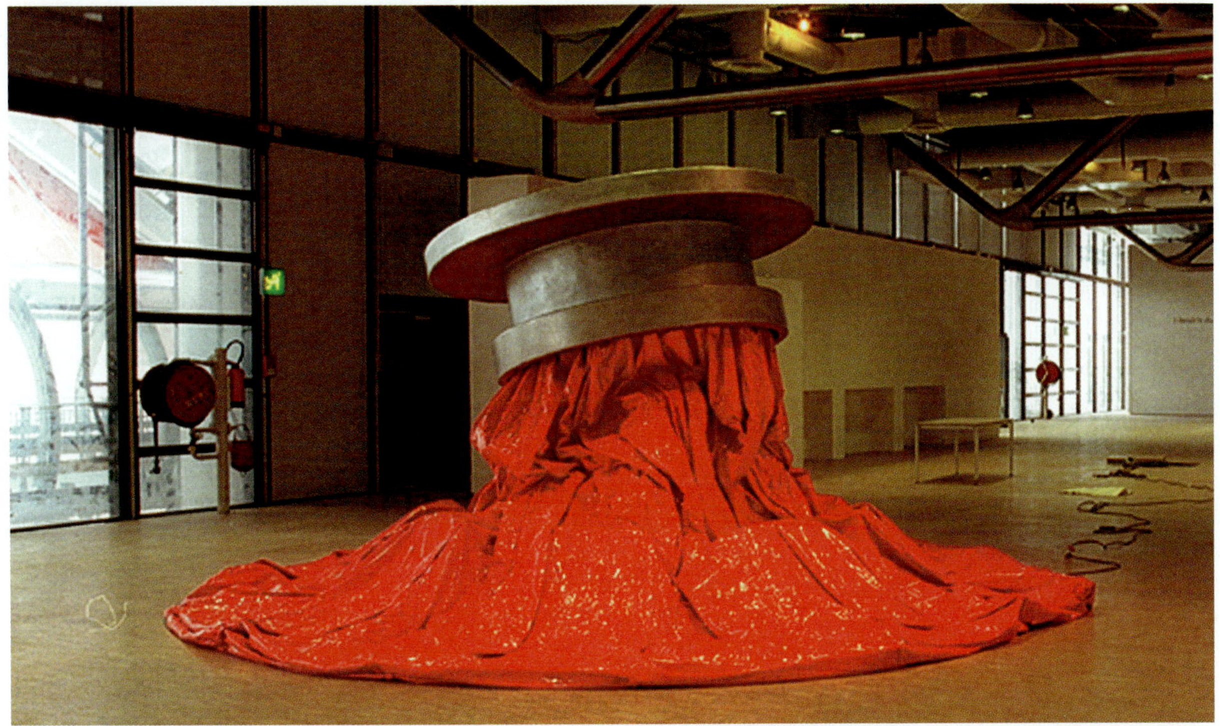

◆ **Figure 12–3** **Oldenburg is famous for making sculptures based on ordinary objects. He has created giant sculptures of clothespins, hamburgers, garden trowels, and lipsticks.**

Claes Oldenburg. *Giant Ice Bag*. 1969–70. Installation: vinyl, steel, motors and fans, fiberglass, lacquer. 600 × 600 cm (19′ 8¼″ × 19′ × 8¼″). Georges Pompidou Center, Paris.

- **Maquettes.** Another type of preliminary artwork used by sculptors is called a maquette. A **maquette** (mah-**ket**) is a *three-dimensional scaled-down study of a larger planned sculpture.* Maquettes are often made from inexpensive materials such as clay or plaster of paris.

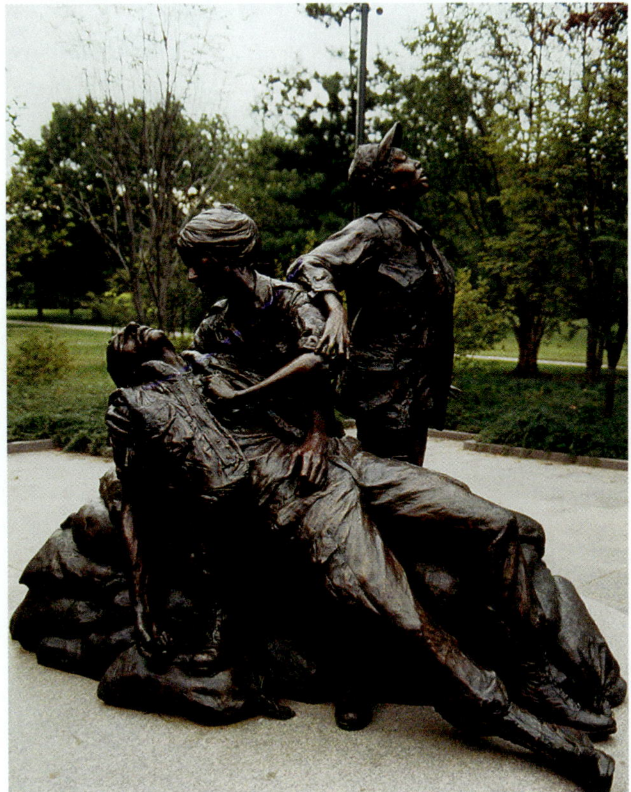

◆ **Figure 12–4** **This is a memorial sculpture honoring the 265,000 women who served in the Vietnam War. Analyze ways that international, historical, and political issues influence artworks. For example, how can art be used as a record of human achievement?**

Glenna Goodacre. *Vietnam Women's Memorial*. 1993. Bronze. Height: 233.7 cm (92″). National Mall, Washington, D.C.

Sculpting Techniques

Sculptors use four basic techniques in their work. These are carving, casting, modeling, and assembling. Some of these techniques are **additive**, *produced by adding to or combining materials.* Other techniques are **subtractive**, *produced by removing or taking away from the original material.*

Carving

Carving is *a sculpting method in which material is cut or chipped away.* The very first carvings were probably nothing more than figures scratched into a flat rock. Since then, sculptors have learned ways of "freeing images" from great blocks of stone. Study the relief carving in **Figure 12–5.** It was carved into the wall of a cave by ancient Chinese artists. Can you tell which of the figures is the empress of the title? What clues suggest this?

In carving, sculptors end up with less material than they start with. For this reason, carving is known as a subtractive method of sculpting.

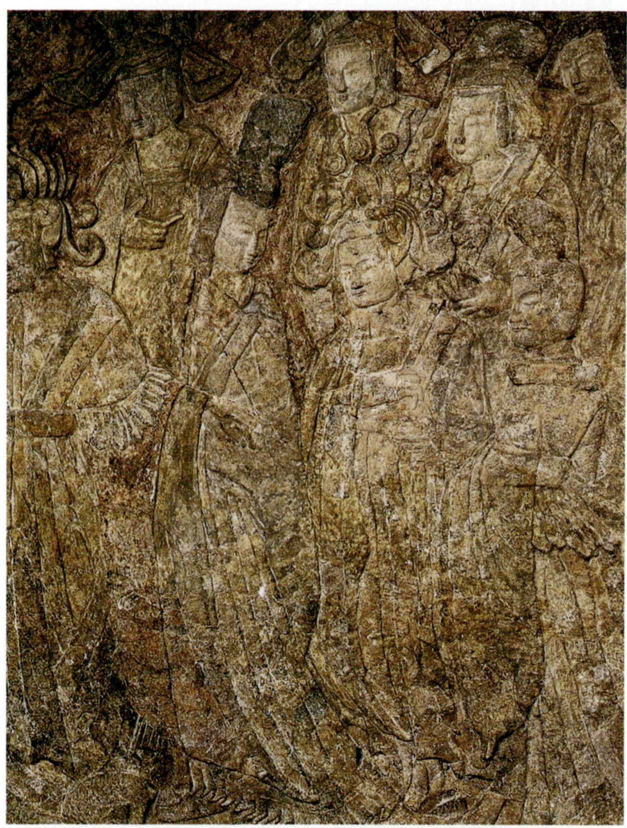

◆ **Figure 12–5** This sculpture was carved onto a cave wall. In the 1930s, looters hacked off pieces of the wall and sold them. An art historian who had studied this work searched all over the world to collect the various pieces. He then spent two years reconstructing it, based on rubbings he had made in the caves.

Chinese, from the Binyang caves. *The Empress as Donor with Attendants.* c. 505–523 A.D. Limestone with traces of color. 278 × 203.2 cm (109 7/16 × 80″). The Nelson-Atkins Museum of Art, Kansas City, Missouri. Purchase: Nelson Trust. 40–38

Casting

The art of casting is over three thousand years old. **Casting** is *a sculpting method in which melted material is poured into a mold.* Usually a metal such as bronze is used for this purpose. When the material cools, it hardens and the mold is removed. The sculpture in **Figure 12–6** was created using the casting method.

This method allows the artist to duplicate an original sculpture done in wax, clay, plaster, or some other material. The technique is practiced today much as it has been for hundreds of years.

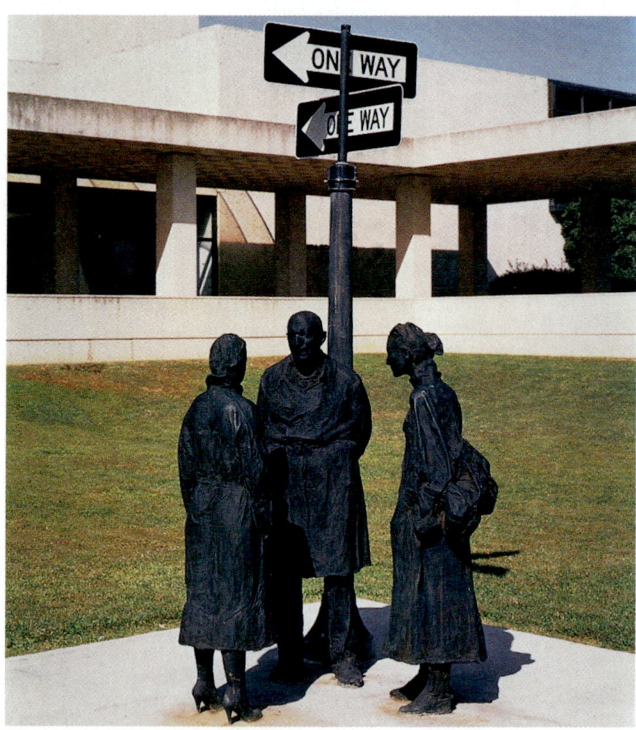

◆ **Figure 12–6** Segal created art depicting ordinary events in ordinary settings. He used friends and family members as models for his works and then added objects, such as this street sign. He believed that events of daily life are mysterious and wonderful.

George Segal. *Chance Meeting.* 1989. Three life-size bronze figures with dark patina, aluminum post, and metal sign. 317.5 × 188 × 147.3 cm (125 × 74 × 58″). The Modern Art Museum of Fort Worth, Fort Worth, Texas. Museum purchase, Sid W. Richardson Foundation Endowment Fund. © The George and Helen Segal Foundation/Licensed byVAGA, New York, NY.

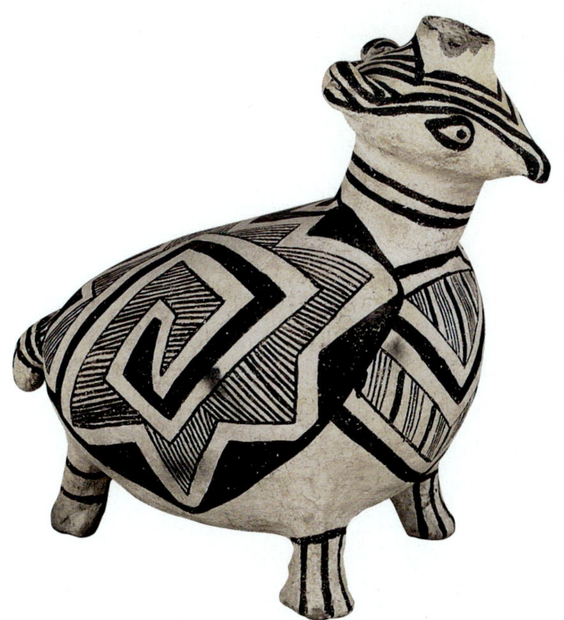

◆ **Figure 12–7** **This vessel is formed in the shape of an antelope. The horns have been carefully modeled as well as the eyes, the tail, and the shortened legs. Why do you think the artist gave an antelope such short legs?**

Native American, Anasazi. *Pronghorn Antelope Effigy Vessel.* 1000–1200. Earthenware, white slip, black mineral paint. 21.6 × 14 x 23 cm. (8½ × 5½ × 9″). Lowe Art Museum, University of Miami, Coral Gables, Florida. Museum purchase through 1987 Acquisitions Funds. 87.0007.

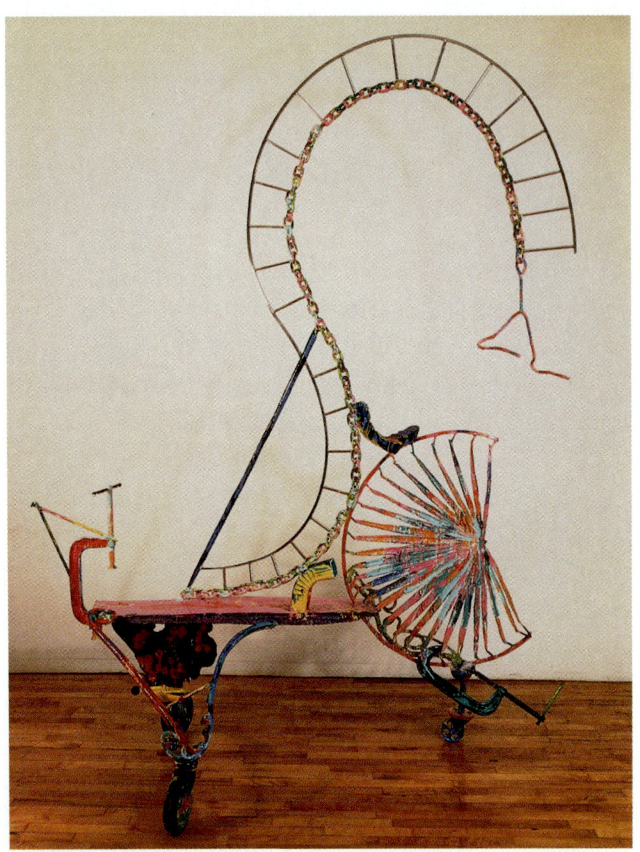

◆ **Figure 12–8** **How many of the parts do you recognize? Stainless steel was used to form the large *S* curve. Why do you think the artist used that material there?**

Nancy Graves. *Wheelabout.* 1985. Bronze and stainless steel with polyurethane paint. 235.6 × 177.8 × 80 cm (92¾ × 70 × 31½″). The Modern Art Museum of Fort Worth, Fort Worth, Texas. Gift of Anne H. Bass and Sid R. Bass. Art © Nancy Graves Foundation/Licensed by VAGA, New York, NY

Modeling

Painters start off with blank canvases. Sculptors sometimes start off with blank space. By adding together bits of material, they create something where nothing was before. Such methods of sculpting are called additive methods.

Modeling, *a sculpting method in which a soft or workable material is built up and shaped,* is an additive method. The material used most often in modeling is clay. Like carving and casting, modeling is a very old method. The clay vessel in **Figure 12–7,** for example was created over a thousand years ago.

Assembling

Not all sculpting methods are old. A second additive method, known as assembling or constructing, came into being only recently. **Assembling** is *a sculpting method in which different kinds of materials are gathered and joined together.* Wood, plastic, wire, string, metal, and found objects are some of the materials used to assemble sculpture. Glue, screws, and nails are a few of the materials used to join the objects together. An example of assembling may be seen in the whimsical sculpture shown in **Figure 12–8.**

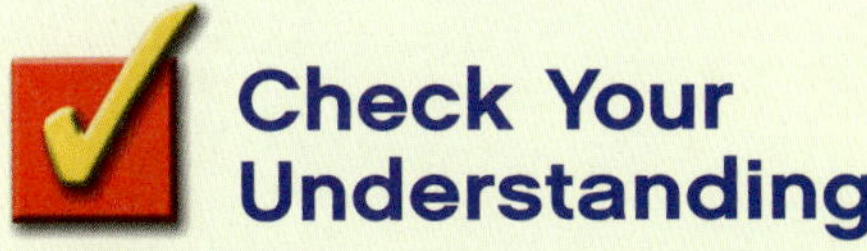

Check Your Understanding

1. Name the four basic techniques of sculpting.
2. Which technique of sculpting is called a subtractive technique? Why is it called this?
3. Which two techniques of sculpting are called additive techniques? Why are they called this?
4. Name three media used in assembling.

Abstract Sculpture

Sculptures created through the method of assembling are often unique and daring. Look at **Figure 12–9.** Can you tell what materials the sculptor used? Can you tell what this sculpture is supposed to be?

This sculpture, by Naum Gabo, is abstract. Artwork is **abstract** if *the subject of the artwork is simplified or stylized.* You probably can see that this sculpture represents a human head even though it is stylized.

Imagine that this sculpture has been taken apart, and all of its pieces are laid in a pile in front of you. Would you be able to tell that these shapes represent the parts of a face? Imagine that you are a sculptor. Could you assemble these same shapes to represent another kind of object?

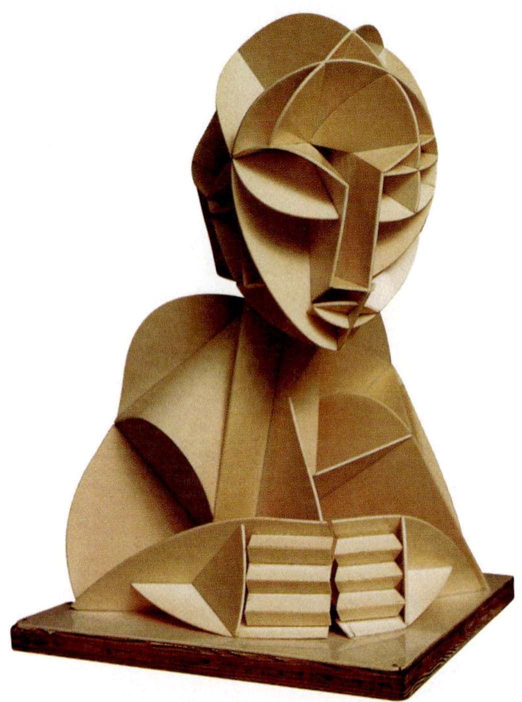

◆ **Figure 12–9** **This sculpture shows a human head. Can you identify any facial features of this figure? Which ones? Why do you think this work was considered to be so daring when it was first created?**

Naum Gabo. *Constructed Head No. 2.* 1916. Reconstructed c.1923–1924. Sculptured celluloid. 43.2 × 31.1 × 31.1 cm (17 × 12¼ × 12¼″). Dallas Museum of Art, Dallas, Texas. Edward S. Marcus Memorial Fund.

What You Will Learn

You will select a variety of appropriate art materials and tools to interpret a subject when producing an abstract sculpture. You will use the traditional method of assembling. You will use cardboard as a building material and glue as a joining material. Your sculpture will be stylized or simplified. It will use a variety of geometric shapes and forms to express the idea of a person's head. Design your sculpture with either a vertical or horizontal emphasis. When finished, paint the sculpture with a coat of black or white paint to give it harmony. (See **Figure 12–10.**)

What You Will Need

- Pencil and sheets of sketch paper
- Sheets of corrugated cardboard cut from boxes or other appropriate materials
- Large scissors and white glue
- Tempera or spray paint

What You Will Do

1. Study Figure 12–9. The facial features appear as simple geometric shapes. The nose is rectangular and the eyes are elliptical, or oval shaped.
2. Select a model for your abstract sculptural portrait. It can be a friend, a family member, or a classmate. Look at your model. Create a main focus by distorting a particular feature, as Gabo has done. You might change the size of the feature or alter its shape in some way. Make several pencil sketches of your model until you have made one that pleases you.
3. Make a revised pencil sketch of your model using simple geometric shapes to symbolize the real shapes. Decide whether your sculpture will be horizontal or vertical.

4. Using scissors, cut a large cardboard shape as a base. Refer to your sketch to cut out smaller geometric shapes to form the facial features of your model. You may cut the shapes in half, or in eighths. Think about different facial expressions. For example, is your model smiling or frowning?
5. Assemble your work by gluing shapes and forms to each other. Work carefully. Look at your sculpture from different angles before joining each new piece. You may choose to cut slits in your cardboard shapes to attach them more securely.
6. Paint your sculpture using either white or black tempera or spray paint. The use of a single color will add harmony to the work. Spray paint works especially well in this case.

Safety Tip

Use spray paint outdoors or in a room with good ventilation. Before spraying, place your sculpture inside a large cardboard box. This will help contain some of the harmful fumes.

Evaluating Your Work

- **Describe** Name the different shapes and forms you used in your work. Show shapes with different textures or patterns.
- **Analyze** Tell whether you used vertical or horizontal emphasis in your work. Explain how shapes and forms add interest to your work.
- **Interpret** Title your work. Explain how you interpreted your subject when producing your abstract head.
- **Judge** Tell whether you feel your work succeeds. Explain your answer.

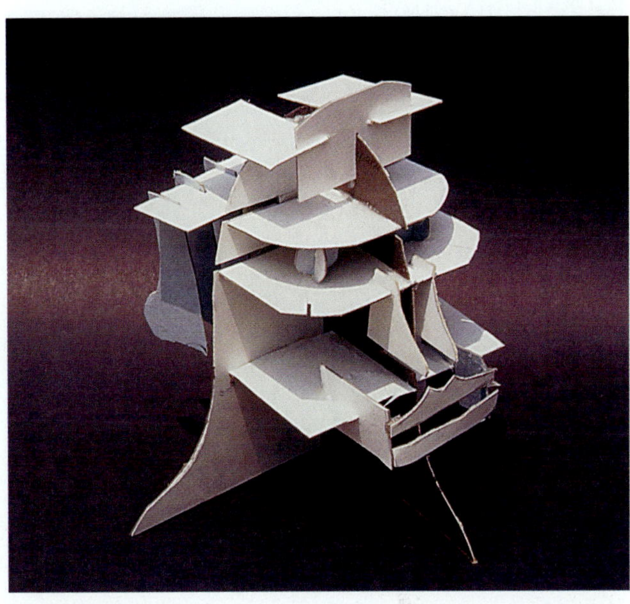

◆ **Figure 12–10** Student work. An abstract sculpture.

STUDIO OPTION

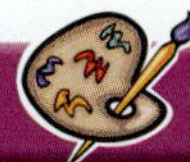

Select and use a variety of appropriate art materials and tools to interpret a subject when producing a second experimental sculpture. Combine found objects to represent an animal, bird, reptile, or amphibian. These odds and ends might include plastic spoons, straws, old door hinges, or other metal parts. Paint your sculpture black, white, or grey to emphasize its overall form.

Visual Art Journal

Define a variety of concepts directly related to the art elements and principles used in your sculpture. How are the elements and principles used to create an abstract style? Write down your thoughts in your journal, using vocabulary accurately.

LESSON 3

Making a Layered Low-Relief Panel

Examine the carving in **Figure 12–11.** This is an example of low-relief sculpture. **Low relief** is *a type of relief sculpture in which the forms project only slightly from a flat background.* In contrast, **high-relief** sculpture is *a type of relief sculpture in which the forms project boldly from a flat background.* Notice how the figures in the art object shown here barely project outward.

What You Will Learn

You will create a low-relief panel by selecting and using a variety of appropriate art materials and tools to interpret a subject in traditional and experimental ways. You will use overlapping to create layers. To do this, you will glue tag board and thick string to a mat board surface. You will create an artwork integrating themes found through direct observation. You will organize the art elements of shape, line, and space using informal balance. Experiment with the elements of line and shape to create a certain mood in your relief. Paint your final piece using two colors to unify the surface of your work.

What You Will Need

- Sketchbook, pencil, and eraser
- Mat board, 9 × 12 inches, scissors
- Tag board, thick string or thin cording
- White glue, paper towels, newspaper
- Spray paint, and/or acrylic paint and brushes
- Rub-and-buff metallic wax (optional)
- Envelope or sandwich bag

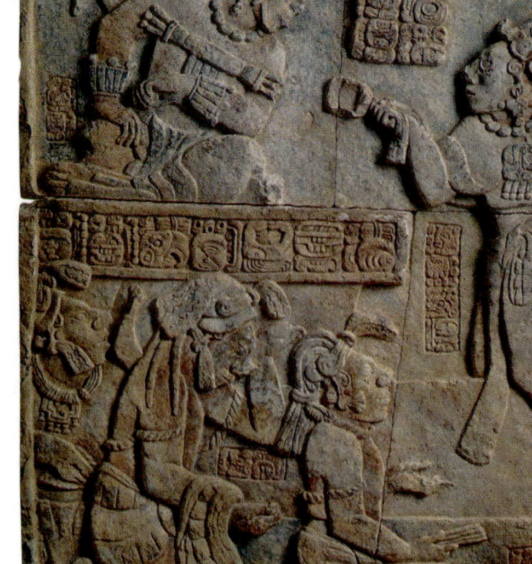

◆ Figure 12–11 **The Mayans had a sophisticated writing system that has recently been deciphered. The glyphs, or picture writing, identify the ruler at that time, the date, and all the people present at that event. Analyze this artwork to form conclusions about historical and cultural contexts.**

Pre-Columbian, Maya. Mexico, Usumacinta River Valley. *Presentation of Captives to a Maya Ruler.* c. 785. Limestone with traces of paint. 115.3 × 88.9 cm (45⅜ × 35″). Kimbell Art Museum, Fort Worth, Texas.

What You Will Do

1. Brainstorm with your class to choose a theme for your work. You might choose a nature scene, a still life, or a scene that tells a story, such as in Figure 12–11. Research and collect images to fit your theme.
2. Illustrate ideas by making several sketches based on your research and by integrating themes found through direct observation. Organize shapes, lines and spaces using informal balance. Keep your sketches simple. Each shape and figure will have to be cut out and glued to the surface.
3. Select your best sketch. Transfer the shapes used in your sketch onto your mat board. Using scissors, cut pieces you plan to use for the background of your scene. Then cut all the pieces you need for the foreground. You can use pieces of thick string or cording to create lines. Before you glue your cut shapes or lines, experiment with different arrangements. Choose the composition you like best.
4. Overlap your cardboard pieces to create a relief. Glue down the background pieces first, and then glue the foreground pieces on top of them. Glue your shapes and lines in place.
5. Select two colors and paint your relief. Display your work with those of your classmates. What similarities and differences can you find in the works produced by your classmates?

Evaluating Your Work

- **Describe** Describe how you made your relief panel. What materials did you use?
- **Analyze** Explain how you experimented with different arrangements. Describe how you arranged your lines, shapes, and spaces to create informal balance.
- **Interpret** Explain what mood your work conveys. What elements and principles help convey that mood? How did you integrate themes found through direct observation?
- **Judge** Do you feel you were able to successfully create a relief panel?

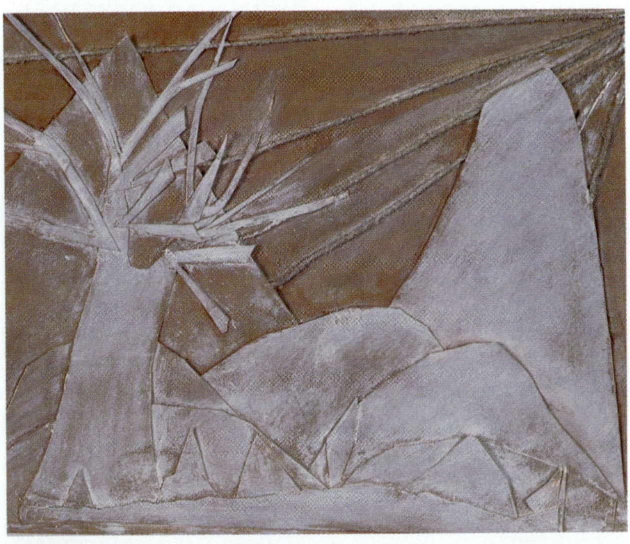

◆ **Figure 12–12** **Student work. A low-relief panel.**

Reflective Thinking

Critical Evaluation. Analyze the relief panels of your peers. Form conclusions about formal properties, such as the way they used line and shape to create informal balance. Form conclusions about intent. For example, does the image match what the artist intended?

Art Online

Click on Web Links at **art.glencoe.com** to learn more about Mayan art and culture. There, you will also find:

- Artist Profiles
- Interactive Games

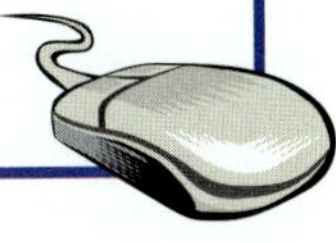

Plaster Carving

Alan Houser was the great-nephew of Geronimo, the renowned Apache chief. Always mindful of his heritage, Houser created beautiful images using Native American subjects. One of these appears in **Figure 12–13.** Notice that the artist uses a variety of textures. These give the sculpture both realistic and abstract qualities. The weight and posture of the figure make it lifelike. The rough textural surface of the body's form adds an abstract quality. Notice how your eye is drawn to the face. Houser used both smooth texture and a contrast in values to emphasize this area.

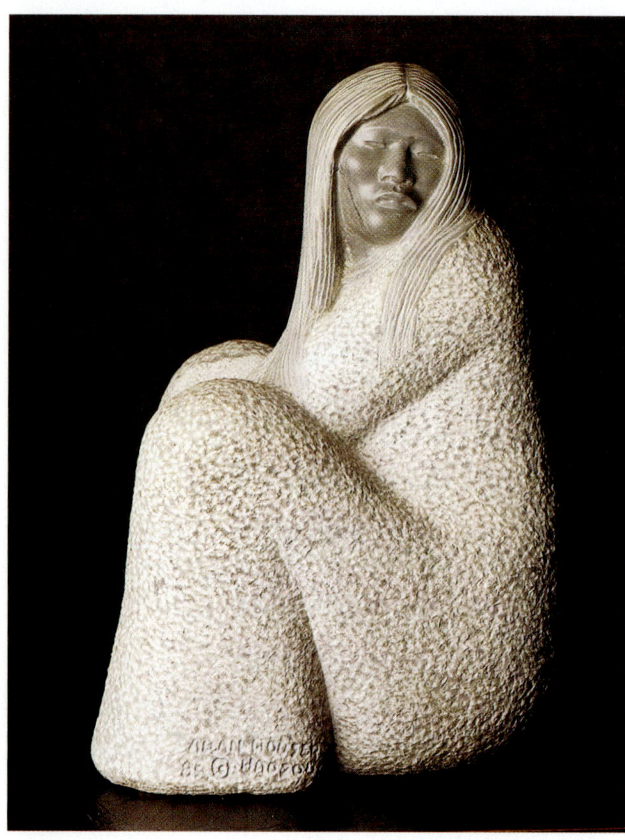

◆ **Figure 12–13** **Houser was known as a sculptor, a painter, and a teacher. He used his childhood memories to convey images of Native American people.**

Allan Houser. *White River Woman.* 1985. Italian gray marble. 57.2 × 35.6 × 40.6 cm (22½ × 14 × 16″). The Genesee County Museum, Rochester, New York.

What You Will Learn

You will carve a plaster sculpture in the round by selecting and using a variety of appropriate art materials and tools in traditional and experimental ways. You will interpret a subject when producing your sculpture. For example, your sculpture can be of a person or an animal. It must be carved on all sides. Plan how your positive form will affect the negative space. Add texture and detail using a variety of tools. Give your work unity through the repetition of shapes, forms, and/or textures.

What You Will Need

- Sketchbook, pencil, eraser
- Images of people and animals
- Modeling plaster, vermiculite
- Plastic bowl or bucket, cold water, mixing stick
- Polystyrene or paper cup or container
- Assorted carving tools such as plastic knives, spoons, paper clips, nails, files
- Spray bottle with water, sandpaper

What You Will Do

1. Begin by deciding whether you will make a sculpture of a person or an animal. Next, collect images of your subject. Make several sketches of what your sculpture will look like from the front, each side, and the back. Plan for repetition of form, shape, and/or texture to create unity. Choose your best set of sketches and set them aside.
2. Pour three parts cold water into a plastic container. Mix in three parts modeling plaster and 1 part vermiculite. Stir the mixture with a stick until it is smooth. When the mixture thickens slightly, pour it carefully into your polystyrene container. (See **Technique Tip** in *Handbook* page 287.)

3. After a few minutes you will notice that the mixture is beginning to dry and set. When the plaster is set, carefully tear the polystyrene container from your mold.
4. Transfer your design onto all four sides of your plaster mold. Using the knife or spoon, begin scraping away the negative areas surrounding your positive form. Your subject will slowly emerge from the form as you carve. Use nails or a paper-clip to carve out small areas. Experiment with different tools to add texture and details. Turn your sculpture as you carve to complete all sides. Periodically spray a light mist of water on your sculpture. This will keep it moist, make it easier to work, and control the dust. When you finish carving, let your sculpture dry completely. Lightly sand the areas you want smooth to give your sculpture a finished look.
5. Display your carving and compare it with those of your classmates.

Safety Tip

If you have breathing problems, tell your teacher. Dry dust from plaster and clay can be harmful. Use a dust mask if necessary.

Evaluating Your Work

- **Describe** What subject did you interpret when producing your sculpture? What tools did you experiment with to add texture and detail?
- **Analyze** How did you use the repetition of shapes, form, or texture to create unity?
- **Interpret** Give your sculpture a title. Write a story and use your sculpture as the main character. Look closely at your sculpture's expressive quality to help you describe its character in your story.
- **Judge** Were you successful in creating a plaster carving?

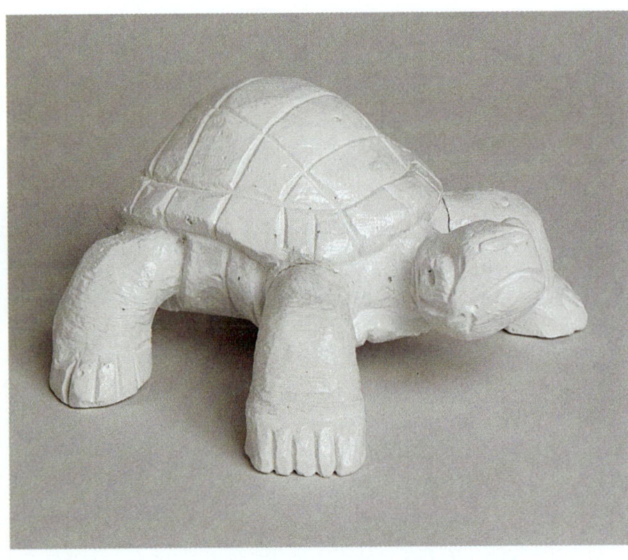

◆ **Figure 12–14** **Student work. A plaster carving.**

STUDIO OPTION

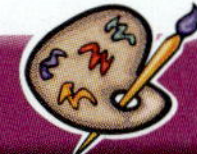

Make several sketches of a monument or building in your community. Choose your best sketch and study it carefully. Using the same steps in this studio lesson, sculpt a model of this structure in traditional ways. For example, use carving tools to add a variety of textures and details. Title your sculpted structure and place it on display.

Visual Art Journal

Analyze Figure 12–13 to determine cultural contexts. For example, what clues does the sculpture give about Native American culture? Write down your thoughts in your journal.

Art Symbols in World Religions

Throughout history, religious belief has driven the art of various cultures. During the Renaissance in Europe, from the 15th to 16th centuries, the Catholic Church was a great patron of the arts. Consequently, much of the art by Michelangelo and Leonardo da Vinci has religious themes. **Figure 12–15** is another artwork that is religious in nature. Do you recognize this figure? More than 700 million followers of the Hindu religion do. This sculpture is the Hindu god Ganesha (guh-**nesh**-uh). Hinduism is the chief religion of India. You can find this nation on the map in **Figure 12–16.** In India, Ganesha is known among children as the *elephant god.* He is a happy figure, whom they associate with receiving gifts and treats. Can you see why?

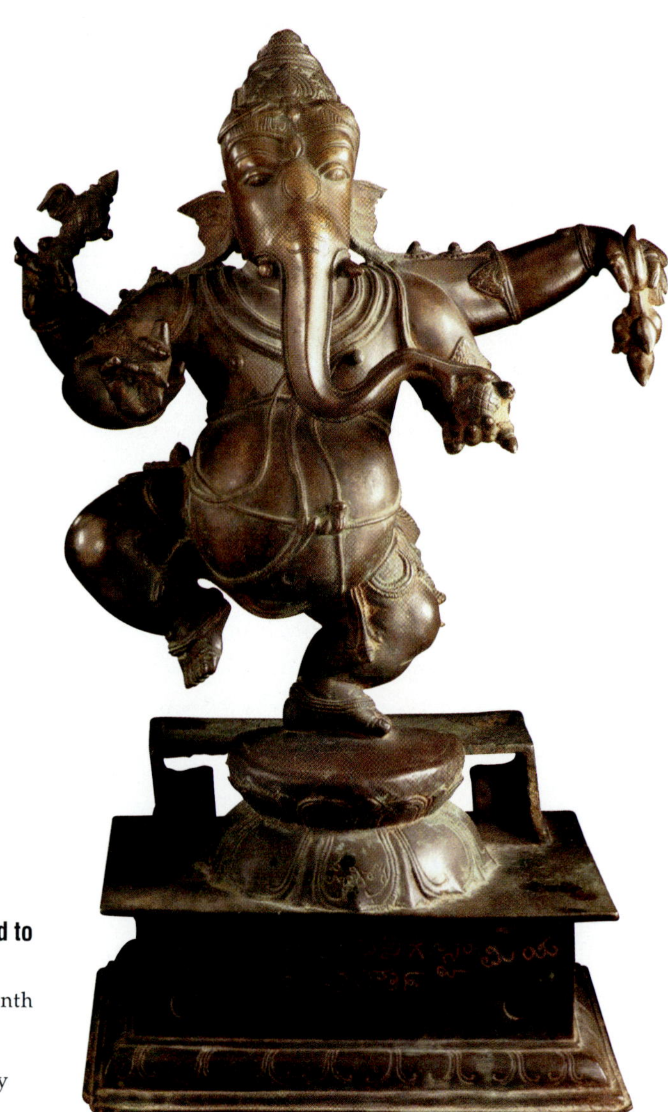

◆ **Figure 12–15** **Which sculpture technique was used to create this work?**

India, Karnataka. *Dancing Ganesha, Lord of Obstacles.* Sixteenth to seventeenth century. Copper alloy. 50.5 × 33 × 19.7cm ($19\frac{7}{8} \times 13 \times 7\frac{3}{4}$″). Los Angeles County Museum of Art, Los Angeles, California. Purchased with funds provided by Harry and Yvonne Lenart.

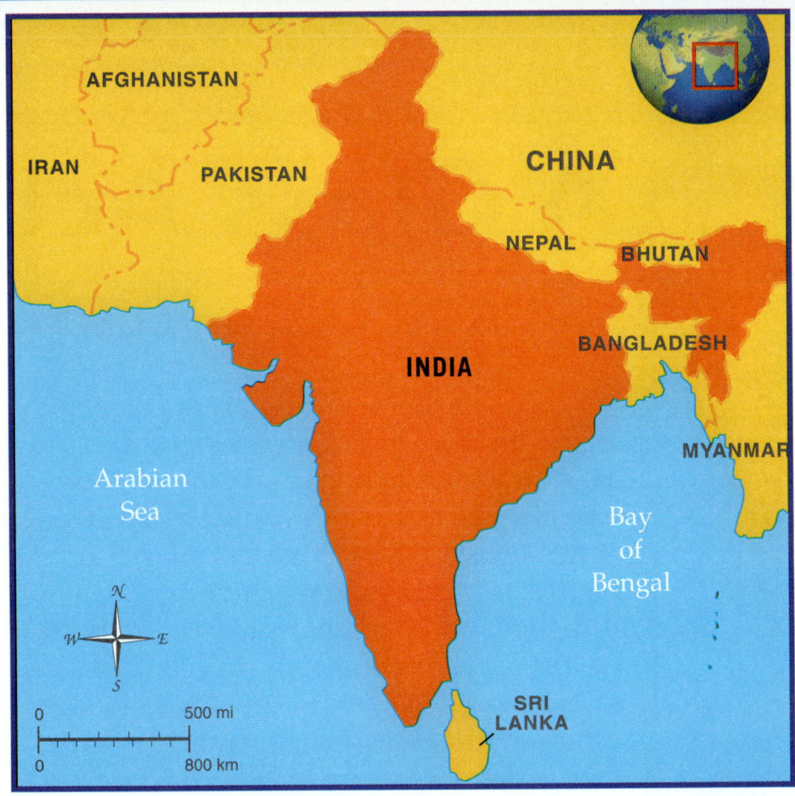

◆ **Figure 12–16** Map of India.

Ganesha: God of Gifts

Ganesha is one of the five gods of worship among Hindus. In India he is one of the most popular of these gods. That is because he is the god of lucky beginnings and good fortune. Notice that the Ganesha in Figure 12–15 is shown dancing. According to tradition, Ganesha loves to dance. Hindu worship often includes sound and music. The following benediction, or blessing, is chanted:

> *May the dancing Ganesha be your aid, copied by the guardian elephants of the horizon, who spring up lightly from the earth that trembles at the stamping of his feet, the while with upraised trunk he drinks and then sprays back like drops of water the great circle of stars.*

In the 1500s, this Ganesha would have been carried in a joyous procession. You can almost see the creature bobbing and swaying to the happy music.

Another version of this god appears in Figure 4–16 on page 81. Compare and contrast these two sculptures. How are they similar? In what ways are they different?

MAKE THE CONNECTION

Take Another Look

1. Analyze the sculpture in Figure 12–15, which depicts a symbol of good fortune in the Hindu religion. Form conclusions about the meaning of this artwork.
2. Compare the artwork in Figure 12–15 with Figure 6–13 on page 125. This figure is a Madonna, an art symbol from Christianity. Analyze and compare relationships, such as function and meaning, in the two artworks.

Art & Social Studies

Other religious art symbols. Research another symbol from a world religion such as Islam, Judaism, Buddhism, or Taoism. How was this symbol depicted by artists? What was the image meant to symbolize? Write down your findings in a paragraph.

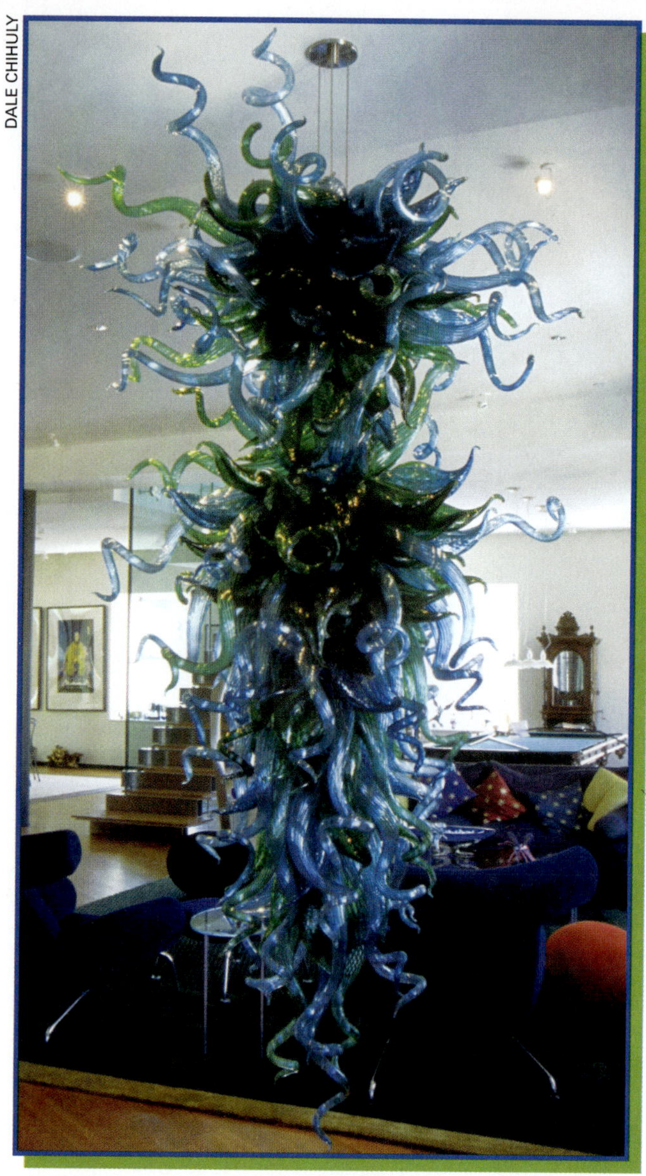
DALE CHIHULY

Dale Chihuly. *Turquoise and Emerald Chandelier.* 1996.

A Glass Act

Dale Chihuly's sculptures depict art with a twist.

For a glassblower, it's actually good to be "full of hot air." After all, it's air that expands a melted glob of glass into fragile works of art. Dale Chihuly (b. 1941) is as "hot"—or popular—as his furnace. His works, including unusually shaped chandeliers and light fixtures, sell for as much as $40,000. One of his pieces is even in the White House, where works of the best American artists are displayed.

Born in Tacoma, Washington, Chihuly first learned about glasswork in graduate school. In 1968, just out of school, Chihuly visited Venice, Italy, a city famous for its exquisite, colorful glass. There, he observed the way teams of people, rather than one lone artist, made a work. Chihuly uses the team approach today. This suits the artist fine: "I was always more interested in the product than in glassblowing itself."

Chihuly sometimes creates large installations. One project involved working in glass factories in Finland, Ireland, and Mexico. In his installation "Chihuly over Venice," 14 chandeliers were hung over some of the canals and squares of Venice. They transformed parts of the watery Italian city into a colorful glass canvas.

Says Chihuly of his glass art, "I want people to be overwhelmed with light and color."

TIME TO CONNECT

- **Why are Chihuly's glassworks considered art but a light bulb is not?**
- **How are Chihuly's glass works different from the glass in your everyday life?**
- **Write a short essay that discusses how function (or usability) relates to an artwork made of glass.**
- **Edit your essay with a partner for clarity of ideas and correct punctuation, grammar, and spelling.**

Chapter 12 Review

BUILDING VOCABULARY

Number a sheet of paper from 1 to 12. After each number, write the term from the list that best matches each description below.

abstract	high relief
additive	low relief
assembling	maquette
carving	modeling
casting	study
cross-section	subtractive

1. A sculpting method in which material is cut or chipped away.
2. A term describing a sculpting method that takes away or removes material.
3. A sculpting method in which melted material is poured into a mold.
4. A term describing a sculpting method that adds together or joins bits of material together.
5. A sculpting method in which a soft or workable material is built up and shaped.
6. Cutaway view.
7. Art in which the subject of the artwork is simplified or stylized.
8. A sculpting method in which different kinds of materials are gathered and joined.
9. Relief sculpture in which the forms project only slightly from a flat background.
10. Relief sculpture that projects boldly from a flat background.
11. A preliminary drawing or painting.
12. A three-dimensional scaled-down study of a larger planned sculpture.

REVIEWING ART FACTS

Number a sheet of paper from 13 to 18. Answer each question in a complete sentence.

13. Name three sculpting media that have been in existence for thousands of years.
14. What are four sculpting techniques?
15. How old is the art of casting in bronze?
16. What material is used most often in modeling?
17. Which method of sculpting is the most recent?
18. Name two building materials used in assembling. Name two fastening materials.

CROSS-CURRICULUM CONNECTIONS

19. **Science.** A method that has been practiced for centuries in the making of castings is the lost-wax method. Using outside resources, learn more about this method and how it is done. Report on your findings in a written paragraph.
20. **Social Studies.** Find examples of relief and freestanding sculptures in your community. Find out who or what the sculptures represent. Using a sketchbook and pencil, illustrate ideas from direct observation. Draw what you see and take photographs of the works of art. Compile a journal using your drawings, photographic imagery, and notes.

Web Museum Activity

Hirshhorn Museum and Sculpture Garden, Smithsonian Institution, Washington, D.C.

Create your own sculpture online by visiting the Hirshhorn Museum and Sculpture Garden. Click on the musem's link at art.glencoe.com to create a virtual sculpture. You can even exhibit your finished piece in the online sculpture garden!

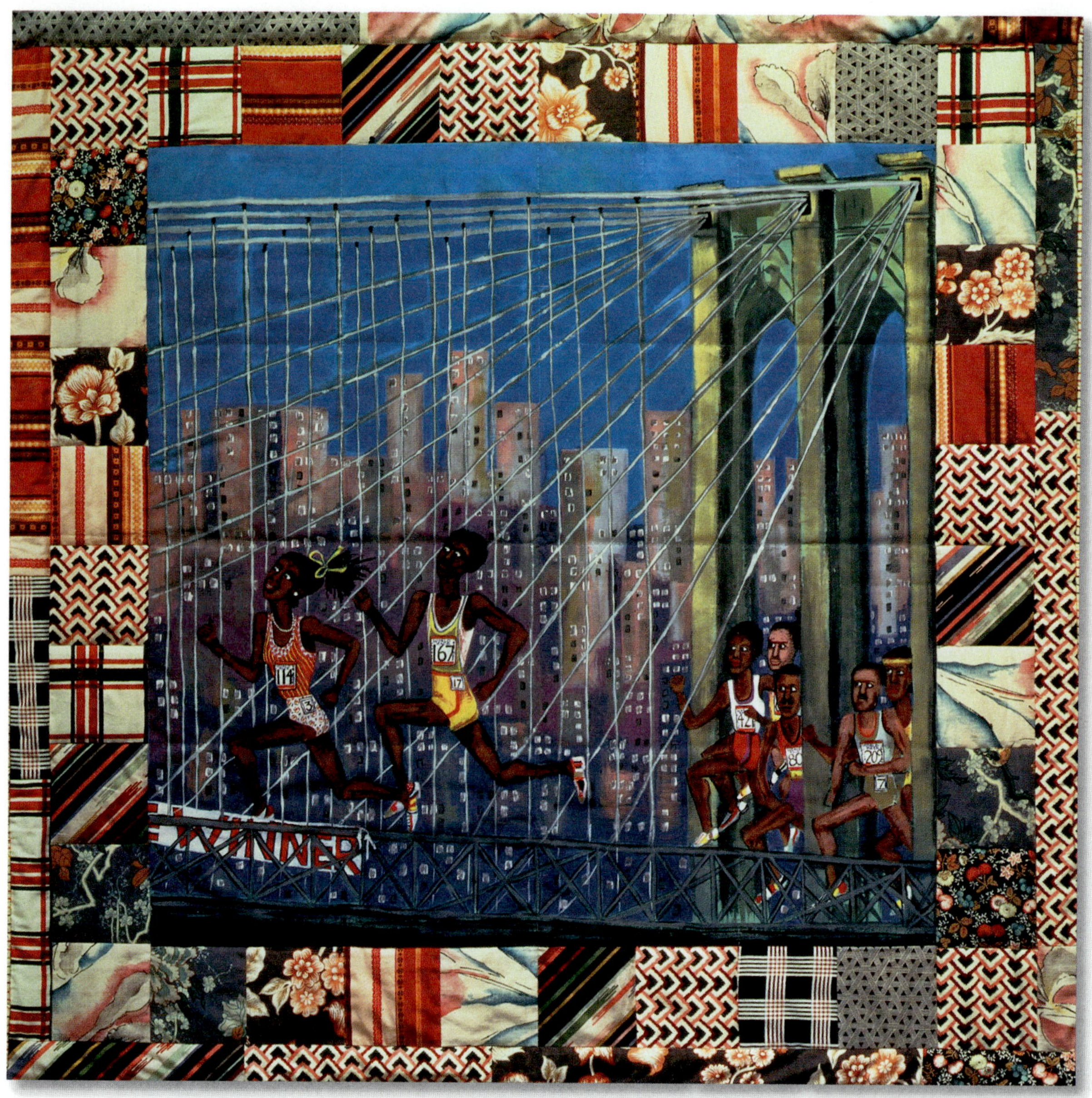

Focus On ◆ **Figure 13–1** **Many of Faith Ringgold's artworks combine fiberart with paint media. Her artworks often carry an inspirational message. What message can you "read" in this artwork?**

Faith Ringgold. *The Winner. (Women on a Bridge #4)*. 1989. Acrylic on canvas with quilted fabric border. 172.7 × 172.7 cm (68 × 68″) Private collection. © Faith Ringgold, 1988.

Chapter 13

Crafts

"Like all artists and writers, I am both enriched and limited by what I know and have experienced. In other words, my books and my art are based on my life's experience."
—Faith Ringgold (b. 1930)

Art is often made to be visually appealing. Some art serves a secondary purpose as well. An example of such art appears at the left. Without looking at the credit line, can you identify this object? Can you explain the practical function of objects of this type? Do you know the name of the area of art this work exemplifies?

In this chapter you will learn what artworks of this type are called. You will learn how—and by whom—they are made.

After completing this chapter, you will be able to:

- Define the terms *crafts* and *craftsperson*.
- Describe the crafts of weaving, glassmaking, and ceramics.
- Identify the different conditions of clay.
- Incorporate design into artworks for use in everyday life by creating a ceramic bank, paper jewelry, and a handmade book.
- Produce fiberart using a variety of materials and tools in traditional and experimental ways.
- Determine cultural contexts in symbols of status.

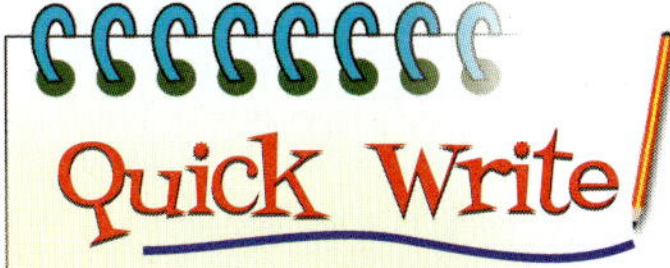

Interpreting the Quote Read the quote. Does the artwork in **Figure 13–1** support the artist's claim in the quote? Explain in a short paragraph.

KEY TERMS

craftspersons
crafts
weaving
fibers
tapestry
loom
glassblowing
ceramics
pottery
plastic clay
leather-hard clay
slip
fired
kiln
glazed

The Art of Crafts

At the beginning of the twentieth century, automaker Henry Ford devised a technological breakthrough. That breakthrough was the *assembly line*. Workers stationed alongside a conveyor belt were each responsible for installing a separate part. By the time the collection of parts reached the end of the line, a car had been built. Ford's method is used today for every imaginable product. The clothing we wear and the dishes we use are mass-produced.

This was not always the case. Before mass production, individual artists made household goods. They wove cloth and sewed clothes by hand. They dug clay from the ground, processed it, and made containers and dishes. They gathered grasses and other fibers to make baskets. They heated glass in furnaces and blew it into usable forms. They took well-deserved pride in their creations. Happily, their breed has not died out. **Craftspersons,** *artists who make useful and aesthetically pleasing goods*, are alive and well. Another name for a craftsperson is *artisan* (**art**-ih-zuhn).

Crafts

Craftspeople use many different media. The unusual bowl in **Figure 13–2**, as an example, was carved from wood. Craftspeople may work in other media, such as metal, fiber, fabric, glass, and clay. In this lesson, you will explore the *different areas of applied art in which craftspeople work*. These areas and their products are better known as **crafts**.

Weaving

Weaving is *a craft in which strands of fiber are interlocked to make cloth or objects*. Some weavers use yarn or rope to create fiberart.

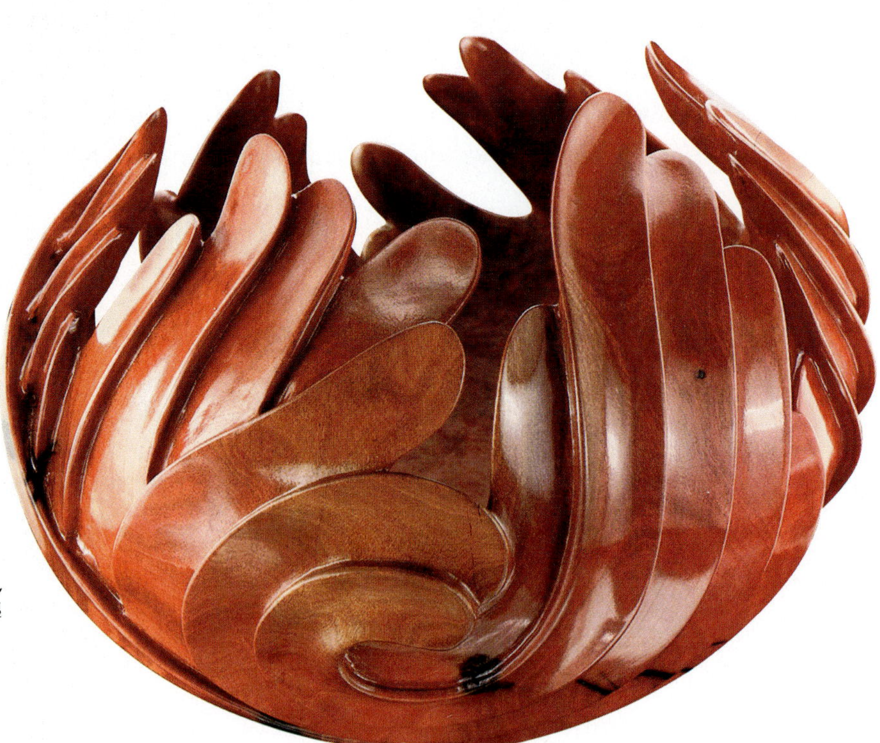

◆ **Figure 13–2** **What makes this bowl different from most is its unusual shape as well as the fact that it was handcarved.**

Ron Fleming. *Firebird*. 1997. Pink ivorywood, lathe turned, carved. 14 × 16.5 × 16.5 cm (5½ × 6½ × 6½″). The Mint Museums, Charlotte, North Carolina. Gift of Jane and Arthur Mason. 1999.69.13.

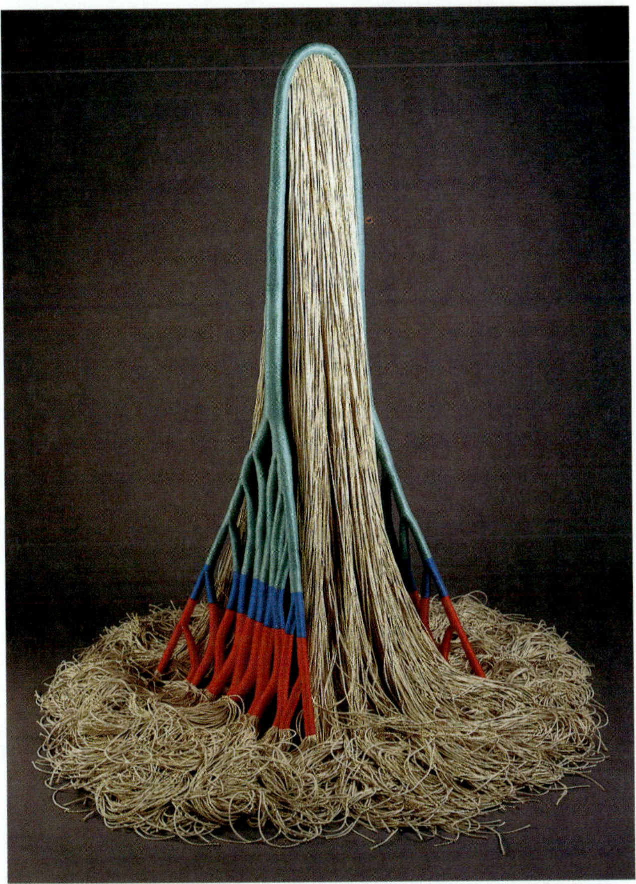

◆ **Figure 13–3** **This artist turned ordinary rope into fiberart.**

Claire Zeisler. *Tri-Color Arch*. 1983–84. Hemp and synthetic fiber. 188 cm (74″) high. The Metropolitan Museum of Art, New York, New York. Gift of Peter Florsheim, Thomas W. Florsheim, and Joan Florsheim-Binkley, 1987. 1987.371

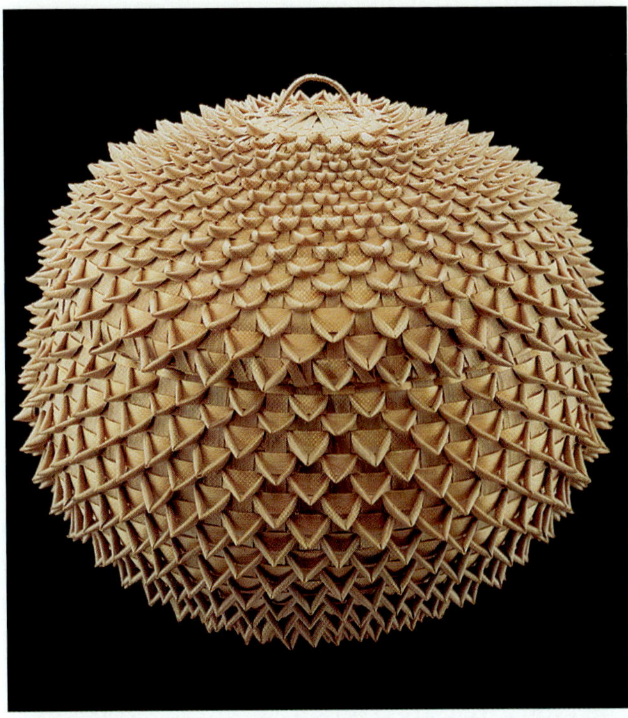

◆ **Figure 13–4** **Does the name of this fiberart seem compatible with its appearance? Why or why not? What other name would you give it?**

Edith Bondie. *Porcupine Basket*. c. 1975. Wood. 20 × 21.4 cm (7⅞ × 8$\frac{7}{16}$″). Museum of American Art, Smithsonian Institution, Washington, D.C. Art Resource, NY.

(**Figure 13–3**). Twigs, reeds, and grasses are among the earliest materials used by weavers. **Figure 13–4** shows an example of a contemporary weaving that uses thin strips of wood. Notice the recurring patterns in this unusual basket.

The majority of weavings are made of **fibers**. These are *strands of any thin, threadlike material*. Artworks that are created with fibers or fabrics such as cotton, wool, and rayon are known as *fiberart*. One such example of fiberart appears in **Figure 13–10** on page 238. This art object is a **tapestry**, a *weaving used as a wall hanging*. Notice that the individual threads are visible.

The earliest fibers used in weaving were derived from animal hair or plant materials. Wool and cotton are two examples. Today, manufactured fibers such as rayon, nylon, and acrylic are used in addition to these traditional weaving materials. Even some sweaters and rugs today are made with fibers produced from recycled plastic bottles!

Cloth weaving is done on a loom. A **loom** is *a frame or machine that holds a set of threads that run vertically*. These are called the "warp" threads. The weaver passes threads from a second set under and over the first set. These threads are called the "weft." This creates a pattern and locks the threads together. In factories, computers are programmed to control large weaving machines. Today some individual artists work on computerized looms.

GLASSMAKING

The practice of melting sand to make glass is thousands of years old. So is the art of glassblowing. **Glassblowing** is *the craft of shaping melted glass by blowing air into it through a tube.* One of the most famous contemporary glassmakers is Dale Chihuly. Notice how the luminous color swirls seem to flow through the design in **Figure 13–5**. Are you reminded of shapes that are natural to the sea? Today glassmakers like Chihuly experiment with designs that, like much art of the day, are daring.

CERAMICS

Ceramics is another craft. **Ceramics** is *the process of creating objects from clay and hardening them by fire.* Clay is found virtually everywhere on the globe. This makes ceramics one of the most widely practiced, not to mention oldest, crafts. The Native American vessel, or pot shown in **Figure 13–6** dates to between 1300 and 1500. Objects made using ceramic techniques are known as **pottery**. This term is also used as a synonym for *ceramics*.

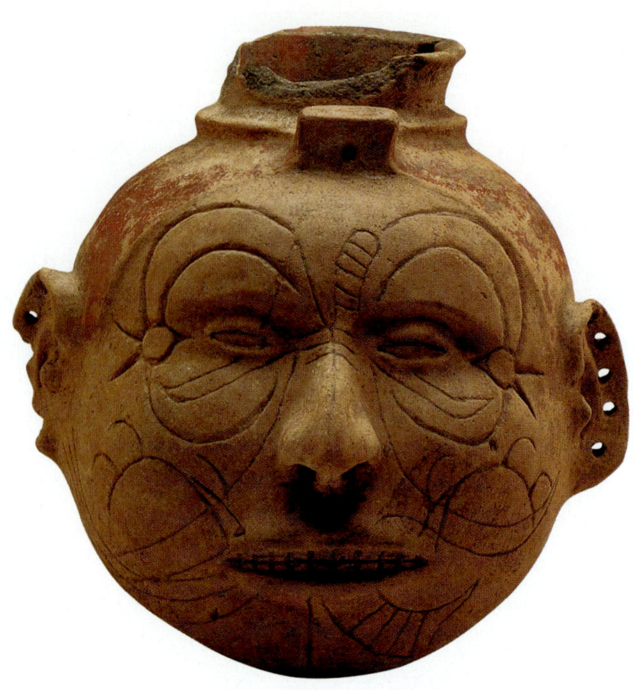

◆ **Figure 13–6 This pot portrays the head of a deceased leader who was spiritually powerful. Analyze this artwork to determine cultural contexts. What does it tell you about the culture that created it?**

Mississippian. *Head Effigy vessel.* 1300–1500. Buffware and pigment. Height: 18 cm (7¼″). The Detroit Institute of Arts, Detroit, Michigan. Founders Society purchase with funds from the Mary G. and Robert H. Flint Foundation. 1986.43.

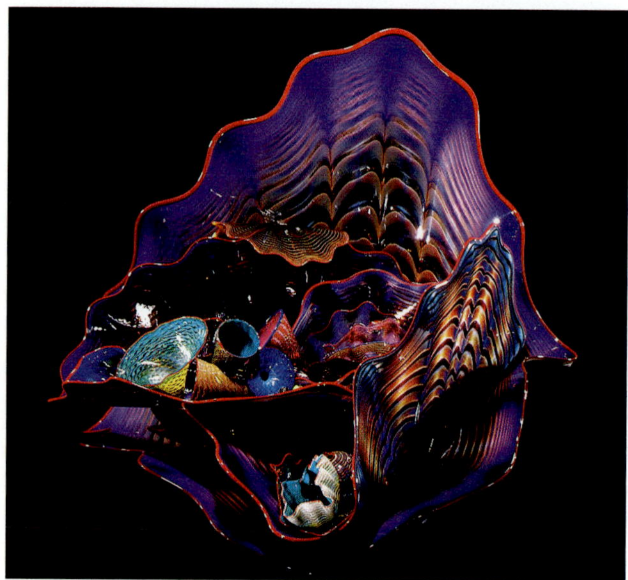

◆ **Figure 13–5 Define a variety of concepts directly related to the art elements and principles in this artwork. In particular, do the flowing lines of color create a sense of rhythm? How?**

Dale Chihuly. *Violet Persian Set with Red Lip Wraps.* 1990. Glass. 76.2 × 66 × 63.5 cm (30 × 26 × 25″). Spencer Museum of Art, The University of Kansas, Lawrence, Kansas. Museum purchase: Peter T. Bohan Art Acquisition Fund.

Preparing the Clay

Making pottery starts with preparing the clay. Water is added so that the clay is wet enough to be worked easily. Potters have special words for the different states clay takes during this process:

- **Plastic clay** is *clay that is wet enough to be worked but firm enough to hold its shape.*
- **Leather-hard clay** is *clay that is still damp but is too dry to shape.*
- **Slip** is *clay that has so much added water that it is liquid and runny.* Slip is used as glue to join together pieces of leather-hard clay. It is also used in decorating a finished work.

When working clay by hand, potters use special methods to shape the clay. Some of these are pinching, coiling, and slab-building. Clay can also be shaped by "throwing" it. This means turning it on a rapidly spinning wheel called a potter's wheel. Throwing a clay object makes a smooth, symmetrical piece. Some finished ceramic objects are made by combining several methods.

Firing the Clay Object

After the clay is shaped and dried, it must be **fired**, or *hardened by applying high heat*. This is done in *a special ceramics furnace* known as a **kiln** (**kil**). The temperature inside a kiln can reach 3000°F (1650°C).

Before clay has been fired, it is called greenware. When it is bone dry it is ready for the kiln. After it has been fired, it is called bisqueware (**bisk**-ware). Sometimes bisqueware is **glazed**. This means *coated with a mixture of powdered chemicals that melt during firing to form a hard, glasslike finish*. Glazes can be made in a wide range of colors. The glaze is painted on the pottery, and the item is fired a second time.

Pottery does not always have to be glazed. Terra-cotta pottery, which is often used to decorate buildings and hold plants, is unglazed (**Figure 13–7**). If a container is designed to hold food or liquid, it must be covered with a nontoxic glaze.

Time & Place

Caddoan Culture (c. 1000)

The term *Caddoan* (**ka**-doh-uhn) denotes a group of Native American cultures of the past. The term is also the family name for the languages the people spoke. The Caddoans lived principally in the upper Missouri Valley in North Dakota, and in the Platto Valley in Nebraska. Other regions they inhabited include southwestern Arkansas, and in neighboring parts of Oklahoma, Louisiana, and Texas. In addition to their finely crafted pottery, the Caddoans are known for the burial mounds they built. Cherokee County, Texas, is home to the Caddoan Mounds State Historic Site. The artwork shown in Figure 13–6 is an example of Caddoan pottery.

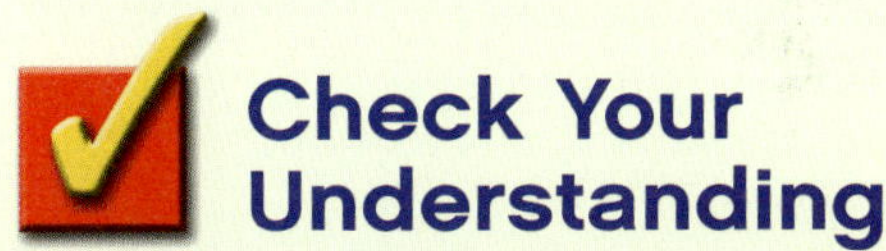

Check Your Understanding

1. What is a *craftsperson*? Define the term *crafts.*
2. What is *weaving*? What is the name of the machine on which cloth is woven?
3. What is glass made of? What is *glassblowing*?
4. Name two ways in which *slip* is used.
5. Describe the difference between plastic clay and leather-hard clay.
6. What is the difference between greenware and bisqueware?

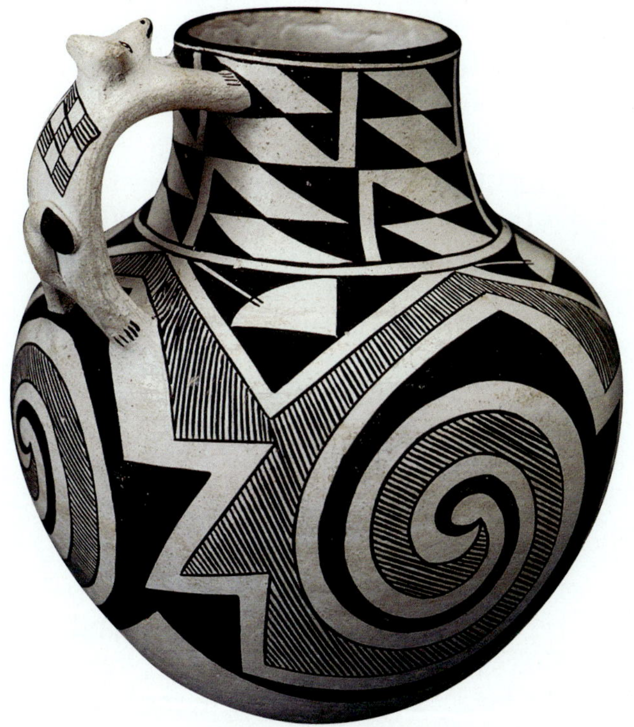

◆ **Figure 13–7 Compare and contrast the use of the art elements in this object with the one shown in Figure 13–6. Using vocabulary accurately, site the differences you detect between the two objects.**

Lucy Lewis. (Acoma Peublo, New Mexico.) *Black-on-white pottery jar*. 1969. 20.3 × 17.8 cm (8 × 7″). National Museum of the American Indian, Smithsonian Institution, Washington, D.C.

Ceramic Animal Banks

Look closely at **Figure 13–8**. What type of animals do you see? What do you notice about the colors and textures used in these sculptures? These are molded ceramic banks used by a child to hold money. These banks were used in ceremonies during The Day of the Dead, a Mexican holiday honoring those who have died. The banks were used during the early twentieth century, but few of them have survived.

What You Will Learn

Select and use a variety of appropriate art materials and tools to create a functional ceramic sculpture of an animal. You will incorporate design into your artwork for use in every-day life. Your ceramic sculpture will be used as a bank modeled after an animal.

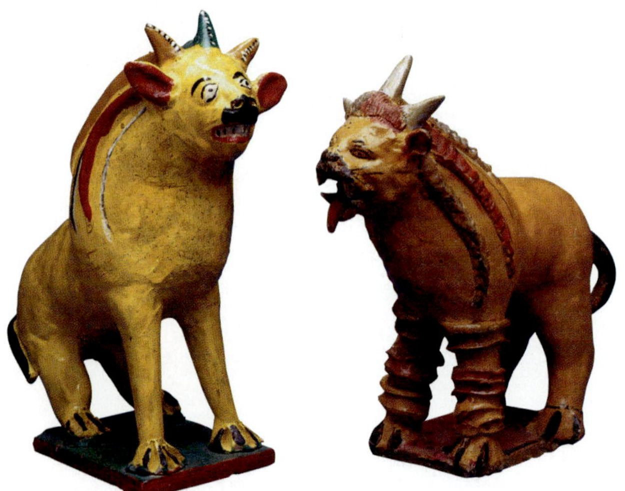

◆ **Figure 13–8** **What elements of art did the artists use effectively in these ceramic banks?**

(Right) Julio Acero. Santa Cruz de las Huertas, Jalisco, Mexico. *Lion Bank*. c. 1930. Single-fired, painted and varnished earthenware. San Antonio Museum of Art, San Antonio, Texas. Nelson A. Rockefeller Folk Art Collection.
(Left) Carlos Medrano. Santa Cruz de las Huertas, Jalisco, Mexico. *Lion Bank*. c. 1970. Single-fired, painted and varnished earthenware. San Antonio Museum of Art, San Antonio, Texas. Gift of Joe Nicholson.

Use the two traditional modeling methods of making coils and a pinch pot to create the body of your bank. Give your bank variety by contrasting the coil and pinch-pot forms. You will also give your animal expressive qualities. Finish your work with glaze or acrylic paint.

What You Will Need

- Sketchbook, pencil, eraser, clay
- Piece of muslin or other smooth cloth
- Clay modeling tools, flat and pointed
- Newspaper, container with slip
- Glaze or acrylic paints (various colors)
- Potter's wheel (optional)

What You Will Do

1. Begin by collecting images of animals, or use personal photos or postcards. In your sketchbook, make several sketches to plan your ideas. Draw your animals sitting upright or standing. You may decide to create a fantasy animal, like a dragon, or a combination animal like a cat with wings. Include textures such as fur, feathers and/or scales in your drawing. Give your animal expressive qualities such as a smile or a snarl. Select your best sketch as a guide.
2. Working on a piece of cloth, roll a ball of clay the size of a softball. Make a pinch pot (or throw a small pot on the potter's wheel). Push your thumb into your ball of clay up to the first joint. With your thumb in place, rest your fingers on the outside of the clay ball. Pinch or press gently, release and turn the clay ball. Repeat the pinching and releasing step, forming a bowl. This is the base of your animal bank. Depending on the animal you chose, your pot will be wide and shallow or tall and deep. Cut a circle a little larger than a quarter in the bottom to allow for the removal of coins.

3. Using more clay, make coils to build the body of your animal. Read **Technique Tip 17,** *Handbook* pages 286–287 about joining clay pieces. Score and apply slip between each coil. Join them to your base. Secure your coils by smoothing the inside of the pot with a flat tool. Stuff crumpled pieces of newspaper inside your bank as you work. This will help hold up the walls as the pot air-dries.
4. Roll a ball of clay the size of a tennis ball. Make a small pinch pot for the head. Cut a small hole in the body where you will attach the head. This will prevent trapped air from expanding and causing breakage during the firing process. Attach the head to the body. As you form the head give your animal an expression. Pinch out the ears and nose. Use a pointed tool to cut into the pot to make the mouth and eyes. Attach thick coils for legs. Add details such as toenails or teeth. Use your tools to add texture for fur, feathers, or scales to create unity. If your animal has a tail, attach it to the back of your bank. Attach it by curling it or twisting it against the back or side. Cut a slit into the back of the bank a little bigger than a quarter.
5. After your bank has been fired, paint or glaze it. Display your finished sculpture in a class "zoo."

Evaluating Your Work

- **Describe** How did you incorporate design into your artwork for everyday life? List the steps used for making the bank.
- **Analyze** Describe the textures and/or colors you used to create unity in your bank. Explain how you used the two modeling methods to create variety.
- **Interpret** Describe your animal's expressive qualities. How did you achieve this? Explain.
- **Judge** Were you successful in creating a functional sculpture? Use the aesthetic theories to defend your decision.

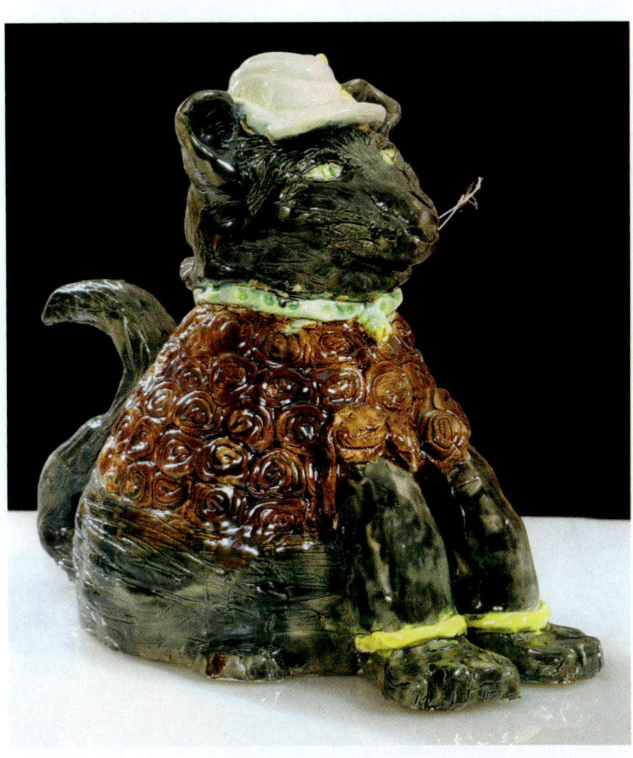

◆ **Figure 13–9** **Student work. Ceramic animal bank.**

PORTFOLIO IDEAS

To include three-dimensional work in your portfolio, take several photographs of your work. Choose the best photographs and attach them to your portfolio. Include the title, date, media, and the process used to create your work. Analyze and compare relationships, such as function and meaning, in your personal artworks.

Visual Art Journal

Analyze portfolios by peers and others to form conclusions about formal properties, historical and cultural contexts, intents, and meanings. Write down your thoughts in your visual art journal.

LESSON 3

Tapestry Weavings

Examine an article of clothing you are wearing. Can you see the individual strands of fiber in the fabric? Your clothing was most likely woven on a machine. At one time, however, all material was handwoven. Today hand weavings are most often used as decorative wall hangings. An example of fiberart appears in **Figure 13–10**. The artist, Maria Nez, blends traditional Navajo weaving techniques with contemporary images. The image is of a dance held in the desert. What clues tell you this is a contemporary work?

Pictorial weaving is very difficult. It often contains curved lines and unusual designs to create a recognizable image. Many of Nez's fiberart weavings take as long as six months to complete.

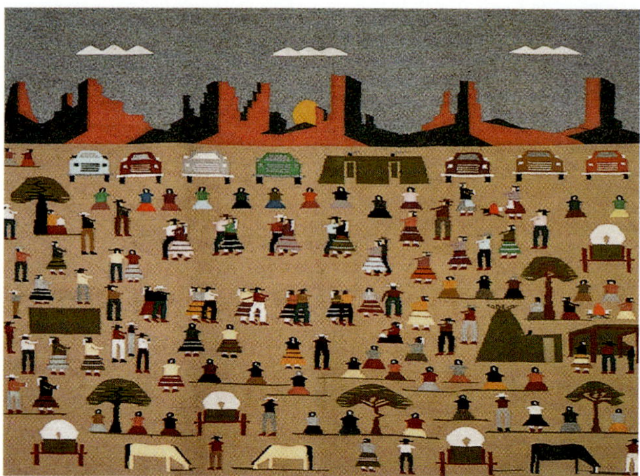

◆ **Figure 13–10** **Identify cultural ideas expressed in this piece of fiberart relating to social themes. What social event is depicted? How does this reflect the artist's culture?**

Maria Nez. Navajo People, Arizona. *Pictorial Weaving*. Tapestry technique, handspun wool yarns. 128.3 × 169.9 cm (50½ × 66½″). Museum of International Folk Art, Santa Fe, New Mexico. Neutrogena Collection.

What You Will Learn

You will select and use a variety of appropriate art materials and tools to interpret subjects when producing fiberart in traditional and experimental ways. You will make a woven wall hanging using a cardboard loom, yarns, strings, and found fibers. You will use a variety of textures and choose a color scheme.

What You Will Need

- Ruler, pencil, scissors, transparent tape
- Sheet of heavy cardboard, 12 × 18 inches
- Spool of strong, thin thread
- Different colored yarns and strings
- Found materials that can be used as fibers, such as grass, strips of paper, and used audiotape
- Tapestry needle, comb, wooden dowel

What You Will Do

1. To make your loom, hold the ruler along the top edge of your cardboard. With the pencil, mark off every ¼-inch.
2. Using the scissors, make a cut about ½-inch deep at each mark. Do the same thing along the bottom of the cardboard.
3. Tape the end of your thread to the back of the cardboard. Bring the spool to the front, passing the thread through the top-left notch. Pull the spool down to the bottom of the loom. Pass the thread through the bottom-left notch and around to the back. Move one notch to the right. Pull the thread through and up the front of the loom. Keep working until you reach the last notch. Bring the spool to the back. Cut the thread, and tape to the cardboard.

4. Decide which color scheme and fibers you will use. Experiment with different textures to add interest to your fiberart.
5. Thread one of your thinner yarns through the eye of the tapestry needle. Start to weave at the bottom of your loom. Move the yarn across the warp, passing over one thread and under the next. Keep working in this over-and-under manner. When you reach the end of the warp, reverse directions. If you wove over the last thread, you must weave under it when you start the next line of the weft. Do not pull the weft too tight. Curve it slightly as you pull it through the warp. This is called ballooning.
6. After weaving a few rows, pack the weft threads tightly with the comb. The tighter the weave, the stronger the fabric will be. Experiment with different weft fibers.
7. Be sure to end with another inch of thin, tightly packed fiber. Break the tabs of your loom to slip the weaving off the cardboard. Fold the weaving over the cardboard. Fold the weaving over the dowel and stitch your weaving together, using a long piece of yarn and a tapestry needle.
8. Make a hanging loop by tying the ends of a piece of string to each end of the dowel.

Evaluating Your Work

- **Describe** Describe how you made the loom. Explain how you attached the warp threads to your loom. Explain ballooning. List the weaving techniques you used.
- **Analyze** What color scheme did you choose? Explain how you experimented by adding a variety of textures to your fiberart.
- **Interpret** In what setting might you hang this weaving?
- **Judge** Tell whether you feel your work succeeds. Explain your answer.

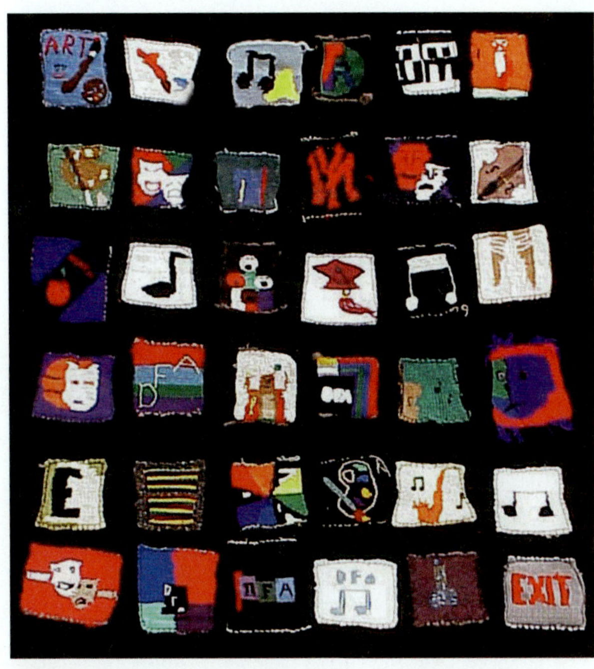

◆ **Figure 13–11** **Student works. Fiberart mural.**

STUDIO OPTIONS

Select and use a variety of appropriate art materials and tools to interpret themes, such as a favorite holiday, when producing a fiberart table placemat. This activity will help you apply design skills to effectively communicate ideas and thoughts in everyday life. Choose colors that best symbolize the holiday you have chosen. Use traditional weft and warp materials of differing textures and weights to create the placemat. Also, experiment with unusual materials such as found objects.

Art Online

Visit **art.glencoe.com** to see more examples of student art at the Student Art Gallery. You will also find:

- Artist Profiles
- Interactive Games
- Web Links

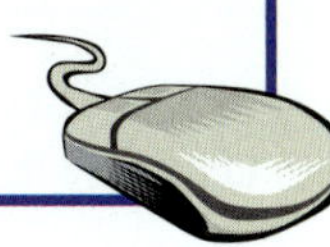

LESSON 4 

Jewelry

Some art is made to be worn. An example of this art used in everyday life appears in **Figure 13–12**. We call this art, and the craft of making it, jewelry.

Some people wear jewelry made of colorful shells and feathers. Other jewelry is created with metal and stones, such as the bracelet shown in Figure 13–12. Can you name any of the stones and metals in this artwork?

What You Will Learn

You will make a piece of paper jewelry with a particular person in mind. You will paint your jewelry with watercolors. You will apply design skills to effectively communicate ideas and thoughts in everyday life. You will choose either geometric or free-form shapes for your design. You will make a pendant, a pin, or a pair of earrings. The item must harmonize with the clothing style of the person for whom it is intended.

◆ **Figure 13–12** **Notice the different materials the artist used to created this unique piece of jewelry.**

Iris Sandkühler. *Blue Moon Beaded Cuff Bracelet.* 1998. Silver, glass, turquoise, pearls. Width: 3.81 cm (1½″). Courtesy of the artist.

What You Will Need

- Pencil and sheets of sketch paper
- Sheet of heavy watercolor paper, 9 × 12 inches
- Sheets of scrap paper, scissors
- Watercolor paints and brushes
- White glue, straight pin
- Pin or earring backs
- Polyurethane spray

What You Will Do

1. Identify the person for whom the piece is intended. Decide whether you will make a pin, a pendant, or a pair of earrings. Make pencil sketches experimenting with different shapes for your jewelry.
2. You may use either geometric or free-form shapes. Transfer your best sketches to the sheet of heavy watercolor paper. Set the paper aside.
3. On scrap paper, experiment with different colors and techniques for applying watercolor paints. (To review the different techniques, see **Technique Tip 14,** *Handbook* page 286.) If you are making the jewelry for yourself, think of your favorite colors. If the jewelry is to be a gift, think about the tastes of the person you have in mind.
4. Tear or cut out the paper shapes and paint them. Choose colors that work together to create a feeling of harmony.
5. When the paint is dry, attach the pieces to a pin or earring backs with glue. For a pendant, poke a hole at the top.

6. To waterproof the jewelry, use polyurethane (pahl-ee-**yuhr**-uh-thane) spray. *Your teacher must be present during this step.*
7. Display your finished jewelry. How did you apply design skills to communicate ideas and thoughts in everyday life?

SAFETY TIP

Polyurethane sprays can be harmful if inhaled. Use these sprays outside or in a room that is well ventilated. Use them only when an adult is present.

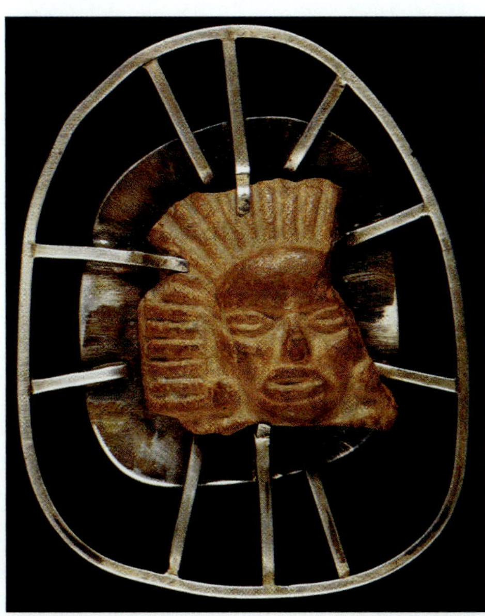

◆ **Figure 13–13** **Compare and contrast the use of art elements and principles in this piece of jewelry with the one shown in Figure 13–12.**

Ramona Solberg. *Mitla* (pendant brooch. c. 1951. Silver, pre-Columbian clay artifact. 7.6 × 5.7 cm (3 × 2¼″). Courtesy of the artist.

Evaluating Your Work

- **Describe** Tell what type of jewelry (pin, pendant, earrings) you made. Identify the materials you used to create the jewelry. Tell what colors you chose.
- **Analyze** Tell whether you chose geometric or free-form shapes. Explain whether the colors and shapes you chose will harmonize with the size and clothing style of the wearer.
- **Interpret** Tell whether the jewelry will appeal to the individual for whom it was made. Explain why.
- **Judge** Explain whether you feel your work succeeds as applied art. Explain your answer.

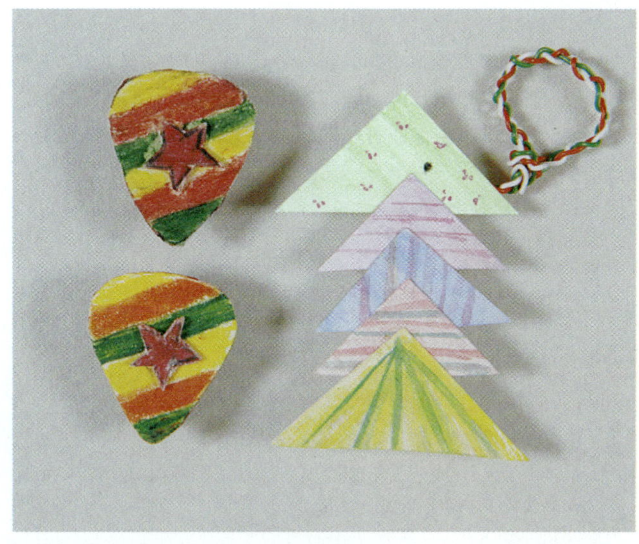

◆ **Figure 13–14** **Student works. Paper pin and earrings.**

STUDIO OPTIONS

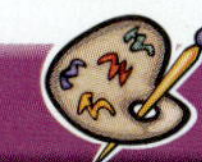

- Add other materials to your paper jewelry to create fiberart. Use a variety of art materials, such as fabric, buttons, string, or feathers, in traditional and experimental ways.
- Produce a ceramic pin using a variety of art materials and tools in traditional and experimental ways. Make your pin using the clay techniques outlined in Lesson 2.

Visual Art Journal

Avocational Choices in Art. What crafts might you create as a hobby? Survey and identify avocational choices or opportunities in art. Review the definition on page 5 and list other choices in your visual art journal.

Bookbinding

Artist's books are a new twentieth century art form. They range from deluxe editions produced by special presses to unique handmade objects. They can be standard rectangles, accordion pleated, or scroll-like.

Dido and Aeneas, shown in **Figure 13–15**, is a handmade book by Canadian-born artist Claire Van Vliet.

What You Will Learn

In this lesson you will incorporate design into an artwork for use in everyday life. You will create this artwork based on personal experience and imagination. You will make a book using a technique called *Japanese binding.* In a Japanese bound book, the pages are stacked between the covers, and there is no spine. The exposed ends of the pages become a part of the design. You will make a unified cover design by using harmony to organize the elements. You will choose a variety of papers to decorate your cover.

What You Will Need

- Ruler, pencil, scissors, white school glue
- Heavy-weight drawing paper, file folder, or card stock, 6 × 9 inches
- Paper: copier, drawing, or handmade, 6 × 9 inches
- Various colors of construction, wrapping, and wallpaper, 6 × 9 inches
- Various colors of tissue paper for endpapers, 6 × 9 inches (optional)
- Tapestry needle and heavy-weight thread
- T-pin, awl, or drill with small bit for making holes
- Large paper clips or binder clips

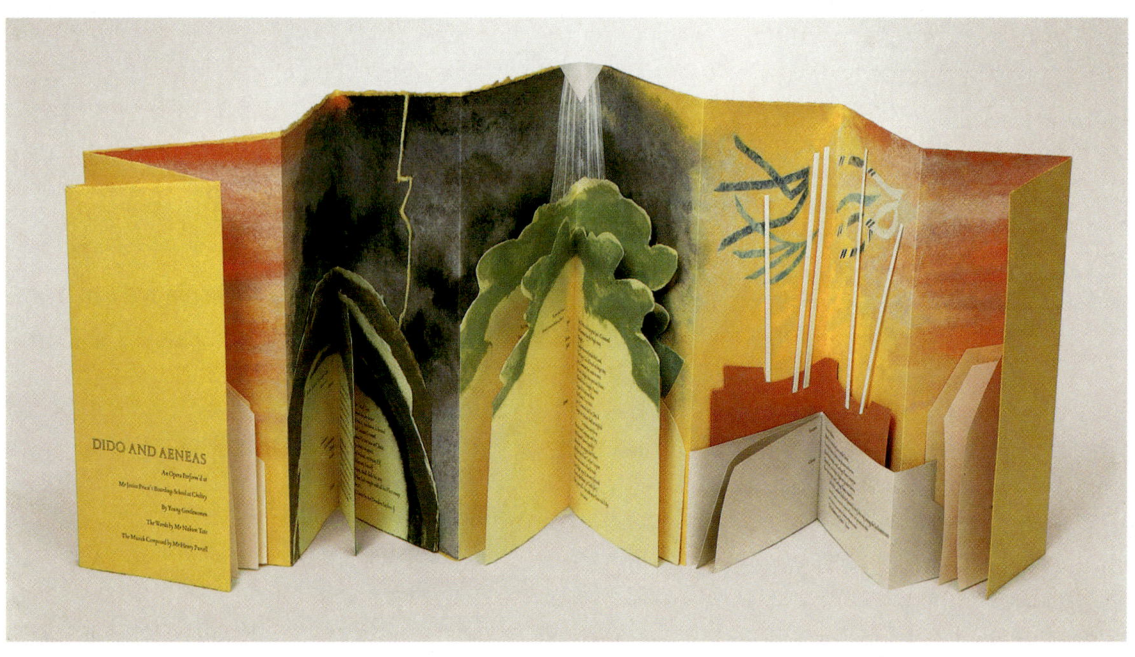

◆ **Figure 13–15** **How does this look similar to other books you have seen? In what ways is it different?**

Claire Van Vliet. *Dido and Aeneas*. 1989. Monoprint on handmade paper. Closed: 35.6 × 17.8 cm (14 × 7″). National Museum of Women in the Arts, Washington, D.C. Gift of Lois Pollard Price.

What You Will Do

1. Think about what you would like your book to hold. It could be a journal, a sketchbook, or a photo album.
2. Plan your front cover. Create your cover design based on your personal experiences or imagination. Your book will be rectangular and will be sewn on the 6-inch side. Use a heavy piece of drawing paper, card stock, or file folder for your cover. Create unity by repeating art elements in the design of your cover. Use color, line, shape, and/or texture. Choose contrasting colors, such as warm and cool, or black and a bright color. Choose a variety of papers to glue onto your cover.
3. Use five to ten pages in your book. Use decorative end sheets, or endpapers, at the front and back of your book.
4. Now prepare your cover. Draw a line lightly with a pencil ½-inch in from the edge on the left side. This is where you will sew your book together. Now, measuring from the top, make a mark every inch along this line. These are your sewing holes. Starting from the top mark, they will be referred to as holes 1, 2, 3, 4, and 5. Stack your papers in this order: back cover, endpaper, pages, second endpaper, and front cover. Use either four large paper clips or binder clips to hold your pages together. Use a T-pin, awl, or drill to make holes through your stack at each mark.
5. Cut a piece of thread 48 inches long. Thread your needle, sew through the holes, and tie both ends together in a knot.

Evaluating Your Work

- **Describe** How did you incorporate design into your artwork for use in everyday life? What will your book be used for?
- **Analyze** Which colors, lines, shapes and/or textures did you use? How does this create unity on your book cover? Explain.
- **Interpret** Did your cover design create a feeling of harmony? How did it convey this feeling?
- **Judge** Were you successful in creating a bound book? Use the aesthetic theories to defend your decision.

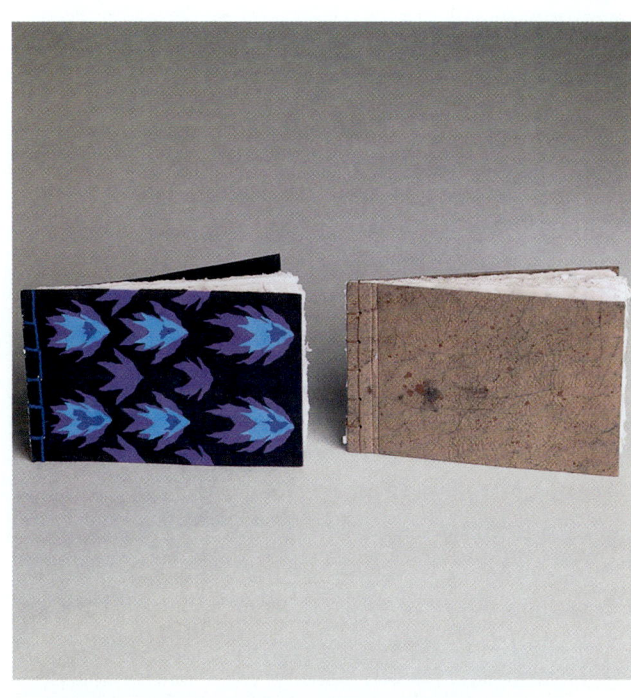

◆ **Figure 13–16** **Student works. Handmade books.**

Reflective Thinking

Critical Response. Analyze and compare relationships, such as function and meaning, in personal artworks and those of your peers. For example, what is the function of your handmade book? How does it differ from those of your classmates?

Art Online

Visit the Career Corner at **art.glencoe.com** to survey and identify career choices or opportunities in art. There you will also find:

- Interactive Games
- Web Links

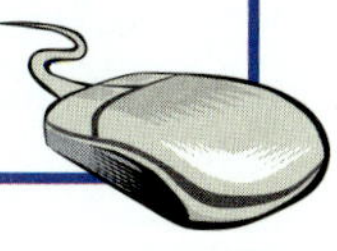

ART & SOCIAL STUDIES

Symbols of Status in Art and Culture

Do you know the term *status symbol?* It refers to an object or item that represents rank or standing in a group. Wearing a certain piece of clothing may be a status symbol among people your age. So may belonging to a certain club or organization. Either shows that you have rank and are accepted by your peers. These are people the same age who share common beliefs and attitudes.

Status in World Cultures

In some societies, including our own, status is often associated with power. The leader of our nation is an elected official with the title *president.* The president is the most powerful figure in the country. He or she enjoys the highest status of any member of government. The *chief executive officer*, or *CEO*, of a large company is another powerful leader. Such an individual has high status in the world of business and industry.

The art object in **Figure 13–17** is associated with yet another leader. In this case, the leader is a ruler of the Yoruba people of Africa. The Yoruba people live today mainly in southwestern Nigeria. (See map in **Figure 13–18**). In centuries past, land controlled by the Yoruba was divided into separate city-states. Each city-state had its own ruler.

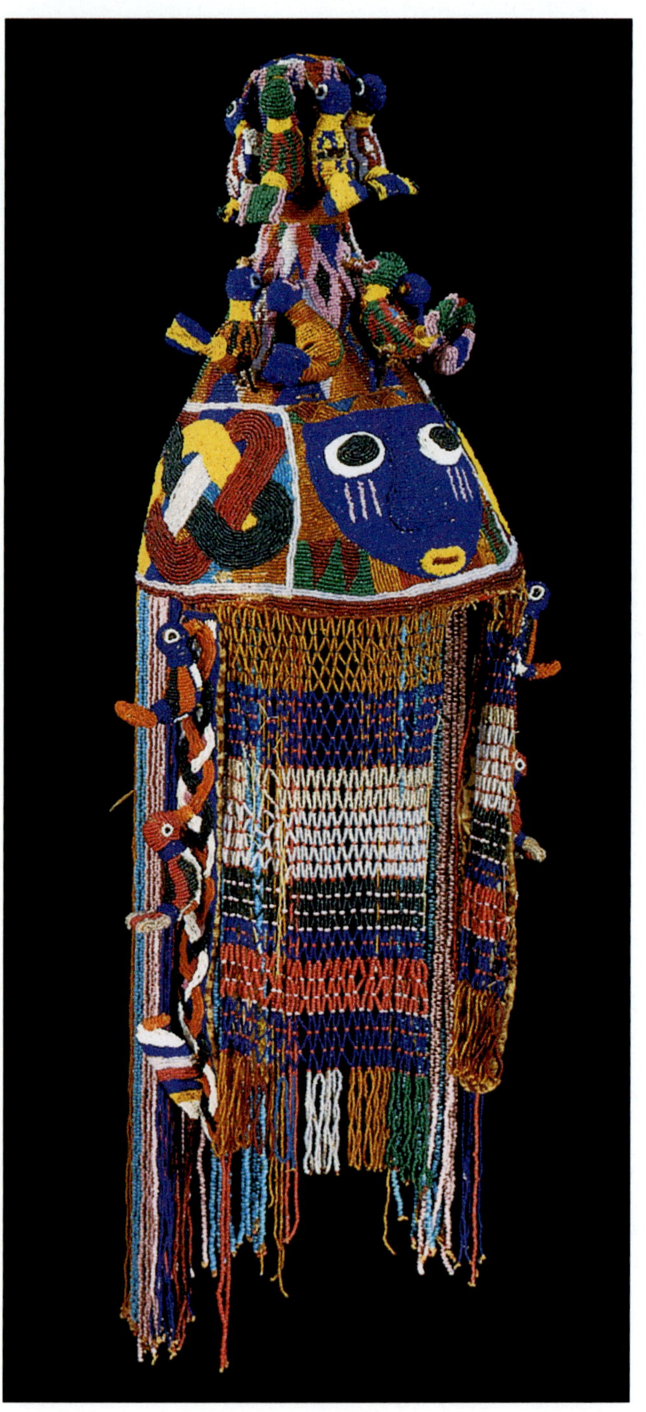

◆ **Figure 13–17 In what way is this object a status symbol? Would it be a sign of status in your own culture? Explain.**

Nigeria, Ijebu region, Yoruba peoples. *Ade* (Crown). ca. 1930. Glass beads, plant fiber, iron, cotton. 76.2 × 33 cm (30 × 13″). National Museum of African Art, Smithsonian Institution, Washington, D.C. Gift of Milton F. and Frieda Rosenthal. 94-1-1.

Art of the Yoruba

The object in Figure 13–17 comes from the ancient city-state of Ijebu (ee-**jay**-boo). Take a moment to study this object. It is an *ade* (**ah**-day), or crown. Did you notice the many beads and longs strands of fiber adorning this crown? These aren't just decorations. They are status symbols, meant to show the power and prestige of the wearer. Unlike crowns in some Western societies, the ade was worn only during special rituals and ceremonies. It was believed to connect the ruler spiritually with the gods.

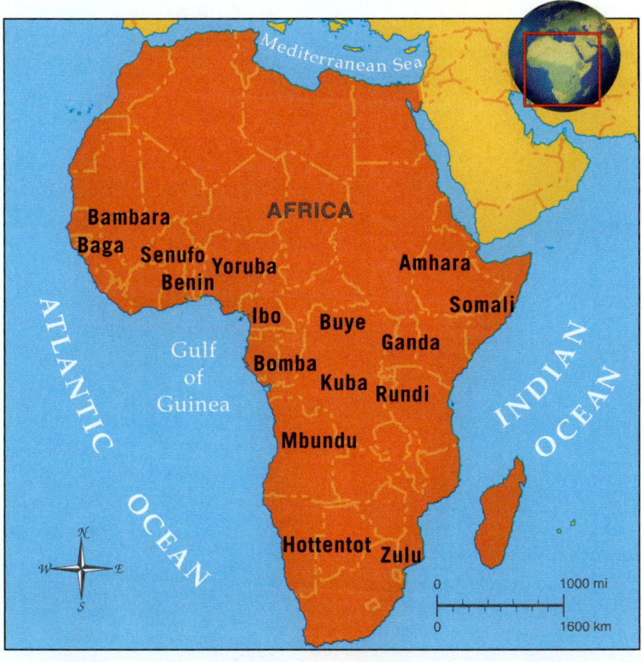

◆ **Figure 13–18** Map of Africa. Major cultural groups.

MAKE THE CONNECTION

Take Another Look

1. Identify cultural ideas expressed in the art object shown in Figure 13–17. What political figure wore the ade, or crown? What do the status symbols express?
2. Yoruba artists were skilled at using textiles, the medium used in Figure 13–17, and were also accomplished weavers. The costume in Figure 1–10 on page 10 depicts this skill. Analyze and compare relationships, such as function and meaning, in that artwork with the one in Figure 13–17.

Art & Social Studies

Using Map Skills. Look at the map shown in Figure 13–18. Using online or print resources, research one of Yoruba's neighboring cultures. Find out what contributions the culture made to the world of art. Analyze selected artworks to determine cultural contexts. For example, what if any, status symbols are used in their rituals and ceremonies?

Unraveling a Secret Code

Were hidden messages stitched in fabric?

The Underground Railroad was neither underground nor a railroad. It was a system of perilous routes to freedom for enslaved persons throughout the first half of the nineteenth century.

Along the routes were "safe houses," which offered help to the desperate runaways. Some people have claimed that women in these houses would hang quilts with special designs out the window or on the wash line. According to stories—none proven—the designs acted as secret codes signaling that the home was a stop on the Underground Railroad. To most people, the quilts were simply hanging out to dry. Those in the know, however, were supposedly able to "read" messages that were sewn into the fabric covers.

It has been said that some colors and patterns in a quilt served as "visual maps" that gave directions for the journey. Few of these quilts exist today. Many of the designs are still popular with quiltmakers, however.

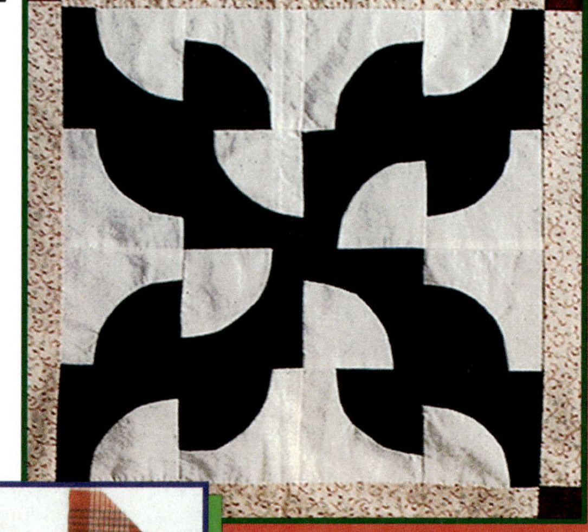

ABOVE: This pattern may have warned enslaved persons to travel in a zigzag pattern, making it harder for them to be followed.

LEFT: A pattern representing geese supposedly gave fleeing enslaved persons these instructions: Like geese, head north, and travel in spring.

BELOW: Known as the Evening Star, this quilt's message may have been to follow the North Star.

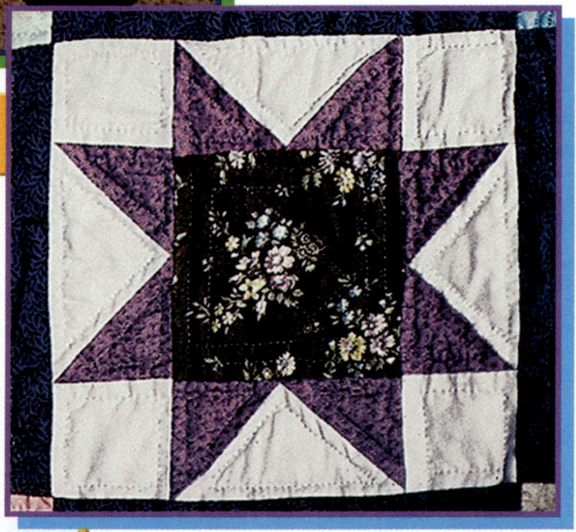

RAYMOND DOBBARD (3)

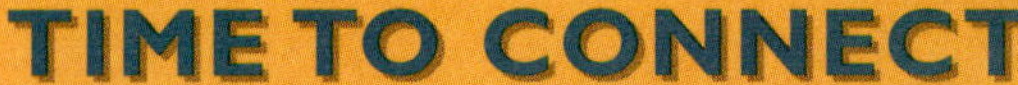

TIME TO CONNECT

- **Debate in two teams whether a quilt that carries messages is more or less successful as a work of art. Make sure to support your arguments in a logical manner with references to the quilts themselves.**
- **Finish this sentence in your journal: "What I found most interesting about debating the artistic aspects versus the symbolic aspects of these quilts was…"**

Chapter 13 Review

BUILDING VOCABULARY

Number a sheet of paper from 1 to 15. After each number, write the term from the list that best matches each description below.

ceramics	leather-hard clay
crafts	loom
craftsperson	plastic clay
fibers	pottery
fired	slip
glassblowing	tapestry
glazed	weaving
kiln	

1. Artists who make useful and aesthetically pleasing goods.
2. The different areas of applied art in which craftspeople work.
3. A craft in which strands of fiber are interlocked to make cloth or objects.
4. Strands of any thin, threadlike material.
5. A weaving used as a wall hanging.
6. A frame or machine that holds a set of threads that run vertically.
7. The craft of shaping melted glass by blowing air into it through a tube.
8. The process of creating objects from clay and hardening them by fire.
9. Objects made using ceramic techniques.
10. Clay that has so much added water that it is liquid and runny.
11. Hardened by applying high heat.
12. A special ceramics furnace.
13. Coated with a mixture of powdered chemicals that melt during firing into a hard, glasslike finish.
14. Clay that is wet enough to be worked but firm enough to hold its shape.
15. Clay that is damp but too dry to shape.

REVIEWING ART FACTS

Number a sheet of paper from 16 to 18. Answer each question in a complete sentence.

16. What materials did the first weavers use as fibers?
17. What is glass made of?
18. Describe how clay pieces are joined in making pottery.

CROSS-CURRICULUM CONNECTIONS

19. **Social Studies.** Based on your research of African culture (page 245), create your own symbolic sculpture. Produce a ceramic sculpture using a variety of art materials and tools in traditional and experimental ways.
20. **Industrial Arts.** Choose one of the handcrafted products discussed in this chapter and find out how a similar product might be manufactured. Explain how the industrial methods differ from those of an individual craftsperson.

Web Museum Activity

Mint Museum of Craft and Design, Charlotte, North Carolina

Participate in the online activities at the Mint Museum of Craft and Design. Simply click on the museum's site at **art.glencoe.com**. Then click on the Hands-On Crafts Activity and choose one of the online studio lessons.

Analyze and compare relationships, such as function and meaning, in the crafts depicted in this chapter with the artworks on the museum's site. For example, the pot shown in Figure 13–6 has a useful function as well as a spiritual meaning.

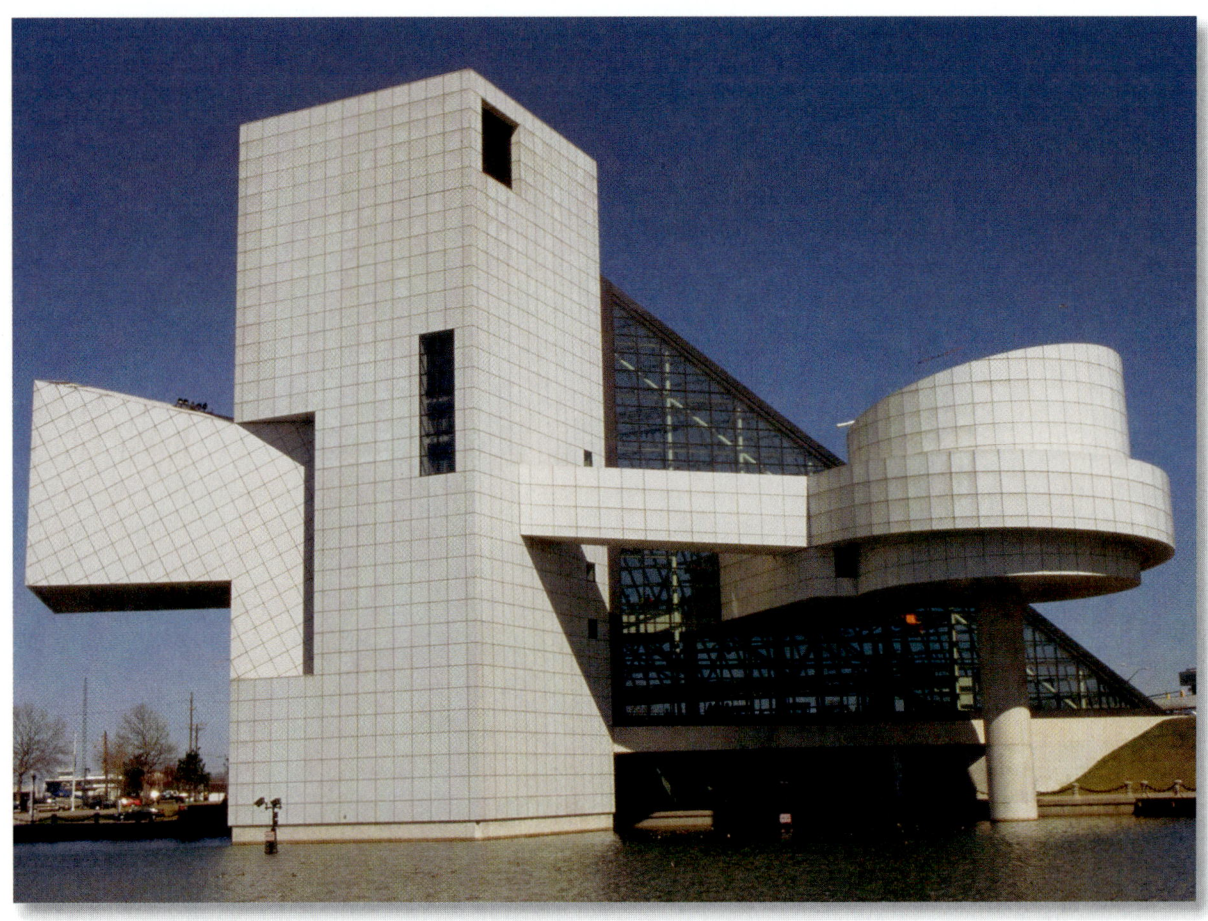

Focus On ◆ **Figure 14–1** **Would you guess that this building houses a museum? Is it similar to museums in your community? How does it differ from them?**

Rock and Roll Hall of Fame. Cleveland, Ohio. 1998.

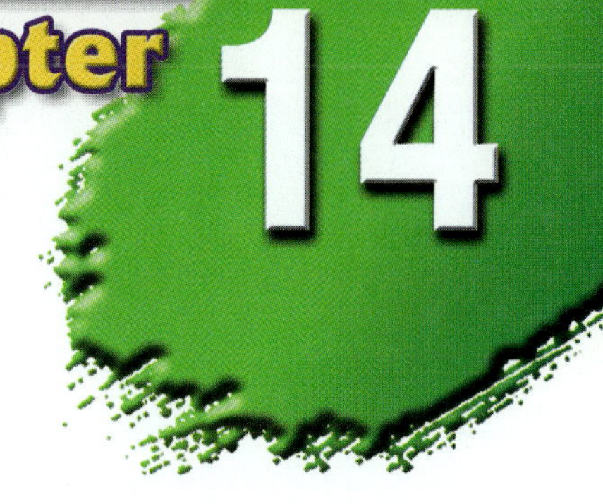

Architecture

> "*Architects . . . search for that special quality that is the spirit of the place as no building exists alone.*"
>
> **—I. M. Pei (b. 1917)**

You will notice many kinds of buildings, whether you live in a town or a city. Do you live in a house? An apartment building? No matter how you answer this question, your home is a product of an area of art known as *architecture.* The same is true of the building on the opposite page. Do you know what type of structure this is or what function it serves?

The answers to these and other questions lie in the pages ahead. There you will learn about and glimpse other examples of architecture, past and present.

After completing this chapter, you will be able to:

- Define *architecture* and explain what architects do.
- Describe four main uses of architecture.
- Explain how architects use floor plans and elevation drawings.
- Use traditional and experimental techniques to design a floor plan for a shopping mall, an elevation of a house, and a drawing using two-point perspective.
- Identify how acoustics and architecture are related, and study a cityscape.

Quick Write

Interpreting the Quote Read the quote by I. M. Pei (**pay**). Look at the building designed by Pei in **Figure 14–1.** What special qualities do you think this building has? Do you think it captures the spirit of its location, or setting? Answer these questions in a short essay.

Key Terms

architecture
architect
dwellings
cathedrals
minarets
amphitheater
floor plan
elevation
façade
columns
vanishing points

The Art of Architecture

Since the dawn of civilization, people have needed a place to live. For the first humans, shelter came ready-made, in the form of caves. Later generations began to recognize that caves were sometimes inconvenient. Reaching water or food sources may have required a long journey. To remedy this problem, these people began building their own shelters from local materials. The art of architecture was born.

In this lesson you will look at the many uses of architecture. In later lessons you will try out some of the methods architects use in their work.

What Is Architecture?

Architecture is *the art of planning and creating buildings. An artist who plans and creates buildings* is known as an **architect**.

Architecture is considered both a fine art and an applied art. Like painters and sculptors, architects use line, color, shape, form, space, and texture. Like craftspeople, architects make works that are functional. They incorporate design into artworks for use in everyday life.

Uses of Architecture

The first architectural works were **dwellings,** or *homes.* Providing people with shelter and privacy has been a key objective of architects ever since. It has not, however, been the sole objective. More recently, architects have been called upon to provide other types of structures. These have included structures for prayer, business, affairs of government, and recreation.

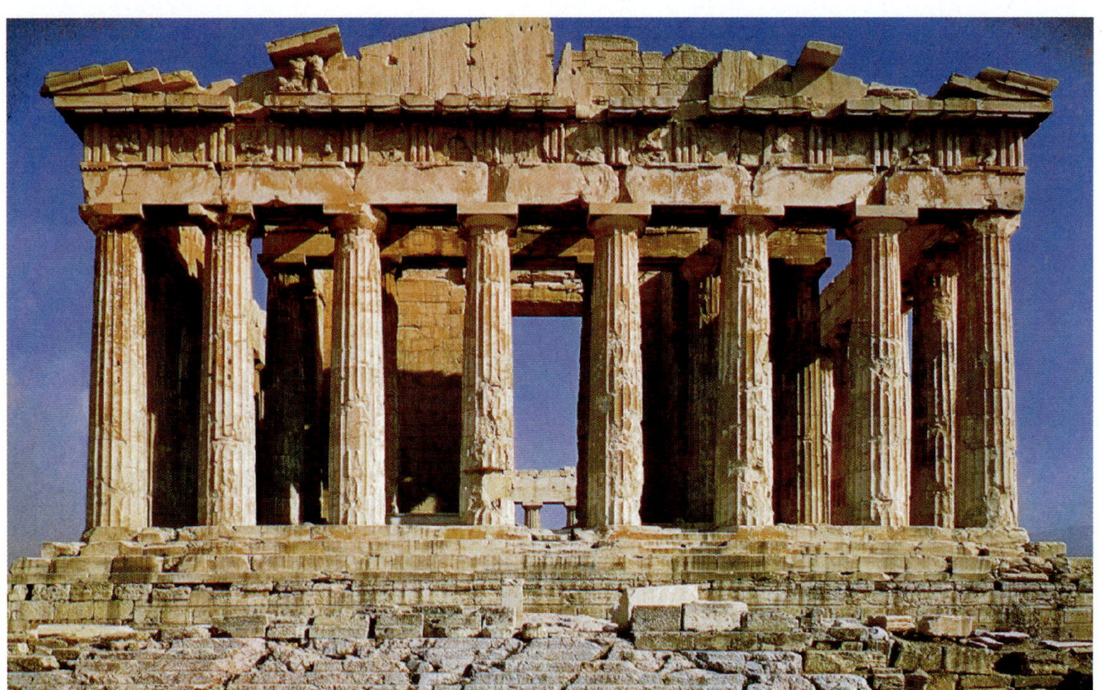

◆ **Figure 14–2 The design of this Greek temple to the goddess Athena is a Golden Rectangle, which means it has perfect mathematical proportions.**

West facade of the Parthenon Temple. Acropolis, Athens, Greece. Begun 447 B.C. Scala/Art Resource, NY.

Structures for Prayer

Structures designed to be used for prayer include temples, churches, synagogues (**sin**-uh-gogz), and mosques. Among the earliest temples were those built by the ancient Greeks. One of these appears in **Figure 14–2.** This famous temple is the Parthenon, in Athens. Temples like this were built as houses for the gods. Only priests and a few helpers were allowed inside. Everyone else prayed in front of the temple. For this reason Greek temples did not have to be large or provide areas for seats. Instead, Greek architects concentrated on making the temples perfectly proportioned.

In Europe in the 1200s and 1300s, *large churches* known as **cathedrals** were built. **Figure 14–3** shows one of the most famous, and largest, cathedrals ever built. It is the Cathedral (*duomo,* in Italian) of Milan. This huge, white marble structure, begun in 1386, rises 350 feet into the air. With a base of 14,000 square yards, the structure accommodates 40,000 worshipers.

The mosque in **Figure 14–4** was built in the early 1600s. This structure, found in the city of Istanbul, Turkey, was built for the Sultan Ahmet (**ah**-met) I. Its architect, Mehmet Aga (**meh**-met **ah**-guh), is considered the greatest architect of the early Ottoman Empire. Notice how the rhythmic repetition of domes carries your eye upward to the spires. The pointed towers on this perfectly symmetrical building are called **minarets**. These are *structures from which the faithful are called to prayer each day.*

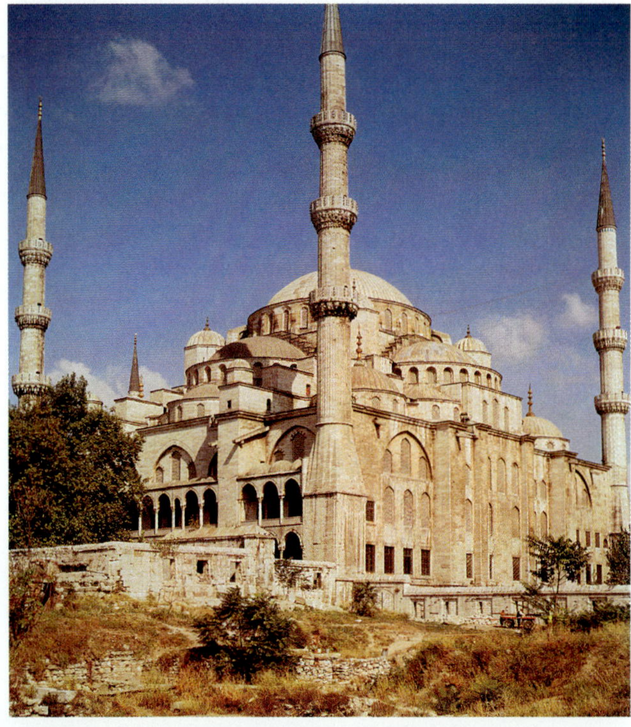

◆ **Figure 14–4** **The popular name for this structure, Blue Mosque, is derived from the blue and green tile work inside.**

Mehmet Aga. Blue Mosque. Istanbul, Turkey. 1609–1616.

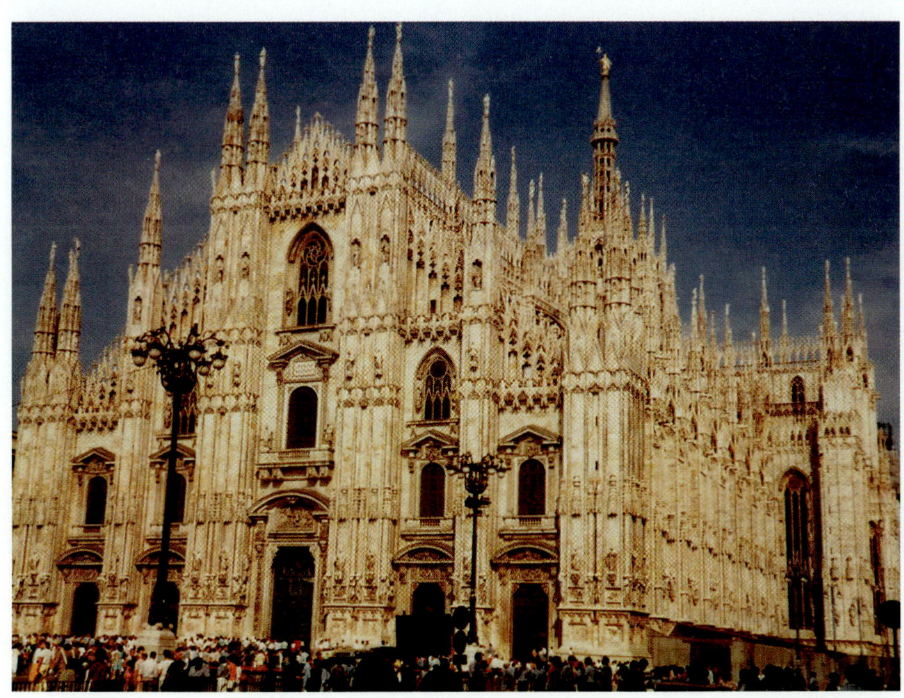

◆ **Figure 14–3** **The roof of this remarkable structure contains hundreds of statues and spires. Visitors can take an elevator up and walk among these sculptures.**

Cathedral of Milan. Milan, Italy. Begun 1386.

Structures for Business and Government

As civilization grew, cities were built. Along with them came new types of buildings. Banks and schools were designed. Government buildings were constructed. An example of this latter type of building is shown in **Figure 14–5**. Do you recognize this building? It is the U.S. Capitol. It is home to our country's Congress in Washington, D.C. The Capitol was built in the mid-1800s, during the Lincoln administration. What feeling do you think the architect intended?

In our own time, buildings used for business have taken a new direction—up. Strong metals such as steel have allowed architects to use space efficiently. The modern skyscraper can be found in major cities throughout the world.

Structures for Recreation

Even in ancient times people needed a break from routine now and then. This need was met as it still is today by leisure-time activities, including sports. **Figure 14–6** shows one of the first sports stadiums. This is the Colosseum, built by the Romans in the first century. This building is an example of an architectural form known as an **amphitheater** (**am**-fuh-**thee**-uh-tuhr.) This is *a circular or oval building with seats rising around an open space.* The Colosseum had seating for 50,000 people. Do you know how this number compares with seating capacity in stadiums today?

Sports arenas, of course, are not the only kinds of buildings designed for recreation. Concert halls and theaters are two others. A third type may be seen in Figure 14–1, which opened this chapter (page 248). This

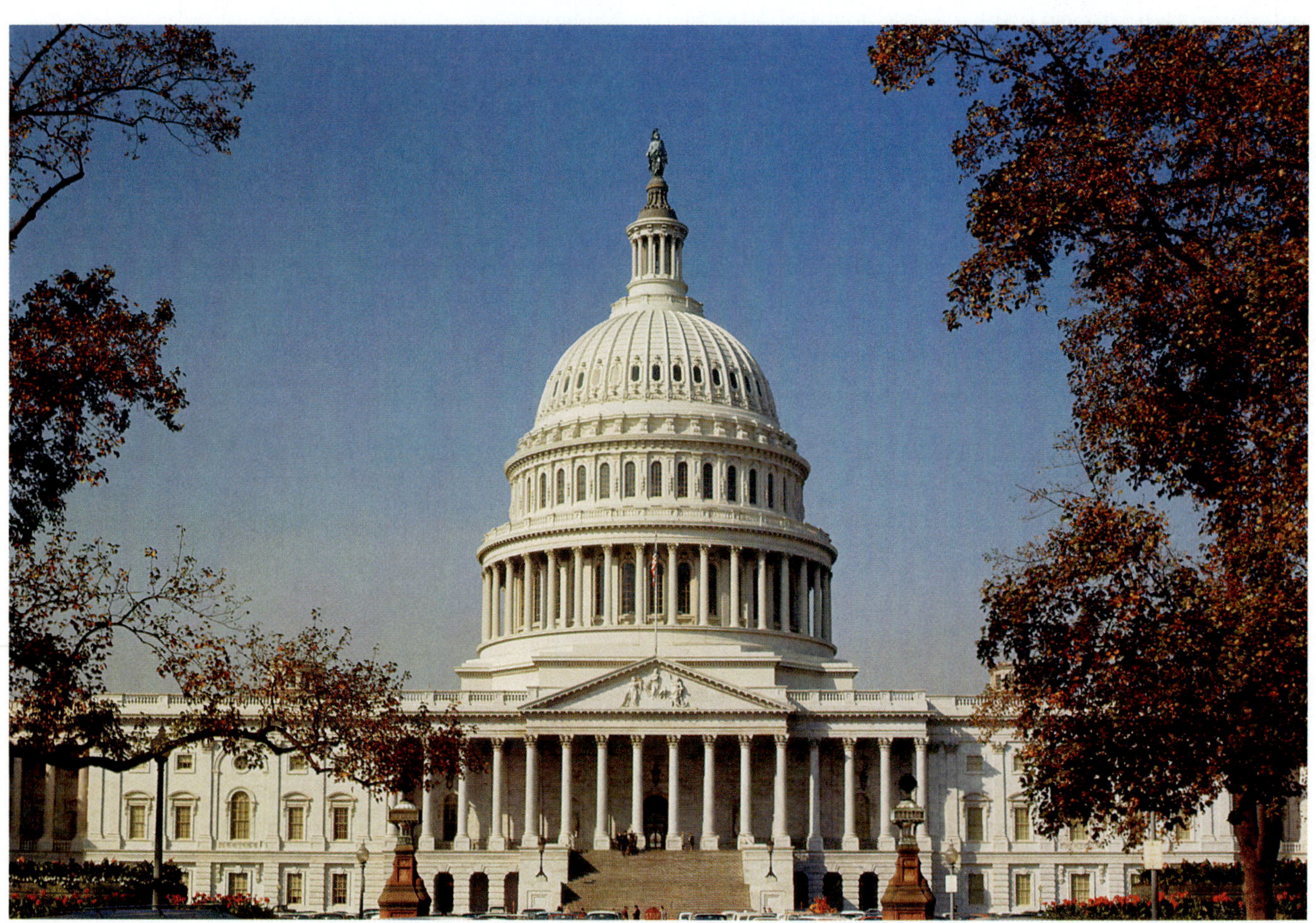

◆ **Figure 14–5** **This famous building was erected while the Civil War raged on nearby.**

United States Capitol, Washington, D.C. Exterior view. Charles Bulfinch and Benjamin Henry Latrobe. 1793–1830. SEF/Art Resource, NY.

structure, the Rock and Roll Hall of Fame, was designed by award-winning Chinese architect I. M. Pei. Does the structure strike you as playful? That is precisely the response Pei was hoping to generate. The sloping glass atrium on the right side of the building illuminates exhibits with natural daylight. What adjectives would you use to describe this modern design?

The Challenge of Architecture

Like other applied artists, architects are faced with a double challenge. That challenge is creating works that are both useful and pleasing to the eye. Since architecture is so much a part of everyday life, the search for new solutions is never-ending. These solutions show up not only in new styles but also in new and exciting building materials.

Take a close look at buildings going up in your town or city. There you are likely to see how architects combine a knowledge of engineering with an understanding of design to create buildings that are both *attractive* and *functional.*

Time & Place

Concrete

The ancient Romans made several important contributions to the field of architecture. One of these was the invention of concrete, a mixture of powdered minerals and small stones. The Colosseum, constructed in the first century A.D., is one of several multistoried buildings the Romans built using this material (Figure 14–6). Recently uncovered records suggest the Romans may have built apartment houses, too. These structures, also made from concrete, may have risen as high as nine stories!

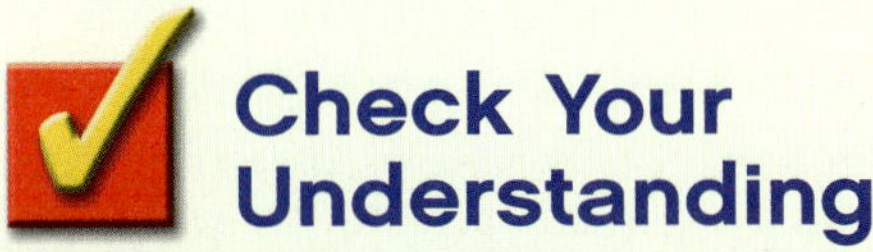

Check Your Understanding

1. What is *architecture?*
2. What are four main purposes of architecture?
3. What is an *amphitheater?*
4. Describe the double challenge facing every architect.

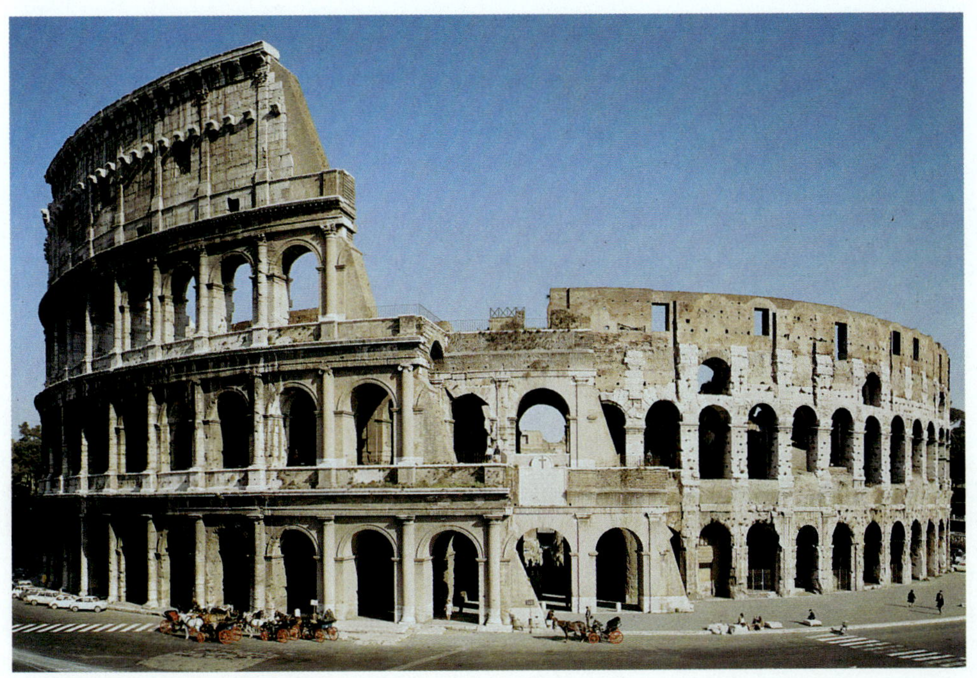

◆ **Figure 14–6** **Eighty arched openings at the ground level enabled 50,000 spectators to leave the Colosseum so efficiently that it could be emptied in minutes.**

Colosseum. Rome. A.D. 72–80.

Drawing Floor Plans

Architects work with and design space. In every instance, their designs must take into account the needs and desires of the people who will use the space. A critical step in designing any structure, therefore, is preparing a detailed floor plan. A **floor plan** is *a diagram, drawn to scale, of a room or building as seen from above.* A floor plan shows the location, size, and shape of rooms. It also pinpoints such features as corridors, windows, doors, and stairs. Another step in the planning process is presenting a sketch of the building's exterior (**Figure 14–7**).

Imagine that your community is planning to build a new shopping mall. You are the architect selected by community leaders to design this new mall. They have asked you to design a unique structure that will provide enough space inside for businesses and shoppers to move about freely. They also want a large parking area for mall visitors. Most important, they want the mall to be an inviting, convenient, and pleasant place for people to shop.

What You Will Learn

You will select and use a variety of art materials and tools to produce an architectural drawing in traditional and experimental ways. You will design a floor plan for a one-story shopping mall. Your mall will have one department store, ten smaller shops, and two restaurants. The department store should be emphasized as the most prominent place of business in the mall. Divide the space in your mall so that large and small shops are created. Your mall will have a wide, roomy, public walkway linking the different stores, and a large parking lot.

What You Will Need

- Pencil, ruler, and eraser
- Sheets of sketch paper
- Sheets of white graph paper, 18 × 24 inches
- Transparent tape

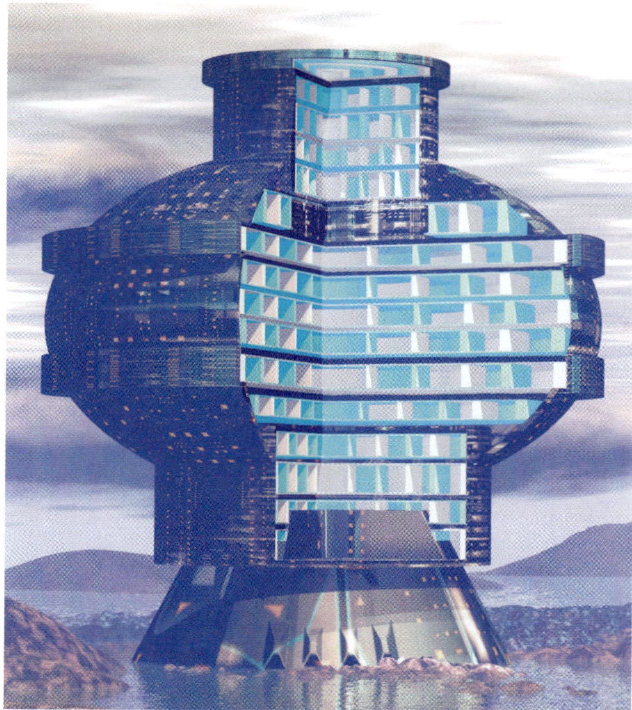

◆ **Figure 14–7** **Have you ever imagined a closed city shaped like this one? How might you design an imaginary structure?**

Computer-drawn elevation of an imaginary city.

WHAT YOU WILL DO

1. Using pencil, ruler, and sketch paper, experiment by creating different possibilities for floor plans. A large department store will be the focal point of the mall. Decide what kinds of businesses you will have among the ten shops. Decide which businesses will be next to each other along the walkway. Decide whether either or both of the restaurants will serve fast food. Decide how much floor space each business will need. Provide a large parking lot. Use the foot as a unit of measurement. Develop a scale for your design, such as 1/4 inch equals 1 foot.
2. Carefully line up two sheets of the white graph paper so their long sides touch. Fasten them where they meet with transparent tape. Turn the paper over. Neatly transfer the final design of your floor plan to the large sheet. Use your ruler. Neatly label each store. Label the walkway and parking area.
3. Show where the entrance to the mall will be. Add any details that will be used as decoration.
4. Display your floor plan in a class exhibition.

Evaluating Your Work

- **Describe** Tell which store in your mall received the most floor space. Explain why.
- **Analyze** Explain how you divided the space in your mall. Point out why some shops received more space than others. Explain how the department store is emphasized in your plan. Tell whether the walkways in your mall are wide and roomy.
- **Interpret** Show what features you added to make your mall inviting to visitors. Tell whether the stores and restaurants will appeal to many different tastes.
- **Judge** Tell whether you think your work succeeds. Explain your answer.

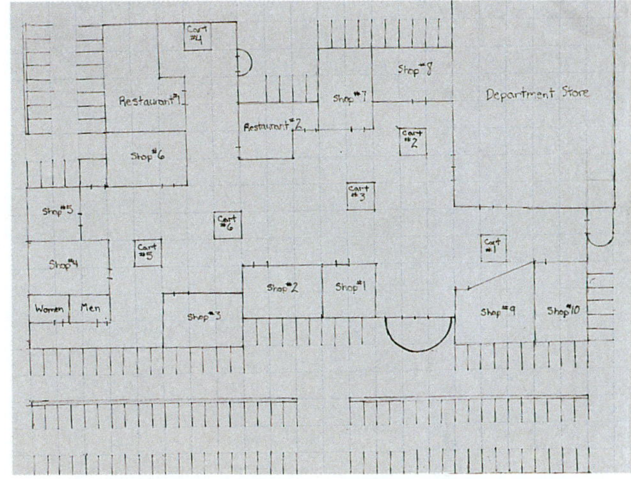

◆ **Figure 14–8** **Student work. A section of a shopping mall floor plan.**

REFLECTIVE THINKING

Critical Evaluation. Analyze the original artworks by your peers in the class exhibition. Form conclusions about formal properties, historical and cultural contexts, and intents. How is the principle of balance used to organize the element of space? What clues do the floor plans provide about our culture?

Art Online

Visit **art.glencoe.com** to survey and identify career and avocational opportunities or choices in architecture at the Career Corner. You will also find:

- Artist Profiles
- Student Art Gallery

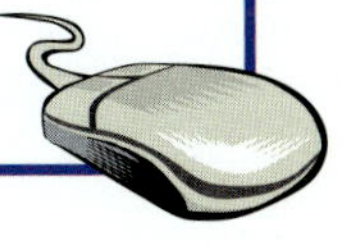

LESSON 3

Creating a Fanciful Exterior

If you thought gingerbread houses were the stuff of fairy tales, think again. The buildings in **Figures 14–9** and **14–10** both look as though they might be made of gingerbread. Yet, both are real structures, made of hard materials. The house in Figure 14–9 represents a style of architecture popular in the 1800s. The building with the onion-shaped domes is even older. It was built in the city of Moscow in Russia during the 1500s. The structure is a cathedral.

What You Will Learn

You will produce a drawing by selecting and using a variety of art materials and tools in traditional and experimental ways. You will interpret an architectural theme by creating an elevation of a house like the one in Figure 14–9. An **elevation** is *a drawing of an outside view of a building.* Your elevation will show the **façade** (fuh-**sahd**). This is *the front of a building.* You will include a porch and other features, using lines and shapes to decorate the surfaces. You will make a decorative border with cut geometric shapes.

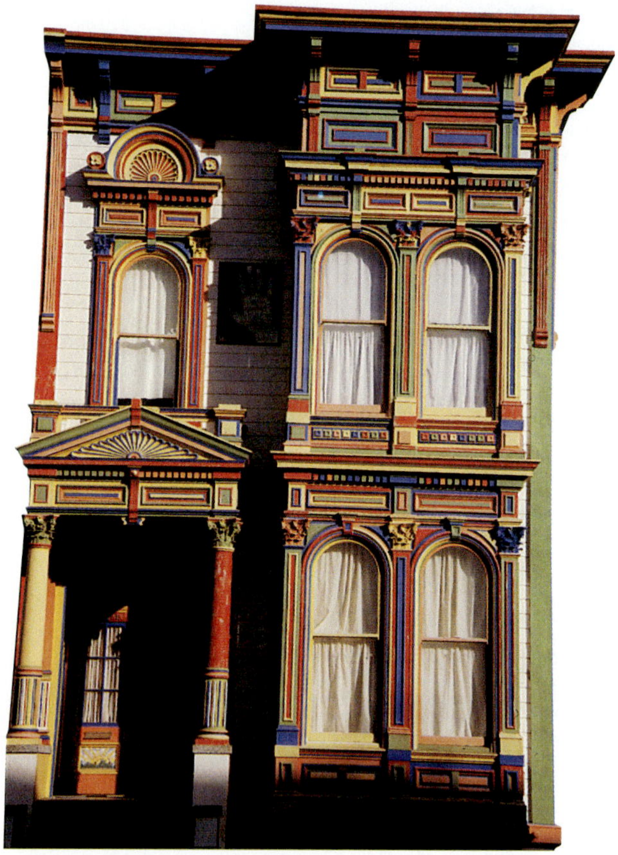

◆ **Figure 14–9** Notice the different shapes used to decorate this house.

Photo of a Victorian "Painted Lady" (gingerbread house).

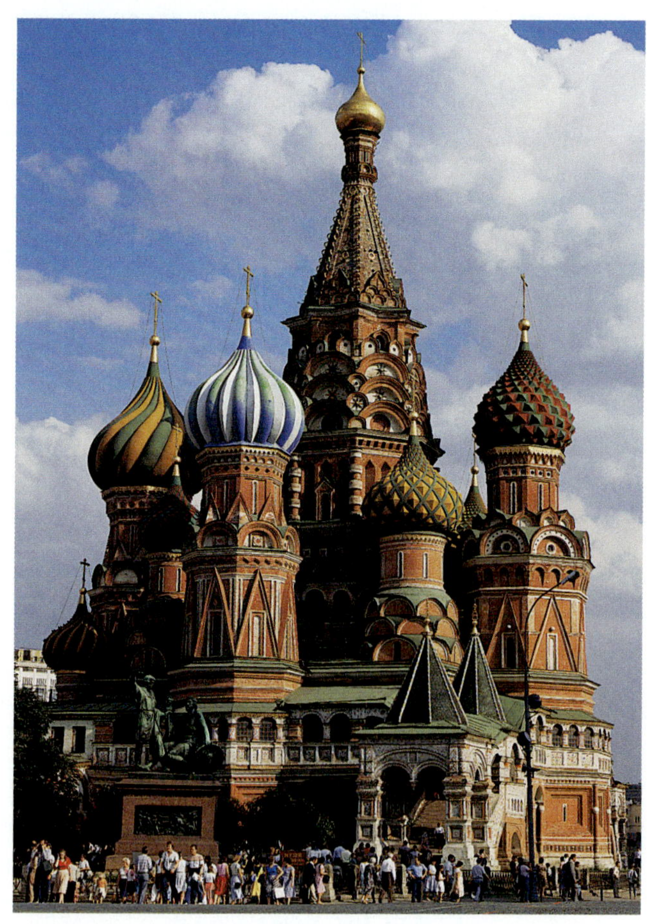

◆ **Figure 14–10** Compare and contrast the use of art elements and principles in this cathedral with the structure shown in Figure 14–9.

St. Basil's Cathedral, Moscow.

What You Will Need

- Pencil, sketch paper, white glue
- Assorted colors of construction paper, 12 × 18 inches
- Oil pastels or crayons
- Small sheet of paper or paper towel
- Scraps of 1-inch square construction paper

What You Will Do

1. Study the house shown in Figure 14–9. Complete several sketches of a similar house. Begin with simple shapes and use these to build arches, towers, and **columns**. These are *vertical posts that rise to support another structure.* Add a porch and a variety of window and door shapes. Look for an architectural theme that you can repeat in your design. The theme could be a building feature such as an arch or column, or it could be a pattern of similar shapes.
2. Choose your best sketch. Using oil pastels, transfer your design to a sheet of construction paper. Begin with a light color of pastel. Use this to draw the lines and shapes of the house, doors, and windows. Emphasize door and window shapes by using double lines.
3. Add railings and decorative touches. Use repeated lines and shapes to invent patterns, natural rhythms, and textures. Decorate every surface of the house. Fill in some areas with colors and add lines, shapes, and textures.

Evaluating Your Work

- **Describe** Does your house have features like those in Figure 14–9?
- **Analyze** Did you use a variety of patterns, textures, and details to decorate all the spaces of the house?
- **Interpret** Explain how you incorporated an architectural theme into your drawing.
- **Judge** Compare your house with the one in Figure 14–9. Is your design successful?

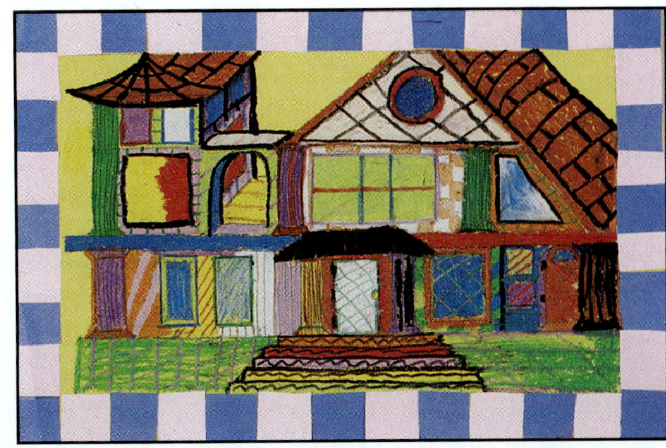

◆ **Figure 14–11** Student work. A fanciful exterior.

Studio Option

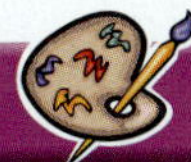

Produce a ceramic version of your fanciful exterior using a variety of art materials and tools in traditional and experimental ways. Use the slab method to create the base of your façade. Attach various architectural details to your base to create a relief. Experiment with different glazes or paints to add color. Refer to Technique Tips on page 286.

Visual Art Journal

Drawing from Direct Observation
Sketch a building in your community as accurately as you can. Then draw a new, imaginary setting for the building. Can your classmates recognize it? In your journal, explain how your sketch illustrates ideas from direct observation and imagination.

Two-Point Perspective

In **Figure 14–12,** artist Edward Hopper uses the technique of linear perspective. Artists use it to make objects in a two-dimensional work appear to have three dimensions. Look closely at Figure 14–12. Notice how the lines that would normally be drawn horizontally are slanted. The corner edge of the building is the part of the building closest to you.

Hopper is using *two-point perspective.* The top and bottom edges of the building meet at two *imaginary points at the horizon.* These points, which are not actually visible in the painting, are called **vanishing points**. (See **Figure 14–13.**)

What You Will Learn

You will select and use a variety of appropriate art materials and tools to create a community-improvement drawing using two-point perspective. You will improve a corner within your community. You will use vertical and diagonal lines in your drawings. Use oil pastels to add color to your drawing in traditional ways.

What You Will Need

- Sketchbook, pencil, eraser, and ruler
- White drawing paper, 12 × 18 inches
- Newsprint, 12 × 18 inches
- Oil pastels, box or cube
- Drawing board (optional)

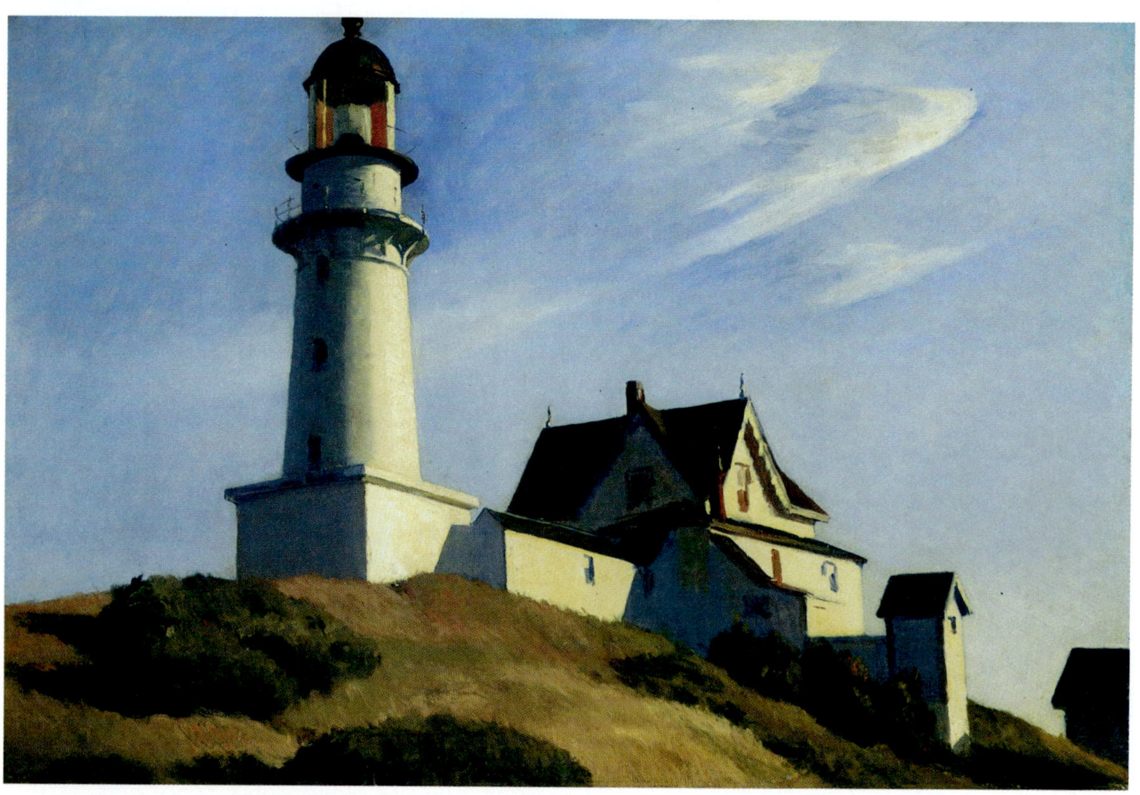

◆ **Figure 14–12** **Notice the angle from which Hopper has chosen to show this lighthouse. Note in particular how the lines of the walls that recede from the viewer appear to slope downward.**

Edward Hopper. *The Lighthouse at Two Lights.* 1929. Oil on canvas. 74.9 × 109.9 cm (29½ × 43¼″). The Metropolitan Museum of Art, New York, New York. Hugo Kastor Fund, 1962.

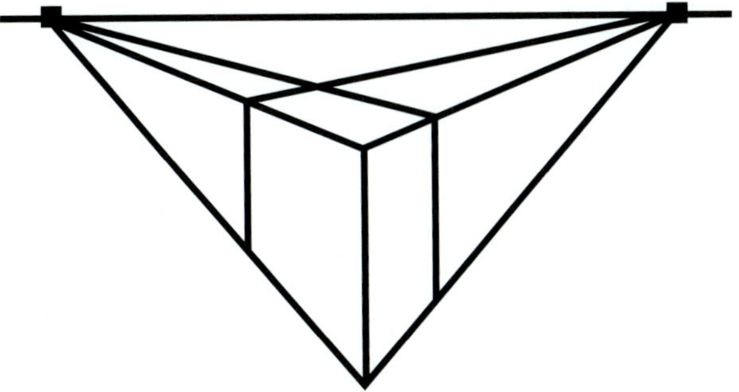

◆ **Figure 14–13** Two-point perspective.

What You Will Do

1. Arrange a box so that a corner points toward you. Place your sketchbook so that your page is opened horizontally. Lightly draw a horizon line at about the middle of your paper. Draw two dots on this line. The first one should be 1 inch in from the left and the second, 1 inch from the right. These will be your two vanishing points. Every line you make will either be vertical or diagonal. Now draw a vertical line about 3 inches tall in the center of your paper. This represents the edge of the box facing you. Look closely at the top and bottom edges of the sides of your box. Using your ruler draw the sides of your box. Draw a diagonal line connecting the top of your vertical line with one dot. Now draw a diagonal line connecting the bottom of your vertical line with the same dot. Draw a vertical line in between your two diagonals. You have just made one side of your box. Repeat these steps to make the other side of your box. Connect the top corners of the sides of your box to the opposite vanishing points. Your lines will cross above your first vertical line making the opposite corner of your box (see diagram). Erase the extra lines.
2. Use the box drawing as a model for your corner. Create a sketch of a corner in your community. Make two sketches showing improvements to this area. Select one of the sketches as your guide. Carefully tape your drawing paper to your newsprint.
3. Lightly draw your horizon line a little above the middle of your paper. Make sure your paper is arranged horizontally. Draw the corner of your building, drawing lightly so extra lines can be erased. Add details such as windows and doors. Add items, such as trees, sidewalks, and signs.
4. Use oil pastels to add color. Display your work with those of your classmates.

Evaluating Your Work

- **Describe** Explain the steps used to make your two-point perspective drawing. What directional lines did you use?
- **Analyze** Which techniques did you use to create the illusion of depth or space in your drawing? Which art elements did you use?
- **Interpret** Explain the changes you made to the corner in your community. How do they improve the corner?
- **Judge** Is your community-improvement drawing successful? Why or why not?

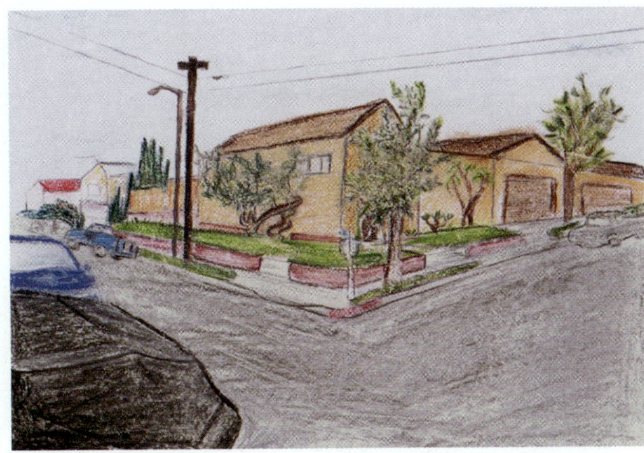

◆ **Figure 14–14** Student work. Two-point perspective drawing.

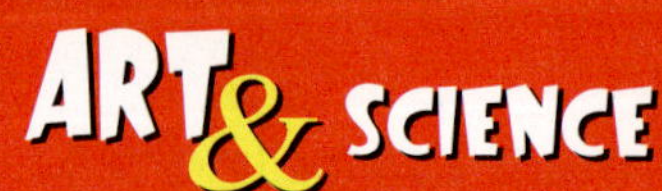

Sound Architecture

As artists, architects face a special challenge. The structures they create must not only be visually appealing. They must also serve a practical function. Nowhere is the truth of this statement more evident than in the unusual structure shown in **Figure 14–15.** This building is the recently completed Walt Disney Concert Hall in Los Angeles. The building is home to the Los Angeles Philharmonic symphony orchestra. The interior of the concert hall appears in **Figure 14–16.**

Architecture Meets Acoustics

The creative force behind this building was cutting-edge American architect Frank Gehry. Like Gehry's other buildings, this one breaks conventional rules of architecture. Unlike his other buildings, this project was the result of a collaborative effort. The structure was a dual effort by Gehry and Japanese acoustical engineer Yasuhisa (ya-soo-**hee**-suh) Toyota. Acoustics is a branch of science that deals with the behavior of sound in enclosed places. Since the building was to house a concert hall, acoustics was a primary consideration. As a result, the structure was built in a sense from the inside out. The starting point was the music hall. Gehry wanted the room to have a sculpted look. Toyota wanted a room in which sound would have exceptional clarity and richness. He added special precast concrete acoustical panels. The result was a concert hall equal or superior to any other. Even the sleek, gleaming curves of the exterior are intended to suggest the natural flow of music.

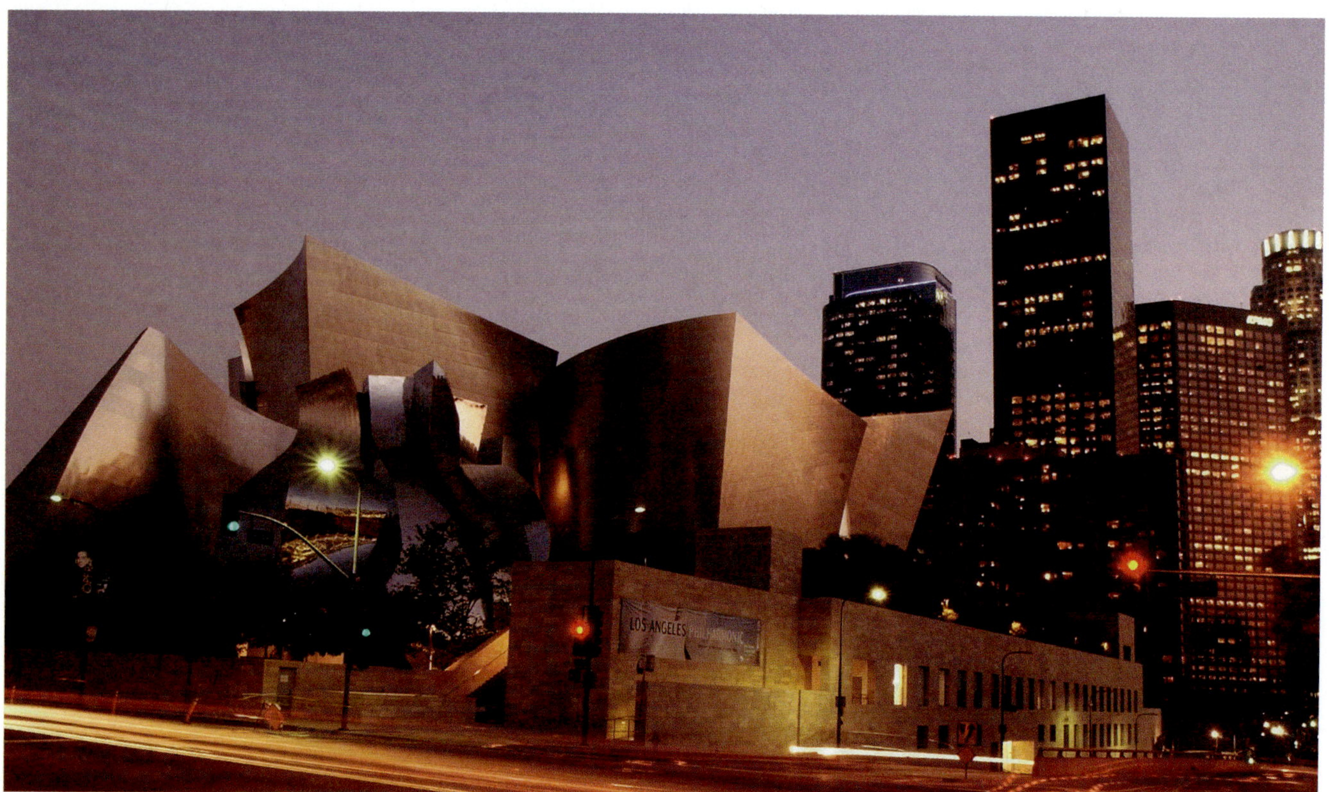

◆ **Figure 14–15** **Frank Gehry built more than 30 small-scale models of this structure. Toyota evaluated the acoustical characteristics of the shapes one by one.**

Walt Disney Concert Hall. Los Angeles, California. 2003.

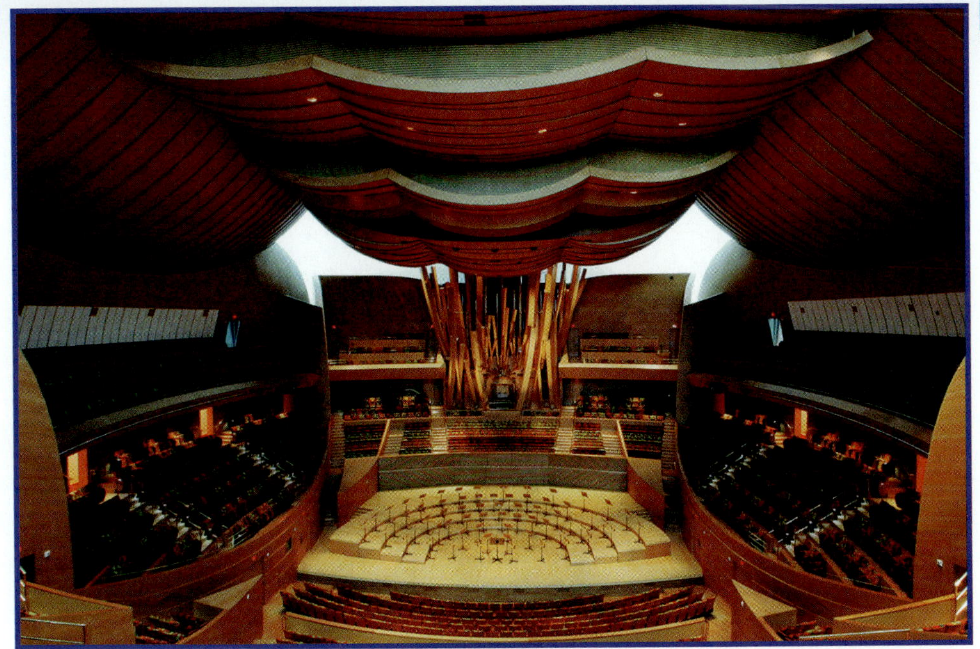

◆ **Figure 14–16** **Acoustical engineer Yasuhisa Toyota added acoustical concrete panels to give the sound inside the concert hall exceptional richness.**

Interior of Walt Disney Concert Hall. Los Angeles, California. 2003.

Making Sense Out of Sound

In a concert hall, sound waves bounce off the walls, ceiling, and other objects. Multiple echoes, called *reverberation,* affect the quality of music. Architects use a variety of materials, such as the acoustical panels shown in Figure 14–16, to reduce reverberation.

The Science of The Cityscape

The Walt Disney Concert Hall is located in the downtown area of a major city. Like other inner-city buildings, it forms part of the *cityscape.* That term refers to the interplay of different works of architecture that are part of the same view. Cityscape design is a science unto itself. One rule of this science is that building designs complement one another. Another is that a newer structure does not block the desirable view of an older structure.

MAKE THE CONNECTION

Take Another Look

1. Define *acoustics.*
2. Gehry and Toyota wanted to create a "physical connection" between the audience and the orchestra. What do you think the creative pair meant by this term?
3. Frank Gehry is noted for his unconventional building designs. Using vocabulary accurately, compare and contrast the use of the art elements and principles in this building with those used in another building from this chapter or with one in your community. Make a list of differences and similarities shared by the structures.

ART & SCIENCE

Study sound waves. Use online resources or your school's media center to research sound waves. What are the characteristics of sound? How does sound travel? Report your findings in a written paragraph.

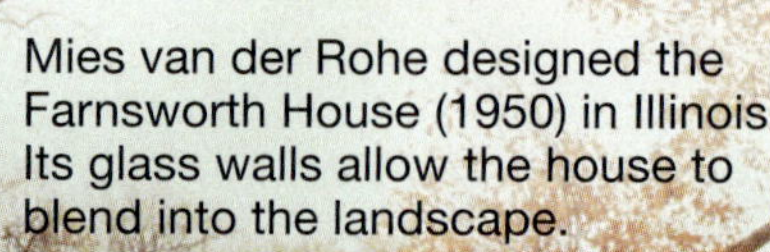

Mies van der Rohe designed the Farnsworth House (1950) in Illinois. Its glass walls allow the house to blend into the landscape.

Less Is More

Mies van der Rohe used glass-and-steel buildings to reflect on nature.

The architect Ludwig Mies van der Rohe (**luhd**-vig meez **van** der roh) (1886–1969) called any kind of decoration on a building "macaroni." He meant that decoration looked too fussy. Mies didn't include any "macaroni" on his buildings. Mies's steel-and-glass structures look like the skin and bones of a building. He used straight-edged rectangles and squares in his sleek designs rather than organic shapes.

Mies actually did incorporate some organic—or natural—elements in his work, but not by adding ornaments. You have to look carefully to see them. Reflections in his glass and steel surfaces show dancing bits of the surrounding natural environment, such as water and light. In this way, Mies' modern-looking buildings establish a fascinating visual dialogue between the human-made and natural world.

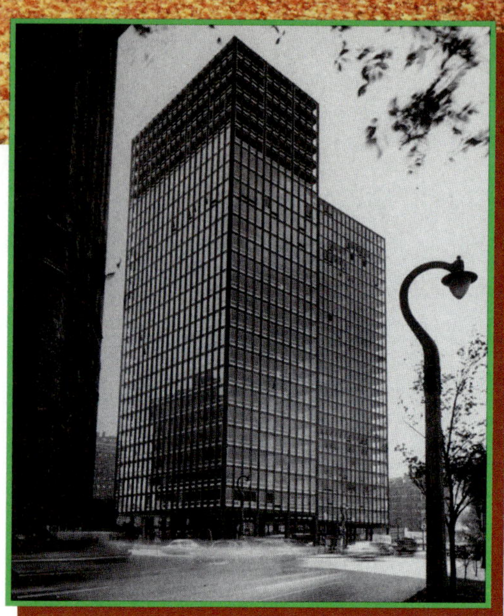

Mies van der Rohe coined the phrase "Less is more," a concept that is evident in his glass-walled apartment house (1951), located in Chicago.

BOTTOM: RALPH CRANE; TOP: JON MILLER/HEDRICH-BLESSING

TIME TO CONNECT

- **Find a building in your neighborhood that has lots of detail and decoration.**
- **Carefully list and describe its ornaments on a sheet of paper. Use as many adjectives and adverbs as possible.**
- **Based on what you observed in this building and in Mies's buildings shown on this page, write a persuasive essay defending why buildings should be built in the style you prefer—ornate or spare. Refer to your visual observations to construct a logical, well-expressed argument.**

Chapter 14 Review

BUILDING VOCABULARY

Number a sheet of paper from 1 to 11. After each number, write the term from the list that best matches each description below.

amphitheater	elevation
architect	façade
architecture	floor plan
cathedrals	minarets
columns	vanishing points
dwellings	

1. Large churches.
2. The art of planning and creating buildings.
3. A drawing of an outside view of a building.
4. An artist who plans and creates buildings.
5. Homes.
6. Imaginary points at the horizon.
7. Vertical posts that rise to support another structure.
8. Structures from which the faithful are called to prayer each day.
9. A circular or oval building with seats rising around an open space.
10. A diagram, drawn to scale, of a room or building as seen from above.
11. The front of a building.

REVIEWING ART FACTS

Number a sheet of paper from 12 to 20. Answer each question in a complete sentence.

12. Why is architecture considered both a fine art and an applied art?
13. What are four main uses for architecture?
14. Why was it not important that Greek temples be large?
15. In what ways were churches of the 1200s and 1300s different from earlier temples?
16. What made it possible for architects to start building upward?
17. For what modern structures did early amphitheaters pave the way?
18. Name three kinds of buildings used for recreation.
19. What challenge faces every architect?
20. What kind of drawing diagrams a building or room as seen from above?

CROSS-CURRICULUM CONNECTIONS

21. **Social Studies.** A zoning law specifies what type of building may be built in a certain part of a city. In teams, research whether there are laws that keep certain types of buildings away from schools. When research is complete, share your results with the class.
22. **Social Studies.** Research famous walls around the world, such as the Great Wall of China, the Berlin Wall, the Vietnam Veterans Memorial in Washington D.C., or Hadrian's Wall in Great Britain. Analyze ways that these architectural creations were influenced by international, historical, and political issues.

Web Museum Activity

National Building Museum, Washington, D.C.

Do you ever wonder what inspires architects? Visit the National Building Museum's site at art.glencoe.com to find out! View different types of architecture at the museum's Building America site. Click on Themes, such as Innovations, Freedom, and Conflict. Discover the inspiration and purpose behind architecture throughout the United States. Analyze the exhibition to form conclusions about formal properties, historical and cultural contexts, intents, and meanings.

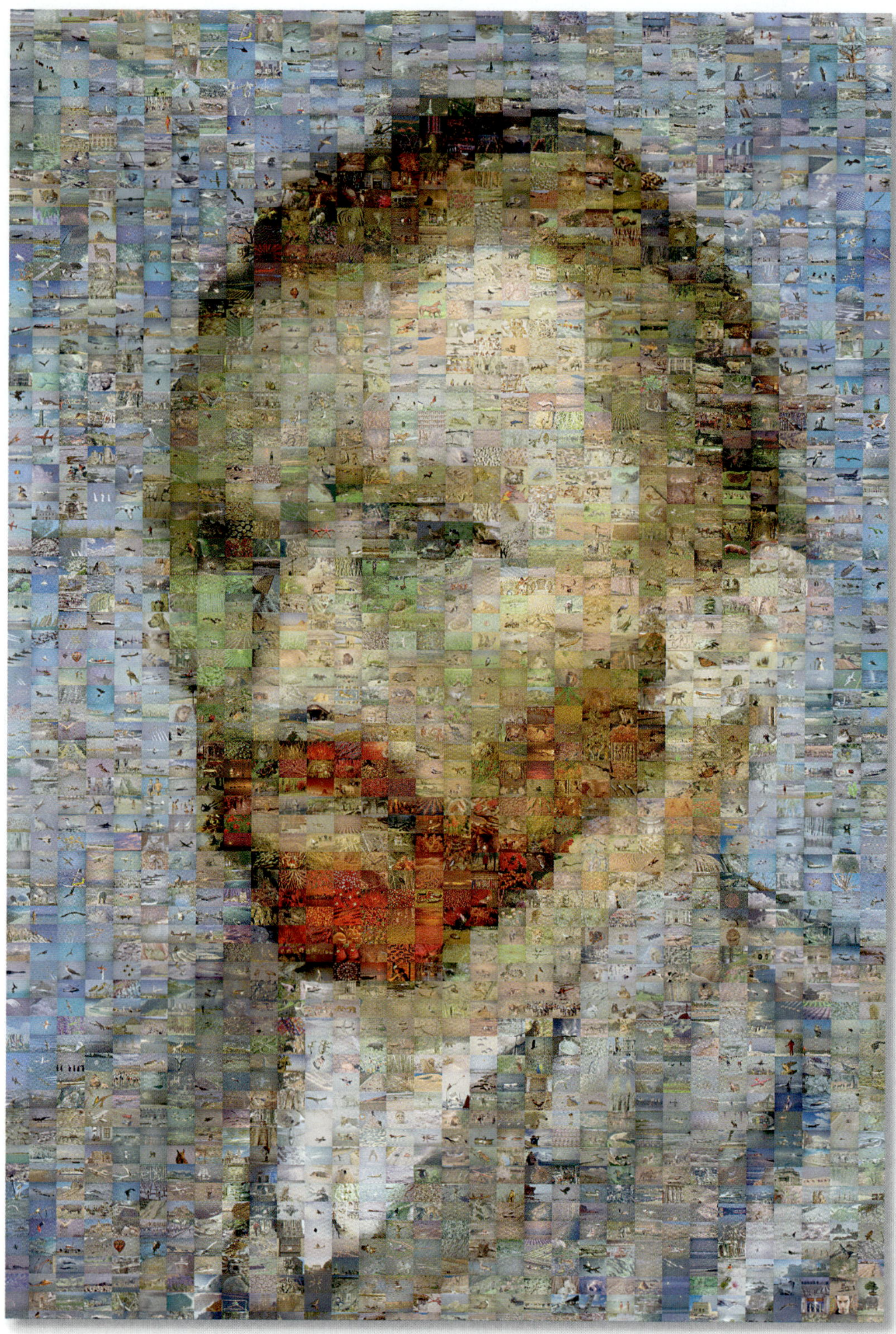

Focus On ◆ **Figure 15–1** **Notice that this image is actually composed of many tiny images. Compare and contrast this artwork with the one in Figure 15–3 on page 267.**

Robert Silvers. Based on Vincent van Gogh's *Self-Portrait.* 1889. The Collection of Musée d'Orsay, Paris. Photomosaic™. 1997.

Chapter 15

Film, Video, and Digital Art

"If Leonardo da Vinci had lived in the computer age, he might have created Photomosaics."

— Cathy Hainer, *USA Today*

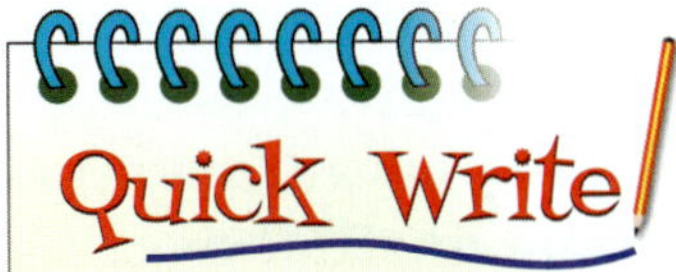

Interpreting the Quote Read the quote. This quote originally appeared in a review of the artist who created the work shown in Figure 15–1. In a paragraph, explain whether you think "Photomosaic" is an appropriate name for this type of art form.

Four centuries ago, the English poet John Donne wrote that no person "is an island." What he meant is that people need each other and influence one another. As you have seen throughout this program, artists are no exception. Each generation learns from and builds on the work of those who came before.

For proof, examine the image in **Figure 15–1.** This image represents an art medium that did not exist until the late 1900s. Do you know what art medium was used to make this image? Do you know what this type of artwork is called? After reading this chapter, you will.

After completing this chapter, you will be able to:

- Tell how movies are made.
- Analyze ways in which electronic media and technologies have influenced art.
- Produce electronic media-generated art, such as a digital frame animation, a digital self-portrait, and a multimedia portfolio.
- Examine how computerized animation is used in motion pictures.

KEY TERMS

motion picture
director
producer
cinematographer
multimedia art
digitizing

LESSON 1

The Art of Motion Pictures and Video

Most artists work on their creations in art studios. These rooms often have large windows to let in plenty of daylight. Over the last few decades, another type of artist's studio has come into existence. In such studios, the pictures that are made give the illusion of real motion. Instead of canvas or other conventional art media, these artists use celluloid film. They are known as filmmakers. In this lesson you will learn about the work they do.

The Beginnings Of Film

Still photographs, as you learned in Chapter 10, trace their roots to the Renaissance during the 1500s. Artists back then knew of and used the *camera obscura* to practice perspective. The art of photography became widespread in the 1900s. Creative inventors have taken the picture-making process an additional step, which ushered in the twentieth century. The result of this step is the **motion picture.** This is *a series of photographs of a moving subject taken a very short time apart and flashed onto a screen.* When projected in this fashion, the image appears to be moving.

Making Films

Every commercial motion picture, or movie, is the combined effort of hundreds of people. The three most important of those people are:

- **The director.** The director is the single most important person in the making of a movie. The **director** is *the person in charge of shooting the film and guiding the actors.* He or she also helps with the script. The director's main job is deciding how every scene should be photographed. To get just the right look, a director may shoot the same scene dozens of times.
- **The producer.** The **producer** is *the person in charge of the business end of making a movie.* The producer is the person who finds the story and hires the director. He or she also figures out how much money it will cost to make the movie. Some producers take part in selecting actors and in writing the script.
- **The cinematographer.** The **cinematographer** (sin-uh-muh-**tahg**-ruh-fuhr) is *the person in charge of running the camera or cameras.* Like other artists, cinematographers are trained in using light and color.

Before filming, or shooting, the director and cinematographer will go over the script together. They will discuss the different camera angles and techniques for shooting each scene.

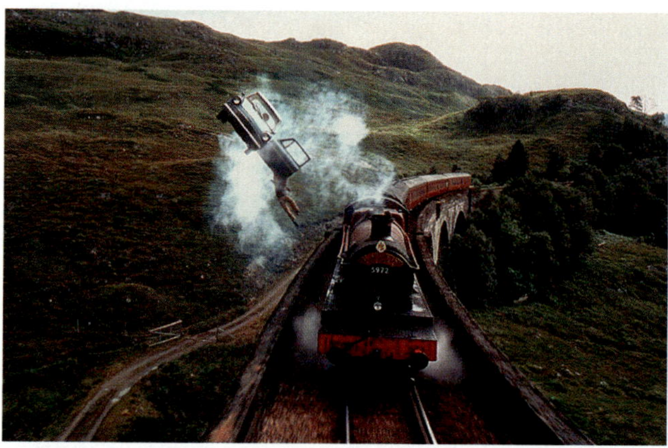

◆ **Figure 15–2** **In what way do the images in this film blur the line between fantasy and reality?**

Harry Potter and the Sorcerer's Stone. Courtesy Warner Brothers, 2002.

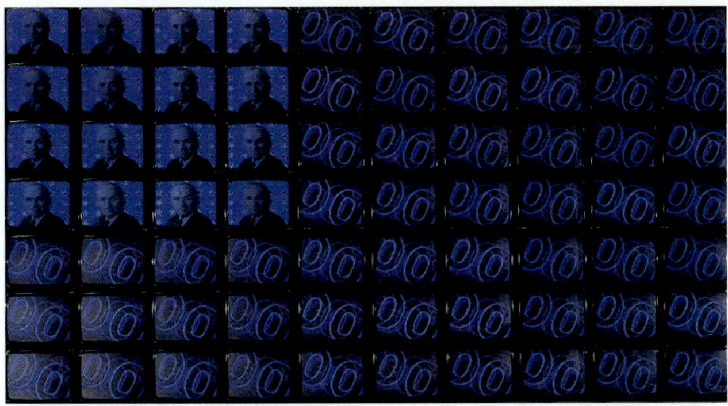

◆ **Figure 15–3 Notice the unconventional art media used by this artist. How do these compare with the media used by other artists whose works you have seen in this book?**

Nam June Paik. *Video Flag.* 1985–96. 70 video monitors, 4 laser disc players, computer, timers, electrical devices, wood and metal housing on rubber wheels. 239.6 × 355 × 121.3 cm (94⅜ × 139¾ × 47¾″). Hirshhorn Museum and Sculpture Garden, Smithsonian Institution, Washington, D.C. Holenia Purchase Fund, in Memory of Joseph H. Hirshhorn, 1996.

The Art of Film

The very first films made were silent. Since these films used no words, strong dramatic acting was required. They could be shown to audiences around the world.

The arrival of sound in the late 1920s opened up new doors to filmmakers. It also closed doors to actors whose voices did not sound right.

One of the most inventive motion pictures ever made was *Citizen Kane*. Orson Welles's use of camera angles and editing were highly praised and are still imitated today. It, like many old classics, was made before color entered the motion picture industry.

The next advance in film, color, made possible the first colored film classics. These were movies such as *The Adventures of Robin Hood* and *The Wizard of Oz.*

The films of today, of course, use dazzling effects the earliest filmmakers probably never dreamed of. Computers and other high-tech equipment have allowed directors to create "the impossible." (See **Figure 15–2.**) One can only guess what astonishing screen images tomorrow's breakthroughs will bring.

Video Art

Film changed the way artists looked at—and recorded—the world. More recently, newer technologies have had a similar impact on artists and their work. One such technology is videotape. First developed for the television industry in the 1960s, videotape allows instant playback of moving images.

In the decades since its arrival, videotape found its way into artworks including the one shown in **Figure 15–3.** This unusual work is by Korean-born American artist Nam June Paik. Like many of his works, this one includes many television monitors playing at once.

Multimedia Art

Video technology has also given rise to an art form known as **multimedia art.** This is *art that simultaneously uses several different electronic media.* One popular form of multimedia art is the music video. This is a medium that combines musical cuts from compact discs with video accompaniment. What other multimedia art forms can you think of?

In the next lesson, you will learn about various electronic media and how they are used to create artworks. To learn more about electronic media and technologies, refer to the **Digital Media Guide**, Handbook pages 293–301. Read the various articles and analyze how these technologies have influenced art.

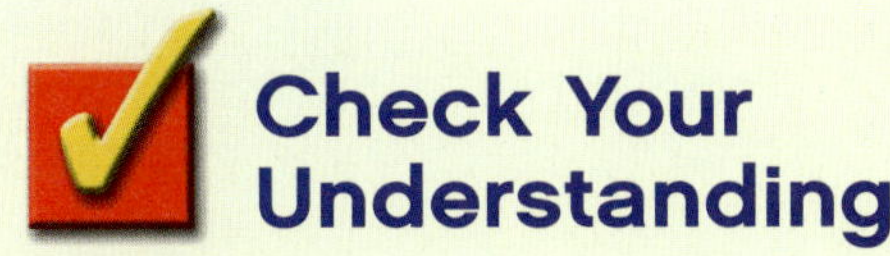

Check Your Understanding

1. What are *motion pictures?*
2. What is a *director?* What are some of the director's tasks?
3. How can videotape be used to create artworks?
4. What is *multimedia art*?

LESSON 2

The Art of Digital Media

Another technological advance that has opened new doors for artists is the digital computer. This invention of the twentieth century redefined the way people work and communicate. It has also had an enormous impact on the art world.

The computer has given artists a new set of virtual tools in the form of software. It has also inspired the development of other art tools, such as the digital camera and scanner. In this lesson, you will examine the kinds of artworks created using these devices.

The History of Computers

The first computers were introduced in the 1950s. These were room-sized machines. Only a handful of technicians with special training had access to them or knew how to use them. Then, in the early 1970s, personal computers, or PCs, were introduced to the public. Computers were now small and inexpensive enough to be a fixture in the home or office. The computer revolution was under way!

The Origin of Computer Art

Computers can only handle visual images in terms of numerical values that describe them. This is accomplished by digitizing. **Digitizing** is *a method of defining the location of points and lines in space by numerical values.* The earliest computerized art consisted of simple digitized photographs (see **Figure 15–4**). Digitized pictures required a camera and computer hooked together with special cables. The resulting pictures were generally black and white, because color printers were not yet

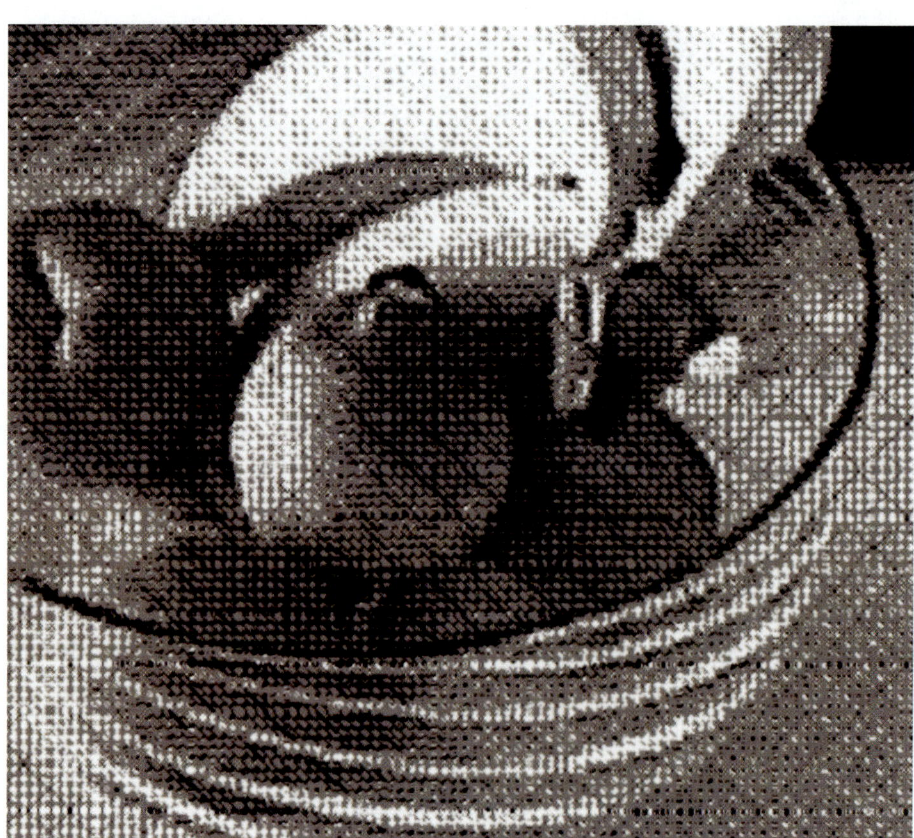

◆ Figure 15–4 **This digitized photograph is made up entirely of black or white dots. See it for yourself by examining the artwork under magnification.**

Pete Serna. *Fruit Bowl.* 1960. Digitized photograph, made using a Nikon camera and IBM computer. © HPES.

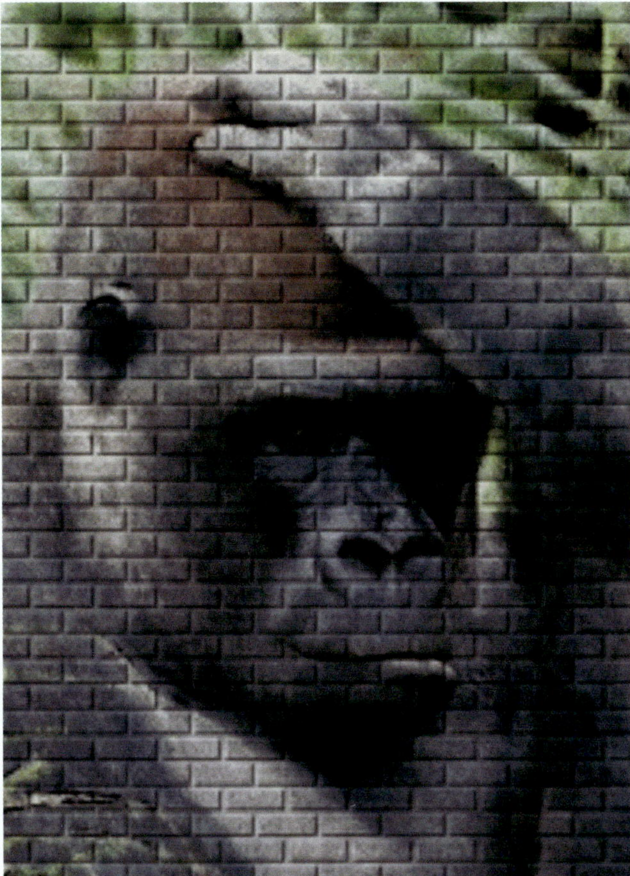

◆ **Figure 15–5** **The digital artist used several filters in a Paint program to achieve this effect. Analyze ways in which electronic media and techniques have influenced art. Could the artist create this work using traditional media?**

Ellen Kemper. *Brickwork Bonzo*. 1987. Adobe Photoshop painting. © HPES.

available. The resolution, or sharpness, of the image was determined by the number of dots in the output image. The more dots used, the longer an image took to process.

Digitizing involved a very basic computer program. The first true art software packages emerged in the 1980s. Artists were at last able to create images directly on the computer using on-screen tools. These early programs, which are still in use, belong to one of two categories of image creation and manipulation software:

- **Paint programs.** Such programs create bitmaps, which result in arrangements of tiny dots similar to those used in digitized photographs. The difference, however, is that these images are now created directly on the computer. An example of a computer painting appears in **Figure 15–5.**
- **Draw programs.** Such programs create vector-based images, pictures based on complex mathematical formulas.

Paint and Draw programs each have strengths and weaknesses not found in the other. Pictures made in Draw programs, for example, can be enlarged indefinitely without distortion. Pictures made in Paint programs cannot. By the same token, pictures made in Paint programs can achieve near-photo quality. Those made in Draw programs are more cartoonlike.

Recent Developments in Hardware and Software

As noted in Lesson 6 of Chapter 4, recent technology has ushered in a host of new digital art tools. Digital cameras and scanners have led to the creation of *photo manipulations* such as the one in Figure 4–20 on page 85. The artwork that opened this chapter (Figure 15–1) also exemplifies the capabilities available to the digital artist in the twenty-first century. The artist, Robert Silvers, calls these original creations *Photomosaics*. Like tile mosaics, the image is composed of small squares. Unlike a tile mosaic, each square contains a tiny reproduction of a photograph. Can you make out the content of any of these miniature photos?

As you create electronic media-generated art in this chapter, experiment with a variety of digital art tools. Think of different ways to create photographic imagery.

Check Your Understanding

1. What is *digitizing?* How were digitized photographs created?
2. Explain the difference between a Paint and a Draw program.

LESSON 3

Digital Frame Animation

Some artists, as explained in Lesson 1, make videos. Others, as noted in Lesson 2, create digital pictures. A new generation of computer programs has combined the two approaches. Digital frame animation software enables the computer artist to create videos directly on his or her desktop. Digital frame animation software can import computer paintings and drawings as well as sound files. A menu of preset effects permits the artist to manipulate these various files, creating the illusion of movement. As in conventional films, images can fade in or out. Objects and actors can move into a scene and then out of it again. Unlike conventional films, digital frame animations can be made by one person.

What You Will Learn

Select appropriate art materials and tools to produce electronic media-generated art. You and at least one other classmate will create an original silent digital frame animation in traditional and experimental ways. Your movie will consist of a single scene that tells a simple story. The story might be humorous or serious in nature. The image files used will include scans, digital photographic imagery, electronic media-generated paintings and/or drawings. Your animation will integrate themes found through personal experience and imagination. You will render and publish your animation to the Internet.

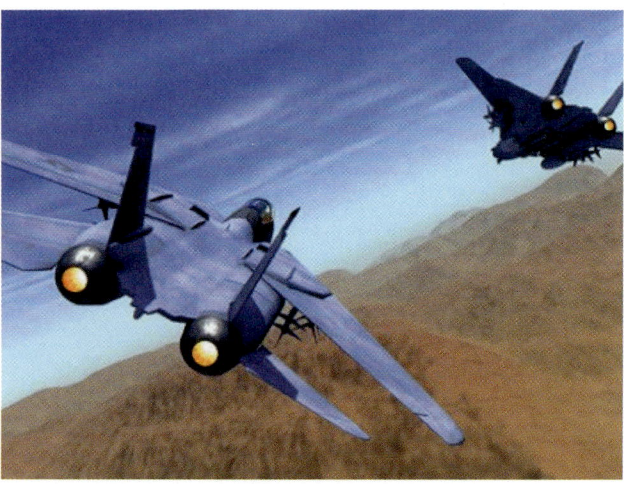

◆ **Figure 15–6** Animation programs make it possible to create 3-D animations, like the one shown here.

What You Will Need

- Digital frame animation program
- Pencil and paper
- Scanner and/or digital camera
- Draw or paint program

What You Will Do

1. Open your digital frame animation program.
2. Use your imagination to brainstorm possible story ideas with a partner. Your animation might be a humorous fantasy about the "life" of an inanimate object such as a pencil. You might also depict a scene based on a personal experience. Another possibility is a public service announcement on school safety or a similar topic. Think about the mood or feeling you are trying to create.
3. Once you have a story idea, create a storyboard on a sheet of paper. A storyboard is a rough drawing of frames in the order in which they will occur. Limit your storyboard to no more than ten frames.
4. Each of you should take on the role of scriptwriter or digital artist, depending on your skills and interests. The scriptwriter is responsible for writing the text of the story. The digital artist will create photographic imagery.

5. When you are ready to work on your animation, decide on a background color. The default color in many animation programs is black.
6. Import the picture file containing the object or actor that will appear first. Use either the "Insert" command from the menu bar or the picture icon from the toolbar.
7. Assign an action or effect to this object, choosing from the "Tools" menu.
8. Repeat steps 6 and 7 to introduce remaining actors and objects. If your layout window becomes overly crowded, try enlarging the window or "hiding" images that are obscuring others. Participate in an in-progress critique of your work with the teacher and your peers. Use critical attributes to analyze the work of your classmates.
9. Type in any text from your storyboard using the "Insert Text" command or icon. Choose a font and color that you like and that fits the context of your movie. Add effects to your text.
10. As you work, periodically play the scene to make sure events occur in the right sequence and at the desired time.
11. Once you are satisfied with your results, publish your movie to the Internet. To do this, select "Export" from the "File," then select "HTML..." Play your movie for classmates.

Evaluating Your Work

- **Describe** What subject did you choose for your digital frame animation? How did you produce photographic imagery in experimental and traditional ways?
- **Analyze** Tell what actions and effects you used in your movie. What problems, if any, did you encounter in the sequence or timing of events? How did you solve those problems?
- **Interpret** Tell what your animation shows. Is it clear and easy to understand? Describe the overall feeling or mood of the animation. Is the feeling or mood the one you set out to communicate to your viewer?
- **Judge** Is there anything about the final animation you would change to make it more effective? What did you change, if anything, after your in-progress critique?

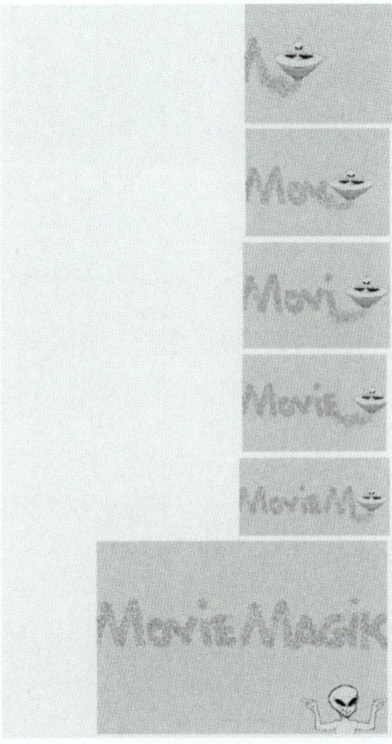

◆ **Figure 15–7** **Student art. A digital frame animation.**

COMPUTER OPTION

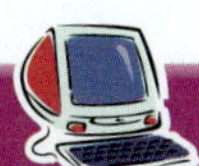

Experimenting with Photographic Imagery
Use the steps in this studio lesson to create another electronic media-generated artwork. Experiment with a variety of "virtual tools" to create photographic imagery.

Visual Art Journal

Analyze ways in which electronic media and technologies have influenced your personal artworks and art in general. Write your thoughts down in your visual art journal.

Digital Self-Portrait

Like traditional photography, digital photography relies on light to create images. A digital camera is used very much like a regular camera. You look through a viewfinder, focus, and take the picture. This is where their similarities end. Digital photography records images digitally. Images can be stored and downloaded into a computer or transferred to a disk. They can be kept as is or using darkroom or graphics software, altered. Best of all, you see your image instantly. This allows you to experiment with shutter speeds, exposure, and lighting. Since your results are immediate, you can make adjustments right away. The images you don't like are easily deleted.

Figure 15–8 shows a digital portrait by photographer Diane Fenster. Does this artwork remind you of a painting? In what ways is it different?

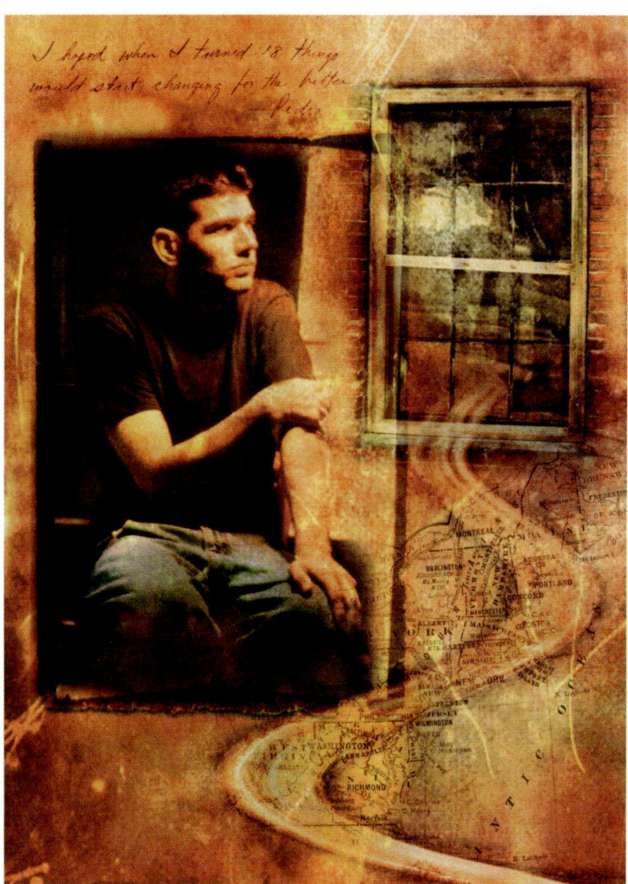

◆ **Figure 15–8** **Analyze this artwork. How have electronic media and technologies influenced this piece?**

Diane Fenster. *Transitions.* 2000. Adobe Photoshop. Private collection.

What You Will Learn

You will experiment with electronic media-generated art to create photographic imagery. You will select from a range of digital options to create several self-portraits. You will experiment with different types of shutter speeds, lighting, and unusual camera angles. You may choose to experiment with computer programs. You will create contrast and texture in at least one photograph. You will select the self-portrait which best portrays your personality.

What You Will Need

- Digital camera (can be disposable)
- Mat board, mat knife or cutter, ruler
- Printer and photography paper (optional)
- Computer and monitor (optional)
- Darkroom or graphic program (optional)

What You Will Do

1. Begin by seeing what tools are available to you. If you do not have a digital camera, use a disposable one.
2. Once you have selected an option, begin experimenting. You will create a self-portrait. Think about your personality, your likes and dislikes, and your environment. This will help you in interpreting your subject and deciding how you will frame or compose your picture.

3. Look through the viewfinder to see what is in your background. A busy or crowded background will distract from your self-portrait. Because this is a self-portrait, most of your shots will be an arm's length away. If your camera has a timer, you can set it to photograph yourself from a distance. Press the shutter-release button halfway down to set the focus and exposure. Your camera will light or beep when it's done. Press the button all the way down to take the picture.
4. Experiment with your shutter speeds. Experiment with lighting. See what happens when you take a photo at night under a neon light. What differences do you see with a fast and slow shutter speed?
5. Try to take your self-portrait from an unusual angle. Try a portion of your face, or shooting from below or above.
6. Explore weather conditions, textures, reflections, and black-and-white images to create a mood. Include some texture in at least one of your self-portraits.
7. After you have taken all your photographs, process them. This can be done at a photo-processing center, or you can print them out on your computer printer. If using a digital camera, analyze your self-portrait in progress with your teacher and peers. Gain feedback by participating in individual and group critiques. A darkroom or graphics program can be used to further manipulate one of your images.
8. Look through your self-portraits and select four images to share with your classmates.

Evaluating Your Work

- **Describe** What digital options did you experiment with to create your self-portraits? Explain how you altered your image.
- **Analyze** Explain the variations you achieved with different lighting and shutter speeds. Explain how you created contrast in one of your images.
- **Interpret** Explain how color and camera angle affected the overall feeling of your self-portrait.
- **Judge** Were you successful at producing at least one self-portrait that best portrays your personality? Use the aesthetic theories in Chapter 5 to defend your decision.

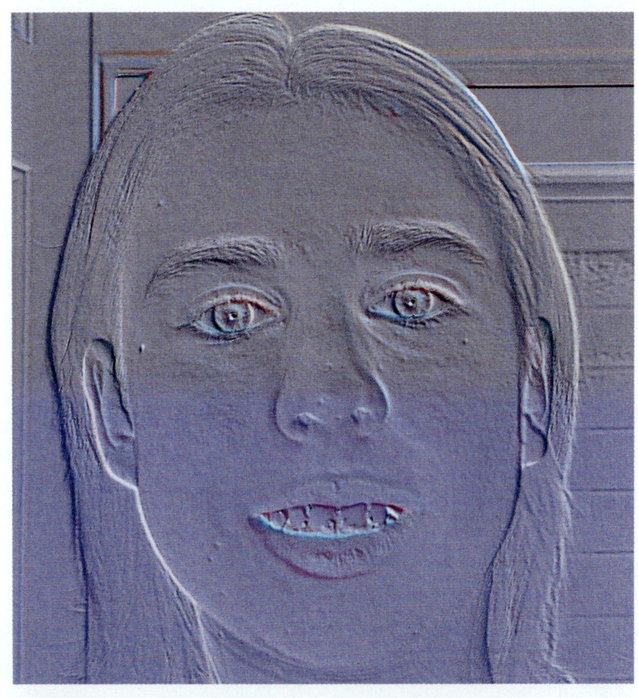

◆ **Figure 15–9** **Student art. A digital self-portrait.**

REFLECTIVE THINKING

Critical Evaluation Analyze the digital self-portraits created by your peers. Form conclusions about formal properties, intents, and meanings. Analyze digital artworks by other artists by searching the Internet. Compare these works to those of your peers to evaluate how digital technology has been used.

Visual Art Journal

Create a self-portrait using traditional photography techniques. Compare your digital self-portrait to the traditional one. Write your thoughts in your journal.

LESSON 5

Presenting a Multimedia Portfolio

In Chapter 1 you learned about how to make a traditional portfolio. In it you have placed your artwork, written observations, favorite reproductions, teacher comments, and sketches. Now you will select your best work to present as a multimedia portfolio. Due to rapid advances in technology, artists often have what is known as a *digital portfolio.* The newest in graphics and multimedia software programs make it easy to do this. Today, when an artist applies for a job, he or she submits a digital portfolio.

What You Will Learn

In this lesson you will learn how to present a multimedia portfolio. You will look through all of your artwork and consider which pieces to select. You will experiment with print and electronic resources to produce digital images of your art. Using presentation software (see **Figure 15–10**), you will organize the images into a multimedia presentation. Your electronic media-generated presentation will show your growth as an artist. You will plan out your presentation by creating a storyboard. Include drawings, paintings, and a three-dimensional work. Experiment by adding photographic imagery, text, and sound to your presentation. You will select one work that you think is your best for your last slide.

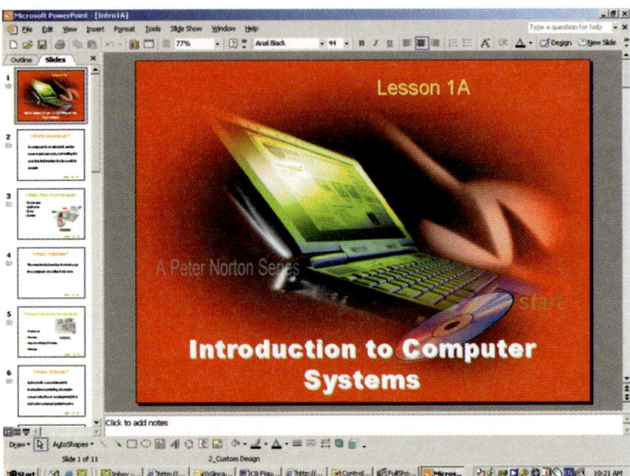

◆ **Figure 15–10 A multimedia portfolio can be displayed using presentation software.**

Microsoft PowerPoint. Screen shot used by permission from Microsoft Corporation.

What You Will Need

- Sketchbook, pencil, and eraser
- Your portfolio with your artwork
- Computer with monitor or projector
- Digital or traditional camera
- Scanner (optional)
- Presentation software

What You Will Do

1. Look through your portfolio and select six to ten of your best pieces of art. If you improved on a piece and have a before-and-after image, use it too. You can also include a sketch. This will help show the process or steps taken to create an artwork.
2. Use a variety of print and electronic resources to produce digital photographic imagery. Use a scanner or digital camera to make copies of your selected artworks. These will then be stored digitally in a file or on a disk or CD. If these methods are not available to you, use traditional photographic methods. Simply take your roll of film to a photo-processing center. They can develop and copy the images onto a disk.

3. Look at your selected pieces and arrange them in order from the first to the last one you made. Choose the one piece you feel is your best work. This will be the last slide in your presentation. In your sketchbook plan out your presentation, referring to your selected images. Make an outline of your presentation by creating a storyboard. Experiment by incorporating text or sound into your presentation.
4. Look back in Chapter 5 and select one of the aesthetic theories to support your decision for selecting your best work. Write out your explanation.
5. Using a graphics or multimedia software program, create a slide show. Select Layout and click on your first saved image from your file. This will add a slide to your presentation. Custom effects will allow you to add text and sound effects. Slide Transition will allow you to change to your next image or slide.
6. Once you have saved your presentation, test it out. To view all of your slides, select Slide Sorter. Have a friend or family member view it. Ask them to critique the presentation and make any necessary adjustments.

Evaluating Your Work

- **Describe** What artworks did you choose? Why? What resources were used to produce digital images? What drawings, paintings and three-dimensional work did you include in your presentation?
- **Analyze** Explain the elements and principles of art that made your selected piece your favorite. What effect did photographic imagery, text, or sound have on your presentation?
- **Interpret** Explain the overall effect that your presentation had on you. What progress as an artist did you see in your work?
- **Judge** Do you feel your multimedia presentation was a success? Using one or more of the aesthetic theories explained in Chapter 5, defend your decision.

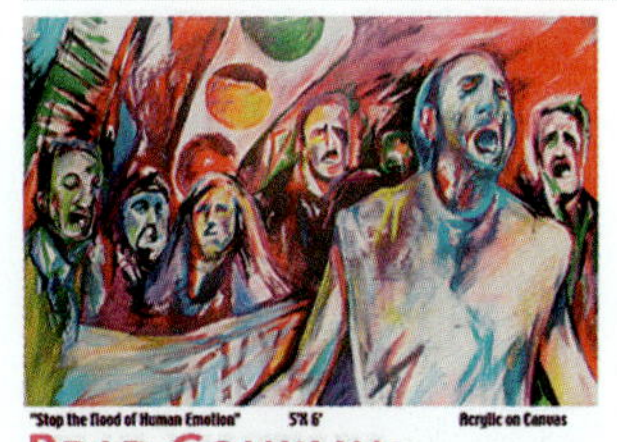

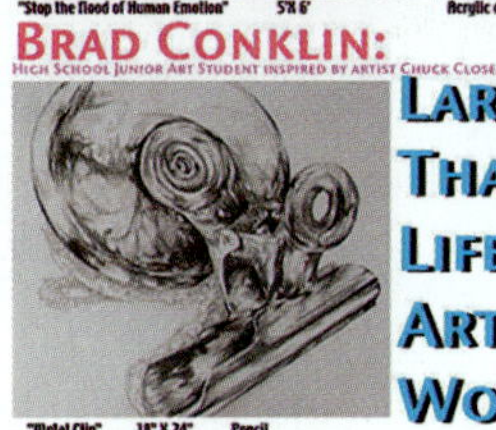

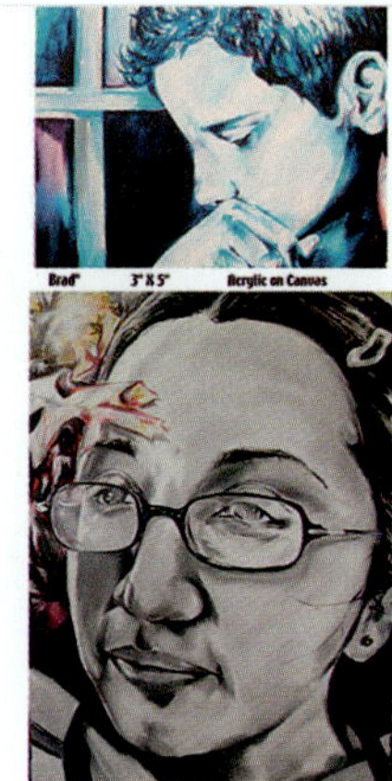

◆ **Figure 15–11** **Student art. A multimedia portfolio.**

PORTFOLIO IDEAS

Analyze digital and traditional portfolios by peers and others, such as high school students or your art teacher. Form conclusions about formal properties, historical and cultural contexts, intents, and meanings. Compare how the digital and traditional portfolios incorporate the elements and principles of art. What clues does each type of portfolio provide about the artist's cultural background and intent? Do they have different meanings?

Art Online

Survey and identify career-choices in art by visiting the Career Corner at **art.glencoe.com**. There you will also find:

- Artist Profiles
- Student Art Gallery
- Web Links

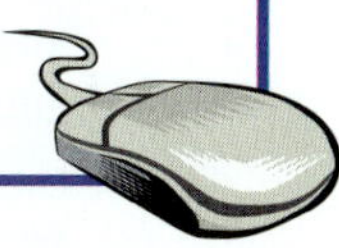

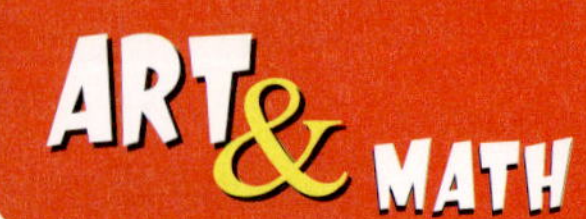

Computerized Animation

The art of animation—bringing cartoon figures to life—dates to the early 1900s. The art of computerized animation is a relatively recent development. The image in **Figure 15–12** is a "still," or frozen image, from one such animation. This particular still is from the movie *Lord of the Rings: The Two Towers.* Do you know this figure?

Computerized 3-D Animation

Computer animation uses specialized computer software known as *3-D rendering software.* As explained in Chapter 4, this type of program involves a multistep process. The first step is modeling figures and objects. As in conventional modeling, the digital sculptor uses sculpting tools to mold forms. A major difference is that in computer modeling, the tools are on-screen. While modeling a form, the digital artist rotates the creation periodically. This permits the artist to view it from different sides and angles.

Once the form is finished, textures are applied by means of visual maps. These are mathematical formulas that create a form-fitting "skin" for the object. Maps determine whether a form appears bumpy or smooth, shiny or dull, and so on. Which of these texture properties do you think were "mapped onto" Figure 15–12?

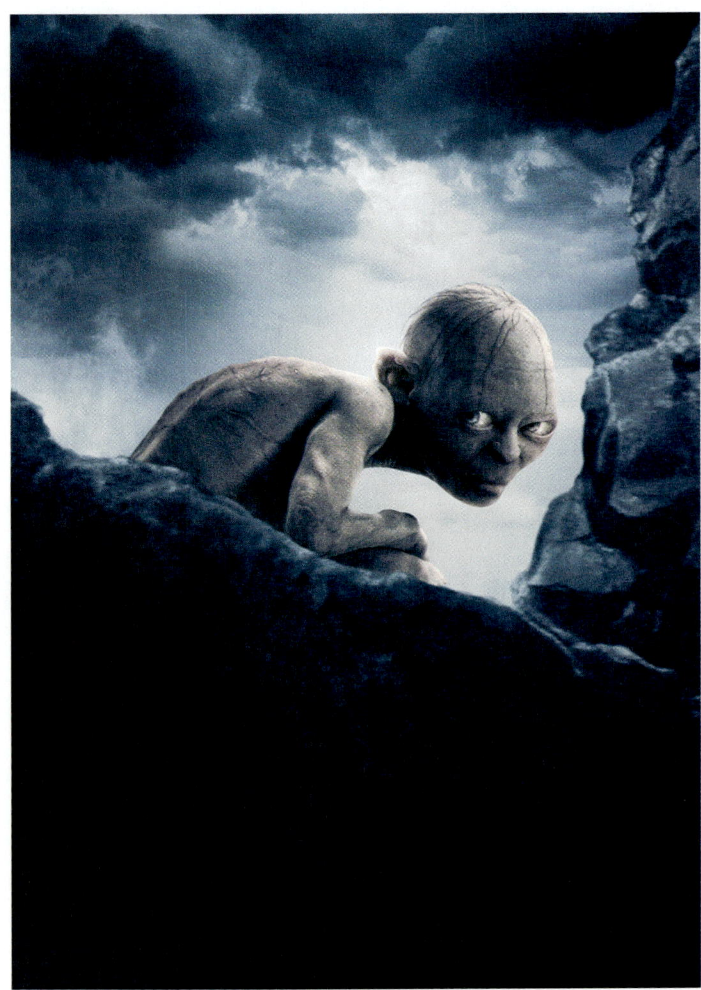

◆ **Figure 15–12** **Does the creature in this image look lifelike? What effects did the digital artist use to achieve this?**

Lord of the Rings: The Two Towers. Courtesy Warner Brothers, 2003.

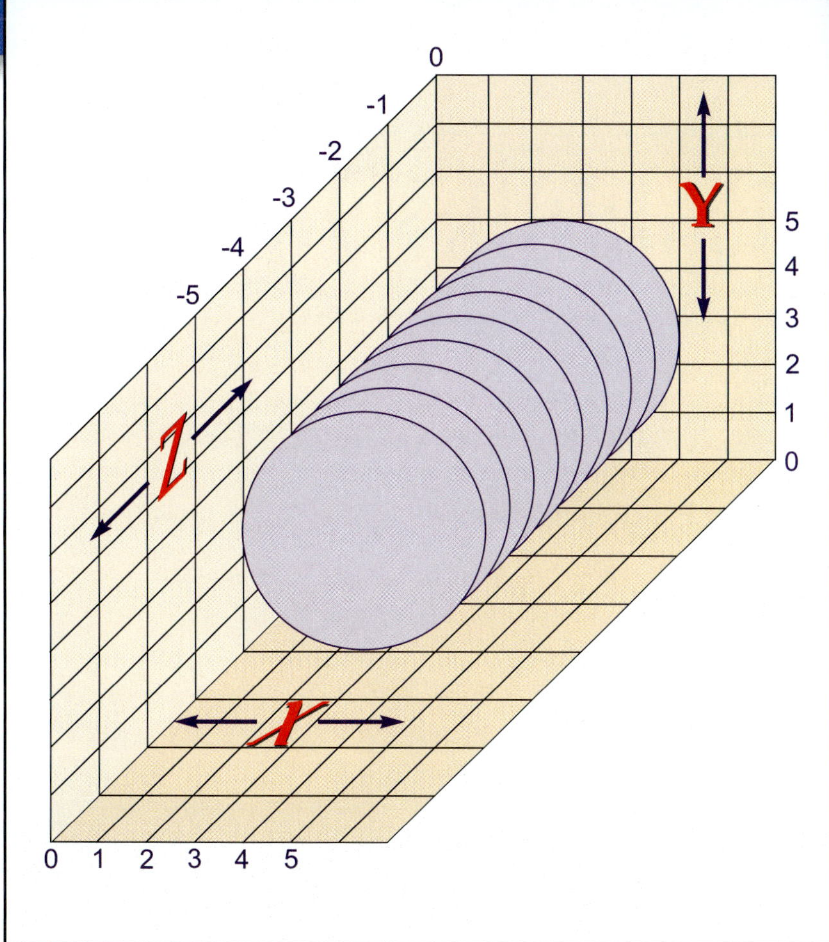

◆ **Figure 15–13** **What is the purpose of the grid lines in this screenshot? What do the three separate grids represent?**

Another step in computer animation is frame development. Like any movie, an animation is made up of a series of frames. The illusion of movement is created by changing a form's frame-to-frame location.

The screen shot in **Figure 15–13** shows a behind-the-scenes glimpse at a single frame. Notice that the object appears in front of three connected surfaces, or planes. Each plane has grid lines like those on graph paper. The form's precise location in any frame is determined by a set of three mathematical coordinates. Notice that there is one coordinate for each dimension. Side-to-side movement is measured along the X axis. Up-and-down motion is computed along the Y axis, front-to-back on the Z axis.

MAKE THE CONNECTION

Take Another Look

1. The facial features and body proportions of the figure in the still shown in Figure 15–12 are stylized. Why do you think the artist has exaggerated these details?
2. In what ways is the work of the digital artist similar to and different from that of the conventional artist? Explain.

ART & MATH

Map out a geometric design. Geometric shapes are made of straight lines, angles, and mathematical curves. In art, geometric shapes can help create a stylized, abstract look. Using Figure 15–13 as a reference, draw a sketch of a three-dimensional animal or object. Now, use geometric shapes to show an abstract version of your design.

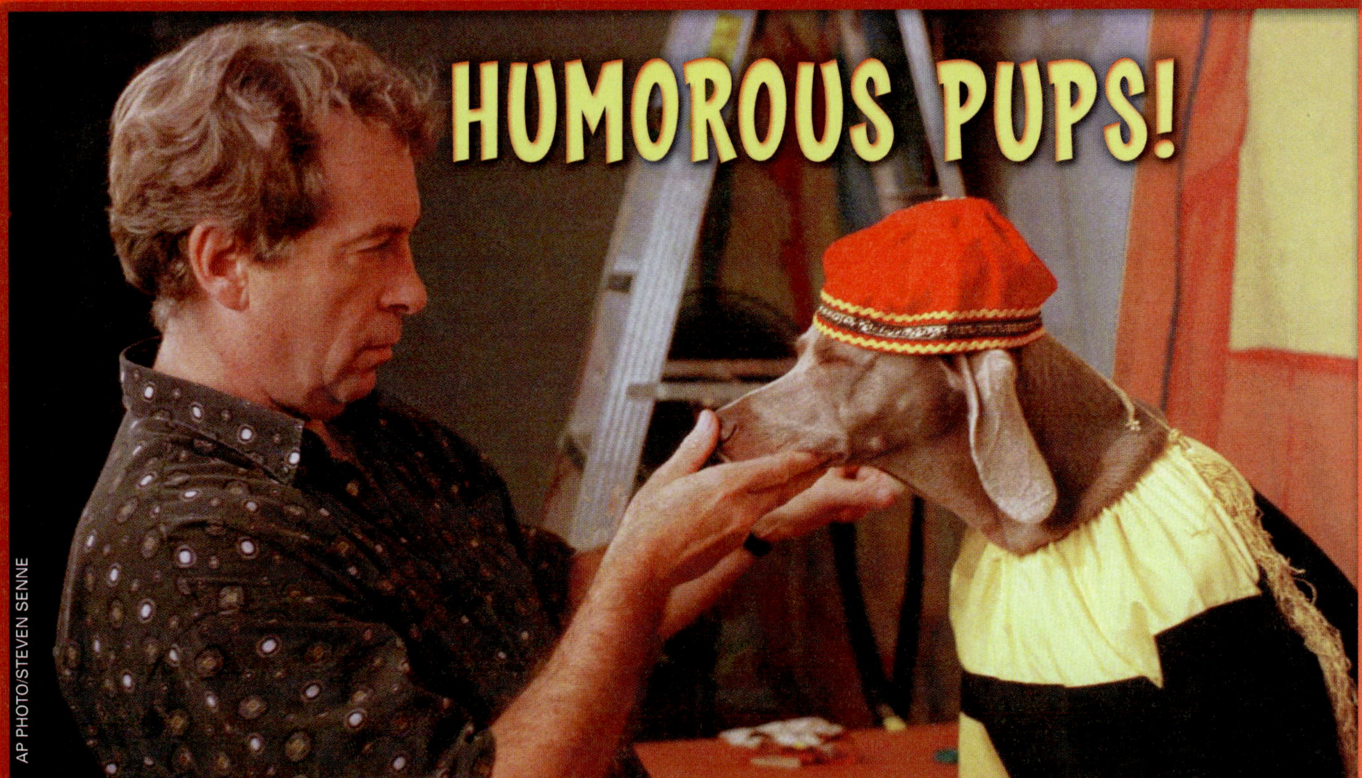

William Wegman prepares his model for a photo shoot. Wegman believes that his dogs like their work:
"They get very competitive to be the one chosen." His costumed canines have gained many fans, appearing regularly on one TV program, and in videos, paintings, and books.

Photographer William Wegman's "pet" subjects

When William Wegman became an artist, he never pictured his career going to the dogs! It all began when Wegman got a Weimaraner puppy. Starting in the early 1970s, Wegman began putting the pooch in his video and photography work. "After a while, it became the strongest element of my work," he says, "and I became kind of known for that."

After he got his next dog, Wegman began photographing his dogs dressed up in different scenes and characters. He often puts them up on modeling stands, and they appear to enjoy being at eye level. They have to remain patient during the time it takes Wegman to set up, focus, and determine the appropriate lighting.

Although Wegman is best known for his humorous dog pictures, he also creates paintings, photographs, and videotapes about a wide range of non-puppy subjects.

TIME TO CONNECT

- **Research more information about Wegman in art books, your school media resource center, or on the Internet.**
- **From what you have learned, write an imaginary interview with Wegman. Write four questions and then, predicting what Wegman might say, write his answers. Make sure to base your predictions on specific information.**

Chapter 15 Review

BUILDING VOCABULARY

Number a sheet of paper from 1 to 6. After each number, write the term from the list that best matches each description below.

cinematographer	motion picture
digitizing	multimedia art
director	producer

1. A series of photographs of a moving subject taken a very short time apart and flashed onto a screen.
2. The person in charge of the business end of making a movie.
3. Art that simultaneously uses several different electronic media.
4. The person in charge of running the camera in the filming of a movie.
5. A method of defining the location of points and lines in space by numerical values.
6. The person in charge of shooting a film and guiding the actors.

REVIEWING ART FACTS

Number a sheet of paper from 7 to 12. Answer each question in a complete sentence.

7. What is a cinematographer? What do they have in common with other artists?
8. Why were the first films made able to be shown to people around the world?
9. How have computers changed since their introduction in the 1950s? How has the software used with them changed?
10. Describe the first images created using computers.
11. What type of image file can be created in Paint programs? In Draw programs? When might a digital artist prefer a Draw program over a Paint program, and vice versa?
12. What are some advantages of using a digital camera to create art compared to a conventional camera?

CROSS-CURRICULUM CONNECTIONS

13. **Technology.** Analyze ways in which electronic media and technologies have influenced art. In particular, what advantages do Paint and Draw programs offer contemporary artists? What is the technological difference between these two types of programs? Explain your thoughts in a paragraph.
14. **Career Opportunities.** Survey career opportunities in the art of filmmaking. If possible, interview a local filmmaker. Find out what kind of preparation is required to become a film director or producer. Are there any courses the individual recalls taking in school that were instrumental in his or her career choice? Share your findings.

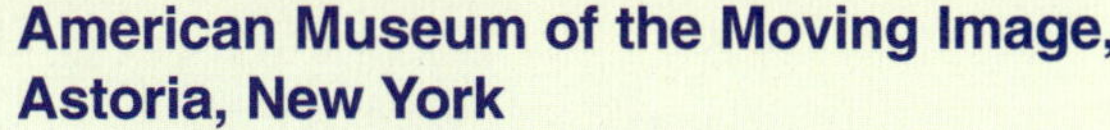

American Museum of the Moving Image, Astoria, New York

Lights, camera, action! Learn about the way movie and television cameras work at the American Museum of the Moving Image. Visit the museum's site at **art.glencoe.com** and click on the interactive lessons. You can also click on Computer Space to learn about the history and development of video games.

Handbook Contents

Technique Tips

DRAWING TIPS

PAINTING TIPS

PRINTMAKING TIPS

SCULPTING TIPS

OTHER TIPS

Digital Media Guide

Career Spotlights

DRAWING TIPS

1. Making Gesture Drawings

Gesture drawing is a way of showing movement in a sketch. Gesture drawings have no outlines or details. You are not expected to draw the figure. Instead, you are expected to draw the movement, or what the figure is doing. Follow these guidelines:

- Use the side of the drawing tool. Do not hold the medium as you would if you were writing.
- Find the lines of movement that show the direction in which the figure is bending. Draw the main line showing this movement.
- Use quickly drawn lines to build up the shape of the person.

2. Making Contour Drawings

Contour drawing is a way of capturing the feel of a subject. When doing a contour drawing, remember the following pointers:

- If you accidentally pick up your pen or pencil, don't stop working. Place your pen or pencil back where you stopped. Begin again from that point.
- If you have trouble keeping your eyes off the paper, ask a friend to hold a piece of paper between your eyes and your drawing paper. Another trick is to place your drawing paper inside a large paper bag as you work.
- Tape your paper to the table, so it will not slide around. With a finger of your free hand, trace an outline of the object. Record the movement with your drawing hand.
- Contour lines show ridges and wrinkles in addition to outlines. Adding these lines gives roundness to the object.

3. Drawing with Oil Pastels

Oil pastels are sticks of pigment held together with an oily binder. The colors are brighter than wax crayon colors. If you press heavily, you will make a brilliant-colored line. If you press lightly, you will create a fuzzy line. You can fill in shapes with the brilliant colors. You can blend a variety of color combinations. For example, you can fill a shape with a soft layer of a hue and then color over the hue with a heavy layer of white to create a unique tint of that hue.

If you use oil pastels on colored paper, you can put a layer of white under the layer of hue to block the color of the paper.

4. Drawing Thin Lines with a Brush

Drawing thin lines with a brush can be learned with a little practice. Just follow these steps:

1. Dip your brush in the ink or paint. Wipe the brush slowly against the side, twirling it between your fingers until the bristles form a point.
2. Hold the brush at the beginning of the metal band near the tip. Hold the brush straight up and down.
3. Imagine that the brush is a pencil with a very sharp point. Pretend that pressing too hard will break the point. Now touch the paper lightly with the tip of the brush and draw a line. The line should be quite thin.

To make a thinner line still, lift up on the brush as you draw. After a while, you will be able to make lines in a variety of thicknesses.

5. Making a Grid for Enlarging

Sometimes the need arises to make a bigger version of a small drawing. An example is when you create a mural based on a small sketch. Follow these steps:

1. Using a ruler, draw evenly spaced lines across and up and down your original drawing (Figure T–1). Count the number of squares you

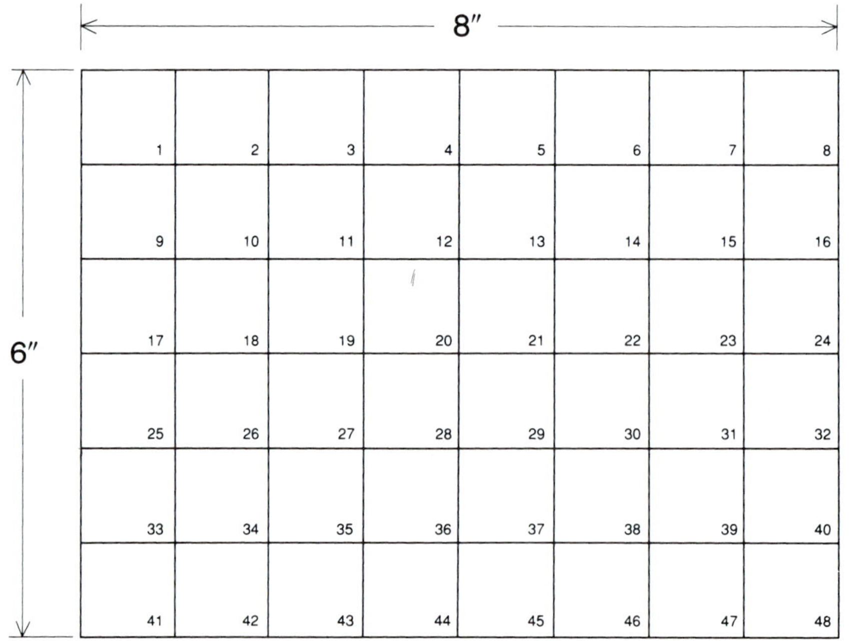

▲ **Figure T–1**

made from side to side. Count the number of squares running up and down.

2. Measure the width of the surface to which the drawing is to be transferred. Divide that figure by the number of side-to-side squares. The resulting number will be the horizontal measure of each square. You may work in inches or centimeters. Using a ruler or yardstick, mark off the squares. Draw in light rules.
3. Measure the height of the surface to which the drawing is to be transferred. Divide that figure by the number of up-and-down squares. The resulting number will be the vertical measure of each square. Mark off the squares. Draw in pencil lines.
4. Starting at the upper left, number each square on the original drawing. Give the same number to each square on the large grid. Working a square at a time, transfer your image. (See Figure T–2.)

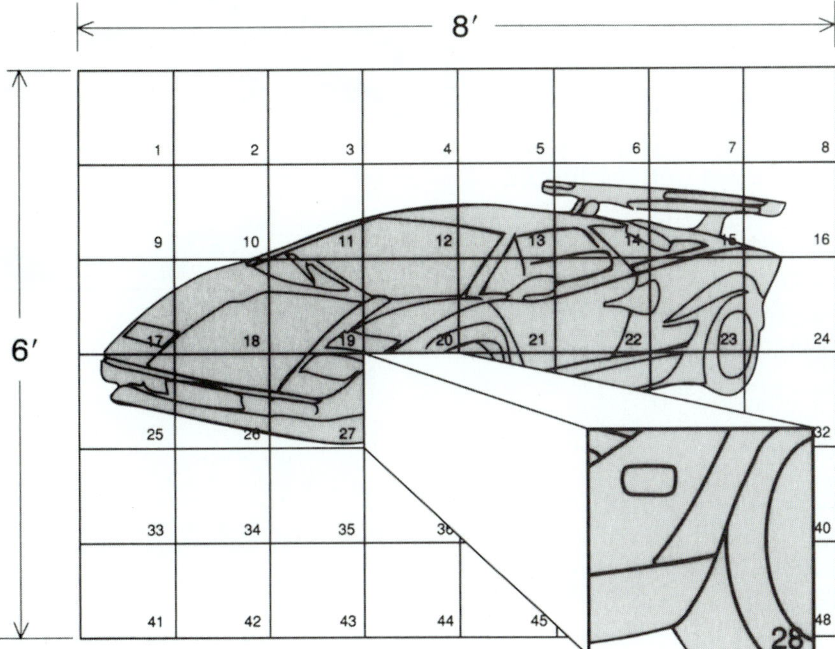

▲ **Figure T–2**

6. Using Shading Techniques

When using shading techniques, keep in mind the following:

- Lines or dots placed close together create dark values.
- Lines or dots placed far apart, on the other hand, create light values. To show a change from light to dark, start with lines or dots far apart and little by little bring them close together.
- Use care also to follow the shape of the object when adding lines. Straight lines are used to shade an object with a flat surface. Rounded lines are used to shade an object with a curved surface.

7. Using Sighting Techniques

Sighting is a technique that will help you draw objects in proportion.

1. Face the object you plan to draw. Hold a pencil straight up and down at arm's length. Your thumb should rest against the side of the pencil and be even with the tip.
2. Close one eye. With your other eye, focus on the object.
3. Slide your thumb down the pencil until the exposed part of the pencil matches the object's height. (See Figure T–3.)

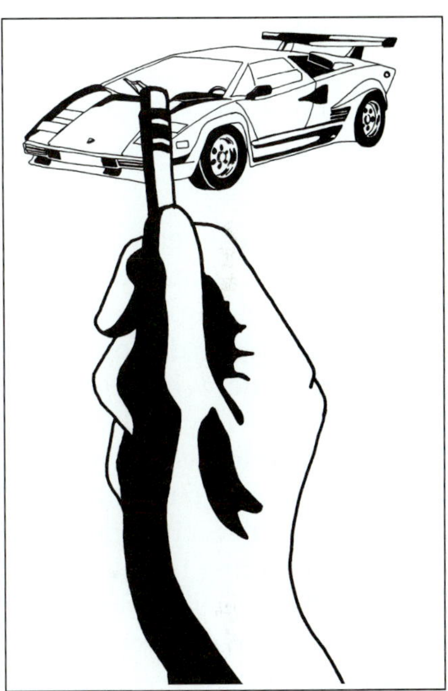

▲ **Figure T–3**

4. Now, without moving your thumb or bending you arm, turn the pencil sideways.
5. Focus on the width of the object. If the height is greater, figure out how many "widths" will fit in one "height." If the width is greater, figure out how many "heights" will fit in one "width."

8. Using a Viewing Frame

Much in the way a camera is used to focus on one area of a scene, you can better zero in on an object you plan to draw by using a viewing frame (Figure T–4). To make a viewing frame, do the following:

1. Cut a rectangular hole in a piece of paper about 2 inches in from the paper's edges.
2. Hold the paper at arm's length and look through the hole at your subject. Imagine that the hole represents your drawing paper.
3. Decide how much of the subject you want to have in your drawing.
4. By moving the frame up, down, sideways, nearer or farther, you can change the focus of your drawing.

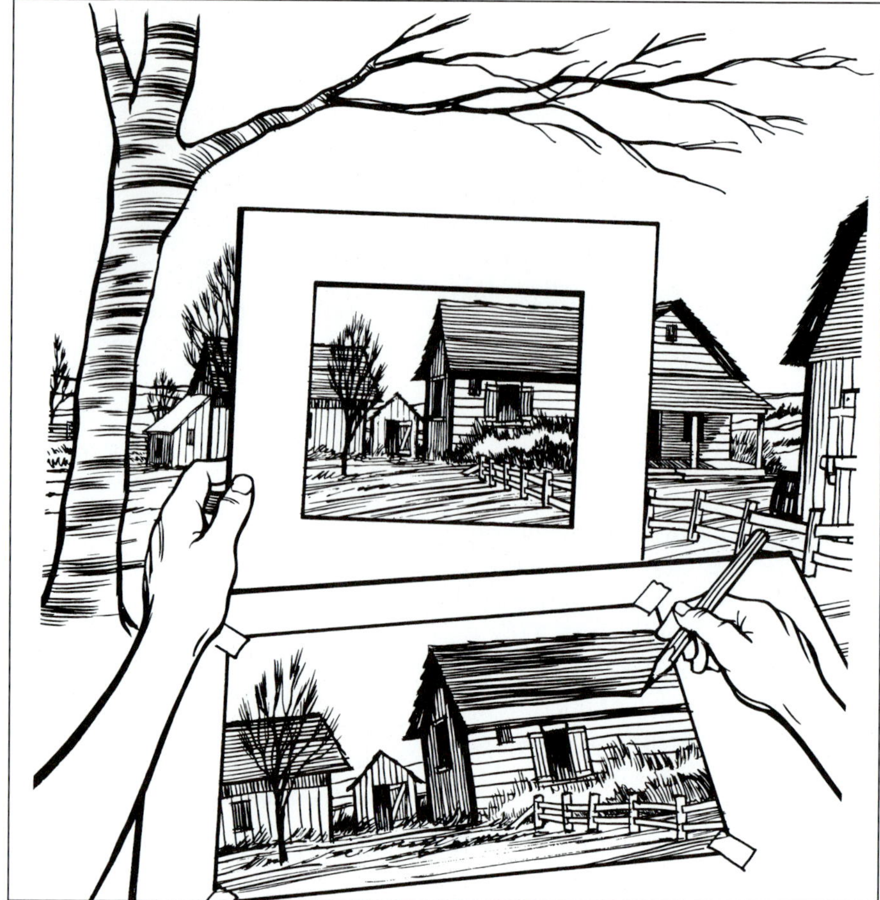

▲ **Figure T–4**

9. Using a Ruler

There are times when you need to draw a crisp, straight line. By using the following techniques, you will be able to do so.

1. Hold the ruler with one hand and the pencil with the other.
2. Place the ruler where you wish to draw a straight line.
3. Hold the ruler with your thumb and first two fingers. Be careful that your fingers do not stick out beyond the edge of the ruler.
4. Press heavily on the ruler so it will not slide while you're drawing.
5. Hold the pencil lightly against the ruler.
6. Pull the pencil quickly and lightly along the edge of the ruler. The object is to keep the ruler from moving while the pencil moves along its edge.

PAINTING TIPS

10. Cleaning a Paintbrush

Cleaning a paint brush properly helps it last a long time. Always:

1. Rinse the thick paint out of the brush under running water. Do not use hot water.
2. Gently paint the brush over a cake of mild soap, or dip it in a mild liquid detergent (Figure T–5).

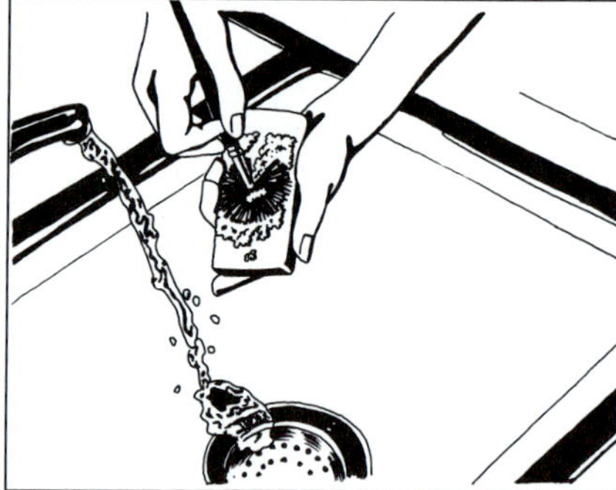

▲ **Figure T–5**

3. Gently scrub the brush against the palm of your hand to work the soap into the brush. This removes paint you may not have realized was still in the brush.
4. Rinse the brush under running water while you continue to scrub your palm against it (Figure T–6).
5. Repeat steps 2, 3, and 4 as needed.

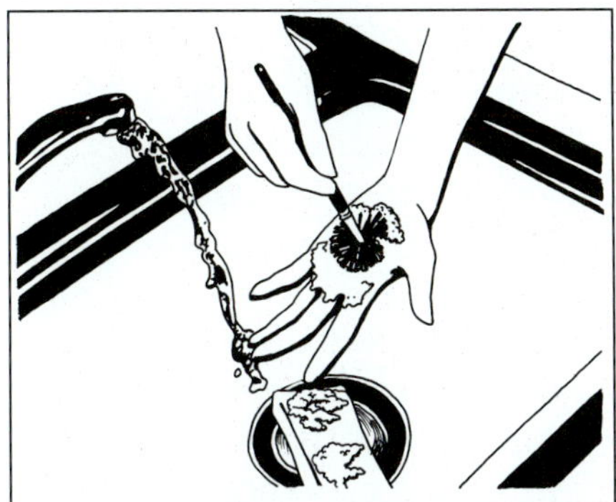

▲ Figure T–6

When it is thoroughly rinsed and excess water has been squeezed from the brush, shape your brush into a point with your fingers (Figure T–7). Place the brush in a container with the bristles up so that it will keep its shape as it dries.

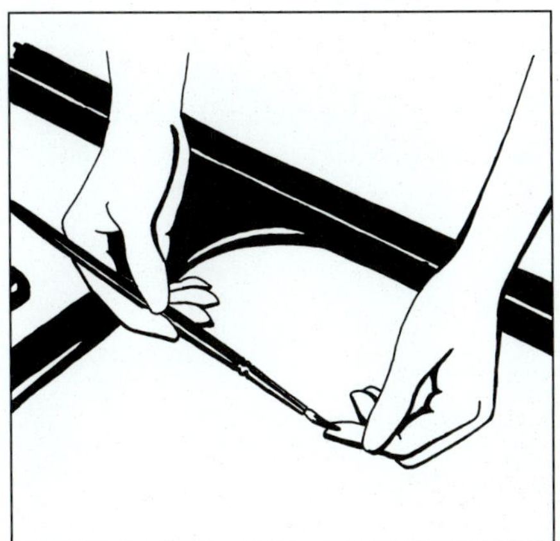

▲ Figure T–7

11. Making Natural Earth Pigments

Anywhere there is dirt, clay, or sand, there is natural pigment. To create your own pigments, gather as many different kinds of earth colors as you can. Grind these as finely as possible. (If you can, borrow a mortar and pestle.) (See Figure T–8.) Do not worry if the pigment is slightly gritty.

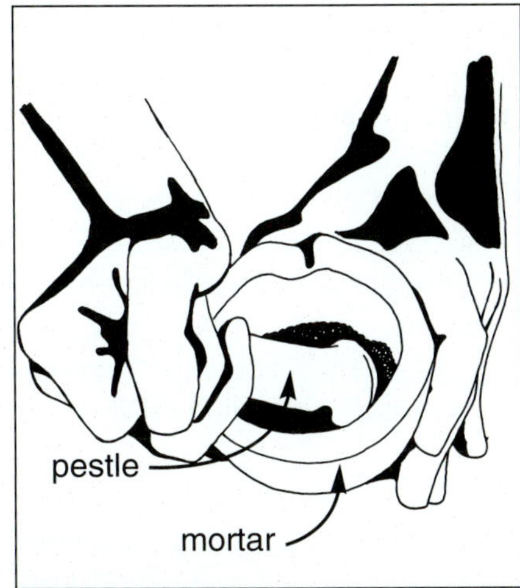

▲ Figure T–8

To make the binder, mix equal parts of white glue and water. Place a few spoonfuls of your powdered pigment into a small jar. Add a little of the binder. Experiment with different amounts of each.

When you work with natural pigments, remember to always wash the brushes before the paint in them has a chance to dry. The glue from the binder can ruin a brush. As you work, stir the paint every now and then. This will keep the grains of pigment from settling to the bottom of the jar.

Make a fresh batch each time you paint.

12. Mixing Paint to Change the Value of Color

You can better control the colors in your work when you mix your own paint. In mixing paints, treat opaque paints (for example, tempera) differently from transparent paints (for example, watercolors).

- *For light values of opaque paints.* Mix only a small amount of the hue to white. The color can always be made stronger by adding more of the hue.
- *For dark values of opaque paints.* Add a small amount of black to the hue. Never add the hue to black.
- *For light values of transparent paints.* Thin a shaded area with water (Figure T–9). This allows more of the white of the paper to show through.
- *For dark values of transparent paints.* Carefully add a small amount of black to the hue.

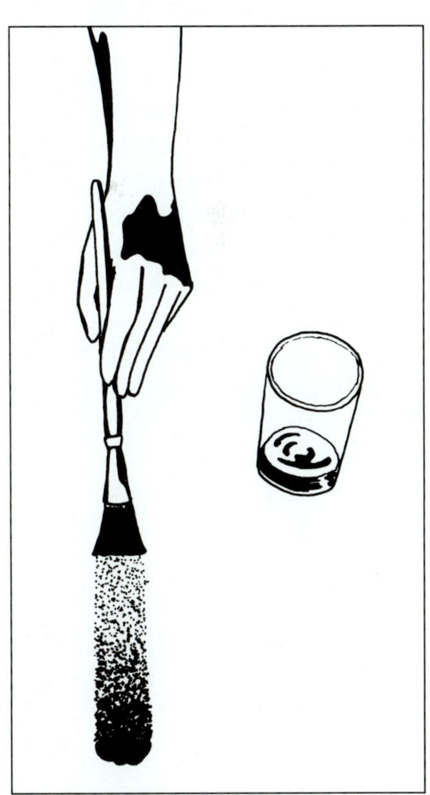

▲ Figure T–9

13. Working with Tempera

When using tempera, remember the following:

- Tempera paints run when wet. To keep this from happening, make sure one shape is dry before painting a wet color next to it.

14. Working with Watercolors

- If you apply wet paint to damp paper, you create lines and shapes with soft edges.
- If you apply wet paint to dry paper, you create lines and shapes with sharp, clear edges.
- If you dip a dry brush into damp paint and then brush across dry paper, you achieve a fuzzy effect.
- School watercolors come in semi-moist cakes. Before you use them, place a drop of water on each cake to let the paint soften. Watercolor paints are transparent. You can see the white paper through the paint. If you want a light value of a hue, dilute the paint with a large amount of water. If you want a bright hue, you must dissolve more pigment by swirling your brush around in the cake of paint until you have dissolved a great deal of paint. The paint you apply to the paper can be as bright as the paint in the cake.

PRINTMAKING TIPS

15. Making a Stamp Printing

A stamp print is an easy way to make repetitive designs. The following are a few suggestions for making a stamp and printing with it. You may develop some other ideas after reading these hints. Remember, printing reverses your design, so if you use letters, be certain to cut or carve them backwards.

- Cut a simple design into the flat surface of an eraser with a knife that has a fine, precision blade.
- Cut a potato, carrot, or turnip in half. Use a paring knife to carve a design into the flat surface of the vegetable.
- Glue yarn to a bottle cap or a jar lid.
- Glue found objects to a piece of corrugated cardboard. Make a design with paper clips, washers, nuts, leaves, feathers, or anything else you can find. Whatever object you use should have a fairly flat surface. Make a handle for the block with masking tape.
- Cut shapes out of a piece of inner tube material. Glue the shapes to a piece of heavy cardboard.

There are several ways to apply ink or paint to a stamp:

- Roll water-based printing ink on the stamp with a soft brayer.
- Roll water-based printing ink on a plate and press the stamp into the ink.
- Apply tempera paint or school acrylic to the stamp with a bristle brush.

SCULPTING TIPS

16. Working with Clay

To make your work with clay go smoothly, always do the following:

1. Dip one or two fingers in water.
2. Spread the moisture from your fingers over your palms.

Never dip your hands in water. Too much moisture turns clay into mud.

17. Joining Clay

If you are creating a piece of sculpture that requires joining pieces, do the following:

1. Gather the materials you will need. These include clay, slip, (a creamy mixture of clay and water), a paint brush, a scoring tool, (perhaps a kitchen fork) and clay tools.
2. Rough up or scratch the two surfaces to be joined (Figure T–10).

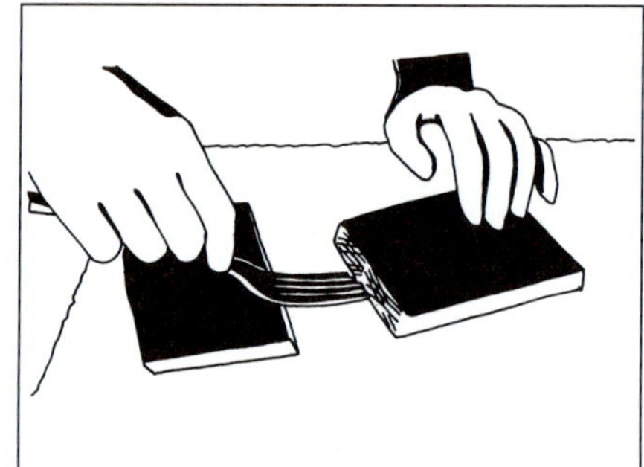

▲ **Figure T–10**

3. Apply slip to one of the two surfaces using a paint brush or your fingers (Figure T–11).

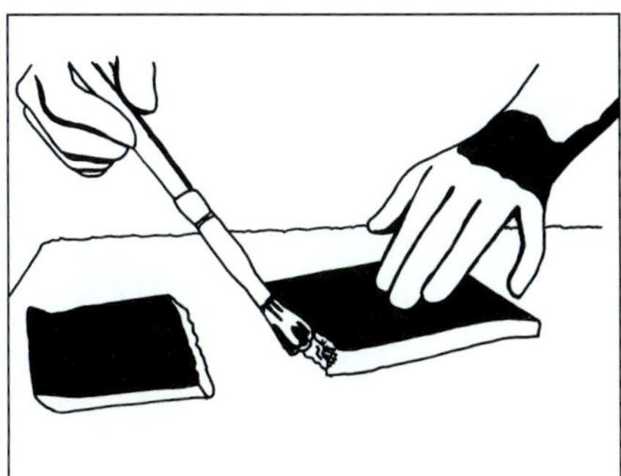

▲ **Figure T–11**

4. Gently press the two surfaces together so the slip oozes out of the joining seam (Figure T–12).

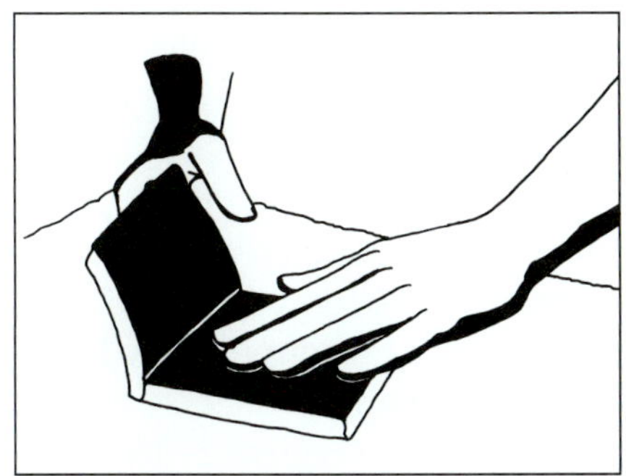

▲ **Figure T–12**

5. Using clay tools and/or your fingers, smooth away the slip that has oozed out of the seam (Figure T–13). You may smooth out the seam as well, or you may leave it for decorative purposes.

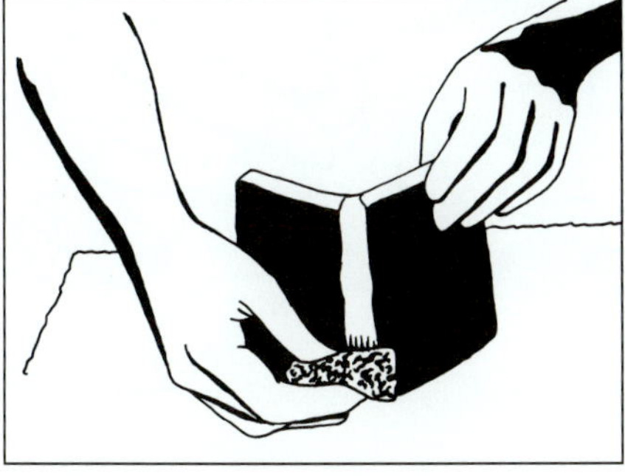

▲ **Figure T–13**

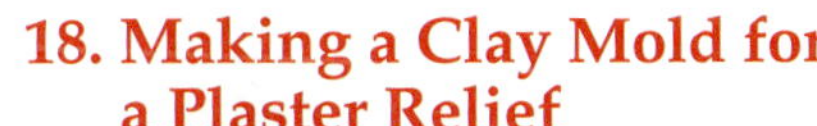

18. Making a Clay Mold for a Plaster Relief

One of the easiest ways to make a plaster relief is with a clay mold. When making a clay mold, remember the following:

- Plaster poured into the mold will come out with the opposite image. Design details cut into the mold will appear raised on the relief. Details built up within the mold will appear indented in the relief.
- Do not make impressions in your mold that have *undercuts* (Figure T–14). Undercuts trap plaster, which will break off when the relief is removed. When cutting impressions, keep the deepest parts the narrowest.
- In carving a raised area in the mold, take care not to create a reverse undercut (Figure T–15).

If you want to change the mold, simply smooth the area with your fingers.

19. Mixing Plaster

Mixing plaster requires some technique and a certain amount of caution. It can also be a very simple matter when you are prepared. Always do the following:

- Use caution when working with dry plaster. Wear a dust mask or work in a well-ventilated room.
- Cover your work space to keep the dust from spreading.
- Always use a plastic bowl and a stick for mixing. Never use silverware you will later eat from.
- Always use plaster that is fine, like sifted flour. Plaster should never be grainy when dry.
- Always add water to the bowl first. Sift in the plaster. Stir slowly.
- Never pour unused plaster down a drain. Allow it to dry in the bowl. To remove the dried plaster, twist the bowl. Crack the loose plaster into a lined trash can.

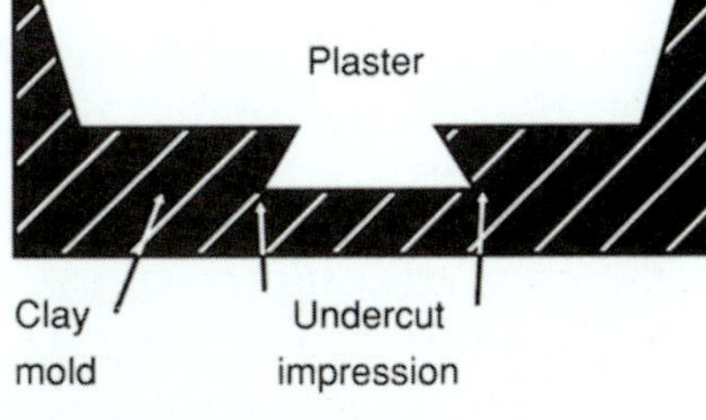

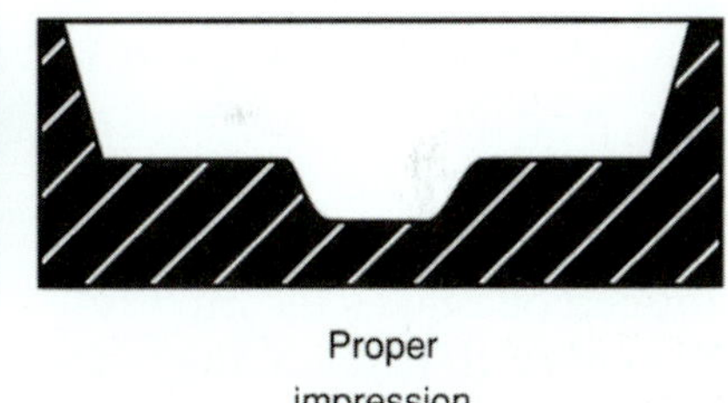

▲ **Figure T–14**

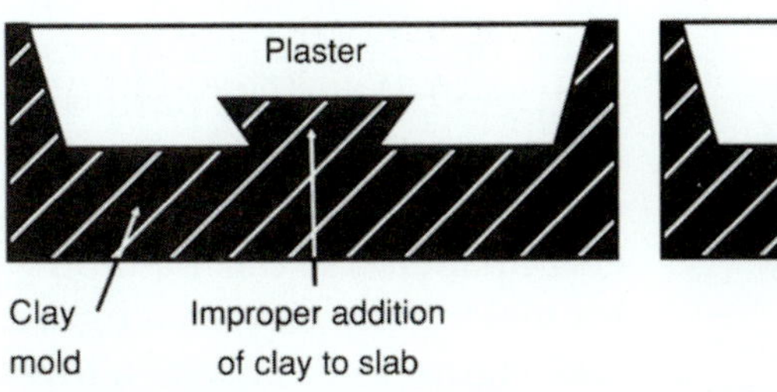

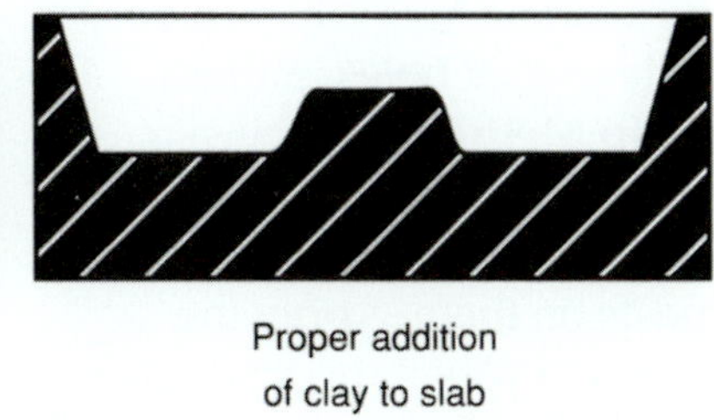

▲ **Figure T–15**

20. Working with Papier-Mâché

Papier-mâché (**pay**-puhr muh-**shay**) is a French term meaning "chewed paper." It is also the name of several sculpting methods using newspaper and liquid paste. These methods can be used to model tiny pieces of jewelry. They can also be used to create life-size creatures.

In creating papier-mâché sculptures, the paper-and-paste mixture is molded over a support. You will learn more about supports shortly. The molded newspaper dries to a hard finish. The following are three methods for working with papier-mâché:

- **Pulp Method**. Shred newspaper, paper towels, or tissue paper into tiny pieces. (Do not use glossy magazine paper: it will not soften.) Soak your paper in water overnight. Press the paper in a kitchen strainer to remove as much moisture as possible. Mix the mashed paper with commercially prepared papier-mâché paste or white glue. The mixture should have the consistency of soft clay. Add a few drops of oil of cloves to keep the mixture from spoiling. A spoonful of linseed oil makes the mixture smoother. (If needed, the mixture can be stored at this point in a plastic bag in the refrigerator.) Use the mixture to model small shapes. When your creations dry, they can be sanded. You will also be able to drill holes in them.
- **Strip Method.** Tear newspaper into strips. Either dip the strips in papier-mâché paste or rub paste on them. Apply the strips to your support (Figure T–16). If you do not want the strips to stick to your support, first cover it with plastic wrap. Use wide strips for large shapes. Use thin strips for smaller shapes. If you plan to remove your finished creation from the support, apply five or six layers. (Change directions with each layer so you can keep track of the number.) Otherwise, two or three layers should be enough. After applying the strips to your support, rub your fingers over the surface.

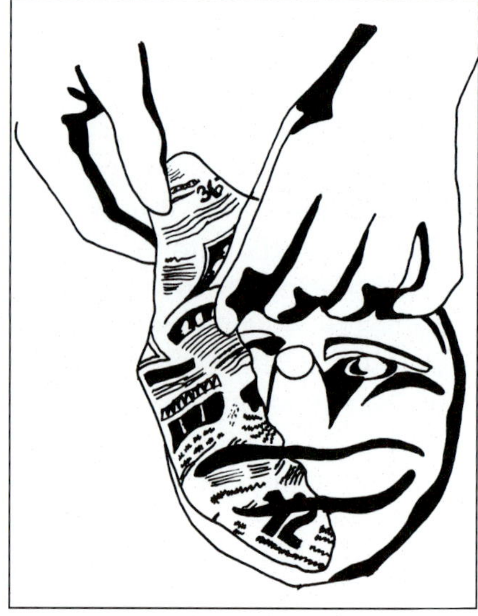

▲ **Figure T–16**

As a last layer, use torn paper towels. The brown paper towels that are found in schools produce an uncomplicated surface on which to paint. Make sure no rough edges are sticking up. Store any unused paste mixture in the refrigerator to keep it from spoiling.

- **Draping Method.** Spread papier-mâché paste on newspaper. Lay a second sheet on top of the first. Smooth the layers. Add another layer of paste and another sheet of paper. Repeat until you have four or five layers of paper. Use this method for making drapery on a figure. (See Figure T–17.) If you allow the layers to dry for a day or two, they will become leathery. They can then be cut and molded as you like. Newspaper strips dipped in paste can be used to seal cracks.

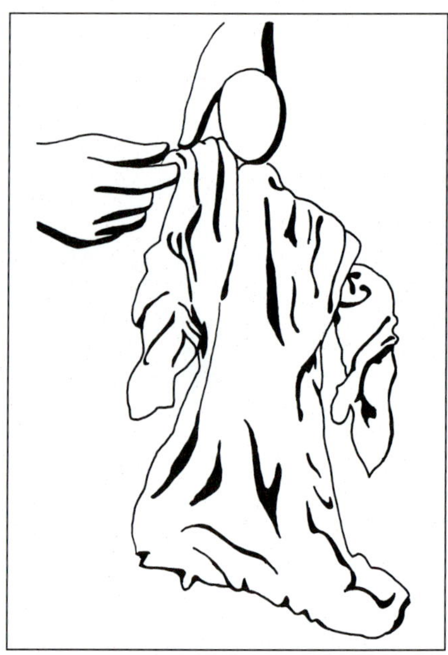

▲ **Figure T–17**

Like papier-mâché, support for papier-mâché creations can be made in several different ways. Dry newspaper may be wadded up and wrapped with string or tape (Figure T–18). Wire coat hangers may be padded with rags. For large figures, a wooden frame covered with chicken wire makes a good support.

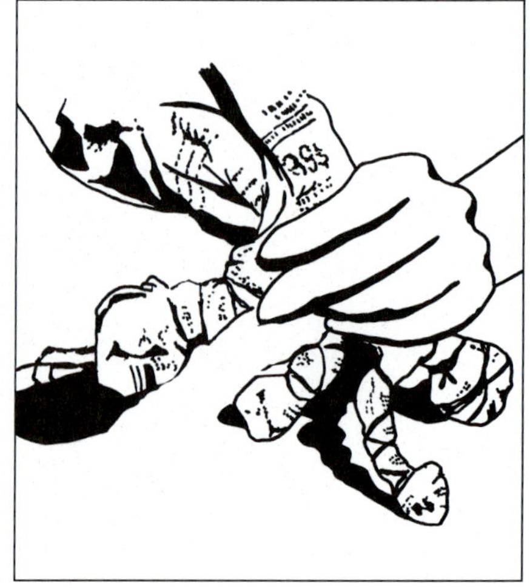

▲ **Figure T–18**

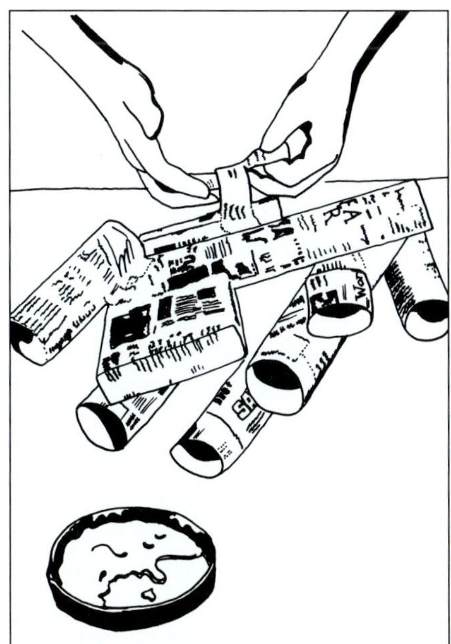

▲ **Figure T–19**

To create a base for your papier-mâché creations, tape together arrangements of found materials. Some materials you might combine are boxes, tubes, and bowls. (See Figure T–19.) Clay can also be modeled as a base. If clay is used, be sure there are no undercuts that would keep the papier-mâché from lifting off easily when dry. (For an explanation of undercuts, see Technique Tip 18, on page 286.)

Always allow time for your papier-mâché creations to dry. The material needs extra drying time when thick layers are used or when the weather is damp. An electric fan blowing air on the material can shorten the drying time.

21. Making a Paper Sculpture

Another name for paper sculpture is origami. The process originated in Japan and means "folding paper." Paper sculpture begins with a flat piece of paper. The paper is then curved or bent to produce more than a flat surface. Here are some ways to experiment with paper.

- **Scoring.** Place a square sheet of heavy construction paper, 12 by 12 inch, on a flat surface. Position a ruler on the paper so that it is close to the center and parallel to the sides. Holding the ruler in place, run the point of a knife or a pair of scissors along one of the ruler's edges. Press down firmly but take care not to cut through the paper. Gently crease the paper along the line you made. Hold your paper with the crease facing upward.
- **Pleating.** Take a piece of paper and fold it one inch from the edge. Then fold the paper in the other direction. Continue folding back and forth.
- **Curling.** Hold one end of a long strip of paper with the thumb and forefinger of one hand. At a point right below where you are holding the strip, grip it lightly between the side of a pencil and the thumb of your other hand. In a quick motion, run the pencil along the strip. This will cause the strip to curl back on itself. Don't apply too much pressure, or the strip will tear. (See Figure T–20.)

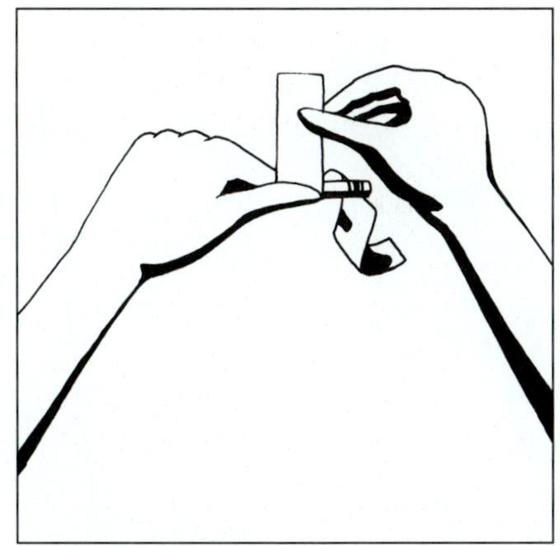

▲ **Figure T–20**

OTHER TIPS

22. Measuring Rectangles

Do you find it hard to create perfectly formed rectangles? Here is a way of getting the job done:

1. Make a light pencil dot near the long edge of a sheet of paper. With a ruler, measure the exact distance between the dot and the edge. Make three more dots the same distance in from the edge. (See Figure T–21.)

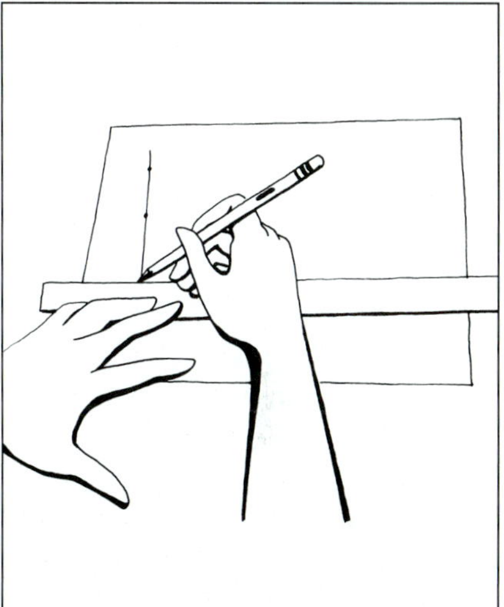

▲ **Figure T–21**

2. Line a ruler up along the dots. Make a light pencil line running the length of the paper.
3. Turn the paper so that a short side is facing you. Make four pencil dots equally distant from the short edge. Connect these with a light pencil rule. Stop when you reach the first line you drew. (See Figure T–22.)
4. Do the same for the remaining two sides. Erase any lines that may extend beyond the box you have made.
5. Trace over the lines with your ruler and pencil.

The box you have created will be a perfectly formed rectangle.

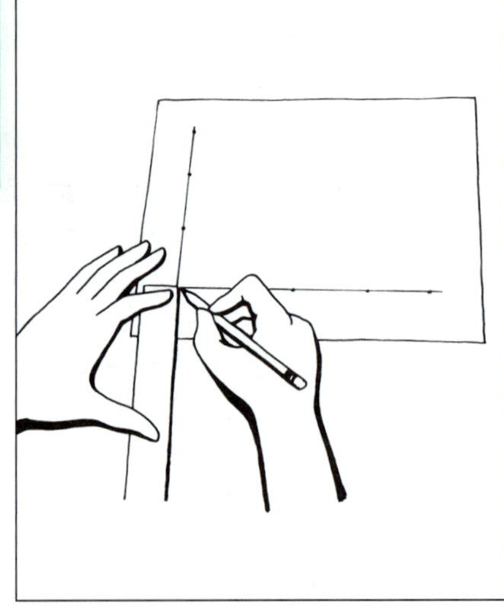

▲ Figure T–22

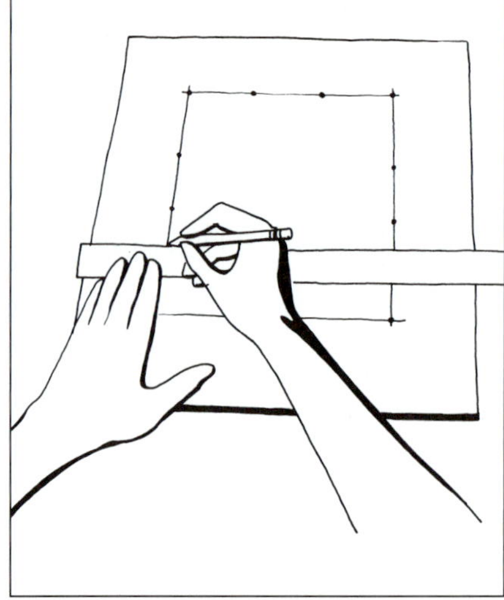

▲ Figure T–23

23. Making a Mat

You can add appeal to an art work by making a mat, using the following steps:

1. Gather the materials you will need. These include a metal rule, a pencil, mat board, cardboard backing, a sheet of heavy cardboard to protect your work surface, a mat knife with a sharp blade, and wide masking tape.
2. Wash you hands. Mat board should be kept very clean.
3. Measure the height and width of the work to be matted. Decide how large a border you want for your work. (A border of approximately 2½ inches on three sides with 3 inches on the bottom is aestheically pleasing.) Your work will be behind the window you will cut.
4. Plan for the opening, or window, to be ¼ inch smaller on all sides than the size of your work. For example, if your work measures 9 by 12 inches, the mat window should measure 8½ inches (9 inches minus ¼ inch times two) by 11½ inches (12 inches minus ¼ inch times two). Using your metal rule and pencil, lightly draw your window rectangle on the back of the board 2½ inches from the top and left edge of the mat. (See Figure T–23.) Add a 2½ inch border to the right of the window and a 3 inch border to the bottom, lightly drawing cutting guidelines.

   Note: If you are working with metric measurements, the window should overlap your work by 0.5 cm (centimeters) on all sides. Therefore, if your work measures 24 by 30 cm, the mat window measures 23 cm (24 – [2 x 0.5]) by 29 cm (30 – [2 x 0.5]).

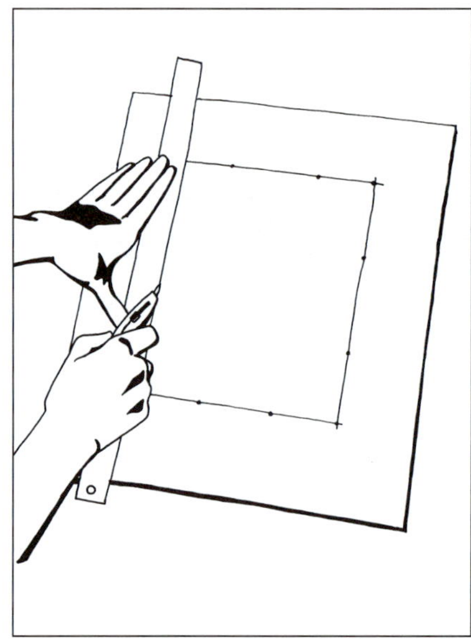

▲ Figure T–24

5. Place the sheet of heavy, protective cardboard on your work surface. Place the mat board, pencil marks up, over the cardboard. Holding the metal rule firmly in place, score the first line with your knife. Always place the metal rule so that your blade is away from the frame. (See Figure T–24.) In case you make an error, you will cut into the window hole or the extra mat that is not used for the frame. Do not try to cut through the board with one stroke. By the third or fourth stroke, you should be able to cut through the board easily.
6. Working in the same fashion, score and cut through the board along all the window lines. Be careful not to go beyond the lines. Remove the window.
7. Cut a cardboard backing for your art work that is slightly smaller than the overall size of your mat. Using a piece of broad masking tape, hinge the back of the mat to the backing. (See Figure T–25.)

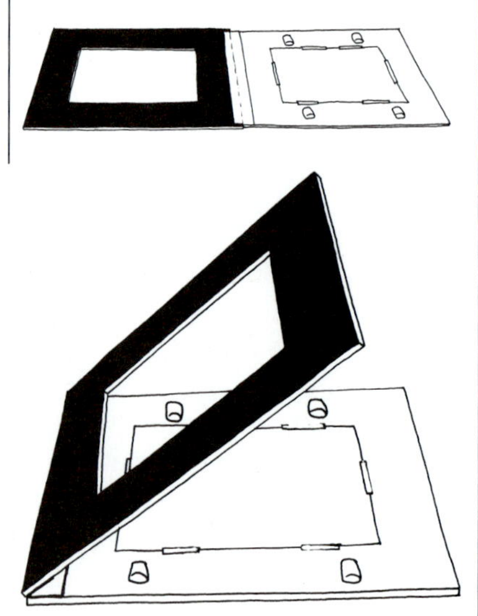

▲ Figure T–25

Position your artwork between the backing and the mat and attach it with tape. Anchor the frame to the cardboard with a few pieces of rolled tape.

24. Mounting a Two-Dimensional Work

Mounting pictures that you make gives them a professional look. To mount a work, do the following:

1. Gather the materials you will need. These include a yardstick, a pencil, poster board, a sheet of heavy cardboard, a knife with a very sharp blade, a sheet of newspaper, and rubber cement.
2. Measure the height and width of the work to be mounted. Decide how large a border you want around the work. Plan your mount size using the work's measurements. To end up with a 3-inch border, for example, make your mount 6 inches wider and higher than your work. Record the measurements for your mount.
3. Using your yardstick and pencil, lightly draw your mount rectangle on the back of the poster board. Measure from the edges of the poster board. If you have a large paper cutter available, you may use it to cut your mount.
4. Place the sheet of heavy cardboard on your work surface. Place the poster board, pencil marks up, over the cardboard. Holding the yardstick firmly in place along one line, score the line with your knife. Do not try to cut through the board with one stroke. By the third try, you should be able to cut through the board.

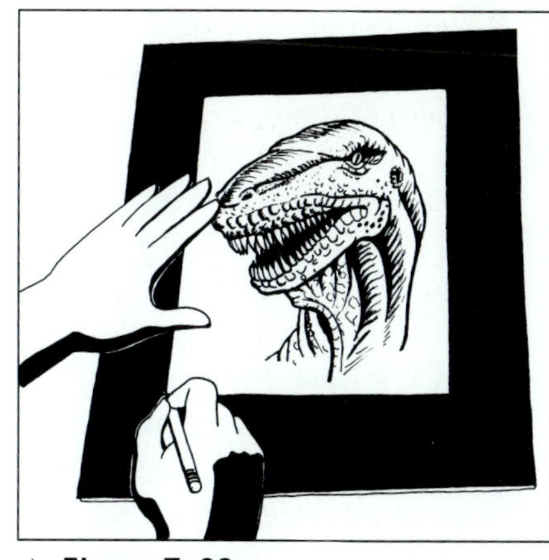

▲ **Figure T–26**

5. Place the artwork on the mount. Using the yardstick, center the work. Mark each corner with a dot. (See Figure T–26.)
6. Place the artwork, face down, on a sheet of newspaper. Coat the back of the work with rubber cement. (*Safety Note:* Always use rubber cement in a room with plenty of ventilation.) *If your mount is to be permanent, skip to Step 8.*
7. Line up the corners of your work with the dots on the mounting board. Smooth the work into place. *Skip to Step 9.*
8. After coating the back of your artwork, coat the poster board with rubber cement. Be careful not to add cement to the border area. Have a partner hold your artwork in the air by the two top corners. Once the two glued surfaces meet, you will not be able to change the position of the work. Grasp the lower two corners. Carefully lower the work to the mounting board. Line up the two corners with the bottom dots. Little by little, lower the work into place (Figure T–27). Press it smooth.

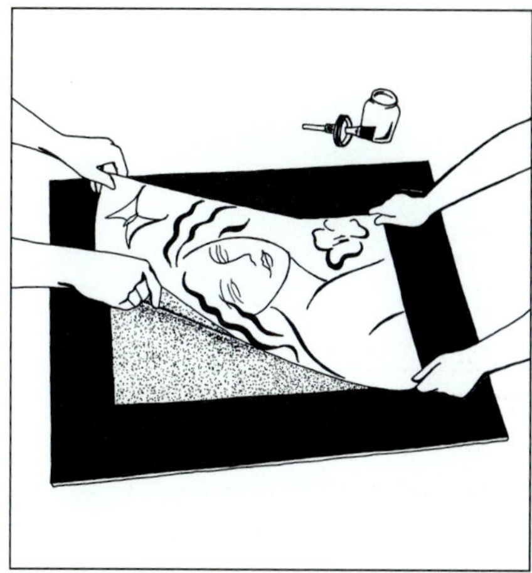

▲ **Figure T–27**

9. To remove any excess cement, create a small ball of nearly dry rubber cement. Use the ball of rubber cement to pick up excess cement.

25. Making Rubbings

Rubbings make interesting textures and designs. They may also be used with other media to create mixed-media art. To make a rubbing, place a sheet of thin paper on top of the surface to be rubbed. Hold the paper in place with one hand. With the other hand, rub the paper with the flat side of an unwrapped crayon. Always rub away from the hand holding the paper. Never rub back and forth, since this may cause the paper to slip.

26. Scoring Paper

The secret to creating neat, sharp folds in cardboard or paper is a technique called scoring. Here is how it is done:

1. Line up a ruler along the line you want to fold.
2. Lightly run a sharp knife or scissors along the fold line. Press down firmly enough to leave a light crease. Take care not to cut all the way through the paper. (Figure T–28).

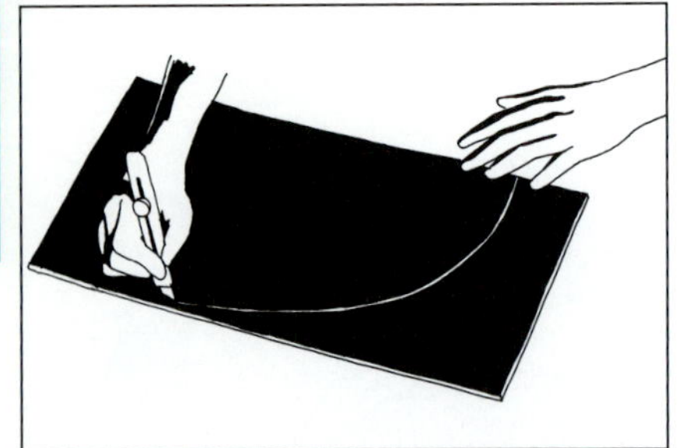

▲ **Figure T–28**

3. Gently crease the paper along the line you made.

To score curved lines, use the same technique. Make sure your curves are wide enough to ensure a clean fold. Too tight a curve will cause the paper to wrinkle (Figure T–29).

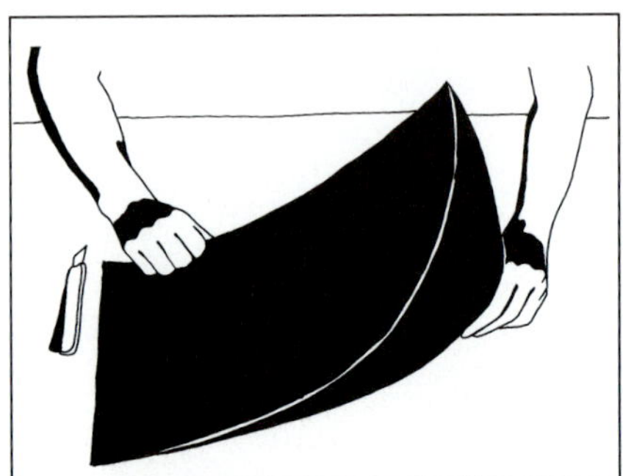

▲ **Figure T–29**

27. Making a Tissue Paper Collage

For your first experience with tissue, make a free design with the tissue colors. Start with the lightest colors of tissue first and save the darkest for last. It is difficult to change the color of dark tissue by overlapping it with other colors. If one area becomes too dark, you might cut out a piece of white paper, glue it over the dark area carefully, and apply new colors over the white area.

1. Apply a coat of adhesive to the area where you wish to place the tissue.
2. Place the tissue down carefully over the wet area (Figure T–30). Don't let your fingers get wet.
3. Then add another coat of adhesive over the tissue. If your brush picks up any color from the wet tissue, rinse your brush in water and let it dry before using it again.
4. Experiment by overlapping colors. Allow the tissue to wrinkle to create textures as you apply it. Be sure that all the loose edges of tissue are glued down.

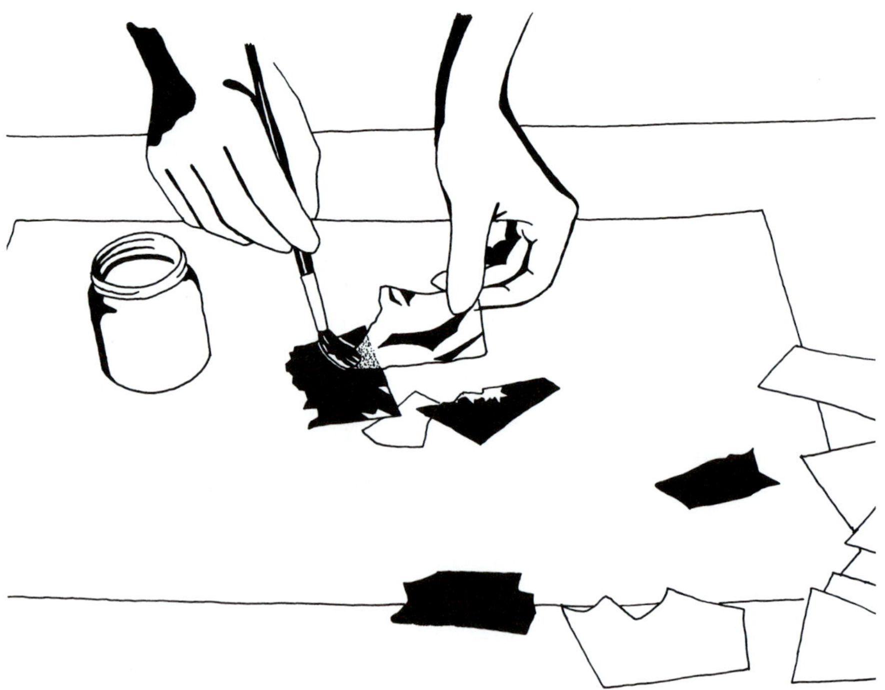

▲ **Figure T–30**

28. Working with Glue

When applying glue, always start at the center of the surface you are coating and work outward.

- When gluing papers together, don't use a lot of glue, just a dot will do. Use dots in the corners and along the edges. Press the two surfaces together. Keep dots at least ½ inch in from the edge of your paper.
- Handle a glued surface carefully with only your fingertips. Make sure your hands are clean before pressing the glued surface into place.
- *Note:* The glue should be as thin as possible. Thick or beaded glue will create ridges on your work.

Scanners

Using Scanners

Whether you need to manipulate an artwork or insert a photo into a report, a scanner can be a useful tool. Scanners allow you to convert documents, illustrations, or photographs into digital image files on your computer. Once stored in a computer, these scanned files can be altered in an image-editing program.

Scanner Basics

Scanners come in a variety of shapes and sizes—from small, handheld devices to full-scaled, professional-quality drum scanners. Flatbed scanners are the most common household or schoolroom models. These machines include a flat, glass panel called the document table glass that is usually large enough to accommodate an 8½ × 11″ image. Many scanners also come with film adapters to let you scan slides and negative or positive filmstrips.

Although individual makes and models will vary, there are some basic guidelines for using a flatbed scanner:

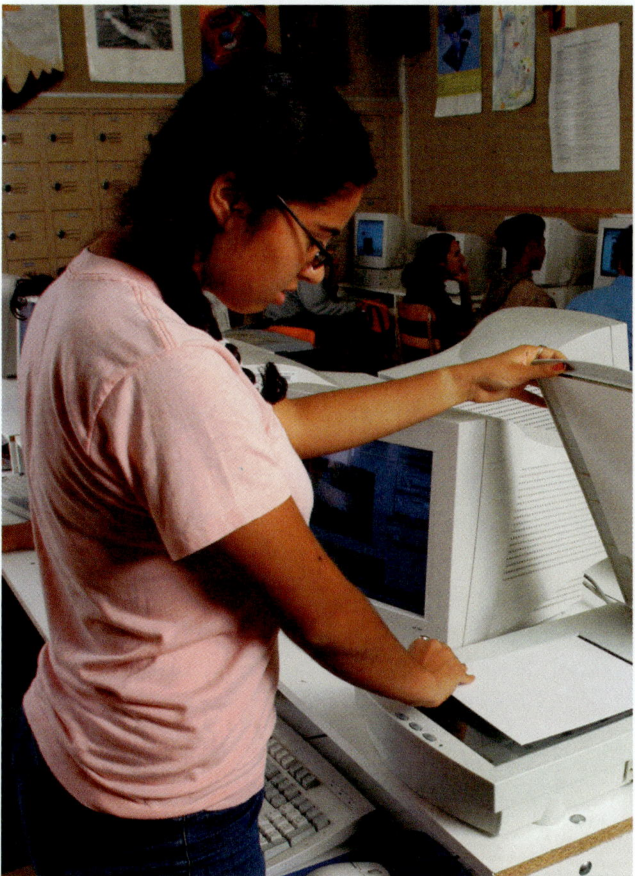

- Clean the glass to make sure there are no smudges or dirt.
- Open a host application on your computer—the program into which you plan to import the scanned image or document.
- Place the image facedown on the glass. Align with the appropriate corner markings.
- Adjust the settings in your host application program to specify the document source, image type, destination, resolution, and desired image size.

Always read the manual that came with your scanner for specific instructions and troubleshooting information.

Technology Notes

Resolution

Resolution is the fineness of detail that can be distinguished in an image. A basic rule of thumb is the finer the detail, the better the quality. In a high-quality image, even the smallest details can be distinguished. The resolution of a scanned image is measured in dpi (dots per inch). On a computer monitor, these dots are referred to as pixels. The more dots or pixels per inch, the better the quality. The recommended settings of dpi depend on the final output. For an image that will be seen on screen via e-mail or the Web, select a dpi between 72 and 96. For printing, the recommended settings vary depending on the type of image. Below are some typical settings which will vary depending upon the printer:

- **Color photo** — **300 dpi**
- **Text** — **400 dpi**
- **Text with images** — **400 dpi**
- **Line art** — **300 to 3200 dpi**

Digital Cameras

Working with Digital Cameras

Digital cameras combine the features of the analog, or conventional, camera and the scanner. Like scanners, digital cameras allow you to download images to your computer's hard drive. Unlike scanners, digital cameras are cordless. They allow you to capture live images. Also, because the images are digital, you never need to buy film.

How Digital Cameras Work

Taking pictures with a digital camera is simple. If it is set on automatic focus, you just aim at your subject and click the shutter. Once you have taken a picture, you can download it to your computer. There, it can be edited, imported into a document, printed, or e-mailed.

Digital cameras vary widely in terms of features. One of the most important features is memory, or storage. The more memory the camera has, the more pictures you can take in a single session. (See "Technology Notes" for more on storage.) Other important features to look for include:

- **Software**. Most cameras come with software for downloading and manipulating images. Some lower-end cameras may not include software. Also, the quality of this software varies. Make sure the output file format is compatible with image-editing programs already installed on your computer.
- **Image quality.** Think about how you intend to use the camera. If you plan to take high-resolution pictures (pictures with very fine detail), you will need a better camera. For most art tasks and other student needs, medium resolution is usually fine.

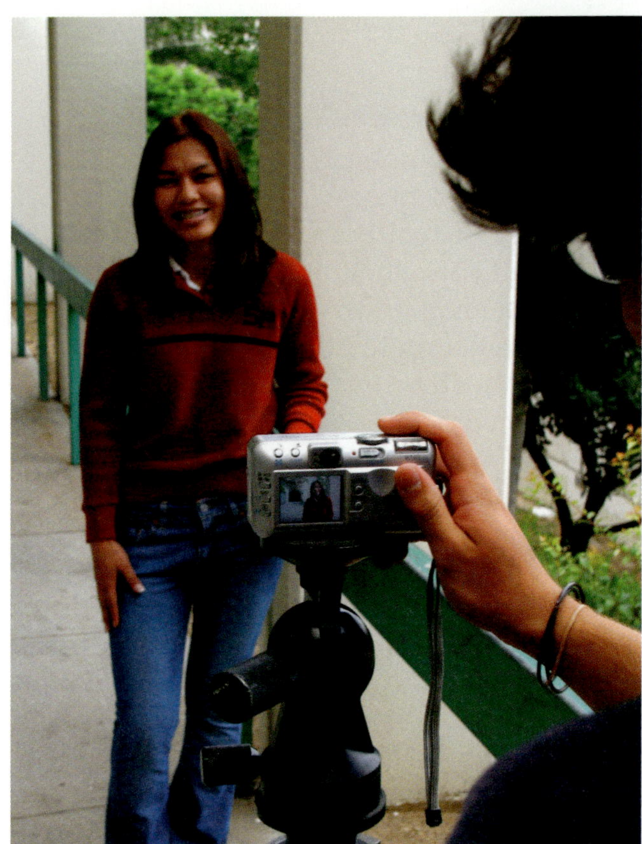

Technology Notes

Storage

Storage is where your digital camera maintains digitized versions of the pictures you take. The least expensive models of digital cameras come with built-in *flash memory*. This type of storage cannot be upgraded. Flash memory can hold up to 25 images. These must be downloaded to your computer or erased before you can take more pictures.

The next step up in storage solutions is the *smart card*. A little like a floppy disk, a smart card is a removable flash memory module. The camera comes with one card, but you can buy additional cards as needed.

Top-of-the-line cameras have built-in hard disks that hold up to a gigabyte of data. Some newer cameras even come with writable CDs and DVDs.

Graphics Tablets

Understanding Graphics Tablets

A graphics tablet is a high-tech version of drawing paper or a painter's canvas. Instead of brushes or other conventional media, you "draw" or "paint" on the tablet with an electronic pen. The image appears simultaneously on the computer screen. If you are unhappy with any pen stroke, you can simply select "Undo" from an on-screen menu. That portion of the drawing will disappear without a trace.

Tablet Fundamentals

Graphics tablets are as easy to install as they are to use. The tablet is plugged into the computer's USB (Universal Serial Bus) or serial port. There is no need to attach the pen, which is cordless. Once the accompanying software is installed, you are ready to draw. Graphics tablets may be used with all major paint and draw applications.

Tablets come in a range of sizes to suit different tasks. The smallest, which measure around 4 × 5″, are often used for sketches or to add objects to larger artworks. The largest tablets, at around 12 ×18″, are the size of a standard sheet of drawing paper. They can be used to create complete artworks.

The electronic pen is pressure sensitive. As with a conventional pen or brush, the harder you press, the darker and thicker the line. Some models boast as many as 1,024 levels of pressure sensitivity. Pressure sensitivity not only controls line thickness, but transparency and color as well. The higher the pressure sensitivity, the more natural your pen and tablet will feel.

Technology Notes

Ergonomics

The term *ergonomics* refers to the application of science to the design of objects and environments for human use. In recent years, ergonomic engineers have been at work, developing computer tools that reduce the risk of repetitive stress injury. This is a type of injury affecting the nerves in the wrist and forearm.

Recent ergonomic developments include the cushioned electronic pen. The cushioned pen has a softer surface and weighs less than earlier pens. These features have been shown to reduce grip effort by up to 40 percent. The cushioned pen, thus, is more comfortable and safer to use.

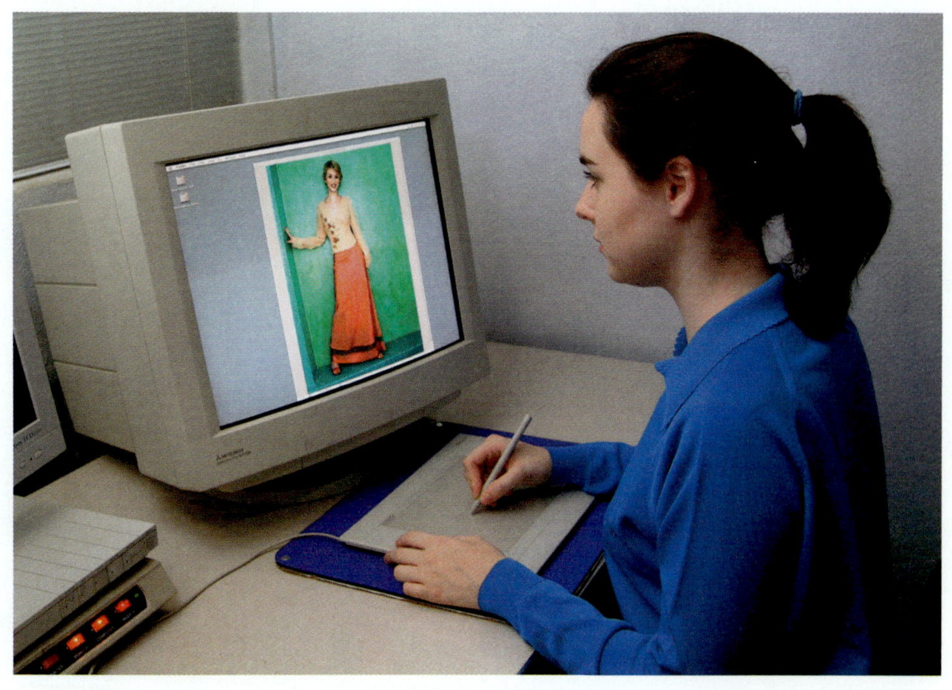

Paint Software

Using Paint Software

Paint software programs offer new conveniences and capabilities to artists. Digital paints do not require any drying time. Not only is there no drying necessary, but paint mixing is a mathematical process. A digital artist has millions of colors in his or her palette. Previously used colors can be duplicated with ease and precision. Also, as with all art software, a painting can be easily erased and altered.

Paint Software Basics

In digital paint programs, images are created and stored as *bitmaps*. These are files made up of tiny dots called *pixels*. Since photographs downloaded to the computer have a similar format, paint programs do double duty as photo editors. A paint program can be used to brighten a dark photo, enhance its contrast, and so forth.

The main features of a paint program are:

- **A menu bar.** The menu bar contains file management commands (such as Open and Save), edit commands (such as Undo and Redo), and view commands (for example, Zoom).
- **The toolbox.** The toolbox contains art tools, such as brushes and pens, and image manipulation tools. These allow you to flip or rotate an image among many other options.
- **Palettes.** These are separate windows that allow you to control colors, brush tip sizes, line thickness, and the like.

Most paint programs also come with a variety of filters. These add special effects to an image or photo. One example is "feathering," which gives an image a wispy, cloudlike look.

Technology Notes

Bitmap File Formats

One important aspect of working with paint programs is understanding file formats. There are many bitmap formats including JPEG, GIF, and PNG. It is worth noting that each of these formats has its own characteristics. JPEG images, for example, are compressed—stored in a smaller size. This means they take up less space on your computer's hard drive. GIF files are used for on-screen images. This format supports up to 256 colors and is often used for Web graphics. GIFs, however do not support print work. Finally, PNG images are increasingly turning up on Web sites and other environments shared by multiple computers and networks.

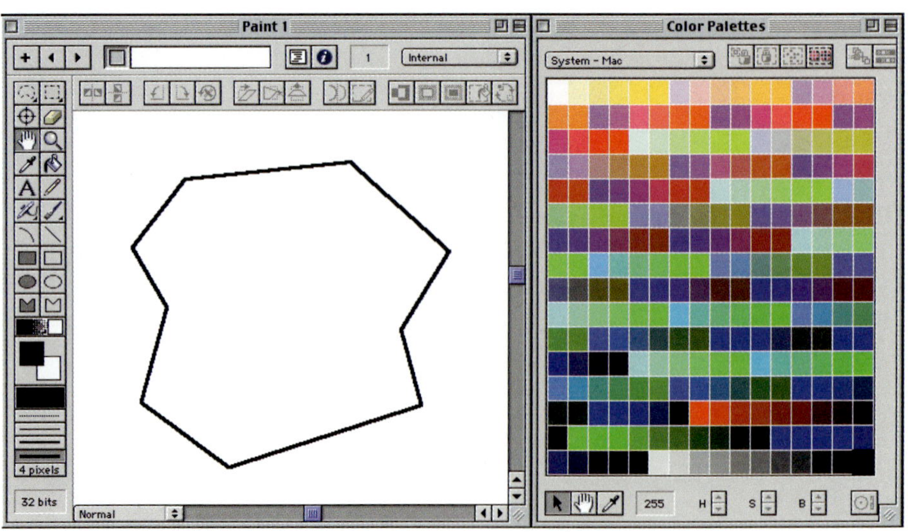

Draw Software

Examining Draw Software

A cousin to paint software, draw software shares many of the same art tools and menus. Although draw programs lack some of the editing capabilities of paint programs, they are ideal for creating original artworks. They are especially well suited for creating logos, book or CD covers, and other art that combines images and text.

Draw Software Fundamentals

In draw programs, images are stored as mathematical formulas called *vectors.* These formulas carry information about the lines and curves that make up a particular drawing. Vector-based formats allow images to be *resized*—shrunk or enlarged—without distortion. This is one advantage of draw programs over paint programs. Paint programs produce images that cannot easily be resized without some loss of image quality.

Every object created by an artist using a draw program contains editable points and handles. By moving or dragging these elements, the artist can alter or smooth out shapes and curves with ease and precision. Digital illustrators often scan and import sketches into draw programs. This allows them to trace over the sketch with a mouse or stylus. They can then refine and color the sketch, creating a digital illustration.

In addition to pens and brushes, the toolbox in a typical draw program contains assorted shape tools. For example, once shapes have been drawn, they can then be extended into three dimensions using an *extrude* command. Draw programs may include a selection of vector-based images that can be manipulated and used in other illustrations.

Recent draw software enhancements enable artists to work with bitmap images. Some sophisticated programs now come with filters, similar to the filters found in paint programs. These filters can be used for adding special effects to bitmap images.

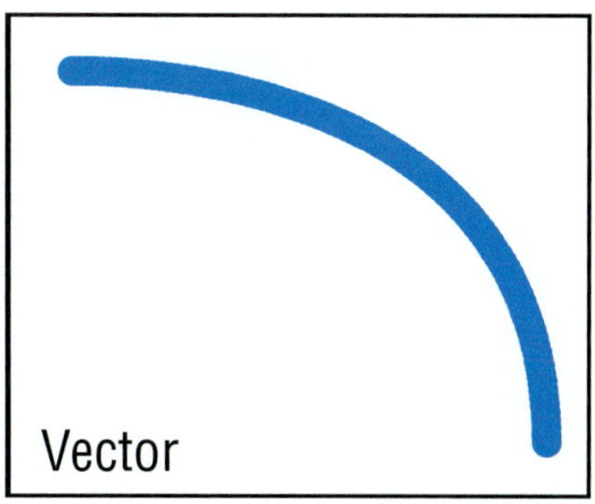

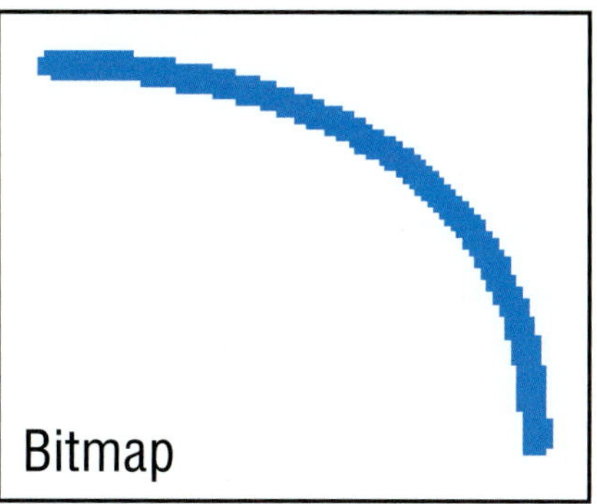

Technology Notes

Color Models

Color models are systems for arranging the colors of the visible spectrum so that they appear as the user intended when the image is viewed. The standard printing color model is CYMK. The letters are short for cyan (a greenish blue), yellow, magenta, and black. Most draw software comes preset for CYMK. Some artists instead work with the RGB (red, green, blue) model. For example, Web designers use the RGB model because their work is viewed on computer monitors. On monitors all the colors of the spectrum are created with only red, green, and blue.

3-D Graphics Software

Examining 3-D Graphics Software

Creating art in three dimensions is nothing new. Creating *digital* art in three dimensions *is* relatively new. The ability to give form to computerized objects only became a reality some 15 years ago. That was when the first 3-D modeling programs arrived on the market. Since that time, the capabilities of these programs have been expanded dramatically. Today, digital artists can create entire animated movies using a single 3-D software package.

How 3-D Software Works

There are many types of 3-D graphics programs. Some are designed specifically for creating and editing 3-D images for use on print materials or on Web sites and CD-ROMs. Other 3-D modeling programs are designed for architects and engineers. These programs are used to create complex digital blueprints for buildings and other structures.

Like draw and paint programs, 3-D programs include tools for creating objects. Once created, objects are placed on a *stage.* The stage is similar to the *work area* in draw and paint programs. The stage has three surfaces, or *planes*—one for width (X), height (Y), and depth (Z). Each plane includes grid lines that allow the user to place objects at exact locations in space.

Similar to movies, 3-D programs include *lighting* and *camera* controls. Lighting allows the user to adjust the intensity and direction of the light source. The camera control determines the view and angle from which the object is seen.

Technology Notes

Rendering

When you see a movie on the big screen, you don't see the lighting, cameras, or film crew. The same is true of 3-D modeling and animation programs. The final product is the *rendered* scene or movie. *Rendering* is a process by which the program mathematically assigns shading, texture, and other art features to one or more bitmaps. Behind-the-scenes details do not appear in the rendered scene or movie.

Rendering can take anywhere from an hour to a day or more, depending on the resolution. If you are previewing a scene or movie, choose a low resolution. Make sure to allow ample rendering time for the final "cut."

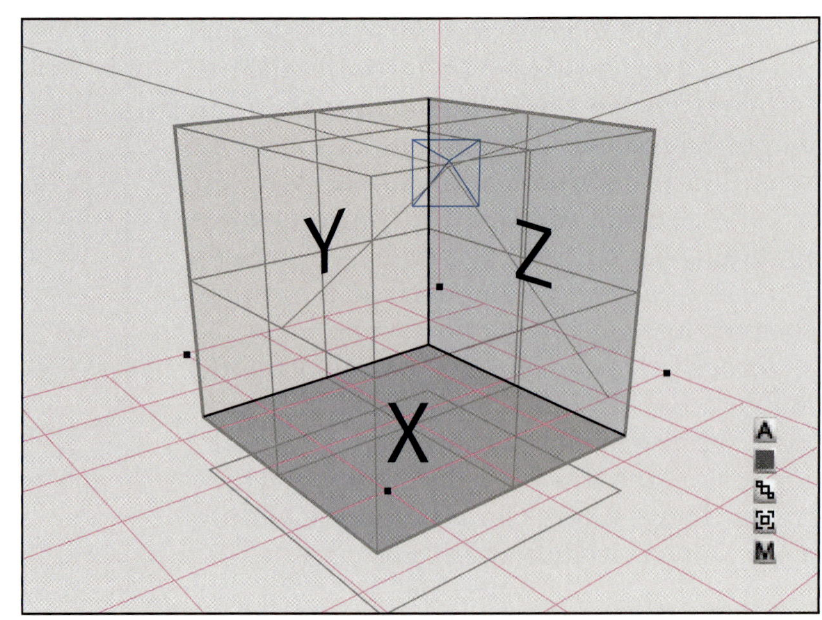

Frame Animation Software

Understanding Frame Animation Software

In comic strips, the action occurs frame by frame. It is precisely this principle that is at work in frame animation software. Using this software, the digital artist is able to animate words and images quickly and easily. The programs even provide tools for "publishing" the finished movie on the Internet.

Frame Animation Basics

The first step in creating a frame animation is choosing your "actors." Objects, created in other graphics programs or by hand, may be imported. Frame animation software also includes tools for creating original simple objects and text.

Once the "cast" has been established, objects are placed on the *timeline.* This is a series of numbered frames beginning at zero. An object's position on the timeline determines the point at which it enters or exits the scene.

The third step in an animation is to create movement. An object can be made to move by means of one of the following:

- **A preset effect.** Animation software comes with a number of preset actions. These include *fade in, fade out, blur,* and *transform.* The last of these controls an object's size, angle, and so on.
- **A motion path.** The software also permits the user to create original motion paths. These tell an object where and how to move at any given moment.

Technology Notes

Sound

Animation software allows the addition of sounds and music to accompany the action. Sound files may be recorded using the computer's microphone. Another source of sounds is clip art Web sites, many of which offer free sound clips. Since sound files tend to be large, they can increase the size of the movie, possibly causing the action to pause. There are two ways of avoiding this:

- Looping sounds. This is having a single sound file, such as background music, repeated over and over.
- Using compressed sound files. AVI sound files tend to be larger because they are not compressed. Choose MPEG-3 files whenever possible. These require far less memory.

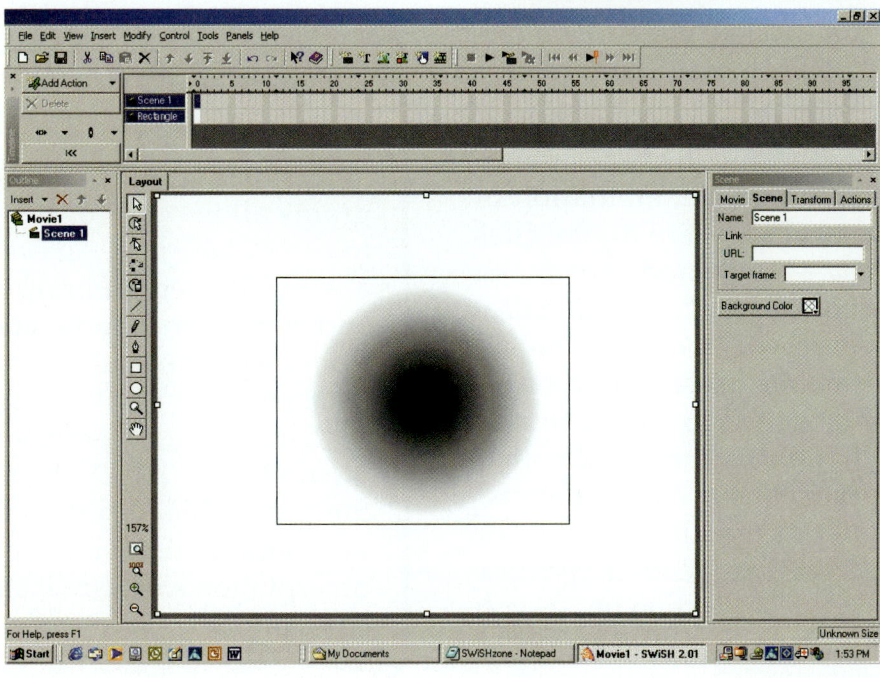

Multimedia Presentation Software

Using Multimedia Presentation Software

Imagine viewing an exhibition of your own portfolio. With multimedia presentation software, there is no need to imagine. These remarkable programs allow you to create digital slideshows right on your computer. You can even add narration, background music, and special visual effects to your presentation.

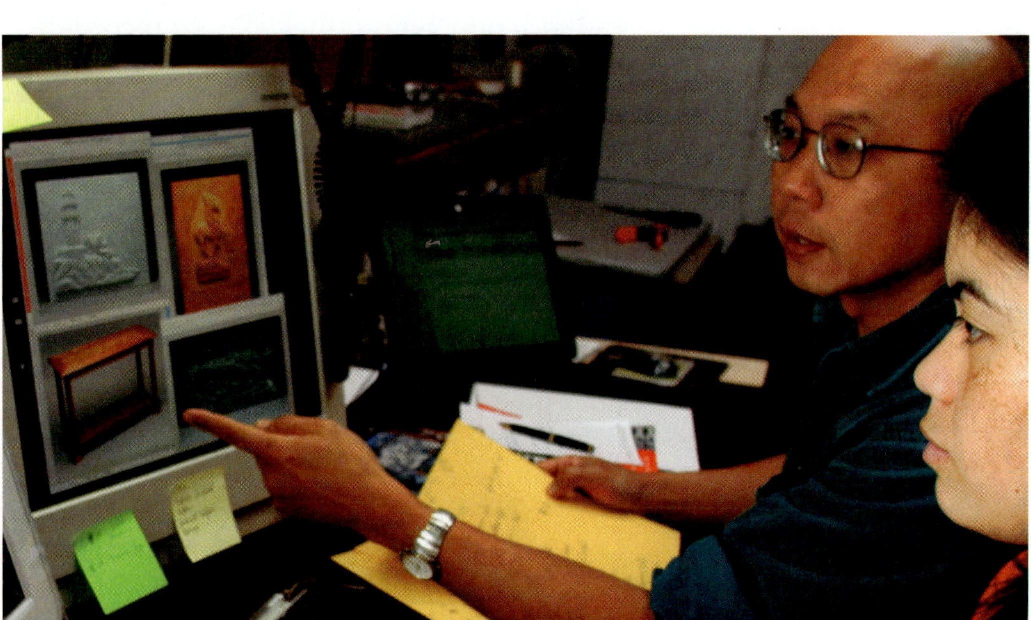

Multimedia Presentation Software Basics

The chief building block of the multimedia presentation is the *slide.* This is an individual screen containing a combination of multimedia *objects.* Objects are digital files that are *embedded*—contained within—a larger file. Sound, image, and animation files are all potential objects in a presentation.

In some multimedia presentation packages, objects can be added to a slide simply by dragging them from an *object bar.* In other programs, you use menus to embed objects.

Once you have created all the slides for your presentation, you are ready to *produce* your show. During the production phase, you attend to details such as the following:

- **Transitions**. *Transitions* are special effects between slides that add visual interest to your show. Known in some packages as "wipes," transitions include *dissolve* (one slide fading into another) and *explode* (a slide appearing to burst apart, revealing the next).
- **Timing.** This is the amount of time any given slide appears on the screen. Timing is one of the most important aspects of a multimedia presentation. If slides change too quickly, your viewers will not have a chance to appreciate each artwork fully. If a slide appears on the screen too long, the presentation may drag.

Technology Notes

Executable Files

Some multimedia presentation programs allow you to turn your shows into *executable files.* An executable file is a self-contained program that will open and run when double-clicked. All the icons on your system's desktop are executable files.

Executable files may be e-mailed or burned onto a CD or other portable medium. This permits viewers to run your slideshow even if they do not have presentation software installed on their computers.

Page Layout Software

Using Page Layout Software

The page you are reading right now was produced using page layout software. In the last two decades, this type of software has replaced earlier manual methods of page layout. It has revolutionized the process whereby printed materials are created.

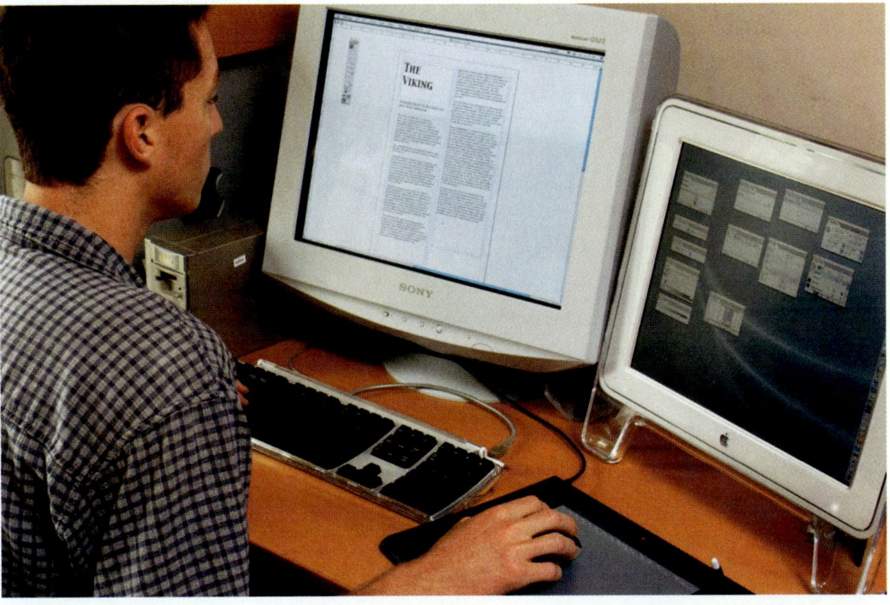

Page Layout Software Basics

Page layout software is one of the chief digital tools of the graphic artist. When the application is opened, a blank text page appears surrounded by *panes.* Panes are windows containing the tools used to manage and arrange text. The text is imported from a word processing program.

The first step in the layout process is to set specifications for the printed page. These include the number of columns, the size of margins, and whether the page will be vertical (portrait) or horizontal (landscape).

Next, the graphic artist adds *frames* to the page. Frames are blank rectangles with dotted outlines used to hold either text or pictures. In the simplest layout, the artist creates a single text frame and "pours in" the text file. This type of layout is used for novels and other books that consist entirely of running text. For more complex page layouts, several frames of different sizes may be added. The page you are looking at right now contains a picture box and several different text boxes.

The typeface, or *font,* used for a particular block of text is chosen from a list of typefaces in the text pane. The text pane also allows the artist to control such features as paragraph indents and line spacing.

Technology Notes

Style Sheets and Libraries

Page layout programs contain several powerful features that further streamline the graphic artist's work. Among these are *style sheets* and *libraries.* Style sheets are sets of user-defined instructions for how to treat a particular block of text or heading. They will include information including the font name, size and color, and the amount of vertical space above and below each line of text.

Libraries contain design elements like logos, and special features that are used repeatedly throughout the document. The artist simply drags a copy of the item from the library window into position on the page.

Advertising Artist

Advertising artists design the artwork that is used in advertisements. They usually work for an advertising agency. They may also work for a publication, such as a magazine or newspaper. Some advertising artists work in the advertising department of a large corporation, such as a store or restaurant chain.

Advertising artists work as part of a design team. This team includes an art director, designers, and copywriters. First, the art director develops a concept, or idea, for an advertisement. The copywriters write the words that will appear in the ad. Then the artist creates a design that works with both the art director's concept and the words. Most advertising artists use computers when creating their artwork.

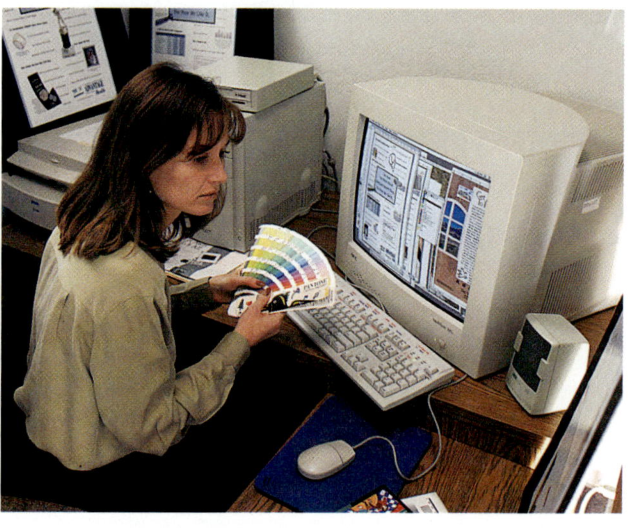

A career as an advertising artist usually requires a college education in art or design. Courses in computer design techniques are essential. Once they are hired, advertising artists may also receive on-the-job training.

Architect

An architect is an artist who designs buildings and other structures. Your home, school, and local shopping mall were all designed by architects. An architect prepares plans that show both the interior and exterior of a building. These sketches include floor plans that show the placement of rooms, hallways, doors, windows, closets, and other features. They also show the exterior walls on all sides of the building and a top-down drawing of the roof.

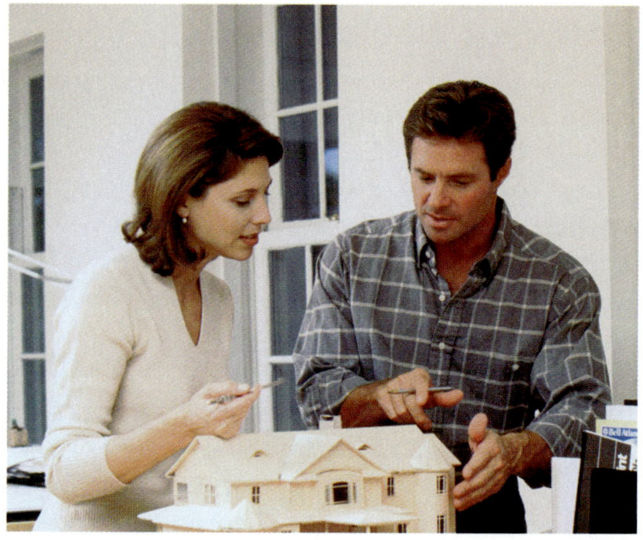

A building design must be not only visually pleasing but also functional and safe. When planning a building, architects must consider how the structure will be used. For example, the design for a home would be very different from the design for a restaurant or hospital. Architects must also keep in mind the needs of the people who will use the building. This includes such subjects as traffic patterns, living and work areas, and storage space. They must also to know about heating and cooling, ventilation, and plumbing.

Architects need a college degree in architecture. They take courses in math, engineering, and drafting. Because most architects use computers to produce their designs, they also take courses in computer-aided design. In addition, they must pass an exam to become licensed.

Art Director

Art directors are responsible for the look of the advertisements that you see in newspapers, in magazines, and on television. They are also responsible for the style and design of magazines, and of books like this one. Art directors most often work in the fields of advertising and publishing.

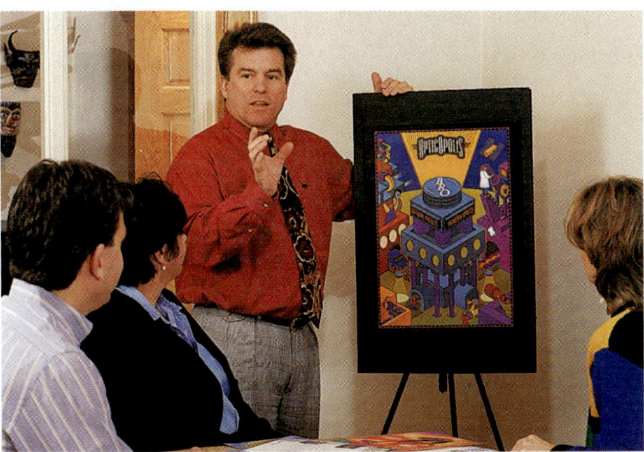

An art director studies the information that needs to be presented. He or she must decide how that information can be shown in a visually appealing way. The art director then works with a design team that includes artists, designers, and copywriters. The art director oversees the team's work and makes sure that the final printed material is satisfactory.

Most art directors have a college education. Courses should provide a well-rounded background in art and design. Art directors study graphic design, drafting, layout, photography, and computer design. Several years of on-the-job training are required before a person can become an art director.

Art Teacher

Art teachers instruct students in the use of various art materials and techniques. They also educate students in the theories and principles of art criticism, aesthetics, and art history. In middle schools, art teachers provide general art instruction. Art teachers in high schools may specialize in a specific area, such as painting, drawing, or crafts.

In a classroom, the art teacher helps students create their own artwork. Students are taught how to use a wide variety of media, such as pencils, charcoal, pastels, paints, and clay. The teacher encourages students to analyze their own work as well as the works of master artists.

Art teachers must have a college degree. Their educational background includes courses in both art and teaching. Many art teachers continue to study and exhibit their own artwork throughout their teaching careers. An essential part of being an art teacher is a love of art and a desire to encourage this appreciation in others.

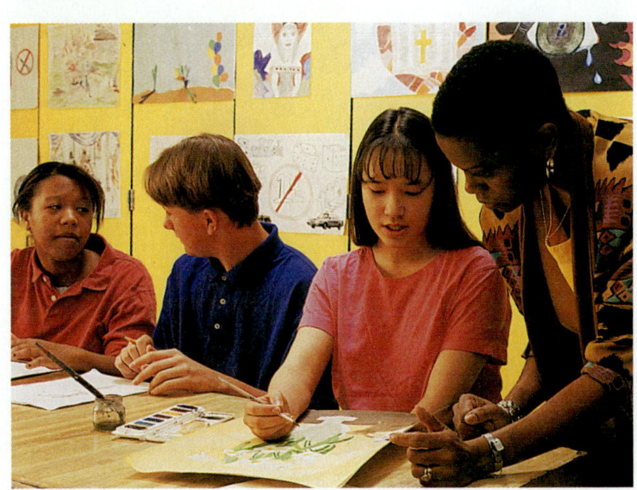

Artist

Artists create works of art. Their work is usually classified as either fine art or applied art. Fine art, such as a painting, is created simply to be viewed and appreciated. Applied art, such as ceramics or other crafts objects, serves a more practical purpose.

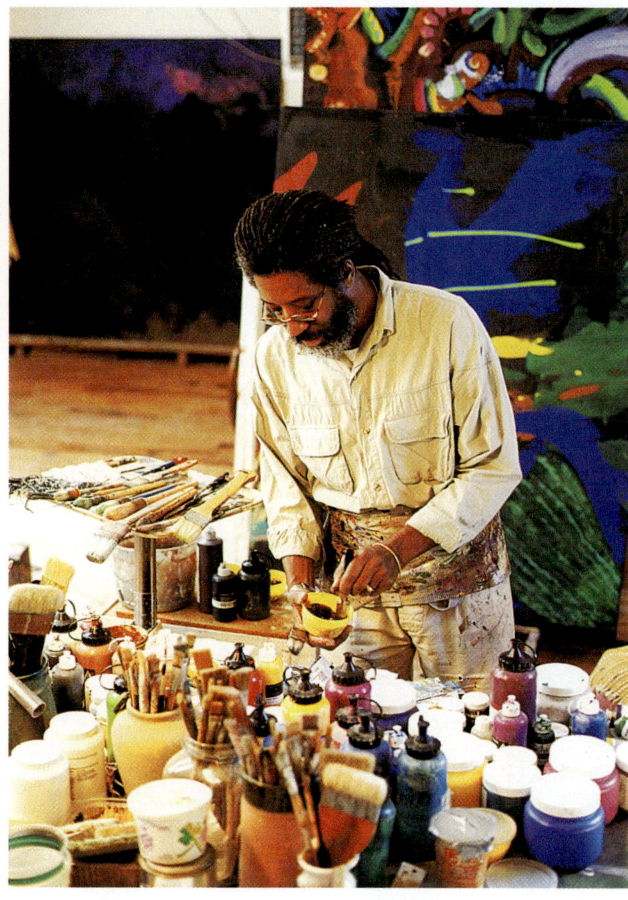

The work of an artist may involve a variety of media. The media are the materials used to create the art. A painter, for instance, might use oil, watercolor, or acrylic paint. A sculptor might create art out of stone, clay, or wood. Other artists might create jewelry, pottery, or furniture from such materials as metal, clay, or plastic.

Although not all artists have a college education, almost all have had formal art instruction. This training includes studio art classes, such as drawing, painting, and design. It also includes courses in art history. One of the most important requirements for a career as an artist is a natural talent in art.

Graphic Artist

Graphic artists design artwork for many types of products. These products might include packaging and promotional displays, brochures, advertisements, magazines, and books like the one you are reading. Graphic artists are often employed in the publishing or advertising fields. However, they may also work in other areas, such as designing the boxes that hold videos and computer games. They frequently work as part of a design team.

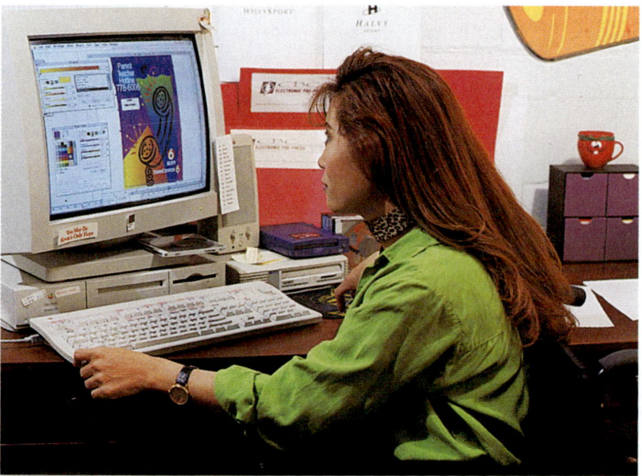

Most graphic artists use computers to help in the creation of their artwork. Computer technology saves time by performing some of the tasks that artists previously had to do by hand. For example, artists can use computer graphics to easily experiment with a variety of colors, shapes, and designs.

A career in graphic art generally requires a college education and formal art training. In addition, graphic artists must have an in-depth knowledge of computer graphics. Because the computer field changes so rapidly, graphic artists must continually learn about new technology.

Illustrator

The work of an illustrator revolves around drawing. Illustrators may create many different types of artwork. Most specialize in one field, such as technical illustration. Illustrators often work in the publishing and advertising industries.

A technical illustrator specializes in drawing diagrams. These might be included in instructional manuals. They help explain how to use appliances or equipment, such as a computer or VCR. A fashion illustrator draws sketches of clothing and accessories. Fashion illustrations might appear in catalogs, advertisements, or magazines. A medical illustrator prepares detailed drawings of the human body. These drawings are often found in medical textbooks and journals.

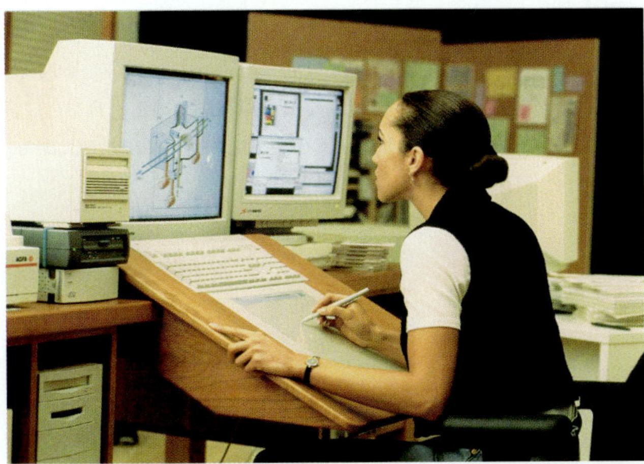

Most illustrators have a college degree in art. Besides drawing, they learn about design, composition, and perspective. Illustrators who want to concentrate on one area must also take courses related to that subject. For example, a medical illustrator must study biology and medicine.

Industrial Designer

Have you ever wondered who designed your favorite toys and electronic games? Those are the work of industrial designers. They design manufactured products, such as computers, kitchen appliances, and cars. Industrial designers usually work for large companies, such as toy or equipment manufacturers.

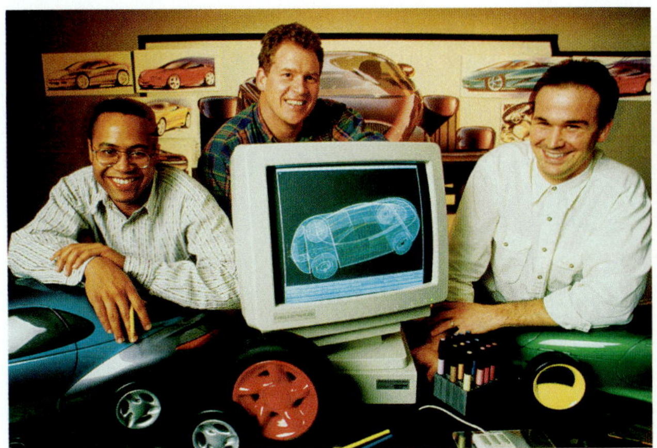

Industrial designers develop new products. They also make improvements to existing products, such as adding new features or changing the design of an automobile. When developing a product, industrial designers first do research. The designers need to know who will use the product and how they will use it. Industrial designers also must evaluate similar products that are already available. Then they combine this knowledge with their artistic ability. Their goal is to create products that will work well and be popular with consumers.

A career in industrial design requires a college education. In addition to art courses, industrial designers study computer-aided design. Many designers use computer technology when developing products.

Interior Designer

Interior designers plan the interior space of buildings. These buildings might include homes, offices, hotels, or restaurants. Sometimes interior designers plan renovations, or upgrades, to existing buildings. In addition to preparing drawings, interior designers choose furniture, carpeting, and window coverings. They also select lighting and color schemes. Interior designers must make sure that all of these individual parts work together as a whole and are aesthetically pleasing.

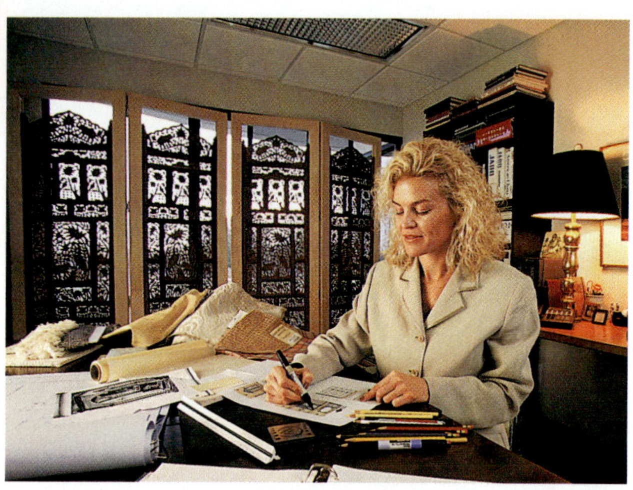

When planning an interior space, the interior designer must always consider the client's needs, tastes, and budget. Many designers use computer programs to create several versions of an interior plan. Using a computer also allows the designer to easily make design changes to suit the client's wishes.

To be an interior designer, you need a college education. Courses include drawing, design, and art history. Interior designers also must show creativity, a flair for color, and an eye for detail.

Landscape Architect

Landscape architects combine their love of nature and the environment with their artistic ability. They design outdoor areas such as those surrounding houses or apartment complexes, shopping centers, and office buildings.

Landscape architects choose which types of trees, bushes, and flowers are best suited for the location. Then they draw sketches of how these plants should be arranged. One goal of a landscape architect is to make sure that the design is not only functional but also attractive. Another goal is to make sure that the design works well with the natural environment. As in all design fields, more and more landscape architects are using computers to complete their work more efficiently.

A career in landscape architecture requires a college education. Courses include landscape design and construction, surveying, and city and regional planning. In addition, landscape architects study science and nature and take studio art courses.

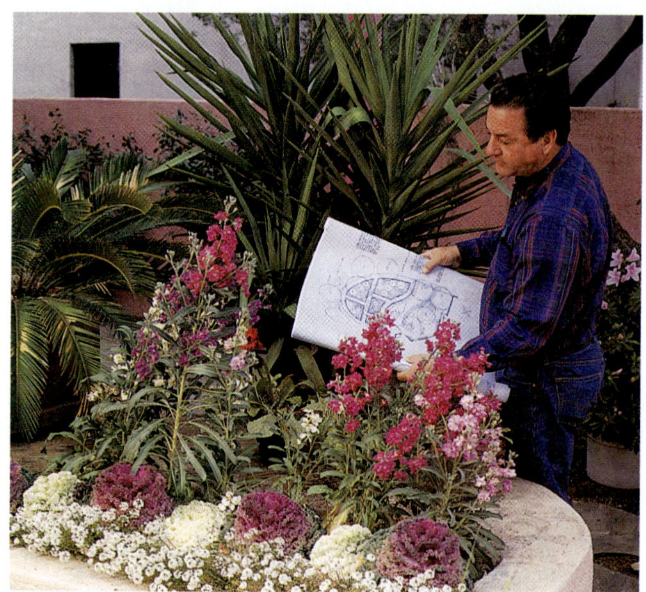

Museum Worker

Some people combine their love of art and museums to become museum workers. There are a wide variety of museums across the country. Some showcase artwork, such as paintings, sculpture, or photographs. Others house objects of historical value, such as antique clothing or furniture. Still others display items related to science or natural history, such as dinosaur skeletons.

People who work in museums may have several different types of jobs. A curator chooses and obtains the objects that will be displayed in the museum. An assistant curator helps the curator set up the museum exhibits. A conservator cares for and preserves the objects kept in the museum. A tour guide provides information about exhibits to the museum's visitors and answers their questions.

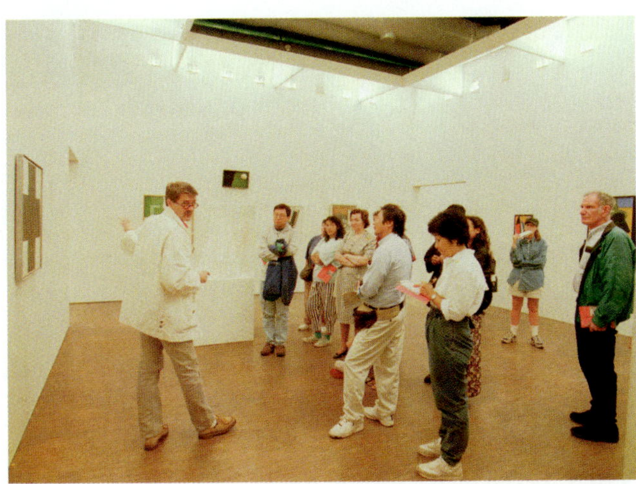

The degree of education required for a museum worker varies depending on the type of work. Most museum workers, however, are highly educated. Many have advanced college degrees and are considered experts in their field.

Photographer

Photographers are skilled artists who use their cameras to create artwork. Their work varies greatly depending on what type of photographs they take. For example, a catalog photographer works in a studio and takes pictures of objects such as food, clothing, or jewelry. A newspaper or magazine photographer works in the field, taking pictures of people and events in the news.

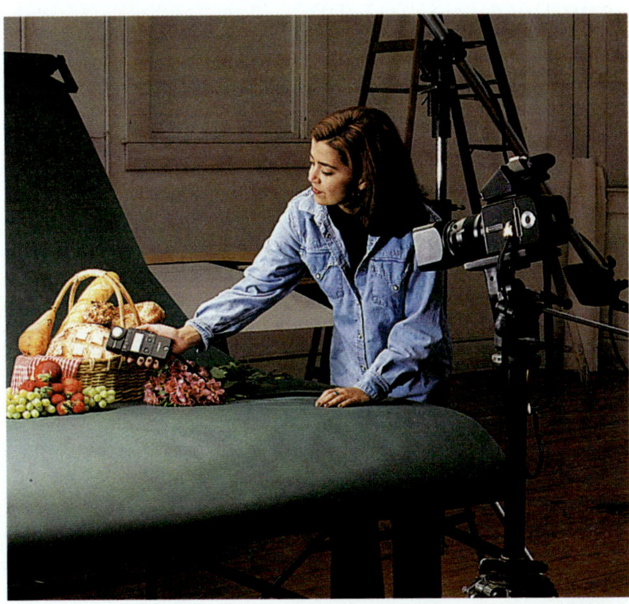

The work of photographers involves more than just taking the pictures. Photographers must first visualize the shot or set it up in an artistic way. After the pictures are taken, many photographers develop their own film in a darkroom. Then they print the slides or photographs.

A career as a photographer requires formal training in photography. Many photographers have a college degree in art. Photographers who specialize in certain areas, such as science, may need additional courses in that field. Beginning photographers sometimes receive training on the job by assisting a professional photographer.

Textile Designer

The fabric of the clothes you are wearing was designed by a textile designer. The word *textile* refers to cloth or fabric. Textile designers create and draw patterns for fabric. The fabric may be used in clothing, furniture upholstery, draperies, or rugs. Textile designers sometimes create their own original designs. At other times, they may adapt a design or develop one based on a certain theme. Textile designers work for companies that manufacture fabric.

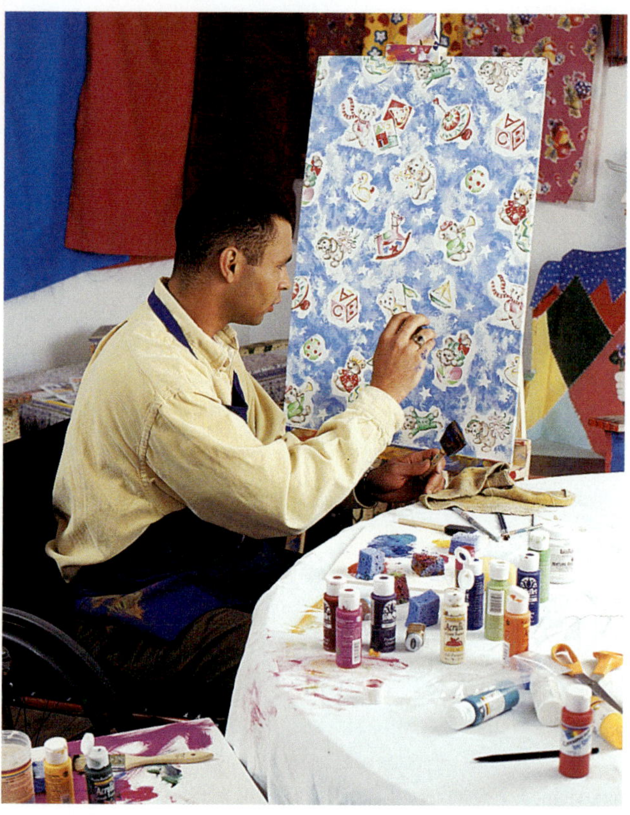

Like other artists, textile designers must have creativity and artistic skill. They must also understand how fabric is constructed and manufactured. In addition, they need to be aware of current fashion trends. With this knowledge, they are better able to create popular designs.

Textile designers generally need a college education. They study art, design, and textiles. Many textile designers also take courses in computer technology, including computer-aided design.

Web Designer

There are countless numbers of sites on the World Wide Web. These sites may be sponsored by companies, organizations, or individuals. They are most often used to provide information, promote products, and answer questions.

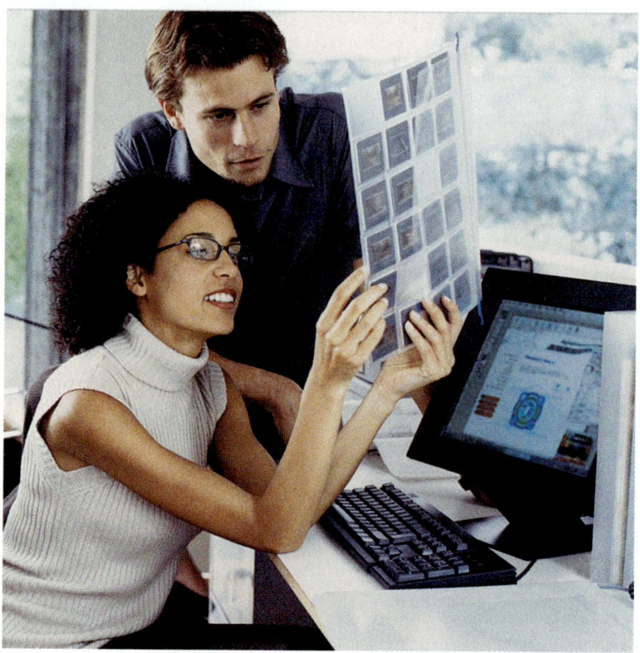

Web designers use computer software to create and maintain these sites. The work involves laying out web pages, designing graphic elements, and creating electronic links to other sites. Web designers may create sites for a large company or organization. They may also work for a design firm that creates sites for many companies.

To be a Web designer, a person must have a background in art, with an emphasis on design. A Web designer must also have technical training in computers and computer programming. Keeping current with the latest technology is an important part of the job.

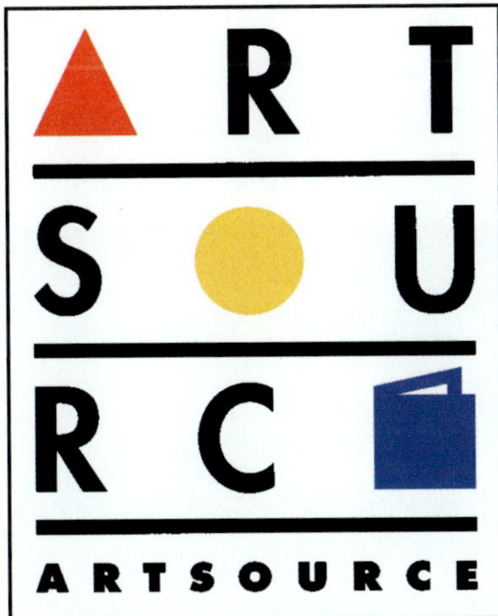

Performing Arts Handbook

The following pages of content were excerpted from *Artsource®: The Center's Study Guide to the Performing Arts*, developed by the Music Center Education Division, an award-winning arts education program of the Music Center of Los Angeles County.

The following artists and groups are featured in the Performing Arts Handbook.

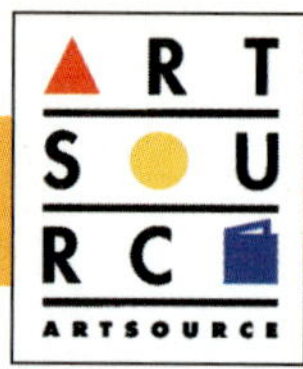

Dance Alvin Ailey American Dance Theater

The Alvin Ailey American Dance Theater performs classical ballet and modern works by well-known choreographers, but the group is best known for dances drawn from Alvin Ailey's African American background. These masterpieces capture the essence of his black experience in America and feature musical themes based on African American cultural heritage such as blues, spirituals, and jazz. "Revelations," the dance shown on this page, has become the "signature piece" for the company because it clearly captures the spirit and aesthetics of the company and its creator. The choreography includes different dances, all of which celebrate the human spirit and its ability to overcome adversity.

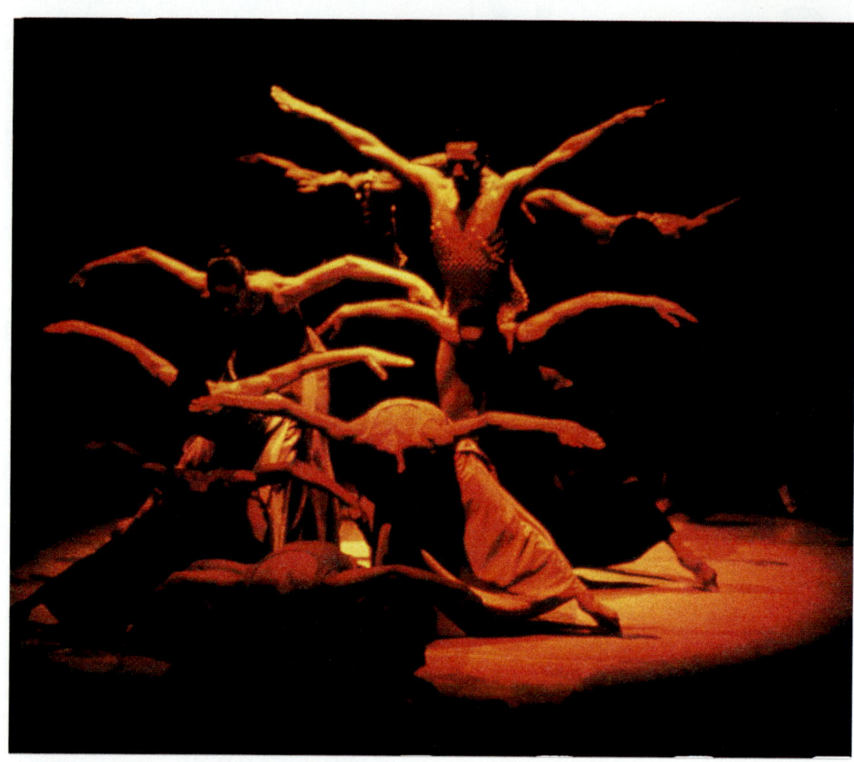

Alvin Ailey American Dance Theater. Alvin Ailey, founder and choreographer. "Revelations." Photo: Bill Hilton.

Discussion Questions

1. The word *revelation* means something that was unknown and is now revealed. Discuss a revelation a person might have while struggling through a difficult situation.
2. Look at the photo on this page. What images come to mind as you study the positions of the dancers? Discuss how unity and variety are demonstrated.
3. Imagine you are going to create a signature piece to represent yourself. Identify three to five traits that describe different aspects of your personality. Demonstrate these traits with a gesture or expressive movement. Which ones seem appropriate for your signature piece? Why?

Creative Expression Activities

Language Arts Think about Discussion Question 1. Write about a time when you or someone you know had a revelation.

Dance/Theatre After discussing Question 3, find gestural movements that can express each of the personal traits you listed. Choose one you like and abstract it in several different ways by exaggerating the size, doing it in slow motion, giving it a rhythmic pattern, adding a turn or change of level, or performing it as you walk. Share ideas with a partner and discuss what worked best.

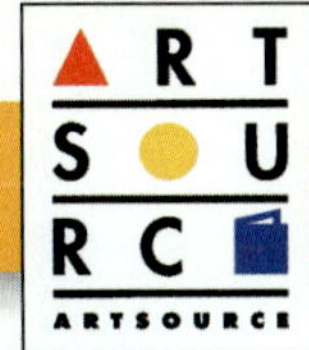

Arco Iris

Danais and Ara Tokatlian, co-directors of Arco Iris, base their persona, and professional lives on the principles of universal brotherhood. They try to help people accept and understand different cultural values and styles of artistic expression. They communicate these ideas through their exciting music. This is accomplished by combining ethnic instruments, rhythms, and melodies from various areas of the Americas with contemporary sounds. Their composition "Peace Pipes" is drawn from the music of the Quechua and Aymara people of Peru and Bolivia.

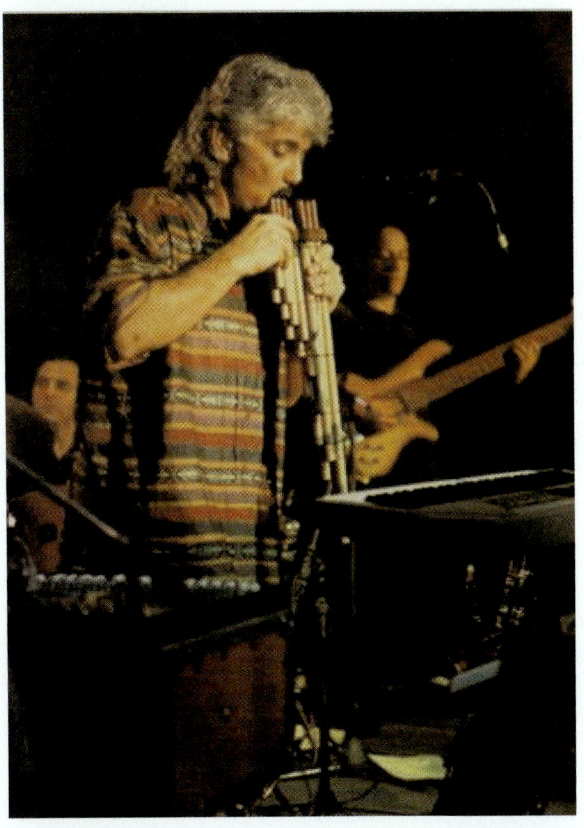

Arco Iris: Ara Tokatlian. Photo by Deborah Allison.

Discussion Questions

1. Think of the titles "Peace Pipes" and "Soaring Over the High Plains." What kind of musical sounds, melody, or rhythms would you create if you were able to compose music to bring these images to life?
2. Arco Iris uses instruments that are made from materials found in the environment. What instruments might you be able to create from natural objects or sources?
3. Think of three different cultures you know about. What instruments from each can you suggest that could combine to form a fusion of new sound?

Creative Expression Activities

Science Explore the scientific basis for sound production of the following instruments: drums, glockenspiel (steel bars), xylophone (wood bars), and flutes.

Language Arts Think of an instrument you find interesting. Write a paragraph, poem, or short story from the point of view of the instrument. Describe yourself in specific detail including shape and color, how you are held, treated, and produce sound to express your feelings. You might ask yourself these questions: How do I make sound? What am I made of? What kind of music do I play? What feelings do I have?

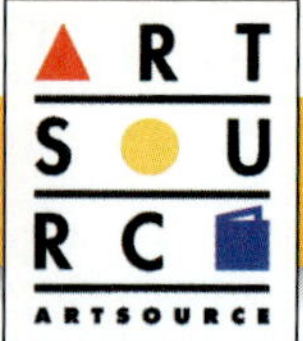

Theatre The Chameleons

Life Cycle follows the relationship of two characters, one female and one male, from infancy through childhood, adolescence, courtship, marriage, parenthood, middle age, old age, death, and finally rebirth. On a bare stage and without costumes or props, The Chameleons—Keith Berger and Sharon Diskin—use pantomime and mime techniques to project a variety of human emotions and enact the rituals of friendship, love, and separation. Their work began with a desire to do a story about universal relationships. They began by improvising ways to create age changes by altering their posture, expressions, and attitudes.

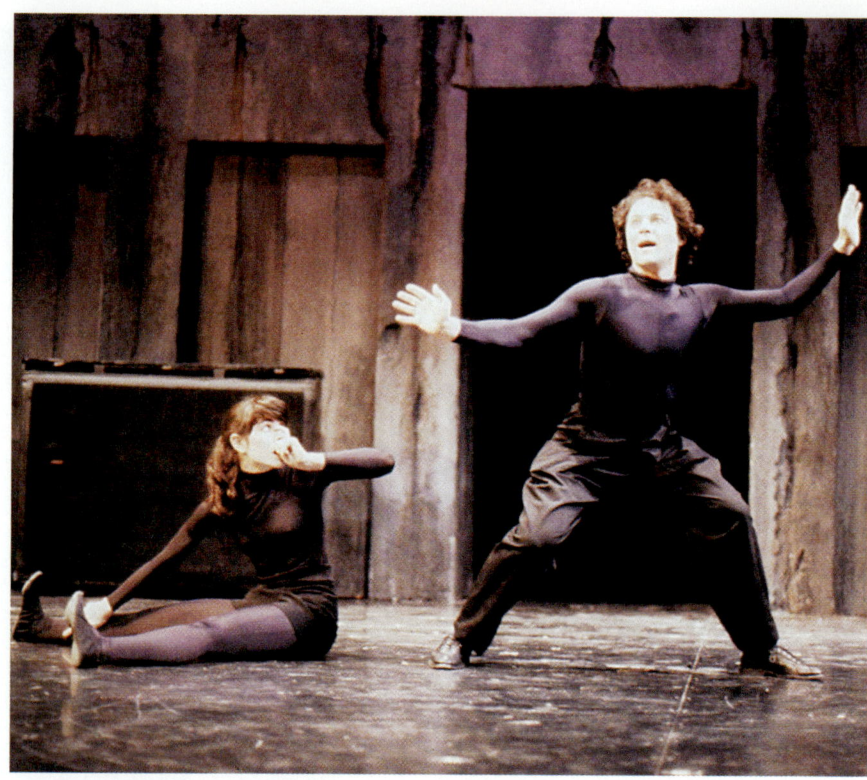

The Chameleons: Keith Berger and Sharon Diskin. *Life Cycle.* Photo © 1990, Craig Schwartz.

ARTSOURCE

Discussion Questions

1. Why do you think Keith Berger and Sharon Diskin titled their mime piece *Life Cycle*? What does the term *cycle* mean, and how does this relate to the stages of life?
2. Study the photo on this page and describe the situation and what you think is being communicated by the two mimes.
3. Identify situations where people use gestures to communicate ideas rather than words. Discuss why this is done in each of the situations.

Creative Expression Activities

Pantomime Imagine that you are watching the following things, using primarily your eyes to show each idea: a tennis match, an airplane flying high, a spider crawling near your toes, and a butterfly flying around you and landing on a part of your body.

Pantomime Show the following ideas in mime movement: fishing, writing a letter, stirring cake batter, dealing cards, getting dressed, sewing a button on a shirt, and bowling.

Playwriting Create a mime scenario about a day in the life of a specific character. Then write an outline of the action to use as a mime script.

Dance Pilobolus Dance Theatre

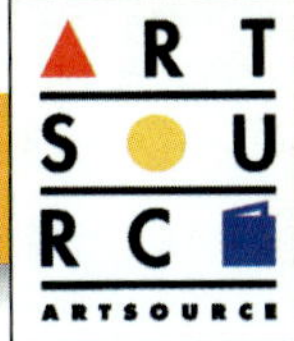

Pilobolus Dance Theatre, an internationally acclaimed American dance company, was formed at Dartmouth College in 1971. Searching for a new dance style, they created a unique and highly original choreographic process that relied on trust, collaboration, and a weight-sharing approach to partnering. Each new dance project begins with several days of improvisation, where the dancers are called upon to find inventive movement through "creative play." This process, which has no rules, is guided by one or more of the four artistic directors. Dances that have emerged from this process feature a startling mixture of humor, artistry, and creativity. The name *Pilobolus* refers to a real-life fungus found in pastures. This small mushroom has an eye that grows or moves in response to light. When ready to reproduce, it can project its spores nearly eight feet into the air. This little organism captures the essence of the way the company works and creates. Now over 30 years old, Pilobolus remains an original, influential, and versatile force in the dance world.

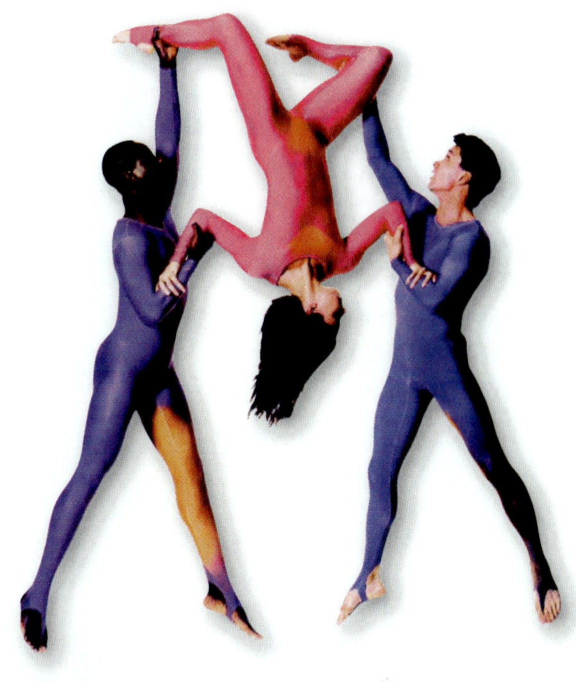

Pilobolus Dance Theatre. "The Brass Ring." Photo: Howard Schatz.

ARTSOURCE

Discussion Questions

1. Discuss how dance can vary so much in purpose and style. Styles include: ceremonial, folk, ballet, jazz, modern, musical theatre, tap, and hip-hop. What do you think is the definition of *dance*? How many different reasons can you think of for why people dance?
2. Pilobolus's dancers collaborate to solve problems and find inventive solutions in order to create their work. Give examples of situations where you have improvised to solve a problem, either alone or in a group. How did collaboration help you and the group in this process? Were you inventive?

Creative Expression Activities

Language Arts/Dance Using verbs (action words) and adverbs (modifiers) as starting points for movement, write a selection of these words on cards. Pair each verb with an adverb. Arrange three to five sets in a sequence and design a small-group dance study. Improvise the words using elements of dance, such as level, size, direction, energy, and tempo to make the movements interesting. Practice working as a team to find solutions to the problem. Verbs delineate the action sequence, and adverbs tell how the action is to be done, e.g., turning slowly or running hesitantly. Prepositions, such as *from* and *in*, can be added to define the relationships between the dancers.

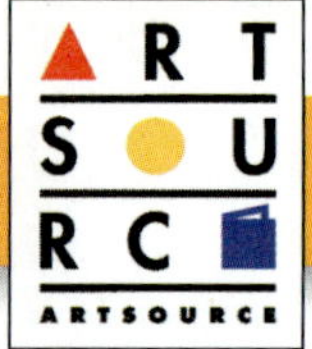

Dance Ballet Folklórico de Mexico

For over 25 years, Ballet Folklórico de Mexico has presented authentic folk dances from different ethnic groups within Mexico. Amalia Hernández, the Artistic Director of the dance company, creates exciting dances based on ancient traditions. From the time of the Olmec Indians to the birth of modern Mexico, more than 30 distinct cultures have influenced Mexican culture. The dance shown in this photo is called "Los Mitos" and features the pageantry and ritual of these cultures before the arrival of the Spaniards.

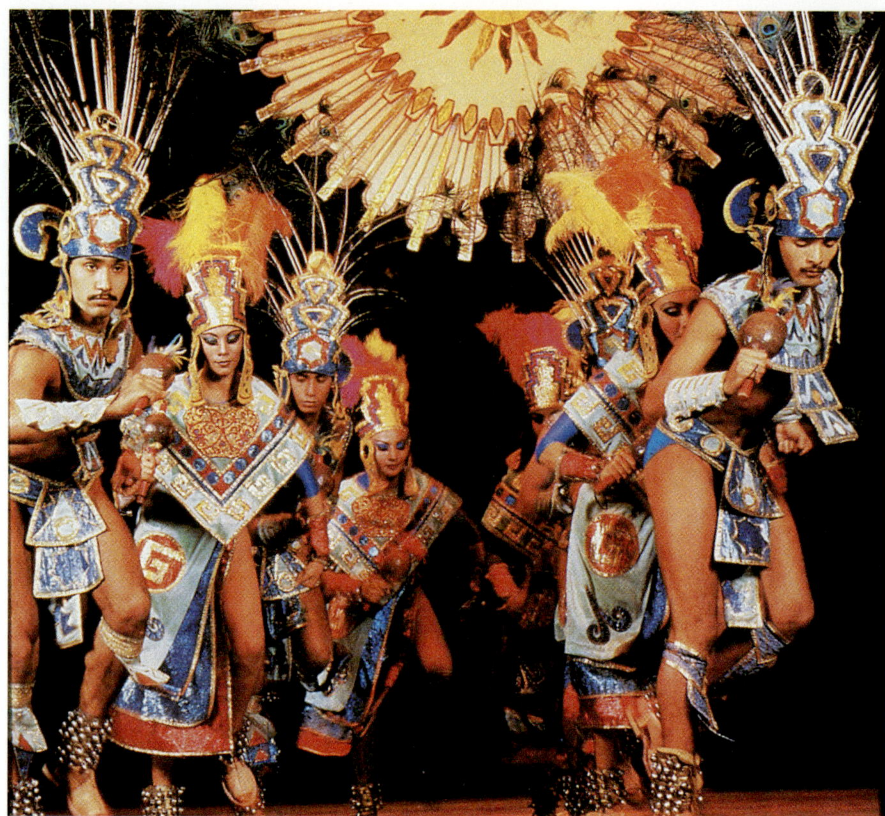

Ballet Folklórico de Mexico. "Los Mitos" from "Los Concheros." Amalia Hernández, Artistic Director. Photo courtesy of Friedson Enterprises.

Discussion Questions

1. What symbolism do you see in the photo on this page? What characteristics of the symbol can you name?
2. After viewing the video, describe how the dancers used geometric spatial designs.

Creative Expression Activities

Dance Stand in an open area with six to eight students and organize yourselves into three different geometric shapes, selecting from a circle, square, triangle, or the letter X. After your designs are organized, choose two that you like and walk or skip from one figure into another using eight counts to travel.

Language Arts Write a personal reflection of your impressions and feelings about either the images you see in the illustration on this page or of the dance in the video.

Dance African American Dance Ensemble

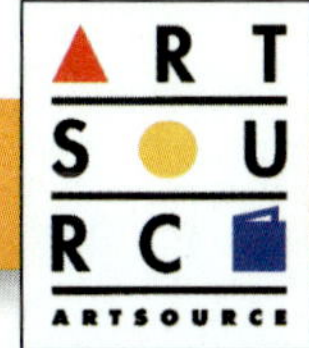

Based on extensive research, the African American Dance Ensemble performances are a blend of traditional African and African American styles. In African cultures, dance is not seen simply as an art form but as an integral part of the economic, political, social, and religious aspects of life. Artistic Director Dr. Chuck Davis and his company use dance and music to bring the message of "peace, love, and respect for everybody." His dance "Balante" is based on a post-initiation dance of the Jolas of the Casamance region of Senegal. It features the joyous, powerful dancing of young men who have completed their rites of passage, attaining the status of manhood.

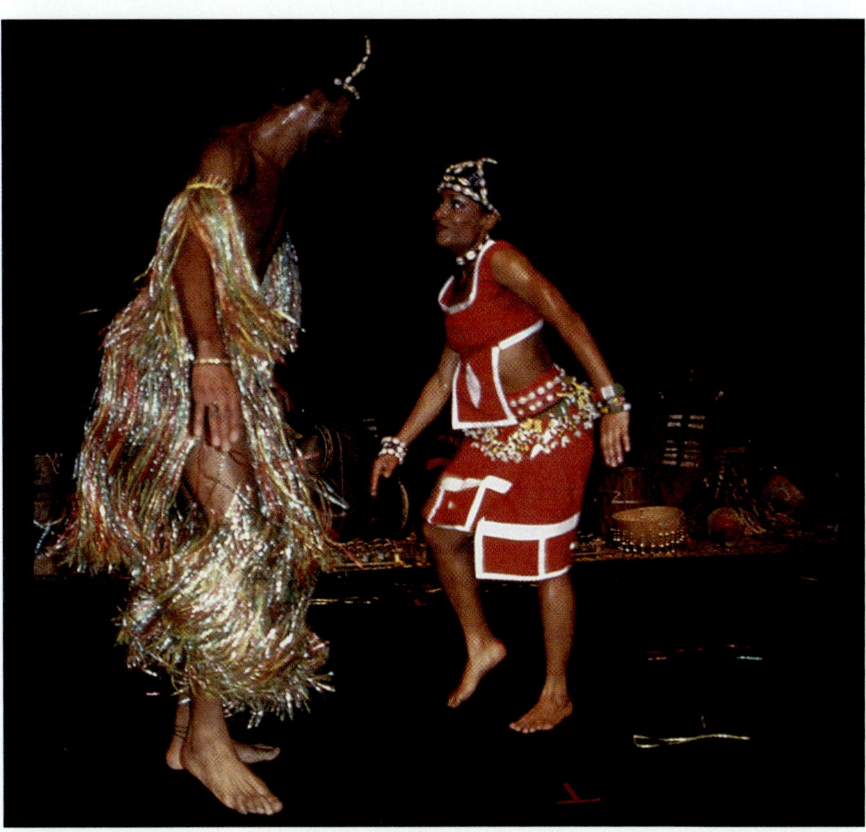

African American Dance Ensemble. "Balante." Dr. Chuck Davis, Artistic Director. Photo: Courtesy of African American Dance Ensemble.

Discussion Questions

1. Initiates, in many traditional African societies, are expected to attain certain moral, intellectual, and spiritual qualities before they attain manhood. This "rite of passage" period is secret, and the boys and girls are separated from their tribe to undergo these instructions and challenges. Identify and discuss any rituals, activities, or accomplishments in our American society that serve as "rites of passage" for young boys or girls.
2. What dance styles do you think have their roots in traditional African cultures? Give reasons for your answers.

Creative Expression Activities

Language Arts In many African ethnic groups, it is believed that wise people speak in proverbs and that everything has a place in life and a reason for being. Read the following proverbs, and then think of English equivalents: "Rain beats a leopard's skin, but it does not wash out the spots." (Ashanti); "When spider webs unite, they can tie up a lion." (Ethiopia); "Cross the river in a crowd and the crocodile won't eat you." (Kenya).

Social Studies Most African groups have ceremonies that celebrate life passages. Create a "Naming Ceremony" for you and your classmates. Select a name for yourself that tells something of your character, appearance, accomplishments, or history. Include a special song and movements.

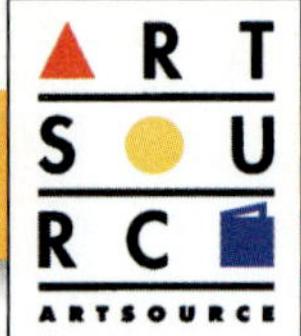

Music Eugene Friesen

World-renowned cellist, Eugene Friesen, uses both his cello and his voice to create new music. Eugene began playing the cello in his elementary school orchestra at age eight, pulling it to school in a little red wagon. By the time he got to high school he played in both school and community orchestras and began experimenting with an amplified cello to play rock and blues styles. A graduate of the Yale School of Music, Eugene moved from the traditional classical world of the cello into a creative, expressive one. The photo captures him playing in a solo performance called "Cello Man," created in collaboration with Faustwork Mask Theater. In this show, Eugene weaves a spellbinding fabric composed of stories, songs, and inventive techniques on both the cello and electric cello. Using masks and costumes, Eugene transforms himself into different characters that integrate with the music he is playing. This use of masks adds a dramatic element to the performance, which includes a duet with the recorded song of a humpback whale.

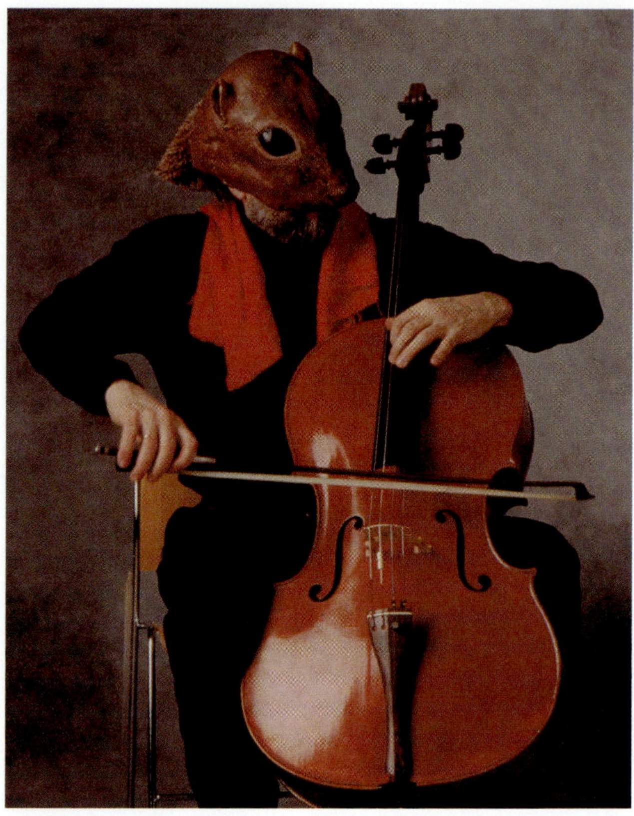

Eugene Friesen. "Cello Man." Photo: Craig Schwartz, © 1998.

ARTSOURCE

Discussion Questions

1. Look at the photo and identify the animal depicted by the mask Eugene is wearing. Think of the characteristics of this animal and think about how they would translate into the tempo, quality, and melody of the music he is playing.
2. Do you know how a cello is played? Can you describe the sound a cello makes? How might this differ from the sound of an electric cello?
3. What other instruments can you name that are in the string family?

Creative Expression Activities

Language Arts Write a story that has a musical instrument as a main character. The instrument's character may be personified so that human traits and emotions are expressed. Also, think about the materials used in making the specific instrument and the way they might be included in describing the character.

Science Sound is produced by vibrations at different frequencies. Each stringed musical instrument produces different levels and speeds of vibrations that are created by bowing or plucking. The type of wood and the material of the strings and bow affect the type of sound that is produced. Research the differences in the sound qualities and textures of the violin, cello, and bass. What things impact the quality, texture, and pitch of the sound?

Dance Donald McKayle

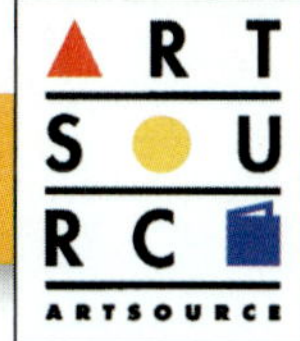

Choreographer Donald McKayle is a performing artist who has broken many barriers. He was the first African American male dancer selected to join the famous Martha Graham Dance Company. He also went with the company on its historic tour of Asia in the late 1950s. Among his many dances is a piece called "Rainbow 'Round My Shoulder," based on prisoners' dreams of freedom. McKayle focuses on prisoners in the South, who were chained together as they worked. In the dance, he incorporates the strong, repetitive rhythm of work movements and prison songs. He believes that the more truthful artists are, the more their art will communicate to others. His dances, as well as his life, reflect this belief.

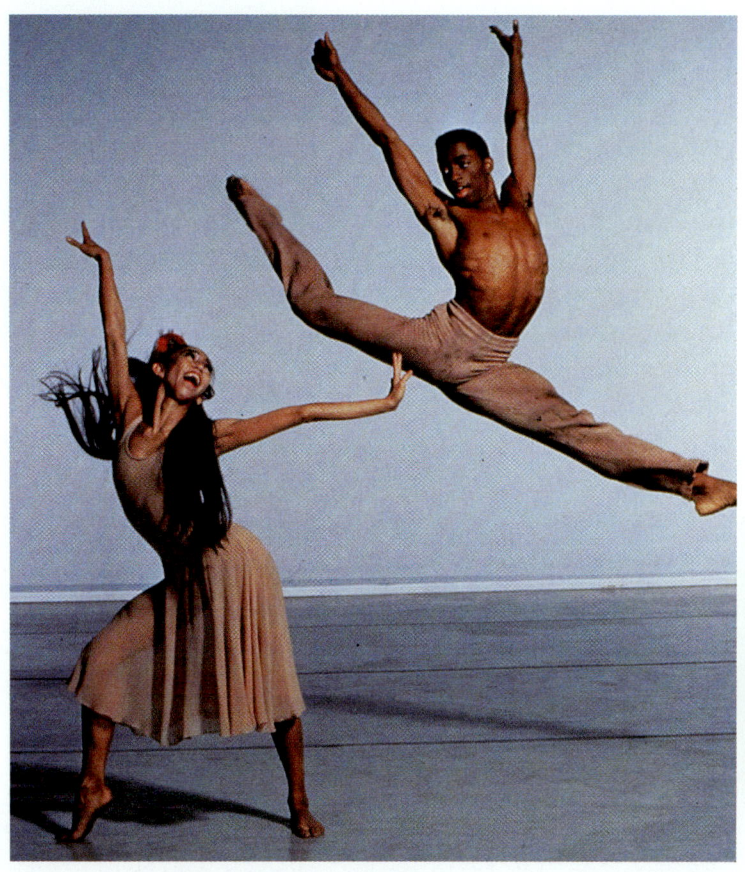

Alvin Ailey American Dance Theater. Donald McKayle, choreographer. "Rainbow 'Round My Shoulder." Featured dancers: Elizabeth Roxas and Desmond Richardson. Photo by Jack Mitchell.

ARTSOURCE

Discussion Questions

1. Share what you know about the life of prisoners working in a chain gang. What kind of movements would a choreographer use to portray a prisoner's hard and repetitive life? Explain your choices.
2. Look at the photo of the dancers on this page. What principles of art can you identify in the photo?
3. Why do you think a choreographer would choose the title "Rainbow 'Round My Shoulder" as a title for a dance about prisoners? What does a rainbow symbolize? What symbols would you choose if you were creating a work of art expressing a wish for freedom?

Creative Expression Activities

Dance Working with a partner or in small groups, think of movements that suggest actions associated with physical work. You might use such repetitive movements as hauling, dragging, pushing, pulling, lifting, carrying, and breaking rocks. Create several variations for each. Perform the movements for the class.

Language Arts List words that describe the feelings of someone who is imprisoned and longs for freedom. Use your list to write a poem or short story about this person and his or her feelings.

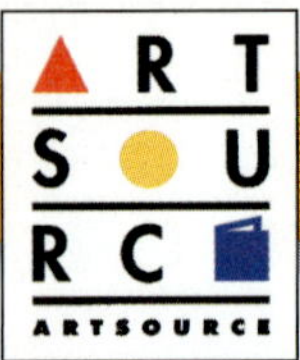

Theatre Blue Palm

Prior to founding *Blue Palm,* Tom Crocker and Jackie Planeix, choreographers and performers, toured the world with the internationally renowned Béjart Ballet. Blue Palm creates original pieces focused on human dreams, fears, and flaws. Using a form called interdisciplinary theatre, they blend drama, dance, and humor. *Childhood* is composed of a series of scenes, each of which gives us a glimpse into the world of children, with its own whimsical logic. Blue Palm holds up a looking glass that lets us see how universal our feelings and struggles are. "The Lot" shows an adult reencountering a childhood friend who became lost in play and never grew up. The dialogue between them reveals each one's perspective and how these influenced the choices they made. The scene in the photo highlights the contrast between a child and an adult perspective, and expresses the enduring bond of friendship.

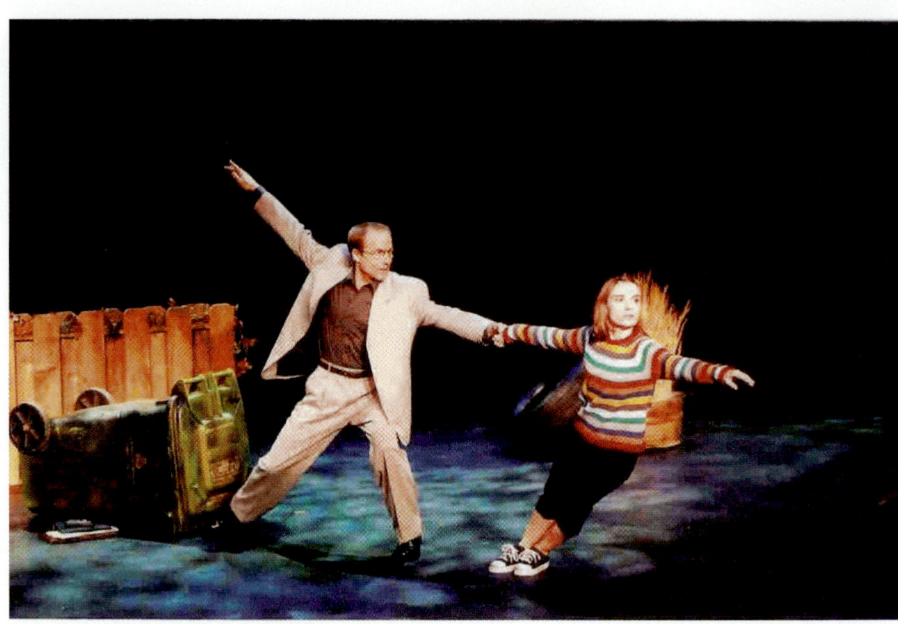

Blue Palm: Tom Crocker and Jackie Planeix. "The Lot" from *Childhood*. Photo: Brigitte Meuwissen.

ARTSOURCE

Discussion Questions

1. This performance examines the magical, yet sometimes complex, process of "growing up." What do you look forward to as you get older? What are the things that frighten you? What do you think will be your biggest strength? What might be your biggest challenge?
2. One of the characters in the play never grew up because she wanted to keep on playing. Imagine you could stop yourself from growing. Where would you choose to stop and stay? What would the advantages and disadvantages be?

Creative Expression Activities

Language Arts Recall a scenario from your own childhood that taught you something. Think of the setting you were in, your age, other people who were involved, and the emotions you were feeling. Imagine the beginning, middle, and ending of the scenario and see what happened and how you felt at the end. Was this feeling different than at the beginning or middle? Did you realize something or make a decision about something because of this event? Use your memory to write a short story that captures the scene, defines the characters, and describes the event. Share this with a partner. Did you learn something new in the writing or telling of your story?

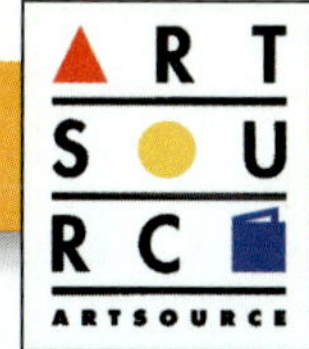

Dance/Theatre Kurt Jooss

"The Green Table," created by choreographer Kurt Jooss in 1932, is a compassionate and powerful dance drama about the horrors of war. It features ten gentlemen in morning coats and spats standing and leaning around a rectangular green table. They posture and disagree until pistols emerge. A shot is fired, and war is declared. After the gun shot, the "Green Table" scene goes black and we see the figure of Death enter. In the scenes that follow, soldiers are called to fight, battles rage, refugees comfort one another, a profit-maker preys on the miseries of his fellow man, and a lone soldier holds watch. Through every scene, Death stalks the stage to find different companions, claiming victim after victim. These characters meet Death in their own ways, some swiftly and some slowly. Because of its universal themes of power, war, and death, "The Green Table" continues to be performed around the world, making it the most performed of all dance works created in the twentieth century.

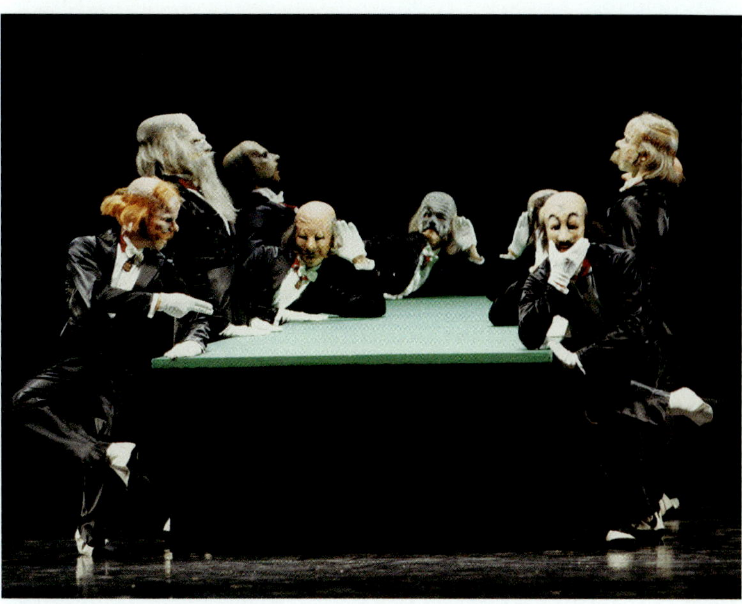

The Joffrey Ballet of Chicago performing "The Green Table." Kurt Jooss, choreographer. Photo: © Robert Migdoll, 1998.

Discussion Questions

1. What do you think a dance drama is? How might this differ from a dance created to express a specific piece of music?
2. Why do you think the choreographer chose to have masks for the men at the green table? How might it have communicated something different without the masks?

Creative Expression Activities

Language Arts Some people feel that dance can't tell a dramatic work as well as a play that has the characters use words and dialogue. However, other people feel that emotions can be portrayed even more strongly when words are taken away and the characters communicate primarily through posture and movement. Write a short essay on the topic of war and how diplomats or statesmen make decisions that impact the ordinary citizen as well as soldiers. How would you portray the character of Death and how he claims his victims? What narration or dialogue would you use?

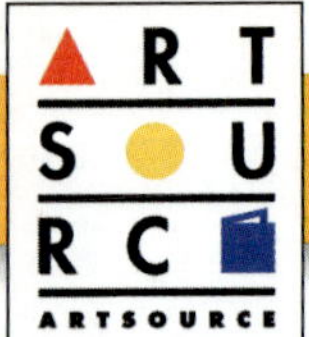

Music Chic Street Man

Chic Street Man is clever at communicating ideas through his music. He often combines storytelling in his compositions, as in *Rag Man*. He skillfully uses his guitar, his singing voice, and his speaking voice to tell the tale of a rag man, as seen through the eyes of a boy. This is a true story-song of an old man who used a horse and wagon to come into Chic's neighborhood looking for rags. The song is sung in a style derived from African cultural traditions, combining storytelling and poetry with music.

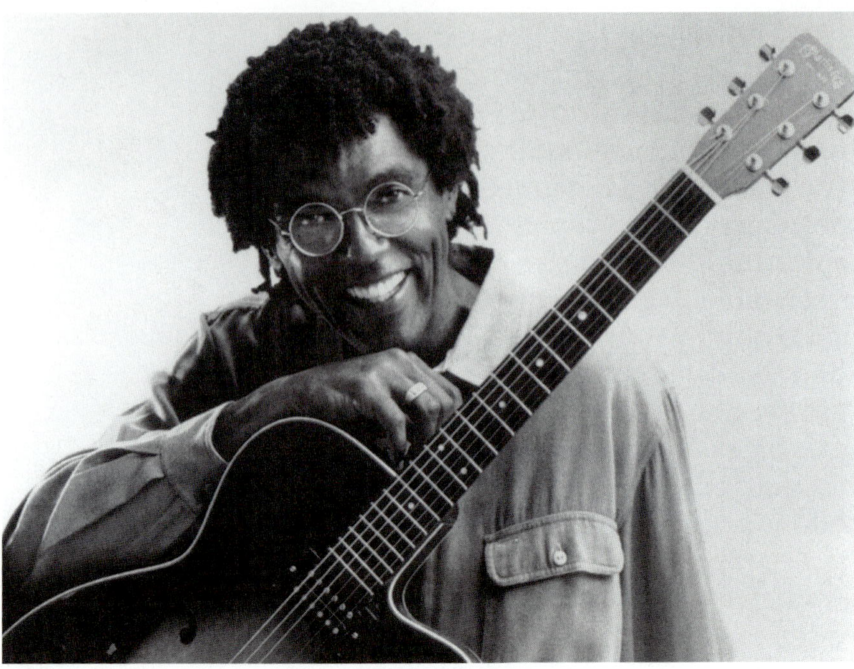

Chic Street Man: *Rag Man.* Photo by Neil Ricklen.

ARTSOURCE

Discussion Questions

1. Chic Street Man calls his *Rag Man* performance a "rap recitation." Why do you think he calls it that?
2. In *Rag Man,* Chic weaves a story about a man who advertised his work by riding though the streets calling and singing to his potential customers. Do vendors still come to your neighborhood? If so, discuss what they sell and how they call to their customers.
3. Discuss how songs and music are used to advertise and sell products. Recall some songs that are memorable or are being currently used.

Creative Expression Activities

Language Arts Select three commercials using music or song that are memorable. Demonstrate and describe them, discuss the various music styles used, and suggest what type of audience the companies wish to reach.

Art/History/Culture Examine the artworks of African American artists who, like their counterparts in music, have portrayed the historical, cultural, social, and political lives of their people. Look for the messages they convey, and describe how the artists communicated their message through visual art.

The Joffrey Ballet of Chicago

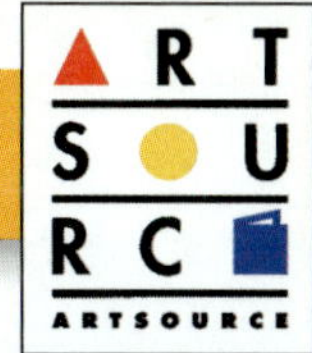

The Joffrey Ballet of Chicago revives major historical ballets and features new choreography that draws from American life. *The Nutcracker,* a traditional ballet, is based on the story *The Nutcracker and The King of the Mice* by E. T. A. Hoffmann. The original ballet premiered in St. Petersburg, Russia, in 1892. Begun by Marius Petipa and completed by Lev Ivanov, it was choreographed to a musical score by Peter Tchaikovsky. Set on Christmas Eve, *The Nutcracker* is a magical story about a young girl named Clara, who receives a nutcracker from her Uncle Drosselmeyer. Fritz, her jealous brother, breaks it. Although angry and sad, she repairs it with her uncle's help. However, when she checks on her nutcracker during the night, she sees him fighting off an attack by the Mouse King and his army. Clara helps the nutcracker he thanks her, then magically turns into a prince. Snow begins to fall and soon they find themselves in "The Land of Sweets," where she meets the Sugar Plum Fairy and a host of toys, flowers, and dolls. After a delightful experience, she returns from her dream and awakens on Christmas morning.

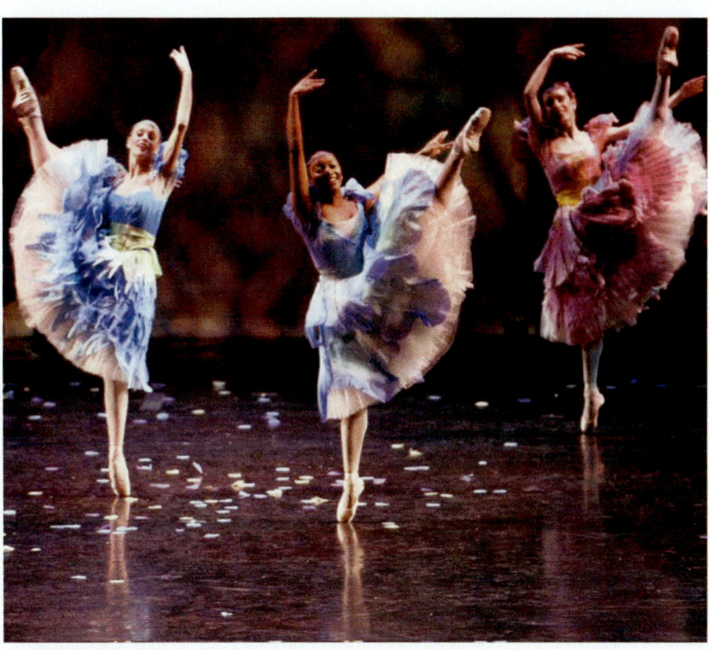

The Joffrey Ballet of Chicago. "Waltz of the Flowers" from *The Nutcracker.* Gerald Arpino, Artistic Director. Photo: Herbert Migdoll.

Discussion Questions

1. Discuss other stories or fairy tales you know that focus on magical transformation. What do you think the role of magical power is in these tales? What purpose, if any, does it serve in our lives?
2. Have you ever seen a story enacted through dance? What would be the main differences between a story that is presented as a play and one that is presented as a dance? Which might be the more powerful? Give reasons why. Be very specific in your responses.

Creative Expression Activities

Language Arts Russian choreographer Michel Fokine said, "Man should and could be expressive from head to foot, yet even the greatest dancer must play his part as one member of a group—the ballet company." In small groups, discuss this idea and find connections to other group efforts such as sports, band, dance teams, and production crews.

Mime Create a mime or movement study based on toys and how they might move if animated. These might include: yo-yos, kites, balls, plastic clay; different types of dolls, jack-in-the-box, or action figures.

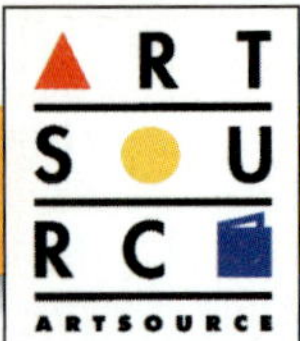

Music Japanese Festival Sounds

Johnny Mori was fascinated by the Taiko drummer who accompanied the folk dancers at the annual Obon Buddhist Festival in Los Angeles, California. This inspired him to learn to play the drums. Today he blends traditional Taiko drumming with a modern Japanese American style. Taiko drumming originated in ancient India as part of religious ceremonies and celebrations. This form eventually found its way to Korea, China, and Japan. Traditionally, Taiko drums were included in ensembles with other instruments. In some cultures, the drums were also used to perform functional roles, such as announcing the time of day or calling people to special gatherings. Today, Taiko is featured in performances with some ensembles composed solely of various sized drums.

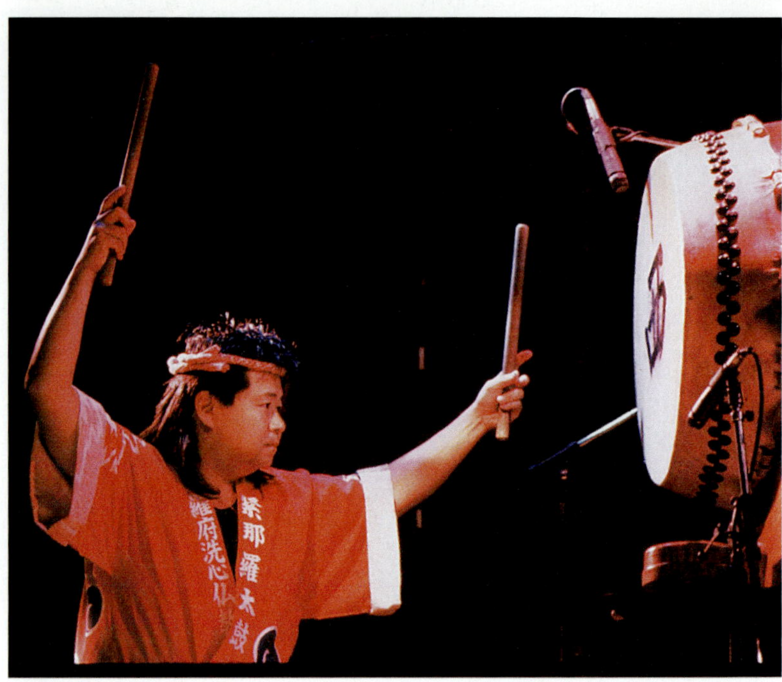

Japanese Festival Sounds. Johnny Mori, Artistic Director. Photo: Craig Schwartz © 1989.

ARTSOURCE

Discussion Questions

1. Where did Taiko drumming originate? To what other countries did it spread?
2. Taiko performers demonstrate great skill and control in movement and drum technique. Their performance skills are a result of many hours of concentrated, vigorous work involving the mind, body, and spirit. Discuss how Taiko drummers are like athletes and dancers.
3. What other cultures place an emphasis on drumming? For what purposes are the drums used?

Creative Expression Activities

Language Arts The technique of learning drum patterns by vocalizing the sounds began in India and was transferred to many Asian cultures. Five basic syllables used in Taiko are: KA; KARA; DON; DOGO; and SU (which means rest). Combine the syllables in different patterns, saying them as you clap or beat out the rhythms. Repeat each pattern several times.

Geography Using a map or globe, trace the geographical and historical route of the Taiko drums from India through Asia to the United States.

Diavolo

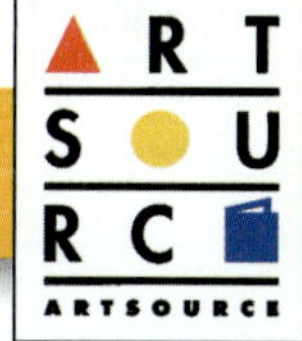

Parisian-born Jacques Heim is the dynamic creator and director of Diavalo, a dance and physical theatre group that takes a daring, compelling, and uncompromising look at contemporary human life. Heim has studied dance, film, and choreography in France, the United States, and England and has an MFA in Theatre, Dance, and Film from the California Institute of the Arts. He created *Diavolo* in 1992 after graduating from Cal Arts in California. He states, "I try to convey an appreciation for movement by breaking down barriers to dance via a vocabulary based on everyday activities." Diavolo is composed of dancers, gymnasts, and actors, who work as teammates. In their collaborations, they work on and around outrageous, surrealistic sets and structures. Everyday items such as benches, doors, and ladders provide the backdrop for dramatic movement. In the dance, "Tête en l'Air," dancers leap from a staircase and roll down its steps, creating metaphors for the challenges of relationships while maintaining balance.

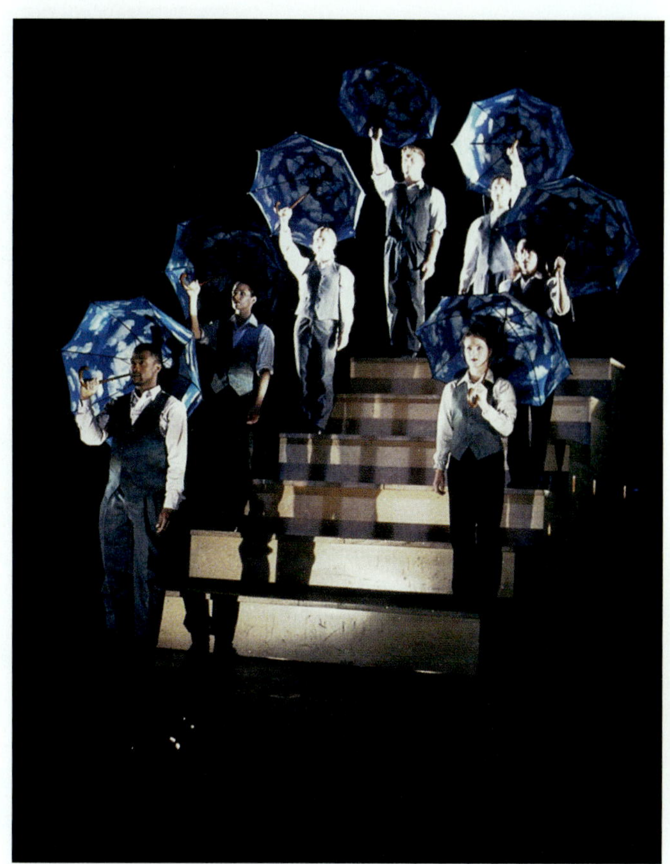

Diavolo performs "Tête en l'Air." Photo: Ed Krieger.

Discussion Questions

1. Can you think of an everyday object that would lend itself to a dance piece? Give reasons why you think this piece or structure would be interesting to dance with or on. How would you have the dancers interact with the object? What thematic ideas come to mind?
2. This dance takes place on and off a staircase structure. If you were the choreographer, how many different actions can you think of that you could incorporate into the dance movements? See if you can list at least ten.

Creative Expression Activities

Language Arts The word *Diavolo* has several possible meanings. A favorite, however, is *dia* (Spanish for "day") and *volo* (Latin for "I will fly"). Write a paragraph titled, "The Day I Will Fly."

Science A theme in Diavolo's work is the relationship between gravity and weight. Choose three different objects of varying size and weight; for example, a ball, a book, a feather, or silk scarf. Drop each object from above your head and observe how each falls to the ground. Is the rate of speed at which they fall constant? What words describe the way each object fell? Floating, bouncing, slamming, forceful, or graceful?

Dance Jiří Kylián

World renowned choreographer Jiří Kylián began his dance training at age nine at the Prague National Theatre, a ballet school. After many years of study he was offered a dancer's contract with the Stuttgart Ballet in Germany. Kylián then became the Artistic Director of the Nederlands Dans Theater, creating over 50 choreographies for the company. During this time he studied the dance and culture of the Aborigines of Australia. They are the only remaining people of a Stone Age culture left undisturbed for 50,000 years. His research led to a powerful suite of dances called, *The Stamping Ground.* These dances are not imitations of the ancient Aboriginal culture, however. They grew out of a new movement vocabulary developed by Kylián that matches the concepts they inspired. His style is difficult to categorize because he blends many elements to create his unique spectrum of expression.

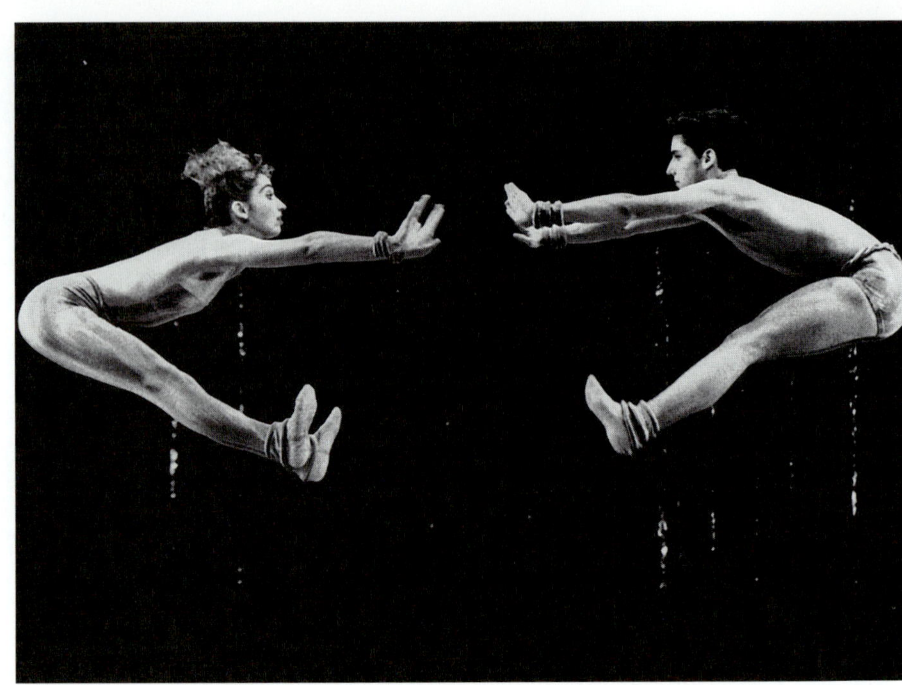

Jiří Kylián - Nederlands Dans Theatre, "Stamping Ground"

Discussion Questions:

1. Why do you think Jiří Kylián did not imitate or try to recreate the ancient Aboriginal dances, but developed his own movement vocabulary and artistic style instead? Discuss why he might choose to study ancient cultures as sources for inspiration.
2. If you were a choreographer, discuss why you might need to do research before you could create a dance. What types of research might a choreographer do if he or she were creating a dance based in a specific historical period? Why would this be necessary?

Creative Expression Activities:

Geography/Science Find Australia on a map and see its global position relative to the United States. Find out what animals are indigenous to Australia. Select one animal, such as the kangaroo, and find out the basic design of its body. Also find what movements the animals make, the things they eat, and their habitat. Design three body shapes or postures that capture your selected animal. Then perform a physical representation of your animal using the postures in sequence. Hold each one for five counts, as if it were a sculpture. Share interpretations with partners or in small groups. A small group improvisation could be structured around each of the animals.

Artists and Their Works

L

M

N

T

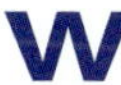

Z

Glossary

A

Abstract Expressionism An art movement that emphasized abstract elements of art and stressed feelings and emotions. (p. 123)

Abstract The subject of the artwork is simplified or stylized. (p. 220)

Acrylic A quick-drying water-based synthetic paint.

Additive A sculpting method produced by adding to or combining materials. (p. 218)

Advertising design An area of graphic art whose goal is to help inform, sell, or promote products or services. (p. 202)

Aesthetic views An idea or school of thought on what is most important in works of art.

Aesthetics The branch of philosophy concerned with the nature and value of art. (p. 106)

Amphitheater A circular or oval building with seats rising around an open space. (p. 252)

Analogous colors Colors that are side by side on the color wheel and share a hue. (p. 31)

Analyzing In art criticism, noting how the art principles are used to organize the elements of art. (p. 98)

Applied art Art made to be functional as well as visually pleasing. (p. 6)

Architect An artist who plans and creates buildings. (p. 250)

Architectural rendering A detailed, realistic, two-dimensional representation of a three-dimensional structure. (p. 136)

Architecture The art of planning and creating buildings. (p. 250)

Art A visual statement that communicates an idea, expresses a feeling, or presents an interesting design. (p. 4)

Art critic A person who practices art criticism. (p. 94)

Art criticism The process of gathering facts and information from artworks in order to make intelligent judgments about them. (p. 94)

Art history The study of art from past to present. (p. 114)

Art media Tools and materials used to create works of art. (p. 68)

Art movement A group of artists with similar styles who have banded together. (p. 118)

Artists People who use imagination, creativity and skill to communicate ideas in visual form. (p. 6)

Assembling A sculpting method in which different kinds of materials are gathered and joined together. (p. 218)

B

Balance The principle of art concerned with arranging art elements in an artwork so no one part of that work overpowers, or seems heavier than, any other part. (p. 49)

Binder A liquid to which the dry pigment is added. (p. 78)

Blending Smoothly drawing dark values little by little by pressing harder on the drawing medium.

Brayer A roller with a handle. (p. 152)

C

Camera A dark box with a hole controlling how much light enters. (p. 184)

Caricature A drawing that exaggerates one or more facial or bodily features.

Carving A sculpting method in which material is cut or chipped away. (p. 218)

Casting A sculpting method in which melted material is poured into a mold. (p. 218)

Cathedrals Large churches. (p. 251)

Ceramics The process of creating objects from clay and hardening them by fire. (p. 234)

Cinematographer The person in charge of running the camera or cameras.

Collage An artwork made up of cut or torn materials pasted to a surface. (p. 12)

Color The element of art that is derived from reflected light. (p. 28)

Color wheel An arrangement of hues in a circular format. (p. 29)

Columns Vertical posts that rise to support another structure. (p. 257)

Complementary colors Colors opposite each other on the color wheel. (p. 30)

Composition How the art principles are used to organize the art elements. (p. 16)

Content The message, feeling, or idea an artwork communicates. (p. 16)

Contour drawing A drawing in which an object is drawn as though your drawing tool is moving along all the edges and the ridges of the form. (p. 142)

Craftspersons Artists who make useful and aesthetically pleasing goods. (p. 232)

Crafts Different areas of applied art in which craftspeople work. (p. 232)

Credit line A listing of important facts about an artwork. (p. 17)

Crosshatching The technique of using lines that crisscross each other to achieve shading. (p. 138)

Cross-section Cutaway view. (p. 216)

Cubism An art style in which a single object is shown simultaneously from multiple points of view. (p. 128)

D

Daguerreotype An image made on copper plates coated with highly polished silver. (p. 185)

Describing In art criticism, making a careful list of all the things you see in the work. (p. 95) In art history, asking when, where, and by whom the work was done. (p. 115)

Desktop publishing The use of a computer and special software to combine text and graphics on a page. (p. 201)

Digital art Art made in part or whole using computer hardware and software. (p. 84)

Digital camera A camera that contains a tiny scanner, which converts visual information into computer-coded form. (p. 184)

Digitizing A method in which basic units of display called pixels were converted to dots. (p. 268)

Director The person in charge of shooting the film and guiding the actors. (p. 266)

Dwellings Homes. (p. 250)

Edition A series of prints that are all exactly alike. (p. 72)

Element of art A basic visual symbol an artist uses to create visual art. (p. 23)

Elevation A drawing of an outside view of a building. (p. 256)

Emphasis The principle of art concerned with making an element or object in an artwork stand out. (p. 53)

Encaustic A painting medium in which pigment is mixed into melted wax. (p. 168)

F

Façade The front of a building. (p. 256)

Fauvism An art movement and painting style that made use of wild intense color combinations. (p. 120)

Fibers Strands of any thin, threadlike material. (p. 233)

Fine art Art valued for its visual appeal or success in communicating ideas or feelings. (p. 6)

Fine art print An artwork created by the printmaking process. (p. 72)

Fine art reproduction High-quality copy of an artwork made using commercial photographic processes. (p. 72)

Fired Hardened by applying high heat. (p. 235)

Floor plan A diagram, drawn to scale, of a room or building as seen from above. (p. 254)

Form An element of art that refers to an object with three dimensions. (p. 36)

Formal properties The way the elements of art are organized by the principle of art. (p. 16)

Freestanding sculpture Sculpture surrounded on all sides by space. (p. 80)

Fresco A painting medium in which pigment is applied to a wall spread with wet plaster. (p. 168)

G

Gesture drawing A drawing in which lines are drawn quickly and loosely to capture the form and actions of a subject. (p. 140)

Glassblowing The craft of shaping melted glass by blowing air into it through a tube. (p. 234)

Glaze A thin, transparent layer. (p. 170)

Glazed Coated with a mixture of powdered chemicals that melt during firing to form a hard, glasslike finish. (p. 235)

Gouache An opaque water-based paint. (p. 170)

Graphic artists Art professionals who work in the field known as graphic design. (p. 200)

Graphic design The field of art that uses pictures and words to instruct or communicate a specific message. (p. 200)

H

Harmony The principle of art concerned with combining similar art elements to create a pleasing appearance. (p. 53)

Hatching Drawing a series of thin lines all running parallel, or in the same direction. (p. 138)

High relief A type of relief sculpture in which the forms project boldly from a flat background. (p. 222)

Hue A color's name. (p. 29)

I

Illuminations Illustrations in early handmade manuscripts. (p. 200)

Impasto Oil paint applied in thick, buttery layers. (p. 170)

Impressionism A style of painting that attempts to capture the rapidly changing effects of sunlight on objects. (p. 119)

Informal balance Involves a balance of unlike objects or elements. (p. 49)

Intaglio Printmaking technique in which the image to be printed is cut or etched into a surface. (p. 153)

Intensity The brightness or dullness of a hue. (p. 30)

Interpreting In art criticism, assigning a meaning or finding a message in an artwork. (p. 102) In art history, noting how time and place affect an artist's style and subject matter. (p. 122)

J

Judging In art criticism, making a decision about a work's success and giving reasons for that decision. (p. 106) In art history, determing an artwork's contribution to the history of art. (p. 128)

K

Kiln A special ceramics furnace. (p. 235)

L

Landscape A drawing or painting of mountains, trees, or other natural scenery. (p. 38)

Layout designers Graphic artists who arrange text and illustrations and prepare the material for printing. (p. 201)

Leather-hard clay Clay that is still damp but is too dry to shape. (p. 234)

Line A continuous mark made on some surface by a moving point. (p. 24)

Lithograph A print made by lithography. (p. 154)

Lithography A printmaking technique in which the image to be printed is drawn on limestone, zinc, or aluminum with a special greasy crayon. (p. 154)

Logo A special image representing a business, group, or product. (p. 202)

Loom A frame or machine that holds a set of threads that run vertically. (p. 233)

Low relief A type of relief sculpture in which the forms project only slightly from a flat background. (p. 222)

M

Madonna A work showing the mother of Christ. (p. 125)

Maquette A three-dimensional scaled-down study of a larger planned sculpture. (p. 217)

Minarets Structures from which the faithful are called to prayer each day. (p. 251)

Mobile A sculptural technique in which painted sheet-metal shapes suspend freely from wires, permitting movement. (p. 129)

Modeling A sculpting method in which a soft or workable material is built up and shaped. (p. 219)

Monochromatic colors Different values of a single hue. (p. 31)

Monoprinting A printmaking technique in which the image to be printed is put on the plate with ink or paint and then transferred to paper by pressing or hand-rubbing. (p. 156)

Motion picture A series of photographs of the same subject taken a very short time apart and flashed onto a screen. (p. 266)

Movement The principle of art used to create the look and feel of action and to guide the viewer's eye throughout a work of art. (p. 58)

Multimedia art Art that simultaneously uses several different electronic media. (p. 267)

N

Negative A reverse image of the object photographed. (p. 186)

Nonobjective art Art having no recognizable subject matter. (p. 15)

O

Oil paint Paint with an oil base. (p. 170)

Opaque A surface or material that does not let light pass through. Opposite of transparent. (p. 169)

P

Palette Any tray or plate on which paints are mixed before use. (p. 169)

Patrons of the arts Sponsors, or supporters, of an artist or art-related events such as exhibitions. (p. 11)

Pattern A principle of art concerned with a two-dimensional decorative effect achieved through the repetition of colors, lines, shapes, and/or textures. (p. 58)

Perceive To become aware through the senses of the special nature of objects. (p. 5)

Perception Awareness of aspects of the environment through the senses. (p. 136)

Photogenic drawing The process of coating a sheet of drawing paper with silver chloride. (p. 185)

Photogram An image made using precoated paper that detects the presence of ultraviolet light. (p. 188)

Photography The art of making images using light and other principles of science. (p. 184)

Photojournalism Reporting a news event mainly or totally through photographic images. (p. 186)

Picture plane The flat surface of a painting or drawing. (p. 98)

Pigment A finely ground, colored powder that gives paint its color. (p. 78)

Plastic clay Clay that is wet enough to be worked but firm enough to hold its shape. (p. 234)

Point of view The angle from which the viewer sees the scene. (p. 38)

Pointillism A technique in which small dots of color are used to create forms. (p. 118)

Portfolio A carefully selected collection of artworks kept by students and professional artists. (p. 11)

Portrait A visual representation of a person. (p. 123)

Pottery Objects made using ceramic techniques. (p. 234)

Presentation drawing Detailed sketches that show the final project in perspective. (p. 144)

Principles of art Guidelines that govern the way artists organize the elements of art. (p. 48)

Printing plate A surface onto or into which the image to be printed is cut or carved. (p. 152)

Printmaking An area of fine art in which an inked image is transferred to a surface. (p. 72)

Producer The person in charge of the business end of making a movie. (p. 266)

Proportion A principle of art concerned with the way in which the parts of a work relate to each other and to the whole. (p. 54)

R

Registration Careful matching up of plates in prints with more than one color. (p. 152)

Relief printing A printmaking method in which the image to be printed is raised from a background. (p. 152)

Relief sculpture A type of sculpture in which forms and figures project only from the front. (p. 81)

Renaissance A period of great cultural awakening. (p. 124)

Rendering A process by which a vector-based image is converted to a bitmap. (p. 87)

Resolution The number of dots per square inch used to produce an image in printing or on a computer display screen. (p. 85)

Rhythm A principle of art concerned with the repetition of an element to make a work seem active. (p. 59)

S

Screen printing A printmaking technique in which a stencil with a design cut into it is placed over a fabric screen. (p. 154)

Sculpture The art of creating three-dimensional works. (p. 80)

Serigraph A screen print that has been handmade by an artist. (p. 154)

Shading The use of light and shadow to give a feeling of depth. (p. 138)

Shape An element of art that refers to an area clearly set off by one or more of the other six visual elements of art. (p. 35)

Slip Clay that has so much added water that it is liquid and runny. (p. 234)

Solvent A liquid that controls the thickness of the paint. (p. 78)

Space An element of art that refers to the distance or area between, around, above, below, and within objects. (p. 36)

Stippling Creating dark values by using a dot pattern. (p. 139)

Studies Preliminary artworks, often done as drawings. (pp. 136, 216)

Style An artist's personal way of expressing ideas in a work. (p. 118)

Subject The image viewers can easily identify in an artwork. (p. 15)

Subtractive Produced by removing or taking away from the original material. (p. 218)

Synthetic paints Manufactured paints with plastic binders. (p. 171)

T

Tapestry A weaving used as a wall hanging. (p. 233)

Tempera A painting medium in which pigment mixed with egg yolk and water is applied with tiny brushstrokes. (p. 169)

Texture The element of art that refers to how things feel, or look as though they might feel, if touched. (p. 40)

Translucent A surface or material in which light is able to pass through. (p. 188)

Transparent Clear. (p. 169)

U

Unity The arrangement of elements and principles with media to create a feeling of completeness. (p. 62)

V

Value An element of art concerned with the lightness or darkness of a hue. (p. 30)

Vanishing points Imaginary points at the horizon. (p. 258)

Variety The principle of art concerned with combining art elements with slight changes to increase visual interest. (p. 52)

W

Watercolor A painting medium in which pigment is blended with gum arabic and water. (p. 169)

Weaving A craft in which strands of fiber are interlocked to make cloth or objects. (p. 232)

Web designers Artists who work with text and pictures to create Web sites. (p. 203)

Glosario

A

Abstract Expressionism/Expresionismo abstracto Movimiento artístico que enfatizaba elementos abstractos del arte y recalcaba los sentimientos y emociones.

Abstract/Abstracto El sujeto de la obra de arte está simplificado o estilizado. (p. 220)

Acrylic/Acrílico Pintura sintética a base de agua que se seca rápidamente.

Additive/Aditivo Se obtiene al añadir o combinar materiales. (p. 218)

Advertising design/Diseño publicitario Área de las artes gráficas cuyo objetivo es de asistir en la difusión de información, venta o promoción de productos o servicios. (p. 202)

Aesthetic views/Opiniones estéticas Ideas u opiniones sobre lo que es el más importante en una obra de arte.

Aesthetics/Estética La rama de la filosofía que trata de la naturaleza y el valor del arte. (p. 106)

Amphitheater/Anfiteatro Edificio circular u ovalado con gradas alrededor de un espacio abierto. (p. 252)

Analogous Colors/Colores Análogo Colores adyacentes en la rueda de colores y que comparten un matiz. (p. 31)

Analyzing/Analizar Notar cómo los principios del arte se usan para organizar los elementos del arte. (p. 98)

Applied art/Arte aplicado Arte creada para ser funcional y a la vez agradable a la vista. (p. 6)

Architect/Arquitecto Artista que diseña y crea edificios. (p. 250)

Architectural rendering/Perspectiva arquitectónica realista Representación bidimensional detallada y realista de una estructura tridimensional. (p. 136)

Architecture/Arquitectura El arte de planear y crear edificios. (p. 250)

Art/Arte Declaración visual que comunica una idea, expresa un sentimiento o presenta un diseño interesante. (p. 4)

Art critic/Crítico de arte Persona que se ha dedicado a la crítica del arte. (p. 94)

Art criticism/Crítica del arte El proceso de recolectar datos e información que pertenecen a obras de arte a fin de juzgarlas de manera inteligente. (p. 94)

Art history/Historia del arte El estudio del arte desde el pasado hasta el presente. (p. 114)

Art media/Elementos artísticos Herramientas y materiales utilizados en la creación de obras de arte. (p. 68)

Art movement/Movimiento artístico Grupo de artistas con estilos similares que han hecho causa común. (p. 118)

Artists/Artistas Personas que usan la imaginación, creatividad y habilidades para comunicar ideas de forma visual. (p. 6)

Assembling/Ensamblar Método de crear esculturas en el cual se reúnen y se combinan varias clases de materiales. (p. 218)

B

Balance/Equilibrio El principio del arte que trata de la disposición de los elementos en una obra de arte de tal manera que ninguna parte de la obra predomine o parezca tener más importancia que otra. (p. 49)

Binder/Aglutinante Líquido al que se le añade el pigmento seco. (p. 78)

Blending/Matizar Dibujar poco a poco de manera uniforme valores oscuros al poner más presión en el instrumento de dibujo.

Brayer/Rodillo Rodillo con mango. (p. 152)

C

Camera/Cámara Caja oscura con un orificio que controla la cantidad de luz que entra. (p. 184)

Caricature/Caricatura Dibujo que exagera uno o más rasgos faciales o características físicas.

Carving/Tallar Método de crear esculturas en el cual se corta o desprende el material. (p. 218)

Casting/Vaciado Método de crear esculturas en el cual un material fundido se vierte en un molde. (p. 218)

Cathedrals/Catedrales Iglesias grandes. (p. 251)

Ceramics/Cerámica Proceso de crear objetos de arcilla y endurecerlos a fuego. (p. 234)

Cinematographer/Director de cinematografía La persona a cargo de operar la cámara o cámaras. (p. 266)

Collage/Collage Obra de arte creada con trozos de material recortados o rotos y pegados en una superficie. (p. 12)

Color/Color El elemento del arte derivado de la luz reflejada. (p. 28)

Color wheel/Rueda de colores La presentación de los colores en formato circular. (p. 29)

Columns/Columnas Postes verticales que sostienen otra estructura. (p. 257)

Complementary colors/Colores complementario Colores que están en posiciones opuestas en la rueda de colores. (p. 30)

Composition/Composición La forma en que se usan los principios del arte para organizar los elementos del arte. (p. 16)

Content/Contenido El mensaje, sentimiento o idea que una obra de arte comunica. (p. 16)

Contour drawing/Dibujo de contorno Dibujo en el cual un objeto se dibuja como si el instrumento para dibujar se moviera por los bordes y relieves de la forma. (p. 142)

Crafts/Artesanías Diferentes áreas de las artes aplicadas en las que trabajan los artesanos. (p. 232)

Craftspersons/Artesanos Artistas que hacen objetos útiles y estéticamente agradables. (p. 232)

Credit line/Resumen de datos Lista de datos importantes sobre una obra de arte. (p. 17)

Crosshatching/Sombreado con líneas cruzadas Técnica de usar líneas que se cruzan para lograr el sombreado de una ilustración. (p. 138)

Cross-section/Corte transversal Vista del interior. (p. 216)

Cubism/Cubismo Estilo de arte en el cual un objeto único se muestra simultáneamente desde múltiples puntos de vista. (p. 128)

D

Daguerreotype/Daguerrotipo Imagen creada en una placa de cobre, y recubierta con plata pulida. (p. 185)

Describing/Describir Hacer una lista minuciosa de todas las cosas que se ven en una obra. (p. 95)

Describing/Describir Cuándo, dónde y quién realizó una obra. (p. 115)

Desktop publishing/Edición electrónica El uso de una computadora y programas especiales para combinar texto y gráficas en una página. (p. 201)

Digital art/Arte digital Obras de arte creadas en parte o en su totalidad con equipo y programas de computadora. (p. 84)

Digital camera/Cámara digital Cámara que contiene sensores diminutos, que convierten información visual en valores digitales de computación. (p. 184)

Digitizing/Digitalizar Método en el cual las unidades básicas de las imágenes, llamadas pixels, se convirtieron en puntos. (p. 268)

Director/Director La persona a cargo de filmar una película y guiar a los actores. (p. 266)

Dwellings/Viviendas Hogares. (p. 250)

E

Edition/Edición Serie de grabados que son exactamente iguales. (p. 72)

Element of art/Elemento del arte Símbolo visual básico que un artista usa para crear obras de arte visuales. (p. 23)

Elevation/Alzado Dibujo de una vista exterior de un edificio. (p. 256)

Emphasis/Énfasis Principio del arte mediante el cual se resalta un elemento o un objeto en una obra de arte. (p. 53)

Encaustic/Encáustico Tipo de pintura en la cual el pigmento se mezcla con cera derretida. (p. 168)

F

Façade/Fachada La parte adelante de un edificio. (p. 256)

Fauvism/Fauvismo Estilo de arte en el cual artistas usaban colores intensos y con frecuencia combinaciones extravagantes en sus pinturas. (p. 120)

Fibers/Fibras Hebras finas de cualquier material filiforme. (p. 233)

Fine art/Bellas artes Arte que se valora exclusivamente por su atractivo visual or por la virtud con que communica ideas o sentimientos. (p. 6)

Fine art print/Grabado de una obra Obra de arte creada mediante el proceso de grabado. (p. 72)

Fine art reproduction/Reproducción de una obra Copia de alta calidad de una obra de arte realizada utilizando procesos fotográficos comerciales. (p. 72)

Fired/Cocido Endurecido mediante la aplicación de calor intenso. (p. 235)

Floor plan/Plano Diagrama, dibujado a escala, de una habitación o edificio visto desde arriba. (p. 254)

Form/Forma Elemento del arte que se refiere a un objeto con tres dimensiones. (p. 36)

Formal properties/Propiedades formales Organización de los elementos del arte según los principios del arte. (p. 16)

Freestanding/De pie Rodeado por espacio vacío en todos sus lados. (p. 80)

Fresco/Fresco Técnica de pintura en la cual el pigmento se aplica a una pared cubierta con yeso mojado. (p. 168)

G

Gesture drawing/Dibujo de gestos Dibujo en el cual se trazan líneas de manera rápida y espontánea para captar la forma y acciones de un sujeto. (p. 140)

Glassblowing/Soplado de vidrio Artesanía de moldear vidrio derretido soplando aire en su interior por medio de un tubo. (p. 234)

Glaze/Glaseado Una capa delgada y transparente. (p. 170)

Glazed/Vidriado Recubierto con una mezcla de químicos pulverizados que se derriten durante la cocción y forman un capa dura de apariencia similar al vidrio. (p. 235)

Gouache/Aguada Un tipo de acuarela opaca. (p. 170)

Graphic artists/Artistas gráficos Artistas que trabajan en el campo conocido como diseño gráfico. (p. 200)

Graphic design/Diseño gráfico Área del arte que usa ilustraciones y palabras para instruir o comunicar un mensaje específico. (p. 200)

H

Harmony/Armonía El principio del arte que trata de la combinación de elementos del arte similares para crear un aspecto agradable. (p. 53)

Hatching/Sombreado con trazos finos Dibujar una serie de líneas delgadas paralelas, u orientadas en la misma dirección. (p. 138)

High relief/Alto relieve Tipo de escultura en relieve en la cual las formas sobresalen de manera destacada de una superficie plana. (p. 222)

Hue/Matiz El nombre de un color. (p. 29)

I

Illuminations/Iluminaciones Ilustraciones en manuscritos antiguos hechos a mano. (p. 200)

Impasto/Empastar Aplicado en capas gruesas y pastosas. (p. 170)

Impressionism/Impresionismo Estilo de pintura que intenta captar los efectos efímeros de la luz solar sobre los objetos. (p. 119)

Informal balance/Equilibrio informal Trata del equilibrio de objetos o elementos no similares. (p. 49)

Intaglio/Entallar Técnica de grabado en la cual la imagen a imprimir se corta o se esculpe en una superficie. (p. 153)

Intensity/Intensidad El brillo u opacidad de un matiz. (p. 30)

Interpreting/Interpretar Asignarle un significado o encontrar un mensaje en una obra de arte. (p. 102)

J

Judging/Evaluar Tomar una decisión acerca del éxito de una obra y dar razones para esa decisión. (p. 106)

K

Kiln/Horno Aparato especial que se usa para la cocción de cerámica. (p. 235)

L

Landscape/Paisaje Dibujo o pintura de montañas, árboles u otras escenas naturales.

Layout designers/Diseñadores de disposición Artistas gráficos que disponen el texto y las ilustraciones y preparan el material para la impresión. (p. 201)

Leather-hard clay/Arcilla de cuero duro Arcilla que aun esta húmedo pero no muy seco para formar.

Line/Línea Raya continua hecha sobre una superficie mediante el movimiento de un punto. (p. 24)

Lithograph/Litografía Grabado hecho mediante el método de litografía.

Lithography/Litografía Técnica de grabado en la cual la imagen a ser impresa se dibuja sobre piedra caliza, zinc o aluminio con un lápiz grasoso especial. (p. 154)

Logo/Logotipo Imagen especial que representa un negocio, grupo o producto. (p. 202)

Loom/Telar Bastidor o máquina que sujeta una serie de hilos verticales.

Low relief/Bajorrelieve Tipo de escultura en relieve en la cual las formas apenas sobresalen de la superficie plana. (p. 222)

M

Madonna/ Madona Una obra que representa a la madre de Cristo.

Maquette/Maqueta Representación tridimensional a escala reducida de una escultura planeada. (p. 217)

Minarets/Minarete Estructuras desde las cuales los fieles son llamados a la oración todos los días. (p. 251)

Mobile/Móvil Técnica de escultura en la cual formas hechas de láminas de metal pintadas cuelgan suspendidas de alambres, y pueden moverse libremente. (p. 129)

Modeling/Modelar Método de escultura en el cual se le da forma a un material suave y moldeable. (p. 219)

Monochromatic colors/Colores monocromáticos Diferentes tonos de un matiz. (p. 31)

Monoprinting/Grabado único Técnica de grabado en la cual la imagen a imprimirse se coloca sobre una placa con tinta o pintura y luego se transfiere al papel presionando o frotando con la mano. (p. 156)

Motion picture/Película cinematográfica Serie de fotografías del mismo sujeto tomadas a intervalos muy breves que se proyectan con rapidez en una pantalla. (p. 266)

Movement/Movimiento El principio del arte que se utiliza para crear la apariencia y sensación de acción y para guiar el ojo del observador en una obra de arte. (p. 58)

Multimedia art/Arte multimedia La combinación de varios medios para crear un nuevo tipo de arte.

N

Negative/Negativo Una imagen al revés de un objeto fotografiado.

Nonobjective art/Arte sin objetivo Arte que no tiene tema que se puede reconocer. (p. 15)

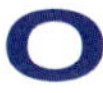

Oil paint/Pintura al óleo Pintura a base de aceite. (p. 170)

Opaque/Opaco Cualidad de un material que no permite que pase la luz. Opuesto de transparente. (p. 169)

P

Palette/Paleta Toda bandeja o placa donde se mezclan las pinturas antes de usarse. (p. 169)

Patrons of the arts/Patrocinadores de las artes Quienes ayudan o apoyan a un artista, o funciones relacionadas con el arte como por ejemplo, exhibiciones. (p. 11)

Pattern/Patrón Un principio del arte que trata de un efecto decorativo bidimensional que se logra mediante la repetición de colores, líneas, formas y texturas. (p. 58)

Perceive/Percibir Tomar conciencia a través de los sentidos de la naturaleza particular de los objetos. (p. 5)

Perception/Percepción Tener conciencia de los aspectos de un ambiente mediante los sentidos. (p. 136)

Photogenic drawing/Dibujo fotogénico El proceso de cubrir una hoja de papel con cloruro de plata. (p. 185)

Photogram/Fotograma Imagen que se hace usando papel laminado especial que detecta la presencia de la luz ultravioleta.

Photography/Fotografía El arte de crear imágenes usando luz y otros principios científicos.

Photojournalism/Periodismo fotográfico Reportar una noticia usando mayormente o en su totalidad imágenes fotográficas. (p. 185)

Picture plane/Plano La superficie plana de una pintura o dibujo. (p. 98)

Pigment/Pigmento Polvo coloreado molido fino que le da a la pintura su color. (p. 78)

Plastic clay/Arcilla de plástico Arcilla que esta suficientemente mojado con cual trabajar pero bastante sólido para que retenga su forma.

Point of view/Punto de vista El ángulo desde el cual el observador ve la escena. (p. 38)

Pointillism/Puntillismo Técnica en la cual se usan pequeños puntos de color para crear formas. (p. 118)

Portfolio/Carpeta de trabajos Colección de obras de arte que un estudiante o artista profesional selecciona cuidadosamente y conserva. (p. 11)

Portrait/Retrato Representación visual de una persona. (p. 123)

Pottery/Alfarería Objetos fabricados utilizando la técnica de la cerámica. (p. 234)

Presentation drawing/Dibujo de presentación Bocetos detallados que muestran el proyecto final en perspectiva. (p. 144)

Principles of art/Principios del arte Las pautas que gobiernan la forma en que los artistas organizan los elementos del arte. (p. 48)

Printing plate/Placa de imprimir Superficie en la cual se corta o talla la imagen que se va a imprimir.

Printmaking/Grabar Área de las bellas artes en la cual una imagen cubierta de tinta se transfiere a otra superficie. (p. 72)

Producer/Productor La persona a cargo de los asuntos financieros en el proceso de hacer una película. (p. 266)

Proportion/Proporción La manera en que las partes de una obra se relacionan entre sí y con el todo. (p. 54)

R

Registration/Registro La alineación cuidadosa de las placas en grabados de más de un color. (p. 152)

Relief/Relieve Tipo de escultura en la cual formas y figuras se proyectan solamente desde el frente. (p. 152)

Relief printing/Grabado en relieve La imagen que se va a imprimir sobresale del fondo. (p. 81)

Renaissance/Renacimiento Periodo caracterizado por un gran despertar cultural. (p. 124)

Rendering/Convertir Proceso en el cual una imagen compuesta por vectores se cambia a una imagen de pixeles.

Resolution/Resolución La cantidad de colores que se puede mostrar simultáneamente en el monitor de una computadora.

Rhythm/Ritmo La repetición de un elemento para crear la sensación de actividad. (p. 59)

S

Screen Printing/Serigrafiado Técnica de hacer grabados en la cual un estarcido con un diseño recortado se coloca encima de a una malla. (p. 154)

Sculpture/Escultura El arte de crear obras tridimensionales.

Serigraph/Serigrafía Grabado hecho por un artista e impreso a mano en una malla. (p. 154)

Shading/Sombrear El uso de la luz y las sombras para dar una sensación de profundidad. (p. 138)

Shape/Forma Un elemento del arte que se refiere a un área claramente demarcada por uno o más de los otros seis elementos visuales del arte. (p. 35)

Slip/Barbotina Arcilla a la que se le ha añadido tanta agua que está líquida. (p. 234)

Solvent/Solvente Líquido que controla el espesor de la pintura. (p. 78)

Space/Espacio Elemento del arte que se refiere a la distancia o área que hay entre, alrededor, encima, debajo o dentro de los objetos. (p. 36)

Stippling/Puntear Crear sombreados usando un patrón de puntos. (p. 139)

Studies/Estudios Obras de arte preliminares, frecuentemente en forma de dibujos. (p. 216)

Style/Estilo La forma personal de un artista de expresar ideas en una obra. (p. 118)

Subject/Sujeto La imagen que el observador puede identificar fácilmente. (p. 15)

Subtractive/Sustraer Se produce al eliminar o quitar parte del material original.

Synthetic paints/Pinturas sintéticas Pinturas fabricadas que contienen aglutinantes plásticos. (p. 171)

T

Tapestry/Tapiz Paño tejido que se cuelga en una pared. (p. 233)

Tempera/Al temple Un tipo de pintura en la cual el pigmento mezclado con yema de huevo y agua se aplica en pequeñas pinceladas. (p. 169)

Texture/Textura El elemento del arte que se refiere a la manera en que las cosas se sienten al tocarlas, o cómo parece que se sentirían al tacto. (p. 40)

Translucent/Traslúcido La luz puede pasar. (p. 188)

Transparent/Transparente Claro. (p. 169)

Unity/Unidad La disposición de los elementos y principios del arte para crear una sensación de que la obra está terminada y completa. (p. 62)

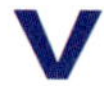

Value/Valor El elemento del arte que trata de la claridad u oscuridad de un matiz. (p. 30)

Vanishing points/Puntos de fuga Puntos imaginarios en el horizonte. (p. 258)

Variety/Variedad El principio del arte que trata de la combinación de elementos del arte efectuando pequeños cambios para intensificar el interés visual de una obra. (p. 52)

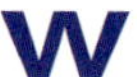

Watercolor/Acuarela Tipo de pintura en la cual el pigmento se mezcla con goma arábiga y agua. (p. 169)

Weaving/Tejeduría Trabajo artesanal en el cual hebras de fibra se entrelazan para hacer tela u objetos. (p. 232)

Web Designers/Diseñadores de web Artistas que trabajan con texto e ilustraciones para crear sitios web. (p. 203)

Index

B

C

D

E

F

G

H

N

O

P

T

U

V

W

Y

Z

Credits

Cover Art
Miriam Schapiro. *High Steppin' Strutter I.* 1985. Paper and acrylic on paper. 203.2 × 138.4 cm (80 × 54½"). Steinbaum-Krauss Gallery, New York, New York. Given anonymously.

Photography Credits
Art Resource 8, 59b, 71, 130, 160, 186r, 206, 233r, 211, 250, 252; Brown Brothers 185b; Digital Images/Getty Images 307b; Tim Fuller Photography. Tucson, AZ 302t, 333(2), 304l, 305b, 306l, 307t; Robert Holmes/Corbis 306r; Charles Jean Marc/Corbis 248; Wolfgang Kaehler/Corbis 217b; Alan Levenson/Getty Images 305t; Robert Llewellyn/Image State 304r; MPTV Archives 266, 276; Darbellay Nathanlie/Corbis Sygma 217t; Michael Newman/Photo Edit 294, 295, 300, 301; Lucy Nicholson/Corbis 260; NASA/Roger Ressmeyer/Corbis; Runaway Technology, Inc. Cambridge, MA 264; Ted Soqui/Corbis 261; Tom Stewart/Corbis 302b; Lee White Photography, Los Angeles, CA 70b, 72, 76, 80, 327 and all student art.